Preterm Birth

Edited by

Hilary Critchley, Phillip Bennett and Steven Thornton

RCOG Press

It was not possible to refer all the material back to the authors or discussants but it is hoped that the proceedings have been reported fairly and accurately.

Hilary OD Critchley MD FRCOG FRANZCOG
Professor of Reproductive Medicine and Consultant Gynaecologist, Centre for Reproductive Biology, University of Edinburgh, The Chancellor's Building, 49 Little France Crescent, Edinburgh EH16 4SB

Phillip Bennett PhD MD FRCOG
Professor of Obstetrics and Gynaecology, Parturition Research Group, Faculty of Medicine, Imperial College London, Institute of Reproductive and Developmental Biology, Hammersmith Hospital Campus, Du Cane Road, London W12 0NN

Steven Thornton DM MRCOG
Professor of Obstetrics and Gynaecology, Department of Biological Sciences and WMS, University of Warwick, Coventry CV4 7AL, Consultant Obstetrician, University Hospitals of Coventry and Warwickshire, Coventry CV2 2DX

Published by the **RCOG Press** at the
Royal College of Obstetricians and Gynaecologists
27 Sussex Place, Regent's Park
London NW1 4RG

www.rcog.org.uk

Registered Charity No. 213280

First published 2004

© Royal College of Obstetricians and Gynaecologists 2004

ISBN 1 900364 92 1

DECLARATION OF INTEREST

All contributors to the Study Group were invited to make a specific Declaration of Interest in relation to the subject of the Study Group. This was undertaken and all contributors complied with this request. Professor Roger Smith holds patents on the use of different ligands to predict preterm delivery, is a director of a company with interests in computer prediction of pregnancy outcomes, and has a consultancy with Eurodiagnostica; Dr Ronald Lamont has chaired sessions at and given lectures and advice to meetings sponsored by unrestricted educational grants from pharmaceutical companies, including Osmotec, Sanofi-Synthélabo and Ferring.

RCOG Editor: Andrew Welsh
Index: Liza Furnival
Design: Karl Harrington, FiSH Books, London
Printed and bound by Antony Rowe Ltd, Eastbourne

PRETERM BIRTH

RCOG Press

Since 1973 the Royal College of Obstetricians and Gynaecologists has regularly convened Study Groups to address important growth areas within obstetrics and gynaecology. An international group of eminent scientists and clinicians from various disciplines is invited to present the results of recent research and to take part in in-depth discussions. The resulting volume, containing the papers presented and also edited transcripts of the discussions, is published within a few months of the meeting and provides a summary of the subject that is both authoritative and up-to-date.

SUPER ARDUA

Some previous Study Group publications available

Infertility
Edited by AA Templeton and JO Drife

Intrapartum Fetal Surveillance
Edited by JAD Spencer and RHT Ward

Early Fetal Growth and Development
Edited by RHT Ward, SK Smith and D Donnai

Ethics in Obstetrics and Gynaecology
Edited by S Bewley and RHT Ward

The Biology of Gynaecological Cancer
Edited by R Leake, M Gore and RHT Ward

Multiple Pregnancy
Edited by RHT Ward and M Whittle

The Prevention of Pelvic Infection
Edited by AA Templeton

Screening for Down Syndrome in the First Trimester
Edited by JG Grudzinskas and RHT Ward

Problems in Early Pregnancy: Advances in Diagnosis and Management
Edited by JG Grudzinskas and PMS O'Brien

Gene Identification, Manipulation and Treatment
Edited by SK Smith, EJ Thomas and PMS O'Brien

Evidence-based Fertility Treatment
Edited by AA Templeton, ID Cooke and PMS O'Brien

Fetal Programming: Influences on Development and Disease in Later Life
Edited by PMS O'Brien, T Wheeler and DJP Barker

Hormones and Cancer
Edited by PMS O'Brien and AB MacLean

The Placenta: Basic Science and Clinical Practice
Edited by JCP Kingdom, ERM Jauniaux and PMS O'Brien

Disorders of the Menstrual Cycle
Edited by PMS O'Brien, IT Cameron and AB MacLean

Infection and Pregnancy
Edited by AB MacLean, L Regan and D Carrington

Pain in Obstetrics and Gynaecology
Edited by AB MacLean, RW Stones and S Thornton

Incontinence in Women
Edited by AB MacLean and L Cardozo

Maternal Morbidity and Mortality
Edited by AB MacLean and J Neilson

Lower Genital Tract Neoplasia
Edited by Allan B MacLean, Albert Singer and Hilary Critchley

Pre-eclampsia
Edited by Hilary Critchley, Allan MacLean, Lucilla Poston and James Walker

Contents

Participants   vii

Preface   xiii

SECTION 1 BASIC SCIENCE

1   **Control of the length of gestation: lessons from animals**
     Peter W Nathanielsz   3

2   **Control of the length of gestation: lessons from women**
     Roger Smith, Sam Mesiano, Richard Nicholson, Tamas Zakar,
     Eng-Cheng Chan, Andrew Bisits, Vicki Clifton and Warwick Giles   13

3   **The preterm parturition syndrome**
     Roberto Romero, Jimmy Espinoza, Moshe Mazor and Tinnakorn
     Chaiworapongsa   28

4   **Fetal growth, maturity and preterm birth**
     Jason Gardosi, Sue M Kady and André Francis   61

5   **Recent trends in the care, complications and outcome**
     of preterm babies
     Denis Azzopardi and Raghuram Mallaiah   73

6   **Discussion**   88

SECTION 2 SCREENING AND DIAGNOSIS I

7   **Cervical physiology**
     Jane E Norman, Andrew J Thomson, Inass Osman and Marie Anne
     Ledingham   99

8   **Inflammatory mediators in the cervix**
     Andrew A Calder and Fiona C Denison   115

9   **Sonographic measurement of cervical length and preterm delivery**
     Kypros H Nicolaides, Elly Tsoi and Meekai S To   124

10   **Cervical cerclage**
     Bryony Jones and Andrew Shennan   140

11   **Discussion**   151

SECTION 3 SCREENING AND DIAGNOSIS II

12   **Bacterial vaginosis**
     Ronald F Lamont   163

13   **Preterm labour and the cervicovaginal fetal fibronectin test**
     Honest and Khalid S Khan   181

14   **Discussion**   188

SECTION 4 MANAGEMENT I

15 **Fetal membrane rupture**
    Stephen C Bell and Penny C McParland   195

16 **Clinical management of preterm prelabour rupture of membranes**
    Sara Brigham and James P Neilson   213

17 **Antimicrobials in the management of preterm parturition**
    David J Taylor   224

18 **Discussion**   231

SECTION 5 MANAGEMENT II

19 **Antiphospholipid syndrome and preterm birth**
    May Backos and Lesley Regan   239

20 **Steroids**
    Patricia Crowley   244

21 **Myometrial physiology**
    Andrés López Bernal   258

22 **Discussion**   277

SECTION 6 MANAGEMENT III

23 **Tocolysis: for and against**
    Azhar Husnain Syed and John J Morrison   287

24 **Nifedipine in the management of preterm labour:**
    evidence from the literature
    Dimitri NM Papatsonis and Guus A Dekker   296

25 **Oxytocin antagonists for tocolysis**
    Roberto Romero, Tinnakorn Chaiworapongsa and Luís F Gonçalves   308

26 **Discussion**   333

SECTION 7 MANAGEMENT IV

27 **Mode of preterm delivery: caesarean section versus vaginal delivery**
    Philip J Steer   341

28 **Postmortem examination and placental pathology in relation**
    to preterm birth
    Neil J Sebire   350

29 **Discussion**   368

SECTION 8 CONSENSUS VIEWS

30 **Consensus views arising from the 46th Study Group: Preterm Birth** 373

Index   377

Participants

Denis Azzopardi
Senior Lecturer in Paediatrics and Neonatal Medicine, Department of Paediatrics, Hammersmith Campus, Imperial College, London W12 0NN, UK.

Stephen C Bell
Professor of Reproductive Science, Reproductive Sciences Section, Department of Cancer Studies and Molecular Medicine, Leicester Medical School, University of Leicester, Leicester, UK.

Phillip Bennett
Professor of Obstetrics and Gynaecology, Parturition Research Group, Faculty of Medicine, Imperial College London, Institute of Reproductive and Developmental Biology, Hammersmith College Campus, Du Cane Road, London W12 0NN, UK.

Andrew A Calder
Head of Division of Reproductive and Developmental Sciences, Simpson Centre for Reproductive Health, Royal Infirmary of Edinburgh, 51 Little France Crescent, Edinburgh EH16 4SA, UK.

Hilary OD Critchley
Professor of Reproductive Medicine and Consultant Gynaecologist, Centre for Reproductive Biology, University of Edinburgh, The Chancellor's Building, 49 Little France Crescent, Edinburgh EH16 4SB, UK.

Patricia Crowley
Senior Lecturer, Trinity College Dublin, Department of Obstetrics and Gynaecology, Coombe Women's Hospital Dublin, Dublin 8, Ireland.

Jason Gardosi
Professor of Maternal and Perinatal Health and Director, West Midlands Perinatal Institute, Crystal Court, Aston Cross, Birmingham B6 5RQ, UK.

Khalid S Khan
Consultant Obstetrician-Gynaecologist and Clinical Sub-dean, Birmingham Women's Hospital, Edgbaston, Birmingham B15 2TG, UK.

Ronald F Lamont
Consultant and Honorary Reader, Imperial College and Northwick Park and St Mark's Hospitals, Harrow HA1 3UJ, UK.

Back row (from left to right): John Morrison, David Taylor, Neil Sebire, Dimitri Papatsonis, Andrés López Bernal, Andrew Shennan, Roger Smith, Roberto Romero, Khalid Khan, Peter Nathanielsz, Philip Steer, Andrew Calder, Kypros Nicolaides, Jason Gardosi, James Neilson, Stephen Bell, Denis Azzopardi

Front row (from left to right): Lesley Regan, Patricia Crowley, Aysun Sapherson, Phillip Bennett, Hilary Critchley, Steven Thornton, Jane Norman, Ronald Lamont, George Saade

Andrés López Bernal
Professor of Human Reproductive Biology, Level D, St Michael's Hospital, Southwell Street, Bristol BS2 8EG, UK.

John J Morrison
Professor, Head of Department and Consultant Obstetrician Gynaecologist, Department of Obstetrics and Gynaecology, National University of Ireland Galway, Clinical Science Institute, University College Hospital Galway, Newcastle Road, Galway, Ireland.

Peter W Nathanielsz
Director, Center for Women's Health Research, Professor of Obstetrics and Gynecology, NYU School of Medicine, 550 First Avenue, 9E2 NBV, New York, NY 10014, USA.

James P Neilson
Professor of Obstetrics and Gynaecology, First Floor, Liverpool Women's Hospital, Crown Street, Liverpool L8 7SS, UK.

Kypros H Nicolaides
Professor and Director, Harris Birthright Research Centre for Fetal Medicine, 9 Jubilee Wing, King's College Hospital, Denmark Hill, London SE5 9RS, UK.

Jane E Norman
Reader, Honorary Consultant in Obstetrics and Gynaecology, University of Glasgow Division of Developmental Medicine, Glasgow Royal Infirmary, Queen Elizabeth Building, 10 Alexandra Parade, Glasgow G31 2ER, UK.

Dimitri NM Papatsonis
Department of Obstetrics and Gynaecology, Amphia Hospital Breda, Langendijk 75, 4819 EV Breda, The Netherlands.

Lesley Regan
Professor and Head of Department of Obstetrics and Gynaecology, Imperial College at St Mary's Hospital, Mint Wing, South Wharf Road, London W2 1NY, UK.

Roberto Romero
Chief, Perinatology Research Branch, NICHD/NIH/DHHS, Hutzel Hospital, Department of Obstetrics and Gynecology, 4707 St. Antoine Boulevard, Detroit, MI 48201, USA.

George R Saade
Professor and Director, Maternal–Fetal Medicine Fellowship Program, The University of Texas Medical Branch, 301 University Boulevard, MR 1062, Galveston, Texas 77555, USA.

Aysun Sapherson
Lay Member, RCOG Consumers' Forum

Neil J Sebire
Consultant in Paediatric Pathology, Department of Histopathology, Camelia Botnar Laboratories, Great Ormond Street Hospital, Great Ormond Street, London WC1N 3JH, UK.

Andrew Shennan
Professor of Obstetrics, Maternal and Fetal Research Unit, Guy's, King's and St Thomas' School of Medicine, 10th Floor, North Wing, St Thomas' Hospital, Lambeth Palace Road, London SE1 7EH, UK.

Roger Smith
Director, Mothers and Babies Research Centre, Endocrine Unit, John Hunter Hospital, Locked Bag 1, Hunter Region Mail Centre, Newcastle NSW 2310, Australia.

Philip J Steer
Professor of Obstetrics, Imperial College London, Academic Department of Obstetrics and Gynaecology, Chelsea and Westminster Hospital, 369 Fulham Road, London SW10 9NH, UK.

David J Taylor
Professor of Obstetrics and Gynaecology, Reproductive Sciences Section, Department of Cancer Studies and Molecular Medicine, Leicester Medical School, University of Leicester, Leicester, UK.

Steven Thornton
Professor of Obstetrics and Gynaecology, Department of Biological Sciences and WMS, University of Warwick, Coventry CV4 7AL, Consultant Obstetrician, University Hospitals of Coventry and Warwickshire, Coventry CV2 2DX, UK.

Additional contributors

May Backos
Associate Specialist, Reproductive Medicine, St Mary's Hospital, Mint Wing, South Wharf Road, London W2 1NY, UK.

Andrew Bisits
Mothers and Babies Research Centre, John Hunter Hospital, Locked Bag 1, Hunter Region Mail Centre, Newcastle NSW 2310, Australia.

Sara Brigham
Clinical Research Fellow, Department of Obstetrics and Gynaecology, Liverpool Women's Hospital, Crown Street, Liverpool L8 7SS, UK.

Tinnakorn Chaiworapongsa
Perinatology Research Branch, NICHD/NIH/DHHS, 4707 St. Antoine Boulevard, Detroit, MI 48201, USA.

Eng-Cheng Chan
Mothers and Babies Research Centre, John Hunter Hospital, Locked Bag 1, Hunter Region Mail Centre, Newcastle NSW 2310, Australia.

Vicki Clifton
Mothers and Babies Research Centre, John Hunter Hospital, Locked Bag 1, Hunter Region Mail Centre, Newcastle NSW 2310, Australia.

Guus A Dekker
Head, Women and Children's Division, Lyell McEwin Health Service, Department of Obstetrics and Gynaecology, University of Adelaide, Adelaide, Australia.

Fiona C Denison
Clinical Lecturer in Obstetrics and Gynaecology, Division of Reproductive and Developmental Sciences, Simpson Centre for Reproductive Health, Royal Infirmary of Edinburgh, 51 Little France Crescent, Edinburgh EH16 4SA, UK.

Jimmy Espinoza
Perinatology Research Branch, NICHD/NIH/DHHS, 4707 St. Antoine Boulevard, Detroit, MI 48201, USA.

André Francis
Statistician, West Midlands Perinatal Institute, Crystal Court, Aston Cross, Birmingham B6 5RQ, UK.

Warwick Giles
Mothers and Babies Research Centre, John Hunter Hospital, Locked Bag 1, Hunter Region Mail Centre, Newcastle NSW 2310, Australia.

Luís F Gonçalves
Perinatology Research Branch, NICHD/NIH/DHHS, 4707 St. Antoine Boulevard, Detroit, MI 48201, USA.

Honest
WellBeing Research Fellow, Department of Obstetrics and Gynaecology, Birmingham Women's Hospital, Edgbaston, Birmingham B15 2TG, UK.

Bryony Jones
Clinical Research Fellow, Parturition Research Group, Imperial College London, Institute for Reproductive and Developmental Biology, Hammersmith Hospital Campus, Du Cane Road, London W12 0HS, UK.

Sue M Kady
Perinatal Research Fellow, West Midlands Perinatal Institute, Crystal Court, Aston Cross, Birmingham B6 5RQ, UK.

Marie Anne Ledingham
Subspecialty Trainee in Maternal Fetal Medicine, Princess Royal Maternity Hospital, Glasgow G31 2ER, UK.

Raghuram Mallaiah
Clinical Fellow in Neonatal Medicine, Hammersmith Hospital, Du Cane Road, London W12 0NN, UK.

Penny C McParland
Lecturer, Reproductive Sciences Section, Department of Cancer Studies and Molecular Medicine, Leicester Medical School, University of Leicester, Leicester, UK.

Moshe Mazor
Division of Obstetrics and Gynecology, Soroka Medical Center, PO Box 151, Beer-Sheva 84101 Israel

Sam Mesiano
Mothers and Babies Research Centre, John Hunter Hospital, Locked Bag 1, Hunter Region Mail Centre, Newcastle NSW 2310, Australia.

Richard C Nicholson
Mothers and Babies Research Centre, John Hunter Hospital, Locked Bag 1, Hunter Region Mail Centre, Newcastle NSW 2310, Australia.

Inass Osman
Clinical Research Fellow, Division of Developmental Medicine, Reproductive and Maternal Medicine, 3rd Floor, Queen Elizabeth Building, Glasgow Royal Infirmary, Glasgow G31 2ER, UK.

Azhar Husnain Syed
Specialist Registrar, Department of Obstetrics and Gynaecology, University College Hospital Galway, Newcastle Road, Galway, Ireland.

Andrew J Thomson
Consultant in Obstetrics and Gynaecology, Department of Obstetrics and Gynaecology, Royal Alexandra Hospital, Corsebar Road, Paisley PA2 9PN, UK.

Meekai S To
Specialist Registrar, c/o Harris Birthright Research Centre for Fetal Medicine, 9 Jubilee Wing, King's College Hospital, Denmark Hill, London SE5 9RS, UK.

Elly Tsoi
Research Fellow, Harris Birthright Research Centre for Fetal Medicine, 9 Jubilee Wing, King's College Hospital, Denmark Hill, London SE5 9RS, UK.

Tamas Zakar
Mothers and Babies Research Centre, John Hunter Hospital, Locked Bag 1, Hunter Region Mail Centre, Newcastle NSW 2310, Australia.

Preface

It is depressing that obstetricians have made little contribution to improving the outcome for preterm babies and that almost all advances have been made in neonatal and paediatric care. There remain many fundamental questions that need to be answered concerning preterm birth, in both basic science and clinical management. We frequently do not know the cause of preterm labour in an individual. The mechanisms of myometrial contraction and cervical ripening and dilatation are poorly understood and there are managements that have been convincingly demonstrated to improve neonatal outcome.

It is therefore timely to review what is currently known about preterm labour and delivery. This 46th RCOG Study Group was designed to bring together some of the field's leaders to inform, debate and discuss the crucial aspects. Short lectures provided an overview of the basic science, epidemiology, prevention, clinical management, investigation and implications of preterm delivery. Adequate time was provided for discussion, which was lively and informative. Examples of issues debated include the lack of consensus on whether tocolysis should be administered in preterm labour, which drug should be used if a tocolytic is given, and even whether the condition can be prevented by administration of progesterone. This book provides a comprehensive summary of the lectures and an overview of the discussions. It will be a valuable reference text for researchers and a key manual for obstetric or midwifery clinicians.

Given the diverse opinion and often apparent lack of consensus highlighted during the Study Group, coupled with the lack of clinical and scientific data, it has been impossible to develop guidelines for many of the clinical aspects of preterm labour. Moreover, a number of guidelines have been recently produced by national organisations. In contrast to previous Study Groups, therefore, we do not provide clinical recommendations.

This Study Group did highlight a critical need to invest in quality basic science and clinical trials relating to prematurity. It would be short-sighted to remove funding from basic science that provides the basis for future trials. Advances must be based on sound scientific principles. Given that this area of medicine causes so much mortality and morbidity, we must support further research if we are to advance clinical management and help these infants.

Hilary Critchley
Phillip Bennett
Steven Thornton

SECTION 1

BASIC SCIENCE

Chapter 1

Control of the length of gestation: lessons from animals

Peter W Nathanielsz

Rationale for integrated physiological studies on animal models

The rationale for the use of animal models to elucidate the many interactive factors that control the length of gestation is the same as the rationale for the use of animal models to study any physiological or pathophysiological process that is important for human health. To understand any complex biological system it is necessary to take both the reductionist approach and the systems approach. Neither approach by itself is adequate to elucidate the complex regulatory mechanisms that control gestation length. Animal models provide the opportunity to collect critical data from both approaches in ways that are not possible in human pregnancy for pragmatic, ethical and economic reasons. Carefully controlled studies using animal models are indispensable to understanding how the whole organism functions. In any system that involves interaction of multiple cell types and organs working in concert there are dangers in placing one's reliance on information obtained solely from the reductionist approach. Reductionist studies only indicate what may happen *in vivo*. They cannot confirm what does happen *in vivo*. This requirement for studies in the whole animal carries with it the need to understand the physiology of the whole animal. Thus, it is important to appreciate the comparative physiology of different species. Collaboration between veterinarians, animal scientists and investigators with human clinical experience is of the utmost importance.

Whole-animal studies conducted in a variety of animal models provide *in vivo* information on the type of *in vitro* laboratory physiometric studies that need to be performed. Thus, the use of uterine muscle myography has provided extensive information on the *in vitro* function of the myometrium and its responses to agonists such as oxytocin and prostaglandins, as well as evaluation of potential antagonists such as betamimetics and oxytocin antagonists.[1-3] *In vivo* studies should both precede and follow the *in vitro* studies.

Physiometric studies inform us of the agonist receptors that need to be studied at the protein (proteomic) and gene expression (genomic) level. Again, the oxytocin receptor system is an excellent example. Many studies have been conducted to show that steroids affect gene expression and translation into protein.[4-6] The availability of reagents for use in several species has enabled investigators to combine a wide variety of different experimental approaches in several animal species – rat, sheep and non-human primate – with tissue retrieval and analysis to demonstrate the ontogenic appearance, regional and tissue distribution and hormonal and local control of the oxytocin receptor. It is important that the information gained both at the proteomic and genomic level is used to design the next *in vivo* studies. As mentioned above, ethical and practical constraints limit the availability of the complete range of human maternal and fetal tissues that must be studied throughout gestation to provide a clear picture of the complex organ, tissue, cellular and subcellular mechanisms that lead to labour. In addition, there is a great need for information on complete time series analyses in sequence.

In addition to providing normative data, the ability to perturb physiological systems in a carefully controlled manner in animal models enables the investigator to isolate the effects of different systems in ways that cannot be performed in human pregnancy. One of the most practical limitations of studies in human pregnancy is the inability to isolate pregnant women from their complex and individual environments. Pregnant women cannot, for example, be followed on a daily basis to evaluate myometrial activity. Even if the methods were available for noninvasive monitoring of myometrial activity in pregnant women in a quantitative and reproducible fashion, the economic and time burden on women would render any study very selective in recruitment. This is one example of the difficulty of obtaining both normative and perturbed data in human pregnancy. In contrast, in both the pregnant sheep and non-human primate it has been possible to record myometrial activity directly from the uterus via electrodes implanted within the myometrium at multiple sites on the uterus. In these studies, it has been possible to describe basic differences in myometrial patterns in the third trimester of gestation and in the days before delivery.

This chapter focuses on three issues that merit study in experimental animals in an attempt to better understand the control of the length of pregnancy. First, it is important to see how animal models have been used to obtain a precise description of the normative endocrine, paracrine and autocrine changes in relation to functional changes that occur as preparations for delivery are being made. Then it is necessary to determine how these endocrine changes in both mother and fetus recruit the various effector hormonal, enzyme, receptor and gene changes in myometrium, decidua, fetal membranes and cervix that must function in concert for safe and timely delivery. This information is best gathered in carefully controlled perturbation experiments in which input variables are altered and the consequences on the various regulators of the length of gestation are determined. Finally, a cautionary tale is described.

Is there value in the concept of a single trigger or a clock that controls the length of gestation?

The mechanisms that initiate labour are not switched on suddenly at the end of gestation. It is important to determine the full sequence of events that form the seamless progression of both the maintenance of normal pregnancy and then its termination in the delivery of viable progeny. Thus, there is no single trigger to parturition, no one clock that times the process. From the time of fertilisation, the programme embodied in the genomic inheritance of the zygote will interact with the environment, with the result that labour will supervene after the integration of all the signals that the conceptus and the mother receive. For example, the observations that fetal hypophysectomy or bilateral lesions of the fetal paraventricular nuclei prolong gestation[7,8] clearly show that these structures are indispensably involved in the process of parturition: they do not show that these individual structures initiate parturition solely themselves. In this author's view, attempts to label individual process as triggers or clocks fails to acknowledge the continuity of the processes that time the length of gestation. It is necessary to remember that phenotype is the ultimate interaction of the genome with the environment. No physiological process occurs in isolation or is spontaneously generated without being influenced by the environment around the organism. The laws of biological causality tell us that every process is the result of the interaction of previously existing processes governed by stored genetic information, with modifying stimuli that are exerted by the environment on the organism. Thus, the regulation of gestation length in a fixed and optimal maternal intrauterine environment is set in most, if not all, mammalian species by the genotype of the fetus. This has been clearly shown by embryo transfer in the sheep.[9] Thus, the trigger to the initiation of parturition in normal pregnancy is fertilisation. As will be discussed elsewhere in this book, length can be significantly shortened by external factors such as maternal infection acting on the developmental programme put in train by the genome of the developing zygote, embryo and fetus.

Normative studies on the control of the length of gestation

Normative data on the endocrine changes that occur throughout pregnancy have been fundamentally important in improving our understanding of the control of the length of gestation. Clear, significant and sometimes dramatic endocrine changes occur several days before parturition. In sheep, the preparturitional increase in fetal cortisol occurs 20 or so days[10,11] rather than three days or so before delivery,[12] as previously considered. In the baboon, a change in the 24-hour rhythms of maternal plasma oestrogen and progesterone can be seen at least ten days before delivery.[13] In this species of primates, ten days before delivery the rise in plasma oestrogen begins earlier in the 24-hour cycle. Since the profile of progesterone remains the same, there is a marked change in the oestrogen to progesterone ratio for a few hours each day. It has become increasingly clear that a commonality between a variety of animal models and human pregnancy is the occurrence of a rise in oestrogen at the end of gestation. This increase in oestrogen occurs relatively early in human pregnancy,[14] later in the rhesus monkey[15] and baboon[13] and very late in the sheep.[16] This relationship of oestrogen to labour and delivery has been confirmed in pregnant women in both term and preterm labour.[17] This chapter focuses on animal studies that have used the non-human primate to investigate the potential role of oestrogen and prostaglandins in regulating the length of gestation.

Advantages of the pregnant rhesus monkey and baboon for the study of mechanisms that control the length of gestation

The pregnant baboon and rhesus monkey present several advantages for both reductionist and systems approaches during gestation and parturition. Pregnancy in the monkey lasts 165 days and in the baboon 185 days. The size of the fetus, fetal membranes and uterine tissues at term in these two species of primate allows for a variety of tissues to be harvested from any area of the uterus in adequate amounts for molecular and cellular studies. The tether and swivel system developed at the Southwest Foundation for Biomedical Research and used extensively by researchers[18,19] allows repeated sampling from both mother and fetus, combined with recording of biophysical variables in the absence of tranquillising pharmacological agents and the stress of physical restraint. Thus, systemic hormonal changes can be linked to fetal and maternal function. One of the major advantages of these two species in relation to parturition is the ability to make precise continuous recordings of the patterns of myometrial activity throughout the 24-hour day for many days. Information on myometrial contractility enables the relation of biological activity in the tissues to the progress through the phases of preparation, activation and stimulation of the uterus that together make up the process of parturition.

The Center for Women's Health Research at NYU School of Medicine studies in these two species of non-human primate have demonstrated that myometrial activity in mid-gestation is of the low-amplitude long-lasting contracture type, which only produces a small rise in intrauterine pressure and recurs periodically with a much longer time interval than the short-lived contractions of delivery (Figure 1.1) This basic activity represents the underlying irritability of smooth muscle. This activity maintains myometrial contractile capability and allows the myometrium to build up its power for labour. A similar contracture pattern exists in pregnant sheep, where contractures switch to contractions late in gestation and myometrial activity remains in the contracture mode until delivery, usually within 12–24 hours.[20] In sheep, the switch from contractures to contractions almost invariably occurs in the early hours of evening. In contrast, in primates contractures switch to contractions in the early hours of the evening but on the night of the first switch the duration of contractions is short and the intrauterine pressure increase resulting from individual contractions is not maximal and within a few hours contractions switch back to contractures.[21] This pattern of switch from contractures to contractions occurs on several nights until labour supervenes. The observations made in the rhesus monkey,[21] cynomologous monkey[22] and baboon[23,24] show that this repetitive nocturnal switch in the days immediately prior to delivery is a characteristic pattern of the primate myometrium. This pattern of increased myometrial activity at night in late gestation is a common one in human pregnancy. There are publications that clearly indicate a 24-hour rhythmicity in human myometrial activity and delivery.[25] This switch from contractures to contractions has been used as a marker of the onset of labour and to follow its progression through to delivery, to evaluate the progression of parturition.

The ability to obtain a detailed record of myometrial activity has enabled us to

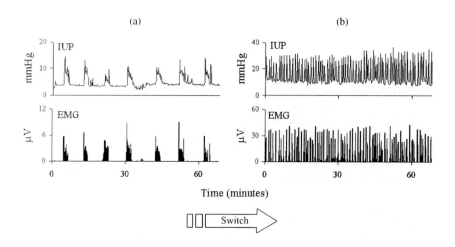

Figure 1.1. Myometrial contractures (a) and contractions (b) as recorded in baboon pregnancy both directly from the myometrium with uterine electrodes (lower trace in each panel) and from a pressure catheter within the uterus (upper trace in each panel); at term, contractures switch to contractions

undertake caesarean section hysterectomy at specific times in relation to the switch from contractures to contractions. Thus, when analysing data on changes in components of key paracrine and autocrine systems such as the prostaglandin system, it is important to be confident of the stage of pregnancy in relation to the onset of labour. This requirement cannot be undertaken with confidence in human pregnancy, since the first few switches from contractures to contractions can be short-lived and lacking in intensity and, hence, may have occurred without being sensed by the pregnant woman. The practical result of the inability to time the final changes that are involved in parturition is clearly demonstrated in many studies by the greater variance in data obtained late in gestation and designated as term not in labour, when compared with data during well-established labour that is clearly discernible and hence precisely determined.

Studies in the non-human primate to evaluate the role of oestrogens

Identification of the relative roles of the many participants in the labour and delivery process is impossible unless each one is changed individually and in a way that mimics the normal gestational changes as closely as possible. The role of oestrogen, for example, has been dismissed by several authorities because of failure to note the normative data in human and animals. There are many studies that provide powerful evidence for increases in maternal plasma oestrogens in late gestation. In particular, the study by Wilson et al.[13] provides some interesting indicators of the role of oestrogen. The opening up of a window each day in which the oestrogen to progesterone ratio changes significantly may be a key to resolution of the continuing controversy of the roles of oestrogen and progesterone and to the problems associated with the failure of non-human primates to show a decline in oestrogen in late gestation. In addition, it is necessary to design studies that mimic normal changes in local production of oestrogen.

There are considerable similarities, as well as many differences, in the changes that occur in activity of the fetal adrenal in primates and ruminants. In both species there is a similar increase in fetal adrenal size and output of steroids. However, the main steroid secreted by the ovine fetal adrenal is cortisol, while in the non-human primate it is androgen.[26] Administration of oestradiol directly to the pregnant rhesus monkey in late gestation does not induce labour and delivery, even when maternal plasma oestradiol concentrations are raised well above the normal term levels.[27] Infusion of oestradiol does, however, induce increased myometrial contractility.[19,28] When the oestrogen precursor androstenedione is infused intravenously to the pregnant rhesus monkey in late gestation, it is converted into oestrogen and induces premature delivery of live young. The delivery appears to be completely normal involving the normal term increase in maternal plasma oxytocin concentration, fetal membrane fibronectin, cervical dilatation and separation of the placenta.[19,28] As in term delivery, maternal plasma progesterone does not fall as a result of androstenedione infusion. Infusion of the aromatase inhibitor 4-hydroxyandrostenedione simultaneously with andro-stenedione will inhibit the effect of androstenedione in precipitating premature labour,[19,28] indicating that the effect is due to the oestrogen produced rather than the androstenedione infused. We can conclude that the circulating oestradiol does play a role in increasing myometrial activity but local paracrine effects of oestradiol are indispensable to the completion of delivery.

Studies in the non-human primate to evaluate the role of prostaglandins

Prostaglandins are a major final common pathway through which other endocrine and paracrine factors exert their influence in initiating the onset of labour. Animal models enable determination of local changes that could not be easily elucidated in human pregnancy. This information can then suggest major underlying concepts. In all species studied in detail there is a positive venoarterial difference for prostaglandin across the uterine and umbilical circulations in late gestation and particularly at the time of delivery. This basic finding demonstrates an overall functional commonality and indicates that intrauterine tissues are the major site of prostaglandin production in late gestation. We have used the baboon as a non-human primate model in which to investigate the key questions of tissue specificity and regional specificity of uterine prostaglandin function.

We have demonstrated gestational length-specific changes in prostaglandin synthesis and metabolism within the myometrium and cervix that lead to delivery, which are both tissue- and topographical site-specific. It is necessary to define the profile of changes in synthesis, metabolism and receptor function to obtain a complete picture of prostaglandin function. Considerable data exist to show that prostaglandin production within the amnion and adjacent chorion and decidua is clearly not uniform throughout the uterus. Prostaglandin concentrations are five to ten times higher in the forebag than in the hindbag, although amnion is distributed throughout the whole uterus and the extent of the amnion surrounding the hindbag is much larger than that surrounding the forebag.[29] Different zones of the uterus have different roles to play and thus alter their function in specific ways in a carefully timed fashion in preparation for delivery. In parturition, the fundus contracts strongly, the lower uterine segment elongates and the cervix effaces each on a different time course. We have conducted a regional analysis within the pregnant baboon uterus to correlate hormonal and paracrine changes with a clear read out of myometrial activity.

The two isozymes of prostaglandin synthase (PGHS), PGHS1 and PGHS2, are responsible for the initial steps in the synthesis of prostaglandins.[30] There are marked changes in PGHS2 in late gestation in the baboon lower uterine segment and cervix. An increase in PGHS2 message occurs well before labour, as recorded by the switch from contractures to contractions.[31] In the baboon, the prelabour increase in PGHS2 mRNA is restricted to the lower uterine segment and cervix. Regulation cannot therefore be completely endocrine but must also involve local factors. Stretch is one potential local factor shown to have powerful interactions with hormones in pregnant rat and sheep studies.[32,33] The lower hindbag prostaglandin concentrations may reflect the failure of fundal PGHS2 production to increase before labour. Engagement of the presenting part acts as a barrier to diffusion of forebag prostaglandin to the hindbag.

Prostaglandin dehydrogenase (PGDH), the enzyme that catalyses the initial oxidative step in the metabolism of prostaglandin E_2 (PGE$_2$) and PGF$_{2\alpha}$ to their biologically inactive 15-keto metabolites,[34–37] is present in the lower uterine segment and fundal myometrium and cervix in the late gestation pregnant baboon.[38] PGDH mRNA decreased significantly in the cervix during late gestation, which would be consistent with the role of prostaglandins in the gradual softening of the cervix in the last days of pregnancy. In contrast, PGDH decreased in the fundus only during spontaneous labour, indicating that local uterine prostaglandin accumulation stimulates the myometrial contractures to contractions switch.

Coleman et al.[39] have identified and characterised several membrane-bound receptors for prostaglandins, each of which is at least ten-fold more selective for a given prostaglandin. Prostanoid receptors are G protein coupled seven transmembrane domain receptors. The individual receptors are named after the native prostaglandin to which they are most sensitive, for example EP receptors for PGE_2, IP receptors for PGI_2, DP receptors for PGD_2, FP receptors for $PGF_2\alpha$ and TP receptors for TxA2. The IP, DP, EP_2 and EP_4 receptors inhibit smooth-muscle contractility and the FP, TP, EP_1 and EP_3 receptors stimulate smooth-muscle contractility.[39,40] The receptor types and subtypes which typically inhibit smooth-muscle contractility are positively coupled to adenylate cyclase, i.e. the IP, DP, EP_2 and EP_4 receptors. The receptors that typically cause smooth-muscle contraction, the EP_1, FP and TP receptors, are usually positively coupled to the phosphatidyl inositol cascade.

Exogenous E and F series prostaglandins can induce delivery of the conceptus at any gestational age in human clinical situations again demonstrating the key role of prostaglandins in the processes that terminate gestation. Studies using caesarean hysterectomy specimens from the baboon demonstrated a weaker contractile response to PGE_2 in myometrial strips from the lower segment compared with those obtained from the fundus. Molecular analysis of paired specimens demonstrated lower expression of the gene encoding the contractile EP_3 receptor and higher expression of the gene encoding the inhibitory EP_2 receptor in myometrium from the lower segment compared with the fundus.[41,42] This finding was specific since the contractile response to $PGF_2\alpha$ and expression of the FP receptor gene showed no regional variation. An example of the importance of conducting studies in non-human primates is the observation of a species difference between primates and nonprimates: both the human and baboon exhibit inhibitory responses to selective EP_2 agonists,[43,44] whereas ovine myometrium does not.[45] Studies in the pregnant baboon caesarean hysterectomy model have demonstrated expression of genes encoding all the main prostanoid receptor types in the myometrium, except the DP receptor. Labour is accompanied by a marked reduction in expression of the inhibitory EP_2 receptor gene, thereby resulting in an increased contractile response to a given concentration of PGE_2.[46–48]

Prostaglandins also have important effects on the cervix. Administration of exogenous synthetic PGE_2 is widespread for the pretreatment of the cervix prior to induction of labour. Prostaglandins are thought to act both to stimulate uterine contraction as well as to produce cervical softening and effacement by decreasing cervical collagen content.[49] The pregnant baboon cervix expresses multiple prostanoid receptor genes: EP_1, EP_2, EP_3, EP_4, FP, IP and TP. Only expression of the gene encoding the EP_1 receptor increased over the last third of pregnancy prior to the onset of labour. Labour was associated with a complex change in the pattern of expression of prostanoid receptor genes in the cervix. As in myometrium, there was a profound decrease in the expression of the EP_2 receptor gene.[47]

A cautionary tale

State-of-the-art techniques for the measurement of small amounts of protein and RNA within tissues have added greatly to our knowledge of the factors that control the length of gestation. However, as with all methodological approaches there are limitations to their use. Measurement of tissue mRNA at a single time point may well miss a peak in altered transcription occurring earlier or later. An additional complexity is the use in different ways of the same cellular transduction techniques by different cells in complex structures. In heterogeneous structures made up of several cell types, measurement of total mRNA as an index of activity of a specific gene within the whole tissue may well miss significant changes in specific cell types that constitute a numerically small yet physiologically significant part of the tissue. We experienced our own example of this problem while evaluating changes in expression of the genes that regulate the endothelin (ET) receptors ET_A and ET_B in response to exposure to glucocorticoids during pregnancy in sheep. Our hypothesis was that the ET_A receptor would be upregulated in fetal placental blood vessels. This hypothesis was based on extensive studies in which we had shown that glucocorticoids upregulate ET_A in different vascular beds in pregnancy.[50] Quantitative reverse transcriptase polymerase chain reaction in whole placentomes from pregnant sheep revealed that, contrary to our hypothesis that the vasoconstrictor ET_A receptor would increase, there was an increase in the ET_B mRNA and a small fall in ET_A mRNA.[51] However, radio-ligand binding studies of frozen sections of the placentome demonstrated that there was indeed an increased binding to the ET_A receptor over the small fetal placental arteries, as we had hypothesised. Subsequent dissection of small fetal arteries and measurement of mRNA for the ET_A receptor in the arteries themselves showed that there was an increase in ET_A receptor mRNA in the arteries masked by the bulk of connective tissue in the placentome. Indeed, the major change in the whole placentome was an increase in the ET_B receptor both at the mRNA and ligand binding levels.[51] These data on the radio-ligand binding and the mRNA in the isolated vessels are consistent with the observation that fetal arteries removed from the placentome showed an increased sensitivity to ET following dexamethasone exposure when studied in the myograph. Although these findings relate to blood vessels, they do demonstrate the care that must be taken when applying specific techniques to heterogeneous tissues.

Summary

The studies reported here illustrate some of the approaches that can be taken in combining systems and reductionist approaches to evaluation of the mechanisms that control the length of gestation. They demonstrate the importance of an understanding of the species that is being studied and a familiarity with the pitfalls that may present themselves.

References

1.   Dayes BA, Lye SJ. Characterization of myometrial desensitization to b-adrenergic agonists. *Can J Physiol Pharmacol* 1990;68:1377–84.

2.   Nathanielsz PW, Honnebier MB, Mecenas C, Jenkins SL, Holland ML, Demarest K. Effect of the oxytocin antagonist atosiban (1-deamino-2-D-tyr(OET)-4-thr-8-orn-vasotocin/oxytocin) on nocturnal myometrial contractions, maternal cardiovascular function, transplacental passage, and fetal oxygenation in the pregnant baboon during the last third of gestation. *Biol Reprod* 1997;57:320–24.

3.   Ivanisevic M, Behrens O, Helmer H, Demarest K, Fuchs AR. Vasopressin receptors in human pregnant myometrium and decidua: interactions with oxytocin and vasopressin agonists and antagonists. *Am J Obstet Gynecol* 1989;161:1637–43.

4.   Umscheid, CA, Wu WX, Gordan P, Nathanielsz PW. Up-regulation of oxytocin receptor messenger ribonucleic acid and protein by estradiol in the cervix of ovariectomized rat. *Biol Reprod* 1998;59:1131–8.

5.   Wu WX, Verbalis JG, Hoffman GE, Derks JB, Nathanielsz PW. Characterization of oxytocin (OT) receptor (OTR) expression and distribution in the late pregnant sheep myometrium and endometrium. *Endocrinology* 1996;137:722–8.

6.   Wu WX, Giussani DA Winter JA, Nathanielsz PW. Characterization of mRNA for steroid receptors and oxytocin receptor (OTR) in rhesus monkey myometrium and placenta during late pregnancy and labor. Society for Gynecologic Investigation Annual Meeting, 1997. Abstract no. 541.

7.   Liggins, GC, Kennedy PC, Holm LW. Failure of initiation of parturition after electrocoagulation of

the pituitary of the fetal lamb. *Am J Obstet Gynecol* 1967;96:1080–6.

8. McDonald TJ, Nathanielsz PW. Bilateral destruction of the fetal paraventricular nuclei prolongs gestation in sheep. *Am J Obstet Gynecol* 1991;1991:764–71.

9. Kitts DD, Stebenfeldt GH, Cupps PT, Bondurant RH, Anderson GB.A preliminary report on the initiation of parturition of ewes carrying fetuses of two different breeds. *Theriogenology* 1982;17:93.

10. Elsner CW, Magyar DM, Fridshal D, Eliot J, Klein A, Glatz T, *et al.* Time-trend analysis of plasma cortisol concentrations in the fetal sheep in relation to parturition. *Endocrinology* 1980;107:155–9.

11. Challis JRG, Brooks AN. Maturation and activation of hypothalamic–pituitary–adrenal function in fetal sheep. *Endocr Rev* 1989;10:182–204.

12. Bassett JM Thorburn GD. Foetal plasma corticosteroids and the initiation of parturition in sheep. *J Endocrinol* 1996;44:285–6.

13. Wilson L, Parsons MT, Flouret G. Forward shift in the initiation of the nocturnal estradiol surge in the pregnant babon: Is this the genesis of labor? *Am J Obstet Gynecol* 1991;165:1487–98.

14. Buster JE, Chang RJ, Preston DL, Elashoff RM, Cousins LM, Abraham GE, *et al.* Interrelationships of circulating maternal steroid concentrations in third trimester pregnancies II. C18 and C19 steroids: estradiol, estriol, dehydroepiandrosterone, dehydroepiandrosterone sulfate, 5-androstenediol, 4-androstenedione, testosterone, and dihydrotestosterone. *J Clin Endocrinol Metab* 1979;48:139–42.

15. Walsh SW, Kittinger GW, Novy MJ. Maternal peripheral concentrations of estradiol, estrone, cortisol, and progesterone during late pregnancy in rhesus monkeys (*Macaca mulatta*) and after experimental fetal anencephaly and fetal death. *Am J Obstet Gynecol* 1979;135:37–42.

16. Challis JRG. Sharp increase in free circulating oestrogens immediately before parturition in sheep. *Nature* 1971;229:208.

17. Germain AM, Kato S, Villarroel LA, Valenzuela GJ, Seron-Ferre M. Human term and preterm delivery is preceded by a rise in maternal plasma 17b-estradiol. *Prenat Neonatal Med* 1996;1:57–63.

18. Daniel SS, James LS, MacCarter G, Morishima HO, Stark RI. Long-term acid-base measurements in the fetal and maternal baboon. *Am J Obstet Gynecol* 1992;166:707–12.

19. Mecenas CA, Giussani DA, Owiny JR, Jenkins SL, Wu WX, Honnebier BO, *et al.* Production of premature delivery in pregnant rhesus monkeys by androstenedione infusion. *Nat Med* 1996;2:443–8.

20. Figueroa JP, Massmann A, Pimentel G, Nathanielsz PW. Characteristics of the electroyogram recorded from the mesometrium of the pregnant ewe from 106 days' gestation to delivery: similarities with and differences from the electromyogram obtained from the myometrium. *Am J Obstet Gynecol* 1987;157:991–8.

21. Honnebier MB, Jenkins SL, Wentworth RA, Figueroa JP, Nathanielsz PW. Temporal structuring of delivery in the absence of a photoperiod: preparturient myometrial activity of the rhesus monkey is related to maternal body temperature and depends on the maternal circadian system. *Biol Reprod* 1991;45:617–25.

22. Germain G, Cabrol D, Visser A, Sureau C. Electrical activity of the pregnant uterus in the cynomolgus monkey. *Am J Obstet Gynecol* 1982;142:513–19.

23. Morgan MA, Silavin SL, Payne GG, Fishburne JI, Nathanielsz PW. 24 hour rhythms in the chronically instrumented baboon during the second half of pregnancy. Society for Perinatal Obstetricians, January 23–27, 1990; Abstract 98.

24. Morgan MA, Silavin SL, Wentworth RA, Figueroa JP, Honnebier BO, Fishburne JI Jr, *et al.* Different patterns of myometrial activity and 24-h rhythms in myometrial contractility in the gravid baboon during the second half of pregnancy. *Biol Reprod* 1992;46:1158–64.

25. Germain AM, Valenzuela GJ, Ivankovic M, Ducsay CA, Gabella C, Seron-Ferre M. Relationship of circadian rhythms of uterine activity with term and preterm delivery. *Am J Obstet Gynecol* 1993;168:1271–7.

26. Nathanielsz PW. *Life Before Birth: The Challenges of Fetal Development*. New York: WH Freeman; 1996.

27. Novy MJ, Walsh SW. Dexamethasone and estradiol treatment in pregnant rhesus macaques: effects on gestational length, maternal plasma hormones, and fetal growth. *Am J Obstet Gynecol* 1983;145:920–31.

28. Nathanielsz PW, Jenkins SL, Tame JD, Winter JA, Guller S, Giussani DA. Local paracrine effects of estradiol are central to parturition in the rhesus monkey. *Nat Med* 1998;4:456–9.

29. MacDonald PC, Casey ML. The accumulation of prostaglandins (PG) in amniotic fluid is an aftereffect of labor and not indicative of a role for PGE2 or PGF2a in the initiation of human parturition. *J Clin Endocrinol Metab* 1993;76,1332–9.

30. Slater DM, Berger LC, Newton R, Moore GE, Bennett PR. Expression of cyclooxygenase types 1 and 2 in human fetal membranes at term. *Am J Obstet Gynecol* 1995;172:77–82.

31.   Wu WX, Ma XH, Smith GCS, Koenen SV, Nathanielsz PW. A new concept of the significance of regional distribution of prostaglandin H synthase 2 throughout the uterus during late pregnancy: investigations in a baboon model *Am J Obstet Gynecol* 2000;183:1287–95.

32.   Ou CW, Chen ZQ, Qi S, Lye SJ. Increased expression of the rat myometrial oxytocin receptor messenger ribonucleic acid during labor requires both mechanical and hormonal signals. *Biol Reprod* 1998;59:1055–61.

33.   Wu WX, Ma XH, Toshi Y, Shinozuka N, Nathanielsz PW. Differential expression of myometrial (Myo) oxytocin receptor (OTR) and prostaglandin H synthase (PGHS)2, but not estrogen receptor (ER) and heat shock protein (Hsp) 90 mRNA between the pregnant horn (PH) and non-pregnant horn (NPH) in sheep during betamethasone induced labor (BL). *Endocrinology,* 1999;140:5712–18.

34.   Hansen HS. 15-hydroxyprostaglandin dehydrogenase. A review. *Prostaglandins* 1976;12:647–9.

35.   Anggard E, Samuelsson B. Prostaglandins and related factors. 28. Metabolism of prostaglandin E1 in guinea pig lung: The structures of two metabolites. *J Biol Chem* 1964;239:4097–102.

36.   Cheung PYC, Walton JC, Tai HH, Rile SC, Challis JRG. Localization of 15-hydroxy prostaglandin dehydrogenase in human fetal membranes, decidua, and placenta during pregnancy. *Gynecol Obstet Invest* 1992;33:142–6.

37.   Sangha RK, Walton JC, Ensor CM, Tai HH, Challis JRG. Immunohistochemical localization, messenger ribonucleic acid abundance, and activity of 15-hydroxyprostaglandin dehydrogenase in placenta and fetal membranes during term and preterm labor. *J Clin Endocrinol Metab* 1994;78:982–9.

38.   Wu WX, Ma XH, Smith GCS, Mecenas CA, Koenen SV, Nathanielsz, PW. Prostaglandin dehydrogenase mRNA in baboon intrauterine tissues in late gestation and spontaneous labor. *Am J Physiol Regul Integr Comp Physiol* 2000; 279:R1082–90.

39.   Coleman RA, Kennedy I, Humphrey PPA, Bunce K, Lumley P. Prostanoids and their receptors. In: Emmett JC, editor. *Comprehensive Medicinal Chemistry: The Rational Design, Mechanistic Study and Therapeutic Application Of Chemical Compounds, Vol. 3. Membranes and Receptors.* Oxford: Pergamon Press; 1990. p. 643–714.

40.   Coleman RA, Grix SP, Head SA, Louttit JB, Mallett A, Sheldrick. A novel inhibitory prostanoid receptor in piglet saphenous vein. *Prostaglandins* 1994;47:151–68.

41.   Smith GCS, Baguma-Nibasheka M, Wu WX, Nathanielsz PW. Regional variations in contractile responses to prostaglandins and prostanoid receptor messenger ribonucleic acid in pregnant baboon uterus. *Am J Obstet Gynecol* 1998;179:1545–52.

42.   Garcia-Villar R, Green LR, Jenkins SL, Wentworth RA, Coleman RA, Nathanielsz PW. Evidence for the presence of AH13205-sensitive EP2 prostanoid receptors in the pregnant baboon but not in the pregnant sheep myometrium near term. *J Soc Gynecol Invest* 1995;2:6–12.

43.   Wikland M, Lindblom B, Wiqvist N. Myometrial response to prostaglandins during labor. *Gynecol Obstet Invest* 1984;17:131–8.

44.   Senior J, Marshall K, Sangha R, Clayton JK. In-vitro characterization of prostanoid receptors on human myometrium at term pregnancy. *Br J Pharmacol* 1993;108:501–6.

45.   Crankshaw DJ, Gaspar V. Pharmacological characterization *in vitro* of prostanoid receptors in the myometrium of nonpregnant ewes. *J Reprod Fertil* 1995;103:55–61.

46.   Smith GC, Wu WX, Nathanielsz PW. Effects of gestational age and labor on expression of prostanoid receptor genes in baboon uterus. *Biol Reprod* 2001;64:1131–7.

47.   Smith GC, Wu WX, Nathanielsz PW. Effects of gestational age and labor on the expression of prostanoid receptor genes in pregnant baboon cervix. *Prostaglandins* 2001;63:153–63.

48.   Smith GC, Wu WX, Nathanielsz PW. Expression of prostanoid receptor genes in baboon chorion and decidua during pregnancy and parturition. *J Endocrinol* 2001; 168:263–72.

49.   Uldbjerg N, Ekman G, Malmstrom A, Sporrong B, Ulmsten U, Wingerup L. Biochemical and morphological changes of human cervix after local application of prostaglandin E2 in pregnancy. *Lancet* 1981;i:267–8.

50.   Docherty CC, Kalmar-Nagy J, Engelen M, Koenen SV, Nijland MJ, Kuc RE, et al. Effect of *in vivo* fetal infusion of dexamethasone at 0.75 GA on fetal ovine resistance artery responses to ET-1. *Am J Physiol* 2001;281:R261–8.

51.   Kutzler MA, Molnar J, Schlafer DH, Kuc RE, Davenport AP, Nathanielsz PW. Maternal dexamethasone increases endothelin-1 sensitivity and endothelin A receptor expression in ovine foetal placental arteries. *Placenta* 2003;24:392–402.

Chapter 2

Control of the length of gestation: lessons from women

Roger Smith, Sam Mesiano, Richard Nicholson,
Tamas Zakar, Eng-Cheng Chan, Andrew Bisits, Vicki Clifton
and Warwick Giles

The clinical problem

Preterm birth occurs in 6–15% of pregnancies, accounts for 70% of neonatal mortality and is a common cause of intellectual handicap among survivors. Unfortunately the rates of preterm birth have not changed for over 30 years due to an inability to predict the event and the lack of effective therapies. This clinical problem has driven research into the mechanisms that regulate the timing of human birth and the disorders that cause preterm birth. For reasons of ethics, most experimental research in the past has focused on animal work, especially in sheep. This research has unfortunately revealed substantial differences between parturition in humans and that in other animals. This difficulty continues to restrict opportunities for interventional experimental studies of relevance to human parturition. Recent observational studies have started to clarify the mechanisms regulating the process and timing of human birth. This chapter outlines some of the progress made over the last decade in this area.

Parturition in mammals – and contrasts with human parturition

Genetic conflict and the evolution of parturition strategies

The astonishing variety of processes observed in mammalian pregnancy has stimulated debate on the evolutionary pressures that have produced this situation. David Haig[1] has cogently argued the paternal–maternal conflict hypothesis to explain the rapid evolutionary divergence that has occurred in reproductive processes. Under this hypothesis, paternal investment in any given pregnancy is restricted to that individual fetus to which he has contributed genetic material, as any other pregnancy carried by that mother may not be his progeny. From the maternal point of view, all of her offspring, current and future, are of equal value. The paternal genome acting through the fetus and placenta therefore has an interest in maximising the maternal resources contributed to that particular fetus even at the expense of other potential offspring of that mother. The mother has a strong interest in the fetus but may wish to modify its demands to preserve resources for future offspring. This setting of paternal–maternal conflict produces rapid evolutionary change as each participant seeks to push the see-saw in a different direction. For every metabolically advantageous mutation developed by the paternal genome the mother will seek a modifying or restricting contrary change. For these reasons, extrapolations from experiments conducted in reproductive processes in one mammal to another are particularly hazardous.

Progesterone withdrawal

In the majority of mammals, parturition is associated with a fall in circulating progesterone concentrations, and often a rise in circulating oestrogens (Figure 2.1). This is seen as a type of switch from the pro-pregnancy environment created by high concentrations of progesterone to the parturition-inducing phenotype created by oestrogen. Progesterone is a 'pro-gestation' hormone: it promotes and sustains the pregnant state. The essential role of progesterone in maintaining pregnancy is unequivocal and remarkably universal. It is aptly referred to as the hormone of pregnancy. In all mammals studied to date, no naturally occurring conditions have been identified in which pregnancy exists in the absence of progesterone. Moreover, labour and delivery rapidly ensue if progesterone synthesis or actions are disrupted. Progesterone maintains pregnancy, in large part, by promoting myometrial relaxation and quiescence. Importantly, progesterone is thought actively to block the trans-formation of the myometrium to a contractile phenotype. In 1956, Csapo[2] proposed that removal of the 'progesterone block' initiates labour and delivery. It is now generally accepted that progesterone withdrawal is a pivotal event in the mammalian parturition cascade.

Different mammals use different mechanisms to create the withdrawal of progesterone. In most mammals, parturition is preceded by a fall in circulating maternal progesterone levels due to decreased placental secretion (sheep, cattle) or regression of the corpus luteum (rats, mice, rabbits, goats and pigs).[3-6] However, in

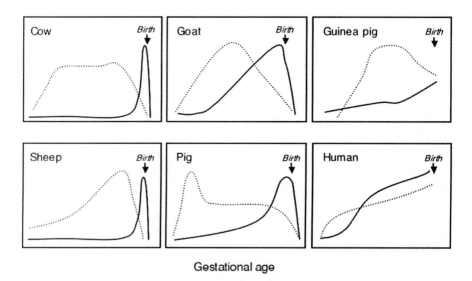

Gestational age

Figure 2.1. Oestrogen (solid line) and progesterone (dotted line) profiles during pregnancy in a range of mammals

humans (and in higher primates and guinea pigs), maternal, fetal and amniotic fluid progesterone levels do not fall prior to labour onset. Instead, progesterone remains elevated and in some cases continues to increase until birth.[7-9] Despite the persistently high levels of progesterone in pregnant women, progesterone withdrawal remains a principal candidate mechanism for the control of human parturition, since synthetic progesterone antagonists (e.g. mifepristone) or agents that decrease progesterone production (e.g. inhibitors of the 3β hydroxysteroid dehydrogenase enzyme) initiate labour and delivery at all stages of pregnancy.[10,11] Clearly, progesterone withdrawal in human parturition cannot be attributed to changes in its circulating progesterone levels. Instead, it is generally accepted that human parturition is precipitated by a 'functional' progesterone withdrawal, whereby actions of progesterone on the pregnant myometrium are nullified.

Role of the fetal hypothalamic–pituitary axis

In sheep, pioneering work by Mont Liggins and colleagues[12-14] demonstrated that the timing of parturition is determined by the activity of the fetal hypothalamic–pituitary–adrenal (HPA) axis. Such an interaction serves to coordinate fetal maturation with the timing of birth. Late in pregnancy, possibly stimulated by placentally derived prostaglandin E2 (PGE_2),[15] the fetal hypothalamus releases increased amounts of the neuropeptide corticotrophin-releasing hormone (CRH), which stimulates fetal pituitary adrenocorticotrophic hormone (ACTH) secretion, leading to increased cortisol production by the fetal adrenals. Rising concentrations of fetal cortisol induce placental expression of 17α hydroxylase leading to conversion of progesterone to oestrogen (Figure 2.2). Maternal progesterone levels consequently fall while oestrogen rises. Rising levels of oestrogen initiate transcription of many contraction-associated genes in the myometrium, such as that coding for the oxytocin receptor (OTr). These changes lead to the onset of labour in the sheep. Damage to the sheep fetal hypothalamus,

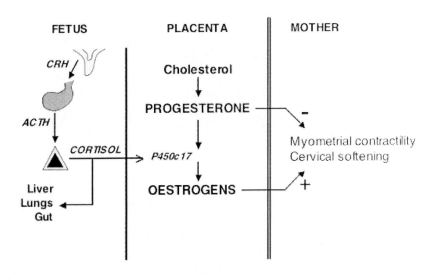

Figure 2.2. Regulation of oestrogen and progesterone production in sheep pregnancy

pituitary or adrenal or administration of a CRH antagonist[16] prevent parturition and prolong pregnancy even to the extent of maternal death due to continued fetal growth and abdominal compression. In contrast, parturition can be initiated prematurely by the administration of ACTH or cortisol to the sheep fetus.

Unlike the sheep, the activity of the human fetal HPA axis does not appear to influence the timing of birth (Figure 2.3). Clinical conditions occur in the human where the fetal hypothalamus, pituitary or adrenal fail to develop or conversely are hyperactive, yet labour occurs close to the normal time. A major difference between human and ovine parturition is that pregnant women do not remain pregnant indefinitely, regardless of the presence of pathology, while preterm delivery is common. Clearly, the sheep is not an ideal experimental model for human parturition.

Parturition in primates

If the sheep is not a particularly good model for the human, surely primates are better? While it is clear that pregnancy among the different primates is more similar than between primates and other mammalian classes, there are intriguing differences. The neuropeptide CRH is produced in the placentas of all primates studied except the lemurs and not at all in nonprimates.[17,18] However, the pattern of production of this peptide and its concentrations in maternal plasma vary considerably across the primates. While an exponential rise is seen across gestation in apes, baboons show a peak in midpregnancy,[19,20] as does the New World marmoset (unpublished observations). In the context of placental CRH production, apes provide a good model of human parturition;[20] however, experimental studies in apes are, if anything, harder to perform than those in humans because of ethical issues, availability of animals, expense and dangers related to human pathogens present in apes.

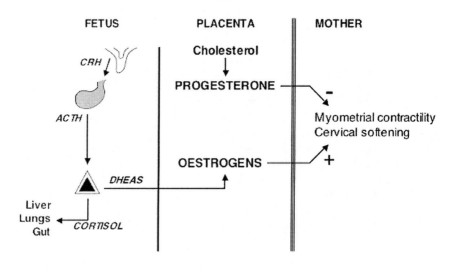

Figure 2.3. Mechanisms leading to production of oestrogens and progesterone throughout human pregnancy

Although animal studies will continue to provide important clues for understanding human reproductive physiology, direct extrapolation is evidently not appropriate in the area of parturition control. Experimental studies in humans are not ethically possible. On some occasions nature's experiments, in the form of naturally occurring mutations, provide valuable insights into physiology but, in general, recent human research has progressed through observational studies.

The timing of human birth

Studies on the regulation of the timing of human birth have addressed two related but different questions: how is the duration of gestation determined and how are the events of labour precipitated? The questions have different clinical corollaries: how can we predict which women are likely to deliver prematurely and how can we prevent preterm labour? Effective methods to identify women at high risk of preterm delivery are lacking. Apart from the obvious benefit for clinical treatment regimens, such a measurement would be helpful to establish trials of methods to prevent preterm delivery since women at low risk of preterm delivery would be saved from needless exposure to experimental protocols.

Predicting the timing of human birth

While many biochemical markers have been examined for their ability to predict preterm delivery the most extensive studies have been conducted on maternal plasma CRH. Placental production and maternal plasma concentrations of CRH increase exponentially through gestation peaking at the time of delivery. Early studies showed that women in preterm labour have elevated maternal plasma CRH concentrations compared with gestational-age matched controls.[21,22] Subsequently, prospective longitudinal studies revealed that women destined to deliver preterm tend to have a more rapid exponential rise in CRH during midpregnancy.[23,24] In contrast, women delivering post-term have a slower rate of rise. Thus, the rate of placental CRH production during mid-gestation appears to be a marker for the length of gestation.

Several important concepts arose from this work. Firstly, it established that, for at least a proportion of women, it is possible to predict the timing of delivery months in advance. This raised the possibility of developing useful diagnostic tests to identify women at high risk of preterm delivery and it may facilitate the establishment of therapeutic trials of treatment to prevent preterm birth. Secondly, the work established that events early in pregnancy have an influence on the subsequent timing of birth. Understanding the regulation of placental CRH expression may therefore provide insights into the determination of gestational length. This is particularly so as additional studies have indicated that the rate of rise of maternal plasma CRH varies in different pathological conditions. For example, a rapid rise occurs in women who require iatrogenic preterm delivery for fetal reasons.[25]

Regulation of placental CRH expression

Regulation of CRH production has been explored in human placental tissue.[26] These studies are largely performed in purified cytotrophoblast cells which differentiate in culture into the syncytiotrophoblast cells that synthesise CRH.[27] Interestingly, *in vitro* studies showed that glucocorticoids, in contrast to their inhibitory effects on CRH production by hypothalamic cells, stimulate CRH secretion by placental cells. Emanuel *et al.*[28] have demonstrated that the exponential increase observed in human pregnancy can be well reproduced using a model that incorporates positive feed forward between CRH and glucocorticoids. Using transfections of CRH promoter constructs, the mechanism for glucocorticoid stimulation of placental CRH expression has been partially elucidated. In placental tissue, glucocorticoids stimulate CRH gene expression by interacting with proteins that bind to the cyclic adenosine monophosphate (cAMP) response element (CRE) of the CRH promoter.[29] The difference in behaviour of the CRH gene in the placenta and hypothalamus appears to be due to the expression of different transcription factors, co-activators and co-repressors in these two cell types.[30] In the placenta, Jun is found binding to the CRE while in the pituitary cell line AtT10 (in which glucocorticoids stimulate CRH expression) Fos is more prominent in its binding. A picture is therefore gradually developing of the multiple protein complex that binds to the CRH promoter and regulates transcription in the placenta (Figure 2.4).

Apart from the stimulatory effect of glucocorticoids, which has been replicated *in vivo*,[31] little is known of the endocrine regulation of placental CRH production. cAMP analogues are potent stimulators of CRH production but it is not clear what external signals may be driving cAMP-stimulated CRH production. Oestrogens have been shown to inhibit CRH secretion and nitric oxide inhibits CRH secretion but not synthesis.[32,33]

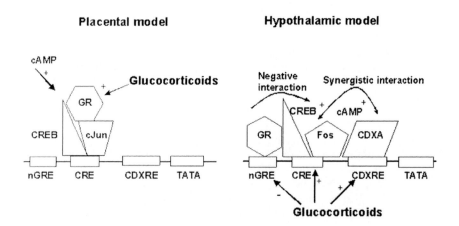

Figure 2.4. Schematic models of CRH promoter regulation. Regulatory interactions on the CRH gene promoter are shown for the placenta (left panel) and the hypothalamus (right panel). The nGRE is a negative glucocorticoid regulatory element, CRE is the cAMP regulatory element, CDXRE is the caudal type homeobox response element, GRR represents the region located between −213 to −99 bps that is stimulated by glucocorticoids in the hypothalamic model, and TATA is the TATA box binding site for basal transcriptional proteins. Stimulatory (+) and inhibitory (−) regulatory effects by cAMP and glucocorticoids through the different elements are shown with thin arrows; negative (thick curved arrow) and synergistic stimulatory (double headed arrow) interactions between sites are also shown. The regulatory proteins identified, so far, are represented by different shapes containing their names

Roles of placental CRH in the initiation of labour

While the association of maternal plasma CRH with the timing of birth is robust, it is unclear how CRH may be directly linked to the onset of labour. CRH receptors have been identified on the myometrium but these are predominantly associated with $G\alpha_s$ proteins which activate adenylyl cyclase and lead to increased cAMP and pathways that promote relaxation rather than contraction.[34] However, different receptor isoforms may be expressed at the end of pregnancy that are less efficient at stimulating cAMP formation and may therefore move the balance within the myometrial cell towards contraction. Alternatively, placental CRH released into the fetal circulation may act on the fetal pituitary to stimulate ACTH production, thereby increasing cortisol synthesis and driving parturition in a manner analogous to that seen in the sheep (possibly by increasing prostaglandin production in the fetal membranes).[35] Finally, CRH may act on the fetal adrenal, and perhaps the maternal adrenal, to drive dehydroepiandrosterone sulphate (DHEA-S) production.[36] In the human, DHEA-S, supplied mainly by the fetal adrenal cortex, is an obligate precursor for placental oestradiol formation. This mechanism may drive a progressively increasing concentration of oestrogen, which activates contraction-associated genes. However, it is also possible that rising concentrations of CRH merely represent a marker of progressive fetoplacental maturation that is itself, through other pathways, associated with the onset of labour.

It appears that conditions at the beginning of pregnancy determine the trajectory of CRH production by the placenta.[37] Once established, this trajectory of exponential increase may be maintained by a positive feed forward system involving glucocorticoids possibly damped by oestrogens. The production of oestrogens may be regulated by CRH stimulation of DHEA-S synthesis by the fetal adrenal cortex which expresses CRH receptors.[36]

The trajectory of CRH production may be increased by an adverse fetal intrauterine environment. Elevated maternal CRH has been observed in pregnancies complicated by pre-eclampsia, reduced Doppler flow studies and where fetal distress has led to elective preterm delivery.[37,38] Whether these increases are due to increased fetal or maternal cortisol production is unclear. Such increases in maternal CRH may have a protective effect since CRH is a powerful vasodilator in both the maternal and placental vascular trees.[39] CRH appears to regulate endothelial function by stimulating mast cell degranulation and increasing release of nitric oxide which produces vasodilatation.

The length of gestation may therefore be determined by factors that set the initial rate of production of CRH or by factors later in pregnancy, which alter the trajectory of CRH.

Not all cases of preterm delivery are associated with elevated concentrations of CRH. Infection does not appear to be associated with increased CRH production. It seems likely that the pathway to delivery can be activated independently of CRH. For these reasons maternal plasma CRH has a relatively high specificity but lower sensitivity.[40,41] That is, if CRH is high, it is likely to be associated with preterm delivery but a low CRH does not preclude preterm birth.

Mechanism for the initiation of labour

The myometrium is the engine of birth and its transformation and activation from a quiescent to a contractile state is a pivotal event in the parturition process. Therefore, a critical issue in understanding the process of human parturition is to determine the biochemical and physiological underpinnings of this remarkable transformation and how it is controlled. In recent years several studies have sought to identify the genes responsible for the initiation of labour by examining differences in protein and gene expression profiles between myometrial tissues obtained at caesarean section either prior to, or after, the onset of labour. An early report identified a reduction in the expression of the $G\alpha_s$ subunit required for pathways leading to myometrial relaxation.[42] This suggested a change in the balance of contractile versus relaxatory forces with the onset of labour. More recent studies have used similar approaches to examine both specific and broad targets. This body of observational data, which is expanding rapidly, is significantly contributing to our understanding of the mechanism by which labour is initiated.

Functional progesterone withdrawal and myometrial contractility

A key difficulty in understanding human labour is to reconcile how labour occurs despite the continued presence of high concentrations of circulating progesterone. In most mammals, labour is associated with a profound fall in circulating progesterone concentrations but this does not occur in humans or the great apes. This conundrum has been addressed by examining the hypothesis that progesterone withdrawal in human parturition is mediated by a functional desensitisation of the myometrium to circulating progesterone. Several studies have shown that changes in progesterone receptor (PR) expression in the myometrium may facilitate this functional progesterone withdrawal.[43,44]

The human PR exists as two major isoforms generated as splice variants of the single gene: the full-length PR-B and the truncated PR-A. Importantly, PR-A lacks a key activating domain and consequently, in most cell systems, including primary cultures of human pregnancy myometrial cells, this PR dominantly represses progesterone actions mediated through PR-B. In fact, it is generally accepted that the target cell progesterone responsiveness is inversely related to the PR-A/PR-B expression ratio. This raises the possibility that functional progesterone withdrawal in human parturition is mediated by increased myometrial expression of PR-A. This issue was investigated and indeed it was found that the onset of labour at term is associated with a significant increase in myometrial expression of PR-A and in the PR-A/PR-B expression ratio.[43,44] Interestingly, in non-labouring term myometrium the PR-A/PR-B expression ratio correlates positively with expression of important contraction-associated genes including oestrogen receptor-α (ERα) and the OTr. Thus, women at term with high levels of myometrial PR-A/PR-B also have high levels of ERα and OTr expression.

These intriguing associations led Mesiano *et al.*[44] to propose a link between functional progesterone withdrawal, mediated by an increase in the myometrial PR-A/PR-B expression ratio, and functional oestrogen activation mediated by an increase in ERα expression. Their model for the control of myometrial contractility in human parturition (Figure 2.5) predicts that for most of pregnancy progesterone acting through PR-B maintains quiescence, in part by desensitising the myometrium to oestrogen via inhibition of ERα expression. At parturition, myometrial PR-A expression gradually rises leading to a rise in PR-A/PR-B and a consequent fall in progesterone responsiveness. This effectively removes the inhibition of ERα expression leading to the observed coordinate increase in ERα mRNA abundance. Increased ERα would then allow circulating oestrogens, which are high for most of human pregnancy, to augment expression of contraction-associated genes such as OTr and transform the myometrium to a contractile phenotype. Importantly, an increase in the PR-A/PR-B

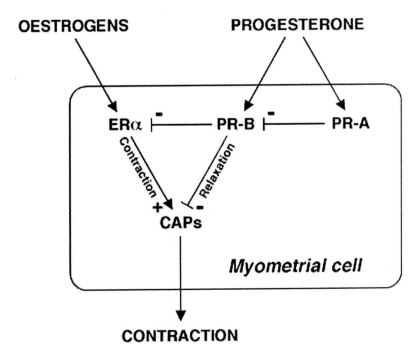

Figure 2.5. A model for the interactions between PR-A and PR-B leading to functional progesterone withdrawal and the onset of parturition in the human myometrium at term; reproduced with permission from Mesiano *et al.*[44]

ratio was also associated with increased concentrations of mRNA for the prostaglandin synthesising enzyme cyclooxygenase 2 (COX-2). Thus, increased myometrial expression of PR-A drives the balance towards contraction by inducing functional progesterone withdrawal and indirectly facilitating functional oestrogen activation. This model explains:

- how progesterone withdrawal and oestrogen activation are coordinated in human parturition even though the uterus is exposed to very high levels of these steroids throughout most of pregnancy
- why the human myometrium is refractory to the high levels of circulating oestrogens for most of pregnancy
- why disruption of progesterone action alone (e.g. with mifepristone) triggers the full parturition cascade
- why birth cannot be prevented by progesterone treatment
- why labour is not induced prematurely by oestrogen treatment or overproduction.

Inflammation

A school of thought has for many years suggested that inflammation is a major component of the pathway to parturition and that it represents the loss of the immune tolerance shown by the mother for the fetal tissues. Inflammation appears to play a major role in the onset of parturition in the murine model.[45] Progesterone is known to have anti-inflammatory properties and perhaps the pathways may be linked by withdrawal of the anti-inflammatory effects of progesterone as PR-A is expressed.

Recent data from Madsen *et al.*,[46] using a human myometrial cell line, suggest that prostaglandins (PGs), and possibly other agonists acting via the protein kinase C pathway, increase the PR-A/PR-B expression ratio and potentially induce functional progesterone withdrawal. These data indicate that in humans PGs have the potential to induce functional progesterone withdrawal by modulating myometrial PR isoform expression. This may be pivotal in the setting of intrauterine infection, since resident or attracted pro-inflammatory cells may produce PGs that promote preterm birth by causing functional progesterone withdrawal. These findings provide important new insights into PG action in the control of human parturition. Prostaglandin production is known to play a key role in parturition in many mammals, for example the prostaglandin-mediated luteolysis that occurs in goats, and, even in humans, prostaglandins are potent stimulators of parturition and they are used clinically.

Several studies have explored the cohort of genes involved in the transformation of the myometrium to a contractile phenotype required for labour and delivery. Chan *et al.*,[47] using a subtraction hybridisation approach, identified a number of genes that are upregulated at the time of labour. Interestingly, many of these genes, such as interleukin-8 (IL-8), are known to be involved in inflammatory activation pathways (Table 2.1). Recent cloning experiments have provided unexpected clues. The breakdown of maternal tolerance for the fetal allograft had been proposed to play a role in parturition, yet the normal birth of a foal born to her genetically identical mother makes this hypothesis less likely.[48]

Interestingly, administration of progesterone to women at high risk of preterm delivery, either intramuscularly or intravaginally, decreases the incidence of preterm birth primarily by increasing the effectiveness of tocolytics.[49–51] Whether this occurs via a non-genomic effect of progesterone (e.g. via the OTr[52]) or by the anti-inflammatory action of progesterone or some other mechanism remains unclear. Nevertheless, these observations represent an important clue as to the nature of human parturition.

Table 2.1. Genes identified by subtractive hybridisation that are upregulated in labour

Gene	GenBank accession no.
Known genes	
Oxytocin receptor	X64878
Matrix metalloproteinase 9 (MMP-9)	NM004994
Fibronectin	U60068
Interleukin-8 (IL-8)	M28130
Genes not previously linked with labour	
MnSOD	M23613
B23	X57351
IFN 1-8d	J04617
EF1α	Y00052
Cyclophilin	X13839
α-Actin	

Four novel genes were also identified with no matching sequences in databases

Prostaglandins from the fetal membranes

Prostaglandin synthesis inhibitors are effective tocolytics and prostaglandin preparations are effective in promoting labour. A model of parturition would therefore be incomplete without addressing the role played by this class of compounds. Intrauterine prostaglandin concentrations critically depend on prostaglandin production by the fetal membranes. The amnion is a major producer of PGE_2 and the capacity of this tissue to generate prostaglandin is controlled by the level of the key prostaglandin biosynthetic enzyme PGHS-2 (prostaglandin endoperoxide H synthase-2), also known as COX-2. COX-2 activity and COX-2 mRNA abundance increases in the amnion at late gestation and labour in conjunction with increasing intrauterine prostaglandin levels. The group led by Tamas Zakar has made significant progress in exploring the mechanisms that regulate amniotic COX-2 expression at labour.[53] COX-2 is an inducible enzyme encoded by a typical immediate-early gene that is transiently induced by cytokines, growth factors, and many other agonists in a cell-specific fashion.[54] By comparing COX-2 gene activity with COX-2 mRNA abundance in a series of amnion samples collected before and after labour, evidence has been produced that suggests that gene activity determines the level of COX-2 mRNA and, in turn, of COX-2 activity, in the tissues. The stability of the COX-2 mRNA corresponded to the stability of constitutively expressed mRNAs, suggesting that COX-2 induction in the amnion is not transient at term. Moreover, short-term explant incubations indicated that factors produced endogenously in the amnion membrane maintain COX-2 gene activity and drive the accumulation of COX-2 mRNA, possibly increasing enzyme expression in a continuous, persistent manner. The results suggest that the expression of COX-2 assumes a constitutive phenotype in the amnion at the time of labour. This phenotype is characterised by an endogenous mechanism maintaining gene activity and by the stabilisation of the resulting mRNA. The consequence is the continually increasing capacity of the amnion membrane to produce the labour-promoting PGE_2, which probably contributes to the clinically irreversible progress of parturition. The mechanism that generates this change in tissue character remains uncertain.

Production of prostaglandins is therefore capable of stimulating production of the shortened form of the progesterone receptor, PR-A. PR-A is, in turn, capable of causing progesterone withdrawal, oestrogen activation and increased production of the mRNA coding for COX-2, the prostaglandin synthetic enzyme. All the components therefore exist to generate a positive feed forward loop driving the process of parturition.

Other factors

Uterine stretch

Work from Steve Lye's laboratory in Toronto, Canada suggests that physical factors in the form of stretch may play a role, perhaps explaining the earlier onset of labour observed in multigravidas and in the presence of a large fetus.[55]

Nutritional state

Recent work in animals has suggested that the nutritional state of the mother at conception can influence the length of gestation.[15,56] This is the type of clue such comparative studies can provide. We should not expect the situation in humans to be identical but parallels may exist. Other data from studies in Israel suggest that nutritional restriction, such as during religious ceremonies, can initiate labour.

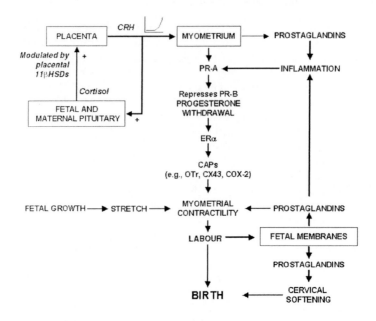

Figure 2.6. Proposed model for the control of human parturition

Conclusions

Although the full picture remains to be assembled, the parts are beginning to take shape (Figure 2.6). While other possibilities exist, one model would incorporate CRH production in early pregnancy linked to the timing of birth. The molecules that interact with the CRH promoter are being defined and glucocorticoids acting through the CRE appear important in driving the exponential increase in placental CRH synthesis. As labour approaches, progesterone withdrawal is achieved by increased production of the shortened progesterone receptor, PR-A, leading to oestrogen receptor expression. Prostaglandins, probably from the chorion, further stimulate PR-A expression, leading to a positive feed forward system linking inflammation and both myometrial activation and cervical softening and the eventual delivery of the fetus. How the events of early pregnancy and labour are linked remains obscure. Greater understanding of this fundamental aspect of human biology may place the treatment of women in preterm labour on a more rational basis and perhaps reduce the frequency of cerebral palsy and other devastating consequences of preterm birth.

References

1. Haig D. Genetic conflicts in human pregnancy. *Q Rev Biol* 1993;68:495–532.
2. Csapo A. Progesterone block. *Am J Anat* 1956;98:273–91.
3. Liggins GC, Fairclough RJ, Grieves SA, Kendall JZ, Knox BS. The mechanism of initiation of parturition in the ewe. *Recent Prog Horm Res* 1973;29:111–59.

4.   Liggins GC. Endocrinology of parturition. In: Novy MJ, Resko JA, editors. *Fetal Endocrinology.* New York: Academic Press, Inc.; 1981. p. 211–37.
5.   Challis JRG and Lye SJ. Parturition. In: Knobil E, Neil JD, editors. *The Physiology of Reproduction.* New York: Raven Press; 1994. p. 985–1031.
6.   Young IR. The comparative physiology of parturition in mammals. *Front Horm Res* 2001;27:10–30.
7.   Tulchinsky D, Hobel CJ, Yeager E, Marshall JR. Plasma estrone, estradiol, estriol, progesterone, and 17-hydroxyprogesterone in human pregnancy. I. Normal pregnancy. *Am J Obstet Gynecol* 1972;112:1095–100.
8.   Boroditsky RS, Reyes FI, Winter JS, Faiman C. Maternal serum estrogen and progesterone concentrations preceding normal labour. *Obstet Gynecol* 1978;51:686–91.
9.   Walsh SW, Stanczyk FZ, Novy MJ. Daily hormonal changes in the maternal, fetal, and amniotic fluid compartments before parturition in a primate species. *J Clin Endocrinol Metab* 1984;58:629–39.
10.   Selinger M, Mackenzie IZ, Gillmer MD, Phipps SL, Ferguson J. Progesterone inhibition in mid-trimester termination of pregnancy: physiological and clinical effects. *Br J Obstet Gynaecol* 1987;94:1218–22.
11.   Haluska GJ, Cook MJ, Novy MJ. Inhibition and augmentation of progesterone production during pregnancy: effects on parturition in rhesus monkeys. *Am J Obstet Gynecol* 1997;176:682–91.
12.   Liggins GC. Fetal influences on myometrial contractility. *Clin Obstet Gynecol* 1973;16:148–65.
13.   Liggins GC. The physiological role of prostaglandins in parturition. *J Reprod Fertil Suppl* 1973;18:143–50.
14.   Liggins GC. Mechanisms of the onset of labour: the New Zealand perspective. *Aust N Z J Obstet Gynaecol* 1994;34:338–42.
15.   Young IR, Loose JM, Kleftogiannis F, Canny BJ. Prostaglandin E2 acts via the hypothalamus to stimulate ACTH secretion in the fetal sheep. *J Neuroendocrinol* 1996;8:713–20.
16.   Chan EC, Falconer J, Madsen G, Rice KC, Webster EL, Chrousos GP, *et al.* A corticotropin-releasing hormone type I receptor antagonist delays parturition in sheep. *Endocrinology* 1998;139:3357–60.
17.   Robinson BG, D'Angio LA Jr, Pasieka KB, Majzoub JA. Preprocorticotropin releasing hormone: cDNA sequence and in vitro processing. *Mol Cell Endocrinol* 1989;61:175–80.
18.   Bowman ME, Lopata A, Jaffe RB, Golos TG, Wickings J, Smith R. Corticotropin-releasing hormone-binding protein in primates. *Am J Primatol* 2001;53:123–30.
19.   Goland RS, Wardlaw SL, Fortman JD, Stark RI. Plasma corticotropin-releasing factor concentrations in the baboon during pregnancy. *Endocrinology* 1992;131:1782–6.
20.   Smith R, Wickings EJ, Bowman ME, Belleoud A, Dubreuil G, Davies JJ, *et al.* Corticotropin-releasing hormone in chimpanzee and gorilla pregnancies. *J Clin Endocrinol Metab* 1999;84:2820–5.
21.   Goland RS, Wardlaw SL, Stark RI, Brown LS Jr, Frantz AG. High levels of corticotropin-releasing hormone immunoactivity in maternal and fetal plasma during pregnancy. *J Clin Endocrinol Metab* 1986;63:1199–203.
22.   Wolfe CD, Patel SP, Campbell EA, Linton EA, Anderson J, Lowry PJ, *et al.* Plasma corticotrophin-releasing factor (CRF) in normal pregnancy. *Br J Obstet Gynaecol* 1988;95:997–1002.
23.   McLean M, Bisits A, Davies J, Woods R, Lowry P, Smith R. A placental clock controlling the length of human pregnancy. *Nat Med* 1995;1:460–3.
24.   Inder WJ, Prickett TC, Ellis MJ, Hull L, Reid R, Benny PS, *et al.* The utility of plasma CRH as a predictor of preterm delivery. *J Clin Endocrinol Metab* 2001;86:5706–10.
25.   McGrath S, McLean M, Smith D, Bisits A, Giles W, Smith R. Maternal plasma corticotropin-releasing hormone trajectories vary depending on the cause of preterm delivery. *Am J Obstet Gynecol* 2002;186:257–60.
26.   Petraglia F, Sutton S, Vale W. Neurotransmitters and peptides modulate the release of immunoreactive corticotropin-releasing factor from cultured human placental cells. *Am J Obstet Gynecol* 1989;160:247–51.
27.   Riley SC, Walton JC, Herlick JM, Challis JR. The localization and distribution of corticotropin-releasing hormone in the human placenta and fetal membranes throughout gestation. *J Clin Endocrinol Metab* 1991;72:1001–7.
28.   Emanuel RL, Robinson BG, Seely EW, Graves SW, Kohane I, Saltzman D, *et al.* Corticotrophin releasing hormone levels in human plasma and amniotic fluid during gestation. *Clin Endocrinol (Oxf)* 1994;40:257–62.
29.   Cheng YH, Nicholson RC, King B, Chan EC, Fitter JT, Smith R. Glucocorticoid stimulation of corticotropin-releasing hormone gene expression requires a cyclic adenosine 3',5'-monophosphate regulatory element in human primary placental cytotrophoblast cells. *J Clin Endocrinol Metab* 2000;85:1937–45.
30.   King BR, Smith R, Nicholson RC. Novel glucocorticoid and cAMP interactions on the CRH gene

promoter. *Mol Cell Endocrinol* 2002;194:19–28.

31.   Korebrits C, Yu DH, Ramirez MM, Marinoni E, Bocking AD, Challis JR. Antenatal glucocorticoid administration increases corticotrophin-releasing hormone in maternal plasma. *Br J Obstet Gynaecol* 1998;105:556–61.

32.   Ni X, Chan EC, Fitter JT, Smith R. Nitric oxide inhibits corticotropin-releasing hormone exocytosis but not synthesis by cultured human trophoblasts. *J Clin Endocrinol Metab* 1997;82:4171–5.

33.   Ni X, Nicholson RC, King BR, Chan EC, Read MA, Smith R. Estrogen represses whereas the estrogen-antagonist ICI 182780 stimulates placental CRH gene expression. *J Clin Endocrinol Metab* 2002;87:3774–8.

34.   Grammatopoulos D, Dai Y, Chen J, Karteris E, Papadopoulou N, Easton AJ, *et al.* Human corticotropin-releasing hormone receptor: differences in subtype expression between pregnant and nonpregnant myometria. *J Clin Endocrinol Metab* 1998;83:2539–44.

35.   Patel FA, Funder JW, Challis JR. Mechanism of cortisol/progesterone antagonism in the regulation of 15-hydroxyprostaglandin dehydrogenase activity and messenger ribonucleic acid levels in human chorion and placental trophoblast cells at term. *J Clin Endocrinol Metab* 2003;88:2922–33.

36.   Smith R, Mesiano S, Chan EC, Brown S, Jaffe RB. Corticotropin-releasing hormone directly and preferentially stimulates dehydroepiandrosterone sulfate secretion by human fetal adrenal cortical cells. *J Clin Endocrinol Metab* 1998;83:2916–20.

37.   McGrath S, McLean M, Smith D, Bisits A, Giles W, Smith R. Maternal plasma corticotropin-releasing hormone trajectories vary depending on the cause of preterm delivery. *Am J Obstet Gynecol* 2002;186:257–60.

38.   Giles WB, McLean M, Davies JJ, Smith R. Abnormal umbilical artery Doppler waveforms and cord blood corticotropin-releasing hormone. *Obstet Gynecol* 1996;87:107–11.

39.   Clifton VL, Read MA, Leitch IM, Giles WB, Boura AL, Robinson PJ, *et al.* Corticotropin-releasing hormone-induced vasodilatation in the human fetal-placental circulation: involvement of the nitric oxide-cyclic guanosine 3',5'-monophosphate-mediated pathway. *J Clin Endocrinol Metab* 1995;80:2888–93.

40.   Inder WJ, Prickett TC, Ellis MJ, Hull L, Reid R, Benny PS, *et al.* The utility of plasma CRH as a predictor of preterm delivery. *J Clin Endocrinol Metab* 2001;86:5706–10.

41.   Ellis MJ, Livesey JH, Inder WJ, Prickett TC, Reid R. Plasma corticotropin-releasing hormone and unconjugated estriol in human pregnancy: gestational patterns and ability to predict preterm delivery. *Am J Obstet Gynecol* 2002;186:94–9.

42.   Europe-Finner GN, Phaneuf S, Watson SP, López Bernal A. Identification and expression of G-proteins in human myometrium: upregulation of G alpha s in pregnancy. *Endocrinology* 1993;132:2484–90.

43.   Pieber D, Allport VC, Hills F, Johnson M, Bennett PR. Interactions between progesterone receptor isoforms in myometrial cells in human labour. *Mol Hum Reprod* 2001;7:875–9.

44.   Mesiano S, Chan EC, Fitter JT, Kwek K, Yeo G, Smith R. Progesterone withdrawal and estrogen activation in human parturition are coordinated by progesterone receptor A expression in the myometrium. *J Clin Endocrinol Metab* 2002;87:2924–30.

45.   Bethin KE, Nagai Y, Sladek R, Asada M, Sadovsky Y, Hudson TJ, *et al.* Microarray analysis of uterine gene expression in mouse and human pregnancy. *Mol Endocrinol* 2003;17:1454–69.

46.   Madsen G, Zakar T, Ku CY, Sanborn BM, Smith R, Mesiano S. Prostaglandins differentially modulate progesterone receptor-A and -B expression in human myometrial cells: evidence for prostaglandin-induced functional progesterone withdrawal. *J Clin Endocrinol Metab* 2004;89:1010–3.

47.   Chan EC, Fraser S, Yin S, Yeo G, Kwek K, Fairclough RJ, *et al.* Human myometrial genes are differentially expressed in labour: a suppression subtractive hybridization study. *J Clin Endocrinol Metab* 2002;87:2435–41.

48.   Galli C, Lagutina I, Crotti G, Colleoni S, Turini P, Ponderato N, *et al.* Pregnancy: a cloned horse born to its dam twin. *Nature* 2003;424:635. Erratum in: *Nature* 2003;425:680.

49.   Meis PJ, Klebanoff M, Thom E, Dombrowski MP, Sibai B, Moawad AH, *et al.* Prevention of recurrent preterm delivery by 17 alpha-hydroxyprogesterone caproate. National Institute of Child Health and Human Development Maternal-Fetal Medicine Units Network. *N Engl J Med* 2003;348:2379–85. Erratum in: *N Engl J Med* 2003;349:1299.

50.   Pomianowski K. Natural progesterone prevents preterm birth in high-risk pregnancies. *J Fam Pract* 2003;52:522–3.

51.   da Fonseca EB, Bittar RE, Carvalho MH, Zugaib M. Prophylactic administration of progesterone by vaginal suppository to reduce the incidence of spontaneous preterm birth in women at increased risk: a randomized placebo-controlled double-blind study. *Am J Obstet Gynecol* 2003;188:419–24.

52.   Zingg HH, Grazzini E, Breton C, Larcher A, Rozen F, Russo C, *et al.* Genomic and nongenomic mechanisms of oxytocin receptor regulation. *Adv Exp Med Biol* 1998;449:287–95.

53.   Johnson RF, Mitchell CM, Giles WB, Walters WA, Zakar T. The in vivo control of prostaglandin H

synthase-2 messenger ribonucleic acid expression in the human amnion at parturition. *J Clin Endocrinol Metab* 2002;87:2816–23.

54. Herschman HR, Reddy ST, Xie W. Function and regulation of prostaglandin synthase-2. *Adv Exp Med Biol* 1997;407:61–6.

55. Lye SJ, Mitchell J, Nashman N, Oldenhof A, Ou R, Shynlova O, *et al*. Role of mechanical signals in the onset of term and preterm labour. *Front Horm Res* 2001;27:165–78.

56. Bloomfield FH, Oliver MH, Hawkins P, Campbell M, Phillips DJ, Gluckman PD, *et al*. A periconceptional nutritional origin for noninfectious preterm birth. *Science* 2003;300:606.

Chapter 3

The preterm parturition syndrome

Roberto Romero, Jimmy Espinoza, Moshe Mazor and
Tinnakorn Chaiworapongsa

Introduction

The implicit paradigm governing the study of preterm parturition is that term and
preterm are fundamentally the same process except for the gestational age at which
they occur. Indeed, both share a common pathway composed of uterine contractility,
cervical dilatation and activation of the membranes.[1] We propose that the fundamental
difference between term and preterm labour is that the former results from
physiological activation of the components of the common pathway while the latter
arises from pathological processes that activate one or more of the components of the
common pathway of parturition. This chapter will review the common pathway of
parturition and then will focus on the evidence that preterm labour is a pathological
condition caused by multiple aetiologies and hence should be considered a syndrome.

The common pathway of parturition: components

The common pathway of human parturition has been defined as the anatomical,
biochemical, physiological and clinical events that occur in the mother and/or fetus in
both term and preterm labour. The components of this pathway include increased
uterine contractility, cervical ripening (dilatation and effacement) and decidual/fetal
membrane activation (Figure 3.1). In addition, systemic processes (endocrinological,
metabolic, etc.) are also part of the pathway. For example, term and preterm parturition
are associated with an increase in the plasma levels of corticotrophin-releasing
hormone (CRH) and cortisol, as well as an increase in the caloric metabolic
expenditures.[2–11]

Increased uterine contractility

Although myometrial activity occurs throughout pregnancy, labour is characterised by
a dramatic change in the pattern of uterine contractility that evolves from
'contractures' to 'contractions'. Nathanielsz and colleagues[12,13] defined contractures as
epochs of myometrial activity lasting several minutes that are associated with a modest
increase in intrauterine pressure and very fragmented bursts of electrical activity on the
electromyogram. In contrast, contractions are epochs of myometrial activity of short
duration, associated with dramatic increases in intrauterine pressure and electromyo-

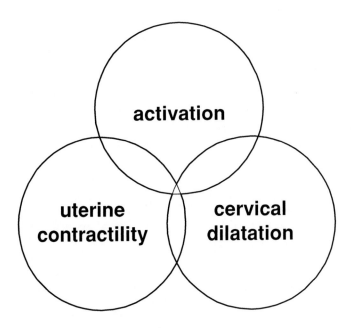

Figure 3.1. The common terminal pathway of preterm and term parturition

graphic activity. The switch from a contracture pattern to a contraction pattern occurs during normal labour[14] or can be induced by pathological events such as food withdrawal, infection and maternal intra-abdominal surgery.[15-17] The switch from a contracture to a contraction pattern is a potentially reversible phenomenon[18-21] The increased birth rate observed immediately after a period of fasting (the 'Yom Kippur effect') suggests that a fasting-induced switch operates in humans.[21,22]

The change from the contracture to the contraction pattern begins at night, and labour is preceded by a progressive nocturnal increase in uterine activity of the contraction pattern.[23,24] The circadian nature of this rhythm suggests that uterine activity is under neural control. Plasma concentrations of oxytocin follow a circadian pattern similar to that of uterine contractility.[23] Oxytocin antagonists blunt the nocturnal increase in uterine activity that precedes the onset of parturition in monkeys,[23-27] suggesting that oxytocin may mediate the circadian rhythm in uterine contractility. Oxytocin is produced by human decidua[28-34] and paraventricular nuclei of hypothalamus, while oxytocin receptors are present in myometrial cells and decidua. This hormone, therefore, may play both an endocrine and a paracrine role in the control of parturition.[29,35-42] .

Labour is characterised by a coordinated and effective generation of mechanical forces by the myometrium, which eventually leads to the expulsion of the conceptus. Increased cell-to-cell communication is thought to be responsible for the effectiveness of myometrial contractility during labour. Gap junctions develop in the myometrium just prior to labour and disappear shortly after delivery.[43-47] Gap junction formation and the expression of the gap junction protein connexin 43 in human myometrium is similar in term and preterm labour.[48-52] These findings suggest that the appearance of gap junctions and increased expression of connexin 43 may be part of the underlying molecular and cellular events responsible for the switch from contractures to contractions prior to the onset of parturition. Oestrogen, progesterone and prostaglandins have been implicated in the regulation of gap junction formation, as well as in influencing the expression of connexin 43.[53-55] Lye *et al.*[49,56,57] have proposed that a set of distinct proteins called 'contraction-associated proteins' is characteristic of this stage of parturition.

Cervical ripening

The ability of the cervix to retain the conceptus during pregnancy is unlikely to depend on a traditional muscular sphincteric mechanism.[58,59] The normal function of the cervix during pregnancy depends on the regulation of the extracellular matrix. The major macromolecular components of the extracellular matrix are collagen, proteoaminoglycans, elastin and various glycoproteins such as fibronectins. Collagen is the most important component of the extracellular matrix and determines the tensile strength of fibrous connective tissue.[60] Changes in cervical characteristics during pregnancy have been attributed to modifications in collagen content and metabolism. Proteoaminoglycans have also been implicated in cervical physiology. The proteoaminoglycan decorin (PG-S2) has a high affinity for collagen and can cover the surface of the collagen fibrils, stabilising them and promoting the formation of thicker bundles of collagen fibres. In contrast, PG-S1 (biglycan) has no affinity for collagen and can therefore disorganise collagen fibrils. The predominant dermatan sulphate proteoglycan in the nonpregnant state is PG-S2, and PG-S1 in the term-pregnant state.[61] The biochemical events that have been implicated in cervical ripening are:

- a decrease in total collagen content
- an increase in collagen solubility (probably indicating degradation or newly synthesised weaker collagen)
- an increase in collagenolytic activity (both collagenase and leucocyte elastase).

Contrary to what is generally believed, extracellular matrix turnover in the cervix is high, and thus the mechanical properties of the cervix can change rapidly. Uldbjerg *et al.*[60] demonstrated the importance of collagen content in cervical dilatation, reporting a strong correlation between the collagen content (measured by hydroxyproline determination) of cervical biopsies obtained after delivery and the time required for the cervix to dilate from 2 to 10 cm.

The changes in extracellular matrix components during cervical ripening have been likened to an inflammatory response.[62] Indeed, during cervical ripening there is an influx of inflammatory cells (macrophages, neutrophils, mast cells, eosinophils, etc.) into the cervical stroma. It has been proposed that these cells produce cytokines (e.g. interleukin-8 [IL-8]) and other mediators (such as prostaglandins), both of which have an effect on extracellular matrix metabolism.[63-67]

The chain of events leading to the physiological cervical ripening has not been defined. However, strong evidence supports a role for sex steroid hormones and includes the following:

- Intravenous administration of 17β-oestradiol induces cervical ripening.[68]
- Oestrogen stimulates collagen degradation *in vitro*.[69]
- Progesterone blocks oestrogen-induced collagenolysis *in vitro*.[69]
- Administration of progesterone receptor antagonist induces cervical ripening in the first trimester of pregnancy.[70]
- IL-8 production by the uterine cervix is downregulated by progesterone.[71]

Prostaglandins have been widely used to ripen the cervix prior to induction of labour or abortion. Within hours of administration, prostaglandin E_2 (PGE$_2$) produces clinical and histological cervical changes resembling physiological ripening that normally develops over several weeks of gestation. The mechanism of action of PGE$_2$ is thought to involve stimulation of collagenolytic activity and synthesis of PG-S1 by cervical tissue.[61]

Another mediator implicated in the mechanisms of cervical ripening is nitric oxide (NO),[72] which accumulates at sites of inflammation and can act as an inflammatory mediator at high concentration.[73–75] Expression of the inducible form of nitric oxide synthase (iNOS) and NO production in the cervix increase during labour in animals.[76] Moreover, the administration of L-nitro-arginine methylester (a nonspecific inhibitor of iNOS) blocks cervical ripening,[76] whereas direct application of sodium nitroprusside, an NO donor, to the cervix can induce cervical ripening.[77] Similar results have been obtained in human clinical trials.[78–81] For a detailed discussion of cervical ripening see Chapter 7.

Cervical changes precede the onset of labour, are gradual, and develop over several weeks.[82] Wood et al.[83] were the first to report that a short cervix was a risk factor for preterm labour and delivery. This observation has been subsequently confirmed by several investigators using both manual and sonographic examination.[84–94]

Although cervical shortening is traditionally considered an irreversible change, anecdotal clinical observations indicate that some women can have a short cervix and remain pregnant for a long time and even deliver at term. Reversibility of cervical ripening has been demonstrated with pharmacological intervention in the pregnant ewe. Dexamethasone administration induces cervical ripening and increased uterine contractility. These effects can be reversed with large doses of progesterone.[95]

Decidual/fetal membrane activation

The term 'decidual/membrane activation' refers to a complex set of anatomical and biochemical events resulting in the separation of the lower pole of the membranes from the decidua of the lower uterine segment and, eventually, in spontaneous rupture of membranes and delivery of the placenta. Untimely activation of this mechanism leads to preterm prelabour rupture of membranes (PROM), which accounts for 40% of all preterm deliveries.

Histological studies of the membranes in women with term PROM indicate that membranes ruptured prematurely have a decrease in the number of collagen fibres and disruption of the normal wavy patterns of these fibres, and deposit amorphous materials among them.[96] Similar changes have been observed in the membranes apposed to the cervix in women undergoing elective caesarean section at term with intact membranes.[97] The implication is that although spontaneous rupture of membranes normally occurs at the end of the first stage of labour, the process responsible for this phenomenon begins before the onset of labour.

Histological studies of the site of rupture have demonstrated a 'zone of altered morphology' (ZAM).[97,98] A significant decrease in the amount of collagen types I, III or V and an increased expression of tenascin have been reported in the ZAM. Tenascin is characteristically expressed during tissue remodelling and wound healing. Its identification in the membranes thus intimates the presence of injury and a wound healing-like response. Observations by Bell et al.[99] and Mallak et al.[100] suggest that the changes in the ZAM are more extensive in the setting of preterm PROM. These morphological and biochemical observations are consistent with the results of biophysical studies suggesting that rupture of membranes results from the application of acute or chronic stress on localised areas of the membranes that are weaker.

Structural extracellular matrix proteins such as collagens have been implicated in the tensile strength of the membranes, while the viscoelastic properties have been attributed to elastin.[101,102] Dissolution of extracellular cements (i.e. fibronectins) is thought to be responsible for the process that allows the membranes to separate from the decidua after the birth of the infant. Fibronectins are a family of important extracellular cements. Oncofetal fibronectin can be found in the vagina during both term and preterm parturition.[103-106] Therefore, degradation of the extracellular matrix, assessed by the detection of oncofetal fibronectin, is part of the common pathway of parturition.

The precise mechanism of membrane/decidual activation remains to be elucidated. However, roles for matrix-degrading enzymes and apoptosis have been proposed. Several studies have demonstrated increased availability of matrix metalloproteinase 1 (MMP-1) (interstitial collagenase),[107] MMP-8 (neutrophil collagenase),[108] MMP-9 (gelatinase-B) and neutrophil elastase[109] in the amniotic fluid of women with preterm PROM compared with that of women in preterm labour with intact membranes. Similar findings have been demonstrated in studies of the chorioamniotic membranes after PROM.[110] Plasmin has also been implicated in this process,[108] as this enzyme can degrade type III collagen, fibronectin and laminin.[111] Other MMPs are likely to be involved but systematic studies have not been conducted to date.[112-114] A role for tissue inhibitors of MMPs (TIMPs) has also been postulated.[115] .

Accumulating evidence suggests that apoptosis is important in the mechanisms of membrane rupture.[116,117] Rupture of membranes has been associated with overexpression of pro-apoptotic genes and decreased expression of anti-apoptotic genes.[118] Some MMPs, such as MMP-9, may induce apoptosis in amnion.[119-121] For a detailed review of this mechanism, see Chapter 15.

A role for the fetus

A role for the fetus in the control of the timing of parturition was demonstrated by the classic studies of Liggins *et al.*[122,123] Subsequent studies showed that destruction of the paraventricular nucleus of the fetal hypothalamus results in prolongation of pregnancy in sheep.[124,125] The human counterpart to this animal experiment is anencephaly, which is also characterised by a tendency to have a prolonged pregnancy (if women with polyhydramnios are excluded).[126] However, the situation in human anencephaly is considerably more complicated than the one described in animal experiments. The discrepancy can be explained by the wide range of central nervous system and pituitary lesions found in human anencephaly.

The current paradigm is that once maturity has been reached, the fetal brain, specifically the hypothalamus, increases CRH secretion, which in turn stimulates adrenocorticotrophic hormone (ACTH) and cortisol production by the fetal adrenals.[127-129] This increase in cortisol in sheep and dehydroepiandrosterone sulphate in primates eventually leads to activation of the common pathway of parturition.[130,131] A role for the human fetus in the onset of preterm labour has been proposed in the context of the fetal inflammatory response syndrome (see below).[132,133]

Premature parturition as a syndrome

The current taxonomy of disease in obstetrics is largely based on the clinical presentation of the mother and not the mechanism of disease responsible for the clinical manifestations. The term 'premature labour', for example, does not inform as to whether the condition is caused by an infection, a vascular insult, uterine overdistension, abnormal allogeneic recognition, stress, or some other pathological process. The same applies to other obstetric complications such as pre-eclampsia, small for gestational age, fetal death, etc. The lack of recognition of the syndromic nature of obstetric diseases is responsible for the prevailing view that one diagnostic test and treatment will detect and cure each of these conditions. The key features of obstetric syndromes[134] are:

- multiple aetiology
- chronicity
- fetal involvement
- clinical manifestations that are often adaptive in nature
- susceptibility owing to gene–environment interaction.

We will review the available evidence to support the concept that premature labour has 'multiple aetiologies'. Clearly, women with a short cervix in the midtrimester of pregnancy or with increased concentrations of fetal fibronectin in vaginal fluid are at increased risk for preterm labour or preterm delivery,[135–138] demonstrating that the pathological disorder leading to these conditions is 'chronic' in nature. For example, intrauterine infection can be detected at the time of routine midtrimester amniocentesis for genetic indications and become clinically evident weeks later with either PROM or preterm labour.[139–141] 'Fetal involvement' has been demonstrated in women with microbial invasion of the amniotic cavity. Fetal bacteraemia has been detected in 30% of women with preterm PROM and a positive amniotic fluid culture for microorganisms.[142] Similarly, neonates born after spontaneous preterm labour or preterm PROM are more likely to be small for gestational age, indicating a pre-existing problem with the supply line.[143–149] The 'adaptive nature' of labour has been proposed in the context of intrauterine infection in which the onset of labour can be considered a mechanism of host defence against infection that enables the mother to eliminate an infected tissue and to allow the fetus to exit from a hostile environment.[132,150] It is possible that other mechanisms of disease in premature labour may also threaten the maternal/fetal pair (i.e. defects of the supply line), and a key question would be why some women resort to fetal growth restriction, others to pre-eclampsia, and yet another group to the onset of preterm labour to deal with this problem. If the clinical manifestations are adaptive, then treatment of the components of the pathway (tocolysis, cerclage, etc.) could be considered as symptomatic in nature and not aimed at the specific pathological process that causes preterm labour. Finally, the predisposition to use a mechanism of host defence may be determined by 'gene–environment interaction' as in other disorders such as atherosclerosis and diabetes. However, complexity is added during pregnancy by the presence, and even perhaps the conflicting interests, of two genomes (maternal and fetal).

The pathological processes implicated in the preterm parturition syndrome include intrauterine infection, uterine ischaemia, uterine overdistension, abnormal allograft reaction, allergy-induced preterm labour, cervical insufficiency and endocrine disorders (Figure 3.2). The following sections review the evidence for each of the potential mechanisms of disease.

Intrauterine infection

Intrauterine infection has been recognised as a frequent and important mechanism of disease in preterm birth.[151–154] Indeed, it is the only pathological process for which a firm

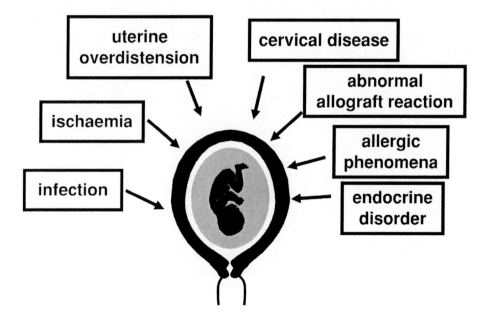

Figure 3.2. The preterm parturition syndrome

causal link with prematurity has been established with a defined molecular pathophysiology. Moreover, fetal infection/inflammation has been implicated in the genesis of fetal or neonatal injury leading to cerebral palsy and chronic lung disease.

Evidence of a role of infection in the aetiology of preterm birth includes:

- Intrauterine infection or systemic administration of microbial products to pregnant animals can result in preterm labour and delivery.[155–164]
- Systemic maternal infections such as pyelonephritis and pneumonia are frequently associated with the onset of premature labour in humans.[165–177]
- Subclinical intrauterine infections are associated with preterm birth.[178]
- Antibiotic treatment of ascending intrauterine infections can prevent prematurity in experimental models of chorioamnionitis.[161,179]
- Treatment of asymptomatic bacteriuria prevents prematurity.[180]

Microbiological and histopathological studies suggest that infection/inflammation may account for 25 to 40% of cases of preterm delivery.[181] Since infection is frequently difficult to confirm, we often refer to women with histological evidence of acute chorioamnionitis/elevated proinflammatory cytokines in the amniotic fluid and with documented microbial invasion of the amniotic cavity as belonging to 'the inflammatory cluster' associated with preterm PROM or preterm labour with intact membranes.

Frequency of intrauterine infection in spontaneous preterm birth

The prevalence of positive amniotic fluid cultures for microorganisms in women with preterm labour and intact membranes is approximately 12.8%.[182] The earlier the gestational age at preterm birth, the more likely that microbial invasion of the amniotic cavity is present.[183] In preterm PROM, the prevalence of positive amniotic fluid cultures for microorganisms is approximately 32.4%.[182] Among women presenting with a dilated cervix in the midtrimester, the prevalence of positive amniotic fluid cultures is 51%.[184] Microbial invasion of the amniotic cavity occurs in 11.9% of twin gestations presenting with preterm labour and delivering a preterm neonate.[185,186] The most common microorganisms found in the amniotic cavity are genital *Mycoplasmas*.

Intrauterine infection as a chronic process

Evidence in support of chronicity of intrauterine inflammation/infection is derived from studies of the microbiological state of the amniotic fluid as well as the concentration of inflammatory mediators at the time of genetic amniocentesis.

Cassell *et al.*[139] were the first to report the recovery of genital *Mycoplasmas* from 6.6% (4/61) of amniotic fluid samples collected by amniocentesis between 16 and 21 weeks of gestation. Two women had positive cultures for *Mycoplasma hominis* and two for *Ureaplasma urealyticum*. Women with *M. hominis* delivered at 34 and 40 weeks without neonatal complications, while those with *U. urealyticum* had premature delivery, neonatal sepsis and neonatal death at 24 and 29 weeks. Subsequently, Gray *et al.*[140] reported a 0.37% prevalence (9/2461) of positive cultures for *U. urealyticum* in amniotic fluid samples obtained during second trimester genetic amniocentesis. After exclusion of a therapeutic abortion case, all women (8/8) with positive amniotic fluid cultures had either a fetal loss within four weeks of amniocentesis (n = 6) or preterm delivery (n = 2). All had histological evidence of chorioamnionitis. These observations suggest that microbial invasion could be clinically silent in the midtrimester of pregnancy and that pregnancy loss/preterm delivery could take weeks to occur. A similar finding was reported by Horowitz *et al.*,[141] who detected *U. urealyticum* in 2.8% (6/214) of amniotic fluid samples obtained between 16 and 20 weeks of gestation. The rate of adverse pregnancy outcome (fetal loss, preterm delivery and low birthweight) was significantly higher in women with a positive amniotic fluid culture than in those with a negative culture (3/6 [50%] versus 15/123 [12%]; $P = 0.035$).

IL-6 concentrations in amniotic fluid are considered to be a marker of intra-amniotic inflammation frequently associated with microbiological infection in the amniotic fluid or the chorioamniotic space.[187–190] Romero *et al.*[191] reported the results of a case–control study in which IL-6 determinations were conducted in stored fluid of women who had a pregnancy loss after a midtrimester amniocentesis and a control group who delivered at term. Women who had a pregnancy loss had a significantly higher median amniotic fluid IL-6 than those with a normal outcome. Similar findings were reported by Wenstrom *et al.*[192] Of note is that maternal plasma concentrations of IL-6 were not associated with adverse pregnancy outcome.

The same approach was subsequently used to test the association between markers of inflammation in midtrimester amniotic fluid of asymptomatic women and preterm delivery. The concentrations of MMP-8,[193] IL-6,[194] tumour necrosis factor-α (TNF-α)[195] and angiogenin[196] in amniotic fluid obtained at the time of midtrimester amniocentesis were significantly higher in women who subsequently delivered preterm than in women who delivered at term.

Collectively, this evidence suggests that a chronic intra-amniotic inflammatory process may be present in early pregnancy and be associated with both miscarriage and spontaneous preterm delivery. Some indirect evidence suggests that such inflammatory processes may be detectable using maternal blood.[197]

Fetal involvement

The most advanced and serious stage of ascending intrauterine infection is fetal infection. The overall mortality rate of neonates with congenital neonatal sepsis ranges between 25 and 90%.[198-202] The wide range of results reflects the effect of gestational age on the likelihood of survival. One study,[202] which focused on infants born before 33 weeks of gestation, found that the mortality rate was 33% for those infected and 17% for noninfected fetuses. Carroll *et al.*[142] have reported that fetal bacteraemia detected by cordocentesis is found in 33% of fetuses with positive amniotic fluid culture and 4% of those with negative amniotic fluid culture. Therefore, subclinical fetal infection is far more common than traditionally recognised.

Preterm labour and preterm PROM as 'adaptive responses'

We have proposed that the onset of preterm labour in the context of intrauterine infection is a host defence mechanisms with survival value . The hosts (mother and/or fetus) would signal the onset of labour for the mother to get rid of infected tissue and maintain reproductive fitness. The molecular mediators involved in parturition are similar to those which have evolved to protect the host against infection (cytokines and other inflammatory mediators).

The current view is that during the course of an ascending intrauterine infection microorganisms may reach the decidua where they can stimulate a local inflammatory reaction as well as the production of proinflammatory cytokines, chemokines and inflammatory mediators (platelet activating factor, prostaglandins, leucotrienes, reactive oxygen species, NO, etc.). If this inflammatory process is not sufficient to signal the onset of labour, microorganisms can then cross intact membranes into the amniotic cavity, where they can also stimulate the production of inflammatory mediators by resident macrophages and other host cells within the amniotic cavity. Finally, microorganisms that gain access to the fetus may elicit a systemic inflammatory response syndrome, characterised by increased concentrations of IL-6[150] and other cytokines,[203-205] as well as cellular evidence of neutrophil and monocyte activation.[206]

Thus far, evidence for the participation of IL-1 and TNF-α in the mechanisms of preterm parturition is persuasive, although the precise role of other pro-inflammatory mediators remains to be elucidated. Evidence supporting a role for IL-1 and TNF-α in preterm parturition include the following:

- IL-1β[207-209] and TNF-α[210,211] stimulate prostaglandin production by amnion, decidua and myometrium.
- Human decidua can produce IL-1β and TNF-α in response to bacterial products.[207,208,212]
- Amniotic fluid IL-1β and TNF-α bioactivity and concentrations are elevated in women with preterm labour and intra-amniotic infection.[213-216]
- In women with preterm PROM and intra-amniotic infection, IL-1β concentrations are higher in the presence of labour.[214,216]
- IL-1β and TNF-α can induce preterm parturition when administered systemically to pregnant animals.[217,218]
- Fetal plasma IL-1β is dramatically elevated in the context of preterm labour with intrauterine infection.[219]
- Placental tissue obtained from women in labour, particularly those with chorioamnionitis, produces larger amounts of IL-1β than that obtained from women not in labour.[220]

There is considerable redundancy in the cytokine network and it is thus not clear that a particular cytokine is required to signal the onset of labour. Results of knockout animal experiments suggest that infection-induced preterm labour and delivery occurs in animals lacking the IL-1 type I receptor.[221] However, a recent observation with a double knockout system indicates that the IL-1 type I and the TNFα type I receptors are essential mediators for bacterially induced preterm birth (E Hirsch, personal communication).

Microbial invasion from the amniotic cavity into the fetus can lead to fetal infection and a systemic inflammatory response: the 'fetal inflammatory response syndrome' (FIRS). FIRS is a subclinical condition originally described in fetuses of mothers presenting with preterm labour and intact membranes and preterm PROM, and operationally defined as a fetal plasma IL-6 concentration above 11 pg/ml.[150] IL-6 is a major mediator of the host response to infection and tissue damage, and is capable of eliciting biochemical, physiological and immunological changes in the host, including stimulation of the production of C-reactive protein by liver cells, activation of T and natural killer cells, etc. Fetuses with FIRS have a higher rate of neonatal complications and are frequently born to mothers with subclinical microbial invasion of the amniotic cavity.[150] It is believed that fetal microbial invasion results in a systemic fetal inflammatory response that can progress towards multiple organ dysfunction,[222] septic shock, and death in the absence of timely delivery. Evidence of multisystemic involvement in cases of FIRS includes increased concentrations of fetal plasma MMP-9,[203] neutrophilia, a higher number of circulating nucleated red blood cells, and higher plasma concentrations of granulocyte colony-stimulating factor (G-CSF).[204] The histological hallmark of FIRS is inflammation in the umbilical cord (funisitis) or chorionic vasculitis.[223] Newborns with funisitis are at increased risk for neonatal sepsis[224] as well as long-term handicap, including bronchopulmonary dysplasia[225] and cerebral palsy.[226,227]

An important observation is that the fetuses with preterm PROM and FIRS are at risk for the impending onset of preterm labour regardless of the inflammatory state of the amniotic cavity (Figure 3.3).[132] This suggests that the human fetus plays a major role in the initiation of preterm labour. Nonetheless, systemic fetal inflammation, and even fetal injury, may occur in the absence of labour when the inflammatory process does not involve the chorioamniotic membranes and decidua. Examples of this are haematogenous viral infections of the fetus and/or alloimmunisation.

Gene–environment interactions

Gene–environment interactions are important in the understanding of many complex disorders such as atherosclerosis, obesity, hypertension etc. A gene–environment interaction is said to be present when the risk of a disease (occurrence or severity) among individuals exposed (to both genotype and an environmental factor) is greater or lower than that which is predicted from the presence of either the genotype or the environmental exposure alone.[228,229] There is now considerable evidence that the inflammatory response is under genetic control and therefore the interaction between the genotype of the host and microorganisms is important in determining the likelihood and course of some infectious diseases. An example of such an interaction has been reported for bacterial vaginosis, an allele for TNFα and preterm delivery.

Bacterial vaginosis (BV) is a risk factor for spontaneous preterm delivery.[135–138] However, randomised clinical trials with antibiotic administration to prevent preterm birth have yielded contradictory results.[230–242] The reasons for this are discussed in Chapter 12. Recently, Macones et al.[243] reported the results of a case–control study in

		n	Procedure-to-delivery interval (median and range, days)
I	AF IL-6 $\leq$ 7.9 ng/ml FP IL-6 $\leq$ 11 pg/ml	 14	5 (0.2–33.6)
II	AF IL-6 > 7.9 ng/ml FP IL-6 $\leq$ 11 pg/ml	 5	7 (1.5–32)
III	AF IL-6 > 7.9 ng/ml FP IL-6 > 11 pg/ml	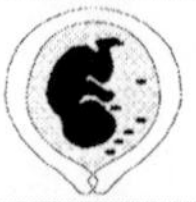 6	1.2 (0.25–2)
IV	AF IL-6 $\leq$ 7.9 ng/ml FP IL-6 > 11 pg/ml	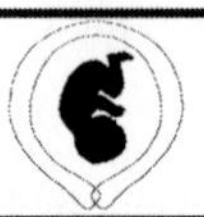 5	0.75 (0.13–1)

Figure 3.3. Classification and procedure-to-delivery interval of women according to amniotic fluid (AF) and fetal plasma (FP) IL-6 concentrations. Analysis was restricted to 30 women with available amniotic fluid. A white colour in the fetal or amniotic fluid compartment represents a low fetal plasma or amniotic fluid IL-6 concentration, respectively. Black in the fetal or amniotic fluid compartment denotes elevated fetal plasma or amniotic fluid IL-6 concentration, respectively

which cases were defined as women who had a spontaneous preterm delivery and controls as women who delivered at term. The environmental exposure was symptomatic BV. The allele of interest was TNF-α allele 2, given that its carriage had been demonstrated to be associated with spontaneous preterm birth.[244] The key observations were: clinically diagnosed BV was associated with an increased risk for preterm delivery (OR 3.3; 95% CI 1.8–5.9); women who carried the TNF-α allele 2 were also at increased risk for preterm delivery (OR 2.7; 95% CI 1.7–4.5); and women with both BV and the TNF-α allele 2 had an odds ratio of 6.1 (95% CI 1.9–21) for spontaneous preterm delivery, suggesting that a gene–environment interaction predisposes to preterm birth. Other gene–environment interactions may determine the susceptibility to intrauterine infection, microbial invasion of the fetus, and the likelihood of perinatal injury.

Uteroplacental ischaemia

Histological studies of the placentas of patients with preterm labour and preterm PROM indicate that, after inflammation, the most common type of lesion are vascular in nature and they can involve the maternal and fetal circulations.[245] Maternal lesions include failure of physiological transformation of the spiral arteries, atherosis, and thrombosis, while those observed in the fetal circulation include a decreased number of arterioles in the villi and fetal arterial thrombosis. The proposed mechanisms linking vascular lesions and preterm labour/delivery is uteroplacental ischaemia.

Evidence supporting a role for vascular disorders/uteroplacental ischaemia as a mechanism of disease leading to preterm parturition include the following:

- Experimental uterine ischaemia in primates is associated with preterm labour and delivery.[246]
- Vascular lesions in decidual vessels attached to the placenta have been reported by Arias *et al.*[247] in 34% of women with spontaneous preterm labour and intact membranes and in 35% of those with preterm PROM, while in only 12% of control women (term gestation without complications).[247]
- Placental abruption is more frequent in women who deliver preterm with intact membranes or rupture of membranes than in those who deliver at term.[247-252]
- Failure of physiological transformation in the myometrial segment of the spiral arteries has been found in women with preterm labour and intact membranes and preterm PROM.[253,254] This developmental abnormality had been previously associated with pre-eclampsia and intrauterine growth restriction (IUGR).
- Women presenting with preterm labour and intact membranes who have an abnormal uterine artery Doppler velocimetry (an index of increased impedance to flow in the uterine circulation) are more likely to deliver preterm than those with normal Doppler velocimetry.[255-257]
- The frequency of small-for-gestational-age infants is increased in women delivering after preterm labour with intact membranes and preterm PROM.[143-149] Vascular lesions leading to compromise of the uterine supply line could account for both IUGR and preterm labour.

The molecular mechanisms responsible for the onset of preterm parturition in cases of ischaemia have not been determined. A role for the renin–angiotensin system has been postulated, as the fetal membranes are endowed with a functional renin–angiotensin system[258] and uterine ischaemia increases the production of uterine renin.[259,260] Angiotensin II can induce myometrial contractility directly[261] or through the release of prostaglandins.[262]

When uteroplacental ischaemia is severe enough to lead to decidual necrosis and haemorrhage, thrombin may activate the common pathway of parturition. Evidence in support of this includes:

- Decidua is a rich source of tissue factor, the primary initiator of coagulation and of thrombin activation.[263]
- Intrauterine administration of whole blood to pregnant rats stimulates myometrial contractility,[264] while heparinised blood does not (heparin blocks the generation of thrombin).[264]
- Fresh whole blood stimulates myometrial contractility *in vitro* and this effect is partially blunted by incubation with hirudin, a thrombin inhibitor.[264]
- Thrombin stimulates myometrial contractility in a dose-dependent manner.[264]
- Thrombin stimulates the production of MMP-1[265] and urokinase type plasminogen activator (uPA) and tissue type plasminogen activator (tPA) by endometrial stromal cells in culture.[266] MMP-1 can digest collagen directly, while uPA and tPA catalyse the transformation of plasminogen into plasmin, which in turn can degrade type III collagen and fibronectin,[267] important components of the extracellular matrix in the chorioamniotic membranes.[268]
- Thrombin/antithrombin (TAT) complexes, a marker of *in vivo* generation of thrombin, are increased in plasma[269] and amniotic fluid[270] of women with preterm labour and preterm PROM.
- An elevation of plasma TAT complex concentration in the second trimester is associated with subsequent preterm PROM.[271]

The recognition that thrombin may play an important role in uterine contractility can explain the clinical observations that retroplacental haematomas in early pregnancy are associated with preterm delivery[272] and also that vaginal bleeding in the first or second trimester is a risk factor for preterm birth[273–276]

Although some investigators have proposed that fetal hypoxaemia is a cause of preterm labour, studies with cordocentesis have indicated that fetal hypoxaemia and metabolic acidaemia are not more frequent in women with preterm labour and intact membranes who deliver preterm than in those who deliver at term.[277] Similarly, Carroll *et al.*[278] have demonstrated that hypoxaemia is not more common in fetuses of women with preterm PROM. Therefore, uterine ischaemia should not be equated with fetal hypoxaemia, and no evidence currently supports that fetal hypoxaemia is a cause of preterm parturition.

Uterine overdistension

The mechanisms responsible for the increased frequency of preterm birth in multiple gestations and other disorders associated with uterine overdistension are unknown.[279–283] The importance of stretch in the initiation of labour is supported by an experiment conducted in humans in which the uterus of pregnant women with a live term fetus or a dead fetus was distended with a balloon inflated with physiological saline (up to 300 ml).[284] Regular uterine contractions occurred in all patients shortly after distension of the balloon, and all delivered within 21 hours. This observation indicated that stretch can induce labour at term, regardless of whether the fetus is alive or dead. Moreover, amniotic fluid concentrations of $PGF_{2\alpha}$ and its stable metabolite in plasma were increased in stretch-induced labour.[284]

Central questions are how the uterus senses stretch, and how these mechanical forces induce biochemical changes that lead to parturition. Investigators have conducted studies which explore the biochemical consequences of stretch on myometrium.[285–310] Increased expression of oxytocin receptor,[292] connexin 43,[52] and the *c-fos* mRNA is consistently demonstrated in the rat myometrium near term.[302–306] However, using a model in which pregnancy is restricted to one of the two uterine horns (by unilateral tubal ligation), the expression of the same genes was substantially lower in the empty horn, but this could be corrected by the distension of the uterus with a 3 mm tube that stretched the horn.[52,292] In another set of studies, progesterone was found to block stretch-induced gene expression in the myometrium.[57] Mitogen-activated protein kinases have been proposed to mediate stretch-induced *c-fos* mRNA expression in myometrial smooth muscle cells.[302–306]

In addition to the effects of stretch on myometrium, recent studies indicate that stretch can have effects on the chorioamniotic membranes.[311–325] For example, *in vitro* studies have demonstrated an increase in the production of collagenase, IL-8,[66,312] and PGE_2,[313] as well as the cytokine pre-B-cell colony-enhancing factor.[314] These observations provide a possible link between the mechanical forces operating in an over-distended uterus and rupture of membranes.

Abnormal allograft reaction

The fetoplacental unit has been considered nature's most successful semi-allograft and abnormalities in the recognition and adaptation to fetal antigens has been proposed as a mechanism of disease in recurrent pregnancy loss, IUGR and pre-eclampsia.[326–328] Chronic villitis has been considered a lesion indicative of 'placental rejection' and such lesions have been found in the placentas of a subset of women who deliver after spontaneous preterm labour.[329] We have observed that some women with preterm labour, in the absence of demonstrable infection, have elevated concentrations of the IL-2 soluble receptor.[245] Such elevations are considered an early sign of rejection in nonpregnant patients with renal transplants.[330] Further studies are required to define the frequency and clinical significance of this pathological process in preterm labour. Recently, allorecognition, in which cytotoxicity and rejection reactions are not inevitable consequences of exposure to foreign antigens,[331] has been proposed as a more accurate means of describing the maternal–fetal relationship and this has implications for the concept of allograft rejection as a mechanism of disease in obstetrics. A role for complement and natural killer cells in adverse pregnancy outcome has been proposed,[332-342] but it is unclear if these systems are deranged in preterm parturition.

Allergy-induced preterm labour

The concept that an allergic-like mechanism (type I hypersensitivity reaction) may be one of the aetiologies of preterm birth was proposed in the early 1990s based upon clinical observations and experimental studies.[343-345] Case reports documented that some women had preterm labour after exposure to an allergen and that a subgroup of patients with preterm labour have eosinophils as the predominant cells in amniotic fluid. Since the presence of eosinophils in body fluids is generally considered an indicator of an allergic reaction, patients with preterm labour and eosinophils as a predominant cell in the amniotic fluid were proposed to represent a form of uterine allergy. Subsequent to this observation, a large body of experimental evidence has accumulated providing biological plausibility to this hypothesis. The key observations have been that mast cells are present in the uterus and their products of degranulation can stimulate uterine contractility. Observations that support a role for a type I hypersensitivity reaction in preterm labour include the following:[346-358]

- The human fetus is exposed to common allergens, such as house dust mite. The allergen Der p 1 has been detected in both amniotic fluid and fetal blood. Moreover, the concentrations of the allergen are higher in fetal than maternal blood.[346]
- Allergen-specific reactivity has been demonstrated in umbilical cord blood at birth and as early as 23 weeks of gestation, indicating that the fetus can recognise the allergen and mount an immune response.[347]
- Pregnancy is considered a state in which there is a preponderance of a TH-2 cytokine response which favours the differentiation of naive CD4+ T cells to the TH-2 phenotype and the production of IgE, the key immunoglobulin required for a type I hypersensitivity reaction.
- The gravid uterus is a rich source of mast cells, the effector cells of allergic responses.[348]
- Several products of mast cell degranulation, such as histamine and prostaglandins, can induce myometrial contractility.[349,350]
- Pharmacological degranulation of mast cells with a compound called '48/80' induces myometrial contractility.[351,352]
- Incubation of myometrial strips from sensitised and nonsensitised animals with an anti-IgE antibody increases myometrial contractility.[351]
- Human myometrial strips obtained from women known to be allergic to ragweed demonstrate increased myometrial contractility when challenged *in vitro* by the allergen.[353] Moreover, sensitivity of the myometrial strips of nonallergic women can be transferred passively by preincubation of the strips with human serum.[353]
- Preterm labour and delivery can be induced by exposure to an allergen in sensitised animals, and can be prevented by treatment with a histamine H1 receptor antagonist.[358]

In summary, there is clinical and experimental evidence that a type I hypersensitivity reaction can induce preterm parturition, although the frequency of this phenomenon in humans is still unknown.

Cervical insufficiency

Although cervical insufficiency (formerly known as cervical incompetence) is traditionally considered a cause of midtrimester miscarriage, accumulating evidence suggests it can also be a cause of spontaneous preterm birth.[359] Cervical insufficiency may be the result of a congenital disorder (e.g. hypoplastic cervix or diethylstilboestrol exposure *in utero*), surgical trauma (e.g. conisation resulting in substantial loss of connective tissue) or traumatic damage to the structural integrity of the cervix (e.g. repeated cervical dilatation associated with termination of pregnancy).[360] Some cases presenting with the clinical characteristics of cervical insufficiency may be due to infection. Indeed, intrauterine infection has been demonstrated in 50% of women presenting with acute cervical insufficiency.[184] The optimal means to diagnose cervical insufficiency, the role of cervical length determination during pregnancy in the prediction of preterm birth, and of cerclage in its prevention are the subject of Chapter 10.

Endocrine disorders

Oestrogen and progesterone play a central role in the endocrinology of pregnancy.[361] Progesterone is thought to maintain myometrial quiescence, downregulate gap junction formation and inhibit cervical ripening.[362–364] Oestrogens have been implicated in increasing myometrial contractility and excitability, as well as in the induction of cervical ripening prior to the onset of labour.[363,364] However, the changes in sex steroids serum concentrations before spontaneous parturition are different among mammalian species .[365] In many species, a fall in maternal serum progesterone concentration occurs prior to spontaneous parturition, but the mechanism for this 'progesterone withdrawal' depends, to a large extent, on whether or not the placenta or the corpus luteum is the major source of progesterone.[365] The reader is referred to the article by Young for a comprehensive review of the comparative physiology of parturition in mammals.[366]

A progesterone withdrawal has not been demonstrated prior to parturition in humans. Nevertheless, this hormone is considered important in pregnancy maintenance because inhibition of progesterone action could result in miscarriage and parturition.[361,362,367,368] Several investigators have proposed alternative mechanisms to explain a suspension of progesterone action without a serum progesterone withdrawal which include:

- binding of progesterone to a high affinity protein and, thus, reduced functional active form[369,370]
- increased cortisol concentration in late pregnancy that can compete with progesterone for binding to the glucocorticoid receptors, resulting in functional progesterone withdrawal[371]
- conversion of progesterone to an inactive form within the target cell before interacting with its receptor.[372,373]

None of these hypotheses, however, has been proven[374] and, therefore, many investigators have shifted their attention to the abundance and modulation of oestrogen–progesterone receptor expression, as well as to progesterone binding, to its nuclear response element.[375–377]

Progesterone receptor subtype and a functional progesterone withdrawal

The human progesterone receptor (PR) exists as two major subtypes, PR-A (94 kDa) and PR-B (116 kDa), both encoded by a single gene independently regulated by separate promoters. PR-A is a truncated form of PR-B that lacks the first 164 N-terminal amino acids. In most human cells, type PR-B is the principal ligand-dependent transcriptional activator of progesterone-responsive genes, whereas PR-A is a ligand-activated repressor of the transcriptional activity mediated by PR-B. The human oestrogen receptor (ER) also exists as two major subtypes, ERα and ERβ. Both are derived from separate genes, each having different ligand binding affinities and tissue distribution.[378] The selective actions of oestrogens and various oestrogen agonists and antagonists are thought to be the result of differential expressions of ERα and ERβ.[379] Mesiano *et al.*[380] have proposed that a functional progesterone withdrawal occurs by increased expression of PR-A in myometrium which suppresses progesterone responsiveness and that functional progesterone withdrawal occurs by increased expression of ERα. There is experimental evidence in support of this hypothesis, namely that mRNA expression of PR-A/PR-B ratio was significantly higher in the myometrium of women in labour than in those not in labour. Moreover, the PR-A/PR-B ratio was correlated with the mRNA expression of ERα.

An alternative mechanism to explain a 'functional progesterone withdrawal' has been proposed by Phillip Bennett's laboratory.[381-385] This group of investigators proposed that the activation of nuclear factor kappa B (NFκB) in amnion represses progesterone function.

Allport *et al.*[383] demonstrated constitutive activity of NFκB in human amnion cells at the time of labour and that activation of NFκB induced cyclooxygenase 2 (COX-2) mRNA expression. The investigators concluded that human labour is associated with increased constitutive NFκB activity within the amnion, the function of which is to increase the expression of COX-2, while contributing to a functional progesterone withdrawal.[383]

Collectively, there is substantial evidence supporting the view that a functional progesterone withdrawal is present locally in intrauterine tissues during human parturition. The changes in oestrogen and progesterone receptor ratio can activate the three components of the common pathway of parturition. The pathological mechanisms responsible for suspension of progesterone action in preterm parturition remain to be elucidated. In the case of infection, IL-1 and TNF-α can induce activation of NFκB and this, in turn, may affect progesterone function.[383]

Randomised clinical trials of progesterone in preventing preterm delivery

Several randomised clinical trials have been conducted to determine the efficacy of progestational agents in preventing preterm delivery or recurrent miscarriage. Three meta-analyses have reported contradictory results.[386-388]

Daya[386] conducted a meta-analysis that included three controlled trials of progesterone treatment in women with recurrent miscarriage and concluded that progesterone treatment was effective in prolonging pregnancy until at least 20 weeks of gestation (OR 3.09; 95% CI 1.28–7.42).

Subsequently, Goldstein *et al.*[387] reported the results of a meta-analysis of 15 trials conducted in women with previous miscarriage, stillbirth or present preterm labour. There was no evidence that progestational agents were beneficial.

The third meta-analysis was conducted by Keirse[388] and included seven trials, six of which enrolled women considered to be at high risk of miscarriage or preterm delivery.

In contrast to previous meta-analyses, this one focused on 17 alpha-hydroxy-progesterone caproate (17P), which is the most widely studied progestational agent. The results showed that 17P administration was associated with a reduction in the rate of preterm labour (OR 0.43; 95% CI 0.2–0.89), preterm delivery (OR 0.5; 95% CI 0.3–0.85) and neonatal birthweight of less than 2500 g (OR 0.46; 95% CI 0.27–0.8). However, there was no significant difference in the rate of perinatal mortality, respiratory distress syndrome and hyperbilirubinaemia between women who received 17P or placebo. Similarly, the administration of 17P did not reduce the rate of miscarriage.

After a long hiatus in clinical investigation, two recent randomised clinical trials have renewed interest in this approach. The first randomised double-blind placebo-controlled study[389] evaluated the effectiveness of prophylactic vaginal progesterone in decreasing the rate of preterm birth. This study included 142 high-risk singleton pregnancies. Women were considered at high risk of preterm delivery if they had at least one previous spontaneous preterm birth, prophylactic cervical cerclage, or a uterine malformation. Patients were randomised to receive either daily progesterone (100 mg) or placebo by vaginal suppository from 24 to 34 weeks of gestation. Patients allocated to progesterone had a lower rate of preterm birth before 34 and 37 weeks of gestation. The rate of preterm delivery at both less than 37 weeks and at less than 34 weeks was lower in the progesterone group than in the placebo group (for 37 weeks: progesterone 13.8% [10/72] versus placebo 28.5% [20/70]; $P=0.03$, and for 34 weeks: progesterone 2.8% [2/72] versus placebo 18.6% [13/70]; $P=0.002$).

The second double-blind placebo-controlled clinical trial was conducted in the USA by Meis *et al.*[390] Women with a history of spontaneous preterm delivery were enrolled at 16 to 20 weeks of gestation and randomly assigned in a 2:1 ratio to receive either weekly injection of 250 mg of 17P or weekly injection of an inert oil placebo until delivery or to 36 weeks of gestation. Treatment with 17P significantly reduced the rate of preterm delivery at less than 37 weeks, less than 35 weeks, and less than 32 weeks of gestation (for 37 weeks: 17P 36.3% [111/306] versus placebo 54.9% [84/153]; RR 0.66; 95% CI 0.54–0.81, for 35 weeks: 17P 20.6% [63/306] versus placebo 30.7% [47/153]; RR 0.67; 95% CI 0.48–0.93, and for 32 weeks: 17P 11.4% [35/306] versus placebo 19.6% [30/153]; RR 0.58; 95% CI 0.37–0.91). Moreover, neonates born from women treated with 17P had significantly lower rates of necrotising enterocolitis, intraventricular haemorrhage and need for supplemental oxygen.

The American College of Obstetricians and Gynecologists Committee on Obstetric Practice issued an opinion[391] in November 2003 stating that further studies are needed to evaluate the use of progesterone in women with other risk factors for preterm delivery, such as multiple gestations, short cervical length or those with positive results for cervicovaginal fetal fibronectin. Despite the benefits of progesterone in women with a history of preterm delivery, the ideal progesterone regimen (formulation) is unknown. The 17P used in the US trial is not commercially available at this time.[391] A formulation for vaginal administration of progesterone is commercially available in Europe and the USA.

Conclusions

The evidence reviewed in this chapter provides compelling support for the concept that preterm parturition is a syndrome caused by multiple aetiologies. The predominant clinical presentation of this syndrome (i.e. uterine contractility, preterm cervical ripening without significant clinical contractility, or PROM) will vary depending upon the type and timing of the insults on the various components of the common pathway of parturition. This conceptual framework has implications for the understanding of the mechanisms responsible for the initiation of preterm parturition, as well as the diagnosis, treatment and prevention of preterm birth. Since preterm labour is a heterogeneous condition, it is unlikely that one diagnostic modality and one therapeutic intervention will prevent all preterm birth. We believe that the way forward requires a systematic examination of the taxonomy of preterm labour which is now possible using genomic and proteomic techniques.

References

1. Romero R, Mazor M, Munoz H, Gomez R, Galasso M, Sherer DM. The preterm labor syndrome. *Ann N Y Acad Sci* 1994;734:414–29.
2. Ohrlander S, Gennser G, Eneroth P. Plasma cortisol levels in human fetus during parturition. *Obstet Gynecol* 1976;48:381–7.
3. Petraglia F, Giardino L, Coukos G, Calza L, Vale W, Genazzani AR. Corticotropin-releasing factor and parturition: plasma and amniotic fluid levels and placental binding sites. *Obstet Gynecol* 1990;75:784–9.
4. Randall NJ, Bond K, Macaulay J, Steer PJ. Measuring fetal and maternal temperature differentials: a probe for clinical use during labour. *J Biomed Eng* 1991;13:481–5.
5. McLean M, Bisits A, Davies J, Woods R, Lowry P, Smith R. A placental clock controlling the length of human pregnancy. *Nat Med* 1995;1:460–3.
6. Challis JR. CRH, a placental clock and preterm labour. *Nat Med* 1995;1:416.
7. Smith R. Alterations in the hypothalamic pituitary adrenal axis during pregnancy and the placental clock that determines the length of parturition. *J Reprod Immunol* 1998;39:215–20.
8. Korebrits C, Ramirez MM, Watson L, Brinkman E, Bocking AD, Challis JR. Maternal corticotropin-releasing hormone is increased with impending preterm birth. *J Clin Endocrinol Metab* 1998;83:1585–91.
9. Leung TN, Chung TK, Madsen G, Lam PK, Sahota D, Smith R. Rate of rise in maternal plasma corticotrophin-releasing hormone and its relation to gestational length. *BJOG* 2001;108:527–32.
10. Florio P, Cobellis L, Woodman J, Severi FM, Linton EA, Petraglia F. Levels of maternal plasma corticotropin-releasing factor and urocortin during labor. *J Soc Gynecol Investig* 2002;9:233–7.
11. Genazzani AR, Petraglia F, Facchinetti F, Galli PA, Volpe A. Lack of beta-endorphin plasma level rise in oxytocin-induced labor. *Gynecol Obstet Invest* 1985;19:130–4.
12. Nathanielsz P, Honnebier M. Myometrial function. In: Drife J, Calder A, editors. *Prostaglandins and the Uterus*. London: Springer-Verlag; 1992. p. 161.
13. Hsu HW, Figueroa JP, Honnebier MB, Wentworth R, Nathanielsz PW. Power spectrum analysis of myometrial electromyogram and intrauterine pressure changes in the pregnant rhesus monkey in late gestation. *Am J Obstet Gynecol* 1989;161:467–73.
14. Taylor NF, Martin MC, Nathanielsz PW, Seron-Ferre M. The fetus determines circadian oscillation of myometrial electromyographic activity in the pregnant rhesus monkey. *Am J Obstet Gynecol* 1983;146:557–67.
15. Binienda Z, Rosen ED, Kelleman A, Sadowsky DW, Nathanielsz PW, Mitchell MD. Maintaining fetal normoglycemia prevents the increase in myometrial activity and uterine 13,14-dihydro-15-keto-prostaglandin F2 alpha production during food withdrawal in late pregnancy in the ewe. *Endocrinology* 1990;127:3047–51.
16. Nathanielsz PW, Poore ER, Brodie A, Taylor NF, Pimentel G, Figueroa JP, *et al*. Update on molecular events of myometrial activity during pregnancy. In: Nathanielsz P, Parer J, editors. *Research in Perinatal Medicine*. Ithaca, NY: Perinatology Press, 1984.p. 87–111.
17. Romero R, Avila C, Sepulveda W. The role of systemic and intrauterine infection in preterm labor. In: Fuchs A, Fuchs F, Stubblefield P, editors. *Preterm Birth: Causes, Prevention, and Management*. New York: McGraw-Hill; 1993.
18. Binienda Z, Rosen ED, Kelleman A, Sadowsky DW, Nathanielsz PW, Mitchell MD. Maintaining fetal normoglycemia prevents the increase in myometrial activity and uterine 13,14-dihydro-15-keto-prostaglandin F2 alpha production during food withdrawal in late pregnancy in the ewe. *Endocrinology* 1990;127:3047–51.
19. Fowden AL, Harding R, Ralph MM, Thorburn GD. The nutritional regulation of plasma prostaglandin E concentrations in the fetus and pregnant ewe during late gestation. *J Physiol* 1987;394:1–12.

20.   Kaplan M, Eidelman AI, Aboulafia Y. Fasting and the precipitation of labor. The Yom Kippur effect. *JAMA* 1983;250:1317–8.
21.   Maymon E, Mazor M, Romero R, Silberstein T, Shoham-Vardi I, Ghezzi F, *et al.* The Yom Kippur effect on human parturition. *Am J Obstet Gynecol* 1997;176:S115.
22.   Kaplan M, Eidelman AI, Aboulafia Y. Fasting and the precipitation of labor. The Yom Kippur effect. *JAMA* 1983;250:1317–8.
23.   Honnebier MB, Jenkins SL, Wentworth RA, Figueroa JP, Nathanielsz PW. Temporal structuring of delivery in the absence of a photoperiod: preparturient myometrial activity of the rhesus monkey is related to maternal body temperature and depends on the maternal circadian system. *Biol Reprod* 1991;45:617–25.
24.   Katz M, Newman RB, Gill PJ. Assessment of uterine activity in ambulatory patients at high risk of preterm labor and delivery. *Am J Obstet Gynecol* 1986;154:44–7.
25.   Owiny JR, Mitchell M, Nathanielsz PW. Effect of 48-hour infusion of the synthetic oxytocin antagonist, [1-beta-mercapto(beta-(CH2)5)1(OMe)Tyr2,Orn8]-oxytocin, on myometrial activity of pregnant sheep at 139-140 days of gestation. *Biol Reprod* 1992;47:436–40.
26.   Wilson L Jr, Parsons MT, Flouret G. Inhibition of spontaneous uterine contractions during the last trimester in pregnant baboons by an oxytocin antagonist. *Am J Obstet Gynecol* 1990;163:1875–82.
27.   Honnebier MB, Figueroa JP, Rivier J, Vale W, Nathanielsz PW. Studies on the role of oxytocin in late pregnancy in the pregnant rhesus monkey: plasma concentrations of oxytocin in the maternal circulation throughout the 24-h day and the effect of the synthetic oxytocin antagonist [1-beta-Mpa(beta-(CH2)5)1,(Me(Tyr2, Orn8] oxytocin on spontaneous nocturnal myometrial contractions. *J Dev Physiol* 1989;12:225–32.
28.   Blanks AM, Vatish M, Allen MJ, Ladds G, de Wit NC, Slater DM, *et al.* Paracrine oxytocin and estradiol demonstrate a spatial increase in human intrauterine tissues with labor. *J Clin Endocrinol Metab* 2003;88:3392–400.
29.   Blanks AM, Thornton S. The role of oxytocin in parturition. *BJOG* 2003;110 Suppl 20:46–51.
30.   Mitchell BF, Wong S. Metabolism of oxytocin in human decidua, chorion, and placenta. *J Clin Endocrinol Metab* 1995;80:2729–33.
31.   Chibbar R, Wong S, Miller FD, Mitchell BF. Estrogen stimulates oxytocin gene expression in human chorio-decidua. *J Clin Endocrinol Metab* 1995;80:567–72.
32.   Mauri A, Argiolas A, Ticconi C, Piccione E. Oxytocin in human intrauterine tissues at parturition. *Reprod Fertil Dev* 1995;7:1481–4.
33.   Mitchell BF, Chibbar R. Synthesis and metabolism of oxytocin in late gestation in human decidua. *Adv Exp Med Biol* 1995;395:365–80.
34.   Mitchell BF. Oxytocin synthesis and metabolism in human decidua. *Reprod Fertil Dev* 1995;7:319–21.
35.   Miller FD, Chibbar R, Mitchell BF. Synthesis of oxytocin in amnion, chorion and decidua: a potential paracrine role for oxytocin in the onset of human parturition. *Regul Pept* 1993;45:247–51.
36.   Chibbar R, Miller FD, Mitchell BF. Synthesis of oxytocin in amnion, chorion, and decidua may influence the timing of human parturition. *J Clin Invest* 1993;91:185–92.
37.   European Atosiban Study Group. The oxytocin antagonist atosiban versus the beta-agonist terbutaline in the treatment of preterm labor. A randomized, double-blind, controlled study. *Acta Obstet Gynecol Scand* 2001;80:413–22.
38.   French/Australian Atosiban Investigators Group. Treatment of preterm labor with the oxytocin antagonist atosiban: a double-blind, randomized, controlled comparison with salbutamol. *Eur J Obstet Gynecol Reprod Biol* 2001;98:177–85.
39.   Moutquin JM, Sherman D, Cohen H, Mohide PT, Hochner-Celnikier D, Fejgin M, *et al.* Double-blind, randomized, controlled trial of atosiban and ritodrine in the treatment of preterm labor: a multicenter effectiveness and safety study. *Am J Obstet Gynecol* 2000;182:1191–9.
40.   Coomarasamy A, Knox EM, Gee H, Khan KS. Oxytocin antagonists for tocolysis in preterm labour – a systematic review. *Med Sci Monit* 2002;8:RA268–73.
41.   Effectiveness and safety of the oxytocin antagonist atosiban versus beta-adrenergic agonists in the treatment of preterm labour. The Worldwide Atosiban versus Beta-agonists Study Group. *BJOG* 2001;108:133–42.
42.   Romero R, Sibai BM, Sanchez-Ramos L, Valenzuela GJ, Veille JC, Tabor B, *et al.* An oxytocin receptor antagonist (atosiban) in the treatment of preterm labor: a randomized, double-blind, placebo-controlled trial with tocolytic rescue. *Am J Obstet Gynecol* 2000;182:1173–83.
43.   Cole WC, Garfield RE, Kirkaldy JS. Gap junctions and direct intercellular communication between rat uterine smooth muscle cells. *Am J Physiol* 1985;249:C20–31.
44.   Garfield RE, Sims S, Daniel EE. Gap junctions: their presence and necessity in myometrium during parturition. *Science* 1977;198:958–60.
45.   Garfield RE, Sims SM, Kannan MS, Daniel EE. Possible role of gap junctions in activation of myometrium during parturition. *Am J Physiol* 1978;235:C168–79.

46. Garfield RE, Hayashi RH. Appearance of gap junctions in the myometrium of women during labor. *Am J Obstet Gynecol* 1981;140:254–60.

47. Garfield RE, Puri CP, Csapo AI. Endocrine, structural, and functional changes in the uterus during premature labor. *Am J Obstet Gynecol* 1982;142:21–7.

48. Balducci J, Risek B, Gilula NB, Hand A, Egan JF, Vintzileos AM. Gap junction formation in human myometrium: a key to preterm labor? *Am J Obstet Gynecol* 1993;168:1609–15.

49. Lefebvre DL, Piersanti M, Bai XH, Chen ZQ, Lye SJ. Myometrial transcriptional regulation of the gap junction gene, connexin-43. *Reprod Fertil Dev* 1995;7:603–11.

50. Orsino A, Taylor CV, Lye SJ. Connexin-26 and connexin-43 are differentially expressed and regulated in the rat myometrium throughout late pregnancy and with the onset of labor. *Endocrinology* 1996;137:1545–53.

51. Chow L, Lye SJ. Expression of the gap junction protein connexin-43 is increased in the human myometrium toward term and with the onset of labor. *Am J Obstet Gynecol* 1994;170:788–95.

52. Ou CW, Orsino A, Lye SJ. Expression of connexin-43 and connexin-26 in the rat myometrium during pregnancy and labor is differentially regulated by mechanical and hormonal signals. *Endocrinology* 1997;138:5398–407.

53. Petrocelli T, Lye SJ. Regulation of transcripts encoding the myometrial gap junction protein, connexin-43, by estrogen and progesterone. *Endocrinology* 1993;133:284–90.

54. Lye SJ, Nicholson BJ, Mascarenhas M, MacKenzie L, Petrocelli T. Increased expression of connexin-43 in the rat myometrium during labor is associated with an increase in the plasma estrogen:progesterone ratio. *Endocrinology* 1993;132:2380–6.

55. Cook JL, Zaragoza DB, Sung DH, Olson DM. Expression of myometrial activation and stimulation genes in a mouse model of preterm labor: myometrial activation, stimulation, and preterm labor. *Endocrinology* 2000;141:1718–28.

56. Lye SJ. The initiation and inhibition of labour: towards a molecular understanding. *Semin Reprod Endocrinol* 1994;12:284–94.

57. Lye SJ, Mitchell J, Nashman N, Oldenhof A, Ou R, Shynlova O, *et al*. Role of mechanical signals in the onset of term and preterm labor. *Front Horm Res* 2001;27:165–78.

58. Schwahn H, Dubrausky V. The structure of the musculature of the human uterus-muscles and connective tissue. *Am J Obstet Gynecol* 1966;94:391.

59. Danforth D, Evanston I. The distribution and functional activity of the cervical musculature. *Am J Obstet Gynecol* 1954;68:1261.

60. Uldbjerg N, Ekman G, Malmstrom A. Ripening of the human uterine cervix related to changes in collagen, glycosaminoglycans and collagenolytic activity. *Am J Obstet Gynecol* 1982;147:662.

61. Uldbjerg N, Forman A, Peterson L, Skajaa K, Svane D.. Biomechanical and biochemical changes of the uterus and cervix during pregnancy. In: Reece E, Hobbins J, Mahoney M, Petrie R, editors. *Medicine of the Fetus and Mother*. Philadelphia: JB Lippincott; 1992. p. 849.

62. Liggins G. Cervical ripening as an inflammatory reaction. In: Ellwood D, Anderson A, editors. *The Cervix in Pregnancy and Labour: Clinical and Biochemical Investigations*. Edinburgh: Churchill Livingstone; 1981. p. 1–9.

63. Ito A, Hiro D, Sakyo K, Mori Y. The role of leukocyte factors on uterine cervical ripening and dilation. *Biol Reprod* 1987;37:511–7.

64. Ito A, Hiro D, Ojima Y, Mori Y. Spontaneous production of interleukin-1-like factors from pregnant rabbit uterine cervix. *Am J Obstet Gynecol* 1988;159:261–5.

65. Ito A, Leppert PC, Mori Y. Human recombinant interleukin-1 alpha increases elastase-like enzyme in human uterine cervical fibroblasts. *Gynecol Obstet Invest* 1990;30:239–41.

66. Maradny EE, Kanayama N, Halim A, Maehara K, Terao T. Stretching of fetal membranes increases the concentration of interleukin-8 and collagenase activity. *Am J Obstet Gynecol* 1996;174:843–9.

67. Osmers RG, Blaser J, Kuhn W, Tschesche H. Interleukin-8 synthesis and the onset of labor. *Obstet Gynecol* 1995;86:223–9.

68. Pinto R, Rabow W, Votta R. Uterine cervix ripening in term pregnancy due to the action of estradiol-17 beta. *Am J Obstet Gynecol* 1965;92:319.

69. Rajabi MR, Dodge GR, Solomon S, Poole AR. Immunochemical and immunohistochemical evidence of estrogen-mediated collagenolysis as a mechanism of cervical dilatation in the guinea pig at parturition. *Endocrinology* 1991;128:371–8.

70. Chwalisz K, Shi Shao O, Neff G, Elger J. The effect of antigestagen ZK 98, 199 on the uterine cervix. *Acta Endocrinol* 1987;283:113.

71. Ito A, Imada K, Sato T, Kubo T, Matsushima K, Mori Y. Suppression of interleukin 8 production by progesterone in rabbit uterine cervix. *Biochem J* 1994;301 (Pt 1):183–6.

72. Chwalisz K, Garfield RE. Role of nitric oxide in the uterus and cervix: implications for the management of labor. *J Perinat Med* 1998;26:448–57.

73. Chwalisz K, Buhimschi I, Garfield RE. The role of nitric oxide in obstetrics. *Prenat Neonatal Med* 1996;4:292–328.

74.   Evans CH, Stefanovic-Racic M, Lancaster J. Nitric oxide and its role in orthopaedic disease. *Clin Orthop* 1995;(312):275–94.

75.   Romero R. Clinical application of nitric oxide donors and blockers. *Hum Reprod* 1998;13:248–50.

76.   Buhimschi I, Ali M, Jain V, Chwalisz K, Garfield RE. Differential regulation of nitric oxide in the rat uterus and cervix during pregnancy and labour. *Hum Reprod* 1996;11:1755–66.

77.   Facchinetti F, Piccinini F, Volpe A. Chemical ripening of the cervix with intracervical application of sodium nitroprusside: a randomized controlled trial. *Hum Reprod* 2000;15:2224–7.

78.   Thomson AJ, Lunan CB, Cameron AD, Cameron IT, Greer IA, Norman JE. Nitric oxide donors induce ripening of the human uterine cervix: a randomised controlled trial. *Br J Obstet Gynaecol* 1997;104:1054–7.

79.   Tschugguel W, Schneeberger C, Lass H, Stonek F, Zaghlula MB, Czerwenka K, Schatten C, Kaider A, Husslein P, Huber JC. Human cervical ripening is associated with an increase in cervical inducible nitric oxide synthase expression. *Biol Reprod* 1999;60:1367–72.

80.   Ekerhovd E, Weijdegard B, Brannstrom M, Mattsby-Baltzer I, Norstrom A. Nitric oxide induced cervical ripening in the human: Involvement of cyclic guanosine monophosphate, prostaglandin F(2 alpha), and prostaglandin E(2). *Am J Obstet Gynecol* 2002;186:745–50.

81.   Ledingham MA, Thomson AJ, Young A, Macara LM, Greer IA, Norman JE. Changes in the expression of nitric oxide synthase in the human uterine cervix during pregnancy and parturition. *Mol Hum Reprod* 2000;6:1041–8.

82.   Bishop E. Pelvic scoring for elective induction. *Obstet Gynecol* 1964;24:266.

83.   Wood C, Bannerman R, Booth R, Pinkerton J. The prediction of premature labor by observation of the cervix and external tocography. *Am J Obstet Gynecol* 1965;91:396.

84.   Anderson AB, Turnbull AC. Relationship between length of gestation and cervical dilatation, uterine contractility, and other factors during pregnancy. *Am J Obstet Gynecol* 1969;105:1207–14.

85.   Papiernik E, Bouyer J, Collin D, Winisdoerffer G, Dreyfus J. Precocious cervical ripening and preterm labor. *Obstet Gynecol* 1986;67:238–42.

86.   Bouyer J, Papiernik E, Dreyfus J, Collin D, Winisdoerffer B, Gueguen S. Maturation signs of the cervix and prediction of preterm birth. *Obstet Gynecol* 1986;68:209–14.

87.   Leveno KJ, Cox K, Roark ML. Cervical dilatation and prematurity revisited. *Obstet Gynecol* 1986;68:434–5.

88.   Stubbs TM, Van Dorsten JP, Miller MC III. The preterm cervix and preterm labor: relative risks, predictive values, and change over time. *Am J Obstet Gynecol* 1986;155:829–34.

89.   Holbrook RH Jr, Falcon J, Herron M, Lirette M, Laros RK Jr, Creasy RK. Evaluation of the weekly cervical examination in a preterm birth prevention program. *Am J Perinatol* 1987;4:240–4.

90.   Catalano PM, Ashikaga T, Mann LI. Cervical change and uterine activity as predictors of preterm delivery. *Am J Perinatol* 1989;6:185–90.

91.   Gomez R, Galasso M, Romero R, Mazor M, Sorokin Y, Goncalves L, *et al.* Ultrasonographic examination of the uterine cervix is better than cervical digital examination as a predictor of the likelihood of premature delivery in patients with preterm labor and intact membranes. *Am J Obstet Gynecol* 1994;171:956–64.

92.   Iams JD, Goldenberg RL, Meis PJ, Mercer BM, Moawad A, Das A, *et al.* The length of the cervix and the risk of spontaneous premature delivery. National Institute of Child Health and Human Development Maternal Fetal Medicine Unit Network. *N Engl J Med* 1996;334:567–72.

93.   Hassan SS, Romero R, Berry SM, Dang K, Blackwell SC, Treadwell MC, *et al.* Patients with an ultrasonographic cervical length < or =15 mm have nearly a 50% risk of early spontaneous preterm delivery. *Am J Obstet Gynecol* 2000;182:1458–67.

94.   Heath VC, Southall TR, Souka AP, Elisseou A, Nicolaides KH. Cervical length at 23 weeks of gestation: prediction of spontaneous preterm delivery. *Ultrasound Obstet Gynecol* 1998;12:312–7.

95.   Stys SJ, Clewell WH, Meschia G. Changes in cervical compliance at parturition independent of uterine activity. *Am J Obstet Gynecol* 1978;130:414–8.

96.   Skinner SJ, Liggins GC. Glycosaminoglycans and collagen in human amnion from pregnancies with and without premature rupture of the membranes. *J Dev Physiol* 1981;3:111–21.

97.   McLaren J, Malak TM, Bell SC. Structural characteristics of term human fetal membranes prior to labour: identification of an area of altered morphology overlying the cervix. *Hum Reprod* 1999;14:237–41.

98.   Malak TM, Bell SC. Structural characteristics of term human fetal membranes: a novel zone of extreme morphological alteration within the rupture site. *Br J Obstet Gynaecol* 1994;101:375–86.

99.   Bell SC, Pringle JH, Taylor DJ, Malak TM. Alternatively spliced tenascin-C mRNA isoforms in human fetal membranes. *Mol Hum Reprod* 1999;5:1066–76.

100.   Malak TM, Mulholland G, Bell SC. Morphometric characteristics of the decidua, cytotrophoblast, and connective tissue of the prelabor ruptured fetal membranes. *Ann N Y Acad Sci* 1994;734:430–2.

101.   Hieber AD, Corcino D, Motosue J, Sandberg LB, Roos PJ, Yu SY, *et al.* Detection of elastin in the human fetal membranes: proposed molecular basis for elasticity. *Placenta* 1997;18:301–12.

102. Bryant-Greenwood GD. The extracellular matrix of the human fetal membranes: structure and function. *Placenta* 1998;19:1–11.

103. Iams JD, Casal D, McGregor JA, Goodwin TM, Kreaden US, Lowensohn R, *et al*. Fetal fibronectin improves the accuracy of diagnosis of preterm labor. *Am J Obstet Gynecol* 1995;173:141–5.

104. Lockwood CJ, Senyei AE, Dische MR, Casal D, Shah KD, Thung SN, *et al*. Fetal fibronectin in cervical and vaginal secretions as a predictor of preterm delivery. *N Engl J Med* 1991;325:669–74.

105. Nageotte MP, Casal D, Senyei AE. Fetal fibronectin in patients at increased risk for premature birth. *Am J Obstet Gynecol* 1994;170:20–5.

106. Oshiro B, Edwin S, Silver R. Human fibronectin and human tenascin production in human amnion cells [abstract]. *J Soc Gynecol Invest* 1996;3:351A.

107. Maymon E, Romero R, Pacora P, Gervasi MT, Bianco K, Ghezzi F, *et al*. Evidence for the participation of interstitial collagenase (matrix metalloproteinase 1) in preterm premature rupture of membranes. *Am J Obstet Gynecol* 2000;183:914–20.

108. Maymon E, Romero R, Pacora P, Gomez R, Athayde N, Edwin S, *et al*. Human neutrophil collagenase (matrix metalloproteinase 8) in parturition, premature rupture of the membranes, and intrauterine infection. *Am J Obstet Gynecol* 2000;183:94–9.

109. Helmig BR, Romero R, Espinoza J, Chaiworapongsa T, Bujold E, Gomez R, *et al*. Neutrophil elastase and secretory leukocyte protease inhibitor in prelabor rupture of membranes, parturition and intra-amniotic infection. *J Matern Fetal Neonatal Med* 2002;12:237–46.

110. Vadillo-Ortega F, Hernandez A, Gonzalez-Avila G, Bermejo L, Iwata K, Strauss JF III. Increased matrix metalloproteinase activity and reduced tissue inhibitor of metalloproteinases-1 levels in amniotic fluids from pregnancies complicated by premature rupture of membranes. *Am J Obstet Gynecol* 1996;174:1371–6.

111. Everts V, van der Zee E, Creemers L, Beertsen W. Phagocytosis and intracellular digestion of collagen, its role in turnover and remodelling. *Histochem J* 1996;28:229–45.

112. Reboul P, Pelletier JP, Tardif G, Cloutier JM, Martel-Pelletier J. The new collagenase, collagenase-3, is expressed and synthesized by human chondrocytes but not by synoviocytes. A role in osteoarthritis. *J Clin Invest* 1996;97:2011–9.

113. Fortunato SJ, Menon R. Screening of novel matrix metalloproteinases (MMPs) in human fetal membranes. *J Assist Reprod Genet* 2002;19:483–6.

114. Velasco G, Pendas AM, Fueyo A, Knauper V, Murphy G, Lopez-Otin C. Cloning and characterization of human MMP-23, a new matrix metalloproteinase predominantly expressed in reproductive tissues and lacking conserved domains in other family members. *J Biol Chem* 1999;274:4570–6.

115. Maymon E, Romero R, Pacora P, Gomez R, Mazor M, Edwin S, *et al*. A role for the 72 kDa gelatinase (MMP-2) and its inhibitor (TIMP-2) in human parturition, premature rupture of membranes and intraamniotic infection. *J Perinat Med* 2001;29:308–16.

116. Lei H, Furth EE, Kalluri R, Chiou T, Tilly KI, Tilly JL, *et al*. A program of cell death and extracellular matrix degradation is activated in the amnion before the onset of labor. *J Clin Invest* 1996;98:1971–8.

117. Fortunato SJ, Menon R, Bryant C, Lombardi SJ. Programmed cell death (apoptosis) as a possible pathway to metalloproteinase activation and fetal membrane degradation in premature rupture of membranes. *Am J Obstet Gynecol* 2000;182:1468–76.

118. Fortunato SJ, Menon R, Lombardi SJ. Support for an infection-induced apoptotic pathway in human fetal membranes. *Am J Obstet Gynecol* 2001;184:1392–7.

119. Lei H, Kalluri R, Furth EE, Baker AH, Strauss JF III. Rat amnion type IV collagen composition and metabolism: implications for membrane breakdown. *Biol Reprod* 1999;60:176–82.

120. McLaren J, Taylor DJ, Bell SC. Increased incidence of apoptosis in non-labour-affected cytotrophoblast cells in term fetal membranes overlying the cervix. *Hum Reprod* 1999;14:2895–900.

121. McLaren J, Taylor DJ, Bell SC. Increased concentration of pro-matrix metalloproteinase 9 in term fetal membranes overlying the cervix before labor: implications for membrane remodeling and rupture. *Am J Obstet Gynecol* 2000;182:409–16.

122. Liggins G, Fairclough RJ, Grieves SA, Forster CS, Knox BS. Parturition in the sheep. In: Knight J, O'Connor M, editors. *The Fetus and Birth*. Amsterdam: Elsevier; 1977. p. 5–25.

123. Liggins GC, Fairclough RJ, Grieves SA, Kendall JZ, Knox BS. The mechanism of initiation of parturition in the ewe. *Recent Prog Horm Res* 1973;29:111–59.

124. McDonald TJ, Nathanielsz PW. Bilateral destruction of the fetal paraventricular nuclei prolongs gestation in sheep. *Am J Obstet Gynecol* 1991;165:764–70.

125. Gluckman PD, Mallard C, Boshier DP. The effect of hypothalamic lesions on the length of gestation in fetal sheep. *Am J Obstet Gynecol* 1991;165:1464–8.

126. Honnebier WJ, Swaab DF. The influence of anencephaly upon intrauterine growth of fetus and placenta and upon gestation length. *J Obstet Gynaecol Br Commonw* 1973;80:577–88.

127.   Kendall JZ, Challis JR, Hart IC, Jones CT, Mitchell MD, Ritchie JW, *et al.* Steroid and prostaglandin concentrations in the plasma of pregnant ewes during infusion of adrenocorticotrophin or dexamethasone to intact or hypophysectomized foetuses. *J Endocrinol* 1977;75:59–71.

128.   Liggins G, Holm LW, Kennedy PC. Prolonged pregnancy following surgical lesions of the foetal lamb pituitary. *J Reprod Fertil* 1966;12:419.

129.   Mecenas CA, Giussani DA, Owiny JR, Jenkins SL, Wu WX, Honnebier BO, *et al.* Production of premature delivery in pregnant rhesus monkeys by androstenedione infusion. *Nat Med* 1996;2:443–8.

130.   Rees LH, Jack PM, Thomas AL, Nathanielsz PW. Role of foetal adrenocorticotrophin during parturition in sheep. *Nature* 1975;253:274–5.

131.   Liggins GC. Premature parturition after infusion of corticotrophin or cortisol into foetal lambs. *J Endocrinol* 1968;42:323–9.

132.   Romero R, Gomez R, Ghezzi F, Yoon BH, Mazor M, Edwin SS, *et al.* A fetal systemic inflammatory response is followed by the spontaneous onset of preterm parturition. *Am J Obstet Gynecol* 1998;179:186–93.

133.   Nathanielsz PW, Jenkins SL, Tame JD, Winter JA, Guller S, Giussani DA. Local paracrine effects of estradiol are central to parturition in the rhesus monkey. *Nat Med* 1998;4:456–9.

134.   Romero R. The child is the father of the man. *Prenat Neonatal Med* 1996;1:8–11.

135.   Eschenbach DA, Gravett MG, Chen KC, Hoyme UB, Holmes KK. Bacterial vaginosis during pregnancy. An association with prematurity and postpartum complications. *Scand J Urol Nephrol Suppl* 1984;86:213–22.

136.   Flynn CA, Helwig AL, Meurer LN. Bacterial vaginosis in pregnancy and the risk of prematurity: a meta-analysis. *J Fam Pract* 1999;48:885–92.

137.   Hillier SL, Nugent RP, Eschenbach DA, Krohn MA, Gibbs RS, Martin DH, *et al.* Association between bacterial vaginosis and preterm delivery of a low-birth-weight infant. The Vaginal Infections and Prematurity Study Group. *N Engl J Med* 1995;333:1737–42.

138.   Meis PJ, Goldenberg RL, Mercer B, Moawad A, Das A, McNellis D, *et al.* The preterm prediction study: significance of vaginal infections. National Institute of Child Health and Human Development Maternal–Fetal Medicine Units Network. *Am J Obstet Gynecol* 1995;173:1231–5.

139.   Cassell GH, Davis RO, Waites KB, Brown MB, Marriott PA, Stagno S, Davis JK. Isolation of *Mycoplasma hominis* and *Ureaplasma urealyticum* from amniotic fluid at 16–20 weeks of gestation: potential effect on outcome of pregnancy. *Sex Transm Dis* 1983;10:294–302.

140.   Gray DJ, Robinson HB, Malone J, Thomson RB Jr Adverse outcome in pregnancy following amniotic fluid isolation of *Ureaplasma urealyticum*. *Prenat Diagn* 1992;12:111–7.

141.   Horowitz S, Mazor M, Romero R, Horowitz J, Glezerman M. Infection of the amniotic cavity with *Ureaplasma urealyticum* in the midtrimester of pregnancy. *J Reprod Med* 1995;40:375–9.

142.   Carroll SG, Papaioannou S, Ntumazah IL, Philpott-Howard J, Nicolaides KH. Lower genital tract swabs in the prediction of intrauterine infection in preterm prelabour rupture of the membranes. *Br J Obstet Gynaecol* 1996;103:54–9.

143.   Zeitlin J, Ancel PY, Saurel-Cubizolles MJ, Papiernik E. The relationship between intrauterine growth restriction and preterm delivery: an empirical approach using data from a European case–control study. *BJOG* 2000;107:750–8.

144.   Tamura RK, Sabbagha RE, Depp R, Vaisrub N, Dooley SL, Socol ML. Diminished growth in fetuses born preterm after spontaneous labor or rupture of membranes. *Am J Obstet Gynecol* 1984;148:1105–10.

145.   Bukowski R, Gahn D, Denning J, Saade G. Impairment of growth in fetuses destined to deliver preterm. *Am J Obstet Gynecol* 2001;185:463–7.

146.   Williams MC, O'Brien WF, Nelson RN, Spellacy WN. Histologic chorioamnionitis is associated with fetal growth restriction in term and preterm infants. *Am J Obstet Gynecol* 2000;183:1094–9.

147.   MacGregor SN, Sabbagha RE, Tamura RK, Pielet BW, Feigenbaum SL. Differing fetal growth patterns in pregnancies complicated by preterm labor. *Obstet Gynecol* 1988;72:834–7.

148.   Ott WJ. Intrauterine growth retardation and preterm delivery. *Am J Obstet Gynecol* 1993;168:1710–5.

149.   Weiner CP, Sabbagha RE, Vaisrub N, Depp R. A hypothetical model suggesting suboptimal intrauterine growth in infants delivered preterm. *Obstet Gynecol* 1985;65:323–6.

150.   Gomez R, Romero R, Ghezzi F, Yoon BH, Mazor M, Berry SM. The fetal inflammatory response syndrome. *Am J Obstet Gynecol* 1998;179:194–202.

151.   Goncalves LF, Chaiworapongsa T, Romero R. Intrauterine infection and prematurity. *Ment Retard Dev Disabil Res Rev* 2002;8:3–13.

152.   Minkoff H. Prematurity: infection as an etiologic factor. *Obstet Gynecol* 1983;62:137–44.

153.   Romero R, Mazor M, Wu YK, Sirtori M, Oyarzun E, Mitchell MD, *et al.* Infection in the pathogenesis of preterm labor. *Semin Perinatol* 1988;12:262–79.

154. Romero R, Sirtori M, Oyarzun E, Avila C, Mazor M, Callahan R, et al. Infection and labor. V. Prevalence, microbiology, and clinical significance of intraamniotic infection in women with preterm labor and intact membranes. Am J Obstet Gynecol 1989;161:817–24.

155. Bang B. The etiology of epizootic abortion. J Comp Anthol Ther 1987;10:125.

156. Fidel PL Jr, Romero R, Wolf N, Cutright J, Ramirez M, Araneda H, et al. Systemic and local cytokine profiles in endotoxin-induced preterm parturition in mice. Am J Obstet Gynecol 1994;170:1467–75.

157. Kullander S. Fever and parturition. An experimental study in rabbits. Acta Obstet Gynecol Scand Suppl 1977;66:77–85.

158. McDuffie RS Jr, Sherman MP, Gibbs RS. Amniotic fluid tumor necrosis factor-alpha and interleukin-1 in a rabbit model of bacterially induced preterm pregnancy loss. Am J Obstet Gynecol 1992;167:1583–8.

159. McKay DG, Wong TC. The effect of bacterial endotoxin on the placenta of the rat. Am J Pathol 1963;42:357–77.

160. Rieder RF, Thomas L. Studies on the mechanisms involved in the production of abortion by endotoxin. J Immunol 1960;84:189–93.

161. Romero R, Munoz H, Gomez R, Ramirez M, Araneda H, Cutright J, et al. Antibiotic therapy reduces the rate of infection-induced preterm delivery and perinatal mortality [abstract]. Am J Obstet Gynecol 1994;170:390.

162. Skarnes RC, Harper MJ. Relationship between endotoxin-induced abortion and the synthesis of prostaglandin F. Prostaglandins 1972;1:191–203.

163. Takeda Y, Tsuchiya I. Studies on the pathological changes caused by the injection of the Shwartzman filtrate and the endotoxin into pregnant rabbits. Jap J Exper Med 1953;21:9–16.

164. Zahl PA, Bjerknes C. Induction of decidua-placental hemorrhage in mice by the endotoxins of certain gram-negative bacteria. Proc Soc Exper Biol Med 1943;54:329–32.

165. Benedetti TJ, Valle R, Ledger WJ. Antepartum pneumonia in pregnancy. Am J Obstet Gynecol 1982;144:413–7.

166. Cunningham FG, Morris GB, Mickal A. Acute pyelonephritis of pregnancy: A clinical review. Obstet Gynecol 1973;42:112–7.

167. Fan YD, Pastorek JG, Miller JM Jr, Mulvey J. Acute pyelonephritis in pregnancy. Am J Perinatol 1987;4:324–6.

168. Finland M, Dublin T. D. Pneumococcic pneumonia complicating pregnancy and the puerperium. JAMA 1939;112:1027–32.

169. Gilles HM, Lawson JB, Sibelas M, Voller A, Allan N. Malaria, anaemia and pregnancy. Ann Trop Med Parasitol 1969;63:245–63.

170. Herd N, Jordan T. An investigtion of malaria during pregnancy in Zimbabwe. Afr J Med 1981;27:62.

171. Hibbard L, Thrupp L, Summeril S, Smale M, Adams R. Treatment of pyelonephritis in pregnancy. Am J Obstet Gynecol 1967;98:609–15.

172. Kass E. Maternal urinary tract infection. N Y State J Med 1962;1:2822–6.

173. Madinger NE, Greenspoon JS, Ellrodt AG. Pneumonia during pregnancy: has modern technology improved maternal and fetal outcome? Am J Obstet Gynecol 1989;161:657–62.

174. McLane CM. Pyelitis of pregnancy: a five-year study. Am J Obstet Gynecol 1939;38:117.

175. Oxhorn H. The changing aspects of pneumonia complicating pregnancy. Am J Obstet Gynecol 1955;70:1057.

176. Stevenson CS, Glasko AJ, Gillespie EC. Treatment of typhoid in pregnancy with chloramphenicol (chloromycetin). JAMA 1951;146:1190.

177. Wing ES, Troppoli D. V. The intrauterine transmission of typhoid. JAMA 1930;95:405.

178. Gomez R, Ghezzi F, Romero R, Munoz H, Tolosa JE, Rojas I. Premature labor and intra-amniotic infection. Clinical aspects and role of the cytokines in diagnosis and pathophysiology. Clin Perinatol 1995;22:281–342.

179. Fidel P, Ghezzi F, Romero R, Chaiworapongsa T, Espinoza J, Cutright J, et al. The effect of antibiotic therapy on intrauterine infection-induced preterm parturition in rabbits. J Matern Fetal Neonatal Med 2003;14:57–64.

180. Romero R, Oyarzun E, Mazor M, Sirtori M, Hobbins JC, Bracken M. Meta-analysis of the relationship between asymptomatic bacteriuria and preterm delivery/low birth weight. Obstet Gynecol 1989;73:576–82.

181. Romero R, Salafia CM, Athanassiadis AP, Hanaoka S, Mazor M, Sepulveda W, et al. The relationship between acute inflammatory lesions of the preterm placenta and amniotic fluid microbiology. Am J Obstet Gynecol 1992;166:1382–8.

182. Romero R, Espinoza J, Chaiworapongsa T, Kalache K. Infection and prematurity and the role of preventive strategies.Semin Neonatol. 2002; 7:259–74.

183. Watts DH, Krohn MA, Hillier SL, Eschenbach DA. The association of occult amniotic fluid infection with gestational age and neonatal outcome among women in preterm labor. Obstet

Gynecol 1992;79:351–7.

184.   Romero R, Gonzalez R, Sepulveda W, Brandt F, Ramirez M, Sorokin Y, *et al.* Infection and labor. VIII. Microbial invasion of the amniotic cavity in patients with suspected cervical incompetence: prevalence and clinical significance. *Am J Obstet Gynecol* 1992;167:1086–91.

185.   Romero R, Shamma F, Avila C, Jimenez C, Callahan R, Nores J, *et al.* Infection and labor. VI. Prevalence, microbiology, and clinical significance of intraamniotic infection in twin gestations with preterm labor. *Am J Obstet Gynecol* 1990;163:757–61.

186.   Romero R, Nores J, Mazor M, Sepulveda W, Oyarzun E, Parra M, *et al.* Microbial invasion of the amniotic cavity during term labor. Prevalence and clinical significance. *J Reprod Med* 1993;38:543–8.

187.   Romero R, Avila C, Santhanam U, Sehgal PB. Amniotic fluid interleukin 6 in preterm labor. Association with infection. *J Clin Invest* 1990;85:1392–400.

188.   Romero R, Sepulveda W, Kenney JS, Archer LE, Allison AC, Sehgal PB. Interleukin 6 determination in the detection of microbial invasion of the amniotic cavity. *Ciba Found Symp* 1992;167:205–20.

189.   Romero R, Yoon BH, Kenney JS, Gomez R, Allison AC, Sehgal PB. Amniotic fluid interleukin-6 determinations are of diagnostic and prognostic value in preterm labor. *Am J Reprod Immunol* 1993;30:167–83.

190.   Yoon BH, Romero R, Kim CJ, Jun JK, Gomez R, Choi JH, *et al.* Amniotic fluid interleukin-6: a sensitive test for antenatal diagnosis of acute inflammatory lesions of preterm placenta and prediction of perinatal morbidity. *Am J Obstet Gynecol* 1995;172:960–70.

191.   Romero R, Munoz H, Gomez R, Sherer DM, Ghezzi F, Ghidini A, *et al.* Two thirds of spontaneous abortion/fetal deaths after genetic amniocentesis are the result of a pre-existing sub-clinical inflammatory process of the amniotic cavity [abstract]. *Am J Obstet. Gynecol* 1995;172:261.

192.   Wenstrom KD, Andrews WW, Tamura T, DuBard MB, Johnston KE, Hemstreet GP. Elevated amniotic fluid interleukin-6 levels at genetic amniocentesis predict subsequent pregnancy loss. *Am J Obstet Gynecol* 1996;175:830–3.

193.   Yoon BH, Oh SY, Romero R, Shim SS, Han SY, Park JS, *et al.* An elevated amniotic fluid matrix metalloproteinase-8 level at the time of mid-trimester genetic amniocentesis is a risk factor for spontaneous preterm delivery. *Am J Obstet Gynecol* 2001;185:1162–7.

194.   Wenstrom KD, Andrews WW, Hauth JC, Goldenberg RL, DuBard MB, Cliver SP. Elevated second-trimester amniotic fluid interleukin-6 levels predict preterm delivery. *Am J Obstet Gynecol* 1998;178:546–50.

195.   Ghidini A, Eglinton GS, Spong CY, Jenkins CB, Pezzullo JC, Ossandon M, *et al.* Elevated mid-trimester amniotic fluid tumor necrosis alpha levels: a predictor of preterm delivery [abstract]. *Am J Obstet Gynecol* 1996;174:307.

196.   Spong CY, Ghidini A, Sherer DM, Pezzullo JC, Ossandon M, Eglinton GS. Angiogenin: a marker for preterm delivery in midtrimester amniotic fluid. *Am J Obstet Gynecol* 1997;176:415–8.

197.   Goldenberg RL, Andrews WW, Mercer BM, Moawad AH, Meis PJ, Iams JD, *et al.* The preterm prediction study: granulocyte colony-stimulating factor and spontaneous preterm birth. National Institute of Child Health and Human Development Maternal–Fetal Medicine Units Network. *Am J Obstet Gynecol* 2000;182:625–30.

198.   Boyer KM, Gadzala CA, Kelly PD, Gotoff SP. Selective intrapartum chemoprophylaxis of neonatal group B streptococcal early-onset disease. III. Interruption of mother-to-infant transmission. *J Infect Dis* 1983;148:810–6.

199.   Gerdes JS. Clinicopathologic approach to the diagnosis of neonatal sepsis. *Clin Perinatol* 1991;18:361–81.

200.   Ohlsson A, Vearncombe M. Congenital and nosocomial sepsis in infants born in a regional perinatal unit: cause, outcome, and white blood cell response. *Am J Obstet Gynecol* 1987;156:407–13.

201.   Placzek MM, Whitelaw A. Early and late neonatal septicaemia. *Arch Dis Child* 1983;58:728–31.

202.   Thompson PJ, Greenough A, Gamsu HR, Nicolaides KH, Philpott-Howard J. Congenital bacterial sepsis in very preterm infants. *J Med Microbiol* 1992;36:117–20.

203.   Romero R, Athayde N, Gomez R, Mazor M, Yoon BH, Edwin SS, *et al.* The fetal inflammatory response syndrome is characterized by the outpouring of a potent extracellular matrix degrading enzyme into the fetal circulation [abstract]. *Am J Obstet Gynecol* 1988;178:S3.

204.   Berry SM, Gomez R, Athayde N, Ghezzi F, Mazor M, Yoon BH, *et al.* The role of granulocyte colony stimulating factor in the neutrophilia observed in the fetal inflammatory response syndrome [abstract]. *Am J Obstet Gynecol* 1998;178:S202.

205.   Romero R, Maymon E, Pacora P, Gomez R, Mazor M, Yoon BH, *et al.* Further observations on the fetal inflammatory response syndrome: a potential homeostatic role for the soluble receptors of tumor necrosis factor alpha. *Am J Obstet Gynecol* 2000;183:1070–7.

206.   Berry SM, Romero R, Gomez R, Puder KS, Ghezzi F, Cotton DB, *et al.* Premature parturition is characterized by *in utero* activation of the fetal immune system. *Am J Obstet Gynecol*

1995;173:1315–20.

207. Romero R, LaFreniere D, Duff G. Human decidua: A potent source of interleukin-1 like activity. 32nd Annual Meeting of the Society for Gynecologic Investigation. Phoenix, Arizona. *J Soc Gynecol Investig* 1985. p. 363. (abstract).

208. Romero R, Durum SK, Dinarello CA, Hobbins JC, Mitchell M. Interleukin-1: A signal for the initiation of labor in chorioamnionitis. 33rd Annual Meeting of the Society for Gynecologic Investigation, Toronto, Ontario, Canada. *J Soc Gynecol Investig* 1986. p. 71. (abstract).

209. Romero R, Durum S, Dinarello CA, Oyarzun E, Hobbins JC, Mitchell MD. Interleukin-1 stimulates prostaglandin biosynthesis by human amnion. *Prostaglandins* 1989;37:13–22.

210. Romero R, Mazor M, Manogue K, Oyarzun E, Cerami A. Human decidua: a source of cachectin-tumor necrosis factor. *Eur J Obstet Gynecol Reprod Biol* 1991;41:123–7.

211. Romero R, Mazor M, Wu YK, Avila C, Oyarzun E, Mitchell MD. Bacterial endotoxin and tumor necrosis factor stimulate prostaglandin production by human decidua. *Prostaglandins Leukot Essent Fatty Acids* 1989;37:183–6.

212. Casey ML, Cox SM, Beutler B, Milewich L, MacDonald PC. Cachectin/tumor necrosis factor-alpha formation in human decidua. Potential role of cytokines in infection-induced preterm labor. *J Clin Invest* 1989;83:430–6.

213. Romero R, Manogue KR, Mitchell MD, Wu YK, Oyarzun E, Hobbins JC, et al. Infection and labor. IV. Cachectin-tumor necrosis factor in the amniotic fluid of women with intraamniotic infection and preterm labor. *Am J Obstet Gynecol* 1989;161:336–41.

214. Romero R, Brody DT, Oyarzun E, Mazor M, Wu YK, Hobbins JC, et al. Infection and labor. III. Interleukin-1: a signal for the onset of parturition. *Am J Obstet Gynecol* 1989;160(5 Pt 1):1117–23.

215. Romero R, Mazor M, Sepulveda W, Avila C, Copeland D, Williams J. Tumor necrosis factor in preterm and term labor. *Am J Obstet Gynecol* 1992;166:1576–87.

216. Romero R, Mazor M, Brandt F, Sepulveda W, Avila C, Cotton DB, et al. Interleukin-1 alpha and interleukin-1 beta in preterm and term human parturition. *Am J Reprod Immunol* 1992;27:117–23.

217. Romero R, Mazor M, Tartakovsky B. Systemic administration of interleukin-1 induces preterm parturition in mice. *Am J Obstet Gynecol* 1991;165:969–71.

218. Silver RM, Lohner S, Daynes RA, Mitchell MD, Branch DW. Lipopolysaccharide-induced fetal death: the role of tumor necrosis factor alpha. *Biol Reprod* 1994;50:1108–12.

219. Gomez R, Ghezzi F, Romero R, Yoon BH, Mazor M, Berry SM. Two thirds of human fetuses with microbial invasion of the amniotic cavity have a detectable systemic cytokine response before birth [abstract]. *Am J Obstet Gynecol* 1997;176:S14.

220. Taniguchi T, Matsuzaki N, Kameda T, Shimoya K, Jo T, Saji F, et al. The enhanced production of placental interleukin-1 during labor and intrauterine infection. *Am J Obstet Gynecol* 1991;165:131–7.

221. Hirsch E, Muhle RA, Mussalli GM, Blanchard R. Bacterially induced preterm labor in the mouse does not require maternal interleukin-1 signaling. *Am J Obstet Gynecol* 2002;186:523–30.

222. Romero R, Gomez R, Ghezzi F, Maymon E, Yoon BH, Mazor M, et al. A novel form of fetal cardiac dysfunction in preterm premature rupture of membranes. *Am J Obstet Gynecol* 1999;180:S27.

223. Pacora P, Chaiworapongsa T, Maymon E, Kim YM, Gomez R, Yoon BH, et al. Funisitis and chorionic vasculitis: the histological counterpart of the fetal inflammatory response syndrome. *J Matern Fetal Med* 2002;11:18–25.

224. Yoon BH, Romero R, Park JS, Kim M, Oh SY, Kim CJ, et al. The relationship among inflammatory lesions of the umbilical cord (funisitis), umbilical cord plasma interleukin 6 concentration, amniotic fluid infection, and neonatal sepsis. *Am J Obstet Gynecol* 2000;183:1124–9.

225. Yoon BH, Romero R, Kim KS, Park JS, Ki SH, Kim BI, et al. A systemic fetal inflammatory response and the development of bronchopulmonary dysplasia. *Am J Obstet Gynecol* 1999;181:773–9.

226. Yoon BH, Romero R, Yang SH, Jun JK, Kim IO, Choi JH, et al. Interleukin-6 concentrations in umbilical cord plasma are elevated in neonates with white matter lesions associated with periventricular leukomalacia. *Am J Obstet Gynecol* 1996;174:1433–40.

227. Yoon BH, Romero R, Park JS, Kim CJ, Kim SH, Choi JH, et al. Fetal exposure to an intra-amniotic inflammation and the development of cerebral palsy at the age of three years. *Am J Obstet Gynecol* 2000;182:675–81.

228. Clayton D, McKeigue PM. Epidemiological methods for studying genes and environmental factors in complex diseases. *Lancet* 2001;358:1356–60.

229. Tiret L. Gene-environment interaction: a central concept in multifactorial diseases. *Proc Nutr Soc* 2002;61:457–63.

230. Morales WJ, Schorr S, Albritton J. Effect of metronidazole in patients with preterm birth in preceding pregnancy and bacterial vaginosis: a placebo-controlled, double-blind study. *Am J Obstet Gynecol* 1994;171:345–7.

231. McGregor JA, French JI, Parker R, Draper D, Patterson E, Jones W, et al. Prevention of premature

birth by screening and treatment for common genital tract infections: results of a prospective controlled evaluation. *Am J Obstet Gynecol* 1995;173:157–67.

232. Hauth JC, Goldenberg RL, Andrews WW, DuBard MB, Copper RL. Reduced incidence of preterm delivery with metronidazole and erythromycin in women with bacterial vaginosis. *N Engl J Med* 1995;333:1732–6.

233. McDonald HM, O'Loughlin JA, Vigneswaran R, Jolley PT, Harvey JA, Bof A, *et al.* Impact of metronidazole therapy on preterm birth in women with bacterial vaginosis flora (*Gardnerella vaginalis*): a randomised, placebo controlled trial. *Br J Obstet Gynaecol* 1997;104:1391–7.

234. Carey JC, Klebanoff MA, Hauth JC, Hillier SL, Thom EA, Ernest JM, *et al.* Metronidazole to prevent preterm delivery in pregnant women with asymptomatic bacterial vaginosis. National Institute of Child Health and Human Development Network of Maternal–Fetal Medicine Units. *N Engl J Med* 2000;342:534–40.

235. Guise JM, Mahon SM, Aickin M, Helfand M, Peipert JF, Westhoff C. Screening for bacterial vaginosis in pregnancy. *Am J Prev Med* 2001;20:62–72.

236. US Preventive Services Task Force. Screening for bacterial vaginosis in pregnancy. Recommendations and rationale. *Am J Prev Med* 2001;20:59–61.

237. Centers for Disease Control and Prevention. Sexually transmitted diseases treatment guidelines 2002. *MMWR Recomm Rep* 2002;51:1–78.

238. Koumans EH, Markowitz LE, Hogan V. Indications for therapy and treatment recommendations for bacterial vaginosis in nonpregnant and pregnant women: a synthesis of data. *Clin Infect Dis* 2002;35:S152–72.

239. Klebanoff MA, Guise JM, Carey JC. Treatment recommendations for bacterial vaginosis in pregnant women. *Clin Infect Dis* 2003;36:1630–1.

240. Leitich H, Brunbauer M, Bodner-Adler B, Kaider A, Egarter C, Husslein P. Antibiotic treatment of bacterial vaginosis in pregnancy: a meta-analysis. *Am J Obstet Gynecol* 2003;188:752–8.

241. McDonald H, Brocklehurst P, Parsons J, Vigneswaran R. Antibiotics for treating bacterial vaginosis in pregnancy. *Cochrane Database Syst Rev* 2003;(2):CD000262.

242. Lamont RF. Infection in the prediction and antibiotics in the prevention of spontaneous preterm labour and preterm birth. *BJOG* 2003;110 Suppl 20:71–5.

243. Macones G, Parry S, Elkousy M, Clothier B, Ural SH, Strauss JF III. A polymorphism in the promoter region of TNF and bacterial vaginosis: preliminary evidence of gene-environment interaction in the etiology of spontaneous preterm birth. *Am J Obstet Gynecol* 2004 (in press).

244. Roberts AK, Monzon-Bordonaba F, Van Deerlin PG, Holder J, Macones GA, Morgan MA, *et al.* Association of polymorphism within the promoter of the tumor necrosis factor alpha gene with increased risk of preterm premature rupture of the fetal membranes. *Am J Obstet Gynecol* 1999;180:1297–302.

245. Romero R, Sepulveda W, Baumann P, Yoon BH, Brandt F, Gomez R, *et al.* The preterm labor syndrome: Biochemical, cytologic, immunologic, pathologic, microbiologic, and clinical evidence that preterm labor is a heterogeneous disease [abstract]. *Am J Obstet Gynecol* 1993;168:288.

246. Combs CA, Katz MA, Kitzmiller JL, Brescia RJ. Experimental preeclampsia produced by chronic constriction of the lower aorta: validation with longitudinal blood pressure measurements in conscious rhesus monkeys. *Am J Obstet Gynecol* 1993;169:215–23.

247. Arias F, Rodriquez L, Rayne SC, Kraus FT. Maternal placental vasculopathy and infection: two distinct subgroups among patients with preterm labor and preterm ruptured membranes. *Am J Obstet Gynecol* 1993;168:585–91.

248. Arias F, Victoria A, Cho K, Kraus F. Placental histology and clinical characteristics of patients with preterm premature rupture of membranes. *Obstet Gynecol* 1997;89:265–71.

249. Gonen R, Hannah ME, Milligan JE. Does prolonged preterm premature rupture of the membranes predispose to abruptio placentae? *Obstet Gynecol* 1989;74:347–50.

250. Major C, Nageotte M, Lewis D. Preterm premature rupture of membranes and placental abruption: is there an association between these pregnancy complications? *Am J Obstet Gynecol* 1991;164:381.

251. Moretti M, Sibai BM. Maternal and perinatal outcome of expectant management of premature rupture of membranes in the midtrimester. *Am J Obstet Gynecol* 1988;159:390–6.

252. Vintzileos AM, Campbell WA, Nochimson DJ, Weinbaum PJ. Preterm premature rupture of the membranes: a risk factor for the development of abruptio placentae. *Am J Obstet Gynecol* 1987;156:1235–8.

253. Kim YM, Chaiworapongsa T, Gomez R, Bujold E, Yoon BH, Rotmensch S, *et al.* Failure of physiologic transformation of the spiral arteries in the placental bed in preterm premature rupture of membranes. *Am J Obstet Gynecol* 2002;187:1137–42.

254. Kim YM, Bujold E, Chaiworapongsa T, Gomez R, Yoon BH, Thaler HT, *et al.* Failure of physiologic transformation of the spiral arteries in patients with preterm labor and intact membranes. *Am J Obstet Gynecol* 2003;189:1063–9.

255. Brar HS, Medearis AL, DeVore GR, Platt LD. Maternal and fetal blood flow velocity waveforms in patients with preterm labor: prediction of successful tocolysis. *Am J Obstet Gynecol* 1988;159:947–50.

256. Brar HS, Medearis AL, De Vore GR, Platt LD. Maternal and fetal blood flow velocity waveforms in patients with preterm labor: relationship to outcome. *Am J Obstet Gynecol* 1989;161:1519–22.

257. Strigini FA, Lencioni G, De Luca G, Lombardo M, Bianchi F, Genazzani AR. Uterine artery velocimetry and spontaneous preterm delivery. *Obstet Gynecol* 1995;85:374–7.

258. Poisner AM. The human placental renin-angiotensin system. *Front Neuroendocrinol* 1998;19:232–52.

259. Woods LL, Brooks VL. Role of the renin-angiotensin system in hypertension during reduced uteroplacental perfusion pressure. *Am J Physiol* 1989;257:R204–R209.

260. Katz M, Shapiro WB, Porush JG, Chou SY, Israel V. Uterine and renal renin release after ligation of the uterine arteries in the pregnant rabbit. *Am J Obstet Gynecol* 1980;136:676–8.

261. Lalanne C, Mironneau C, Mironneau J, Savineau JP. Contractions of rat uterine smooth muscle induced by acetylcholine and angiotensin II in Ca2+-free medium. *Br J Pharmacol* 1984;81:317–26.

262. Campos GA, Guerra FA, Israel EJ. Angiotensin II induced release of prostaglandins from rat uterus. *Arch Biol Med Exp (Santiago)* 1983;16:43–9.

263. Lockwood CJ, Krikun G, Papp C, Toth-Pal E, Markiewicz L, Wang EY, *et al*. The role of progestationally regulated stromal cell tissue factor and type-1 plasminogen activator inhibitor (PAI-1) in endometrial hemostasis and menstruation. *Ann N Y Acad Sci* 1994;734:57–79.

264. Elovitz MA, Saunders T, Ascher-Landsberg J, Phillippe M. Effects of thrombin on myometrial contractions *in vitro* and *in vivo*. *Am J Obstet Gynecol* 2000;183:799–804.

265. Rosen T, Schatz F, Kuczynski E, Lam H, Koo AB, Lockwood CJ. Thrombin-enhanced matrix metalloproteinase-1 expression: a mechanism linking placental abruption with premature rupture of the membranes. *J Matern Fetal Neonatal Med* 2002;11:11–7.

266. Lockwood CJ, Krikun G, Aigner S, Schatz F. Effects of thrombin on steroid-modulated cultured endometrial stromal cell fibrinolytic potential. *J Clin Endocrinol Metab* 1996;81:107–12.

267. Lijnen HR. Matrix metalloproteinases and cellular fibrinolytic activity. *Biochemistry (Mosc)* 2002;67:92–8.

268. Aplin JD, Campbell S, Allen TD. The extracellular matrix of human amniotic epithelium: ultrastructure, composition and deposition. *J Cell Sci* 1985;79:119–36.

269. Chaiworapongsa T, Espinoza J, Yoshimatsu J, Kim YM, Bujold E, Edwin S, *et al*. Activation of coagulation system in preterm labor and preterm premature rupture of membranes. *J Matern Fetal Neonatal Med* 2002;11:368–73.

270. Gomez R, Athayde N, Pacora P, Mazor M, Yoon BH, Romero R. Increased thrombin in intrauterine inflammation. *Am J Obstet Gynecol* 1998;178:S62.

271. Rosen T, Kuczynski E, O'Neill LM, Funai EF, Lockwood CJ. Plasma levels of thrombin-antithrombin complexes predict preterm premature rupture of the fetal membranes. *J Matern Fetal Med* 2001;10:297–300.

272. Nagy S, Bush M, Stone J, Lapinski RH, Gardo S. Clinical significance of subchorionic and retroplacental hematomas detected in the first trimester of pregnancy. *Obstet Gynecol* 2003;102:94–100.

273. Signore CC, Sood AK, Richards DS. Second-trimester vaginal bleeding: correlation of ultrasonographic findings with perinatal outcome. *Am J Obstet Gynecol* 1998;178:336–40.

274. Williams MA, Mittendorf R, Lieberman E, Monson RR. Adverse infant outcomes associated with first-trimester vaginal bleeding. *Obstet Gynecol* 1991;78:14–18.

275. Funderburk SJ, Guthrie D, Meldrum D. Outcome of pregnancies complicated by early vaginal bleeding. *Br J Obstet Gynaecol* 1980;87:100–5.

276. Ghezzi F, Ghidini A, Romero R, Gomez R, Galasso M, Cohen J, *et al*. Doppler velocimetry of the fetal middle cerebral artery in patients with preterm labor and intact membranes. *J Ultrasound Med* 1995;14:361–6.

277. Gomez R, Romero R, Ghezzi F, David C, Field S, Berry SM. Are fetal hypoxia and acidemia causes of preterm labor and delivery [abstract]? *Am J Obstet Gynecol* 1997;176:S115.

278. Carroll SG, Papaioannou S, Nicolaides KH. Assessment of fetal activity and amniotic fluid volume in the prediction of intrauterine infection in preterm prelabor amniorrhexis. *Am J Obstet Gynecol* 1995;172:1427–35.

279. Ludmir J, Samuels P, Brooks S, Mennuti MT. Pregnancy outcome of patients with uncorrected uterine anomalies managed in a high-risk obstetric setting. *Obstet Gynecol* 1990;75:906–10.

280. Hill LM, Breckle R, Thomas ML, Fries JK. Polyhydramnios: ultrasonically detected prevalence and neonatal outcome. *Obstet Gynecol* 1987;69:21–5.

281. Phelan JP, Park YW, Ahn MO, Rutherford SE. Polyhydramnios and perinatal outcome. *J Perinatol* 1990;10:347–50.

282.   Besinger R, Carlson N. The physiology of preterm labor. In: Keith L, Papiernik E, Keith D, Luke B, editors. *Multiple Pregnancy: Epidemiology, Gestation and Perinatal Outcome.* London: Parthenon Publishing; 1995. p. 415.

283.   Weiner CP, Heilskov J, Pelzer G, Grant S, Wenstrom K, Williamson RA. Normal values for human umbilical venous and amniotic fluid pressures and their alteration by fetal disease. *Am J Obstet Gynecol* 1989;161:714–17.

284.   Manabe Y, Sagawa N, Mori T. Fetal viability does not affect the onset of stretch-induced labor and the increase in amniotic fluid prostaglandin F2 alpha and plasma prostaglandin F2 alpha metabolite levels. Prostaglandins 1992; 44:119–28.

285.   Fuchs AR, Periyasamy S, Alexandrova M, Soloff MS. Correlation between oxytocin receptor concentration and responsiveness to oxytocin in pregnant rat myometrium: effects of ovarian steroids. *Endocrinology* 1983;113:742–9.

286.   Sideris IG, Nicolaides KH. Amniotic fluid pressure during pregnancy. *Fetal Diagn Ther* 1990;5:104–8.

287.   Fisk NM, Ronderos-Dumit D, Tannirandorn Y, Nicolini U, Talbert D, Rodeck CH. Normal amniotic pressure throughout gestation. *Br J Obstet Gynaecol* 1992;99:18–22.

288.   Speroff L, Glass RH, Kase NG. The endocrinology of pregnancy. In: Mitchell C, editor. *Clinical Gynecologic Endocrinology and Infertility.* Baltimore: Williams & Wilkins; 1994. p. 251–90.

289.   Sladek SM, Westerhausen-Larson A, Roberts JM. Endogenous nitric oxide suppresses rat myometrial connexin 43 gap junction protein expression during pregnancy. *Biol Reprod* 1999;61:8–13.

290.   Laudanski T, Rocki W. The effects on stretching and prostaglandin F2alpha on the contractile and bioelectric activity of the uterus in rat. *Acta Physiol Pol* 1975;26:385–93.

291.   Kloeck FK, Jung H. *In vitro* release of prostaglandins from the human myometrium under the influence of stretching. *Am J Obstet Gynecol* 1973;115:1066–9.

292.   Ou CW, Chen ZQ, Qi S, Lye SJ. Increased expression of the rat myometrial oxytocin receptor messenger ribonucleic acid during labor requires both mechanical and hormonal signals. *Biol Reprod* 1998;59:1055–61.

293.   Ticconi C, Lye SJ. Placenta and fetal membranes in human parturition and preterm delivery – a workshop report. *Placenta* 2002;23 Suppl A:S149–52.

294.   Watson PA, Hannan R, Carl LL, Giger KE. Contractile activity and passive stretch regulate tubulin mRNA and protein content in cardiac myocytes. *Am J Physiol* 1996;271:C684–9.

295.   Barany K, Rokolya A, Barany M. Stretch activates myosin light chain kinase in arterial smooth muscle. *Biochem Biophys Res Commun* 1990;173:164–71.

296.   Steers WD, Broder SR, Persson K, Bruns DE, Ferguson JE, Bruns ME, *et al.* Mechanical stretch increases secretion of parathyroid hormone-related protein by cultured bladder smooth muscle cells. *J Urol* 1998;160:908–12.

297.   Farrugia G, Holm AN, Rich A, Sarr MG, Szurszewski JH, Rae JL. A mechanosensitive calcium channel in human intestinal smooth muscle cells. *Gastroenterology* 1999;117:900–5.

298.   Tzima E, del Pozo MA, Shattil SJ, Chien S, Schwartz MA. Activation of integrins in endothelial cells by fluid shear stress mediates Rho-dependent cytoskeletal alignment. *EMBO J* 2001;20:4639–47.

299.   Holm AN, Rich A, Sarr MG, Farrugia G. Whole cell current and membrane potential regulation by a human smooth muscle mechanosensitive calcium channel. *Am J Physiol Gastrointest Liver Physiol* 2000;279:G1155–61.

300.   Li C, Xu Q. Mechanical stress-initiated signal transductions in vascular smooth muscle cells. *Cell Signal* 2000;12:435–45.

301.   Hu Y, Bock G, Wick G, Xu Q. Activation of PDGF receptor alpha in vascular smooth muscle cells by mechanical stress. *FASEB J* 1998;12:1135–42.

302.   Piersanti M, Lye SJ. Increase in messenger ribonucleic acid encoding the myometrial gap junction protein, connexin-43, requires protein synthesis and is associated with increased expression of the activator protein-1, c-fos. *Endocrinology* 1995;136:3571–8.

303.   Mitchell JA, Lye SJ. Regulation of connexin43 expression by c-fos and c-jun in myometrial cells. *Cell Commun Adhes* 2001;8:299–302.

304.   Mitchell JA, Lye SJ. Differential expression of activator protein-1 transcription factors in pregnant rat myometrium. *Biol Reprod* 2002;67:240–6.

305.   Oldenhof AD, Shynlova OP, Liu M, Langille BL, Lye SJ. Mitogen-activated protein kinases mediate stretch-induced c-fos mRNA expression in myometrial smooth muscle cells. *Am J Physiol Cell Physiol* 2002;283:C1530–9.

306.   Shynlova OP, Oldenhof AD, Liu M, Langille L, Lye SJ. Regulation of c-fos expression by static stretch in rat myometrial smooth muscle cells. *Am J Obstet Gynecol* 2002;186:1358–65.

307.   Wu WX, Ma XH, Yoshizato T, Shinozuka N, Nathanielsz PW. Differential expression of myometrial oxytocin receptor and prostaglandin H synthase 2, but not estrogen receptor alpha and

heat shock protein 90 messenger ribonucleic acid in the gravid horn and nongravid horn in sheep during betamethasone-induced labor. *Endocrinology* 1999;140:5712–18.

308. Lee HS, Millward-Sadler SJ, Wright MO, Nuki G, Al Jamal R, Salter DM. Activation of Integrin-RACK1/PKCalpha signalling in human articular chondrocyte mechanotransduction. *Osteoarthritis Cartilage* 2002;10:890–7.

309. Shyy JY, Chien S. Role of integrins in endothelial mechanosensing of shear stress. *Circ Res* 2002;91:769–75.

310. Ravens U. Mechano-electric feedback and arrhythmias. *Prog Biophys Mol Biol* 2003;82:255–66.

311. Millar LK, Stollberg J, DeBuque L, Bryant-Greenwood G. Fetal membrane distention: determination of the intrauterine surface area and distention of the fetal membranes preterm and at term. *Am J Obstet Gynecol* 2000;182:128–34.

312. Maehara K, Kanayama N, Maradny EE, Uezato T, Fujita M, Terao T. Mechanical stretching induces interleukin-8 gene expression in fetal membranes: a possible role for the initiation of human parturition. *Eur J Obstet Gynecol Reprod Biol* 1996;70:191–6.

313. Kanayama N, Fukamizu H. Mechanical stretching increases prostaglandin E2 in cultured human amnion cells. *Gynecol Obstet Invest* 1989;28:123–6.

314. Nemeth E, Tashima LS, Yu Z, Bryant-Greenwood GD. Fetal membrane distention: I. Differentially expressed genes regulated by acute distention in amniotic epithelial (WISH) cells. *Am J Obstet Gynecol* 2000;182:50–9.

315. Nemeth E, Millar LK, Bryant-Greenwood G. Fetal membrane distention: II. Differentially expressed genes regulated by acute distention *in vitro. Am J Obstet Gynecol* 2000;182:60–7.

316. Sennstrom MK, Brauner A, Lu Y, Granstrom LM, Malmstrom AL, Ekman GE. Interleukin-8 is a mediator of the final cervical ripening in humans. *Eur J Obstet Gynecol Reprod Biol* 1997;74:89–92.

317. Chwalisz K, Benson M, Scholz P, Daum J, Beier HM, Hegele-Hartung C. Cervical ripening with the cytokines interleukin 8, interleukin 1 beta and tumour necrosis factor alpha in guinea-pigs. *Hum Reprod* 1994;9:2173–81.

318. el Maradny E, Kanayama N, Halim A, Maehara K, Sumimoto K, Terao T. Interleukin-8 induces cervical ripening in rabbits. *Am J Obstet Gynecol* 1994;171:77–83.

319. Barclay CG, Brennand JE, Kelly RW, Calder AA. Interleukin-8 production by the human cervix. *Am J Obstet Gynecol* 1993;169:625–32.

320. Rajabi M, Solomon S, Poole AR. Hormonal regulation of interstitial collagenase in the uterine cervix of the pregnant guinea pig. *Endocrinology* 1991;128:863–71.

321. Stjernholm YM, Sahlin L, Eriksson HA, Bystrom BE, Stenlund PM, Ekman GE. Cervical ripening after treatment with prostaglandin E2 or antiprogestin (RU486). Possible mechanisms in relation to gonadal steroids. *Eur J Obstet Gynecol Reprod Biol* 1999;84:83–8.

322. Denison FC, Calder AA, Kelly RW. The action of prostaglandin E2 on the human cervix: stimulation of interleukin 8 and inhibition of secretory leukocyte protease inhibitor. *Am J Obstet Gynecol* 1999;180:614–20.

323. Calder AA. Prostaglandins and biological control of cervical function. *Aust N Z J Obstet Gynaecol* 1994;34:347–51.

324. Mazor M, Hershkovitz R, Ghezzi F, Maymon E, Horowitz S, Leiberman JR. Intraamniotic infection in patients with preterm labor and twin pregnancies. *Acta Obstet Gynecol Scand* 1996;75:624–7.

325. Yoon BH, Park KH, Koo JN, Kwon JH, Jun JK, Syn HC, et al. Intra-amniotic infection of twin pregnancies with preterm labor [abstract]. *Am J Obstet Gynecol* 1997;176:535.

326. McLean JM. Early embryo loss. *Lancet* 1987;1:1033–4.

327. Aksel S. Immunologic aspects of reproductive diseases. *JAMA* 1992;268:2930–4.

328. Kilpatrick DC. Immune mechanisms and pre-eclampsia. *Lancet* 1987;2:1460–1.

329. Benirschke K, Kaufmann P. Villitis of unknown etiology. In: Benirschke K, Kaufmann P, editors. *Pathology of the Human Placenta.* New York: Springer-Verlag; 1995. p. 596.

330. Soulillou JP, Peyronnet P, Le Mauff B, Hourmant M, Olive D, Mawas C, et al. Prevention of rejection of kidney transplants by monoclonal antibody directed against interleukin 2. *Lancet* 1987;1:1339–42.

331. Loke YW, King A. Immunology of human implantation: an evolutionary perspective. *Hum Reprod* 1996;11:283–6.

332. Holmes CH, Simpson KL. Complement and pregnancy: new insights into the immunobiology of the fetomaternal relationship. *Baillieres Clin Obstet Gynaecol* 1992;6:439–60.

333. Holmes CH, Simpson KL, Okada H, Okada N, Wainwright SD, Purcell DF, et al. Complement regulatory proteins at the feto-maternal interface during human placental development: distribution of CD59 by comparison with membrane cofactor protein (CD46) and decay accelerating factor (CD55). *Eur J Immunol* 1992;22:1579–85.

334. Hagmann M. Embryos attacked by mom's natural defenses. *Science* 2000;287:408.

335. Simpson KL, Jones A, Norman S, Holmes CH. Expression of the complement regulatory proteins

decay accelerating factor (DAF, CD55), membrane cofactor protein (MCP, CD46) and CD59 in the normal human uterine cervix and in premalignant and malignant cervical disease. *Am J Pathol* 1997;151:1455–67.

336.   Xu C, Mao D, Holers VM, Palanca B, Cheng AM, Molina H. A critical role for murine complement regulator crry in fetomaternal tolerance. *Science* 2000;287:498–501.

337.   Vanderpuye OA, Labarrere CA, McIntyre JA. The complement system in human reproduction. *Am J Reprod Immunol* 1992;27:145–55.

338.   Cunningham DS, Tichenor JR Jr Decay-accelerating factor protects human trophoblast from complement-mediated attack. *Clin Immunol Immunopathol* 1995;74:156–61.

339.   Gonzalez NC, Chairez JA, Cueto SM. [Immunology of the fetal-maternal relationship]. [Spanish]. *Rev Alerg Mex* 1996;43:18–22.

340.   Nishikori K, Noma J, Hirakawa S, Amano T, Kudo T. The change of membrane complement regulatory protein in chorion of early pregnancy. *Clin Immunol Immunopathol* 1993;69:167–74.

341.   Pham TQ, Goluszko P, Popov V, Nowicki S, Nowicki BJ. Molecular cloning and characterization of Dr-II, a nonfimbrial adhesin-I-like adhesin isolated from gestational pyelonephritis-associated Escherichia coli that binds to decay-accelerating factor. *Infect Immun* 1997;65:4309–18.

342.   Girardi G, Berman J, Redecha P, Spruce L, Thurman JM, Kraus D, *et al.* Complement C5a receptors and neutrophils mediate fetal injury in the antiphospholipid syndrome. *J Clin Invest* 2003;112:1644–54.

343.   Romero R, Mazor M, Avila C, Quintero R, Munoz H. Uterine "allergy": A novel mechanism for preterm labor [abstract]. *Am J Obstet Gynecol* 1991;164:375.

344.   Holgate ST. The epidemic of allergy and asthma. *Nature* 1999;402:B2–4.

345.   Corry DB, Kheradmand F. Induction and regulation of the IgE response. *Nature* 1999;402:B18–23.

346.   Holloway JA, Warner JO, Vance GH, Diaper ND, Warner JA, Jones CA. Detection of house-dust-mite allergen in amniotic fluid and umbilical-cord blood. *Lancet* 2000;356:1900–2.

347.   Jones AC, Miles EA, Warner JO, Colwell BM, Bryant TN, Warner JA. Fetal peripheral blood mononuclear cell proliferative responses to mitogenic and allergenic stimuli during gestation. *Pediatr Allergy Immunol* 1996;7:109–16.

348.   Rudolph MI, Reinicke K, Cruz MA, Gallardo V, Gonzalez C, Bardisa L. Distribution of mast cells and the effect of their mediators on contractility in human myometrium. *Br J Obstet Gynaecol* 1993;100:1125–30.

349.   Padilla L, Reinicke K, Montesino H, Villena F, Asencio H, Cruz M, *et al.* Histamine content and mast cells distribution in mouse uterus: the effect of sexual hormones, gestation and labor. *Cell Mol Biol* 1990;36:93–100.

350.   Rudolph MI, Bardisa L, Cruz MA, Reinicke K. Mast cells mediators evoke contractility and potentiate each other in mouse uterine horns. *Gen Pharmacol* 1992;23:833–6.

351.   Garfield RE, Bytautiene E, Vedernikov YP, Marshall JS, Romero R. Modulation of rat uterine contractility by mast cells and their mediators. *Am J Obstet Gynecol* 2000;183:118–25.

352.   Bytautiene E, Vedernikov YP, Saade GR, Romero R, Garfield RE. Endogenous mast cell degranulation modulates cervical contractility in the guinea pig. *Am J Obstet Gynecol* 2002;186:438–45.

353.   RE Garfield, personal commmunication.

354.   Shingai Y, Nakagawa K, Kato T, Fujioka T, Matsumoto T, Kihana T, *et al.* Severe allergy in a pregnant woman after vaginal examination with a latex glove. *Gynecol Obstet Invest* 2002;54:183–4.

355.   Bulmer JN, Pace D, Ritson A. Immunoregulatory cells in human decidua: morphology, immunohistochemistry and function. *Reprod Nutr Dev* 1988;28:1599–613.

356.   Lachapelle MH, Miron P, Hemmings R, Roy DC. Endometrial T, B, and NK cells in patients with recurrent spontaneous abortion. Altered profile and pregnancy outcome. *J Immunol* 1996;156:4027–34.

357.   Kammerer U, Schoppet M, McLellan AD, Kapp M, Huppertz HI, Kampgen E, *et al.* Human decidua contains potent immunostimulatory CD83(+) dendritic cells. *Am J Pathol* 2000;157:159–69.

358.   Bytautiene E, Romero R, Vedernikov Y, Saade G, Garfield R. An allergic reaction can induce premature labor and delivery, which can be prevented by treatment with antihistaminics and chromolyn sodium [abstract]. *Am J Obstet Gynecol* 2004;189:S71.

359.   Iams JD, Johnson FF, Sonek J, Sachs L, Gebauer C, Samuels P. Cervical competence as a continuum: a study of ultrasonographic cervical length and obstetric performance. *Am J Obstet Gynecol* 1995;172:1097–103.

360.   Romero R, Mazor M, Gomez R. Cervix, incompetence and premature labor. *Fetus* 1993;3:1.

361.   Mesiano S. Roles of estrogen and progesterone in human parturition. *Front Horm Res* 2001;27:86–104.

362.   Chwalisz K. The use of progesterone antagonists for cervical ripening and as an adjunct to labour

and delivery. *Hum Reprod* 1994; 9 Suppl 1:131–61.

363. Gorodeski IG, Geier A, Lunenfeld B, Beery R, Bahary CM. Progesterone (P) receptor dynamics in estrogen primed normal human cervix following P injection. *Fertil Steril* 1987;47:108–13.

364. Stjernholm Y, Sahlin L, Akerberg S, Elinder A, Eriksson HA, Malmstrom A, *et al*. Cervical ripening in humans: potential roles of estrogen, progesterone, and insulin-like growth factor-I. *Am J Obstet Gynecol* 1996;174:1065–71.

365. Bernal AL. Overview of current research in parturition. *Exp Physiol* 2001;86:213–22.

366. Young IR. The comparative physiology of parturition in mammals. In: Smith R, editor. *The Endocrinology of Parturition.* Basel: Reinhardt Druck; 2001. p. 10–30.

367. Bygdeman M, Swahn ML, Gemzell-Danielsson K, Gottlieb C. The use of progesterone antagonists in combination with prostaglandin for termination of pregnancy. *Hum Reprod* 1994;9 Suppl 1:121–5.

368. Puri CP, Patil RK, Elger WA, Pongubala JM. Effects of progesterone antagonist ZK 98.299 on early pregnancy and foetal outcome in bonnet monkeys. *Contraception* 1990;41:197–205.

369. McGarrigle HH, Lachelin GC. Increasing saliva (free) oestriol to progesterone ratio in late pregnancy: a role for oestriol in initiating spontaneous labour in man? *BMJ* 1984;289:457–9.

370. Westphal U, Stroupe SD, Cheng SL. Progesterone binding to serum proteins. *Ann N Y Acad Sci* 1977;286:10–28.

371. Karalis K, Goodwin G, Majzoub JA. Cortisol blockade of progesterone: a possible molecular mechanism involved in the initiation of human labor. *Nat Med* 1996;2:556–60.

372. Milewich L, Gant NF, Schwarz BE, Chen GT, MacDonald PC. Initiation of human parturition. VIII. Metabolism of progesterone by fetal membranes of early and late human gestation. *Obstet Gynecol* 1977;50:45–8.

373. Mitchell BF, Wong S. Changes in 17 beta,20 alpha-hydroxysteroid dehydrogenase activity supporting an increase in the estrogen/progesterone ratio of human fetal membranes at parturition. *Am J Obstet Gynecol* 1993;168:1377–85.

374. Pieber D, Allport VC, Hills F, Johnson M, Bennett PR. Interactions between progesterone receptor isoforms in myometrial cells in human labour. *Mol Hum Reprod* 2001;7:875–9.

375. Rezapour M, Backstrom T, Lindblom B, Ulmsten U. Sex steroid receptors and human parturition. *Obstet Gynecol* 1997;89:918–24.

376. How H, Huang ZH, Zuo J, Lei ZM, Spinnato JA, Rao CV. Myometrial estradiol and progesterone receptor changes in preterm and term pregnancies. *Obstet Gynecol* 1995;86:936–40.

377. Henderson D, Wilson T. Reduced binding of progesterone receptor to its nuclear response element after human labor onset. *Am J Obstet Gynecol* 2001;185:579–85.

378. Gustafsson JA. An update on estrogen receptors. *Semin Perinatol* 2000;24:66–9.

379. Warner M, Nilsson S, Gustafsson JA. The estrogen receptor family. *Curr Opin Obstet Gynecol* 1999;11:249–54.

380. Mesiano S, Chan EC, Fitter JT, Kwek K, Yeo G, Smith R. Progesterone withdrawal and estrogen activation in human parturition are coordinated by progesterone receptor A expression in the myometrium. *J Clin Endocrinol Metab* 2002;87:2924–30.

381. Pieber D, Allport VC, Bennett PR. Progesterone receptor isoform A inhibits isoform B-mediated transactivation in human amnion. *Eur J Pharmacol* 2001;427:7–11.

382. Bennett P, Allport V, Loudon J, Elliott C. Prostaglandins, the fetal membranes and the cervix. *Front Horm Res* 2001;27:147–64.

383. Allport VC, Pieber D, Slater DM, Newton R, White JO, Bennett PR. Human labour is associated with nuclear factor-kappaB activity which mediates cyclo-oxygenase-2 expression and is involved with the 'functional progesterone withdrawal'. *Mol Hum Reprod* 2001;7:581–6.

384. Belt AR, Baldassare JJ, Molnar M, Romero R, Hertelendy F. The nuclear transcription factor NF-kappaB mediates interleukin-1beta-induced expression of cyclooxygenase-2 in human myometrial cells. *Am J Obstet Gynecol* 1999;181:359–66.

385. Kalkhoven E, Wissink S, Van der Saag PT, van der Burg B. Negative interaction between the RelA(p65) subunit of NF-kappaB and the progesterone receptor. *J Biol Chem* 1996;271:6217–24.

386. Daya S. Efficacy of progesterone support for pregnancy in women with recurrent miscarriage. A meta-analysis of controlled trials. *Br J Obstet Gynaecol* 1989;96:275–80.

387. Goldstein P, Berrier J, Rosen S, Sacks HS, Chalmers TC. A meta-analysis of randomized control trials of progestational agents in pregnancy. *Br J Obstet Gynaecol* 1989;96:265–74.

388. Keirse MJ. Progestogen administration in pregnancy may prevent preterm delivery. *Br J Obstet Gynaecol* 1990;97:149–54.

389. da Fonseca EB, Bittar RE, Carvalho MH, Zugaib M. Prophylactic administration of progesterone by vaginal suppository to reduce the incidence of spontaneous preterm birth in women at increased risk: a randomized placebo-controlled double-blind study. *Am J Obstet Gynecol* 2003;188:419–24.

390.   Meis PJ, Klebanoff M, Thom E, Dombrowski MP, Sibai B, Moawad AH, *et al.* Prevention of recurrent preterm delivery by 17 alpha-hydroxyprogesterone caproate. *N Engl J Med* 2003;348:2379–85.

391.   ACOG Committee Opinion. Use of progesterone to reduce preterm birth. *Obstet Gynecol* 2003;102:1115–16.

Chapter 4

Fetal growth, maturity and preterm birth

Jason Gardosi, Sue M Kady and André Francis

Introduction

Prematurity is the leading cause of neonatal morbidity and mortality. According to UK figures, it is responsible for 56% of neonatal deaths.[1] Preterm delivery can be iatrogenic or spontaneous. In this chapter, the clinical associations of spontaneous onset of labour are reviewed, with special emphasis on the epidemiological links between fetal growth, maturity and preterm birth.

Prepregnancy predictors of preterm birth

There is a large aetiological heterogeneity in prematurity,[2] with many factors known even prior to pregnancy that are associated with subsequent preterm birth. These include maternal characteristics such as low maternal age, nulliparity, high parity, low maternal weight, obesity, ethnic origin, social class and cigarette smoking (Table 4.1).[3-6]

The effect of smoking on spontaneous preterm birth is dose related.[6,7] However, the association is somewhat complex as smoking is also known to be protective of pre-eclampsia in primiparae.[8] Measures of social class (including indicators of socio-economic status, education, marital status and low income) are also linked to preterm birth.[3,9-11]

Another factor is ethnic origin. Each of the main ethnic minority groups represented in the UK has an increased likelihood of preterm delivery.[6,12] It is uncertain as to what degree this difference is due to physiological variation. There is interaction with other confounders, in particular social class, and different interactions are found in different ethnic groups.[13] In Afro-Caribbean women, half of the excess in prematurity rates can be explained by deprivation and marital status, while in Asian women from the Indian subcontinent, the increased risk of preterm delivery may not be related to deprivation.[13] The link between prepregnancy obesity and preterm delivery is well established.[5] Obese women also have a higher incidence of pre-eclampsia.[14-16] Previous obstetric history is also relevant: miscarriage[17] and preterm birth[18,19] are strongly linked. In fact, the risk is higher the earlier the previous preterm birth has occurred.[20] Previous preterm birth associated with pre-eclampsia is a risk factor for subsequent indicated preterm delivery associated with pre-eclampsia.[21,22]

Many of these factors are interrelated and require assessment by multivariate analysis. Table 4.2 shows adjusted odds ratios for primiparae and multiparae in an English population.[6]

Table 4.1. Univariate analysis of factors associated with preterm birth; adapted with permission from Gardosi and Francis[6]

		Column %	Preterm birth (<37 weeks)		
			Rate (%)	Odds ratio	95% CI
Parity	nulliparae	43.1	7.5	1.14	1.03–1.27
	multiparae[a]	56.9	6.7		
Delivery	iatrogenic	21.7	9.2	1.47	1.30–1.65
	spontaneous[a]	78.3	6.5		
Maternal age	<20	7.8	10.4	1.60	1.35–1.90
	20–34[a]	84.8	6.7		
	≥35	7.4	7.0	1.03	0.84–1.27
	other[b]	0.05			
Maternal height (cm)	≤155	11.8	9.3	1.41	1.21–1.64
	156–171[a]	78.2	6.8		
	≥172	10.1	6.5	0.96	0.79–1.15
	other[b]	2.1			
Maternal weight (kg)	<52	9.9	11.3	1.80	1.55–2.10
	52–80[a]	79.0	6.6		
	>80	11.1	6.7	1.02	0.86–1.21
	other[b]	1.8			
Body mass index (kg/m²)	<20.0	10.0	10.0	1.56	1.33–1.83
	20.1–29.4[a]	78.3	6.6		
	>29.4	11.7	7.3	1.11	0.94–1.31
	other[b]	3.4			
Ethnic group	European[a]	89.2	6.8		
	Non-European	10.8	8.8	1.32	1.13–1.54
	Indian/Pakistani	6.3	9.0	1.34	1.10–1.64
	Afro-Caribbean	2.1	9.8	1.48	1.08–2.03
	other	2.4	7.5	1.11	0.80–1.55
Cigarettes per day	1–9	9.1	7.9	1.26	1.05–1.50
	10+	14.9	10.1	1.65	1.45–1.88
	any	24.0	9.2	1.50	1.34–1.68
	none[a]	76.0	6.4		
Alcohol consumption	regular/heavy	0.1			
	moderate	31.6	6.6	0.89	0.80–1.00
	none[a]	68.4	7.3		
History of abortion	yes	22.0	8.0	1.20	1.06–1.36
	no[a]	78.0	6.8		
History of preterm delivery (11 983 multiparae)	yes	3.7	18.8	3.51	2.74–4.50
	no[a]	96.3	6.2		
Menstrual–scan dates discrepancy	<−7 days	4.8	5.4	0.86	0.65–1.14
	within ±7 days[a]	71.9	6.2		
	>+7 days	23.3	10.2	1.72	1.54–1.93
	other[b]	1.4			

Total n = 21 069; [a] baseline category for odds ratios; [b] excluded because of missing data or likelihood of erroneous entry

Dating pregnancies: menstrual history versus ultrasound biometry

The proportion of births which falls into the 'preterm' category depends on the method of dating used. Over the last two decades, this has changed as ultrasound scanning has gradually been introduced into routine practice. Before the advent of ultrasound, pregnancy dating (expected date of confinement and the length of pregnancy at any one time) had to be determined by menstrual history, and 'gestational age' had become synonymous with menstrual age.

Table 4.2. Adjusted odds ratios for spontaneous preterm birth for primiparae and multiparae, including prevalence and aetiological fraction (population attributable risk, PAR); reproduced with permission from Gardosi and Francis[6]

	Prevalence (%)	Adjusted odds ratio	PAR[a] (%)
Early preterm (< 34 weeks)			
Nulliparae:			
Maternal weight ≥ 80 kg	9.08	1.78	6.61
Prolonged MCI	22.76	1.45	9.26
Multiparae:			
Cigarette smoker	24.00	1.47	10.14
History of abortion	21.97	1.55	10.72
History of preterm delivery	2.12	5.07	7.93
Prolonged MCI	22.99	1.91	17.27
All preterm (< 37 weeks)			
Nulliparae:			
Age < 20 years	15.01	1.34	4.79
Weight < 52 kg	10.89	1.40	4.21
Weight ≥ 80 kg	9.08	1.31	2.77
Non-European	9.50	1.30	2.78
Prolonged MCI	22.76	1.52	10.66
Multiparae:			
Age < 20 years	2.36	1.54	1.27
Height < 155 cm	12.63	1.24	2.92
Weight < 52 kg	9.15	1.69	5.91
Non-European	11.73	1.31	3.53
Cigarette smoker	25.68	1.82	17.38
History of abortion	26.43	1.21	5.35
History of preterm delivery	3.66	3.27	7.69
Prolonged MCI	23.17	1.86	16.57

[a] population attributable risk, $PAR = 100 \times (AOR - 1)/[AOR + (100/Pr) - 1]$, where AOR = adjusted odds ratio and Pr = prevalence); MCI = menstruation–conception interval, based on the difference in gestational age between menstrual dates and ultrasound dates

However, accuracy of recollection of menstrual history varies and can be wrong in 10-45% of cases.[23] Furthermore, Naegele's rule assumes that conception occurs on day 14 of the follicular phase, but this is in fact often not the case. The error has a wide distribution and positive skewness[24] which tends not to be predictable. For example, over 50% of the cycles in which ovulation was later than day 18 were not predicted by a preceding irregularity or abnormal length of menstrual cycles.[25] In contrast, the error in ultrasound biometry is narrower and more normally distributed. The 95% confidence interval was 5–6 days when performed by one or a few operators in a single unit,[26-28] and 8 days when performed in multiple units as part of a routine service.[29] Ultrasound is a better predictor of the date of confinement, even when the discrepancy between the two methods of prediction is small.[30] The resultant clinical recommendation is that (as long as a first or second trimester dating scan is available) it should be used as the method of choice for establishing the pregnancy dates.[31,32]

Improved pregnancy dating by fetal age (as assessed by ultrasound biometry) in contrast to menstrual age and its associated error gives us new perspectives at both extremes of gestation.[33] Many apparent post-term pregnancies are in fact misdated and not post-term by scan dates, as conception occurred later than mid-cycle and the actual gestational age was overstated by the menstrual history.[34] Accurate dating is even more important in the preterm period, where small dating errors can have substantial effects. Menstrual dates systematically underestimate the prevalence of preterm delivery and the 'left shift' along the gestational age axis results in more pregnancies being recognised as preterm.[35,36] For example, in a cohort of over 23 000 pregnancies dated by menstrual and scan dates, the preterm rate (less than 37 weeks of gestation) by menstrual dates was 6.3%, and by scan dates 7.0%; below 34 weeks, the rate is similarly higher: 1.7% (menstrual dates) versus 1.9% (scan dates).[6]

Unlike the error in the post-term period, where menstrual history often overestimates the true length of gestation, many preterm babies are older than their menstrual dates would suggest: menstrual dates of babies considered preterm by last menstrual period (LMP) underestimated their scan-based gestational age by more than one week in 27.5%, and overestimated it in 14.2% of cases.[37] Together, the dating error was more than a week in over 40% of cases. This is clearly of importance when decisions are made on the basis of gestational age, for both clinical management and for counselling parents.

The menstruation–conception interval

While ultrasound is more accurate in establishing the actual age of conception, the menstrual history still has a role to play, as a discrepancy between menstrual and scan dates has associations with outcome. This could be due to several factors, including irregular periods, uncertain recall of menstrual history, social class, or an unfavourable milieu for implantation. However, a negative difference, i.e. early ovulation within the conception cycle, has no appreciable effect. A positive discrepancy, as would arise from delayed ovulation or a prolonged follicular phase, increases the risk of preterm delivery significantly (Table 4.1).[6] As it occurs in a substantial proportion of cases (26% in an unselected population), the aetiological fraction or 'population attributable risk' is one of the highest of all variables studied.

Other adverse outcome indicators have also been described for a menstrual–scan dates discrepancy, including fetal growth restriction and stillbirth.[38–40]

Adverse outcome following an unexpectedly low crown rump measurement in the first trimester has also been reported.[41] This was described as being due to early, severe fetal growth restriction. Alternatively, it could be interpreted as another example of the effect of an increased menstruation to conception interval affecting pregnancy outcome.

Fetal growth

Many factors that affect length of gestation also affect fetal growth. The advantage of good pregnancy dating is that it allows a distinction to be made between 'low birthweight' due to fetal growth restriction and due to prematurity. A number of investigators have reported a link between small-for-gestational-age (SGA) babies and preterm labour.[42–47]

The birthweight distribution at preterm gestations is negatively skewed,[12] while the distribution of fetal weight at the same gestation is close to normal (Figure 4.1). Ultrasound studies can provide more appropriate preterm weight limits, as they can be based on pregnancies that have proceeded to normal term delivery.[48,49]

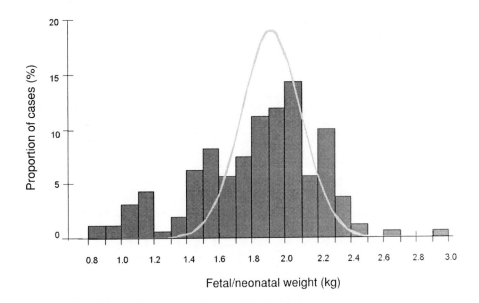

Figure 4.1. Ultrasound fetal weight versus birthweight standard at 32 weeks of gestation. The line shows ultrasound weight estimations derived from pregnancies that have proceeded to normal term delivery, according to Hadlock.[48] The curve is characterised by a relatively narrow normal distribution. The histogram shows birthweights of babies born at this same, preterm gestation in a data set of approximately 40 000 cases in the Midlands.[12] The distribution has a lower median, a wider range and negative skewness

In addition to using fetal instead of neonatal weight, the standard also needs to exclude pathological factors (such as smoking) to assess the effect of the relationship between fetal growth and prematurity. Furthermore, as maternal physiological and constitutional variables such as parity, height, weight and ethnic origin are also associated with preterm birth (Table 4.1), they need to be adjusted for. This is done by using a standard which can calculate the optimal growth potential and can 'customise' the normal limits for each pregnancy.[50,51] This tool for assessing birthweight and fetal growth has been found to improve the differentiation between normal and abnormal outcome, in low- as well as high-risk populations.[52,53] Applying such an individually optimised standard would seem particularly relevant in preterm births. Customised centiles have been applied to birthweights of preterm babies born after spontaneous onset of labour in case–controlled studies in Europe[10] and the USA.[54] After adjustment for a variety of confounders, spontaneous preterm birth was found to be significantly associated with an increased risk of the fetus's not having reached its growth potential.[55]

It has also been suggested that failure of tocolysis may be linked to a baby's being smaller than expected at that gestation.[56,57]

The association between spontaneous preterm birth and growth restriction suggests that the widespread use of neonatal standards to assess the weight of preterm babies should be discouraged, as they are derived from a (preterm) population which is, by definition, not normal. The application of appropriate standards also allows a better understanding of 'unexplained' antepartum stillbirths. Fetal growth restriction has a strong association with antepartum stillbirths.[40,58] A recently completed multivariate analysis[59] of physiological and pathological factors in a Swedish database of over 300 000 unselected pregnancies showed that fetal growth restriction (< 10th customised centile) had the highest aetiological fraction or 'population attributable risk' (PAR) for stillbirths in the preterm period: 62.7. Other significant factors were antepartum haemorrhage (PAR 5.5), maternal weight greater than the 90th centile (PAR 4.4) and cord accidents (PAR 1.3). For neonatal deaths after preterm birth, the analysis showed two significant factors – congenital anomalies (PAR 39.9) and fetal growth restriction less than the third customised centile (PAR 22.0).[59]

Such considerations may go some way to explaining why in many instances tocolysis is unsuccessful.[57] The strong associations between growth failure, spontaneous preterm birth and stillbirth raise the question whether preterm labour should not, at times, be seen as an adaptive response to an unfavourable intrauterine environment, initiated by the fetoplacental unit. It is tempting to speculate further that, in instances where this response is not initiated or is delayed, stillbirth may supervene. The clinical implication is that the assessment of a mother in spontaneous preterm labour should include a careful assessment of the growth status of the fetus.

Prematurity, fetal growth restriction and neonatal survival

Within low-birthweight categories, growth restricted infants do better than their non-growth restricted counterparts whose low weight is more likely due to earlier gestation.[44] Gestational age is the key predictor of survival at the limits of viability.[60] Nevertheless, when corrected for length of gestation, growth restricted preterm infants have a significantly higher perinatal morbidity and mortality than appropriately grown infants.[61,62] The relative contributions of maturity and growth on survival are, however, uncertain, and studies are hampered by different dating methods which can have a substantial effect at the extremes of gestation.

To study the effects of pregnancy dating on the assessment of weight, we plotted 1608 unselected East Midlands preterm birthweights on a standard growth curve, comparing scan and menstrual dates (Figure 4.2). Birthweights plotted according to menstrual history had a much wider distribution and were more likely to be outside normal weight limits. 50.3% of preterm babies which are SGA by menstrual history were in fact appropriate for gestational age (AGA) when scan dates were used, and 39.8% of babies plotted as large for gestational age (LGA) by LMP dates were AGA.

The question, therefore, is whether, at any given preterm gestation, a deficit of weight or maturity is more important in affecting survival. We examined an ultrasound-dated data set of more than 400 000 births in Sweden (Figure 4.3), and plotted the survival rates of SGA (defined as below the 10th customised centile) and non-SGA neonates. The figure shows that there was a difference in survival between these two weight groups between 24 and 32 weeks of gestation.

Pre-eclampsia

Hypertension and proteinuria in pregnancy is linked to SGA babies as well as spontaneous preterm birth.[16,63] It is common in clinical parlance to suggest that pre-eclampsia 'causes' fetal growth restriction. However, as the baby is often already SGA at the time pre-eclampsia manifests clinically, it is likely that the process of diminished growth has gone on for some time.

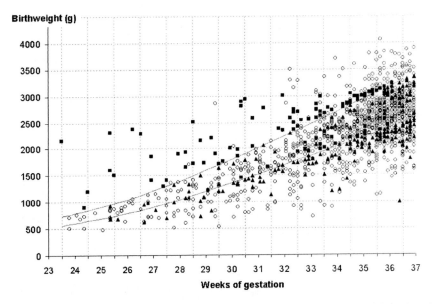

Figure 4.2. Dating error and its effect on weight-for-gestation; the data set comprised 1608 unselected singleton preterm births, from pregnancies with dates by 'certain' menstrual history as well as by ultrasound scan in the first or second trimester; birthweights plotted by last menstrual period (LMP) with 90th and 10th centile lines, with points falling into large, appropriate, or small for gestational age categories; recalculating gestational age by scan would result in no change in cases marked (o); however, many datapoints would shift along the gestation axis sufficiently for the birthweight to end up in either a smaller (■) or a larger (▲) weight-for-gestation category

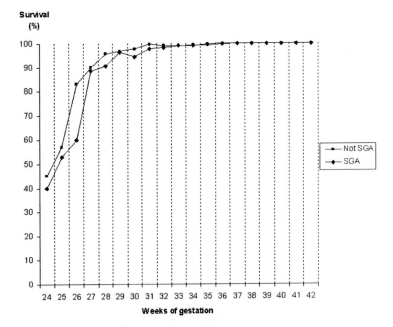

Figure 4.3. Survival rates of small-for-gestational-age (SGA) versus non-SGA babies in an unselected, ultrasound-dated Swedish population, 1992–1995, n > 400 000

This notion is supported by preliminary results from a longitudinal, blinded ultrasound study of primiparous women in Amsterdam.[64] Thirty-seven of a total of 220 women scanned serially developed clinical pre-eclampsia, of which 38% had babies who were SGA at birth (smaller than the 10th customised centile). In the majority of these cases (79%), the growth curve crossed below the 10th centile *before* the clinical manifestation of pre-eclampsia, and the average delay between crossing of the curve and clinical pre-eclampsia was 12 days (Figure 4.4).[64]

Multifetal pregnancies

The recent increase in multifetal pregnancies is largely due to fertility treatments and assisted reproduction techniques.[65,66] Twin pregnancies provide a fascinating insight into associations between gestation length and growth. They are almost ten times more likely to be low birthweight (less than 2500 or less than 1500 g), and their mean birthweight is approximately 1000 g less than that of singletons.[66] This weight difference is caused by both slower growth and by birth at earlier gestations.

As in singletons, growth restriction in twins is mostly an effect of placental failure. This applies to both mono- and dichorionic twin pregnancies. Although monochorionic twins are at risk of twin–twin transfusion and associated growth problems, mono- and dichorionic pregnancies do not differ significantly in inter-twin disparity in fetal size.[67]

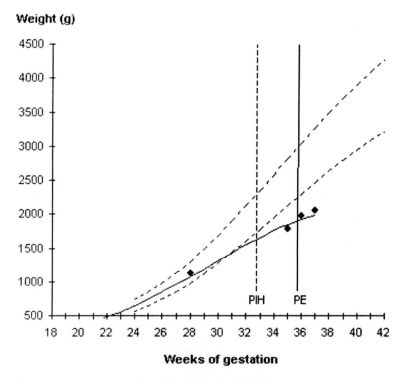

Figure 4.4. An example of a growth curve crossing the 10th centile before the clinical manifestation of pregnancy induced hypertension (PIH) and supervening proteinuria (pre-eclampsia, PE)

Twin birthweight discordance is a risk factor for preterm birth and is usually attributable to fetal growth restriction.[68] Most twins are not born with discordant weight, yet their gestation length after spontaneous-onset labour is on average three weeks shorter than that of singletons,[69] which means that half of all twins are born preterm. About 70% of women with an 'ideal' twin pregnancy gave birth between 35 and 38 weeks of gestation.[70] There is a higher mortality rate among twins born after 37 weeks when compared with singleton infants at a similar gestational age.[71] The increased risk of stillbirth and neonatal death after 38 weeks of gestation corresponded to that observed in singleton pregnancies at 43 weeks of gestation.[72] Elective delivery in twins needs to be planned for earlier gestations than in singletons.[69]

Longitudinal analysis of intrauterine weight suggests that the optimal weight curve for twins follows that of singletons, until a relatively late slowing of growth before labour.[73] This is supported by studies of ultrasound biometry in pregnancies following assisted conception, which showed that twins were the same size as singletons in the second trimester, while being born earlier in the third trimester, and significantly smaller than singletons.[74] These findings are again consistent with the notion that, in twins as in singletons, intrauterine growth restriction is an antecedent to spontaneous preterm birth.

Conclusions

Prematurity has heterogeneous causes which include demographic characteristics as well as the timing of conception and subsequent growth. Fetal growth restriction is usually associated with failure of early placentation. It can be demonstrated to precede, in many instances, the clinical manifestation of pregnancy-induced hypertension and pre-eclampsia. Growth failure is strongly associated with antepartum stillbirths as well as preterm birth. In the absence of other obvious causes, spontaneous preterm labour with evidence of growth restriction could be seen as a fetal adaptive response to escape an unfavourable intrauterine environment. In other words, not only is the size of the baby dependent on its length of gestation, but the length of gestation is also determined by the baby's size and growth *in utero*. These concepts have implications for the understanding of the pathophysiology of preterm labour, as well as clinical management.

References

1.   *Confidential Enquiry into Stillbirths and Deaths in Infancy: 8th Annual Report*. London: Maternal and Child Health Research Consortium; 2001.
2.   Savitz DA, Blackmore CA, Thorp JM. Epidemiologic characteristics of preterm delivery: etiologic heterogeneity. *Am J Obstet Gynecol* 1991;164:467–71.
3.   Meis PJ, Michielutte R, Peters TJ, Wells HB, Sands RE, Coles EC, et al. Factors associated with preterm birth in Cardiff, Wales. II. Indicated and spontaneous preterm birth. *Am J Obstet Gynecol* 1995;173:597–602.
4.   Kramer MS, Coates AL, Michoud MC, Dagenais S, Hamilton EF, Papageorgiou A. Maternal anthropometry and idiopathic preterm labor. *Obstet Gynecol* 1995;86:744–8.
5.   Cnattingius S, Bergstrom R, Lipworth L, Kramer MS. Prepregnancy weight and the risk of adverse pregnancy outcomes. *N Engl J Med* 1998;338:147–52.
6.   Gardosi J, Francis A. Early pregnancy predictors of preterm birth: the role of the menstruation–conception interval. *BJOG* 2000;107:228–37.
7.   Kyrklund-Blomberg NB, Cnattingius S. Preterm birth and maternal smoking: risks related to gestational age and onset of delivery. *Am J Obstet Gynecol* 1998;179:1051–5.
8.   Marcoux S, Brisson J, Fabia J. The effect of cigarette smoking on the risk of preeclampsia and gestational hypertension. *Am J Epidemiol* 1989;130:950–7.
9.   Kramer MS, Seguin L, Lydon J, Goulet L. Socio-economic disparities in pregnancy outcome: why

do the poor fare so poorly? *Paediatr Perinat Epidemiol* 2000;14:194–210.

10.   Zeitlin J, Ancel PY, Saurel-Cubizolles MJ, Papiernik E. The relationship between intrauterine growth restriction and preterm delivery: an empirical approach using data from a European case–control study. *BJOG* 2000;107:750–8.

11.   Peacock JL, Bland MJ, Anderson HR. Preterm delivery: effects of socio-economic factors, psychological stress, smoking, alcohol, and caffeine. *BMJ* 1995;311:531–5.

12.   Wilcox M, Gardosi J, Mongelli M, Ray C, Johnson I. Birth weight from pregnancies dated by ultrasonography in a multicultural British population. *BMJ* 1993;307:588–91.

13.   Aveyard P, Cheng KK, Manaseki S, Gardosi J. The risk of preterm delivery in women from different ethnic groups. *BJOG* 2002;109:894–9.

14.   Eskenazi B, Fenster L, Sidney S. A multivariate analysis of risk factors for preeclampsia. *JAMA* 1991;266:237–41.

15.   Stone JL, Lockwood CJ, Bekowitz GS, Alvarez M, Lapinski R, Berkowitz RL. Risk factors for severe preeclampsia. *Obstet Gynecol* 1994;83:357–61.

16.   Zeitlin JA, Ancel P-Y, Saurel-Cubizolles MJ, Papiernik E. Are risk factors the same for small for gestational age versus other preterm births? *Am J Obstet Gynecol* 2001;185:208–15.

17.   Goldenberg RL, Mayberry SK, Copper RL, Dunard MB, Hauth JC. Pregnancy outcome following a second trimester loss. *Obstet Gynecol* 1993;81:444–6.

18.   Bakketeig LS, Hoffman HJ, Harley EE. The tendency to repeat gestational age and birthweight in successive births. *Am J Obstet Gynecol* 1979;135:1086–103.

19.   Goldenberg RL, Hoffman HJ, Cliver SP, Cutter GR, Nelson KG, Copper RL. The influence of previous low birth weight on birth weight, gestational age, and anthropometric measurements in the current pregnancy. *Obstet Gynecol* 1992;79:276–80.

20.   Mercer BM, Goldenberg RL, Moawad AH, Meis PJ, Iams JD, *et al.* The preterm prediction study: effect of gestational age and cause of preterm birth on subsequent obstetric outcome. National Institute of Child Health and Human Development Maternal-Fetal Medicine Units Network. *Am J Obstet Gynecol* 1999;181(5 Pt 1):1216–21.

21.   Meis PJ, Goldenberg RL, Mercer BM, Iams JD, Moawad AH, Miodovnik M, *et al.* The preterm prediction study: risk factors for indicated preterm births. Maternal-Fetal Medicine Units Network of the National Institute of Child Health and Human Development. *Am J Obstet Gynecol* 1998;178:562–7.

22.   Koike T, Minakami H, Izumi A, Watanabe T, Matsubara S, Sato I. Recurrence risk of preterm birth due to preeclampsia. *Gynecol Obstet Invest* 2002;53:22–7.

23.   Geirsson RT, Busby-Earle RMC. Certain dates may not provide a reliable estimate of gestational age. *Br J Obstet Gynaecol* 1991;98:108–9.

24.   Guerrero R, Florez PE. The duration of pregnancy. *Lancet* 1969;(ii):268–9.

25.   Walker EM, Lewis M, Cooper W, Marnie M, Howie PW. Occult biochemical pregnancy: fact or fiction? *Br J Obstet Gynaecol* 1988;95:659–63.

26.   Persson PH, Weldner BM. Reliability of ultrasound fetometry in estimating gestational age in the second trimester. *Acta Obstet Gynecol Scand* 1986;65:481–3.

27.   Geirsson RT, Have G. Comparison of actual and ultrasound estimated second trimester gestational length in *in-vitro* fertilized pregnancies. *Acta Obstet Gynecol Scand* 1993;72:344–6.

28.   Chervenak FA, Skupski DW, Romero R, Myers MK, Smith-Levitin M, Rosenwaks Z, *et al.* How accurate is fetal biometry in the assessment of fetal age? *Am J Obstet Gynecol* 1998;178:678–87.

29.   Mul T, Mongelli M, Gardosi J. A comparative analysis of second-trimester ultrasound dating formulae in pregnancies conceived with artificial reproductive techniques. *Ultrasound Obstet Gynecol* 1996;8:397–402.

30.   Mongelli M, Wilcox M, Gardosi J. Estimating the date of confinement: ultrasonographic biometry versus certain menstrual dates. *Am J Obstet Gynecol* 1996;174:278–81.

31.   Gardosi J. Dating of pregnancy: time to forget the last menstrual period [editorial]. *Ultrasound Obstet Gynecol* 1997;9:367–8.

32.   Gardosi J, Geirsson RT. Routine ultrasound is the method of choice for dating pregnancy. *Br J Obstet Gynaecol* 1998;105:933–6.

33.   Goldenberg RL, Davis RO, Cutter GR, Hoffman HJ, Brumfield CG, Foster JM. Prematurity, postdates, and growth retardation: the influence of use of ultrasonography on reported gestational age. *Am J Obstet Gynecol* 1989;160:462–70.

34.   Gardosi J, Vanner T, Francis A. Gestational age and induction of labour for prolonged pregnancy. *Br J Obstet Gynaecol* 1997;104:792–7.

35.   Mongelli M, Gardosi J. Birth weight, prematurity and accuracy of gestational age. *Int J Gynaecol Obstet* 1997;56:251–6.

36.   Yang H, Kramer MS, Platt RW, Blondel B, Breart G, Morin I, *et al.* How does early ultrasound scan estimation of gestational age lead to higher rates of preterm birth? *Am J Obstet Gynecol* 2002;186:433–7.

37. Gardosi J, Francis A. Effect of menstrual dating error in the assessment of gestational age in premature babies. *Am J Obstet Gynecol* 1999;180 Suppl 1:A334.

38. Larsen T, Nguyen TH, Greisen G, Engholm G, Moller H. Does a discrepancy between gestational age determined by biparietal diameter and last menstrual period sometimes signify early intrauterine growth retardation? *BJOG* 2000;107:238–44.

39. Nguyen TH, Larsen T, Engholm G, Moller H. A discrepancy between gestational age estimated by last menstrual period and biparietal diameter may indicate an increased risk of fetal death and adverse pregnancy outcome. *BJOG* 2000;107:1122–9.

40. Gardosi J, Francis A, Settatree R. Association between fetal growth restriction and unexplained stillbirth at term. *Am J Obstet Gynecol* 1999;180 Suppl 1:S157.

41. Smith GC, Smith MF, McNay MB, Fleming JE. First-trimester growth and the risk of low birth weight. *N Engl J Med* 1998;339:1817–22.

42. Tamura RK, Sabbagha RE, Depp R, Vaisrub N, Dooley SL, Socol ML. Diminished growth in fetuses born preterm after spontaneous labor or rupture of membranes. *Am J Obstet Gynecol* 1984;148:1105–10.

43. Weiner C, Sabbagha RE, Vaisrub N, Depp R. A hypothetical model suggesting suboptimal intrauterine growth in infants delivered preterm. *Obstet Gynecol* 1985;65:323–6.

44. Goldenberg RL, Nelson KG, Koski JF, Cutter GR. Low birth weight, intrauterine growth retardation and preterm delivery. *Am J Obstet Gynecol* 1985;152:980–4.

45. Secher NJ, Hansen PK, Thomsen B, Keiding N. Growth retardation in preterm infants. *Br J Obstet Gynaecol* 1987;94:115–20.

46. Ott WJ. Intrauterine growth retardation and preterm delivery. *Am J Obstet Gynecol* 1993;168:1710–7.

47. Doubilet PM, Benson CB, Wilkins-Haug L, Ringer S. Fetuses subsequently born premature are smaller than gestational age-matched fetuses not born premature. *J Ultrasound Med* 2003;22:359–63.

48. Hadlock FP, Harrist RB, Martinez-Poyer J. In-utero analysis of fetal growth: a sonographic weight standard. *Radiology* 1991;181:129–33.

49. Mongelli M, Gardosi J. Longitudinal study of fetal growth in subgroups of a low risk population. *Ultrasound Obstet Gynecol* 1995;6:340–4.

50. Gardosi J, Chang A, Kalyan B, Sahota D, Symonds EM. Customised antenatal growth charts. *Lancet* 1992;339:283–7.

51. Gardosi J, Mongelli M, Wilcox M, Chang A. An adjustable fetal weight standard. *Ultrasound Obstet Gynecol* 1995;6:168–74.

52. Mongelli M, Gardosi J. Longitudinal study of fetal growth in subgroups of a low risk population. *Ultrasound Obstet Gynecol* 1995;6:340–4.

53. de Jong CLD, Gardosi J, Baldwin C, Francis A, Dekker GA, van Geijn HP. Fetal weight gain in a serially scanned high-risk population. *Ultrasound Obstet Gynecol* 1998;11:39–43.

54. Bukowski R, Gahn D, Denning J, Saade G. Impairment of growth in fetuses destined to deliver preterm. *Am J Obstet Gynecol* 2001;185:463–7.

55. Gardosi J. Abnormal fetal growth is associated with spontaneous preterm labour. *Fetal Diagn Ther* 1998;13 Suppl 1:117.

56. Hediger ML, Scholl TO, Schall JI, Miller LW, Fischer RL. Fetal growth and the etiology of preterm delivery. *Obstet Gynecol* 1995;85:175–82.

57. MacGregor SN, Sabbagha RE, Tamura RK, Pielet BW, Feigenbaum SL. Differing fetal growth patterns in pregnancies complicated by preterm labor. *Obstet Gynecol* 1988;72:834–7.

58. Clausson B, Gardosi J, Francis A, Cnattingius S. Perinatal outcome in SGA births defined by customised versus population-based birthweight standards. *BJOG* 2001;108:830–4.

59. Kady SM, Gardosi J. Perinatal mortality and fetal growth restriction. In: *Fetal Surveillance. Best Practice and Research in Clinical Obstetrics and Gynaecology.* Arulkumaran S, Gardosi J, editors. London: Elsevier; 2004. (in press).

60. Draper ES, Manktelow B, Field DJ, James D. Prediction of survival for preterm births by weight and gestational age: retrospective population based study. *BMJ* 1999;319:1093–7.

61. Piper JM, Xenakis EM, McFarland M, Elliott BD, Berkus MD, Langer O. Do growth-retarded premature infants have different rates of perinatal morbidity and mortality than appropriately grown premature infants? *Obstet Gynecol* 1996;87:169–74.

62. Heinonen K, Matilainen R, Koski H, Launiala K. Intrauterine growth retardation (IUGR) in pre term infants. *J Perinat Med* 1985;13:171–8.

63. Clausson B, Cnattingius S, Axelsson O. Preterm and term births of small-for-gestational age infants: a population based study of risk factors amongst nulliparous women. *Br J Obstet Gynaecol* 1998;105:1011–7.

64. Gardosi J, de Jong CLD. Temporal relationship between onset of preeclampsia and fetal growth restriction. *Am J Obstet Gynecol* 1999;180 Suppl 1:A127.

65.   Callahan TL, Hall JE, Ettner SL, Christiansen CL, Greene MF, Crowley WF Jr. The economic impact of multiple-gestation pregnancies and the contribution of assisted-reproduction techniques to their incidence. *N Engl J Med* 1994;331:244–9.

66.   Gardosi J. Multifetal pregnancy. In: Ransom S, Dobrowski MP, Moghissi KS, McNeeley SG, Munkarah AR. editors. *Practical Strategies in Obstetrics and Gynecology*. Philadelphia: WB Saunders; 2000. p. 337–43.

67.   Sebire NJ, D'Ercole C, Soares W, Nayar R, Nicolaides KH. Intertwin disparity in fetal size in monochorionic and dichorionic pregnancies. *Obstet Gynecol* 1998;91:82–5.

68.   Cooperstock MS, Tummaru R, Bakewell R, Schramm W. Twin birth weight discordance and risk of preterm birth. *Am J Obstet Gynecol* 2000;183:63–7.

69.   Mahomoud-Kady S, Francis A, Gardosi J. Timing for elective Caesarean section for twin pregnancy. *J Obstet Gynaecol* 2004;24 (Suppl 1):48.

70.   Luke B, Minogue J, Witter FR, Keith LG, Johnson TR. The ideal twin pregnancy: patterns of weight gain, discordancy, and length of gestation. *Am J Obstet Gynecol* 1993;169:588–97.

71.   Cheung YB, Yip P, Karlberg J. Mortality of twins and singletons by gestational age: a varying-coefficient approach. *Am J Epidemiol* 2000;152:1107–16.

72.   Minakami H, Sato I. Reestimating date of delivery in multifetal pregnancies. *JAMA* 1996;275:1432–4. Erratum in: *JAMA* 1996;276:452.

73.   Min SJ, Luke B, Gillespie B, Min L, Newman RB, Mauldin JG, *et al*. Birth weight references for twins. *Am J Obstet Gynecol* 2000;182:1250–7.

74.   Gardosi J, Mul T, Francis A, Hall J, Fishel S. Comparison of second trimester biometry in singleton and twin pregnancies conceived by assisted reproduction techniques. *Br J Obstet Gynaecol*;1997:104:737–40.

Chapter 5

Recent trends in the care, complications and outcome of preterm babies

Denis Azzopardi and Raghuram Mallaiah

Introduction

The burden of preterm birth has increased in recent years. The rise in multiple births following assisted conception and the tendency towards earlier intervention in high-risk pregnancies have resulted in an increase in preterm births. In addition, more extremely premature or sick babies are surviving. Although mortality following preterm birth has reduced, preterm babies remain at a high risk of developing major complications. Outcome following preterm birth may be affected by several factors, including antenatal events, the physiological immaturity of the neonate and the effects of therapeutic interventions. An overview of the complications of preterm birth was published in 2003.[1] This paper will focus on recent trends in the care, complications and outcome for preterm babies.

The changing rate of preterm birth

An increase of 17% in the rate of preterm birth was recorded in the USA between 1980 and 2000 and similar increases have been observed in other countries.[2-6] Much of this increase was due to the rise in multiple births as a consequence of assisted conception techniques.[7-9] More than half of multiple births are born preterm and these babies have substantially increased mortality and long-term morbidity, especially if conceived by *in vitro* fertilisation. The risk of cerebral palsy is increased three- to seven-fold in twins compared with singletons and the risk is even greater in higher order multiples or where a co-sibling has died *in utero*.[10] Improved identification of at-risk pregnancies, closer monitoring of the fetus and earlier intervention may also have contributed to the increase in preterm births. For example, in the UK the lower segment caesarean section (LSCS) rate increased between 1990 and 1997 from 11% to 18%, and some of this increase is likely to have been due to earlier intervention in pregnancy.[11] Coincidental with the increase in preterm birth has been a marked reduction in neonatal mortality: for England and Wales, the neonatal mortality fell by 54% between 1975 and 1988 and by a further 20% between 1988 and 2000.[11] Unfortunately, however, there is as yet no evidence that the major adverse long-term outcomes of preterm birth have lessened. As a consequence of improved survival, the proportion of children with cerebral palsy and other neurodevelopmental problems who were born preterm has increased. These trends may now have stabilised. In England and Wales, the rate of births weighing less than

2500 g remained at 7.9% between 1997 and 2001, perhaps because of a reduction in the number of pregnancies resulting in multiple births, which fell by 5% in this period.[11]

Trends in the management of the preterm baby

Protocol-directed clinical care

Preterm babies are especially susceptible to harm, both as a result of their physiological immaturity and from therapeutic interventions. Their clinical course is often very unstable and even small changes in metabolic and biochemical parameters may have severe adverse consequences.[12-15] In addition, the evidence supporting many practices and treatments is weak. For example, many therapies in common use in neonatal care have not been adequately evaluated or licensed for use in neonates, mainly because pharmaceutical companies perceive little benefit in carrying out the required studies. As a result, there have been instances of harmful consequences following the introduction of new therapies in babies.[16,17] It is thus appropriate that current clinical practice should be scrutinised and reassessed.

Clinical practice is often guided by the opinion of experts.[18] However, in recent years, as in other branches of clinical medicine, there has been an increasing desire among neonatologists to standardise clinical management by developing protocols that are supported by high-quality evidence whenever possible.[19] One such successful example is in retinopathy of prematurity (ROP), where a broad consensus has been reached in the definition, assessment and management, and this has facilitated clinical research into the condition.[20] Unfortunately, for many aspects of neonatal care the development of clinical guidelines has been haphazard. Many neonatal intensive care units have individually produced protocols but few have been adequately researched or subjected to peer review. Perhaps because of the cost involved, specialty groups, such as the British Association of Perinatal Medicine, have produced only a limited number of evidence-based clinical guidelines. Despite the current enthusiasm for developing protocols and defining standards of care, there has so far been little assessment of their impact on clinical outcomes. In the UK, the imminent introduction of managed clinical networks may be an opportunity to standardise and audit clinical care.

One of the most valuable resources available for guiding clinical practice is the Cochrane Collaboration [www.cochrane.org]. This has carried out more than 100 systematic reviews of clinical trials of neonatal care, and they are widely accessible to neonatologists. However, the fact that currently fewer than 60% of the Cochrane reviews of neonatal care are able to make conclusive recommendations is evidence of the dearth of good-quality studies in neonates. Despite the difficulties of performing clinical research in babies, especially the unique ethical situation and lack of pharmaceutical company financial support, it is clearly essential that clinical research be supported if the care of preterm babies and their outcome is to improve.

Management at birth

The management of a preterm baby immediately after birth is critically important. Neonatal outcome is improved if the baby is managed in a well-resourced tertiary neonatal centre and if transfer to another hospital after birth can be avoided.[21,22] Inadequate ventilatory, cardiovascular or metabolic support and temperature instability may have deleterious effects and precipitate major neurological complications. Adequately trained and experienced personnel should attend the delivery of preterm babies. There is now an expectation that those attendants should have completed an accredited course in resuscitation of newborn babies.

The severity of respiratory distress syndrome can be reduced by early administration of intra-tracheal surfactant after birth. In babies of less than 30 weeks of gestation, the most benefit is achieved if surfactant is administered immediately after birth.[23,24] The more general use of antenatal steroids and the lessening severity of respiratory distress have led some to question the need for routine prophylactic treatment with surfactant, and to reserve surfactant for the most immature babies or those with significant respiratory distress after birth.[25] However, experimental studies indicate that even a few positive-pressure breaths may initiate pulmonary inflammation and increase the risk of developing chronic lung disease. Lung injury may be reduced if surfactant is administered before initiating positive-pressure ventilation.[26] Therefore, current recommendations are to have a low threshold for administering surfactant, to use the least possible amount of positive-pressure ventilation and to attempt to apply nasal continuous positive airway pressure (CPAP) as soon as possible after birth.[25,27]

Very premature babies rapidly lose heat and fluid through the skin, resulting in hypothermia and dehydration, and this may be minimised by rapidly placing the baby into a polyethylene bag following birth. The bag can be removed after admission to the nursery when the infant can be placed in a high-humidity environment. There is no evidence to support the common practice of giving intravenous fluid boluses for fluid expansion in the absence of evidence of cardiovascular compromise.[28,29]

Respiratory management following birth

Preterm babies frequently require respiratory support. Until recently, many babies born before 30 weeks of gestation would have received a period of mechanical ventilation after birth. However, the reduction in the severity of respiratory distress syndrome, together with a greater concern about the adverse effects of even brief periods of mechanical ventilation, has led to a change in practice. The majority of preterm babies, including those born before 26 weeks of gestation, now receive nasal CPAP as the only respiratory support during the first few days after birth.[25,30] Although this policy has been associated with a lower incidence of chronic lung disease in some centres, there is as yet little evidence that the incidence of chronic lung disease has reduced generally.[30-32] Even though most babies may be successfully managed with nasal CPAP initially, the smallest infants often ultimately require periods of mechanical ventilation, often in association with the occurrence of infection.

When mechanical ventilation is required, a number of different techniques are now available, such as volume-cycled ventilation, high-frequency jet or oscillatory ventilation and various types of patient assist modes with conventional ventilation.[33-44] However, despite the impressive experimental evidence suggesting that these techniques reduce pulmonary inflammation and improve lung function, there is at present little evidence of clinical benefit over conventional ventilation, particularly in reducing the risk of chronic lung disease.[45]

Complications following preterm birth

Pulmonary complications

Pulmonary complications are among the most common complications of preterm birth. It is thus not surprising that over 70% of the Cochrane neonatal reviews deal with respiratory-related issues. The dramatic reduction in severe surfactant-deficiency respiratory distress syndrome that followed the general introduction of antenatal steroids and postnatal surfactant therapy is widely known.[23,46-48] However, some preterm babies continue to present with severe acute lung disease. Often there is a clinical history of chorioamnionitis or evidence of fetal infection and immune activation. These babies are often seriously ill and may develop cystic lung disease with air leaks, acute renal failure, cerebral white matter injury and necrotising enterocolitis.[49] In the past, such babies would have died before birth.

Despite the reduction in the severity of surfactant-deficiency-associated respiratory distress, chronic lung disease remains a common complication in preterm babies, its incidence closely related to the degree of prematurity.[50] The terms bronchopulmonary dysplasia and chronic lung disease have become synonymous in recent years, but the nature and definition have changed with increasing survival of extremely premature babies.[45] The classic findings of pulmonary inflammation and fibrosis are less frequently observed in very premature babies, who appear instead mainly to have impaired acinar development and less alveolar septal fibrosis, a process probably induced by pro-inflammatory cytokines.[51,52] Studies using magnetic resonance imaging (MRI) of the lung show that persisting atelectasis and excessive lung water are frequently present in affected babies.[53,54] Although chronic lung disease is usually defined as persisting oxygen requirement at 36 weeks post-conceptional age, with abnormal chest radiograph and following mechanical ventilation, many preterm babies who only receive support with CPAP also have prolonged oxygen requirement.

There is currently no effective therapy or strategy for prevention and treatment of chronic lung disease but the trend towards less severe respiratory distress at birth and less intensive forms of ventilatory support may have lessened the severity of the condition.[55] Although postnatal steroids reduce the incidence and severity of chronic lung disease, the reported associated adverse neurological complications limit their use to desperately ill babies.[56-60] There is very little evidence that the newer styles of mechanical ventilation significantly reduce the incidence of chronic lung disease, although they may benefit long-term pulmonary function.[61,62]

Necrotising enterocolitis

Necrotising enterocolitis remains one of the most serious complications of preterm birth. Its incidence varies between centres and over time; some outbreaks may be so serious as to prompt closure of the neonatal centre. Although there has been a greater understanding of the epidemiology and pathophysiology, its management has not changed substantially. Most cases are treated with antibiotics and withholding feeding, and surgery is reserved for cases of perforation or clinical deterioration.[63,64] Catastrophic cases involving a large area of the bowel are increasingly observed. Although such cases may be 'rescued' with intensive care and surgical intervention, they often succumb later from recurrent infection and intestinal failure. Experimental studies[65,66] indicate that inflammatory mediators and loss of protective growth factors are critically important in the development of necrotising enterocolitis. These findings point to likely future therapeutic approaches but none have so far been tested in neonates.[67] There is limited evidence that enteral antibiotics and oral immunoglobulins reduce the risk.[68,69] Limiting feeding volumes during the first 7–10 days after birth and feeding wholly with breast milk are probably the best preventive measures that can be recommended at present.[70,71]

Sepsis

Almost every preterm baby requiring intensive care will be treated with antibiotics on at least one occasion because of suspected sepsis. Sepsis is a leading cause of mortality in preterm babies and of chronic morbidity hindering growth and development.[72-75] The most common pathogens are currently group B streptococcus (GBS), coagulase-negative staphylococci, *Staphylococcus aureus*, Gram-negative bacteria and fungi.

Early-onset GBS sepsis is a leading cause of death from infection in babies. Babies born to mothers with GBS bacteriuria, with chorioamnionitis or with another child with GBS disease are at greatest risk of early-onset infection.[76] Antenatal screening and treatment with penicillin can prevent neonatal GBS infection, but the appropriate screening strategy remains uncertain. The Centers for Disease Control and Prevention guidelines[77] revised in 2002 recommend universal screening in pregnant women at 35–37 weeks of gestation. In the UK, interim 'good practice' guidelines have been published by the Public Health Laboratory Service [www.phls.org.uk] but clinical practice probably varies widely. Most centres have a policy of selective screening targeted towards women at high risk of GBS carriage and neonatal sepsis. However, a study[78] published in 2003 found that the incidence of probable neonatal GBS infection in London is similar to that of countries prior to the introduction of a screening programme, suggesting that the current UK practice is inadequate.

Coagulase-negative staphylococci are the most commonly isolated organisms in preterm babies. They are often associated with parenteral nutrition and intravascular catheters and may cause chronic low-grade illness.[79] Infection with *Staphylococcus aureus* has been observed more frequently recently; it is often serious and may be fatal. Infection with methicillin-resistant *Staphylococcus aureus* is also observed in neonatal intensive care units.[80,81] Extremely premature babies are also susceptible to fungal infections, which usually present with renal, hepatic or cerebral abscesses. Prolonged treatment and drainage of the abscess is often required to eradicate infection. Prophylactic treatment with antifungal agents may reduce the incidence of fungal infections in high-risk babies.[82]

Preterm babies have low plasma immunoglobulins and may have an impaired cellular immune response, which partly explains their susceptibility to infection. A number of studies have investigated the role of treatment with immunoglobulins and growth factors such as granulocyte colony stimulating factor and granulocyte macrophage colony stimulating factor to prevent and treat infections. However, the results are so far inconclusive and their use is limited to specific situations.[83-86] Several studies are continuing.

Retinopathy of prematurity

Retinopathy of prematurity (ROP) is a process of abnormal vascularisation of the premature retina and is probably due to abnormal regulation of vascular endothelial growth factor mediated by episodes of hyperoxia and hypoxia in the presence of low insulin-like growth factor I levels.[87,88] Its incidence and severity is inversely proportional to the gestational age. If untreated, ROP can lead to retinal detachment and blindness but these can be avoided by timely treatment with laser photocoagulation. There is an international consensus on the definition, classification, screening and treatment of ROP, but uncertainties remain about optimal oxygen therapy for prevention and reducing the rate of progression. Win Tin *et al.*[89] reported that the incidence of ROP requiring treatment was much less in one UK centre with a policy of limiting oxygen saturation to 80–90% compared with four other centres with higher limits. Pulmonary outcome was also apparently better, with a reduction in days of ventilatory support and oxygen supplementation. In another study,[90] the introduction of clear guidelines aimed at minimising episodes of hyperoxia and hypoxia was associated with a dramatic reduction in the rate of severe ROP. Many neonatal centres are now introducing more restrictive policies for oxygen therapy in very premature babies during the first few weeks after birth. In contrast, other studies have examined whether maintaining high oxygen saturation in very premature babies after a few weeks of age reduces progression of ROP. Neither the STOP-ROP[91] nor the BOOST[92] study demonstrated significant benefits with this policy in babies with established ROP.

Early neurological complications

The introduction of neonatal cranial ultrasonography in the 1980s helped to characterise the major early neurological complications in preterm babies: germinal matrix intraventricular haemorrhage and cystic periventricular leukomalacia. More recently, cohort studies of MRI have identified new patterns of injury: the most common findings are abnormal signals in the white matter and dilatation of the ventricles. In one study,[93] abnormalities were already present in more than 60% of a cohort of babies born before 30 weeks of gestation on the initial scans done at median 48 hours after birth, suggesting an antenatal origin of these findings. Further examinations done at term-corrected age showed further progression of these abnormalities.

Severe perinatal germinal matrix intraventricular haemorrhage leading to porencephalic cysts and/or post-haemorrhagic hydrocephalus, previously a major cause of severe neurological morbidity in preterm babies, is now much less common. This is probably a consequence of preterm maternal antenatal steroid therapy.[46] Preterm babies are now less likely to have severe acute cardio-respiratory problems during the early perinatal period, and they are thus at less risk of developing cerebral vascular instability, an important factor leading to germinal matrix intraventricular haemorrhage.[94] Additionally, treatment with antenatal steroids may augment neonatal haemostasis and reduce the risk of bleeding. Other treatments given soon after birth, such as vitamin E, ethamsylate and indomethacin, also appear to reduce the risk of severe haemorrhage but these therapies do not seem to influence long-term neurological outcome.[95–97] Severe germinal matrix intraventricular haemorrhage with periventricular infarction is now observed mostly in extremely premature babies particularly if antenatal steroids were not administered or in babies with evidence of intrauterine infection.

The pattern of cerebral white matter injury in preterm babies has also altered in recent years. Subtle forms of injury as evidenced by slight abnormalities or mildly dilated cerebral ventricles on neuroimaging are now more frequently observed than cystic leukomalacia.[98,99] Whereas periventricular leukomalacia has been considered to be primarily an ischaemic injury related to anatomical factors such as arterial end zones and border zones, or as a result of a reduction in cerebral blood flow because of hypotension or hypocarbia, other factors may be more important in infants with the more subtle forms of cerebral white matter injury. Recent studies have focused on the role of intrauterine infection and inflammation. Intrauterine infection increases the risk of preterm delivery, and markers of infection may be present in women with preterm onset of labour.[100,101] Chorioamnionitis is associated both with cerebral white matter injury and the development of cerebral palsy in preterm and perhaps also in full-term babies, and this association is present irrespective of whether the diagnosis of chorioamnionitis is made on clinical grounds or is confirmed by histological analysis.[102,103] It has also been demonstrated that babies with evidence of fetal immune activation and inflammation are more likely to have MRI abnormalities soon after birth.[104]

The relationship between immunity and cerebral injury is complex. Experimental studies confirm that the immune response is directly involved in cerebral injury: for example, increased cytokine levels and lymphocytes are detected in injured cerebral tissue.[105] This inflammatory response may exacerbate glutamate-mediated brain injury or impair mitochondrial function resulting in impaired energy metabolism.[106] Experimental studies indicate that there may be a close synergy between inflammation and hypoxia ischaemia: cerebral damage is greatest when sub-lethal ischaemia is combined with sub-lethal infection.[107]

A striking observation from recent MRI studies is impairment of brain growth after birth. Brain volume, surface area and cortical complexity appear to be reduced in preterm babies by term-corrected age compared with full-term controls.[108] Brain growth appears to be further impaired in preterm babies exposed to multiple courses of steroids, whether administered antenatally or postnatally.[59,109] The clinical correlates of these findings are as yet uncertain but treatment with steroids after birth is associated with an increased risk of cerebral palsy.[110] New image manipulation techniques can indicate differential growth of specific brain areas. Future studies should provide interesting data on the relationship between these structural alterations and later behavioural and functional outcome.

The developing brain may also be critically affected by hormonal disturbances. One example is the thyroid hormone system, which is essential for normal human development. The observation that low levels of thyroid hormones may be associated with impaired neurodevelopmental outcome[111,112] and that transient hypothyroxinaemia in preterm babies is common has led to studies of supplementation with thyroid hormones. However, these have not consistently shown benefit.[113,114] Further studies are needed to determine the importance of the endocrine system in neurodevelopment during the perinatal period.[115]

Survival and outcome following preterm birth

Survival following very preterm birth

Mortality is one of the more clearly defined outcomes of preterm birth. Most outcome studies of infants following very premature birth are based on birthweight as opposed to gestation. There are only a few studies based on gestation alone, although obstetricians are more likely to make decisions based on this than estimated fetal weight. In infants of very low birthweight it has been shown that gestational age is a much better predictor of survival than estimated fetal weight.[116] Improved antenatal care and advances in ultrasound dating are overcoming this problem and outcomes should in future be reported based on both gestation and birthweight.

There are a number of perinatal and neonatal factors that may influence mortality, such as birthweight, sex of the infant, multiple pregnancy, intrauterine growth restriction, maternal chorioamnionitis, antenatal steroids, hypothermia and subsequent management following birth.[117,118]

Among infants of 24–28 weeks of gestation there is a wide range of survival reported (Table 5.1). The data[118] published by the NICHD Neonatal Research Network suggest an improving trend in survival among very low-birthweight infants (less than 1000 g at birth) in 1996 compared with 1991. This improvement in survival may be attributed to advancements in antenatal and neonatal care, especially the increasing use

Table 5.1. Summary of survival by gestation; figures are based on survival to discharge for liveborn infants

Place	Year of birth	23 weeks	24 weeks	25 weeks	26 weeks	27 weeks
Detroit[148]	1988–91	5/27	17/29	17/26		
Cambridge (UK)[149]	1985–92	2/9	13/28	26/55	43/80	
Montreal[150]	1978–92	0/25	9/39	31/62	44/69	91/117
Trent (UK)[151]	1991–93	1/37	27/95	38/104	73/132	132/186
Northern Region (UK)[152]	1991–94	1/49	13/78	36/103		
Melbourne[153]	1992–94	2/19	18/34	43/61	47/58	48/55
Wales[154]	1993–94	1/22	6/31	19/41	40/59	39/57
EPICure* (UK)[117]	1995	26/131	100/298	186/357		

* Survival figures are based on admissions to neonatal intensive care units

of antenatal steroids and surfactant. However, there was no improvement in survival at the lower limits of viability, at 21–23 weeks of gestation, where mortality remained high. The EPICure study, [117] a national study of infants born before 26 weeks of gestation, also reported a very high mortality rate among the lowest gestational ages: for admissions to the neonatal unit mortality was 100%, 90% and 80% at 21, 22 and 23 weeks of gestation respectively.

Long-term outcomes

It has long been recognised that preterm birth is associated with an increased risk of cerebral palsy and other adverse neurodevelopmental outcomes. Determining current trends in the outcome of preterm babies from published studies can be difficult because in recent years the pattern of neonatal illness has changed: more extremely premature babies survive and obstetric intervention in high-risk pregnancies is more common. However, studies that report outcome over long time intervals suggest that there has been little change in neurodevelopmental outcomes in recent years. The studies consistently indicate that about 10% of surviving infants of less than 28 weeks of gestation or with birthweight less than 1000 g develop severe neuromotor disabilities, mostly spastic diplegia or quadriplegia. In addition, some infants with a normal neuromotor examination will have severe cognitive or sensory impairments, so that the total incidence of severe disability is about 25%, although there is some variation between centres.[117,119–125] It is probably higher at the limit of viable gestation (23 weeks or birthweight less than 500 g), but the number of survivors is too small to be certain. Babies who develop bronchopulmonary dysplasia or retinopathy of prematurity or who have abnormal findings on cranial ultrasonography also have a greatly increased risk of later neurodevelopmental abnormalities. Those with a combination of these complications fare worst.[126]

Of increasing concern are reports of neurobehavioural problems and poor school performance at school age. Extremely low-birthweight infants are reported to have more attention difficulties, internalising behaviour problems and immature adaptive skills than their full-term peers, and perform worse in reading, comprehension, spelling and arithmetic.[127–130] Similar but less severe problems have also been noted in more mature infants, born at 32–35 weeks of gestation.[131]

When assessing long-term outcome, it is important also to take into account the children's perception of quality of life. Donohue[132] found that although children who were born preterm have more health-related problems the majority do not perceive their quality of life differently from others their own age. It appears that children with milder problems underestimate their difficulties compared with those with more serious health-related problems.[133]

Possible strategies for improving the outcome of preterm babies

Apart from efforts aimed at preventing preterm birth and better recognition of problems and their management before birth, there is a need to examine opportunities for intervention during the neonatal period and throughout growth and development of the child.

Improving the quality of neonatal care

The care of preterm babies is not particularly difficult or complex but it does need to be carried out meticulously. This is difficult to achieve consistently because of the large number of carers involved, the high turnover of staff and poor provision of training. In the UK, the introduction of managed networks should prompt an evaluation of current practice and lead to better use of human resources, more-structured training and standardised practice. Identifying improvements in clinical care and altering practice are achievable and result in improved outcomes.[90,134-138]

Targeting pathophysiology

As described previously, many of the major complications that occur during the neonatal period share common pathophysiological processes. There is increasingly robust evidence that an altered immune response leading to increased levels of pro-inflammatory cytokines is directly implicated. This suggests that interventions with anti-inflammatory cytokines, cytokine receptor antibodies or with specific growth factors will be considered in the future. Some of these approaches have shown promise in adults[139] but none have so far been reported in neonates. A major concern is the possible adverse effects of these agents on developing tissues.

Social and educational interventions

The relationship between the social gradient, preterm birth and poor educational achievement is well recognised. Although targeted social programmes can reduce the rate of preterm birth and educational intervention will improve school performance, the difficulty is to find ways of achieving these benefits more widely.[140-147] The increasing awareness of the health, behavioural and psychological problems of children who were born preterm calls for more support for these children. The provision of effective social, educational and specialist health support can determine whether a child is merely impaired or will be handicapped by these problems.

Summary and conclusion

The rise in preterm births in wealthy countries may have been halted very recently because of changes in fertility treatment practices, although wider provision of these treatments may alter this in the future. Preterm babies are uniquely susceptible to injury because of the possibility of antenatal exposure to insults, impaired development, their unstable clinical course and exposure to several potentially harmful interventions. Social disadvantages compound the problems. However, effective interventions can be introduced at all stages in this process; if implemented, outcomes for preterm babies will steadily improve in the future.

References

1. Ward RM, Beachy JC. Neonatal complications following preterm birth. *BJOG* 2003;110 Suppl 20:8–16.
2. Alexander GR, Slay M. Prematurity at birth: trends, racial disparities, and epidemiology. *Ment Retard Dev Disabil Res Rev* 2002;8:215–220.
3. Ventura SJ, Martin JA, Curtin SC, Mathews TJ, Park MM. Births: final data for 1998. *Natl Vital Stat Rep* 2000;48:1–100.
4. Joseph KS, Kramer MS. Recent versus historical trends in preterm birth in Canada. *CMAJ* 1999;161:1409.
5. Joseph KS, Kramer MS, Marcoux S, Ohlsson A, Wen SW, Allen A, *et al*. Determinants of preterm birth rates in Canada from 1981 through 1983 and from 1992 through 1994. *N Engl J Med* 1998;339:1434–9.
6. Mcfarlane A, Mugford M. *Birth Counts, Statistics of Pregnancy and Childbirth*. London: Stationery Office; 2000.
7. Roberts CL, Algert CS, Raynes-Greenow C, Peat B, Henderson-Smart DJ. Delivery of singleton preterm infants in New South Wales, 1990–1997. *Aust N Z J Obstet Gynaecol* 2003;43:32–7.
8. Roberts CL, Algert CS, Morris JM, Henderson-Smart DJ. Trends in twin births in New South Wales, Australia, 1990–1999. *Int J Gynaecol Obstet* 2002;78:213–9.
9. Blondel B, Kaminski M. Trends in the occurrence, determinants, and consequences of multiple births. *Semin Perinatol* 2002;26:239–49.
10. Bryan E. The impact of multiple preterm births on the family. *BJOG* 2003;110 Suppl 20:24–8.
11. National Statistics Online [www.statistics.gov.uk].
12. Hawdon JM. Hypoglycaemia and the neonatal brain. *Eur J Pediatr* 1999;158 Suppl 1:S9–12.
13. Erickson SJ, Grauaug A, Gurrin L, Swaminathan M. Hypocarbia in the ventilated preterm infant and its effect on intraventricular haemorrhage and bronchopulmonary dysplasia. *J Paediatr Child Health* 2002;38:560–2.
14. Vannucci RC, Vannucci SJ. Hypoglycemic brain injury. *Semin Neonatol* 2001;6:147–55.
15. Collins MP, Lorenz JM, Jetton JR, Paneth N. Hypocapnia and other ventilation-related risk factors for cerebral palsy in low birth weight infants. *Pediatr Res* 2001;50:712–9.
16. Silverman WA. *Retrolental Fibroplasia: A Modern Parable*. New York: Grune and Stratton; 1980.
17. Silverman WA. 'Acceptable' and 'unacceptable' risks. *Paediatr Perinat Epidemiol* 2002;16:2–3.
18. Klaus MA, Fanaroff AA. *Care of the High-Risk Neonate*. 5th ed. London: WB Saunders; 2001.
19. Soll RF, Andruscavage L. The principles and practice of evidence-based neonatology. *Pediatrics* 1999;103(1 Suppl E):215–24.
20. Committee for the Classification of Retinopathy of Prematurity. An international classification of retinopathy of prematurity. *Br J Ophthalmol* 1984;68:690–7.
21. Lee SK, McMillan DD, Ohlsson A, Boulton J, Lee DS, Ting S, *et al*. The benefit of preterm birth at tertiary care centers is related to gestational age. *Am J Obstet Gynecol* 2003;188:617–22.
22. Chien LY, Whyte R, Aziz K, Thiessen P, Matthew D, Lee SK. Improved outcome of preterm infants when delivered in tertiary care centers. *Obstet Gynecol* 2001;98:247–52.
23. Soll RF, Morley CJ. Prophylactic versus selective use of surfactant in preventing morbidity and mortality in preterm infants. *Cochrane Database Syst Rev* 2001;(2):CD000510.
24. Walti H, Paris-Llado J, Egberts J, Brand R, Bevilacqua G, Gardini F, *et al*. Prophylactic administration of porcine-derived lung surfactant is a significant factor in reducing the odds for peri-intraventricular haemorrhage in premature infants. *Biol Neonate* 2002;81:182–7.
25. Dunn MS, Reilly MC. Approaches to the initial respiratory management of preterm neonates. *Paediatr Respir Rev* 2003;4:2–8.
26. Wada K, Jobe AH, Ikegami M. Tidal volume effects on surfactant treatment responses with the initiation of ventilation in preterm lambs. *J Appl Physiol* 1997;83:1054–61.
27. Jobe AH, Ikegami M. Prevention of bronchopulmonary dysplasia. *Curr Opin Pediatr* 2001;13:124–9.
28. Kecskes ZB, Davies MW. Rapid correction of early metabolic acidaemia in comparison with placebo, no intervention or slow correction in LBW infants. *Cochrane Database Syst Rev* 2002;(1):CD002976.

29. Osborn DA, Evans N. Early volume expansion for prevention of morbidity and mortality in very preterm infants. *Cochrane Database Syst Rev* 2001;(4):CD002055.

30. Polin RA, Sahni R. Newer experience with CPAP. *Semin Neonatol* 2002;7:379–89.

31. Avery ME, Tooley WH, Keller JB, Hurd SS, Bryan MH, Cotton RB, *et al.* Is chronic lung disease in low birth weight infants preventable? A survey of eight centers. *Pediatrics* 1987;79:26–30.

32. Van Marter LJ, Allred EN, Pagano M, Sanocka U, Parad R, Moore M, *et al.* Do clinical markers of barotrauma and oxygen toxicity explain interhospital variation in rates of chronic lung disease? The Neonatology Committee for the Developmental Network. *Pediatrics* 2000;105:1194–201.

33. Baumer JH. Patient-triggered ventilation in premature neonates. *Acta Paediatr Suppl* 2001;90:22–4.

34. Beresford MW, Shaw NJ, Manning D. Randomised controlled trial of patient triggered and conventional fast rate ventilation in neonatal respiratory distress syndrome. *Arch Dis Child Fetal Neonatal Ed* 2000;82:F14–8.

35. Bhuta T, Henderson-Smart DJ. Rescue high frequency oscillatory ventilation versus conventional ventilation for pulmonary dysfunction in preterm infants. *Cochrane Database Syst Rev* 2000;(2):CD000438.

36. Bhuta T, Henderson-Smart DJ. Elective high frequency jet ventilation versus conventional ventilation for respiratory distress syndrome in preterm infants. *Cochrane Database Syst Rev* 2000;(2):CD000328.

37. Calvert S. Prophylactic high-frequency oscillatory ventilation in preterm infants. *Acta Paediatr Suppl* 2002;91:16–8.

38. Cheema IU, Ahluwalia JS. Feasibility of tidal volume-guided ventilation in newborn infants: a randomized, crossover trial using the volume guarantee modality. *Pediatrics* 2001;107:1323–8.

39. Davies MW, Woodgate PG. Tracheal gas insufflation for the prevention of morbidity and mortality in mechanically ventilated newborn infants. *Cochrane Database Syst Rev* 2002;(2):CD002973.

40. Greenough A, Milner AD, Dimitriou G. Synchronized mechanical ventilation for respiratory support in newborn infants. *Cochrane Database Syst Rev* 2001;(1):CD000456.

41. Henderson-Smart DJ, Wilkinson A, Raynes-Greenow CH. Mechanical ventilation for newborn infants with respiratory failure due to pulmonary disease. *Cochrane Database Syst Rev* 2002;(4):CD002770.

42. Olsen SL, Thibeault DW, Truog WE. Crossover trial comparing pressure support with synchronized intermittent mandatory ventilation. *J Perinatol* 2002;22:461–6.

43. Pianosi PT, Fisk M. High frequency ventilation trial. Nine year follow up of lung function. *Early Hum Dev* 2000;57:225–34.

44. Woodgate PG, Davies MW. Permissive hypercapnia for the prevention of morbidity and mortality in mechanically ventilated newborn infants. *Cochrane Database Syst Rev* 2001;(2):CD002061.

45. Jobe AH, Bancalari E. Bronchopulmonary dysplasia. *Am J Respir Crit Care Med* 2001;163:1723–9.

46. Crowley P. Prophylactic corticosteroids for preterm birth. *Cochrane Database Syst Rev* 2000;(2):CD000065.

47. Crowley P. Antenatal corticosteroids – current thinking. *BJOG* 2003;110 Suppl 20:77–8.

48. Soll RF. Synthetic surfactant for respiratory distress syndrome in preterm infants. *Cochrane Database Syst Rev* 2000;(2):CD001149.

49. Rimensberger PC. Neonatal respiratory failure. *Curr Opin Pediatr* 2002;14:315–21.

50. Van Marter LJ, Allred EN, Leviton A, Pagano M, Parad R, Moore M. Antenatal glucocorticoid treatment does not reduce chronic lung disease among surviving preterm infants. *J Pediatr* 2001;138:198–204.

51. Husain AN, Siddiqui NH, Stocker JT. Pathology of arrested acinar development in postsurfactant bronchopulmonary dysplasia. *Hum Pathol* 1998;29:710–7.

52. Jobe AJ. The new BPD: an arrest of lung development. *Pediatr Res* 1999;46:641–3.

53. Adams EW, Counsell SJ, Hajnal JV, Cox PN, Kennea NL, Thornton AS, *et al.* Magnetic resonance imaging of lung water content and distribution in term and preterm infants. *Am J Respir Crit Care Med* 2002;166:397–402.

54. Adams EW, Counsell SJ, Cox P, Al Nakhib L, Hajnal JV, Allsop J, *et al.* Investigation of the role of lung liquid in the pathogenesis of lung disease in the preterm infant using magnetic resonance imaging. *Early Hum Dev* 2000;58:76.

55. Charafeddine L, D'Angio CT, Phelps DL. Atypical chronic lung disease patterns in neonates. *Pediatrics* 1999;103(4 Pt 1):759–65.

56. Halliday HL, Ehrenkranz RA, Doyle LW. Early postnatal (<96 hours) corticosteroids for preventing chronic lung disease in preterm infants. *Cochrane Database Syst Rev* 2003;(1):CD001146.

57. Halliday HL, Ehrenkranz RA, Doyle LW. Delayed (>3 weeks) postnatal corticosteroids for chronic lung disease in preterm infants. *Cochrane Database Syst Rev* 2003;(1):CD001145.

58. Halliday HL, Ehrenkranz RA, Doyle LW. Moderately early (7–14 days) postnatal corticosteroids for preventing chronic lung disease in preterm infants. *Cochrane Database Syst Rev* 2003;(1): CD001144.

59.   Murphy BP, Inder TE, Huppi PS, Warfield S, Zientara GP, Kikinis R, *et al.* Impaired cerebral cortical gray matter growth after treatment with dexamethasone for neonatal chronic lung disease. *Pediatrics* 2001;107:217–21.

60.   Postnatal corticosteroids and sensorineural outcome at 5 years of age. *J Paediatr Child Health* 2000;36:256–61.

61.   Greenough A. Respiratory support techniques for prematurely born infants: new advances and perspectives. *Acta Paediatr Taiwan* 2001;42:201–6.

62.   Gerstmann DR, Wood K, Miller A, Steffen M, Ogden B, Stoddard RA, *et al.* Childhood outcome after early high-frequency oscillatory ventilation for neonatal respiratory distress syndrome. *Pediatrics* 2001;108:617–23.

63.   Chandler JC, Hebra A. Necrotizing enterocolitis in infants with very low birth weight. *Semin Pediatr Surg* 2000;9:63–72.

64.   Camberos A, Patel K, Applebaum H. Laparotomy in very small premature infants with necrotizing enterocolitis or focal intestinal perforation: postoperative outcome. *J Pediatr Surg* 2002;37:1692–5.

65.   Hsueh W, Caplan MS, Qu XW, Tan XD, De Plaen IG, Gonzalez-Crussi F. Neonatal necrotizing enterocolitis: clinical considerations and pathogenetic concepts. *Pediatr Dev Pathol* 2003;6:6–23.

66.   Hsueh W, Caplan MS, Tan X, MacKendrick W, Gonzalez-Crussi F. Necrotizing enterocolitis of the newborn: pathogenetic concepts in perspective. *Pediatr Dev Pathol* 1998;1:2–16.

67.   Caplan MS, Hedlund E, Adler L, Lickerman M, Hsueh W. The platelet-activating factor receptor antagonist WEB 2170 prevents neonatal necrotizing enterocolitis in rats. *J Pediatr Gastroenterol Nutr* 1997;24:296–301.

68.   Bury RG, Tudehope D. Enteral antibiotics for preventing necrotizing enterocolitis in low birthweight or preterm infants. *Cochrane Database Syst Rev* 2001;(1):CD000405.

69.   Foster J, Cole M. Oral immunoglobulin for preventing necrotizing enterocolitis in preterm and low birth-weight neonates. *Cochrane Database Syst Rev* 2001;(3):CD001816.

70.   Berseth CL, Bisquera JA, Paje VU. Prolonging small feeding volumes early in life decreases the incidence of necrotizing enterocolitis in very low birth weight infants. *Pediatrics* 2003;111:529–34.

71.   McGuire W, Anthony MY. Donor human milk versus formula for preventing necrotising enterocolitis in preterm infants: systematic review. *Arch Dis Child Fetal Neonatal Ed* 2003;88:F11–4.

72.   Bergstrom S. Infection-related morbidities in the mother, fetus and neonate. *J Nutr* 2003;133(5 Suppl 2):1656S–60S.

73.   Dammann O, Kuban KC, Leviton A. Perinatal infection, fetal inflammatory response, white matter damage, and cognitive limitations in children born preterm. *Ment Retard Dev Disabil Res Rev* 2002;8:46–50.

74.   Lott JW. Neonatal bacterial sepsis. *Crit Care Nurs Clin North Am* 2003;15:35–46.

75.   Resch B, Vollaard E, Maurer U, Haas J, Rosegger H, Muller W. Risk factors and determinants of neurodevelopmental outcome in cystic periventricular leucomalacia. *Eur J Pediatr* 2000;159:663–70.

76.   Benitz WE, Gould JB, Druzin ML. Risk factors for early-onset group B streptococcal sepsis: estimation of odds ratios by critical literature review. *Pediatrics* 1999;103:e77.

77.   Schrag S, Gorwitz R, Fultz-Butts K, Schuchat A. Prevention of perinatal group B streptococcal disease. Revised guidelines from CDC. *MMWR Recomm Rep* 2002;51(RR-11):1–22.

78.   Luck S, Torny M, d'Agapeyeff K, Pitt A, Heath P, Breathnach A, *et al.* Estimated early-onset group B streptococcal neonatal disease. *Lancet* 2003;361:1953–4.

79.   Isaacs D. A ten year, multicentre study of coagulase negative staphylococcal infections in Australasian neonatal units. *Arch Dis Child Fetal Neonatal Ed* 2003;88:F89–93.

80.   Nambiar S, Herwaldt LA, Singh N. Outbreak of invasive disease caused by methicillin-resistant *Staphylococcus aureus* in neonates and prevalence in the neonatal intensive care unit. *Pediatr Crit Care Med* 2003;4:220–6.

81.   Wilcox MH, Fitzgerald P, Freeman J, Denton M, Gill AB, Hoy C, *et al.* A five year outbreak of methicillin-susceptible *Staphylococcus aureus* phage type 53,85 in a regional neonatal unit. *Epidemiol Infect* 2000;124:37–45.

82.   McGuire W, Clerihew L, Austin N. Prophylactic intravenous antifungal agents to prevent mortality and morbidity in very low birth weight infants. *Cochrane Database Syst Rev* 2003;(1):CD003850.

83.   Carr R, Modi N, Dore CJ, El Rifai R, Lindo D. A randomized, controlled trial of prophylactic granulocyte-macrophage colony-stimulating factor in human newborns less than 32 weeks gestation. *Pediatrics* 1999;103(4 Pt 1):796–802.

84.   La Gamma EF, De Castro MH. What is the rationale for the use of granulocyte and granulocyte-macrophage colony-stimulating factors in the neonatal intensive care unit? *Acta Paediatr Suppl* 2002;91:109–16.

85.   Miura E, Procianoy RS, Bittar C, Miura CS, Miura MS, Mello C, *et al.* A randomized, double-masked, placebo-controlled trial of recombinant granulocyte colony-stimulating factor

administration to preterm infants with the clinical diagnosis of early-onset sepsis. *Pediatrics* 2001;107:30–5.

86.   Ohlsson A, Lacy JB. Intravenous immunoglobulin for preventing infection in preterm and/or low-birth-weight infants. *Cochrane Database Syst Rev* 2001;(2):CD000361.

87.   Hellstrom A, Perruzzi C, Ju M, Engstrom E, Hard AL, Liu JL, et al. Low IGF-I suppresses VEGF-survival signaling in retinal endothelial cells: direct correlation with clinical retinopathy of prematurity. *Proc Natl Acad Sci U S A* 2001;98:5804–8.

88.   Smith LE. Pathogenesis of retinopathy of prematurity. *Acta Paediatr Suppl* 2002;91:26–8.

89.   Tin W, Milligan DW, Pennefather P, Hey E. Pulse oximetry, severe retinopathy, and outcome at one year in babies of less than 28 weeks gestation. *Arch Dis Child Fetal Neonatal Ed* 2001;84:F106–10.

90.   Chow LC, Wright KW, Sola A. Can changes in clinical practice decrease the incidence of severe retinopathy of prematurity in very low birth weight infants? *Pediatrics* 2003;111:339–45.

91.   Supplemental Therapeutic Oxygen for Prethreshold Retinopathy Of Prematurity (STOP-ROP), a randomized, controlled trial. I: primary outcomes. *Pediatrics* 2000;105:295–310.

92.   Askie L, Henderson-Smart D, Irwig L. The effect of differing oxygen saturation targeting ranges on long term growth and development of extremely preterm, oxygen dependent infants: the BOOST trial. *Pediatr Res* 2002;51:378A.

93.   Maalouf EF, Duggan PJ, Rutherford MA, Counsell SJ, Fletcher AM, Battin M, et al. Magnetic resonance imaging of the brain in a cohort of extremely preterm infants. *J Pediatr* 1999;135:351–7.

94.   Volpe JJ. *Neurology of the Newborn*. 4th ed. WB Saunders; 2001.

95.   Chiswick M, Gladman G, Sinha S, Toner N, Davies J. Vitamin E supplementation and periventricular hemorrhage in the newborn. *Am J Clin Nutr* 1991;53(1 Suppl):370S–2S.

96.   Elbourne D, Ayers S, Dellagrammaticas H, Johnson A, Leloup M, Lenoir-Piat S. Randomised controlled trial of prophylactic etamsylate: follow up at 2 years of age. *Arch Dis Child Fetal Neonatal Ed* 2001;84:F183–7.

97.   Ment LR, Vohr B, Allan W, Westerveld M, Sparrow SS, Schneider KC, et al. Outcome of children in the indomethacin intraventricular hemorrhage prevention trial. *Pediatrics* 2000;105(3 Pt 1):485–91.

98.   Felderhoff-Mueser U, Rutherford MA, Squier WV, Cox P, Maalouf EF, Counsell SJ, et al. Relationship between MR imaging and histopathologic findings of the brain in extremely sick preterm infants. *AJNR Am J Neuroradiol* 1999;20:1349–57.

99.   Maalouf EF, Duggan PJ, Counsell SJ, Rutherford MA, Cowan F, Azzopardi D, et al. Comparison of findings on cranial ultrasound and magnetic resonance imaging in preterm infants. *Pediatrics* 2001;107:719–27.

100. Dammann O, Leviton A. Maternal intrauterine infection, cytokines, and brain damage in the preterm newborn. *Pediatr Res* 1997;42:1–8.

101. Romero R, Gomez R, Ghezzi F, Yoon BH, Mazor M, Edwin SS, et al. A fetal systemic inflammatory response is followed by the spontaneous onset of preterm parturition. *Am J Obstet Gynecol* 1998;179:186–93.

102. Grether JK, Nelson KB. Maternal infection and cerebral palsy in infants of normal birth weight. *JAMA* 1997;278:207–11.

103. Wu YW, Colford JM Jr. Chorioamnionitis as a risk factor for cerebral palsy: A meta-analysis. *JAMA* 2000;284:1417–24.

104. Duggan PJ, Maalouf EF, Watts TL, Sullivan MH, Counsell SJ, Allsop J, et al. Intrauterine T-cell activation and increased proinflammatory cytokine concentrations in preterm infants with cerebral lesions. *Lancet* 2001;358:1699–700.

105. Bona E, Andersson AL, Blomgren K, Gilland E, Puka-Sundvall M, Gustafson K, et al. Chemokine and inflammatory cell response to hypoxia-ischemia in immature rats. *Pediatr Res* 1999;45(4 Pt 1):500–9.

106. Dommergues MA, Patkai J, Renauld JC, Evrard P, Gressens P. Proinflammatory cytokines and interleukin-9 exacerbate excitotoxic lesions of the newborn murine neopallium. *Ann Neurol* 2000;47:54–63.

107. Eklind S, Mallard C, Leverin AL, Gilland E, Blomgren K, Mattsby-Baltzer I, et al. Bacterial endotoxin sensitizes the immature brain to hypoxic–ischaemic injury. *Eur J Neurosci* 2001;13:1101–6.

108. Ajayi-Obe M, Saeed N, Cowan FM, Rutherford MA, Edwards AD. Reduced development of cerebral cortex in extremely preterm infants. *Lancet* 2000;356:1162–3.

109. Modi N, Lewis H, Al Naqeeb N, Ajayi-Obe M, Dore CJ, Rutherford M. The effects of repeated antenatal glucocorticoid therapy on the developing brain. *Pediatr Res* 2001;50:581–5.

110. Shinwell ES, Karplus M, Reich D, Weintraub Z, Blazer S, Bader D, et al. Early postnatal dexamethasone treatment and increased incidence of cerebral palsy. *Arch Dis Child Fetal Neonatal Ed* 2000;83:F177–81.

111. Leviton A, Paneth N, Reuss ML, Susser M, Allred EN, Dammann O, et al. Hypothyroxinemia of

prematurity and the risk of cerebral white matter damage. *J Pediatr* 1999;134:706–11.

112.   van Wassenaer AG, Briet JM, van Baar A, Smit BJ, Tamminga P, de Vijlder JJ, *et al.* Free thyroxine levels during the first weeks of life and neurodevelopmental outcome until the age of 5 years in very preterm infants. *Pediatrics* 2002;110:534–9.

113.   Briet JM, van Wassenaer AG, Dekker FW, de Vijlder JJ, van Baar A, Kok JH. Neonatal thyroxine supplementation in very preterm children: developmental outcome evaluated at early school age. *Pediatrics* 2001;107:712–8.

114.   Osborn DA. Thyroid hormones for preventing neurodevelopmental impairment in preterm infants. *Cochrane Database Syst Rev* 2001;(4):CD001070.

115.   Yeung MY, Smyth JP. Hormonal factors in the morbidities associated with extreme prematurity and the potential benefits of hormonal supplement. *Biol Neonate* 2002;81:1–15.

116.   Bottoms SF, Paul RH, Mercer BM, MacPherson CA, Caritis SN, Moawad AH, *et al.* Obstetric determinants of neonatal survival: antenatal predictors of neonatal survival and morbidity in extremely low birth weight infants. *Am J Obstet Gynecol* 1999;180(3 Pt 1):665–9.

117.   Costeloe K, Hennessy E, Gibson AT, Marlow N, Wilkinson AR. The EPICure study: outcomes to discharge from hospital for infants born at the threshold of viability. *Pediatrics* 2000;106:659–71.

118.   Lemons JA, Bauer CR, Oh W, Korones SB, Papile LA, Stoll BJ, *et al.* Very low birth weight outcomes of the National Institute of Child health and human development neonatal research network, January 1995 through December 1996. NICHD Neonatal Research Network. *Pediatrics* 2001;107:E1.

119.   Cloonan HA, Maxwell SR, Miller SD. Developmental outcomes in very low birth weight infants: a six-year study. *W V Med J* 2001;97:250–2.

120.   LeBlanc MH, Graves GR, Rawson TW, Moffitt J. Long-term outcome of infants at the margin of viability. *J Miss State Med Assoc* 1999;40:111–4.

121.   Monset-Couchard M, de Bethmann O, Kastler B. Mid- and long-term outcome of 166 premature infants weighing less than 1,000 g at birth, all small for gestational age. *Biol Neonate* 2002;81:244–54.

122.   Msall ME, Tremont MR. Measuring functional outcomes after prematurity: developmental impact of very low birth weight and extremely low birth weight status on childhood disability. *Ment Retard Dev Disabil Res Rev* 2002;8:258–72.

123.   Sweet MP, Hodgman JE, Pena I, Barton L, Pavlova Z, Ramanathan R. Two-year outcome of infants weighing 600 grams or less at birth and born 1994 through 1998. *Obstet Gynecol* 2003;101:18–23.

124.   Walther FJ, den Ouden AL, Verloove-Vanhorick SP. Looking back in time: outcome of a national cohort of very preterm infants born in The Netherlands in 1983. *Early Hum Dev* 2000;59:175–91.

125.   Yu VY. Developmental outcome of extremely preterm infants. *Am J Perinatol* 2000;17:57–61.

126.   Schmidt B, Asztalos EV, Roberts RS, Robertson CM, Sauve RS, Whitfield MF. Impact of bronchopulmonary dysplasia, brain injury, and severe retinopathy on the outcome of extremely low-birth-weight infants at 18 months: results from the trial of indomethacin prophylaxis in preterms. *JAMA* 2003;289:1124–9.

127.   Sullivan MC, Margaret MM. Perinatal morbidity, mild motor delay, and later school outcomes. *Dev Med Child Neurol* 2003;45:104–12.

128.   Anderson P, Doyle LW. Neurobehavioral outcomes of school-age children born extremely low birth weight or very preterm in the 1990s. *JAMA* 2003;289:3264–72.

129.   Bohm B, Katz-Salamon M. Cognitive development at 5.5 years of children with chronic lung disease of prematurity. *Arch Dis Child Fetal Neonatal Ed* 2003;88:F101–5.

130.   Bohm B, Katz-Salamon M, Institute K, Smedler AC, Lagercrantz H, Forssberg H. Developmental risks and protective factors for influencing cognitive outcome at 5 1/2 years of age in very-low-birthweight children. *Dev Med Child Neurol* 2002;44:508–16.

131.   Huddy CL, Johnson A, Hope PL. Educational and behavioural problems in babies of 32–35 weeks gestation. *Arch Dis Child Fetal Neonatal Ed* 2001;85:F23–8.

132.   Donohue PK. Health-related quality of life of preterm children and their caregivers. *Ment Retard Dev Disabil Res Rev* 2002;8:293–7.

133.   Feingold E, Sheir-Neiss G, Melnychuk J, Bachrach S, Paul D. HRQL and severity of brain ultrasound findings in a cohort of adolescents who were born preterm. *J Adolesc Health* 2002;31:234–9.

134.   Kaempf JW, Campbell B, Sklar RS, Arduza C, Gallegos R, Zabari M, *et al.* Implementing potentially better practices to improve neonatal outcomes after reducing postnatal dexamethasone use in infants born between 501 and 1250 grams. *Pediatrics* 2003;111(4 Pt 2):e534–41.

135.   Vohr BR, McKinley LT. The challenge pays off: early enhanced nutritional intake for VLBW small-for-gestation neonates improves long-term outcome. *J Pediatr* 2003;142:459–61.

136.   Walker MW, Shoemaker M, Riddle K, Crane MM, Clark R. Clinical process improvement: reduction of pneumothorax and mortality in high-risk preterm infants. *J Perinatol* 2002;22:641–5.

137. Kuzma-O'Reilly B, Duenas ML, Greecher C, Kimberlin L, Mujsce D, Miller D, *et al*. Evaluation, development, and implementation of potentially better practices in neonatal intensive care nutrition. *Pediatrics* 2003;111(4 Pt 2):e461–70.
138. Kilbride HW, Wirtschafter DD, Powers RJ, Sheehan MB. Implementation of evidence-based potentially better practices to decrease nosocomial infections. *Pediatrics* 2003;111(4 Pt 2):e519–33.
139. Off-label use of tumor necrosis factor inhibitors on ankylosing spondylitis, ulcerative colitis, and psoriasis. *TEC Bull (Online)* 2003;20:9–18.
140. Barlow J, Parsons J. Group-based parent-training programmes for improving emotional and behavioural adjustment in 0–3 year old children. *Cochrane Database Syst Rev* 2003;(1):CD003680.
141. Hall RT, Santos SR, Cofield F, Brown MJ, Teasley SL, Cai J. Perinatal outcomes in a school-based program for pregnant teen-agers. *Mo Med* 2003;100:148–52.
142. Armstrong MA, Gonzales Osejo V, Lieberman L, Carpenter DM, Pantoja PM, Escobar GJ. Perinatal substance abuse intervention in obstetric clinics decreases adverse neonatal outcomes. *J Perinatol* 2003;23:3–9.
143. Blair C. Early intervention for low birth weight, preterm infants: the role of negative emotionality in the specification of effects. *Dev Psychopathol* 2002;14:311–32.
144. Linver MR, Brooks-Gunn J, Kohen DE. Family processes as pathways from income to young children's development. *Dev Psychol* 2002;38:719–34.
145. Melnyk BM, Alpert-Gillis L, Feinstein NF, Fairbanks E, Schultz-Czarniak J, Hust D, *et al*. Improving cognitive development of low-birth-weight premature infants with the COPE program: a pilot study of the benefit of early NICU intervention with mothers. *Res Nurs Health* 2001;24:373–89.
146. Reece EA, Lequizamon G, Silva J, Whiteman V, Smith D. Intensive interventional maternity care reduces infant morbidity and hospital costs. *J Matern Fetal Neonatal Med* 2002;11:204–10.
147. Villar J, Merialdi M, Gulmezoglu AM, Abalos E, Carroli G, Kulier R, *et al*. Nutritional interventions during pregnancy for the prevention or treatment of maternal morbidity and preterm delivery: an overview of randomized controlled trials. *J Nutr* 2003;133(5 Suppl 2):1606S–25S.
148. Holtrop PC, Ertzbischoff LM, Roberts CL, Batton DG, Lorenz RP. Survival and short-term outcome in newborns of 23 to 25 weeks' gestation. *Am J Obstet Gynecol* 1994;170(5 Pt 1):1266–70.
149. Rennie JM. Perinatal management at the lower margin of viability. *Arch Dis Child Fetal Neonatal Ed* 1996;74:F214–8.
150. Lefebvre F, Glorieux J, Laurent-Gagnon T. Neonatal survival and disability rate at age 18 months for infants born between 23 and 28 weeks of gestation. *Am J Obstet Gynecol* 1996;174:833–8.
151. Bohin S, Draper ES, Field DJ. Impact of extremely immature infants on neonatal services. *Arch Dis Child Fetal Neonatal Ed* 1996;74:F110–3.
152. Tin W, Wariyar U, Hey E. Changing prognosis for babies of less than 28 weeks' gestation in the north of England between 1983 and 1994. Northern Neonatal Network. *BMJ* 1997;314:107–11.
153. Gultom E, Doyle LW, Davis P, Dharmalingam A, Bowman E. Changes over time in attitudes to treatment and survival rates for extremely preterm infants (23–27 weeks' gestational age). *Aust N Z J Obstet Gynaecol* 1997;37:56–8.
154. Cartlidge PH, Stewart JH. Survival of very low birthweight and very preterm infants in a geographically defined population. *Acta Paediatr* 1997;86:105–10.

Chapter 6

Basic science

Discussion

Shennan: Dr Romero, I see that we are not talking much about progesterone. I sense this is potentially an interesting and controversial area. From a clinical perspective, the two trials that you mentioned are interesting. The *American Journal of Obstetrics and Gynecology* trial[1] had a high incidence of preterm delivery (about 28%). To me that seemed plausible. What seemed implausible was the *New England Journal of Medicine* trial,[2] which had an over-50% prematurity rate with bland entry criteria. I am just wondering about a type I error. Firstly, do you think that they are plausible trials? Secondly, I would really like Dr Nathanielsz and Professor Smith to tell us what they think about the mechanisms behind the effects.

Romero: On the question as to whether they are plausible, I have to accept the evidence presented. We have two meta-analyses that are consistent, indicating a reduction in the rate of preterm birth, and now two very large trials. The high rate of preterm birth in the control group is something that has been aired in the *New England Journal of Medicine*. One of the questions was whether the placebo (castor oil) could have accounted for it. The reply from the investigators was that progesterone was given in the same vehicle so that could not account for the difference. I believe the effect is real. It has the potential for a major impact on intervention for prevention of preterm birth.

Saade: There are a number of reasons for the higher rate of preterm birth in the placebo group in the *New England Journal of Medicine* trial. Women were given weekly intramuscular injections so, for the patients to agree to the study, they probably had a worse history of preterm birth. In other words, they were the ones who delivered very early preterm, or their babies died. Professor Smith questioned whether progesterone changes the response of the myometrium to tocolytics. We have such data for nitric oxide.

Smith: Dr Romero, one of the things I was intrigued by in both of the trials was that the rate of premature birth was reduced but the rate of premature labour was the same. This suggests that the progesterone sensitised individuals to the tocolytics used.

Romero: Yes, that seems to be the case for both trials.

Smith: But not in your meta-analysis.

Romero: Not in the meta-analysis of Mark Keirse's.[3] There was also a reduction in preterm birth.

Nathanielsz: We were debating why these investigators used 17 alpha-hydroxyprogesterone caproate. Does anyone know the binding characteristics of 17 alpha-hydroxyprogesterone caproate to the various steroid receptors? Given the amount of time clinicians and researchers have invested over the last few years in looking at the potential adverse effects exerted by antenatal glucocorticoids, and knowing some of the effects of progesterone in early gestation, one wonders whether this is another instance of having to be cautious about the law of unintended consequences.

Bennett: We have been using progesterone for people at high risk of preterm delivery for some years. This is based on Mark Keirse's meta-analysis and biochemical evidence that progesterone downregulates a whole range of things important for cervical ripening. One of the problems I had with the *New England Journal of Medicine* study was that progesterone was administered systemically. I could not see how systemic administration could elevate progesterone any higher than it already was since it is enormously high in normal pregnancy. The South American study[1] administered a vaginal preparation which is what we have been doing. It strikes me that the two studies present the dilemma that if people want to introduce progesterone clinically how are they going to administer it and do we understand how it worked in the *New England Journal of Medicine* study.

Thornton: Can I get a feeling for who uses progesterone?

Lamont: We have been using it for about ten years, again based largely on Mark Keirse's meta-analysis.

Nathanielsz: Perhaps this is not the time to go into the meta-analysis (here is a non-clinician talking). Has anyone produced any data to evaluate its efficacy?

Lamont: Not at all, it is the old problem. There are so many variables there is no way that you are going to be able to test them in the traditional randomised double-blind placebo-controlled trial.

Calder: While we are on the subject of progesterone, I wonder if the speakers might comment on what seems to me an important clinical observation that the use of antiprogesterones in early and mid pregnancy seems to have a much more dramatic effect on our ability to interrupt pregnancy than it does at term. It may be that the sensitivity has changed so that progesterone is no longer so important in the last few weeks of pregnancy.

Critchley: I was particularly interested in Professor Smith's comments on the steroid receptors. You spoke about genomic receptors but there are membrane-bound progesterone receptors. It is probably too early to ask the question but is there information on their expression?

Bennett: We are just starting to do those experiments so we will know soon but I do not have any data at the moment.

Lamont: I was going to change the subject: a question for Professor Gardosi on epidemiology. For years we have tried to get people to separate single and multiple pregnancies when they are quoting data on premature birth. Do you think we should be further dividing the twins into monochorionic diamniotic and dichorionic diamniotic because this will influence gestational age at delivery, complication rates and risk of preterm birth?

Gardosi: The endocrinology of twin pregnancies is different to singletons. You have two placentae. The human placental lactogen and corticotrophin-releasing hormone (CRH) levels are higher in twin pregnancies. In monochorionic twin pregnancies, in addition to the higher incidence of fetal growth restriction, you also have the chance of twin–twin transfusion which can lead to abnormal outcome.

Smith: We have been studying the marmoset recently and marmosets usually have twins. Sometimes they have singletons or triplets. They have a gradation in their CRH levels depending whether they are singletons, twins or triplets.

Sebire: To return to Dr Lamont's point, I think it is important that we separate dichorionic and monochorionic twins. It is clear that the monochorionic group have complications of twin to twin transfusion and deliver prematurely. I think it makes it much easier to understand the mechanisms when those groups are separated.

Gardosi: They need to be recorded separately but many comparisons include induced preterm births. I think you might find that there is little difference in spontaneous preterm rates between mono- and dichorionic twin pregnancies.

Regan: Dr Romero, I was fascinated to hear that you found raised levels of thrombin-antithrombin complexes in women delivering preterm. Have you been able to identify these complexes in women before or during pregnancy and if so at what gestation? There is a cheap ELISA and it would be useful to identify a group who are at risk.

Romero: Our data was on blood samples obtained at the time of diagnosis of preterm labour with intact membranes or PPROM. There is a study in the *Journal of Maternal-Fetal and Neonatal Medicine* in which complexes were measured in the middle trimester and patients who had elevated levels were more likely to have PPROM.[4] The potential explanation is that thrombin can induce matrix metalloproteinase 1 (MMP-1) so the mechanism would be thrombin, MMP-1 followed by membrane rupture.

Regan: We have shown that you can group women with late miscarriage (up to 24 weeks) into those with raised complexes (who will benefit by being given prophylaxis) and those without. It would be interesting if you could take this forward and identify a subgroup prepregnancy.

Romero: I think the concept is that thrombosis may be a mechanism for premature labour and PPROM. I think there is evidence in the placentae of women who have preterm labour and PPROM of thrombotic lesions in both the maternal and fetal sides. If we look at the placentae there are three distinct groups: women with inflammation, women with vascular lesions, and a group with a mixture of vascular lesions and inflammation. I think that we need to remember that pro-inflammatory cytokines stimulate the production of tissue factors and may activate the coagulation system.

Taylor: I have a question about classification of spontaneous preterm birth and PPROM, which are often regarded as the same condition but they are not. The Aberdeen database of over 60 000 pregnancies had a significant incidence of small-for-gestational-age infants but the spontaneous preterm birth group had normal birthweights. Have you been able to interrogate your databases and, if not, could you please?

Gardosi: I think this is a good point but any database is only as good as the quality of the information which has been put in, especially with regard to timing of PPROM. I have not really convinced myself that people have been able to separate out the two but it would be nice to make these comparisons.

Nathanielsz: Professor Smith, that was tremendous data that you provided on the gene associations. Did you look at these in a multiplicity of tissues or just placenta? Also, was it at mRNA, protein or binding?

Smith: We looked at mRNA in the placenta, myometrium and membranes. The data I showed today was myometrium and it is the myometrium where the major changes in progesterone receptor A and B occur.

Nathanielsz: That is lower segment?

Smith: Yes, but we also have tissue from the fundus and we have not seen any differences.

Steer: It is traditional when considering a discussion of this nature to start off with some definitions. I would like to propose that we distinguish gestational length, preterm delivery and prematurity because they are not all the same thing. We all know that some babies born at 35 weeks of gestation do extremely well and others at 38 weeks get severe respiratory distress. I think we need to bear in mind that statistics do not necessarily apply to individuals. The parallel is that for many years we talked about growth restriction as less than the tenth centile whereas now we realise that it is growth velocity that matters. I would like to propose that the true definition of prematurity is neonatal dysfunction typical of abnormally short gestation. I think this has practical significance. For example, Professor Gardosi mentioned that the gestational length is different in different ethnic groups. In my view, the majority of that is physiological. For example, babies of African mothers on average will be born five days earlier but have lower rates of respiratory distress and jaundice. Their perinatal mortality starts increasing a week earlier, and in Indian babies the mortality increases up to two weeks earlier than Europeans. It is therefore clearly a mistake to assume that different groups have the same gestational length. I think we need to distinguish between these physiological variations in gestational length (which, if we are not careful, get called prematurity) and the pathological causes. I agree with Dr Romero that we need to start looking at the multiple pathological causes of preterm delivery and stop getting quite so hung up on gestational length.

Lamont: Looking at the St Mary's Maternity Information System database, there are almost 600 000 births of which about 70 000 were preterm. Whether the midwives recorded the gestational age as completed weeks or rounded up or rounded down made a huge difference to the incidence. A second point that I wanted to make to Dr Romero was that you raised the point that prematurity is an adaptive process so the feto-maternal unit responds by preterm birth. I remember reading Dr Romero's papers saying that preterm birth due to infection was a host response with the mother trying to empty the uterus for her own protection. I wonder whether this is the case or the fetus jumps a burning ship, or perhaps a combination of the two.

Romero: The obvious case for the mother providing value in terms of species survival is that she can get rid of the infected conceptus and placenta, thereby having the opportunity to reproduce again. Recently we have considered survival value for the fetus, not at 24 weeks of gestation when survival will be nil, but in late gestation where survival would be possible. Infection would be sufficient to signal the onset of labour and there would be survival of both mother and infant.

López Bernal: My comment is about the first presentation by Dr Nathanielsz. I agree with you about the importance of comparative physiology. I like your model that local production of oestrogen is important but how does that fit with the clinical observation of placental sulphatase deficiency? How can you have a situation where oestrogens are not being produced and yet pregnancy and delivery are almost completely normal?

Nathanielsz: That always comes up and is very difficult to answer. I have often always asked myself whether these pregnancies are normal. I cannot believe they are, in so far as we all know that one of the major factors that regulates uterine blood flow is oestrogen. There may also be adequate oestrogen produced on the fetal side and we do not know too much about that. I suppose we have to fall back on the fact that parturition is a multifactorial system with a huge number of back-ups.

I have a question for Professor Smith. I was fascinated that, in one of your later graphs, you extrapolated the CRH concentrations back to the nonpregnant state and there were measurable levels of CRH. I would like you to comment on whether one can measure circulating maternal prepregnancy CRH concentrations.

Smith: We did not have levels very early in pregnancy and I extrapolated to show how the curves were different. We can measure CRH by about 12 to 14 weeks.

Calder: I am not sure that women with placental sulphatase deficiency have a normal course. I am one of the few people around who can remember diagnosing that condition because we used to measure oestriol as a presumed index of placental function. The primigravid women were extremely difficult to deliver and most of them ended up with caesarean section.

I remember old data suggesting that preterm deliveries were clustered into two particular groups that seem to have different aetiologies. In the ones before 30 weeks, infection was perhaps the main driver and later they were perhaps a placental clock. What I wonder is whether in pregnancies provoked to deliver early by sudden events such as haemorrhage or infection, the whole mechanism is bypassed to drive labour quite quickly.

Romero: My view is that there are really three clusters. There is an inflammatory cluster and a noninflammatory cluster. The inflammatory is defined by elevated cytokines in the amniotic fluid. In the absence of inflammation there are two subgroups of women: those who have a history of bleeding and a group of women that deliver very close to term whose babies do fine.

Smith: I agree that there is a basic framework of physiological and abnormal events. The latter can set off the feed-forward mechanisms that drive parturition independently. I would put infection amongst these. I think the important lesson in trying to predict preterm delivery is that this is a syndrome with multiple causes and you cannot expect any diagnostic test to predict a multitude of different pathological events.

Gardosi: As concerns the 'placental clock' there is a very strong epidemiological link between preterm delivery, growth restriction and unexplained stillbirths. I suspect that sometimes the birth response has for some reason failed or was not initiated before fetal demise.

Romero: I would just like to share this idea with you to see what you think. I believe that in pregnancy there are fundamentally three responses. One is for the fetus to slow down growth, the second is to increase maternal blood pressure as a compensatory mechanism and the other is to labour. Perhaps the critical nature and state of the baby will determine which of the mechanisms occurs.

Thornton: Could I ask Dr Nathanielsz and Professor Smith to comment on tocolysis given the comments that they made about the events occurring so long before labour?

Nathanielsz: Several important changes may occur a long time before; on the other hand some key processes may be late events. However, I think there will be differences with different aetiologies. One issue, which I never got the time to talk about, is that of polyunsaturated fatty acids. We have very strong evidence in our sheep models that the animal's dietary regimen can alter uterine contractility and prevent certain forms of prematurity.

Smith: I think it is a syndrome so it follows that the treatment is likely to be different for different components of the syndrome. The work I presented illustrates that the CRH trajectory can be changed. I also think that the more we understand about the processes of labour the better our likelihood of achieving effective tocolysis. We are currently exploring the idea that there are several pathways active in labour and, unless you block the majority, tocolysis will not be effective.

Nielson: An important statement that Dr Azzopardi made was to highlight the state of crisis in clinical research in this country. In some instances, local studies are submitted to a multicentre research ethics committee (MREC) in London. This committee decreed that all women have to give full written consent at 36 weeks even though the incidence of the condition studied is about 1%. So to recruit 100 women you have to obtain written consent from 10000 women, which is impossible. I think that this is something that consumer organisations need to get involved in, since if this becomes the norm then we are not going to be able to do trials on tocolytics. I think it is really important that we point out that the quality of clinical care is improved by appropriate research. If this does not happen, the clinical care of women in premature or term labour or the care of their babies is going to be adversely affected.

Lamont: The other constraint is medico-legal litigation. Indemnity cover is huge and pharmaceutical companies now cannot afford the indemnity to do the trials.

Smith: We have similar problems in Australia. We are not allowed to get informed consent at emergency caesarean section so we have to consent all women who may in future have an emergency caesarean. You have to consent hundreds in order to get a few biopsies.

Lamont: I have no problems at all with the principle of women being informed during the course of the pregnancy about studies in labour but to seek universal consent during pregnancy for something that has quite a low incidence is impossible.

Steer: While we are on that topic it might be appropriate to put on record the problems created by the Health and Social Care Act 2001 (section 60), which came into force in the UK on 1 June 2002. This is part of a European initiative which means that it is illegal to use routinely collected clinical data for epidemiological purposes without the signed consent of the person involved. We have now got over half a million well-validated pregnancies on our database but we are currently unable to add to it because our application for exemption from this requirement has been turned down by the committee that is policing it (the Patient Information Advisory Group – see section 61 of the Act). At the moment, there is no clear guidance as to what forms proper informed consent for people to have routine clinical data used for epidemiological purposes. Most of the work has come to a halt while we try to sort out the legal difficulties of using the information. I think the majority of people in this country would be appalled if they realised that we are prevented from benefiting from this data for entirely bureaucratic reasons.

Gardosi: I would second that. It also affects data for trying to analyse what went wrong. It is affecting care prospectively in trials but also retrospectively when trying to audit what is happening.

Saade: Initially it was as restrictive in the USA but then, through pressure and education, it was changed. Now we can do the epidemiological studies.

Thornton: I suspect that many people do not quite realise what difficulties we have. The well-meaning pressure from some individuals is affecting research and clinical care.

Sapherson: I strongly support research and trials because they will eventually save us if we are going to be a patient in hospital. When there is no treatment we get upset and we complain but do not really know the details of what you need to do to set up research or a trial. I am sure my committee will be divided because some of my colleagues would say if you do not give consent then what is the difference between other animals and us. I think that if it is anonymous the data should be used for good purposes.

Regan: I think it is so ironic that all these organisations are attempting to assure that participants of studies are in a position to give informed consent yet the thing they really need information about is what the outcome will be for people if they do not participate. I wonder whether it would be possible to make some sort of presentation to the RCOG Consumers' Forum on this and see whether this group could cascade it down to other organisations. Is it possible to circulate every ethics committee with the comments so they can cascade to the local ones since it is such an important point?

Critchley: I think a lot of organisations are very conscious of this, given the public interest in research. There is an imperative to engage the public because people have misconceptions about what research is, what is happening to their data, and whether it is anonymised properly.

Norman: I think there are two issues. One is that women in labour are not able to know their own mind to give consent and I think this is an offensive statement. I think the other thing is that we have to have a more robust dialogue and sit on MRECs so that when these issues arise we can take part in the discussion.

Steer: I have some anxieties as to whether just to inform women is acceptable. We have been told that we have to get signed consent or at least an indication that the woman has consented before we can use her data for epidemiological purposes. I have taken this to the national user group of the maternity system that I chair, which covers about 26 trusts. Without exception, they declined to introduce such a consent process because they did not have the time, money or staff to do so. Furthermore, they did not know what they would do if a significant proportion of women declined to consent because the data would have to be embargoed so it could not be used. Because of this, they are not prepared to introduce a formal consent process and therefore we cannot use the data they are currently collecting. It is not simply agreeing that women should be asked to sign a consent but the practicality of doing it which is at the moment defeating us.

Calder: I would like to bring the discussion back to the control of labour. There are a number of reports of twins where the second is delivered a long time (weeks) after the first. There are also animals with double uteri where labour occurs in each at a different time. These suggest that labour is an intrauterine event rather than a systemic one.

Bennett: We have a case where the cervix reformed after the first twin, which demonstrates that this process is reversible.

Nathanielsz: These clinical cases fit with the distinction I tried to make between local and systemic oestradiol. Everyone wants to find the unifying hypotheses and we have agreed there is no single unifying factor.

Thornton: Getting back to tocolysis and progesterone, I think that just stopping uterine contractions may not always pay dividends and it is interesting that we are considering how we could be preventing labour. There is a slight onus upon us now to consider progesterone in someone who has had preterm deliveries yet we are a bit doubtful about the current data. We should make recommendations at the end of this meeting as to what should happen next in the progesterone story.

Sebire: Can I make a practical point? It is unbelievable how many trials of interventions for preterm labour have no placental pathology component. I think it is exceedingly important to better define the groups. I suggest that a pathologist examines all placentae from preterm deliveries in future trials.

Crowley: Could I ask Professor Gardosi why he excluded any mention whatsoever of social class? Many of your population-attributable risks could be surrogates for poverty, such as age under twenty and body mass index.

Gardosi: There are a number of studies relating to the importance of social class and deprivation. Deprivation is linked to not only preterm birth but also a whole host of other adverse outcomes. It depends on how well the information is recorded in the data set being studied, but I accept that it is an important consideration.

Nathanielsz: Just a very small point: in our research it is becoming clear that events happening during fetal life are fetal sex dependent. What about prematurity and fetal sex?

Smith: We have looked at this and found no effect. We did see very profound effects of asthma on fetal growth if the fetus was female but not if it was male.

Lamont: Just a couple of small points. I was interested in the question of medically assisted conception and *in vitro* fertilisation (IVF). There is an excess of preterm birth in IVF pregnancies compared to natural conceptions. Historically we have said that this is due to the number of fetuses but even if you correct for the number there is still an excess of preterm births. My own feeling is that it is due to infection. This may be the reason they are having IVF in the first place. Some work from Leeds has shown that bacterial vaginosis and abnormal colonisation result in early miscarriage with embryo transfers or IVF pregnancies compared to natural conceptions. The second thing is that we were talking about medically assisted conception contributing to the preterm birth rate. We must not forget that it is not just IVF but induction of ovulation that influences risk. Another point that needs to be made is that the number of embryos implanted should be limited.

Romero: I wanted to thank Dr Azzopardi for his talk and ask two specific questions. You mentioned that there may be two sorts of babies who have inflammation. One group has inflammation *in utero* – a fetal systemic inflammatory response. These babies are born and the inflammatory process goes away. The other group has persisting inflammation and presumably will be at a greater risk for complications. My question is do you have evidence that these two groups exist?

Azzopardi: I have no data to support it and I was hypothesising based on clinical observations. We have babies where there is clear evidence of inflammation. The baby is born with a syndrome compatible with systemic inflammatory disease. They have a progressive illness characterised by severe lung disease, white matter injury that develops into periventricular cysts, renal failure and gut problems. Giving antibiotics does not stop the syndrome from progressing to its natural termination. There is a suggestion that there could be some underlying genetic basis for this but I have not come across any supporting data.

References

1.   da Fonseca EB, Bittar RE, Carvalho MH, Zugaib M. Prophylactic administration of progesterone by vaginal suppository to reduce the incidence of spontaneous preterm birth in women at increased risk: a randomized placebo-controlled double-blind study. *Am J Obstet Gynecol* 2003;188:419–24.

2.   Meis PJ, Klebanoff M, Thom E, Dombrowski MP, Sibai B, Moawad AH, *et al*. National Institute of Child Health and Human Development Maternal–Fetal Medicine Units Network. Prevention of recurrent preterm delivery by 17 alpha-hydroxyprogesterone caproate. *N Engl J Med* 2003;348: 2379–85. Erratum in *N Engl J Med* 2003;349:1299.

3.   Keirse MJ. Progestogen administration in pregnancy may prevent preterm delivery. *Br J Obstet Gynaecol* 1990;97:149–54.

4.   Rosen T, Kuczynski E, O'Neill LM, Funai EF, Lockwood CJ. Plasma levels of thrombin-antithrombin complexes predict preterm premature rupture of the fetal membranes. *J Matern Fetal Med* 2001;10:297–300.

SECTION 2

SCREENING AND DIAGNOSIS I

Chapter 7

Cervical physiology

Jane E Norman, Andrew J Thomson, Inass Osman and
Marie Anne Ledingham

Introduction

The importance of cervical dysfunction as a factor in preterm delivery is increasingly
recognised.[1] During pregnancy the primary function of the cervix is to stay closed, thus
retaining the baby within the uterus until fetal maturity. A secondary (and perhaps
neglected) function is to prevent infection ascending from the vagina into the uterus.
Later in pregnancy, in the weeks prior to normal delivery at term, the cervix softens
and becomes more distensible (a process known as ripening) to facilitate cervical
dilation by myometrial contractions during labour. This softening, distensibility and
associated cervical shortening can be detected clinically, and quantified using the
Bishop score. Research in sheep suggests that cervical ripening (softening) can occur
independently of any vascular or mechanical connection with the uterus.[2] During
labour the cervix is pulled open passively by myometrial contractions.[3,4] Although there
is some smooth muscle in the cervix, which enables it to contract,[4] the passive
biomechanical strength of the cervix is 10 times its active muscular contractile ability.[5]

There are two obvious manifestations of cervical dysfunction. In the most common
scenario, the cervix fails to ripen at the end of pregnancy or in early labour, and thus
contractions of the myometrium in labour are unable to pull the cervix open. This
presents clinically as slow progress or arrest in labour in the absence of obvious
cephalopelvic disproportion. In the second scenario, the tensile strength of the cervix
is reduced (either permanently or temporarily), and thus modest myometrial
contractions (or merely the weight of the uterine contents) force open the cervix,
leading to preterm delivery. This presents clinically as actual or imminent preterm
delivery in the absence of painful uterine contractions, and is called cervical weakness.

In this chapter, we focus on the biochemistry of the cervix and the physiology of
cervical function. It is clear that there are significant gaps in our understanding of the
process of human cervical ripening. These relate primarily to the difficulties inherent
in studying a dynamic process by taking 'snapshots' of cervical state at a single
moment in time using cervical biopsies. It is possible to examine a partially ripened
pregnant cervix (by taking a biopsy from a woman at term having an elective caesarean
section before the onset of labour) and a fully ripened cervix (by taking a biopsy from
a woman having a caesarean section in labour, ideally because of suspected fetal
compromise and not slow progress in labour [which might imply cervical
dysfunction]). It is also possible to take biopsies of a first-trimester pregnant cervix,
well before the ripening process starts. However, it is almost impossible to determine

the events occurring between these time points. Furthermore, many groups have been unwilling to take cervical biopsies and have used lower uterine segment to represent cervix, since the lower uterine segment is more readily accessible. We have tried to avoid this strategy: in our view, the lower uterine segment has much more in common biologically and anatomically with upper uterine segment myometrium than with cervical tissue.[6] Many studies have used postpartum cervical biopsies when examining the ripened cervix. In this scenario, it is not possible solely to ascribe the structural and biochemical changes observed to the process of cervical ripening, as the passage of the baby through the cervix may also have had an effect.

Notwithstanding these caveats, we shall aim to describe the changes in cervical biochemistry observed in association with cervical ripening and attempt to integrate the known pathways into an overarching scheme. Where possible, we shall focus on human cervical physiology *in vitro* and *in vivo*, although where animal data are informative these will also be included.

Cervical structure

Anatomy

The human uterine cervix is continuous with and distal to the uterine body, and projects into the vagina. It is cylindrical in shape and around 2 cm long and 1–2 cm wide in the nonpregnant stage, with some growth during pregnancy. During labour the cervix dilates, to a maximum diameter of 10 cm, to allow the baby to pass through during delivery (Figure 7.1). The blood supply to the cervix is from a descending branch of the uterine artery. The innervation of the cervix is mostly from branches of the inferior hypogastric plexus. The endocervical canal is lined with columnar epithelium, containing many large, highly branched glands. At the external cervical os, the epithelium changes in type, so that the portion of the cervix protruding into the vagina is covered by stratified squamous epithelium. Underlying the epithelial layer is the cervical stroma, which has received most attention in terms of cervical physiology during pregnancy. Its biochemistry is described below.

Normal cervical biochemistry

The uterine cervix is composed of connective tissue. The principal collagens in the cervix are types I (70%) and III (30%),[7,8] with a tiny proportion of type IV collagen in the basement membranes. The collagen fibres of the cervix are embedded in a ground substance made up of proteoglycans. These proteoglycans contain a variety of glycosaminoglycans (GAGs) – long chains of negatively charged repeating disaccharides with one hexosamine (glucosamine or galactosamine) or uronic acid (glucuronic or iduronic). In cervical tissue, the most abundant proteoglycans are chondroitin sulphates (such as the large chondroitin sulphate versican) and dermatan sulphates (such as biglycan and the small dermatan sulphate decorin).[9–12] The keratan sulphate fibromodulin and heparan sulphates have also been demonstrated.[10,13] In addition to the collagen fibres and proteoglycans, the cervix has a significant water content, a cellular component composed mainly of fibroblasts,[14] and smooth muscle that is capable both of spontaneous and drug-induced contractions.[15]

The collagen fibres and proteoglycans, and the interactions between them, together confer on the cervix its unique characteristics. The collagen fibres resist pulling forces (which would dilate the cervix), and the ground substance of proteoglycans resist

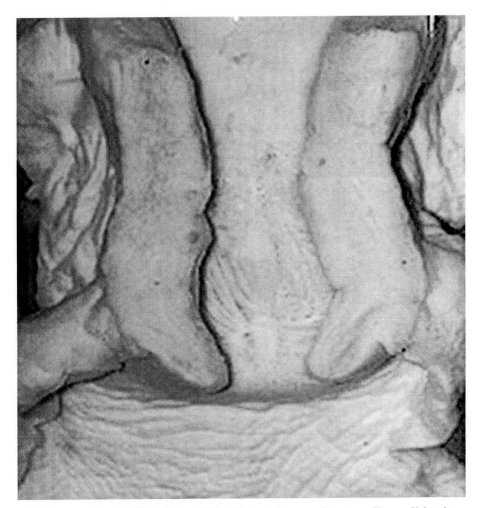

Figure 7.1. Dissection by William Hunter (1718–1783, in the Museum of Anatomy, Glasgow University, showing fully effaced and partially dilated cervix in a woman who died during labour

compressive forces.[16] Additionally, some GAGs also resist pulling forces, help to maintain the shape of the cervix, and interact with collagen fibrils to maintain their organisation. The last of these is particularly important under the action of tensile forces. Of the specific proteoglycans discovered in the cervix so far, decorin (and possibly also fibromodulin) orient collagen fibres and allow collagen fibril growth, while inhibiting new fibrillogenesis.[17] The importance of decorin in maintaining the tensile strength of collagen is highlighted by the demonstration that decorin-null animals have abnormal collagen fibre formation in the skin with markedly reduced tensile strength. Furthermore, it has been shown *in vitro* that decorin incorporation increases the tensile strength of uncrosslinked collagen fibres.[18]

Biochemistry of disordered cervical function

The functional importance of each of the biochemical components of the cervix is demonstrated by studies of cervical dysfunction. Lower cervical hydroxyproline concentrations and increased collagen extractability (implying decreased collagen stability) have been demonstrated in cervices of nonpregnant women with a history of cervical weakness when compared with apparently normal nonpregnant controls.[19] In another study,[20] second-trimester biopsies from women with cervical weakness had normal collagen concentrations but high collagen extractabilities and collagenolytic activity (suggesting high collagen turnover), with associated low strength and high extensibility. Another study[21] of cervical weakness found decreased concentration of elastic fibres, compared with controls. In contrast, higher collagen concentrations and lower collagen extractability were found in cervical biopsies from women undergoing caesarean section due to failure to progress in labour, compared with women who were progressing normally in labour (the latter group being delivered by caesarean section due to fetal distress).[22]

Changes in structural composition of the cervix during ripening

Collagen concentrations

During pregnancy cervical collagen content is reduced, and the extractability of collagen decreases progressively in labour.[10,11,23,24] A recent study[25] examined this in detail and found (using SDS-PAGE) that solubilised collagen type 1 levels are lower in cervical biopsies from the third trimester (36–38 weeks), compared with the first trimester (9–14 weeks). Alpha 1 chains from each of collagen types I, III and V were expressed as a ratio of total $\alpha 1$ density. The ratio of $\alpha 1(I)$ fell in the third trimester to around 60% of the first trimester value ($P < 0.05$ between the two ratios). In contrast, the ratio of $\alpha 1(III)$ increased by 80% ($P < 0.01$). There was no change in $\alpha 1(V)$ ratio.[25] Although SDS-PAGE is only able to examine solubilised collagen, further analysis demonstrated that the solubilisation methods used solubilised 75–85% of total collagen, suggesting that the collagen examined would be representative of all the collagen in the cervical biopsy.

In parallel with the decrease in type I collagen levels, a fall in $\alpha 1(I)$ mRNA expression was observed, so that in the third trimester $\alpha 1(I)$ mRNA levels were around one-tenth of that in the first trimester.[25] In another study,[10] collagen 1 and III mRNA levels were compared in cervical biopsies from women nonpregnant, at term, immediately postpartum and involuting (2–4 days postpartum): postpartum mRNA levels for both collagen 1 and III were similar in women at term and nonpregnant but lower in women postpartum. Taken together, these studies imply a progressive decrease in collagen I synthesis during pregnancy, with a further decline in collagen 1 and III synthesis in the late phase of cervical ripening and during labour.

Collagen organisation

In addition to changes in collagen concentration, cervical ripening is associated with changes in collagen organisation. Collagen fibres maintain the tensile strength of the cervix best when arranged in parallel, with tight crosslinks effected by binding of ground substance.[26] Studies in rat cervix using polarised light and electron microscopy indicate that in early pregnancy collagen fibres are packed tightly with a regular arrangement.[27] This arrangement breaks down later in pregnancy so that, as the cervix softens, collagen fibril alignment becomes much more disordered. In the human cervix, a similar process of collagen fibril disorganisation has been observed during the ripening process, using both histochemistry and electron microscopy.[25,28] Although the changes observed in collagen fibre organisation appear substantial, the techniques used have not allowed or been supported by statistical analysis of these differences.

A device called a colloscope, which measures crosslinked cervical collagen *in vivo* using light-induced fluorescence, has been developed by Garfield's group. In rats, colloscope-measured changes in light-induced autofluorescence from the cervix correlate with previously observed changes in cervical collagen content.[29] A more recent study[30] by the same group in humans has now also shown a significant inverse correlation between light-induced fluorescence and gestational age and between light-induced fluorescence and the interval between cervical measurements and eventual delivery. These studies infer a progressive decrease in collagen content and/or organisation in the human cervix as delivery approaches.

Proteoglycan concentrations

Proteoglycan concentrations in the cervix are also altered with ripening. The overall concentration is lower in pregnancy than in the nonpregnant state.[11,31] However, within this general trend, some proteoglycans increase and some decrease.[32]

In rats, concentrations of the proteoglycan decorin are greatest at term and fall progressively postpartum towards the nadir nonpregnant level.[33,34] While this is perhaps counter-intuitive, since decorin strengthens the cervix, it is proposed that excess decorin production competes with the decorin already bound to collagen, thus disrupting and dissociating the collagen fibres.[35] In support of this, cervical ripening agents such as onapristone and prostaglandin E (PGE) both increase rat cervical decorin concentrations in parallel with cervical ripening.[35]

In humans, however, potential changes in decorin concentration associated with ripening are less clear. One study[36] showed greater decorin concentrations at term compared with nonpregnant or first-trimester samples, suggesting that, as in the rat, cervical ripening is associated with increased decorin concentrations. In contrast, in other studies, human cervical decorin concentrations were lower immediately postpartum compared with nonpregnant women[32] and lower during labour than before.[37] Another study[10] has further added to the confusion by failing to demonstrate a difference in decorin concentration (assessed by agarose gel electrophoresis) or decorin mRNA concentration between nonpregnant, term and postpartum biopsies.

The proteoglycans biglycan and versican fill up the space between collagen fibres and disperse them.[38] Cervical biglycan, versican protein and mRNA concentrations appear to increase in association with cervical ripening[10,32,39] The effect of the increased biglycan and versican concentration on collagen fibril dispersal will be to decrease cervical tensile strength.

Cellular components of the cervix

In addition to changes in the collagen and GAG/proteoglycan composition of the cervix, the cellular component also changes during cervical ripening. The fibroblasts present in cervical biopsies of nonpregnant women appear to have proliferated and differentiated into myofibroblasts (cells with features of both fibroblasts and smooth muscle) by the end of pregnancy.[14] The function of these cervical myofibroblasts is not clear – in other tissues they are involved in wound healing and wound contraction. The authors speculate that the myofibroblasts may form a 'purse string' around the lumen of the cervix that may help to close the cervical canal post delivery. Further work is needed to investigate this hypothesis.

The other obvious change in cellular composition of the cervix observed in association with ripening is the profound cellular inflammatory infiltrate, principally of neutrophils and macrophages[28,40,41] (Figure 7.2). These are reviewed in more detail in Chapter 8.

Biochemical factors mediating changes in cervical structure during ripening

Collagen breakdown

Collagen breakdown is largely mediated by the collagenases, principally matrix metalloproteinases MMP-1 and MMP-8.[42] Studies using functional assays have shown collagenase activity to be increased in human cervix in association with cervical ripening.[43,44] (Indeed, in studies where lower segment is used to represent human uterine cervix, there is a progressive increase in MMP-8, MMP-9 and tissue inhibitor of metalloproteinases 1 (TIMP-1) expression with progress in labour.[45])

Additionally, mRNA levels of the gelatinases MMP-2 and MMP-9 (which break down proteoglycans and denatured collagen and activate procollagenases[46]) are also greater in term and postpartum cervical samples, compared with those from nonpregnant women.[47] However, since MMP activity is regulated not only by gene expression and secretion but also by zymogen activation and other proteinase inhibitors in the extracellular matrix,[42] demonstration of increased gelatinase mRNA expression in association with cervical ripening does not, by itself, confirm increased activity. Further studies are required to explore the precise nature of the matrix metalloproteinases involved in cervical ripening and their concentration–activity profile at various stages of the ripening process.

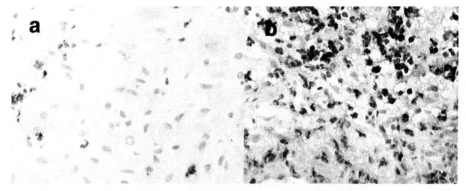

Figure 7.2. Identification of polymorphonuclear leucocytes (neutrophils) in human cervix before (a) and after (b) the onset of labour at term. Neutrophils are identified using immunohistochemistry with an antibody directed against the enzyme human neutrophil elastase. Cervical ripening is associated with a massive influx of neutrophils into the cervical stroma

Endogenous regulators of cervical MMP activity

Inflammatory mediators such as cytokines, prostaglandins and nitric oxide synthase

Pro-inflammatory cytokines, specifically tumour necrosis factor-α (TNF-α) and interleukin-1β (IL-1β), stimulate MMP expression in human cervical smooth muscle cells.[48] In culture *in vitro*, TNF-α and IL-1β stimulated mRNA and protein for MMP-1, -3 and -9 in a time- and (for TNF-α) dose-dependent manner, while mRNA and protein concentrations for TIMP-1 and -2 remained unchanged.[48] The functional effects of the increase in MMP production were confirmed by casein (MMP-1 and -3) and gelatin (MMP-9) zymography respectively. The potential effects of other cytokines were not determined.

Other studies have shown that IL-1β stimulates collagenase activity in human cervical fibroblasts in culture.[49–51]

The human data showing that metalloproteinase activity is stimulated by cytokine production is paralleled by rabbit data, both *in vitro*[52] and *in vivo*,[53,54] showing that pro-inflammatory cytokines such as IL-1, IL-8 and TNF-α stimulate MMP activity and/or production. Additionally, *in vivo*, cervical administration of pro-inflammatory cytokines to both rabbits and guinea pigs has been shown to stimulate changes which occur during ripening, such as neutrophil invasion and decreased collagen concentration.[54,55]

The effect of the cytokines in stimulating MMP activity is important, since we have now shown increased IL-1, -6 and -8 mRNA and protein expression in the cervix in association with cervical ripening (Figures 7.3 and 7.4).[40,56] Additionally, IL-1 levels in cervicovaginal secretions also increase as parturition approaches.[57] The role of TNF-α

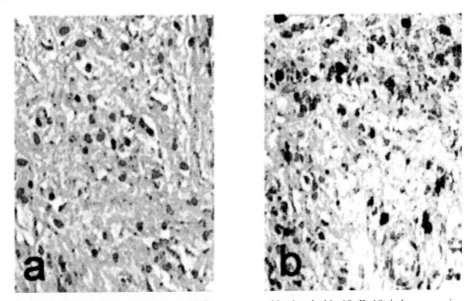

Figure 7.3. Immunolocalisation of the pro-inflammatory cytokine interleukin-1β (IL-1β) in human cervix. There is little staining for IL-1β in cervical biopsies taken before the onset of labour (a). IL-1β is identified within leucocytes abundant in cervical biopsies collected during labour (b)

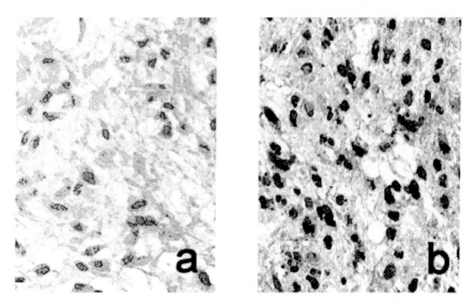

Figure 7.4. Immunolocalisation of the pro-inflammatory cytokine interleukin-6 (IL-6) in human cervix. In cervix, IL-6 is restricted to a subpopulation of leucocytes, the density of which appeared greater in labouring (b) than in non-labouring tissue (a)

is less clear, with no clear increase in association with parturition in either cervical or lower segment biopsies.[58] Platelet aggregating factor (PAF) has been shown to stimulate MMP-1 mRNA and protein concentration in human uterine fibroblasts *in vitro*, while having no effect on TIMP-1 production.[59] A functional effect of PAF *in vitro* is supported by data showing PAF receptor mRNA expression on human uterine cervical fibroblasts.[59] PAF is also known to be produced by leucocytes such as macrophages and neutrophils,[60] which others have shown to invade the cervix during parturition. Again, these data suggest that endogenous PAF production, derived from invading leucocytes, might stimulate MMP activity during cervical ripening.

Of the other inflammatory mediators, both prostaglandin $F_2\alpha$ and nitric oxide (NO) produced by the enzyme nitric oxide synthase (NOS) stimulate MMP-1 protein and mRNA production from human uterine cervical fibroblasts *in vitro*.[51,61] We and others have described the increased expression of some of the NOS isoforms in the cervix in association with labour (Figure 7.5).[4,62–65] This increased NOS expression generates increased NO production, which stimulates MMP expression and activity. Endogenous prostaglandin production also increases in the cervix in association with ripening[66] and again this will stimulate MMP activity.

Hormones

In vitro studies of human lower uterine segment fibroblasts suggest that progesterone inhibits pro MMP-1 and -3 expression, while having no significant effect on MMP-2 and TIMP-1 expression.[67] Although this study did not use fibroblasts obtained from the cervix, it is in keeping with an immunohistochemical study in the first trimester,[68] where the antiprogesterone mifepristone stimulated expression of MMP-1, -8 and -9,

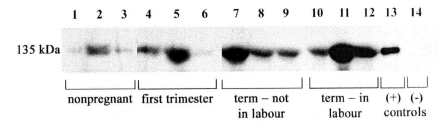

Figure 7.5. We and others (see text) have shown an increased expression of some of the nitric oxide synthase (NOS) isoforms in the cervix in association with labour. This figure shows Western blot analysis of cervical samples collected from nonpregnant and pregnant women using an antibody directed against endothelial NOS (lanes 1–3, nonpregnant; lanes 4–6, pregnant first trimester; lanes 7–9, term pregnant not in labour; lanes 10–12, term pregnant in spontaneous labour). The putative endothelial NOS band is seen at 135 kDa. Positive and negative controls are shown in lanes 13 and 14 respectively. The figure shows representative bands from a larger study group[63]

while having no effect on TIMP expression. In addition to progesterone-inhibiting MMP activity, *in vitro* data suggest that sulphated oestrogens also stimulate collagenase in human cervical cells in culture.[69] In contrast, an *in vitro* study of fibroblasts obtained from nonpregnant human cervix failed to demonstrate an effect of either progesterone (1 µmol/l) or oestradiol (40 nmol/l) on MMP activity.[70]

Similar inhibitory effects of progesterone on MMP expression and activity, and stimulatory effects on TIMP expression and activity have been found in animal studies.[71,72] Furthermore, the antiprogesterone onapristone has been found to stimulate MMP-3 expression.[73]

Taken together, these studies suggest that an increase in oestrogen or a decrease in progesterone levels might stimulate MMP activity in the cervix and thus promote cervical ripening. It might be argued that these potential regulatory activities are not involved in human cervical ripening, since there is no rise in oestrogen or fall in progesterone levels in association with parturition. However, increasing evidence points to a 'functional progesterone withdrawal' occurring in human parturition via changes in steroid receptor concentration and function in the lower segment myometrium.[74] Similar events may occur in the cervix. When biopsies from women not pregnant, at term and postpartum were examined, oestrogen receptor alpha (ERα) mRNA expression was found to be lower postpartum than in the nonpregnant and term-pregnant state. In contrast, ERβ mRNA receptor expression was higher in term-pregnant than in nonpregnant or postpartum uterus.[75] Protein concentrations were not assessed, but immunohistochemistry suggested that changes in protein expression of the receptors paralleled that of mRNA. Taken together, these data imply a switch from ERα to ERβ dominance during late pregnancy and labour. This switch might downregulate progesterone receptor expression, with functional progesterone withdrawal, even if progesterone concentrations are unchanged.[76] In support of this, one study has suggested a decrease in progesterone receptor protein expression in association with cervical ripening, although this study did not differentiate between the receptor subtypes.[37] If these findings are confirmed, decrease in functional endogenous progesterone receptor concentration in the cervix in association with cervical ripening will be shown to be yet another stimulus to increased MMP activity.

Relaxin stimulates pro MMP-1 and pro MMP-3 mRNA and protein expression, and pro MMP-2 expression while decreasing TIMP-1 protein concentration in human lower uterine segment fibroblasts *in vitro.*[67] In human uterine cervical stromal cells, relaxin has also been shown to stimulate proteinase activity.[70] Similar stimulatory effects of relaxin on collagen remodelling and/or metalloproteinase activity has been found in the pig,[77] guinea pig,[78] and rat.[79] In humans, there is no obvious change in serum relaxin levels in association with parturition[80] although elevated serum relaxin is associated with increased risk of preterm delivery.[81–83] Thus it is possible that in the abnormal situation of preterm delivery relaxin stimulates MMP activity in the cervix, but there is no evidence that this mechanism is also important during physiological cervical ripening.

Other hormones, such as dehydroepiandrosterone sulphate (DHAS), have been found to stimulate collagenase in human cervical fibroblasts *in vitro.*[69] The physiological importance of this finding in human cervical ripening is unclear.

Stretch

The importance of mechanical stimuli on the physiology of both the myometrium and cervix is increasingly recognised. *In vitro* studies suggest that mechanical stretch stimulates MMP-1 mRNA and protein production from human uterine cervical fibroblasts.[51] Since stretch is known to stimulate endogenous prostaglandin release in nonpregnant cervix,[84] it is possible that passive mechanical stretch of the cervix has some or all of its effect on stimulating MMP activity via an increase in prostaglandin production. Whatever the mechanism, it is clear that the cervix is increasingly subject to stretch as term approaches, as uterine activity increases and the lower segment forms. In this scenario, stretch increases MMP activity, which promotes collagen breakdown, which in turn allows further stretch – a feed-forward loop thus emerges.

GAG breakdown and synthesis

Agents that regulate GAG production may also be important in cervical ripening, since GAG concentrations change in association with this process. As discussed above, ripening-associated changes in GAG concentration are more complex than those of collagen since, although total GAG concentration increases in association with cervical ripening, within this overall effect some GAGs are increased and some decreased.

Inflammatory mediators

In vitro studies using cultured human cervical fibroblasts have suggested a stimulatory effect of IL-1β on total GAG synthesis (measured as radiolabelled glucosamine incorporation).[85] Similarly, prostaglandin E_2 (PGE$_2$) induces GAG synthesis *in vitro,*[86,87] although an *in vitro* study[32] in organ culture published in 1993 did suggest an inhibitory effect. With the exception of this latter study, the data suggest that agents known to be increased in the cervix in association with cervical ripening (IL-1β and prostaglandins) may contribute to the mechanism of cervical ripening via an increase in GAG synthesis.

Hormones

In vitro studies suggest that progesterone induces a dose-dependent increase in GAG synthesis.[87] Again, at first sight, this is counterintuitive if labour is considered to be associated with progesterone withdrawal. However, at high concentrations progesterone was also shown to inhibit the stimulatory effect of PGE$_2$ on GAG synthesis. The authors propose that the dominant effect of progesterone during pregnancy is to inhibit PGE$_2$-induced GAG synthesis, an effect that is presumably reversed as term approaches and functional progesterone levels fall.

In vitro studies in humans[85] suggest that relaxin stimulates GAG synthesis, and similar effects have been reported in the rat.[88] As described above for collagen breakdown, this may be a mechanism by which high serum relaxin levels predispose to preterm delivery.

Cellular elements

Cervical ripening is associated with fibroblast differentiation and increased density of inflammatory cells. We have assumed that the latter is caused by invasion of inflammatory cells from the peripheral circulation, rather than increased proliferation or decreased degradation locally. Leucocyte invasion from the peripheral circulation is promoted by both increased adhesion molecule and IL-8 expression. Both events occur in the cervix in association with spontaneous cervical ripening.[40,89] We are not aware of any data on agents that might promote myofibroblast proliferation.

Apoptosis

Apoptosis has been conclusively demonstrated in the smooth muscle cells of the rat cervix in association with parturition,[90,91] and a similar process has been shown during human cervical ripening.[92] Further studies are needed to investigate this but apoptosis may be another event that could be targeted to inhibit cervical changes that predispose to preterm delivery.[93]

Agents that induce cervical ripening *in vivo*

Information on agents that effect cervical ripening when administered *in vivo* can aid understanding of the physiology of this process. Each of the agents prostaglandins (particularly those of the E series), antiprogesterones and nitric oxide donors can induce cervical ripening in humans *in vivo*[94–96] Whether vaginally applied oestrogen is an effective cervical ripening agent is uncertain, with some studies indicating that it is effective[97] although a recent meta-analysis suggested that its efficacy is inconclusive.[98] The (limited) data on the oestrogen precursor DHAS suggest that it ripens the cervix.[99]

Other than the effects on Bishop score or cervical resistance, there is (for obvious reasons) little data on the effect of these agents administered *in vivo* on cervical composition, although mifepristone administration is associated with collagen fibre dissolution.[100]

In animal experiments, exogenous application of cytokines such as IL-1β, IL-8,[53] hyaluronic acid,[101] heparin sulphate and hyaluronic acid,[102] relaxin[103] and DHAS[53] also stimulate cervical ripening *in vivo*. In addition to physical softening, histological examination post application of these agents showed collagen fibre dissolution and a leucocytic infiltration.

Conclusions

Changes in cervical physiology, principally decreased collagen concentration and organisation, changes in GAG synthesis and changes in the cellular component (influx of leucocytes and development of myofibroblasts), are integral to the process of cervical ripening. Increased endogenous cytokine, prostaglandin and nitric oxide synthase expression, a decrease in functional progesterone receptor concentration, and increased cell adhesion molecule expression all promote the physiological changes observed in cervical ripening at term, although it is not yet clear which of these pathways are most important.

There are few data on cervical pathophysiology, although the limited data available suggest that derangements in collagen synthesis and organisation may also be important. Further work on cervical function in preterm delivery may prompt novel therapeutic developments in the prevention of prematurity.

Acknowledgements

We are grateful to Anne Young for technical assistance and expertise in immuno-histochemistry. We are grateful to SHERT and to Wellbeing for funding of some of our work discussed in this review. The photograph in Figure 7.1 was taken by David Russell at the Museum of Anatomy, University of Glasgow, under the supervision of Dr Stuart MacDonald, and we are grateful to them for their assistance.

References

1.   Olah KS, Gee H. The prevention of preterm delivery – can we afford to continue to ignore the cervix? *Br J Obstet Gynaecol* 1992;99:278–80.
2.   Ledger WL, Webster M, Harrison LP, Anderson AB, Turnbull AC. Increase in cervical extensibility during labor induced after isolation of the cervix from the uterus in pregnant ewes. *Am J Obstet Gynecol* 1985;151:397–402.
3.   Leppert P. Anatomy and physiology and cervical ripening. *Clin Obstet Gynecol* 1995;38:267–79.
4.   Ekerhovd E, Brannstromm M, Weijdegard B, Norstrom A. Nitric oxide synthases in the human cervix at term pregnancy and effects of nitric oxide on cervical smooth muscle contractility. *Am J Obstet Gynecol* 2000;183:610–6.
5.   Petersen LK, Oxlund H, Uldbjerg N, Forman A. *In vitro* analysis of muscular contractile ability and passive biomechanical properties of uterine cervical samples from nonpregnant women. *Obstet Gynecol* 1991;77:772–6.
6.   Thomson A, Telfer J, Kohnene G, Young A, Cameron I, Greer I, *et al.* Nitric oxide synthase activity and localisation do not change in uterus and placenta during human parturition. *Hum Reprod* 1997;12:2546–52.
7.   Kleissl HP, van der Rest M, Naftolin F, Glorieux FH, de Leon A. Collagen changes in the human uterine cervix at parturition. *Am J Obstet Gynecol* 1978;130:748–53.
8.   Minamoto T, Arai K, Hirakawa S, Nagai Y. Immunohistochemical studies on collagen types in the uterine cervix in pregnant and nonpregnant states. *Am J Obstet Gynecol* 1987;156:138–44.
9.   Fischer DC, Henning A, Winkler M, Rath W, Haubeck HD, Greiling H. Evidence for the presence of a large keratan sulphate proteoglycan in the human uterine cervix. *Biochem J* 1996;320(Pt 2):393–9.
10. Westergren-Thorsson G, Norman M, Bjornsson S, Endresen U, Stjernholm Y, Ekman G, *et al.* Differential expressions of mRNA for proteoglycans, collagens and transforming growth factor-beta in the human cervix during pregnancy and involution. *Biochim Biophys Acta* 1998;1406:203–13.
11. Uldbjerg N, Ekman G, Malmstrom A, Olsson K, Ulmsten U. Ripening of the human uterine cervix related to changes in collagen, glycosaminoglycans, collagenolytic activity. *Am J Obstet Gynecol* 1983;147:662–6.
12. von Maillot K, Stuhlsatz HW, Mohanaradhakrishnan V, Greiling H. Changes in the glycosaminoglycans distribution pattern in the human uterine cervix during pregnancy and labor. *Am J Obstet Gynecol* 1979;135:503–6.
13. Kitamura K, Ito A, Mori Y, Hirakawa S. Glycosaminoglycans of human uterine cervix: heparan sulfate increase with reference to cervical ripening. *Biochem Med* 1980;23:159–66.
14. Montes GS, Zugaib M, Joazeiro PP, Varayoud J, Ramos JG, Munoz-de-Toro M, *et al.* Phenotypic modulation of fibroblastic cells in the mucous layer of the human uterine cervix at term. *Reproduction* 2002;124:783–90.

15. Hillier K, Karim SM. The human isolated cervix: a study of its spontaneous motility and responsiveness to drugs. *Br J Pharmacol* 1970;40:576P+.

16. Scott JE. Structure and function in extracellular matrices depend on interactions between anionic glycosaminoglycans. *Pathol Biol (Paris)* 2001;49:284–9.

17. Iozzo RV. Matrix proteoglycans: from molecular design to cellular function. *Annu Rev Biochem* 1998;67:609–52.

18. Pins GD, Christiansen DL, Patel R, Silver FH. Self-assembly of collagen fibers. Influence of fibrillar alignment and decorin on mechanical properties. *Biophys J* 1997;73:2164–72.

19. Petersen LK, Uldbjerg N. Cervical collagen in non-pregnant women with previous cervical incompetence. *Eur J Obstet Gynecol Reprod Biol* 1996;67:41–5.

20. Rechberger T, Uldbjerg N, Oxlund H. Connective tissue changes in the cervix during normal pregnancy and pregnancy complicated by cervical incompetence. *Obstet Gynecol* 1988;71:563–7.

21. Leppert P, Yu S, Keller S, Cerreta J, Mandl I. Decreased elastic fibers and desmosine content in incompetent cervix. *Am J Obstet Gynecol* 1987;157:1134–9.

22. Granstrom L, Ekman G, Malmstrom A. Insufficient remodelling of the uterine connective tissue in women with protracted labour. *Br J Obstet Gynaecol* 1991;98:1212–6.

23. Danforth DN, Veis A, Breen M, Weinstein HG, Buckingham JC, Manalo P. The effect of pregnancy and labor on the human cervix: changes in collagen, glycoproteins, and glycosaminoglycans. *Am J Obstet Gynecol* 1974;120:641–51.

24. Ito A, Kitamura K, Mori Y, Hirakawa S. The change in solubility of type I collagen in human uterine cervix in pregnancy at term. *Biochem Med* 1979;21:262–70.

25. Iwahashi M, Muragaki Y, Ooshima A, Umesaki N. Decreased type I collagen expression in human uterine cervix during pregnancy. *J Clin Endocrinol Metab* 2003;88:2231–5.

26. Aspden RM. Collagen organisation in the cervix and its relation to mechanical function. *Coll Relat Res* 1988;8:103–12.

27. Yu SY, Tozzi CA, Babiarz J, Leppert PC. Collagen changes in rat cervix in pregnancy–polarized light microscopic and electron microscopic studies. *Proc Soc Exp Biol Med* 1995;209:360–8.

28. Junqueira L, Zugaib M, Montes G, Toledo O, Krisztan R, Shigihara K. Morphologic and histochemical evidence for the occurrence of collagenolysis and for the role of neutrophilic polymorphonuclear leukocytes during cervical dilation. *Am J Obstet Gynecol* 1980;138:273–81.

29. Glassman W, Byam-Smith M, Garfield RE. Changes in rat cervical collagen during gestation and after antiprogesterone treatment as measured *in vivo* with light-induced autofluorescence. *Am J Obstet Gynecol* 1995;173:1550–6.

30. Maul H, Olson G, Fittkow CT, Saade GR, Garfield RE. Cervical light-induced fluorescence in humans decreases throughout gestation and before delivery: Preliminary observations. *Am J Obstet Gynecol* 2003;188:537–41.

31. Norman M, Ekman G, Ulmsten U, Barchan K, Malmstrom A. Proteoglycan metabolism in the connective tissue of pregnant and non-pregnant human cervix. An *in vitro* study. *Biochem J* 1991;275(Pt 2):515–20.

32. Norman M, Ekman G, Malmstrom A. Changed proteoglycan metabolism in human cervix immediately after spontaneous vaginal delivery. *Obstet Gynecol* 1993;81:217–23.

33. Kokenyesi R, Woessner JF Jr. Relationship between dilatation of the rat uterine cervix and a small dermatan sulfate proteoglycan. *Biol Reprod* 1990;42:87–97.

34. Leppert PC, Kokenyesi R, Klemenich CA, Fisher J. Further evidence of a decorin-collagen interaction in the disruption of cervical collagen fibers during rat gestation. *Am J Obstet Gynecol* 2000;182:805–11;discussion 811-2.

35. Rechberger T, Abramson SR, Woessner JF Jr. Onapristone and prostaglandin E2 induction of delivery in the rat in late pregnancy: a model for the analysis of cervical softening. *Am J Obstet Gynecol* 1996;175:719–23.

36. Fischer DC, Kuth A, Winkler M, Handt S, Hauptmann S, Rath W, *et al.* A large keratan sulfate proteoglycan present in human cervical mucous appears to be involved in the reorganization of the cervical extracellular matrix at term. *J Soc Gynecol Investig* 2001;8:277–84.

37. Stjernholm Y, Sahlin L, Malmstrom A, Barchan K, Eriksson H, Ekman G. Potential roles for gonadal steroids and insulin-like growth factor I during final cervical ripening. *Obstet Gynecol* 1997;90:375–80.

38. Lindahl U, Hook M. Glycosaminoglycans and their binding to biological macromolecules. *Annu Rev Biochem* 1978;47:385–417.

39. Norman M, Ekman G, Malmstrom A. Prostaglandin E2-induced ripening of the human cervix involves changes in proteoglycan metabolism. *Obstet Gynecol* 1993;82:1013–20.

40. Osman I, Young A, Ledingham M, Thomson A, Jordan F, Greer I, *et al.* Leukocyte density and pro-inflammatory cytokine expression in human fetal membranes, decidua, cervix and myometrium before and during labour at term. *Mol Hum Reprod* 2003;9:41–5.

41. Bokstrom H, Brannstrom M, Alexandersson M, Norstrom A. Leukocyte subpopulations in the

human uterine cervical stroma at early and term pregnancy. *Hum Reprod* 1997;12:586–90.

42. Woessner JF Jr. The family of matrix metalloproteinases. *Ann N Y Acad Sci* 1994;732:11–21.

43. Osmers R, Rath W, Adelmann-Grill BC, Fittkow C, Severenyi M, Kuhn W. Collagenase activity in the cervix of non-pregnant and pregnant women. *Arch Gynecol Obstet* 1990;248:75–80.

44. Rath W, Adelmann-Grill BC, Pieper U, Kuhn W, Osmers R. Collagenase activity in cervical tissue of the non-pregnant and pregnant human cervix. *Acta Physiol Hung* 1988;71:491–5.

45. Winkler M, Oberpichler A, Tschesche H, Ruck P, Fischer DC, Rath W. Collagenolysis in the lower uterine segment during parturition at term: correlations with stage of cervical dilatation and duration of labor. *Am J Obstet Gynecol* 1999;181:153–8.

46. Hulboy DL, Rudolph LA, Matrisian LM. Matrix metalloproteinases as mediators of reproductive function. *Mol Hum Reprod* 1997;3:27–45.

47. Stygar D, Wang H, Vladic YS, Ekman G, Eriksson H, Sahlin L. Increased level of matrix metalloproteinases 2 and 9 in the ripening process of the human cervix. *Biol Reprod* 2002;67:889–94.

48. Watari M, Watari H, DiSanto ME, Chacko S, Shi GP, Strauss JF 3rd. Pro-inflammatory cytokines induce expression of matrix-metabolizing enzymes in human cervical smooth muscle cells. *Am J Pathol* 1999;154:1755–62.

49. Ito A, Sato T, Ojima Y, Chen LC, Nagase H, Mori Y. Calmodulin differentially modulates the interleukin 1-induced biosynthesis of tissue inhibitor of metalloproteinases and matrix metalloproteinases in human uterine cervical fibroblasts. *J Biol Chem* 1991;266:13598–601.

50. Ito A, Leppert PC, Mori Y. Human recombinant interleukin-1 alpha increases elastase-like enzyme in human uterine cervical fibroblasts. *Gynecol Obstet Invest* 1990;30:239–41.

51. Yoshida M, Sagawa N, Itoh H, Yura S, Takemura M, Wada Y, *et al.* Prostaglandin F(2alpha), cytokines and cyclic mechanical stretch augment matrix metalloproteinase-1 secretion from cultured human uterine cervical fibroblast cells. *Mol Hum Reprod* 2002;8:681–7.

52. Ito A, Goshowaki H, Sato T, Mori Y, Yamashita K, Hayakawa T, *et al.* Human recombinant interleukin-1 alpha-mediated stimulation of procollagenase production and suppression of biosynthesis of tissue inhibitor of metalloproteinases in rabbit uterine cervical fibroblasts. *FEBS Lett* 1988;234:326–30.

53. El Maradny E, Kanayama N, Halim A, Maehara K, Sumimoto K, Terao T. Biochemical changes in the cervical tissue of rabbit induced by interleukin-8, interleukin-1beta, dehydroepiandrosterone sulphate and prostaglandin E2: a comparative study. *Hum Reprod* 1996;11:1099–104.

54. el Maradny E, Kanayama N, Halim A, Maehara K, Sumimoto K, Terao T. The effect of interleukin-1 in rabbit cervical ripening. *Eur J Obstet Gynecol Reprod Biol* 1995;60:75–80.

55. Chwalisz K, Benson M, Scholz P, Daum J, Beier HM, Hegele-Hartung C. Cervical ripening with the cytokines interleukin 8, interleukin 1 beta and tumour necrosis factor alpha in guinea-pigs. *Hum Reprod* 1994;9:2173–81.

56. Young A, Thomson A, Ledingham M, Jordan F, Greer I, Norman J. Immunolocalization of pro-inflammatory cytokines in myometrium, cervix and fetal membranes during human parturition at term. *Biol Reprod* 2002;66:445–9.

57. Imai M, Tani A, Saito M, Saito K, Amano K, Nisijima M. Significance of fetal fibronectin and cytokine measurement in the cervicovaginal secretions of women at term in predicting term labor and post-term pregnancy. *Eur J Obstet Gynecol Reprod Biol* 2001;97:53–8.

58. Maul H, Nagel S, Welsch G, Schafer A, Winkler M, Rath W. Messenger ribonucleic acid levels of interleukin-1 beta, interleukin-6 and interleukin-8 in the lower uterine segment increased significantly at final cervical dilatation during term parturition, while those of tumor necrosis factor alpha remained unchanged. *Eur J Obstet Gynecol Reprod Biol* 2002;102:143–7.

59. Sugano T, Nasu K, Narahara H, Kawano Y, Nishida Y, Miyakawa I. Platelet-activating factor induces an imbalance between matrix metalloproteinase-1 and tissue inhibitor of metalloproteinases-1 expression in human uterine cervical fibroblasts. *Biol Reprod* 2000;62:540–6.

60. Chao W, Olson MS. Platelet-activating factor: receptors and signal transduction. *Biochem J* 1993;292(Pt 3):617–29.

61. Yoshida M, Sagawa N, Itoh H, Yura S, Korita D, Kakui K, *et al.* Nitric oxide increases matrix metalloproteinase-1 production in human uterine cervical fibroblast cells. *Mol Hum Reprod* 2001;7:979–85.

62. Tschugguel W, Schneeberger C, Lass H, Stonek F, Zaghlula M, Czerwenka K, *et al.* Human cervical ripening is associated with an increase in cervical inducible nitric oxide synthase expression. *Biol Reprod* 1999;60:1367–72.

63. Ledingham M, Thomson A, Macara L, Young A, Greer I, Norman J. Changes in the expression of nitric oxide synthase in the human uterine cervix during pregnancy and parturition. *Mol Hum Reprod* 2000;6:1041–8.

64. Bao S, Rai J, Schreiber J. Brain nitric oxide synthase expression is enhanced in the human cervix in labor. *J Soc Gynecol Investig* 2001;8:158–64.

65. Vaisanen-Tommiska M, Nuutila M, Aittomaki K, Hiilesmaa V, Ylikorkala O. Nitric oxide metabolites in cervical fluid during pregnancy: further evidence for the role of cervical nitric oxide in cervical ripening. *Am J Obstet Gynecol* 2003;188:779–85.

66. Ellwood DA, Mitchell MD, Anderson AB, Turnbull AC. The *in vitro* production of prostanoids by the human cervix during pregnancy: preliminary observations. *Br J Obstet Gynaecol* 1980;87:210–4.

67. Palejwala S, Stein DE, Weiss G, Monia BP, Tortoriello D, Goldsmith LT. Relaxin positively regulates matrix metalloproteinase expression in human lower uterine segment fibroblasts using a tyrosine kinase signaling pathway. *Endocrinology* 2001;142:3405–13.

68. Denison FC, Riley SC, Elliott CL, Kelly RW, Calder AA, Critchley HO. The effect of mifepristone administration on leukocyte populations, matrix metalloproteinases and inflammatory mediators in the first trimester cervix. *Mol Hum Reprod* 2000;6:541–8.

69. Yoshida K, Tahara R, Nakayama T, Yanaihara T. Effect of dehydroepiandrosterone sulphate, oestrogens and prostaglandins on collagen metabolism in human cervical tissue in relation to cervical ripening. *J Int Med Res* 1993;21:26–35.

70. Hwang JJ, Macinga D, Rorke E. Relaxin modulates human cervical stromal cell activity. *J Clin Endocrinol Metab* 1996;81:3379–84.

71. Imada K, Ito A, Sato T, Namiki M, Nagase H, Mori Y. Hormonal regulation of matrix metalloproteinase 9/gelatinase B gene expression in rabbit uterine cervical fibroblasts. *Biol Reprod* 1997;56:575–80.

72. Imada K, Ito A, Itoh Y, Nagase H, Mori Y. Progesterone increases the production of tissue inhibitor of metalloproteinases-2 in rabbit uterine cervical fibroblasts. *FEBS Lett* 1994;341:109–12.

73. Imada K, Sato T, Hashizume K, Tanimoto A, Sasaguri Y, Ito A. An antiprogesterone, onapristone, enhances the gene expression of promatrix metalloproteinase 3/prostromelysin-1 in the uterine cervix of pregnant rabbit. *Biol Pharm Bull* 2002;25:1223–7.

74. Mesiano S, Chan EC, Fitter JT, Kwek K, Yeo G, Smith R. Progesterone withdrawal and estrogen activation in human parturition are coordinated by progesterone receptor A expression in the myometrium. *J Clin Endocrinol Metab* 2002;87:2924–30.

75. Wang H, Stjernholm Y, Ekman G, Eriksson H, Sahlin L. Different regulation of oestrogen receptors alpha and beta in the human cervix at term pregnancy. *Mol Hum Reprod* 2001;7:293–300.

76. Weihua Z, Saji S, Makinen S, Cheng G, Jensen EV, Warner M, *et al.* Estrogen receptor (ER) beta, a modulator of ERalpha in the uterus. *Proc Natl Acad Sci U S A* 2000;97:5936–41.

77. Lenhart JA, Ryan PL, Ohleth KM, Palmer SS, Bagnell CA. Relaxin increases secretion of tissue inhibitor of matrix metalloproteinase-1 and -2 during uterine and cervical growth and remodeling in the pig. *Endocrinology* 2002;143:91–8.

78. Mushayandebvu TI, Rajabi MR. Relaxin stimulates interstitial collagenase activity in cultured uterine cervical cells from nonpregnant and pregnant but not immature guinea pigs; estradiol-17 beta restores relaxin's effect in immature cervical cells. *Biol Reprod* 1995;53:1030–7.

79. Luque EH, Munoz de Toro MM, Ramos JG, Rodriguez HA, Sherwood OD. Role of relaxin and estrogen in the control of eosinophilic invasion and collagen remodeling in rat cervical tissue at term. *Biol Reprod* 1998;59:795–800.

80. Petersen LK, Vogel I, Agger AO, Westergard J, Nils M, Uldbjerg N. Variations in serum relaxin (hRLX-2) concentrations during human pregnancy. *Acta Obstet Gynecol Scand* 1995;74:251–6.

81. Iams JD, Goldsmith LT, Weiss G. The preterm prediction study: maternal serum relaxin, sonographic cervical length, and spontaneous preterm birth in twins. *J Soc Gynecol Investig* 2001;8:39–42.

82. Vogel I, Salvig JD, Secher NJ, Uldbjerg N. Association between raised serum relaxin levels during the eighteenth gestational week and very preterm delivery. *Am J Obstet Gynecol* 2001;184:390–3.

83. Petersen LK, Skajaa K, Uldbjerg N. Serum relaxin as a potential marker for preterm labour. *Br J Obstet Gynaecol* 1992;99:292–5.

84. Hillier K, Coad N. Synthesis of prostaglandins by the human uterine cervix *in vitro* during passive mechanical stretch. *J Pharm Pharmacol* 1982;34:262–3.

85. Schmitz T, Leroy MJ, Dallot E, Breuiller-Fouche M, Ferre F, Cabrol D. Interleukin-1beta induces glycosaminoglycan synthesis via the prostaglandin E(2) pathway in cultured human cervical fibroblasts. *Mol Hum Reprod* 2003;9:1–8.

86. Carbonne B, Jannet D, Dallot E, Pannier E, Ferre F, Cabrol D. Synthesis of glycosaminoglycans by human cervical fibroblasts in culture: effects of prostaglandin E2 and cyclic AMP. *Eur J Obstet Gynecol Reprod Biol* 1996;70:101–5.

87. Carbonne B, Dallot E, Haddad B, Ferre F, Cabrol D. Effects of progesterone on prostaglandin E(2)-induced changes in glycosaminoglycan synthesis by human cervical fibroblasts in culture. *Mol Hum Reprod* 2000;6:661–4.

88. Vasilenko P, Mead JP. Growth-promoting effects of relaxin and related compositional changes in the uterus, cervix, and vagina of the rat. *Endocrinology* 1987;120:1370–6.

89.   Ledingham M, Thomson A, Jordan F, Young A, Crawford M, Norman J. Cell adhesion molecule expression in cervix and myometrium during pregnancy and parturition. *Obstet Gynecol* 2001;97:235–42.

90.   Leppert P, Yu S. Apoptosis in the cervix of pregnant rats in assocation with cervical softening. *Gynecol Obstet Invest* 1994;37:150–4.

91.   Leppert P. Proliferation and apoptosis of fibroblasts and smooth muscle cell in rat uterine cervix throughout gestation and the effect of the antiprogesterone onapristone. *Am J Obstet Gynecol* 1998;178:713–25.

92.   Allaire AD, D'Andrea N, Truong P, McMahon MJ, Lessey BA. Cervical stroma apoptosis in pregnancy. *Obstet Gynecol* 2001;97:399–403.

93.   Thomson A, Norman J, Greer I, The cervix. In: Elder MG, Romero R, Lamont RF, editors. *Preterm Labor*. Edinburgh: Churchill Livingstone; 1997. p. 445–55.

94.   Radestad A, Christensen N, Stromberg L. Induced cervical ripening with mifepristone in first trimester abortion. A double-blind, randomised, biomechanical and biochemical study. *Contraception* 1988;38:301–12.

95.   Thomson A, Lunan C, Cameron A, Cameron I, Greer I, Norman J. Nitric oxide donors induce ripening of the human uterine cervix: a randomised controlled trial. *Br J Obstet Gynaecol* 1997;104:1054–7.

96.   Kelly A, Kavanagh J, Thomas J. Vaginal prostaglandin (PGE2 and PGF2a) for induction of labour at term. *Cochrane Database Syst Rev* 2003;(4):CD003101.

97.   Gordon AJ, Calder AA. Oestradiol applied locally to ripen the unfavourable cervix. *Lancet* 1977;ii:1319–21.

98.   Thomas J, Kelly AJ, Kavanagh J. Oestrogens alone or with amniotomy for cervical ripening or induction of labour. *Cochrane Database Syst Rev* 2001;(4):CD003393.

99.   Mochizuki M, Maruo T. Effect of dehydroepiandrosterone sulfate on uterine cervical ripening in late pregnancy. *Acta Physiol Hung* 1985;65:267–74.

100.   Radestad A, Thyberg J, Christensen N. Cervical ripening with mifepristone (RU486) in first trimester abortion. An electron microscope study. *Hum Reprod* 1993;8:1136–42.

101.   El-Maradny E, Kanayama N, Kobayashi H, Hossain B, Khatun S, Liping S, *et al.* The role of hyaluronic acid as a mediator and regulator of cervical ripening. *Hum Reprod* 1997;12:1080–8.

102.   Belayet HM, Kanayama N, Khatun S, Sumimoto K, Kobayashi T, Terao T. Binding of interleukin-8 to heparan sulphate enhances cervical maturation in rabbits. *Mol Hum Reprod* 1999;5:261–9.

103.   Shi L, Shi SQ, Saade GR, Chwalisz K, Garfield RE. Studies of cervical ripening in pregnant rats: effects of various treatments. *Mol Hum Reprod* 2000;6:382–9.

Chapter 8

Inflammatory mediators in the cervix

Andrew A Calder and Fiona C Denison

Introduction

In the preceding chapter, Jane Norman and her colleagues have provided a clear and authoritative account of the current state of knowledge of the physiology of the cervix, especially in relation to pregnancy and parturition. They have described the roles and interactions of the complex array of structural elements, cellular components, enzymes, hormones and other mediators that are involved in inflammation. In recent years, inflammatory mediators have commanded increasing attention from investigators interested in the control of human labour and it is therefore justified to concentrate specifically on such substances and how they might contribute to the birth process in its normal and complicated manifestations.

Fifty years ago the cervix was largely neglected as an object of special study in the context of human parturition. It was perhaps regarded rather as the Cinderella of the genital tract, the passive handmaiden of her ugly sister the uterine corpus, simply waiting to yield to the latter's muscular demands during labour. However, as the story has unfolded she has metamorphosed into a princess with a prominent and active role and a staff of servants in the form of biological participants among whom inflammatory mediators are increasingly favoured.

There was not even a clear consensus concerning the structural composition of the cervix and several eminent anatomists and clinicians[1,2] were reluctant to accept Danforth's observation[3] that the uterine cervix was principally a connective tissue structure rather than one composed mostly of smooth muscle and that its understanding would have to be pursued in that context. The past five decades have witnessed a steady process of cervical enlightenment as a result of extensive human and animal research that has carried investigators into the realms of collagen biology and ground substance biochemistry. The same period has witnessed a similar illumination of some of the dark corners of myometrial physiology and even more intriguingly has shed light on those triggering and controlling mechanisms that determine the onset and progression of human labour.

Three or four decades ago it seemed sufficient (at least for clinicians) to accept that labour began when oxytocin – known to derive from the mother's posterior pituitary gland – stimulated the generation of contractions in the myometrium which in turn brought about cervical dilatation and expulsion of the offspring. Such a simplistic notion was partially excusable because oxytocin (in its synthetic form of Syntocinon® or Pitocin®) was widely and effectively employed to induce or augment myometrial contractions that appeared more or less identical to those of spontaneous labour.[4] From those blissfully simple far-off days, the cast list of biological players that participate in that grand performance that is human parturition has steadily expanded. They have been recruited from a wide variety of sectors in physiology and biochemistry as the emphasis has shifted from an attempt to see the control of labour as a purely endocrine phenomenon to one that embraces a much wider range of biological processes and substances. Amidst this, probably the most significant shift in thinking has embraced an entirely new category of players that can best be described as 'inflammatory mediators'. Such substances that might impact on human labour are:

- prostaglandins
- nitric oxide
- interleukins
- colony stimulating factors
- interferons
- growth factors
- cytokines
- pro- and anti-inflammatory chemokines (especially interleukin-8)
- monocyte chemotactic peptide-1
- natural antimicrobials (including defensins and cathelicidins).

It is now widely acknowledged that 'inflammatory' mechanisms play a prominent role in a number of facets of parturition, including cervical function. Indeed, Liggins[5] went so far to suggest that cervical ripening, the essential prerequisite of successful cervical dilatation in labour, might usefully be described as an 'inflammatory process'. Against this background it has become popular to label a wide variety of reproductive processes as inflammatory in their nature. These include ovulation, luteal regression, menstruation, fetal membrane rupture and even myometrial contractility.

The nature of inflammation

Inflammation can be seen as a response to a number of stimuli including infection, tissue injury, immunological stimulation and foreign or altered host antigen. The response may be local when it is characterised by vasodilatation, increased vascular permeability and directional accumulation and extravasation of effector cells such as neutrophils, monocytes, B cells and T cells or as a systemic response characterised by pyrexia and release of acute-phase proteins. Celsus[6] defined the cardinal signs of what might be regarded as 'classical inflammation' as *rubor et tumor cum calor et dolor* (redness and swelling with heat and pain) and to these four Galen[7] added a fifth, namely *functio laesa* (loss of function). A moment of reflection will serve to emphasise that if indeed those reproductive processes can be considered inflammatory in nature, then they do not all demonstrate all five features of classical inflammation although clearly most show some of them. For instance, menstruation is preceded by some degree of tissue swelling and is often characterised by pain, and ovulation has long been recognised as being associated with a systemic rise in temperature. On the other hand while myometrial contractions are clearly painful, there is nothing to suggest that pain is a feature of cervical ripening. As regards Galen's fifth classical feature of inflammation, if those reproductive processes listed above do exploit inflammatory mechanisms they do so in order to achieve a gain rather than a loss of function. Indeed, as Liggins himself observed, 'The rapid remodelling of tissue is not peculiar to pathological processes but may be observed in a variety of strictly physiological situations such as shedding of epidermal structures (deciduous teeth, antlers, feathers, or skin), uterine involution, and, of course, cervical ripening.'

An inflammatory reaction is dependent on the presence of inflammatory cells. The process of leucocyte chemotaxis requires five separate steps, beginning with the activity of cell adhesion molecules (selectins) that cause the leucocytes to adhere to the endothelial lining of the blood vessels.[8] They then appear to roll along the surface before being arrested by integrins.[9] This is followed by extravasation into the extravascular tissue under the influence of chemokines and, finally, migration within the tissue to their preferred site of action.[10]

If Liggins's 'inflammatory hypothesis of cervical ripening' is correct then there should be evidence of chemotaxis of inflammatory cells prior to and during cervical ripening. There should be a plausible mechanism by which such cells could infiltrate the cervix and, finally, once in the cervical stroma they should be capable of contributing to cervical ripening. In this chapter we will address each of these points in turn, citing studies in human subjects and in animal models where appropriate.

The role of inflammatory cells

The process of cervical ripening begins long before the onset of labour. The mucous seal surrounding the cervical plug opens about a month before the onset of labour, thus exposing the cervix to the microbial environment and vaginal secretions.[11] Studies conducted on vaginal washings have demonstrated that the number of viable polymorphonuclear leucocytes and the concentration of interleukin-8 (IL-8) increase significantly towards the end of pregnancy.[12]

Junqueira et al.[13] were the first to demonstrate that a massive immigration of resident neutrophils and macrophages occurred in the cervical stroma at term. These were located predominantly near capillaries and small veins within the cervical stroma. Further morphological analysis demonstrated that the leucocytes contained collagenases and elastase and on degranulation created a 'halo of fluorescence' around collagen fibres. It has since been demonstrated that the number of activated polymorphonuclear cells increases as pregnancy progresses[14] with a further increase during labour[15] and with cervical dilatation.[16]

Similar findings have been observed in the guinea pig[17-19] and rabbit[20,21] with cervical ripening being accompanied by significant leucocytic invasion of the cervical stroma.

Macrophages are also present in the human cervix and the number of resident macrophages increases ten-fold between the first and third trimester of pregnancy.[22] These macrophages appear to be activated, as evidenced by increased concentrations of intercellular adhesion molecule-1 (ICAM-1), the macrophage activation marker, in the cervices of women in labour.[23] Moreover, concentrations of cytokines such as IL-1, IL-6 and IL-8, which are released by macrophages, increase in cervical stroma and mucus, coinciding with cervical dilatation and leucocytic infiltration of the cervix.[24-26]

These findings are supported by studies in the mouse[27] on cervical macrophages, which have demonstrated that four days before birth (day 15), numbers are no different to the nonpregnant state. However, on the day before birth (day 18) macrophage numbers increase by a factor of three compared with the nonpregnant state before falling on the first day postpartum.

Eosinophils, granulocytes demonstrating degranulation, have also been found in human cervices after spontaneous vaginal delivery, whereas very few were seen in the biopsies from nonpregnant or early pregnant women or those having a planned caesarean section.[28] However, unlike in the rat,[29] eosinophils are probably not the principal inflammatory cells involved in cervical ripening in women because their numbers are small in comparison to the numbers of neutrophils in ripening cervices.

Mechanism of inflammatory cell infiltration

There are a number of potential mechanisms whereby inflammatory cells may infiltrate the cervix at term.

The activated macrophages, resident in the cervix, may participate in recruitment of leucocytes by release of proinflammatory and immunomodulatory cytokines such as IL-1, IL-6, IL-8 and platelet activating factor (PAF). The levels of these macrophage-related cytokines increase at term and this correlates with cervical dilatation and cellular infiltration. IL-8,[30] otherwise known as neutrophil chemoattractant, could synergise with prostaglandin E_2 (PGE$_2$)[31] and possibly nitric oxide (NO),[32] both potent vasodilators, to effect cellular extravasation from the capillaries into the cervical stroma.

During pregnancy, the chorion has high levels of the enzyme prostaglandin dehydrogenase (PGDH) which degrades PGE$_2$ produced by the amnion. At parturition, the activity of this enzyme falls dramatically, particularly in the area of the fetal membrane overlying the internal cervical os.[33] This rich source of PGE$_2$ may therefore cross to the internal os and participate in cellular recruitment to effect tissue remodelling and cervical dilatation. PGE$_2$ may in addition further stimulate IL-8 release from endothelial cells and upregulate adhesion molecules,[34] thereby augmenting the inflammatory cascade.

The activity of nitric oxide and its synthetic enzymes, specifically the inducible form, also increases at term within the cervical stroma.[35,36] In addition to synergising with IL-8,[37] nitric oxide stimulates the release of PGE$_2$.[38]

Finally, there is evidence suggesting that the innervation of the cervix may have a role in cervical ripening. Unlike the uterine corpus, the cervix is richly innervated. Cervical biopsies at term and postpartum have demonstrated that there is increased peri-arterial nerve fibre density and arborisation.[39] The sensory afferents could release neuropeptides that potentially might have a role in leucocyte chemoattraction and cellular trafficking. Indirect evidence to support this hypothesis is found in rats where transection of the sensory afferent supply to the cervix disrupts parturition by interfering with cervical remodelling.[40]

Role of inflammatory cells

Given that leucocytes are present in the ripening cervix, what role could they play in this process? As has been detailed in the preceding chapter, the cervix is mainly composed of connective tissue,[41] with the collagen being predominantly type I (70%) and type III (30%). In order for the cervix to change from a rigid unyielding barrier to delivery into a compliant one that can be fully dilated across a few hours of labour, the stroma of the cervix must undergo radical remodelling. This is principally effected by collagenolysis, mediated by the metalloproteinases. Matrix metalloproteinases 1, 8 and 13 degrade intact collagen,[42,43] whereas MMP-2 and MMP-9 break down proteoglycans, denatured collagen and basement membrane (type IV collagen).[44,45]

Neutrophils predominantly produce MMP-8 and MMP-9. MMP-8 (human neutrophil collagenase) degrades type I collagen whereas MMP-9 breaks down gelatinases and basement membrane (type IV collagen).[46,47] The activity of MMP-8 and MMP-9 increases in the cervix during ripening and this correlates with cervical dilatation and neutrophil counts.[16,48,49] MMP-1 is released by cervical stromal fibroblasts.[50] Although its release is stimulated by mechanical stretch, prostaglandin F$_2\alpha$ (PGF$_2\alpha$) and IL-1,[51] studies have not demonstrated that its activity rises significantly with cervical dilatation. MMP-13, which also degrades collagen, has not been studied in women, although its message has been found in the rat cervix.[52]

It is therefore proposed that MMP-8 released by neutrophils could be responsible for collagen degradation during cervical ripening and that MMP-9, by breaking down the basement membrane, could facilitate leucocyte egress from the capillaries into the cervical stroma.

In contemplating these concepts it may be helpful to examine closely Figures 8.1 and 8.2. These are photographs of human anatomical dissections made more than 200 years ago by the great anatomist and obstetrician William Hunter. They were very probably prepared for his monumental work of 1774, *The Anatomy of the Human Gravid Uterus.*[53]

Figure 8.1 shows a sagittal section bisecting the lower part of the uterus, the cervix, the vagina, the bladder and the urethra in the midline in a woman who died 'in the ninth month of pregnancy'. Hunter described it as 'a side view of the cervix uteri in its short state, also of the vagina and bladder' implying that he considered that the cervix was already partially effaced.

Figure 8.2 shows 'the cervix and os uteri in the last month of pregnancy' viewed, as it were, from inside the uterine cavity. This beautifully illustrates the extent to which the process of effacement of the cervix has progressed. The landmark described by Danforth[54] as the fibromuscular junction has migrated from the internal cervical os towards the periphery of the specimen.

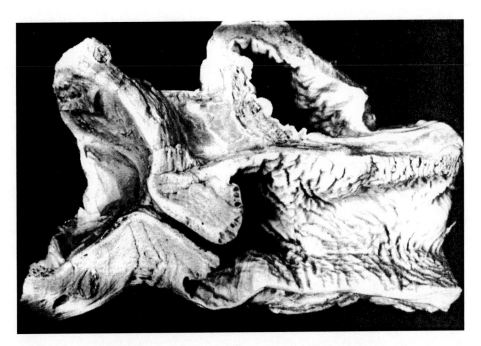

Figure 8.1. A photograph of one of William Hunter's anatomical dissections. This shows 'the cervix uteri in the ninth month of pregnancy'. Hunter described it as 'a side view of the cervix uteri in its short state, also of the vagina and bladder' (from the Hunterian Anatomical Museum in the Anatomy Department of the University of Glasgow by kind permission of Professor RJ Scothorne)

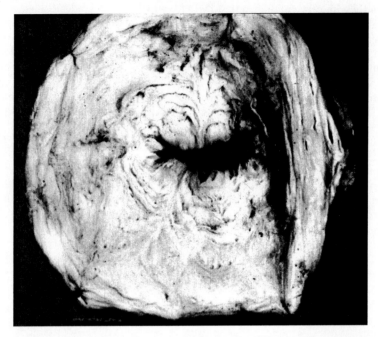

Figure 8.2. A photograph of another of Hunter's dissections, 'the cervix and os uteri in the last month of pregnancy'. The mucosal pattern of the cervix, forming the *plicae palmatae* (literally palm-like folds) is clearly seen and shows the progress of effacement or 'taking up' of the cervix in late pregnancy, this mucosa having hitherto occupied the endocervical canal. The fibromuscular junction described in the text will by this stage have demonstrated a centrifugal migration towards the periphery of the specimen (from the Hunterian Anatomical Museum in the Anatomy Department of the University of Glasgow by kind permission of Professor RJ Scothorne)

Hypothesis for cervical ripening

It would seem logical that the process of cervical effacement, an essential prerequisite for cervical ripening and dilatation, should depend on remodelling of the cervical tissue that lies at the internal os. From a clinical perspective, it is worth observing that in pregnancies in which the fetal membranes are ruptured when the cervix is not properly effaced, labour is often dysfunctional and ineffective. Wherever else inflammatory mediators exert their influence, they must do so at this critical anatomical focus.

The following 'inflammatory' mechanism for cervical ripening is therefore proposed. A reduction in PGDH in the chorion overlying the internal os permits high levels of PGE$_2$, synthesised by the amnion, to permeate the internal os. The combination of high levels of PGE$_2$ and NO may then facilitate capillary vasodilatation in the cervical stroma. Activated resident macrophages, in conjunction with circulating leucocytes, could release proinflammatory chemotactic cytokines. Synergy between cytokines and vasodilators and upregulation of adhesion molecules may then promote directional chemotaxis and emigration of leucocytes from the capillaries into the cervical stroma. Finally, degranulation of leucocytes releases MMPs which degrade collagen, activate fibroblasts to release inflammatory mediators and break down the capillary basement membrane, facilitating further leucocyte emigration. Thus, a positive proinflammatory feedback may be initiated, with the end result being collagenolysis, cervical effacement and dilatation.

Conclusions

It seems probable that inflammatory processes play a key role in the control of cervical function in both normal and dysfunctional labour, especially preterm labour. Although long recognised as a feature of some cases of premature labour or premature rupture of the fetal membranes, it has been increasingly accepted that infection at a subclinical level may play a role in many more cases of premature delivery than has hitherto been recognised.[55] Infection may not only provoke myometrial contractions but it may also have a role in bringing about cervical ripening at an earlier stage of pregnancy than is appropriate. In doing so it may facilitate ingress of pathological organisms into the chorio-decidual space whereby a cascade of cytokine and chemokine production makes premature delivery inevitable. In this context, a future profitable line of investigation is likely to focus on the importance of innate defences in pregnancy that are provided by natural antimicrobial proteins such as α- and β-defensins and cathelicidins.[56] The journey to find the holy grail of human parturition and its perturbations is set to take several more fascinating turns.

References

1.   Danforth, DN. The distribution and functional activity of the cervical musculature. *Am J Obstet Gynecol* 1954;68:1261–71.
2.   Hughesden PC. The fibromuscular nature of the cervix and its changes during pregnancy and labour. *J Obstet Gynaecol Br Emp* 1952;59:763–76.
3.   Danforth DN. The fibrous nature of the uterine cervix. *Am J Obstet Gynecol* 1947;53:541–60.
4.   Turnbull AC, Anderson AB. Uterine contractility and oxytocin sensitivity during human pregnancy in relation to the onset of labour. *J Obstet Gynaecol Br Cwlth* 1968;75:278–88.
5.   Liggins GC. Cervical ripening as an inflammatory reaction. In: Ellwood DA and Anderson ABM, editors. *The Cervix in Pregnancy and Labour, Clinical and Biochemical Investigations.* Edinburgh: Churchill Livingstone; 1983. p. 1–9.
6.   Lyons AS and Petracelli R, editors. *Medicine: An Illustrated History.* New York: Abradale Press; 1987. p. 248.
7.   Lyons AS and Petracelli R, editors. *Medicine: An Illustrated History.* New York: Abradale Press; 1987. p. 259.
8.   McIntyre TM, Prescott SM, Weyrich AS, Zimmerman GA. Cell–cell interactions: leukocyte–endothelial interactions. *Curr Opin Hematol* 2003;10:150–8.
9.   Alon R, Grabovsky V, Feigelson S. Chemokine induction of integrin adhesiveness on rolling and arrested leukocytes local signaling events or global stepwise activation? *Microcirculation* 2003;10:297–311.
10.   Liu L, Kubes P. Molecular mechanisms of leukocyte recruitment: organ-specific mechanisms of action. *Thromb Haemost* 2003;89:213–20.
11.   Hendricks CH, Brenner WE, Kraus G. Normal cervical dilatation pattern in late pregnancy and labor. *Am J Obstet Gynecol* 1970;106:1065–82.
12.   Yamada T, Minakami H, Matsubara S, Kohmura Y, Aoya T, Sato I. Changes in the number of polymorphonuclear leukocytes and concentrations of IL-8 and granulocyte elastase in the vaginas of normal pregnant women. *Am J Reprod Immunol* 2002;47:98–103.
13.   Junqueira LC, Zugaib M, Montes GS, Toledo OM, Krisztan RM, Shigihara KM. Morphologic and histochemical evidence for the occurrence of collagenolysis and for the role of neutrophilic polymorphonuclear leukocytes during cervical dilation. *Am J Obstet Gynecol* 1980;138:273–81.
14.   Okamura K, Yonemoto Y, Hamazaki Y, Higashiiwai H, Yajima A. Nitroblue tetrazolium reduction by leukocytes in the cervix of pregnant women. *Am J Obstet Gynecol* 1988;159:417–20.

15.   Thomson AJ, Telfer JF, Young A, Campbell S, Stewart CJ, Cameron IT, *et al*. Leukocytes infiltrate the myometrium during human parturition: further evidence that labour is an inflammatory process. *Hum Reprod* 1999;14:229–36.

16.   Winkler M, Oberpichler A, Tschesche H, Ruck P, Fischer DC, Rath W. Collagenolysis in the lower uterine segment during parturition at term: correlations with stage of cervical dilatation and duration of labor. *Am J Obstet Gynecol* 1999;181:153–8.

17.   Chwalisz K, Benson M, Scholz P, Daum J, Beier HM, Hegele-Hartung C. Cervical ripening with the cytokines interleukin 8, interleukin 1 beta and tumour necrosis factor alpha in guinea-pigs. *Hum Reprod* 1994;9:2173–81.

18.   Chwalisz K, Shao-Qing S, Garfield RE, Beier HM. Cervical ripening in guinea-pigs after a local application of nitric oxide. *Hum Reprod* 1997;12:2093–101.

19.   Hegele-Hartung C, Chwalisz K, Beier HM, Elger W. Ripening of the uterine cervix of the guinea-pig after treatment with the progesterone antagonist onapristone (ZK 98.299): an electron microscopic study. *Hum Reprod* 1989;4:369–77.

20.   El Maradny E, Kanayama N, Halim A, Maehara K, Sumimoto K, Terao T. Biochemical changes in the cervical tissue of rabbit induced by interleukin-8, interleukin-1beta, dehydroepiandrosterone sulphate and prostaglandin E2: a comparative study. *Hum Reprod* 1996;11:1099–104.

21.   El Maradny E, Kanayama N, Halim A, Maehara K, Sumimoto K, Terao T. The effect of interleukin-1 in rabbit cervical ripening. *Eur J Obstet Gynecol* 1995;60:75–80.

22.   Bokstrom H, Brannstrom M, Alexandersson M, Norstrom A. Leukocyte subpopulations in the human uterine cervical stroma at early and term pregnancy. *Hum Reprod* 1997;12:586–90.

23.   Ledingham MA, Thomson AJ, Jordan F, Young A, Crawford M, Norman JE. Cell adhesion molecule expression in the cervix and myometrium during pregnancy and parturition. *Obstet Gynecol* 2001;97:235–42.

24.   Barclay CG, Brennand JE, Kelly RW, Calder AA. Interleukin-8 production by the human cervix. *Am J Obstet Gynecol* 1993;169:625–32.

25.   Winkler M, Ruck P, Horny HP, Wehrmann M, Kemp B, Kaiserling E, *et al*. Expression of cell adhesion molecules by endothelium in the human lower uterine segment during parturition at term. *Am J Obstet Gynecol* 1998;178:557–61.

26.   Maul H, Nagel S, Welsch G, Schafer A, Winkler M, Rath W. Messenger ribonucleic acid levels of interleukin-1 beta, interleukin-6 and interleukin-8 in the lower uterine segment increased significantly at final cervical dilatation during term parturition, while those of tumor necrosis factor alpha remained unchanged. *Eur J Obstet Gynecol Reprod Biol* 2002;102:143–7.

27.   Mackler AM, Iezza G, Akin MR, McMillan P, Yellon SM. Macrophage trafficking in the uterus and cervix precedes parturition in the mouse. *Biol Reprod* 1999;61:879–83.

28.   Knudsen UB, Uldbjerg N, Rechberger T, Fredens K. Eosinophils in human cervical ripening. *Eur J Obstet Gynecol Reprod Biol* 1997;72:165–8.

29.   Luque EH, Munoz de Toro MM, Ramos JG, Rodriguez HA, Sherwood OD. Role of relaxin and estrogen in the control of eosinophilic invasion and collagen remodeling in rat cervical tissue at term. *Biol Reprod* 1998;59:795–800.

30.   Carveth HJ, Bohnsack JF, McIntyre TM, Baggiolini M, Prescott SM, Zimmerman GA. Neutrophil activating factor (NAF) induces polymorphonuclear leukocyte adherence to endothelial cells and to subendothelial matrix proteins. *Biochem Biophys Res Commun* 1989;162:387–93.

31.   Kelly RW. Inflammatory mediators and cervical ripening. *J Reprod Immunol* 2002;57:217–24.

32.   Thomson AJ, Lunan CB, Cameron AD, Cameron IT, Greer IA, Norman JE. Nitric oxide donors induce ripening of the human uterine cervix: a randomised controlled trial. *Br J Obstet Gynaecol* 1997;104:1054–7.

33.   Van Meir CA, Ramirez MM, Matthews SG, Calder AA, Keirse MJ, Challis JR. Chorionic prostaglandin catabolism is decreased in the lower uterine segment with term labour. *Placenta* 1997;18:109–14.

34.   Winkler M, Kemp B, Hauptmann S, Rath W. Parturition: steroids, prostaglandin E2, and expression of adhesion molecules by endothelial cells. *Obstet Gynecol* 1997;89:398–402.

35.   Ledingham MA, Thomson AJ, Young A, Macara LM, Greer IA, Norman JE. Changes in the expression of nitric oxide synthase in the human uterine cervix during pregnancy and parturition. *Mol Hum Reprod* 2000;6:1041–8.

36.   Vaisanen-Tommiska M, Nuutila M, Aittomaki K, Hiilesmaa V, Ylikorkala O. Nitric oxide metabolites in cervical fluid during pregnancy: further evidence for the role of cervical nitric oxide in cervical ripening. *Am J Obstet Gynecol* 2003;188:779–85.

37.   Denison FC, Calder AA, Kelly RW. The action of prostaglandin E2 on the human cervix: stimulation of interleukin 8 and inhibition of secretory leukocyte protease inhibitor. *Am J Obstet Gynecol* 1999;180:614–20.

38.   Meijer F, Tak C, van Haeringen NJ, Kijlstra A. Interaction between nitric oxide and prostaglandin synthesis in the acute phase of allergic conjunctivitis. *Prostaglandins* 1996;52:431–46.

39. Stjernholm Y, Sennstrom M, Granstrom L, Ekman G, Johansson O. Protein gene product 9.5-immunoreactive nerve fibers and cells in human cervix of late pregnant, postpartal and non-pregnant women. *Acta Obstet Gynecol Scand* 1999;78:299–304.

40. Renegar RH, Steel M, Burden HW, Hodson CA. Endocrine parameters associated with disruption of parturition after bilateral pelvic neurectomy. *Proc Soc Exp Biol Med* 1992;201:28–33.

41. Minamoto T, Arai K, Hirakawa S, Nagai Y. Immunohistochemical studies on collagen types in the uterine cervix in pregnant and nonpregnant states. *Am J Obstet Gynecol* 1987;156:138–44.

42. Seiki M. Membrane-type 1 matrix metalloproteinase: a key enzyme for tumor invasion. *Cancer Lett* 2003;194:1–11.

43. Herman MP, Sukhova GK, Libby P, Gerdes N, Tang N, Horton DB, *et al.* Expression of neutrophil collagenase (matrix metalloproteinase-8) in human atheroma: a novel collagenolytic pathway suggested by transcriptional profiling. *Circulation* 2001;104:1899–904.

44. Roach DM, Fitridge RA, Laws PE, Millard SH, Varelias A, Cowled PA. Up-regulation of MMP-2 and MMP-9 leads to degradation of type IV collagen during skeletal muscle reperfusion injury; protection by the MMP inhibitor, doxycycline. *Eur J Vasc Endovasc Surg* 2002;23:260–9.

45. Morgan M, Kniss D, McDonnell S. Expression of metalloproteinases and their inhibitors in human trophoblast continuous cell lines. *Exp Cell Res* 1998;10:18–26.

46. Van Wart HE. Human neutrophil collagenase. *Matrix Suppl* 1992;1:31–6.

47. Delclaux C, Delacourt C, D'Ortho MP, Boyer V, Lafuma C, Harf A. Role of gelatinase B and elastase in human polymorphonuclear neutrophil migration across basement membrane. *Am J Respir Cell Mol Biol* 1996;14:288–95.

48. Rath W, Winkler M, Kemp B. The importance of extracellular matrix in the induction of preterm delivery. *J Perinat Med* 1998;26:437–41.

49. Sennstrom MB, Brauner A, Bystrom B, Malmstrom A, Ekman G. Matrix metalloproteinase-8 correlates with the cervical ripening process in humans. *Acta Obstet Gynecol Scand* 2003;82:904–11.

50. Yoshida M, Sagawa N, Itoh H, Yura S, Korita D, Kakui K, *et al.* Nitric oxide increases matrix metalloproteinase-1 production in human uterine cervical fibroblast cells. *Mol Hum Reprod* 2001;7:979–85.

51. Yoshida M, Sagawa N, Itoh H, Yura S, Takemura M, Wada Y, *et al.* Prostaglandin F(2alpha), cytokines and cyclic mechanical stretch augment matrix metalloproteinase-1 secretion from cultured human uterine cervical fibroblast cells. *Mol Hum Reprod* 2002;8:681–7.

52. Wolf K, Sandner P, Kurtz A, Moll W. Messenger ribonucleic acid levels of collagenase (MMP-13) and matrilysin (MMP-7) in virgin, pregnant, and postpartum uterus and cervix of rat. *Endocrinology* 1996;137:5429–34.

53. Hunter W. *The Anatomy of the Human Gravid Uterus.* Birmingham: Baskerville; 1774.

54. Danforth DN, Henricks CH. In: Danforth DN, editor. *Obstetrics and Gynecology.* 3rd ed. Maryland: Harper Row; 1977.

55. Romero R, Avila C, Sepulveda W. The role of systemic and intra-uterine infection in preterm labor. In: Fuchs AR, Fuchs F, Stubblefield PG, editors. *Preterm Birth.* New York: McGraw-Hill; 1993. p. 97–136.

56. Ganz T. Defensins: antimicrobial peptides of innate immunity. *Nat Rev Immunol* 2003;3:710–20.

Chapter 9

Sonographic measurement of cervical length and preterm delivery

Kypros H Nicolaides, Elly Tsoi and Meekai S To

Introduction

Routine sonographic measurement of cervical length at mid-gestation in both high-risk and low-risk pregnancies provides a useful method for prediction of the likelihood of subsequent preterm delivery. In women who present with threatened preterm labour measurement of cervical length can help distinguish between true and false labour. This chapter reviews the evidence that supports the clinical introduction of transvaginal sonography in both the prediction and management of preterm labour.

Transvaginal sonographic measurement of cervical length

Technique

In the sonographic measurement of cervical length it is important to avoid the exertion of undue pressure on the cervix and to identify the internal and external os by the presence of the echogenic endocervical mucosa along the length of the canal (Figure 9.1).

The woman is asked to empty her bladder, is placed in the dorsal lithotomy position and the transvaginal probe is placed in the anterior fornix of the vagina. A sagittal view of the cervix is obtained and the calipers are used to measure the distance between the triangular area of echodensity at the external os and the V-shaped notch at the internal os.[1-3] The cervix is often curved and there is an inevitable disparity of measurements between the internal and external os taken as a straight line or along the cervical canal. However, the method of measurement is not clinically important because when the cervix is short it is always straight.[4] Each examination should be performed over a period of about three minutes. In about 1% of cases dynamic cervical changes, due to uterine contractions, are observed. In such cases the shortest measurement is recorded.

Transvaginal measurement of cervical length is highly reproducible and in 95% of occasions the difference between two measurements by the same observer and by two observers is 3.5 mm or less and 4.2 mm or less, respectively.[1]

The best approach for measurement of cervical length is by transvaginal sonography. In transabdominal scanning, the cervix may not be visualised in up to 50% of cases unless the bladder is full, but bladder filling significantly increases the length of the cervix.[5-7] The transperineal route is limited both by the inconsistency in

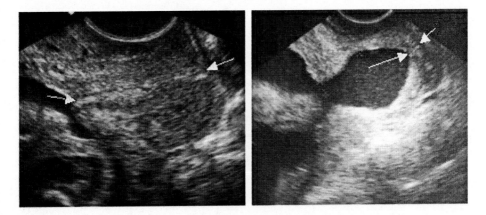

Figure 9.1. Ultrasound scan of a long (left) and short (right) cervix

correlation between transvaginal and transperineal measurements and the inadequate visualisation of the cervix in up to 25% of cases.[8–10]

Acceptability

A survey of 755 women who had agreed to undergo screening for preterm delivery by transvaginal sonographic measurement of cervical length at 22–24 weeks of gestation found that more than 95% of women felt it to be an acceptable and worthwhile procedure.[11] The women rated the scan to be significantly less difficult than undergoing a cervical smear, dental filling or venepuncture. The women who had declined screening were found to be significantly less likely to be worried about preterm delivery and more likely to be multiparous.

Cervical assessment in asymptomatic pregnancies

Singleton pregnancies

Cervical length in high-risk women

High-risk pregnancies include those in women with a previous history of spontaneous mid-trimester miscarriage or preterm birth, cervical surgery, uterine anomaly, or maternal exposure to diethylstilboestrol. Several studies have demonstrated that the risk of preterm delivery is substantially higher in women with cervical length less than 25 mm, at 14–24 weeks of gestation, than in those with a longer cervix (Table 9.1).[12–16] In five such studies in a combined total of 1265 pregnancies, preterm delivery occurred in 14% of cases, and 41% of these women had a short cervix. The incidence of preterm delivery was 29% in the group with a short cervix and 11% in those women with a long cervix.

These studies reported that neither funnelling nor dynamic shortening of the cervix provided significant additional contribution to cervical length in the prediction of preterm delivery.[15,16] In terms of the best time for screening, Guzman *et al.*[15] found that assessment at 21–24 weeks of gestation was better than at 15–20 weeks. Additionally,

Table 9.1. Studies in asymptomatic high-risk pregnancies reporting on the association between sonographically measured cervical length at 14–24 weeks of gestation and the incidence of subsequent preterm delivery

Study	Women (n)	Gestation (weeks)	Short cervix Definition (mm)	Short cervix Incidence (n)	Preterm delivery Definition (weeks)	Preterm delivery Incidence (n) Overall	Preterm delivery Incidence (n) Short cervix	Preterm delivery Incidence (n) Long cervix
Watson et al.[12] (1997)	407	24	≤25	26 (6.4%)	<35	39/407 (9.6%)	9/26 (34.6%)	30/381 (7.9%)
Berghella et al.[13] (1997)	96	14–22	≤25	22 (22.9%)	<35	17/96 (17.7%)	10/22 (45.5%)	7/74 (9.5%)
Andrews et al.[14] (2000)	110	15–24	≤25	15 (13.6%)	<35	18/110 (16.4%)	10/15 (66.7%)	18/95 (19.0%)
Guzman et al.[15] (2001)	469	15–24	≤25	172 (36.7%)	<34	55/469 (11.7%)	34/172 (19.8%)	21/297 (7.1%)
Owen et al.[16] (2001)	183	16–24	<25	12 (6.6%)	<35	48/183 (26.2%)	9/12 (75.0%)	39/171 (22.8%)
Total	1265			247 (19.5%)		177/1265 (14.0%)	72/247 (29.1%)	115/1018 (11.3%)

Table 9.2. Studies in asymptomatic low-risk pregnancies reporting on the association between sonographically measured cervical length at 18–24 weeks of gestation and the incidence of subsequent preterm delivery

Study	Women (n)	Gestation (weeks)	Short cervix Definition (mm)	Short cervix Incidence (n)	Preterm delivery Definition (weeks)	Preterm delivery Incidence (n) Overall	Preterm delivery Incidence (n) Short cervix	Preterm delivery Incidence (n) Long cervix
Iams et al.[17] (1996)	2915	22–24	≤25	264 (9%)	<35	126/2915 (4.3%)	47/264 (17.8%)	79/2651 (3.0%)
Heath et al.[18] (1998)	1252	22–24	≤25	100 (8%)	<35	29/1252 (2.3%)	14/100 (14.0%)	15/1152 (1.3%)
Taipale et al.[19] (1998)	3694	18–22	≤25	13 (0.3%)	<35	31/3694 (0.8%)	2/13 (15.0%)	29/3681 (0.8%)
Total	7861			377 (4.8%)		186/7861 (2.4%)	63/377 (16.7%)	123/7607 (1.6%)

for women with a previous mid-trimester loss 15 mm, rather than 25 mm, was the optimal threshold for the prediction of preterm delivery. Owen *et al.*[16] reported that prediction of preterm delivery was better with serial measurements at 16–23 weeks than a single measurement at 16–18 weeks.

Cervical length in low-risk women

More than half of all spontaneous preterm births occur in low-risk women. Several studies have demonstrated that the risk of preterm delivery is substantially higher in women with cervical length less than 25 mm than in those with a longer cervix (Table 9.2). Thus, in three large screening studies at 18–24 weeks of gestation in a combined total of 7861 pregnancies, preterm delivery before 35 weeks occurred in 2.4% of cases, and 40% of those had a short cervix. The incidence of preterm delivery was 17% in the group with a short cervix and 2% in those with a long cervix.[17–19]

Two screening studies were carried out at 26–30 weeks of gestation with the aim of predicting delivery before 37 weeks (Table 9.3).[20,21] In the combined data on a total of 1413 pregnancies, preterm delivery occurred in 8% of cases, and 11% of those had a short cervix. The incidence of preterm delivery was 17% in the group with a short cervix and 8% in those with a long cervix.

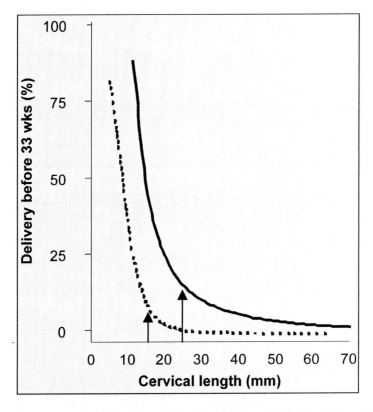

Figure 9.2. Relation between cervical length at 23 weeks of gestation and rate of spontaneous delivery before 33 weeks in singleton (dotted line) and twin or triplet (solid line) pregnancies[18,30,34]

Table 9.3. Studies in asymptomatic low-risk pregnancies reporting on the association between sonographically measured cervical length at 26–30 weeks of gestation and the incidence of subsequent preterm delivery

Study	Women (n)	Gestation (weeks)	Short cervix Definition (mm)	Short cervix Incidence (n)	Definition (weeks)	Preterm delivery Incidence (n) Overall	Preterm delivery Incidence (n) Short cervix	Preterm delivery Incidence (n) Long cervix
Tongsong et al.[30] (1995)	730	28–30	≤25	16 (2.1%)	<37	91/730 (12.5%)	5/16 (31.0%)	86/714 (12.0%)
Arinami et al.[21] (1999)	683	26–28	≤25	60 (8.8%)	<37	28/683 (4.1%)	8/60 (13.3%)	20/623 (3.2%)
Total	1413			76 (5.4%)		119/1413 (8.4%)	13/76 (17.1%)	106/1337 (7.9%)

Table 9.4. Studies in asymptomatic twin pregnancies reporting on the association between sonographically measured cervical length at 18–26 weeks of gestation and the incidence of subsequent preterm delivery

Study	Women (n)	Gestation (weeks)	Short cervix Definition (mm)	Short cervix Incidence (n)	Definition (weeks)	Preterm delivery Incidence (n) Overall	Preterm delivery Incidence (n) Short cervix	Preterm delivery Incidence (n) Long cervix
Goldenburg et al.[26] (1996)	147	24	≤25	21 (14.3%)	<32	13/147 (8.8%)	6/21 (26.9%)	7/126 (5.6%)
Imseis et al.[27] (1997)	85	24–26	≤20	11 (12.9%)	<32	5/85 (5.9%)	2/11 (18.1%)	3/74 (4.1%)
Yang et al.[28] (2000)	65	18–26	≤25	6 (9.2%)	<32	6/65 (9.2%)	3/6 (50.0%)	3/59 (5.1%)
Guzman et al.[29] (2000)	131	21–24	≤20	23 (17.6%)	<32	12/131 (9.2%)	5/23 (21.7%)	7/108 (6.5%)
Skentou et al.[30] (2001)	434	22–24	≤20	37 (8.0%)	<33	36/434 (7.8%)	14/37 (37.8%)	22/397 (5.5%)
Vayssiere et al.[31]	250	22–24	≤20	8 (3.2%)	<32	13/250 (5.2%)	3/8 (37.5%)	10/240 (4.2%)
Total	1112			108 (9.5%)		85/1112 (7.6%)	33/108 (30.6%)	52/1004 (5.2%)

The sensitivity of mid-trimester cervical screening is better at predicting delivery before 33 weeks of gestation rather than 37 weeks. In the study by Heath et al.,[18] the rate of spontaneous preterm delivery at less than 33 weeks was 1.5% and the risk of such delivery increased exponentially with decreasing cervical length from about 0.2% at 60 mm to 1% at 25 mm, 4% at 15 mm and 78% at 5 mm (Figure 9.2). Furthermore, demographic characteristics, previous obstetric history or funnelling of the internal cervical os do not have a significant additional contribution to that of cervical length in the prediction of preterm delivery.[1,22]

In addition to the above prospective studies, a large retrospective study of 6877 pregnancies in which cervical length had been measured at 14–24 weeks of gestation reported that preterm delivery before 33 weeks occurred in 5% of cases. The risk of delivery before 33 weeks was 48% in the subgroup of 0.6% of women with cervical length less than 15 mm and 4% in the 99.4% of women with a longer cervix.[23]

Cervical length and fetal fibronectin

Two screening studies in asymptomatic women with singleton pregnancies have examined the value of short cervix and a positive fetal fibronectin test at 22–24 weeks of gestation in the prediction of spontaneous delivery before 32 and 33 weeks respectively.[24,25]

Goldenberg et al.[24] examined 2915 pregnancies at 24–26 weeks and Heath et al.[25] examined 5146 women at 22–24 weeks. A positive fetal fibronectin test was reported in 6.6%[24] and 3.5%[25] of women respectively and cervical length of 25 mm or less in 9.1%[24] and 8.4%.[25] Heath et al.[25] reported that fetal fibronectin positivity increased exponentially with decreasing cervical length, from 3% to 19% and 57% for respective cervical lengths of 31–40 mm, 11–15 mm and 0–5 mm. Similarly, in Goldenberg et al.,[24] the incidence of a positive fetal fibronectin test was 6% in those women with a cervical length of more than 25 mm and 16% for a cervical length of 25 mm or less.

In these studies, short cervix and a positive fetal fibronectin test provided significant independent contributions for the prediction of preterm delivery with similar odds ratios (12.5 versus 12.2,[24] and 8.7 versus 9.8 in nulliparous women and 10.0 versus 4.6 for multiparous women[25]).

Twin pregnancies

Cervical length in low-risk women

In six studies of cervical assessment at 18–26 weeks of gestation, on a combined total of 1112 twin pregnancies, early preterm delivery occurred in 85 cases (7.6%), and in 33 (30.6%) of these the cervical length was less than 20 mm or less than 25 mm (Table 9.4).[26-31] The incidence of preterm delivery was 31% in those women with a short cervix and 5% in those with a long cervix.

In the largest screening study, involving 434 women, the rate of spontaneous delivery before 33 weeks was inversely related to cervical length at 22–24 weeks (Figure 9.2).[30] The median cervical length in twins was similar to that in singleton pregnancies but a higher proportion of twins had a cervical length of 25 mm or less (13% in twins compared with 8% in singletons) and 15 mm or less (5% in twins compared with 1.5% in singletons).[18,30] This is not surprising because the rate of preterm delivery in twins is much higher than in singletons. Thus, the rate of spontaneous delivery before 33 weeks was about 8% in twins compared with 1.5% in singletons.

Table 9.5. Studies in asymptomatic triplet pregnancies reporting on the association between sonographically measured cervical length at 21–26 weeks of gestation and the incidence of subsequent preterm delivery

Study	Women (n)	Gestation (weeks)	Short cervix Definition (mm)	Short cervix Incidence (n)	Preterm delivery Definition (weeks)	Preterm delivery Incidence (n) Overall	Preterm delivery Incidence (n) Short cervix	Preterm delivery Incidence (n) Long cervix
Guzman et al.[33] (2000)	47	21–24	≤25	14/47 (29.8%)	<32	15/47 (31.9%)	9/14 (64.3%)	6/33 (18.2%)
To et al.[34] (2000)	38	22–24	≤25	6/38 (15.8%)	<33	6/38 (15.8%)	3/6 (50.0%)	3/32 (9.4%)
Maymon et al.[35] (2001)	34	26	≤25	11/34 (32.4%)	<34	17/34 (50.0%)	10/11 (90.9%)	7/23 (30.4%)
Total	119			31/119 (26.1%)		38/119 (31.9%)	22/31 (71.0%)	16/88 (18.2%)

Table 9.6. Studies in pregnancies with threatened preterm labour reporting on the association between sonographically measured cervical length at presentation and the incidence of subsequent preterm delivery

Study	Women (n)	Gestation (weeks)	Short cervix Definition (mm)	Short cervix Incidence (n)	Preterm delivery Definition (weeks)	Preterm delivery Incidence (n) Overall	Preterm delivery Incidence (n) Short cervix	Preterm delivery Incidence (n) Long cervix
Bartolucci et al.[36] (1982)	38	2	26–32	≤30	<37 weeks	14/38 (36.8%)	14/27 (51.9%)	0/11 (0%)
Rizzo et al.[37] (1996)	108	0	24–36	≤20	<37 weeks	47/108 (43.5%)	32/45 (71.1%)	15/63 (23.8%)
Hincz et al.[38] (2002)	82	0	24–34	≤20	<28 days[a]	14/82 (17.1%)	8/13 (61.5%)	6/69 (8.7%)

a delivery within 28 days of presentation

In singleton pregnancies the exponential increase in risk for early preterm delivery is observed in women with a cervical length below 15 mm, whereas in twins this threshold is 25 mm.[18,30]

Cervical length and fetal fibronectin

A study of 101 asymptomatic women with twin pregnancies examined the value of short cervix and fetal fibronectin postivity at 24 weeks of gestation in the prediction of spontaneous delivery before 35 weeks, which occurred in 22% of cases.[32] Fetal fibronectin was present in 15% of the women. The incidence of spontaneous preterm delivery was 54% in the fibronectin-positive group and 16% in those with a negative result. Cervical length was a poor predictor of preterm delivery, and a cervical length of less than 25 mm had no predictive value for preterm birth.

Triplet pregnancies

Prospective studies in triplet pregnancies have shown that in women with a short cervix at 21–26 weeks of gestation the risk of early preterm delivery is increased. In combined data from three studies with a total of 119 women, delivery at less than 32–34 weeks occurred in 32% of cases, and 58% of these women had a cervical length of less than 25 mm (Table 9.5). The incidence of preterm delivery was 71% in the group with a short cervix and 18% in those with a long cervix.[33–35]

In triplet pregnancies the risk of spontaneous preterm delivery before 33 weeks increases exponentially with decreasing cervical length at 22–24 weeks (Figure 9.2).[34] As in the case of twin pregnancies, the threshold for exponential increase in risk is 25 mm.

Cervical assessment in women with threatened preterm labour

Several studies in women with threatened preterm labour have examined the value of sonographic measurement of cervical length in the prediction of preterm delivery.

Cervical length at presentation in the prediction of preterm delivery

Bartolucci et al.[36] performed transabdominal sonography in 38 women with threatened preterm labour at 26–32 weeks of gestation and reported that delivery before 37 weeks occurred in 51.9% of those with a cervical length of less than 30 mm and in none of those with a longer cervix (Table 9.6). In all subsequent studies the cervix was measured transvaginally or transperineally. Rizzo et al.[37] and Hincz et al.[38] examined women with threatened preterm labour at presentation and reported that the incidence of preterm delivery was considerably higher in those with cervical length of less than 20 mm compared with those with a longer cervix (Table 9.6). Timor-Trisch et al.[39] examined 70 women presenting at 20–35 weeks of gestation and reported that in those delivering before 37 weeks the mean cervical length was shorter than in those delivering at term (16.9 mm versus 31.9 mm). Cetin and Cetin[40] examined 65 women presenting at 26–35 weeks and reported that the mean cervical length on admission in those with successful tocolysis was 27 (range 9–45) mm, compared with 9 (6–12) mm in the unsuccessful group.

Table 9.7. Studies in pregnancies with threatened preterm labour reporting on the association between sonographically measured cervical length after the administration of tocolytics and the incidence of subsequent preterm delivery

Study	Women (n)	Gestation (weeks)	Short cervix Definition (mm)	Short cervix Incidence (n)	Preterm delivery Definition (weeks)	Overall	Incidence (n) Short cervix	Incidence (n) Long cervix
Murakawa et al.[41] (1993)	32	0	18–36	≤30	<37	11/32 (34.4%)	11/17 (64.7%)	0/15 (0%)
Iams et al.[42] (1994)	60	12	24–35	≤30	<36	24/60 (40.0%)	24/44 (54.5%)	0/16 (0%)
Gomez et al.[43] (1994)	59	0	20–35	≤18	<36	22/59 (37.3%)	16/18 (89.0%)	6/41 (14.6%)
Crane et al.[44] (1997)	136	0	23–33	≤30	<37	37/139 (27.2%)	30/65 (46.1%)	7/71 (9.8%)
Onderoglu[45] (1997)	90	0	25–36	≤28	<37	32/90 (35.6%)	25/35 (71.4%)	7/55 (12.7%)
Goffinet et al.[46] (1997)	108	0	24–34	≤26	<37	24/108 (22.2%)	19/47 (40.4%)	5/61 (8.2%)
Venditelli et al.[47] (2001)	200	26	18–36	≤30	<37	82/200 (41.0%)	68/127 (53.5%)	14/73 (19.2%)
Total	685					232/685 (33.9%)	193/353 (54.7%)	39/332 (11.8%)

Table 9.8. Studies in singleton pregnancies with threatened preterm labour reporting on the association between sonographically measured cervical length at presentation and the incidence of subsequent delivery within seven days of presentation

Study	Women (n)	Gestation (weeks)	Cervix (mm)	Incidence of delivery within seven days (n) Overall	Short cervix	Long cervix
Tsoi et al.[48] (2003)	216	24–36	≤15	17/216 (7.9%)	16/43 (37.2%)	1/173 (0.6%)
Fuchs et al.[49] (2004)	253	24–36	≤15	21/253 (8.2%)	17/36 (47.2%)	4/217 (1.8%)
Tsoi et al.[50] (2004)	63	24–34	≤15	20/63 (31.7%)	20/30 (66.7%)	0/33 (0%)
Total	532			58/532 (10.9%)	53/109 (48.6%)	5/423 (1.2%)

Cervical length after tocolysis in the prediction of preterm delivery

In seven studies sonographic measurement of cervical length was performed in women with threatened preterm labour after the administration of tocolytics (Table 9.7).[41–47] The outcome measure was delivery before 36–37 weeks, which occurred in 34% of the total of 685 women. These studies demonstrated that a short cervix, usually less than 30 mm, identifies a group at a particularly high risk of preterm delivery.

Cervical length at presentation in the prediction of delivery within seven days

In pregnancies presenting with threatened preterm labour the outcome measure of relevance to clinical management is delivery within the subsequent seven days, rather than preterm delivery as such. The clinical dilemma revolves around the issue of whether the woman is truly in labour and therefore in need of, firstly, hospitalisation in a unit with facilities for neonatal intensive care and, secondly, administration of tocolytics with the potentially achievable objective of short-term prolongation of pregnancy for the effective administration of corticosteroids to improve fetal lung maturity.

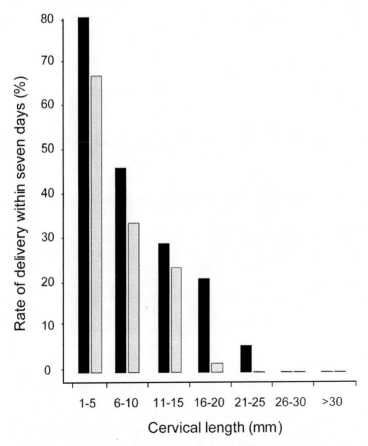

Figure 9.3. Relation between cervical length at presentation with threatened preterm labour and rate of delivery within seven days in singleton (grey) and twin (black) pregnancies

It could be argued that, in the absence of reliable ways to distinguish between true and false labour, the high mortality and handicap rates associated with early preterm delivery justify treatment of all women with threatened preterm labour, because such risks outweigh the economic cost of hospitalisation, the maternal risks associated with tocolytics, and the potential fetal risks associated with corticosteroids (see Chapters 20 and 23).

This concept of 'treatment for all' has been challenged by evidence that sonographic measurement of cervical length at presentation can help distinguish between those women who do and those who do not deliver within the subsequent seven days. In the combined data from three sonographic studies in a total of 532 singleton pregnancies presenting with threatened preterm labour, delivery within seven days occurred in 49% of those women with a cervical length less than 15 mm and in 1% of those with cervical length of 15 mm or more (Table 9.8; Figure 9.3).[48–50] Hospitalisation and the administration of tocolytics and steroids should be reserved for women that are truly in labour and these women can be identified by sonographic measurement of cervical length at presentation.

Two of the studies were in Europe and the incidence of delivery within seven days of presentation was 8%.[48,49] The third study was in South Africa and the incidence of delivery within seven days was 32%.[50] However, in all three studies sonographic measurement of cervical length was equally effective in distinguishing between true and false labour.

Cervical length and fetal fibronectin

Two studies have investigated the effect of combining cervical length and fetal fibronectin in cervicovaginal secretions, in 108[51] and 76[52] singleton pregnancies respectively presenting with threatened preterm labour. In both studies the performance of the two tests was similar with a screen positive rate for a positive fetal fibronectin test and short cervix of about 40% and detection rates for preterm delivery of about 70–75%.[51,52] In one study, 70% of the women with a short cervix were also fetal fibronectin positive and a combination of the two tests did not provide a substantial improvement in the prediction of preterm delivery,[52] whereas the other study[51] reported that combining the two tests provided a significant improvement in the prediction of preterm delivery.

One study investigated the effect of combining cervical length and fetal fibronectin in the prediction of delivery within seven days of presentation.[53] In 195 singleton pregnancies with threatened preterm labour at 24–36 weeks of gestation, fetal fibronectin positivity in cervicovaginal secretions was determined and transvaginal sonographic measurement of cervical length was carried out. Delivery within seven days occurred in 51% of the 35 women with a cervical length of less than 15 mm and 0.6% of the 160 women with a cervical length of 15 mm or more, in 21% of the 85 women with a fibronectin positive result and in 1% of the 110 women with a fibronectin negative result.

The findings of this study demonstrated that, firstly, in women with threatened preterm labour, the risk of delivery within the following seven days is less than 1% if at presentation the cervical length is longer than 15 mm or the fetal fibronectin test is negative. Secondly, the incidence of a positive fetal fibronectin test is inversely related to cervical length (Figure 9.4). Thirdly, the prediction of the likelihood of delivery within seven days provided by cervical length is not improved by the addition of fetal fibronectin testing.

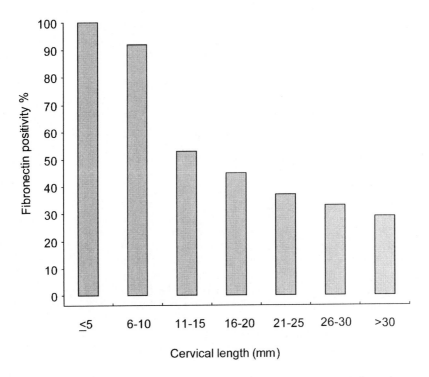

Figure 9.4. Relation between cervical length and incidence of a positive fetal fibronectin test in women with threatened preterm labour

Cervical length and ruptured membranes

Studies in women with preterm prelabour rupture of the membranes (PPROM) have demonstrated that, firstly, in about one-third of such pregnancies there is evidence of intrauterine infection and the incidence is inversely related to the gestation at membrane rupture. Secondly, the interval between membrane rupture and delivery is substantially shorter in women with evidence of intrauterine infection than in those with no infection. Thirdly, in women with no infection there is an inverse correlation between gestation at membrane rupture and the interval to delivery.[54–58] Delivery within seven days of PPROM occurs in about 60% of cases.[59]

Three studies have examined the relation between sonographic measurement of cervical length and the latency period in PPROM. Rizzo et al.[60] examined 92 women and reported that the median interval to delivery was two days in those with cervical length below 20 mm, compared with six days in those with a longer cervix. In contrast, Carlan et al.[61] examined 45 women and found no significant difference in latency period between those with cervical length of more than 30 mm and those with a shorter cervix at presentation. Tsoi et al.[62] measured cervical length in 101 women with singleton pregnancies presenting with PPROM at 24–36 weeks of gestation. Delivery within seven days of presentation occurred in 57% of the pregnancies and significant independent contribution in the prediction of such delivery was provided by cervical length, gestation and presence of contractions at presentation.

In women presenting with PPROM clinical examination is directed at the confirmation of membrane rupture but is not useful in assessing the likelihood of delivery within the next few days.[63] Furthermore, there is evidence to suggest that digital vaginal assessment of the cervix shortens the latency period and is therefore contraindicated in the absence of active labour.[64] In contrast, transvaginal ultrasound has been proven to be safe in cases with PPROM.[65] In the management of such women prediction of the risk of delivery within the subsequent seven days can help optimise the neonatal care for the potentially preterm infant, through referral to a specialist centre. However, in PPROM, unlike preterm labour with intact membranes, measurement of cervical length needs to be combined with other parameters in order to derive a reliable risk.

Cervical length in twin pregnancies

The incidence of preterm delivery in twin pregnancies is 5–10 times higher than in singletons. Crane et al.[44] examined sonographic cervical length after spontaneous or tocolytic-induced arrest of contractions in 26 twin pregnancies presenting with threatened preterm labour at 23–33 weeks of gestation. The outcome measure of the study was subsequent delivery before 34 weeks and this occurred in 5 of the 14 women (36%) with a cervical length of less than 30 mm and none of the 12 women with a cervical length of 30 mm or greater. Fuchs et al.[66] examined 87 twin pregnancies presenting with threatened labour at 24–36 weeks of gestation. Delivery within seven days of presentation occurred in 22% of the pregnancies and the incidence of such delivery was inversely related to cervical length (Figure 9.3). The threshold in cervical length that apparently distinguishes between false and true labour in twin pregnancies presenting with threatened preterm labour was 25 mm, compared with 15 mm in singletons.

The findings of these studies suggest that sonographic measurement of cervical length in twin pregnancies presenting with threatened preterm labour can define the risk of delivery within seven days and may help distinguish between true and false labour.

Conclusions

- Transvaginal measurement of cervical length is highly reproducible and is acceptable to women.
- Routine measurement of cervical length at 20–24 weeks of gestation provides sensitive prediction of spontaneous preterm delivery. The risk of such delivery increases exponentially with decreasing cervical length from less than 1% at 25 mm or longer to about 5% at 15 mm and 80% at 5 mm. In twin and triplet pregnancies, the threshold cervical length for the exponential increase in risk is 25 mm.
- In pregnancies presenting with threatened preterm labour the outcome measure of relevance to clinical management is delivery within the subsequent seven days, rather than preterm delivery as such. In singleton pregnancies, delivery within seven days occurs in about 50% of women with a cervical length of less than 15 mm and in 1% of women with a cervical length of 15 mm or more. The threshold in cervical length that apparently distinguishes between false and true labour in twin pregnancies is 25 mm.
- The incidence of a positive fetal fibronectin test is inversely related to cervical length. In asymptomatic women fibronectin testing improves the prediction of

preterm delivery provided by measurement of cervical length. In women with threatened preterm labour, the prediction of the likelihood of delivery within seven days provided by cervical length is not improved by the addition of fetal fibronectin testing.

References

1. Heath VCF, Southall TR, Souka AP, Novakov A, Nicolaides KH. Cervical length at 23 weeks of gestation: relation to demographic characteristics and previous obstetric history. *Ultrasound Obstet Gynecol* 1998;12:304–11.
2. Andersen HF, Nugent CE, Wanty SD, Hayashi RH. Prediction of risk for preterm delivery by ultrasonographic measurement of cervical length. *Am J Obstet Gynecol* 1990;163:859–67.
3. Sonek J, Shellaas C. Cervical sonography: a review. *Ultrasound Obstet Gynecol* 1998;11:71–8.
4. To MS, Skentou C, Chan C, Zagaliki A, Nicolaides KH. Cervical assessment at the routine 23-week scan: standardizing techniques. *Ultrasound Obstet Gynecol* 2001;17:217–9.
5. Podobnik M, Bulic M, Smiljanic N, Bistricki J. Ultrasonography in the detection of cervical incompetency. *J Clin Ultrasound* 1988;13:383–91.
6. Andersen HF. Transabdominal and transvaginal ultrasonography of the uterine cervix during pregnancy. *J Clin Ultrasound* 1991;19:77–83.
7. To MS, Skentou C, Cicero S, Nicolaides KH. Cervical assessment at the routine 23-weeks' scan: problems with transabdominal sonography. *Ultrasound Obstet Gynecol* 2000;15:292–6.
8. Kurtzman JT, Goldsmith LJ, Gall SA, Spinnato JA. Transvaginal versus transperineal ultrasonography: a blinded comparison in the assessment of cervical length at midgestation. *Am J Obstet Gynecol* 1998;179:852–7.
9. Owen J, Neely C, Northen A. Transperineal versus endovaginal ultrasonographic examination of the cervix in the midtrimester: a blinded comparison. *Am J Obstet Gynecol* 1999;181:780–3.
10. Cicero S, Skentou C, Souka A, To MS, Nicolaides KH. Cervical length at 22–24 weeks of gestation: comparison of transvaginal and transperineal-translabial ultrasonography. *Ultrasound Obstet Gynecol* 2001;17:335–40.
11. Clement S, Candy B, Heath V, To M, Nicolaides KH. Transvaginal ultrasound in pregnancy: its acceptability to women and maternal psychological morbidity. *Ultrasound Obstet Gynecol* 2003;22:508–14.
12. Watson WJ, Stevens D, Welter S, Day D. Observations on the sonographic measurement of cervical length and the risk of premature birth. *J Matern Fetal Med* 1999;8:17–9.
13. Berghella V, Tolosa JE, Kuhlman K, Weiner S, Bolognese RJ, Wapner RJ. Cervical ultrasonography compared with manual examination as a predictor of preterm delivery. *Am J Obstet Gynecol* 1997;177:723–30.
14. Andrews WW, Copper R, Hauth JC, Goldenberg RL, Neely C, Dubard M. Second-trimester cervical ultrasound: associations with increased risk for recurrent early spontaneous delivery. *Obstet Gynecol* 2000;95:222–6.
15. Guzman ER, Walters C, Ananth CV, O'Reilly-Green C, Benito CW, Palermo A, *et al.* A comparison of sonographic cervical parameters in predicting spontaneous preterm birth in high-risk singleton gestations. *Ultrasound Obstet Gynecol* 2001;18:204–10.
16. Owen J, Yost N, Berghella V, Thom E, Swain M, Dildy GA 3rd, Miodovnik M, Langer O, Sibai B, McNellis D; National Institute of Child Health and Human Development, Maternal-Fetal Medicine Units Network. Mid-trimester endovaginal sonography in women at high risk for spontaneous preterm birth. *JAMA* 2001;286:1340–8.
17. Iams JD, Goldenberg RL, Meis PJ, Mercer BM, Moawad A, Das A, *et al.* The length of the cervix and the risk of spontaneous premature delivery. National Institute of Child Health and Human Development Maternal Fetal Medicine Unit Network. *N Engl J Med* 1996;334:567–72.
18. Heath VCF, Southall TR, Souka AP, Elisseou A, Nicolaides KH. Cervical length at 23 weeks of gestation: prediction of spontaneous preterm delivery. *Ultrasound Obstet Gynecol* 1998;12:312–7.
19. Taipale P, Hilesmaa V. Sonographic measurement of uterine cervix at 18–22 weeks' gestation and the risk of preterm delivery. *Obstet Gynecol* 1998;92:902–7.
20. Tongsong T, Kamprapanth P, Srisomboon J, Wanapirak C, Piyamongkol W, Sirichotiyakul S. Single transvaginal sonographic measurement of cervical length early in the third trimester as a predictor of preterm delivery. *Obstet Gynecol* 1995;86:184–7.
21. Arinami Y, Hasegawa I, Takakuwa K, Tanaka K. Prediction of preterm delivery by combined use of simple clinical tests. *J Matern Fetal Med* 1999;8:70–3.
22. To MS, Skentou C, Liao AW, Cacho A, Nicolaides KH. Cervical length and funneling at 23 weeks

of gestation in the prediction of spontaneous early preterm delivery. *Ultrasound Obstet Gynecol* 2001;18:200–3.

23.   Hassan SS, Romero R, Berry SM, Dang K, Blackwell SC, Treadwell MC, *et al*. Patients with an ultrasonographic cervical length < or =15 mm have nearly a 50% risk of early spontaneous preterm delivery. *Am J Obstet Gynecol* 2000;182:1458–67.

24.   Goldenberg RL, Iams JD, Mercer BM, Meis PJ, Moawad AH, Copper RL, Das A, Thom E, Johnson F, McNellis D, Miodovnik M, Van Dorsten JP, Caritis SN, Thurnau GR, Bottoms SF. The Preterm Prediction Study: The value of new vs standard risk factors in predicting early and all spontaneous preterm births. *Am J Public Health* 1998;88:233–8.

25.   Heath V, Daskalakis G, Zagaliki A, Carvalho M, Nicolaides KH. Cervicovaginal fibronectin and cervical length at 23 weeks of gestation: relative risk of early preterm delivery. *Br J Obstet Gynaecol* 2000;107:1276–81.

26.   Goldenberg RL, Iams JD, Miodovnik M, Van Dorsten JP, Thurnau G, Bottoms S, *et al*. The preterm prediction study: risk factors in twin gestations. National Institute of Child Health and Human Development Maternal-Fetal Medicine Units Network. *Am J Obstet Gynecol* 1996;175:1047–53.

27.   Imseis HM, Albert TA, Iams JD. Identifying twin gestations at low risk for preterm birth with a transvaginal ultrasonographic cervical measurement at 24 to 26 weeks' gestation. *Am J Obstet Gynecol* 1997;177:1149–55.

28.   Yang JH, Kuhlman K, Daly S, Berghella V. Prediction of preterm birth by second trimester cervical sonography in twin pregnancies. *Ultrasound Obstet Gynecol* 2000;15:288–91.

29.   Guzman ER, Walters C, O'reilly-Green C, Kinzler WL, Waldron R, Nigam J, *et al*. Use of cervical ultrasonography in prediction of spontaneous preterm birth in twin gestations. *Am J Obstet Gynecol* 2000;183:1103–7.

30.   Skentou C, Souka AP, To MS, Liao AW, Nicolaides KH. Prediction of preterm delivery in twins by cervical assessment at 23 weeks. *Ultrasound Obstet Gynecol* 2001;17:7–10.

31.   Vayssiere C, Favre R, Audibert F, Chauvet MP, Gaucherand P, Tardif D, *et al*. Cervical length and funneling at 22 and 27 weeks to predict spontaneous birth before 32 weeks in twin pregnancies: a French prospective multicenter study. *Am J Obstet Gynecol* 2002;187:1596–604.

32.   Wennerholm UB, Holm B, Mattsby-Baltzer I, Nielsen T, Platz-Christensen J, Sundell G, Hosseini N, Hagberg H. Fetal fibronectin, endotoxin, bacterial vaginosis and cervical length as predictors of preterm birth and neonatal morbidity in twin pregnancies. *Br J Obstet Gynaecol* 1997;104:1398–404.

33.   Guzman ER, Walters C, O'reilly-Green C, Meirowitz NB, Gipson K, Nigam J, *et al*. Use of cervical ultrasonography in prediction of spontaneous preterm birth in triplet gestations. *Am J Obstet Gynecol* 2000;183:1108–13.

34.   To MS, Skentou C, Cicero S, Liao AW, Nicolaides KH. Cervical length at 23 weeks in triplets: prediction of spontaneous preterm delivery. *Ultrasound Obstet Gynecol* 2000;16:515–8.

35.   Maymon R, Herman A, Jauniaux E, Frenkel J, Ariely S, Sherman D. Transvaginal sonographic assessment of cervical length changes during triplet gestation. *Hum Reprod* 2001;16:956–60.

36.   Bartolucci L, Hill WC, Katz M, Gill PJ, Kitzmiller JL. Ultrasonography in preterm labor. *Am J Obstet Gynecol* 1984;149:52–6.

37.   Rizzo G, Capponi A, Arduini D, Lorido C, Romanini C. The value of fetal fibronectin in cervical and vaginal secretions and of ultrasonographic examination of the uterine cervix in predicting premature delivery for patients with preterm labor and intact membranes. *Am J Obstet Gynecol* 1996;175:1146–51.

38.   Hincz P, Wilczynski J, Kozarzewski M, Szaflik K. Two-step test: the combined use of fetal fibronectin and sonographic examination of the uterine cervix for prediction of preterm delivery in symptomatic patients. *Acta Obstet Gynecol Scand* 2002;81:58–63.

39.   Timor-Tritsch I, Boozarjomehri E, Masakowski Y, Monteagudo A, Chao C. Can a "snapshot" sagittal view of the cervix by transvaginal ultrasonography predict active preterm labour? *Am J Obstet Gynecol* 1996;174:990–5.

40.   Cetin M, Cetin A. The role of transvaginal sonography in predicting recurrent preterm labour in patients with intact membranes. *Eur J Obstet Gynecol Reprod Biol* 1997;74:7–11.

41.   Murakawa H, Utumi T, Hasegawa I, Tanaka K, Fuzimori R. Evaluation of threatened preterm delivery by transvaginal ultrasonographic measurement of cervical length. *Obstet Gynecol* 1993;82:829–32.

42.   Iams JD, Paraskos J, Landon MB, Teteris JN, Johnson FF. Cervical sonography in preterm labor. *Obstet Gynecol* 1994;84:40–6.

43.   Gomez R, Galasso M, Romero R, Mazor M, Sorokin Y, Goncalves L, Treadwell M. Ultrasonographic examination of the uterine cervix is better than cervical digital examination as a predictor of the likelihood of premature delivery in patients with preterm labor and intact membranes. *Am J Obstet Gynecol* 1994;171:956–64.

44.   Crane JM, Van den Hof M, Armson BA, Liston R. Transvaginal ultrasound in the prediction of preterm delivery: singleton and twin gestations. *Obstet Gynecol* 1997;90:357–63.

45. Onderoglu LS. Digital examination and transperineal ultrasonographic measurement of cervical length to assess risk of preterm delivery. *Int J Gynaecol Obstet* 1997;59:223–8.

46. Goffinet F, Rozenberg P, Kayem G, Perdu M, Philippe HJ, Nisand I. The value of intravaginal ultrasonography of the cervix uteri for evaluation of the risk of premature labor. *J Gynecol Obstet Biol Reprod (Paris)* 1997;26:623–9.

47. Vendittelli F, Mamelle N, Munoz F, Janky E. Transvaginal ultrasonography of the uterine cervix in hospitalized women with preterm labor. *Int J Gynaecol Obstet* 2001;72:117–25.

48. Tsoi E, Akmal S, Rane S, Otigbah C, Nicolaides KH. Ultrasound assessment of cervical length in threatened preterm labour. *Ultrasound Obstet Gynecol* 2003;21:552–5.

49. Fuchs IB, Henrich W, Osthues K, Dudenhausen JW. Sonographic cervical length in singleton pregnancies with intact membranes presenting with threatened preterm labor. *Ultrasound Obstet Gynecol* 2004. In press.

50. Tsoi E, Geerts L, Jeffery B, Odendaal HJ, Nicolaides KH. Sonographic cervical length in threatened preterm labour in a South African population. *Ultrasound Obstet Gynecol* 2004. In press.

51. Rizzo G, Capponi A, Arduini D, Lorido C, Romanini C. The value of fetal fibronectin in cervical and vaginal secretions and of ultrasonographic examination of the uterine cervix in predicting premature delivery for patients with preterm labor and intact membranes. *Am J Obstet Gynecol* 1996;175:1146–51.

52. Rozenberg P, Goffinet F, Malagrida L, Giudicelli Y, Perdu M, Houssin I, et al. Evaluating the risk of preterm delivery: a comparison of fetal fibronectin and transvaginal ultrasonographic measurement of cervical length. *Am J Obstet Gynecol* 1997;176:196–9.

53. Tsoi E, Akmal S, Geerts L, Jeffery B, Nicolaides KH. Sonographic measurement of cervical length and fetal fibronectin testing in threatened preterm labour. *Ultrasound Obstet Gynecol* 2004. In press.

54. Carroll SG, Ville Y, Greenough A, Gamsu H, Patel B, Philpott-Howard J, et al. Preterm prelabour amniorrhexis: intrauterine infection and interval between membrane rupture and delivery. *Arch Dis Child Fetal Neonatal Ed* 1995;72:F43–6.

55. Romero R, Yoon BH, Mazor M, Gomez R, Gonzalez R, Diamond MP, et al. A comparative study of the diagnostic performance of amniotic fluid glucose, white blood cell count, interleukin-6, and Gram stain in the detection of microbial invasion in patients with premature rupture of membranes. *Am J Obstet Gynecol* 1993;169:839–51.

56. Hillier SL, Martius J, Krohn M, Kiviat N, Holmes KK, Eschenbach DA. A case–control study of chorioamniotic infection and histologic chorioamnionitis in prematurity. *N Engl J Med* 1988;319:972–7.

57. Kitajima H, Nakayama M, Miyano A, Shimizu, Taniguchi T, Shimoya K, et al. Significance of chorioamnionitis. *Early Hum Dev* 1992;29:125–30.

58. Seo K, McGregor JA, French JI. Preterm birth is associated with increased risk of maternal and neonatal infection. *Obstet Gynecol* 1992;79:75–80.

59. Kenyon SL, Taylor DJ, Tarnow-Mordi W for the ORACLE Collaborative Group. Broad spectrum antibiotics for preterm, prelabour rupture of fetal membranes: The ORACLE I randomised controlled trial. *Lancet* 2001;357:979–88.

60. Rizzo G, Capponi A, Angelini E, Vlachopoulou A, Grassi C and Romanini C. The value of transvaginal ultrasonographic examination of the uterine cervix in predicting preterm delivery in patients with preterm premature rupture of membranes. *Ultrasound Obstet Gynecol* 1998;11:23–9.

61. Carlan SJ, Richmond LB, O'Brien WF. Randomized trial of endovaginal ultrasound in preterm premature rupture of membranes. *Obstet Gynecol* 1997;89:458–61.

62. Tsoi E, Fuchs I, Henrich W, Dudenhausen JW, Nicolaides KH. Sonographic measurement of cervical length in preterm prelabour amniorrhexis. *Ultrasound Obstet Gynecol*. In press.

63. Nelson LH, Anderson RL, O'Shea TM, Swain M. Expectant management of premature rupture of membranes. *Am J Obstet Gynecol* 1994;171:350–8.

64. Lewis DF, Major CA, Towers CV, Asrat T, Harding JA, Garite TJ. Effects of digital vaginal examination on latency period in preterm premature rupture of membranes. *Obstet Gynecol* 1992;80:630–4.

65. Carlan SJ, Richmond LB, O'Brien WF. Randomized trial of endovaginal ultrasound in preterm premature rupture of membranes. *Obstet Gynecol* 1997;89:458–61.

66. Fuchs I, Tsoi E, Henrich W, Dudenhausen , Nicolaides KH. Sonographic measurement of cervical length in twin pregnancies in threatened preterm labour. *Ultrasound Obstet Gynecol* 2004;23:42–5.

Chapter 10

Cervical cerclage

Bryony Jones and Andrew Shennan

Introduction

Acute tocolysis has been disappointing in the prevention of preterm delivery.[1] Interventions targeted at asymptomatic women are more likely to tackle initiating factors, and are potentially more efficacious. However, mechanisms are poorly understood. Recent prophylactic strategies, such as the use of progesterone or the treatment of abnormal vaginal flora, have shown some potential. Cervical cerclage is a common prophylactic intervention that has been used for many decades. The data to support its use are not extensive and, in contrast to other interventions such as antenatal steroid use, only a few randomised controlled trials evaluating its efficacy have been published. More recent developments in prediction, such as cervical length, have allowed women at high risk to be targeted with cerclage. As cervical length is relatively good at predicting early birth, cerclage may have the best potential to reduce morbidity as it allows those most at risk to be targeted.[2,3]

Preterm labour is the end result of many different processes. Some are of maternal origin, some fetal. Maternal factors include infection (systemic or intrauterine), uteroplacental ischaemia, uterine overdistension (multiple gestation, polyhydramnios) and müllerian duct abnormalities. All of these could result in cervical change. It is unclear whether cerclage can influence this process but, as there is likely to be an interaction between cervical dilatation and ascending infection, regardless of whether the primary problem is in the cervical tissue, cerclage remains a logical intervention to consider in all women at risk of preterm delivery (Figure 10.1). The relative importance of each of the above factors varies between individuals and may even differ between successive pregnancies in the same woman.

True cervical insufficiency is probably rare but it is classically defined as painless dilatation and shortening of the cervix in the second trimester of pregnancy, resulting in pregnancy loss or delivery. Cervical insufficiency has a wide spectrum of aetiologies including congenital cervical anomalies, cervical trauma or other unknown factors. The diagnosis is often made in retrospect after exclusion of other causes of uterine activity. However, as term pregnancies are common even after these classical histories, the actual pathophysiology remains obscure.

Although some cases of cervical insufficiency are primarily mechanical (cervical surgery, trauma or congenital anomalies), most women diagnosed with cervical insufficiency have normal cervical anatomy. Consequently, a model of a continuum of cervical integrity has been proposed.[4,5] In this model, the cervix and the endocervical canal are considered to be the chief mechanical barriers that separate the vaginal bacteria from the fetus and the fetal membranes. Against the background of the

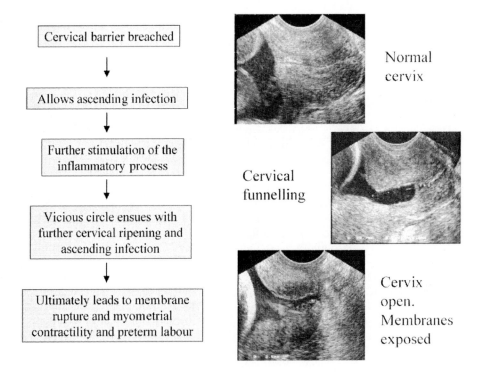

Cervical barrier breached

↓

Allows ascending infection

↓

Further stimulation of the inflammatory process

↓

Vicious circle ensues with further cervical ripening and ascending infection

↓

Ultimately leads to membrane rupture and myometrial contractility and preterm labour

Normal cervix

Cervical funnelling

Cervix open. Membranes exposed

Figure 10.1. Events amenable to prevention by cervical cerclage

individual's risk factors, this mechanical barrier may be breached. Once this happens, it is hypothesised that abnormal colonisation by vaginal bacteria, infection and inflammatory processes may all occur. As a consequence, there is an upregulation of labour-associated pathways. These may be within the cervix or uterus and are likely to lead to a further increase in uterine activity or cervical ripening, causing second trimester loss or preterm birth. A proportion of women with apparent cervical incompetence have evidence of subclinical infection detected by precerclage amniocentesis.[6,7] It is not known whether the bacteriological findings are the cause of or a result of premature dilatation of the cervix.

Cervical cerclage has been used in the management of second trimester loss and preterm delivery for almost 50 years with the intention of stopping this cascade. However its use and efficacy is still surrounded by considerable controversy.

Incidence of cervical insufficiency

Approximately 25% of women who have had a previous spontaneous preterm delivery (24–27 weeks of gestation) will deliver preterm in a subsequent pregnancy (the relative risk of preterm delivery is more than 20).[8] As there are essentially no proven objective criteria for cervical insufficiency, the clinical diagnosis is often made in retrospect, after a poor obstetric outcome. Consequently, the incidence of cervical insufficiency is almost impossible to ascertain, but estimates often suggest about 1% of all women are affected.

Elective cerclage

The efficacy of elective cerclage has been studied in three significant randomised controlled trials. The first study included 194 women with singleton pregnancies at high risk of preterm delivery at 15–21 weeks of gestation with at least two pregnancies that had ended spontaneously before 37 weeks.[9] Women were excluded from the study if they had a history of cervical surgery, cervical cerclage or with the cervix length less than 2.0 cm or dilated at trial entry. Randomisation allocated 98 women to a McDonald cerclage and 96 to no cerclage. Both groups were comparable for demographic characteristics and obstetric history. No significant differences in preterm delivery rate, neonatal morbidity and mortality were found between the two groups. Women in the cerclage group spent significantly longer in hospital.

The second study included 506 singleton pregnancies at moderate risk of preterm delivery.[10] Women at higher risk of cervical insufficiency were excluded from the study. Randomisation allocated 268 women to a McDonald cerclage and 238 to no cerclage. Women in the cerclage group had significantly more first and second trimester losses. This difference was focused around differences in groups from one participating centre in the study but even when results from this centre were excluded it did not affect the conclusion. Both studies found no significant improvement in outcomes in women treated with cerclage. Furthermore, both studies found that women in the cerclage group were more likely to receive tocolytic drugs and had more antenatal admissions than women without cerclage. It has been argued that both these trials could not show a difference between cerclage or not as women who might benefit from cerclage were not included in the study.[11]

In the third study, 1292 women with singleton pregnancies at risk of preterm delivery were enrolled into an international, randomised controlled trial.[12] Women were recruited if their obstetrician was uncertain whether to advise her to have cervical cerclage. Randomisation allocated 647 women to cerclage and 645 to no cerclage. The frequency of delivery prior to 33 weeks of gestation was lower in the cerclage group compared with controls when looking at the entire study population (83/647 versus 110/645; RR 0.75).

The authors provided subgroup analyses of six different cohorts of pregnancies:

1. 554 singleton pregnancies with one previous second trimester loss or preterm delivery (no history of cervical surgery)
2. 196 singleton pregnancies with two previous second trimester losses or preterm deliveries (no history of cervical surgery)
3. 107 singleton pregnancies with three or more previous second trimester losses or preterm deliveries (no history of cervical surgery)
4. 138 singleton pregnancies with history of cervical surgery
5. 28 twin pregnancies
6. 269 singleton pregnancies with 'other indications'.

Only in the subgroup of women who had had three or more second trimester losses was there a significant benefit in reducing the preterm delivery rate prior to 33 weeks of gestation with treatment with elective cerclage. There was, however, an increased incidence of postpartum fever in the cerclage cohort. The authors concluded that the

Table 10.1. Meta-analysis of randomised controlled trials showing the effect of elective cerclage on preterm delivery[9,10,12]

	Difference (%)	Odds ratio (95% confidence interval)
Delivery <33 weeks	9.8 versus 12.3	0.77 (0.58–1.02)
Delivery <37 weeks	21.8 versus 24.7	0.85 (0.68–1.05)

benefit of cerclage remained small because of the relatively low prevalence of preterm delivery even in the highest risk group. This amounted to approximately one saved pregnancy for every 25 women treated with elective cerclage. This study forms the basis of the current recommendations of the Royal College of Obstetricians and Gynaecologists. However, the flexible entry criteria and the obstetricians' perception of risk of adverse outcome rather than actual risk may have diluted the number of cases of cervical insufficiency in the study and may have partially obscured a possibly greater benefit from cerclage.[13]

Meta-analyses published in 2003 of the studies of elective cerclage have shown a possible significant effect[14] and a trend[15] towards reducing preterm births before 34 weeks of gestation. Further work is needed to identify women who would most benefit from cervical cerclage. One can conclude that the magnitude of benefit demonstrated by these different meta-analyses is clinically important but that the numbers studied are insufficient to show statistical certainty that this benefit is real. Table 10.1 shows the overall relative risk reduction in preterm delivery from our interpretation of these studies. There is obviously a need for more research in this area to confirm this potential benefit.

Ultrasound-indicated cerclage

The use of transvaginal ultrasound assessment of cervical length has been demonstrated to be a good predictor of risk of preterm delivery in both low-risk[5,16,17] and high-risk populations.[18,19] Some clinicians are now using this as a screening test and only performing cerclage if cervical changes occur, although it is not clear whether this reduces the risk of preterm delivery. Nonrandomised studies comparing ultrasound-indicated cerclage with conservative management for a short cervix have shown conflicting results.[20–24]

Some of those studies favouring cerclage[20,21,25–27] and those not favouring cerclage[22–24,28] are listed in Table 10.2. Unfortunately, the literature is very hetero-geneous with a wide variety of gestations, populations and cut-offs for cervical length at which cerclage is suggested. Interpretation of the multiple studies of cerclage is thus difficult. The speed and timing of cervical shortening may be influenced by factors other than cervical insufficiency, and by different pathologies for which cerclage may be of no benefit. Cervical shortening may be a final common pathway for preterm delivery, and whether this is amenable to intervention or not is unknown.

There have been two randomised controlled clinical trials studying the benefit of ultrasound-indicated cerclage versus conservative management.[26,28] The CIPRACT study[26] included women who were at high risk for spontaneous birth with a past obstetric history suggestive of cervical insufficiency. Randomisation allocated women to a prophylactic cerclage or not based on the finding of cervical length of less than

Table 10.2. The main studies investigating the use of cervical cerclage in women with changes in cervical length on ultrasound

Study	Type of study	Criterion for cerclage	Outcome	Favour treatment
Heath et al.[20] 1998	Nonrandomised	<15 mm	Delivery <32 weeks: Cerclage 5% No cerclage 50%	Yes
Berghella et al.[23] 1999	Nonrandomised	<25 mm	Odds ratio 1.1 for preterm delivery with cerclage	No
Novy et al.[21] 2001	Historical cohort	<30 mm	Mean 4 week improvement in gestational age with cerclage	Yes
Hibbard et al.[27] 2000	Nonrandomised	<30 mm	Mean 2 week improvement in gestational age with cerclage	Yes
Hassan et al.[22] 2000	Historical cohort	<15 mm	Delivery <34 weeks: Cerclage 68% No cerclage 44%	No
Althuisius et al.[26] 2001	RCT	<25 mm	Delivery <34 weeks: Cerclage 0% No cerclage 44%	Yes
Rust et al.[28] 2000	RCT	<25 mm	Delivery <34 weeks: Cerclage 35% No cerclage 36%	No

RCT = randomised controlled trial

25 mm on ultrasound cervical surveillance. Women underwent serial ultrasound cervical assessment and, in the group without prophylactic cerclage, if a cervical length less than 25 mm was found before 27 weeks of gestation, randomisation allocated women to therapeutic cerclage with bed rest or bed rest alone. Thirty-six women developed a cervical length less than 25 mm before 27 weeks, and 35 were randomised. Of the 19 women who received cerclage, none delivered before 34 weeks, which was significantly less (statistically) then the 7/16 who were on bed rest alone.

Rust et al.[28] randomly assigned 138 women who were found to have a sonographic cervical length of less than 25 mm or greater than 25 mm funnelling at 16–24 weeks of gestation to cerclage or no cerclage. The cohort included 12% multiple gestations. Preterm birth occurred in 35% of the cerclage group and in 36% of controls.

The differences in methodology may have contributed to the differences in result. Rust et al. used precerclage amniocentesis to exclude infection, thus delaying the intended cerclage by 48–72 hours. The effect of a delay when the processes leading to cervical ripening have been established is unknown. Different suture materials were used in each study.[29] There was a greater incidence of reported placental abruption in the Rust et al.[28] study, perhaps suggesting that other pathologies were responsible for preterm labour in that population.

The appropriate threshold for an ultrasound-indicated suture has not been established. It is known, however, that once cervical length has reached 15 mm the relative risk of preterm delivery is 14.[5] A preoperative cervical length of less than 15 mm is associated with the presence of visible fetal membranes.[30] The presence of visible fetal membranes at the time of suture insertion is associated with a poor outcome. Consequently, the threshold for cerclage should probably be above 15 mm. A requirement for the cervical length to be less than 15 mm for cerclage to be indicated might explain the lack of significant effect of cerclage seen in some studies.[22]

Overall, the data available are far too limited to draw any conclusions, and further studies are required. Ultrasound-indicated sutures should probably not be inserted in routine clinical practice until more evidence is available.

Transabdominal sonography is not favoured for cervical surveillance, as successful visualisation requires a full bladder which may falsely elongate the cervix.[31] Ultrasound follow-up once the suture is *in situ* may be useful in predicting continuing pregnancy. Funnelling of fetal membranes to the level of the suture is significantly associated with earlier preterm delivery.[32,33] Cerclage is associated with an increase in cervical length post procedure.[34] The increase in cervical length seen post cervical cerclage is greater than seen by bed rest alone.[35] However, the degree of increase is not predictive of term delivery.[36] The best predictor of outcome is the length of cervix closed above the suture; the best prognosis is associated with lengths of greater than 10 mm.[30]

It is not known whether there is any benefit in inserting a repeat cerclage in those women with a cervical suture *in situ* who have cervical shortening and/or funnelling of the fetal membranes below the level of the suture on ultrasound. An observation study of 26 women with a McDonald cerclage, followed up by serial cervical sonography, revealed 12 women to have significant cervical changes.[37] Of the 12 women who had a repeat suture inserted, 11 women delivered viable infants. The authors proposed that repeat cerclage delayed delivery by an average of 7 weeks. There are few data to guide the decision on inserting a second suture and the possibility of prolonging the pregnancy must be weighed against the potential risks of membrane rupture, preterm delivery and infection.

Emergency 'rescue cerclage'

No randomised study has prospectively documented the benefits of emergency cervical cerclage. One small prospective, nonrandomised study showed that, in women with viable singleton pregnancies with cervical dilatation greater than 4 cm and in the absence of uterine activity, cerclage resulted in the birth of infants of significantly higher mean birthweight compared with those whose mothers had had bed rest alone.[38] There was no statistical difference in the frequency of chorioamnionitis, maternal morbidity or perinatal mortality. Nulliparity, the presence of membranes prolapsing beyond the level of the external os, and gestational age less than 22 weeks of gestation at cerclage placement are associated with a decreased chance of delivery at or after 28 weeks.[39] Other studies have suggested that insertion of a suture prior to 20 weeks has a more favourable outcome.[34] The median pregnancy prolongation for emergency cervical cerclage is approximately 7 weeks.[40] The benefit of perioperative antibiotics has not been established.[41]

Transabdominal cerclage and preconception cerclage

The treatment for women with a history of cervical insufficiency that resulted in a preterm delivery or midtrimester loss despite placement of a cervical suture is uncertain. Transabdominal cervical cerclage (TAC) was first described in the 1960s.[42] A number of case reports and series have since been described. TAC insertion is usually recommended either prior to conception or during early pregnancy. Insertion of the suture later in pregnancy may be more difficult owing to the increase in uterine dimensions. A review of the literature suggested a combined success rate of TAC of 89%.[43] There has only been one retrospective cohort series that compared TAC with vaginal suture in early pregnancy in women with previous 'failed' vaginal sutures.[44] Transabdominal cerclage is associated with a lower incidence of preterm delivery and preterm premature rupture of membranes (PPROM) in comparison with transvaginal cerclage. This may be due to insertion of the suture at the level of the internal os in the case of TAC. The disadvantage of the procedure is the need for two laparotomies. At caesarean section the woman is delivered by a transverse uterine incision above the level of the suture. The suture is usually left in place for future pregnancies. The need for major surgery may be avoided by the insertion of the suture laparoscopically.[45] The cerclage may be removed by posterior colpotomy, thereby permitting vaginal delivery. The major complication of TAC is bleeding at the time of insertion. Other complications include pregnancy loss and intrauterine growth restriction from inadvertent ligation of the uterine arteries.[43] There is a theoretical risk of subfertility with preconception cerclage.

A transvaginal cervicoisthmic cerclage as an alternative to TAC has been proposed.[46] A systematic review published in 2002 found that TAC may be associated with a lower risk of perinatal death or delivery at less than 24 weeks of gestation but it is also associated with a higher operative morbidity than a transvaginal procedure.[47]

Role for cerclage in multiple pregnancy

In many developed countries, the number of multifetal pregnancies has increased dramatically in the past 20 years as a result of the progress in assisted reproductive techniques. As a result, preterm labour, PROM of one fetus and single fetal demise are now more frequently encountered. There are reports, however, that there are more cervical sutures being performed in multiple pregnancies arising in assisted reproductive technology as well as after ultrasonographic evidence of cervical dilatation.[48]

Prophylactic cerclage in multifetal pregnancies has failed to show any benefit.[9,10,12,28] In twin pregnancies, cervical length decreases with advancing gestation and after 20 weeks the cervix is shorter than in singleton pregnancies.[49] Likelihood ratios associated with cervical lengths of 15–20 mm at around 20 weeks of gestation are in the range 8–40.[50–54] Results for triplet pregnancies are even more variable.[55,56] Cervical length may be at least as good as other ultrasound variables to predict delivery at less than 34 weeks in twins and triplets.[50,55] Cervical length of less than 30 mm and funnelling were independently associated with delivery at less than 34 weeks of gestation. A cervix greater than 35 mm is associated with a 4% risk of preterm labour.[51]

Case reports have demonstrated that delayed interval delivery between twins can be successfully achieved in some cases with cerclage. Studies in which cerclage was infrequently used reported a shorter inter-delivery interval (9 days) compared with studies where cerclage was used in all cases (26 days).[57] Despite routine use of prophylactic antibiotics, the overall incidence of clinical intrauterine infection was 36% and maternal sepsis 4.5%. After controlling for other factors, the use of cerclage did not appear to increase the risk of intrauterine infection significantly (adjusted risk 1.1).

Types of cerclage

There has not yet been a randomised controlled trial comparing Shirodkar cerclage and McDonald types of cerclage. Compared with McDonald sutures, the Shirodkar suture is associated with a greater increase in the cervical length measured by ultrasound.[58] Small retrospective studies comparing Shirodkar and McDonald methods of cerclage did not reveal any statistical differences in mean gestational age at delivery[58-60] or rate of admission to the neonatal intensive care unit.[59] A randomised trial of management of women directly after suture insertion did not show a statistically significant difference between outpatient and inpatient procedures.[61] There are differences in the material used for cerclage but no trials of potential benefits of polyester tape over monofilament suture material have been undertaken.[29] A very small retrospective study has reported the use of an absorbable suture (PDS) as efficacious as other suture materials.[62]

Reported adverse events associated with cervical cerclage

Early complications of cervical cerclage include abdominal pain, vaginal bleeding, PROM and pregnancy loss. Late complications include chorioamnionitis (16%[28] and 20%[24]), suture displacement, preterm labour, PROM (15%[12] and 18%[9]), uterine rupture and cervical dystocia.[63] The incidence of cervical trauma and difficulty in cerclage removal have each been reported at 1%.[12] Retrospective studies have associated cervical scarring and caesarean section with cervical cerclage.[60] The policy of cervical ultrasound surveillance is not thought to carry any infective risk. Endovaginal sonography is not associated with increased risks of infection.[64]

When to remove the suture?

The management of PPROM in the presence of a cervical suture varies. There is concern over the potential infectious complications and that the suture may be an additive focus for infection and increase neonatal mortality rate.[65] In the absence of intra-amniotic infection, current recommendations favour expectant management of pregnancies complicated by PPROM remote from term, in an effort to prolong latency to delivery and improve perinatal outcome.[66-68] Clinicians may balance the risk of infection against that of precipitating an extremely premature delivery with the cerclage removal itself.

Other factors

Dual pathology has been found responsible in 5% of women with a previous second trimester loss. One series (n = 158) with high risk of second trimester loss (25%) found an incidence of 33% for antiphospholipid antibodies.[69]

Conclusions

Cerclage remains a widely used clinical intervention, although there are limited data on which to base clinical practice. Advances in assessing changes in the cervix, such as the use of cervical ultrasound, may help to direct clinicians to those women who would benefit most from this intervention. Until further research is done, it is difficult to make firm recommendations as to who should receive a cervical suture. The evidence suggests that a careful risk benefit of suture placement needs to be considered in every case and that there are few absolute indications for suture insertion. Given the relative safety of the procedure, it seems reasonable to continue to offer cervical cerclage on an elective basis to women most at risk; this assessment of risk has to be a pragmatic judgement until further data become available. Ultrasound-indicated sutures should only be performed as part of an evaluation programme, such as within a randomised controlled trial.

References

1. King JF, Flenady VJ, Papatsonis DN, Dekker GA, Carbonne B. Calcium channel blockers for inhibiting preterm labour. *Cochrane Database Syst Rev* 2003;(1):CD002255.
2. Wood NS, Marlow N, Costeloe K, Gibson AT, Wilkinson AR. Neurologic and developmental disability after extremely preterm birth. EPICure Study Group. *N Engl J Med* 2000;343:378–84.
3. Escobar GJ, Littenberg B, Petitti DB. Outcome among surviving very low birthweight infants: a meta-analysis. *Arch Dis Child* 1991;66:204–11.
4. Iams JD. Cervical ultrasonography. *Ultrasound Obstet Gynecol* 1997;10:156–60.
5. Iams JD, Johnson FF, Sonek J, Sachs L, Gebauer C, Samuels P. Cervical competence as a continuum: a study of ultrasonographic cervical length and obstetric performance. *Am J Obstet Gynecol* 1995;172(4 Pt 1):1097–106.
6. Hillier S, Martins J, Krohn M, Kiviat N, Holmes K, Eschenbach D. A case–control study of chorio-amniotic infection and histologic chorioamnionitis in prematurity. *N Engl J Med* 1988;319:972–8.
7. Mays JK, Figueroa R, Shah J, Khakoo H, Kaminsky S, Tejani N. Amniocentesis for selection before rescue cerclage. *Obstet Gynecol* 2000;95:652–5.
8. Mercer BM, Goldenberg RL, Moawad AH, Meis PJ, Iams JD, Das AF, *et al*. The preterm prediction study: effect of gestational age and cause of preterm birth on subsequent obstetric outcome. National Institute of Child Health and Human Development Maternal-Fetal Medicine Units Network. *Am J Obstet Gynecol* 1999;181(5 Pt 1):1216–21.
9. Rush RW, Isaacs S, McPherson K, Jones L, Chalmers I, Grant A. A randomized controlled trial of cervical cerclage in women at high risk of spontaneous preterm delivery. *Br J Obstet Gynaecol* 1984;91:724–30.
10. Lazar P, Gueguen S, Dreyfus J, Renaud R, Pontinnier G, Papiernik E. Multicentered controlled trial of cervical cerlcage in women at moderate risk of preterm delivery. *Br J Obstet Gynaecol* 1984;91:731–5.
11. Althuisius SM, Dekker GA, van Geijn HP. Cervical incompetence: a reappraisal of an obstetric controversy. *Obstet Gynecol Surv* 2002;57:377–87.
12. MRC/RCOG Working Party on Cervical Cerclage. Final report of the Medical Research Council/Royal College of Obstetricians and Gynaecologists multicentre randomised trial of cervical cerclage. *Br J Obstet Gynaecol* 1993;100:516–23.
13. Lamont RF. New approaches in the management of preterm labour of infective aetiology. *Br J Obstet Gynaecol* 1998;105:134–7.
14. Bachmann LM, Coomarasamy A, Honest H, Khan KS. Elective cervical cerclage for prevention of preterm birth: a systematic review. *Acta Obstet Gynecol Scand* 2003;82:398–404.
15. Odibo AO, Elkousy M, Ural SH, Macones GA. Prevention of preterm birth by cervical cerclage compared with expectant management: a systematic review. *Obstet Gynecol Surv* 2003;58:130–6.
16. Heath VCF, Southall TR, Souka AP, Elisseou A, Nicolaides KH. Cervical length at 23 weeks gestation: prediction of spontaneous preterm delivery. *Ultrasound Obstet Gynecol* 1998;12:312–7.
17. Hassan SS, Romero R, Berry SM, Dang K, Blackwell SC, Treadwell MC, *et al*. Patients with an ultrasonographic cervical length < or =15 mm have nearly a 50% risk of early spontaneous preterm delivery. *Am J Obstet Gynecol* 2000;182:1458–67.
18. Andrews WW, Copper R, Hauth JC, Goldenberg RI, Neely C, Dubard M. Second trimester cervical ultrasound: associations with increased risk for recurrent early spontaneous delivery. *Obstet Gynecol* 2000;95:222–6.
19. Iams JD, Goldenberg RL, Mercer BM, Moawad A, Thom E, Meis PJ, *et al*. The Preterm Prediction Study: recurrence risk of spontaneous preterm birth. National Institute of Child Health and Human Development Maternal-Fetal Medicine Units Network. *Am J Obstet Gynecol* 1998;178:1035–40.
20. Heath VCF, Souka AP, Erasmus D, Gibb DMF, Nicolaides KH. Cervical length at 23 weeks gestation: the value of Shirodkar suture for the short cervix. *Ultrasound Obstet Gynecol* 1998;12:318–22.
21. Novy MJ, Gupta A, Wothe DD, Gupta S, Kennedy KA, Gravett MG. Cervical cerclage in the second trimester of pregnancy: a historical cohort study. *Am J Obstet Gynecol* 2001;184:1447–56.
22. Hassan SS, Romero R, Maymon E, Berry SM, Blackwell SC, Treadwell MC, *et al*. Does cervical cerclage prevent preterm delivery in patients with a short cervix? *Am J Obstet Gynecol* 2001;184:1325–31.

23. Berghella V, Daly SF, Tolosa JE, DiVito MM, Chalmers R, Garg N, *et al*. Prediction of preterm delivery with transvaginal ultrasonography of the cervix in patients with high-risk pregnancies: does cerclage prevent prematurity? *Am J Obstet Gynecol* 1999;181:809–15.

24. Rust OA, Atlas RO, Reed J, van Gaalen J, Balducci J. Revisiting the short cervix detected by transvaginal ultrasound in the second trimester: why cerclage therapy may not help. *Am J Obstet Gynecol* 2001;185:1098–105.

25. To MS, Erasmus I, Palma Dias R, Pusenjak S, Heath VCF, Nicolaides KH. A prospective randomised controlled trial of Shirodkar suture insertion in women with a short cervix. *J Soc Gynecol Investig* 2003;10:103A.

26. Althuisius SM, Dekker GA, Hummel P, Bekedam DJ, van Geijn HP. Final results of the Cervical Incompetence Prevention Randomized Trial (CIPRACT): therapeutic cerclage with bed rest versus bed rest alone. *Am J Obstet Gynecol* 2001;185:1106–12.

27. Hibbard JU, Snow J, Moawad AH. Short cervical length by ultrasound and cerclage. *J Perinatol* 2000;20:161–5.

28. Rust OA, Atlas RO, Jones KJ, Benham BN, Balducci J. A randomized trial of cerclage versus no cerclage among patients with ultrasonographically detected second-trimester preterm dilatation of the internal os. *Am J Obstet Gynecol* 2000;183:830–5.

29. Zalar RW. Differences in cerclage management lead to different outcomes. *Am J Obstet Gynecol* 2002;187:514.

30. Groom KM, Shennan AH, Bennett PR. Ultrasound indicated cervical cerclage: outcome depends on preoperative cervical length and presence of visible fetal membranes at time of cerclage. *Am J Obstet Gynecol* 2002;187:445–9.

31. To MS, Skentou C, Cicero S, Nicolaides KH. Cervical assessment at the routine 23-weeks' scan: problems with transabdominal sonography. *Ultrasound Obstet Gynecol* 2000;15:292–6.

32. O'Brien JM, Barton JR, Milligan DA. Funnelling to the stitch: an informative ultrasonographic finding after cervical cerclage. *Ultrasound Obstet Gynecol* 2002;20:252–5.

33. Guzman ER, Houlihan C, Vintzileos A, Ivan J, Benito C, Kappy K. The significance of transvaginal ultrasonographic evaluation of the cervix in women treated with emergency cerclage. *Am J Obstet Gynecol* 1996;175:471–6.

34. O'Connell MPO, Lindow SW. Reversal of asymptomatic cervical length shortening with cervical cerclage: a preliminary study. *Hum Reprod* 2001;16:172–3.

35. Althuisius S, Dekker G, Hummel P, Bekedam D, Kuik D, van Geijn H. Cervical Incompetence Prevention Randomized Cerclage Trial (CIPRACT): effect of therapeutic cerclage with bed rest vs. bed rest only on cervical length. *Ultrasound Obstet Gynecol* 2002;20:163–7.

36. Dijkstra K, Funai EF, O'Neill L, Rebarber A, Paidas MJ, Young BK. Change in cervical length after cerclage as a predictor of preterm delivery. *Obstet Gynecol* 2000;96:346–50.

37. Fox R, Holmes R, James N, Tuohy J, Wardle P. Serial transvaginal ultrasonography following McDonald cerclage and repeat suture insertion. *Aust N Z J Obstet Gynaecol* 1998;38:27–30.

38. Olatunbosun OA, al-Nuaim L, Turnell RW. Emergency cerclage compared with bed rest for advanced cervical dilatation in pregnancy. *Int Surg* 1995;80:170–4.

39. Terkildsen MFC, Parilla BV, Kumar P, Grobman W. Factors associated with success of emergent second-trimester cerclage. *Obstet Gynecol* 2003;101:565–9.

40. Hordnes K, Askvik K, Dalaker K. Emergency McDonald cerclage with application of stay sutures. *Eur J Obstet Gynecol Reprod Biol* 1995;64:43–9.

41. O'Brien KE, Silver H, Heber W. Effect of prophylactic antibiotic therapy upon time gained in patients undergoing emergency cervical cerclage. *J Soc Gynecol Investig* 2003;9(1 Suppl):120.

42. Benson RC, Durfee RB. Transabdominal cervicouterine cerclage during pregnancy for the treatment of cervical incompetence. *Obstet Gynecol* 1965;25:145–55.

43. Novy MJ. Transabdominal cervicoisthmic cerclage for the management of repetitive abortion and premature delivery. *Am J Obstet Gynecol* 1991;143:1982.

44. Davis G, Berghella V, Talucci M, Wapner RJ. Patients with a prior failed transvaginal cerclage: a comparison of obstetric outcomes with either transabdominal or transvaginal cerclage. *Am J Obstet Gynecol* 2000;183:836–9.

45. Lesser KB, Childers JM, Survit EA. Transabdominal cerclage: a laparoscopic approach. *Obstet Gynecol* 1998;91:855–6.

46. Golfier F, Bessai K, Paparel P, Cassignol A, Vaudoyer F, Raudrant D. Transvaginal cervicoisthmic cerclage as an alternative to the transabdominal technique. *Eur J Obstet Gynecol Reprod Biol* 2001;100:16–21.

47. Zaveri V, Aghajafari F, Amankwah K, Hannah M. Abdominal versus vaginal cerclage after a failed transvaginal cerclage: a systematic review. *Am J Obstet Gynecol* 2002;187:868–72.

48. Al-Azemi M, Al-Qattan F, Omu A, Taher S, Al-Busiri N, Abdulaziz A. Changing trends in the obstetric indications for cervical cerclage. *J Obstet Gynaecol* 2003;23:507–11.

49. Kushnir O, Izquierdo LA, Smith JF, Blankstein J, Curet LB. Transvaginal sonographic

measurement of cervical length. Evaluation of twin pregnancies. *J Reprod Med* 1995;40:380–2.

50.   Guzman ER, Walters C, O'reilly-Green C, Kinzler WL, Waldron R, Nigam J, *et al.* Use of cervical ultrasonography in prediction of spontaneous preterm birth in twin gestations. *Am J Obstet Gynecol* 2000;183:1103–7.

51.   Yang JH, Kuhlman K, Daly S, Berghella V. Prediction of preterm birth by second trimester cervical sonography in twin pregnancies. *Ultrasound Obstet Gynecol* 2000;15:288–91.

52.   Imseis HM, Albert TA, Iams JD. Identifying twin gestations at low risk for preterm birth with a transvaginal ultrasonographic cervical measurement at 24 to 26 weeks' gestation. *Am J Obstet Gynecol* 1997;177:1149–55.

53.   Skentou C, Souka AP, To MS, Liao AW, Nicolaides KH. Prediction of preterm delivery in twins by cervical assessment at 23 weeks. *Ultrasound Obstet Gynecol* 2001;17:7–10.

54.   Souka AP, Heath V, Flint S, Sevastopoulou I, Nicolaides KH. Cervical length at 23 weeks in twins in predicting spontaneous preterm delivery. *Ultrasound Obstet Gynecol* 1999;94:450–4.

55.   Guzman ER, Walters C, O'reilly-Green C, Meirowitz NB, Gipson K, Nigam J, *et al.* Use of cervical ultrasonography in prediction of spontaneous preterm birth in triplet gestations. *Am J Obstet Gynecol* 2000;183:1108–13.

56.   To MS, Skentou C, Cicero S, Liao AW, Nicolaides KH. Cervical length at 23 weeks in triplets: prediction of spontaneous preterm delivery. *Ultrasound Obstet Gynecol* 2000;16:515–8.

57.   Zhang J, Johnson C, Hoffman M. Cervical cerclage in delayed interval delivery in a multifetal pregnancy: a review of seven case series. *Eur J Obstet Gynecol Reprod Biol* 2003;108:126–30.

58.   Rozenberg P, Senat MV, Gillet A, Ville Y. Comparison of two methods of cervical cerclage by ultrasound cervical measurement. *J Matern Fetal Neonatal Med* 2003;13:314–7.

59.   Perrotin F, Marret H, Ayeva-Derman M, Alonso AM, Lansac J, Body G. Second trimester cerclage of short cervixes: which technique to use? A retrospective study of 25 cases. *J Gynecol Obstet Biol Reprod (Paris)* 2002;31:640–8.

60.   Harger JH. Comparison of the success and morbidity in cervical cerclage procedures. *Obstet Gynecol* 1980;36:543–8.

61.   Blair O, Fletcher H, Kulkarni S. A randomised controlled trial of outpatient versus inpatient cervical cerclage. *J Obstet Gynecol* 2002;22:493–7.

62.   Abdelhak YE, Sheen JJ, Kuczynski E, Bianco A. Comparison of delayed absorbable suture v nonabsorbable suture for treatment of incompetent cervix. *J Perinat Med* 1999;27:250–2.

63.   Jongen VH, van Roosmalen J. Complications of cervical cerclage in rural areas. *Int J Gynaecol Obstet* 1997;57:23–6.

64.   Krebs-Jimenez J, Neubert AG. The microbiological effects of endovaginal sonographic assessment of cervical length. *J Ultrasound Med* 2002;21:727–9.

65.   Ludmir J, Bader T, Chen L, Lindenbaum C, Wong G. Poor perinatal outcome associated with retained cerclage in patients with premature rupture of membranes. *Obstet Gynecol* 1994;84:823–6.

66.   McElrath TF, Norwitz ER, Lieberman ES, Heffner LJ. Management of cervical cerclage and preterm premature rupture of the membranes: should the stitch be removed? *Am J Obstet Gynecol* 2000;183:840–6.

67.   McElrath TF, Norwitz ER, Lieberman ES, Heffner LJ. Perinatal outcome after preterm premature rupture of membranes with *in situ* cervical cerclage. *Am J Obstet Gynecol* 2002;187:1147–52.

68.   Jenkins TM, Berghella V, Shlossman PA, McIntyre CJ, Maas BD, Pollock MA, *et al.* Timing of cerclage removal after preterm premature rupture of membranes: maternal and neonatal outcomes. *Am J Obstet Gynecol* 2000;183:847–52.

69.   Drakeley AJ, Quenby S, Farquharson RG. Mid-trimester loss-appraisal of a screening protocol. *Hum Reprod* 1998;13:1975–80.

Chapter 11

Screening and diagnosis I

Discussion

Thornton: I was just trying to tie up the link between myometrial contractility, changes in the cervix and prostanoid receptors in the cervix. Dr Nathanielsz's presentation yesterday talked about prostanoid receptors throughout the uterus in non-human primates. What about prostanoid receptors in the cervix? Is there a link between some of the changes that Dr Norman and others described earlier with differential expression of the prostanoid receptors?

Nathanielsz: Gordon Smith, when he was with us, did a fairly extensive regional study of distribution of prostanoid receptors using Northern analysis. We came to the conclusion that the major cervical prostanoid receptor was EP2. We are now doing a much more extensive analysis, admittedly in the sheep, and we will also study the baboon. We will look at message, which is always a good starting point but is never really enough, and look also at protein. It is very interesting and I was going to bring up this point in relation to Dr Norman's talk. If cervical dilatation is an inflammatory condition perhaps we ought to think of it as a vascular condition because one of the things that has really surprised us in the sheep is the density of prostaglandin receptors on the endothelium of the blood vessels. Perhaps we need to develop some functional measurements of permeability in the vessels and look at prostaglandins. Certainly as far as the sheep is concerned every single prostaglandin receptor is present in the cervix and vascular endothelium, vascular smooth muscle, stromal cells and the myometrial cells. They are on every single tissue type which is a bit disappointing in a way because you're looking for specificity but it does perhaps open up some opportunities.

Critchley: Are you now bringing into the discussion vascular mediators and changes in permeability? I appreciate that the prostaglandins influence permeability but vascular permeability factor is also known as vascular endothelial growth factor and nobody has yet mentioned VEGF. I wonder if there are data in the cervix on VEGF and again where the receptors are because most of the time they are endothelial.

Nathanielsz: I can't think of any data on VEGF in the cervix.

Critchley: Prostaglandins are obviously major mediators of permeability change but so too is VEGF and, depending on the steroid environment, you will get changes in expression of the receptors for VEGF and also the cell type in which VEGF is expressed, either at the message or at the protein level.

Nathanielsz: I don't think it's been looked at but it's certainly worth doing.

Romero: At the last Society for Gynecologic Investigation meeting there was an abstract reporting that VEGF applied to the cervix was able to induce dramatic cervical ripening.

Calder: I think there is a problem about this though. I think almost everything you apply to the cervix will induce ripening.

Romero: There was a control group.

Calder: What was being applied to the control group?

Romero: I don't remember.

Bennett: Both Dr Norman and Professor Calder were quite pessimistic about the possibility of influencing cervical ripening because of the multiplicity of different factors that are involved. I could not help noticing that pretty much everything on that slide is potentially regulated by nuclear factor kappa B (NFκB). Actually, I feel quite optimistic, that particularly in terms of modulating cervical function, we might be able to get somewhere with strategies that are aimed at inhibition of NFκB. I was also quite pleased that Professor Calder made the point that the tissue in the lower segment of the uterus might well be more like the cervix than the myometrium. We have been doing studies on fibroblasts taken from the lower segment as a model for the cervix and one of the things that quite powerfully inhibits NFκB in lower segment fibroblasts and also in the amnion, which then has a knock-on affect on cyclooxygenase-2 (COX2), is progesterone. In the context of the effect of stretch in amnion cells, it turns out that, unlike in the myometrium, stretch very powerfully activates NFκB and leads to increased NFκB DNA binding. Is the difference between those women with a short cervix and no visible fetal membranes and those with a short cervix where you can see the membranes perhaps that the membranes are actually prolapsing down into the cervix where they are being stretched? Thus NFκB is being turned on and there is thus going to be increased production of prostaglandins, cytokines and so on. My final comment then is that perhaps one of the things that cervical cerclage might do is not, as we think classically, to support some sort of failing weak cervix that is not functioning because it is damaged or because its congenitally weak, but that the purpose of a possible rescue treatment is to support the top of the cervix and prevent fetal membrane prolapse and reduce the mechanical stresses and therefore switch off activated NFκB and lead to resolution.

Steer: I would like to follow on from what Professor Bennett has just said and try to bring together some of the things all the speakers have said. One of the important messages that I think we need to highlight is, as you pointed out, that the cervix is not just a mechanical structure; it has a very wide variety of functions. If we look at it as cervical dysfunction rather than cervical incompetence then we might make slightly more progress. One of the issues that has also been highlighted by Dr Norman is the importance of the immunological response of the cervix and indeed the function of the cervical mucus. I think, again referring to Professor Nicolaides's data, that what we have seen is that there is a progressive change in the cervix and he has done fantastic work showing when that becomes irreversible. I think we should also be cautious about trying to shut the stable door after the horse has bolted and put in rescue sutures and so on. Most of the evidence currently suggests this is not effective. Neither would you necessarily expect it to be once the ripening is well under way.

We have thus been looking at a slightly different concept that brings in all those factors, and it originated in a woman in whom I put in a high Shirodkar suture. She refused a transabdominal cerclage, and had a very bad history with three or four previous midtrimester losses. We put in a high Shirodkar suture and then she presented at 26 weeks of gestation with prolapse of membranes. I know from experience before that when trying to put in repeat sutures it is difficult to get the cervix closed enough to prevent them prolapsing again. In this case, I simply pushed them back and then occluded the external os with multiple sutures of fine prolene, much as Saling[1] did in the 1960s by cutting off the end of the cervix and allowing it to heal over completely. This is a problem for future pregnancies, which is why we do not do that. In our case, the woman then progressed to 38 weeks and when we took the suture out suddenly this great mucus plug came out. It occurred to us that what we had allowed to happen was for the mucus plug to reform.

Since then we have done 53 of these combined sutures in women, some of whom have had 14 previous midtrimester losses and many of whom have almost anatomically absent cervix. We have had three losses only, all due to factors independent of preterm labour. The key is to put one stitch high and one low, to allow the cervix to recreate a proper internal environment that then acts as the appropriate barrier to infection. We have actually reached the situation where we warn these women when we take the sutures out at 37 to 38 weeks not to expect to go into labour. One of the problems is that these women often, as we have already heard anecdotally, do not go into labour.

In summary I would firstly like to suggest that we talk about cervical dysfunction rather than cervical incompetence. Secondly, we should look at it in a functional way and any surgical intervention should be prompt, with the objective being to prevent rather than reverse the ripening process. Thirdly, we should think about trying to recreate a more physiological function of the cervix perhaps by using this double-suture technique.

Shennan: I agree with the philosophy of having to move away from cervical incompetence but I am not sure cervical dysfunction is an all-encompassing term. Maybe the term that has been coined in the literature now of 'premature cervical shortening' captures all dysfunction and other causes of cervical change and takes away the emphasis from a disease entity of incompetence, which I think is a good thing.

Steer: But I think shortening does not necessarily incorporate the message because some of these cervices, as you pointed out, may not be too short but the internal os is often too wide. Those of us who do a lot of this type of surgery see that.

Romero: A number of years ago, we did a simple experiment which consisted of placing a mucus plug on an agar plate with bacteria.[2] The cervical mucus had strong antimicrobial properties. Subsequently, a group from Denmark was able to systematically demonstrate this biological effect and identify a number of antimicrobial peptides in cervical mucus including defensins.[3,4] Therefore, I think that the concept that the cervical mucus plug can prevent ascending infection is an important one and Professor Steer has made an interesting suggestion that part of the benefit of a cervical cerclage may derive from favouring the presence and maintenance of a cervical mucus plug.

On a different subject, I have one comment and a question for Professor Shennan. The cervix is fundamentally an extracellular matrix organ with high collagen turnover.

It is possible that a cerclage may work in some selected patients by providing support for the structure of the cervix to reconstitute itself, such as a cast would support the healing of a fractured bone, another extracellular matrix structure. My question is whether you have any data to suggest that cervical length after the placement of a cerclage has any prognostic value.

Shennan: Yes it does. We scan people longitudinally after cervical cerclage, really as a data-gathering exercise. When analysed, the total length of the cervix was not predictive of outcome but the length closed above the suture was predictive of outcome. If the cervix is closed 10 mm above the suture, this has a significantly improved prognosis. To me, this implies a remodelling and a reversal of some process. Should the membranes continue through or down to the suture, then this implies a progressive process. Delivery often occurs within a few weeks. We have published our data on this and find it very useful when counselling women.[5]

López Bernal: I wanted to say again how useful this session has been because everything that has been discussed is so clinically relevant. I have a question about the idea that leucocyte and macrophage activation in the cervix is involved in the process of ripening. How can you explain reversibility and remodelling through an inflammatory process. Presumably, if the leucocytes enter the cervix, that is a terminal process, so how would that fit into this process of changes throughout pregnancy if the cervix was opening and closing with contractions? Is that a mechanism that only applies at term during the real onset of labour or are the leucocytes involved in earlier stages?

Norman: We have really shown a change in leucocyte density from term women not in labour to mid-labour. We have not shown a difference from term to the early pregnant stage. There are a couple of other reports in the literature about leucocyte density and they say there is increased leucocyte density from early pregnancy to term. When you actually go and look at the data you would not come to that conclusion as there are no statistics to show a difference. So certainly in our hands the change in leucocytes are from before to during labour. I think the cervix is still remodelling at that stage but you may be right that it is an irreversible process and that is what I meant when I was saying that I think part of this process is a reversible one. If we want to prevent it, we need to try to prevent it at the very early stage because by the time you have got leucocyte invasion I do not think that it is going to be reversed.

Critchley: Dr Norman, you showed in your final diagram the potential for several feed forward loops. Various components produce mediators that recruit leucocytes and then these leucocytes secrete the same mediators. So although you could not reverse it, you may be able to halt it.

Norman: That is possible. The other problem in this analogy is that we are comparing a lot of the scientific data from the physiological process of cervical ripening in late pregnancy and labour and we are trying to use that data to explain what is happening in the pathological process of preterm cervical ripening or cervical incompetence. No one, not surprisingly, has been brave enough to take cervical tissue from women with cervical incompetence and it might be that the processes are very different.

Critchley: Well that was certainly suggested by Dr Romero yesterday when he showed those very different patterns with the gene arrays from the different groups. There may be a physiological process and there may be a disease process and that is what is happening in some women with preterm labour.

Romero: I agreed with you, Professor Critchley. There are probably two populations of patients with a short cervix: those in whom cervical ripening has occurred, and those who have a short, but unripe, cervix. The former group is probably at risk for preterm delivery, while the latter are more likely to deliver close to term. So, Dr Norman, your point is well taken.

Thornton: One way of tying up some of the clinical data is that different groups of women were admitted into the different studies. Professor Nicolaides very nicely demonstrated that if the cervix was short, this increased the risk of preterm delivery. In those studies where a short cervix followed by a suture has been beneficial it is likely that those women have, possibly due to their history, had an underlying problem with the cervix. Professor Nicolaides also showed us that if a short cervix is treated in the absence of cervical pathology, then a stitch is not very helpful. So, we are probably looking at two different populations in the different studies, those with and those without intrinsic cervical pathology. Also, it may be that Professor Nicolaides's group with a short cervix (which were not helped by a stitch) may be improved by other methods such as progesterone. So my question is: you nicely justified why you had done cervical length at 23 weeks of gestation but do you have cervical length data for earlier in pregnancy to see if it predicts patients more likely to be helped by other prophylaxis such as progesterone?

Nicolaides: You summarised the two types of studies well. The argument is centring around whether on the basis of the history alone you introduce an elective cerclage at 12 weeks immediately, after the nuchal scan to at least confirm that the fetus looks normal, or whether you follow such patients and only insert a stitch when the cervix becomes shorter than 25 mm. The argument is that with the latter management you will only be required to put in a stitch roughly in half of the women that you would otherwise have stitched if you had a policy of elective cerclage for everybody. The evidence is inconclusive as to which is the best management. On the issue of the interrelation between short cervix and infection, we know from pregnancies with PPROM that those with infection will deliver within the next three to five days. You do not really catch an infection several weeks later unless introduced by our clinical management. So an inflammatory process as I understood it in medicine resolves itself in the next three to five days. I cannot imagine that you have an inflammatory process starting several weeks before 23 weeks resulting in a short cervix at 23 weeks and about 5% of these go on to deliver in the next two months. The work of Professor Shennan suggests that in women with a short cervix and visible membranes there may be a process of irreversible inflammation while in those with nonvisible membranes there is a functional shortening of the cervix. It is possible that, if you put in a stitch and a few hours later the cervix above the stitch appears to be lengthening, the cervix would have lengthened in any case. What had made it short at the time that you measured it was a functional event at that time and a few hours later it may have lengthened. Therefore, visualisation of the membranes in women with a short cervix may actually be a test distinguishing between the 95% that will not deliver and the 5% that will deliver irrespective of what we do.

Calder: I would like to pick up on the point of this dynamic situation where if you scan at one point it looks one way and then later on it changes. We have tended to assume that the thing that really matters in the cervix is the collagen and clearly it is of fundamental importance but I think we should not lose sight of the fact that there is elastic tissue and muscle in the cervix which must be there for some purpose. Some of the dynamic changes we are seeing are probably the result of the activities of those tissues.

Norman: It was just to disagree with you, inflammation is not always an acute process. I think there are good examples of many diseases that are chronic – inflammatory arthritis or some of the rheumatoid arthritis conditions, systemic lupus erythematosus (SLE) for instance. The other thing is I think there are data, correct me if I am wrong, looking at the amniotic fluid showing that you can have elevated interleukin-6 (IL-6) in amniotic fluid many weeks before preterm delivery and that elevated IL-6 is predictive of preterm delivery. So I think there is evidence that inflammatory processes or things we would associate with inflammation can take a more chronic time course.

Nicolaides: Could I ask a question about the so-called chronic inflammatory diseases? Do you have an acute process continuing chronically or do you have repeated acute episodes followed by remission? Do you have a constant acute inflammation for many years? Is that not what chronic means?

Sebire: The answer to your question is that you very, very rarely have an acute inflammatory process that continues for a long time. The two processes of acute and chronic inflammation are often quite different and one of the issues that is becoming increasingly clear is that actually almost every disease now involves an inflammatory component, in that interleukins or matrix metalloproteinases, etc., have been identified. We need to be quite clear when we are talking about 'inflammation' that here we may be talking about different pathological processes.

Shennan: I think Professor Nicolaides has made a very important point in response to Professor Thornton's question which is we have to distinguish between pathology and what could be physiology. I think it would be wrong to extrapolate the large surveys which pick up the short cervix and look at intervention to what is a much more practical issue, which is identifying these women in the context of a high-risk prematurity clinic. Like it or not, this is a common practice now people out there in many hospitals are scanning and putting in stitches when the cervix is short. The value is we are going to remove unnecessary elective stitches and one has to do the studies to show what that does in comparison to current practice. I think we should not say we should not be doing elective cerclage based on the work that has been suggested by Professors Steer and Nicolaides. We have to move forward and look at what is going on in clinical practice and answer a different question in the high-risk setting.

Critchley: We might come back to that but I think Dr Romero wanted to add a comment in the context of the pathology, physiology, inflammation term that is being used.

Romero: I think that inflammation can occur in a physiological or pathological context. For example, some degree of inflammation is important in some physiological reproductive processes such as ovulation, implantation and parturition at term. But overt inflammation, pathological inflammation, has been implicated in the mechanism of preterm parturition in the presence of infection.

Some inflammatory mediators, such as proinflammatory cytokines, were discovered when studying macrophage biology in response to microbial products. Subsequently, the production of these proinflammatory cytokines has been demonstrated in other cells and in other pathological processes such as atherosclerosis and neoplasia (i.e. tumours). Professor Calder raised the issues appropriately during his talk. When is inflammation part of physiology and when is it part of pathology? Perhaps we can consider that inflammatory mediators and inflammatory cells are part of homeostasis, and as such they participate in physiological responses. However, an intense and sustained physiological response can lead to disease and this would represent pathological inflammation. The spectrum of inflammation is broad even in the same tissue. For example, physiological inflammation can be present in the chorioamniotic membranes during normal parturition at term and pathological inflammation in the same tissue in preterm labour associated with infection. The infiltration of inflammatory cells in a tissue in which they are not considered a normal constituent would suggest 'pathological inflammation' (e.g. inflammation of the umbilical cord).

Another issue is the difference between acute and chronic inflammation, which was raised by Professor Nicolaides. The cellular infiltrate is key to diagnosing acute or chronic inflammation in many organs such as the lung. However, the situation in the amniotic cavity may be different from that of other tissues. Specifically, infection elicits an inflammatory response with infiltration of neutrophils and proinflammatory cytokines and chemokines. However, although these infections may persist for weeks and thus be 'chronic' in nature, the inflammatory cells and even cytokine profile resembles that of an acute infection both in the membranes and in the amniotic fluid.

Smith: Just a slightly different view perhaps on what has been going on. We have been working with one of our professors of engineering and discussing human parturition from an engineering perspective. David Smith has proposed to me that we should be thinking of the process of human pregnancy as a multi-dimensional trajectory eventually leading to a surface in multi-dimensional space and when you hit that surface that is when you deliver. We have changes going on in the cervix, changes going on in the fetus, changes going on in the myometrium and these were all following a certain pathway to eventually hit a critical surface that leads to delivery. In relation to perhaps Dr Nathanielsz's discussions going in and out of labour of the primate model as it approaches so you can imagine a trajectory that is oscillating towards a critical event and other factors too may determine when the critical event actually occurs from the levels of the hormones changing to structural events in the cervix. To me most of these things are reversible until they all combine together to be so powerful that they are insuperable and delivery occurs. So, I am as optimistic as Professor Bennett is that we will be able to change these trajectories and move the critical surface away when we understand more of the physiology and we can change more of the different factors that are impinging on the process.

Lamont: We have talked a lot about infection but we have not actually mentioned anything about antibiotics. A while ago I was very reluctant and resistant to cervical cerclage. I am now less reluctant to use cervical cerclage, for a number of reasons. I can sterilise the vagina and give a three day course of intravaginal antibiotics before I put a stitch in. No one has mentioned that today and I also give the patients a seven day course of systemic antibiotics afterwards to prevent any ascending infection. Very early in pregnancy there may already be abnormal colonisation in the vagina by the time you put the stitch in which may explain why the stitch is successful in some cases but not in others. It is not the stitch, it is the question of whether or not there is already some infection. So I think that if we are going to talk about doing any studies on cervical cerclage, we talked about this in 1985 at the last study group and then it was thought to be impossible, I think if there are going to be any studies that need to be done they need to be small and focused, not huge multicentre studies, and it would be very difficult particularly bearing in mind the variables there because I think antibiotics has to be a consideration so you have then got cervical cerclage and antibiotics and I think also we should be looking at prophylactic-tocolytics, be it progesterone or other interventions. There are three variables: cervical cerclage, antibiotics and prophylactic-tocolytics. I think we can exclude bed rest. That is going to make any trial all the more difficult with these variables for what is thankfully a very rare condition at the present time. And another point I wanted to make about emergency cerclage is that in the UK we are very reluctant to do amniocentesis under those circumstances whereas it is commonplace in many centres in the USA. There is certainly good evidence that if you are going to insert an emergency cervical cerclage, amniocentesis would be helpful to differentiate those in whom it might work or those in whom it might not work. Certainly if there is evidence of infection there the chances of that rescue suture working are greatly reduced. You can get quite rapid results from amniocentesis. Very soon there may be side room tests for interleukins but even just a Gram stain or a white cell count or even a glucose concentration.

Nielson: To address some clinical issues it is important to have very substantial numbers. That is a large part of the rationale for meta-analyses as part of systematic reviewing: to increase the power of your conclusions. I think what you are addressing is the difference between failure to demonstrate an effect and demonstration of no effect. If the trial were bigger that might be demonstrable so I think you need to take that range of uncertainty into account. I think that the meta-analysis of cervical cerclage requires individual patient data meta-analysis and I think Professor Shennan made that point pretty clear that this is a technique that is quite person-intensive and expensive but has been used a lot in cancer and cardiovascular fields but has not really been used in the perinatal field. It does allow a much more sophisticated investigation of the effects of an intervention in specific sub-groups and I think that is very important. I think the MRC trial was very important because it stopped obstetricians putting stitches into women who were inappropriate for cervical cerclage, for example, women who had had a couple of previous anembryonic pregnancies. Historically I think it was a very important study but I agree entirely with Professor Shennan that we need to move on from that.

Morrison: Just a clinical question for Professor Shennan in relation to his high-risk prematurity clinic and a question for which there is no evidence base. I am sure that there is a group of women who have had one previous preterm delivery and for whom you do not obviously give a stitch but in whom you would keep a regular intermittent monitoring on cervical length. Suddenly at 26 weeks of gestation there is a cervical length of 10 mm and the question is, basically, do you entertain later stitches than would be traditionally used?

Shennan: Up until recently we have as a data-collecting exercise had the policy of not putting in elective sutures although some women have them because there is no other way to manage them because of their and their clinician's wishes. We longitudinally scan all risk cases so with one previous 36 week delivery they would have longitudinal scanning and if the cervix went very short we have put in a stitch and our policy is to put it in a bit sooner or when it is not so short following our evidence of the visible fetal membranes. The thing is all this is very un-evidenced-based and we are now doing a clinical trial and we are no longer offering longitudinal scanning and sutures outside the randomised controlled trial. That is my brief: to try to convince other people who are doing that to follow suit because I think they should only do it in the context of a trial because there is no evidence, and the NICE guidelines concur. There is no evidence that inserting a suture on the basis of cervical length is appropriate and yet the only alternative is to fall back to old practice, which I think is equally uncertain, so the logical thing is to do a trial of old versus new, at least to get some answers.

Calder: I want to make an observation which I think is very important for clinical staff. You have heard very interesting data about visible membranes at the cervix but I think we often encounter the situation where it looks as if the cervix is very dilated when it is not because the membranes have actually prolapsed right down into the vagina in a sort of hour glass arrangement. The rescue suture data from Miles Novy's experience to me seems to be the most impressive, albeit it is not randomised: he has put in rescue sutures to women with really pretty hopeless looking situations. In some of his cases he has done an amniocentesis not simply to look for infection but to reduce the liquor and allow the membranes to go back through and into the cervix. He also bombarded them with every conceivable pharmacological agent following that but got very good results with many women going on to term or post-term.

Critchley: I think that Mr Lamont raised a number of quite interesting points. Obviously there is an issue about the type of suture and Professor Steer has suggested a dual approach to try and retain the mucus plug for its potential antibacterial properties. Dr Lamont then addressed the role for antibiotics.

Romero: To answer your question, we did a study looking at patients with cervical dilatation and no contractions before 24 weeks of gestation. We did an amniocentesis before taking the patients to the operating room and the amniotic fluid cultures were positive in 50% women at less than 24 weeks of gestation and 2 cm dilation. The women who had a cervical cerclage (because the Gram stain was negative) all developed clinical chorioamnionitis, bleeding or ruptured their membranes.

Steer: I would support the view that all this scanning followed by rescue cerclages is becoming an epidemic, and I am not convinced that there is any very good basis for it. I am concerned that there is a lot of over-intervention. I think that if one good recommendation could come out of this study group it should be that it is almost unethical to be just scanning people at random and then putting stitches in when they have a short cervix. It is causing a huge amount of concern and anxiety and upset. I think we should say that it should only be done in the context of a trial. The next point about trials is that we see many women who come from abroad, who have had dozens of midtrimester miscarriages, who would never accept to be in a randomised trial because they want treatment. One of the difficulties with women with strong indications for cerclage is that it is very difficult for us not to put a suture in, especially when we are quoting success rates of in excess of 90%. I'd like to suggest one particular group, however, which could be looked at quite easily, and that is women who get preterm prelabour rupture of the membranes (PPROM) without any evidence of obvious cervical change at that point. PPROM is relatively common. We know from historical studies that the recurrence rate is likely to be about 20% in a successive pregnancy so they are quite a high-risk group. At the present time I am not aware that anyone is doing anything very active about prevention in subsequent pregnancies. Now if our hypothesis about the importance of ascending infection, the mucus plug etc., is valid then simply putting in an occlusion suture (which is just a fine prolene suture to close the external os and retain the mucus plug) is likely to be effective. The hypothesis is that that it will reduce the recurrence rate of ruptured membranes by about 50% and that would only require 200 women in each group for an adequately powered prospective randomised trial. I think such a trial is possible, firstly because PPROM is relatively common, secondly because we currently do not do anything to prevent recurrence, and thirdly because the intervention is relatively simple with few if any significant complications.

References

1.   Saling E. Early total occlusion of os uteri prevent habitual abortion and premature deliveries. [German]. *Z Geburtshilfe Perinatol* 1981;185:259–61.

2.   Romero, R, Gomez, R, Araneda, H, Ramirez, M, Cotton, DB. Cervical mucus inhibits microbial growth: a host defense mechanism to prevent ascending infection in pregnant and non-pregnant women [abstract]. *Am J Obstet Gynecol* 1993;168:312.

3.   Hein M, Valore EV, Helmig RB, Uldbjerg N, Ganz T. Antimicrobial factors in the cervical mucus plug. *Am J Obstet Gynecol* 2002;187:137–44.

4.   Hein M, Helmig RB, Schonheyder HC, Ganz T, Uldbjerg N. An in vitro study of antibacterial properties of the cervical mucus plug in pregnancy. *Am J Obstet Gynecol* 2001;185:586–92.

5.   Groom KM. Shennan AH, Bennett PR. Ultrasound-indicated cervical cerclage: outcome depends on preoperative cervical length and presence of visible membranes at time of cerclage. *Am J Obstet Gynecol* 2002;187:445–9.

SECTION 3

SCREENING AND DIAGNOSIS II

Chapter 12

Bacterial vaginosis

Ronald F Lamont

Introduction

Bacterial vaginosis (BV) is a polymicrobial condition of unknown aetiology which is increasingly associated with adverse sequelae in both obstetrics and gynaecology. While many women remain asymptomatic, BV is a clinical syndrome associated with characteristic pathophysiological changes in the microbiology and biochemistry of the delicate vaginal micro-ecosystem. BV is difficult to treat, frequently recurs and is a co-factor for sexually transmitted infections (STI) and acquisition of HIV in women. When diagnosed early in pregnancy, BV is associated with a 5- to 7.5-fold increased risk of preterm prelabour rupture of the membranes (PPROM), spontaneous preterm labour (SPTL) and preterm birth (PTB). Treatment of high-risk women[1] or early treatment of low-risk women[2,3] in pregnancy is associated with a statistically significant reduction in the incidence of PTB.

History and nomenclature

In 1892, Albert Döderlein considered vaginal flora to be homogeneous, and composed mainly of Gram-positive rods (*Lactobacillus* spp.). Between that time and 1954, any abnormal vaginal discharge not due to pathogens such as *Chlamydia trachomatis* or *Neisseria gonorrhoeae* was known as nonspecific vaginitis. In 1954, Gardner and Dukes[4] isolated a new organism thought to be the cause of nonspecific vaginitis. Initially, this was thought to be of the genus *Haemophilus* then the genus *Corynebacterium*. Further identification revealed this to be a new genus renamed *Gardnerella vaginalis* in recognition of the role of Gardner's research in the field and the condition became known as *Gardnerella* vaginitis. Unfortunately, *Gardnerella vaginalis* can be isolated from up to 50% of women without signs or symptoms of vaginitis, indicating that many organisms other than *Gardnerella vaginalis* are also associated with the condition.[5] In the early 1980s, the importance of anaerobes became apparent (anaerobic vaginosis),[6] and the term bacterial vaginosis was adopted to reflect the polymicrobial nature of the condition with characteristic clinical findings, microbiology and biochemistry but lacking any cellular inflammatory response;[7] hence vaginosis rather than vaginitis.

Prevalence

BV is the most common cause of vaginal discharge in the developed world and, in young women of reproductive age, accounts for 10 million clinic visits annually in the USA.[8] The incidence of BV varies according to the population studied and the range is shown in Table 12.1. In pregnancy, BV was detected in 15% of unselected women in an antenatal clinic in a middle-class area of London.[9] In contrast, BV was detected in 33% of women from an inner-city area of Denver, Colorado, USA.[10]

Associated factors

A number of factors have been associated with the change from a *Lactobacillus* spp. dominated flora to BV-associated flora and these have been reviewed elsewhere.[11] Age at first sexual intercourse, change in sexual partner, greater number of lifetime sexual partners and concurrent STI have all been associated with BV. Cigarette smoking, intrauterine contraceptive device (IUCD) usage and vaginal douching are also linked to an increased risk of acquiring BV. There is also a racial disparity in the development of BV: it is more common in Afro-Caribbean compared with white women. After adjusting for confounding variables, in the third trimester of pregnancy black women were 2.6 times more likely to have BV than their white counterparts. Each BV-related organism was also found more frequently in black compared with white women.[12]

BV has also been linked to lesbian activity,[13–15] with a prevalence greater than 50% in a group of lesbians attending a genitourinary medicine clinic. This figure appeared to be related to the lifetime number of female sexual partners rather than frequency of sexual activity. The higher prevalence found in the lesbian compared with the heterosexual population raises the possibility of sexual transmission between women due to oral sex.

Aetiology

The aetiology of BV remains unclear.

Sexual transmission

Notwithstanding the evidence pertaining to lesbians, there is some evidence that BV behaves like an STI.[16] Evidence against such a cause is the fact that there is no difference in the incidence of BV between virginal and nonvirginal adolescent girls.[8] In addition, there is no evidence of any benefit of treating male partners.[17–19]

Phage viruses

Bacteriophages are viruses that infect or parasitise bacteria. They may remain dormant by parasitising the bacteria and affecting their function but they also have the potential to be transmissible by destroying 99% of the lactobacilli and releasing more bacteriophages to infect/parasitise other lactobacilli. In this way, they are noxious agents of *Lactobacillus* spp. causing dysfunction and depletion. *Lactobacillus* spp. phage viruses are known to the food industry, being found in meat processing factories and affecting yoghurt culture in dairy products. In meat processing, *Lactobacillus* spp. starter culture delays acid production, reduces *Lactobacillus* spp. numbers and slows down ripening. With respect to vaginal lactobacilli, decreased acid production and numbers of *Lactobacillus* spp. may lead to an overgrowth of anaerobes and other BV-related organisms. Phage viruses have now been isolated from human lactobacilli

Table 12.1. Incidence of bacterial vaginosis (BV) in different populations

Study	Year	Country	Population Studied	Incidence of BV
Eschenbach et al.[7]	1988	USA	Asymptomatic college students	4%
Lamont et al.[111]	2000	UK	Women attending GP for routine cervical cytology	9%
Hay et al.[44]	1992	UK	General gynaecological clinic	11%
Bump and Buesching[112]	1988	USA	Virginal post-menarchial girls	12%
Hay et al.[9]	1994	UK	General antenatal clinic	15%
Eschenbach et al.[7]	1988	USA	Symptomatic college students	16%
Ralph et al.[68]	1999	UK	*In vitro* fertilisation clinic	25%
Blackwell et al.[113]	1993	UK	Termination of pregnancy clinic	28%
McGregor et al.[10]	1995	USA	Inner-city pregnant women	33%
Paxton et al.[114]	1995	Uganda	Rural population	51%
Embree et al.[115]	1984	USA	Sexually transmitted infections clinic	64%

found in the vagina and the gut and from lactobacilli in yoghurt. Phages from vaginal lactobacilli have the potential to infect the vaginal lactobacilli of other women.[20] Phage viruses from yoghurt have been shown to inhibit vaginal lactobacilli.[21] In an analysis of products containing *Lactobacillus* spp. strains, 43 different types of *Lactobacillus* spp. were detected, from 11 of which phages were isolated and seven of these phages were found to inhibit vaginal lactobacilli.[21]

Endocrine changes

In women with recurrent BV, the symptoms are frequently cyclical.[22] When a relationship between the menstrual cycle and BV can be demonstrated, changes in microbial flora occur more often during the follicular phase of the cycle when oestrogen concentration is relatively high compared with progesterone. Relative oestrogen dominance favours candida colonisation/infection of the vagina.[23,24] Whether due to absolute hormone levels or the oestrogen/progesterone concentration ratio, this change in endocrine status may influence the development of BV.[25] In the rodent model, administration of oestrogen increases susceptibility to infection by *Mycoplasma hominis*[26,27] and *Neisseria gonorrhoeae*[28] to which mice are not normally susceptible and during which time there is a large increase in the number of organisms in the genital tract.[29] This change is accompanied by the appearance of vaginal epithelial cells with many adherent coccobacilli described as clue cells. The prevalence of BV decreases as pregnancy progresses yet the concentration of oestrogen remains elevated throughout. However, the oestrogen/progesterone ratio alters as pregnancy progresses suggesting that a relative excess of progesterone may inhibit the development of BV.

Enzymes

Mucinase and sialidase concentrations in vaginal secretions are significantly elevated in women with BV compared with those with *Lactobacillus* spp. dominated flora. It is possible that the presence of these enzymes facilitates the entry of pathogens by promoting breakdown of the mucosal barrier.[30]

Pathophysiology

The aetiology of BV remains unclear, but the condition is polymicrobial with no single organism responsible. However, the condition is associated with characteristic symptomatological abnormalities and changes in the microbiology and biochemistry of the vaginal ecosystem.

Microbiology

Normal vaginal flora is dominated by *Lactobacillus* spp. which, by producing lactic acid from glycogen in vaginal secretions, render the pH of the vagina acid at less than 4.5. At this low pH, the adherence of bacteria to the vaginal epithelium is reduced and the growth of other organisms such as *G. vaginalis* and anaerobes is suppressed[31] so that normal vaginal secretions contain 10^8 organisms per millilitre[32] with a ratio of anaerobes to aerobes between 2 to 1 and 5 to 1. At low pH, lactobacilli produce compounds such as lactacin B,[33] acidolin[34] and hydrogen peroxide,[35] which are toxic to bacteria. In BV, the quantity and quality of lactobacilli is poor so that the pH of the vagina drifts upwards, resulting in a 1000-fold increase in the number of organisms per millilitre and an anaerobe to aerobe ratio of between 100 to 1 and 1000 to 1.[36]

There are many important facultative organisms such as *Escherichia coli* and Group B haemolytic streptococcus (GBS) or anaerobic organisms such as *Peptostreptococcus* spp. and *Bacteroides* spp. which can be found in the vagina of healthy women. The same bacteria are found in women with BV although in much higher numbers and ratios. It is thus not possible to identify any single species as the cause of BV. Synergism also exists, whereby a mixed colonisation of aerobes and anaerobes potentiate the growth and virulence of the others. In low numbers, *G. vaginalis* can be isolated from the vagina of 30% of women without BV[37] and *Mobiluncus* spp. can also be isolated from women without BV.[38] While these organisms are undoubtedly associated with BV, the routine culture of *Mobiluncus* spp. or *G. vaginalis* for the diagnosis of BV is not recommended. *Bacteroides* spp. in large numbers are commonly found in association with BV and between 60 and 75% of women with BV will be colonised by *M. hominis*.

Biochemistry

Mobiluncus spp. and *Bacteroides* spp. produce succinate as a major biochemical metabolite. At a pH of 5.5, succinate blunts the chemotactic response of polymorphonuclear leucocytes and also their killing ability. This may be why, despite large numbers of potentially pathogenic bacteria, there is no cellular inflammatory response (hence vaginosis not vaginitis) albeit that there may be a chemical inflammatory response mediated through cytokines (*vide infra*). This is an excellent way for a condition to establish itself within the host organism by rendering itself undetected. At a higher pH caused by conditions such as bleeding, vaginal douching or sexual intercourse, lactobacilli lose their ability to produce hydrogen peroxide, which increases the numbers of organisms 1000-fold.

Gas–liquid chromatography of normal vaginal secretions shows a preponderance of lactic acid produced by lactobacilli. In BV, owing to decreased numbers of lactobacilli, lactate levels are low but there is a corresponding increase in the concentration of other keto-acids produced by those organisms associated with BV such as *Bacteroides* spp. (succinate), *G. vaginalis* (acetate) and *Peptostreptococcus* spp. (propionate and butyrate). Although a research tool, it is interesting to note that the gas–liquid chromatography profile associated with BV returns to normal after successful treatment.[5] Chen and co-workers[39] detected the presence of amines in the vaginal secretions of women with BV but not in women without a clinical diagnosis of BV. Amine production by a mixed group of BV-associated organisms was examined with and without metronidazole added to culture. Amines were only produced in the metronidazole-deficient culture, suggesting that anaerobes were mainly responsible for the production of amines. While not appearing to increase amine production, *G. vaginalis* has a symbiotic and synergistic relationship with anaerobes. By producing keto-acids, the growth of anaerobes is stimulated synergistically. By producing decarboxylases and aminopeptidases, peptides are broken down to amino acids and then to amines. At low pH these amines are stable. At high pH these amines become volatile, giving off the characteristic amine odour associated with BV.

Vaginal flora in pregnancy

During pregnancy, there is a rise in the overall numbers of vaginal flora compared with the nonpregnant state, owing mainly to a ten-fold increase in the number of lactobacilli. There is a concurrent reduction in the number of anaerobes but relatively stable numbers of aerobes. With increasing gestational age, the vaginal flora tends to become more benign, mainly owing to increased numbers of lactobacilli, such that at term the vaginal flora is dominated by organisms of low virulence which pose no threat to the fetus. Any alteration of this balance, such as BV, may result in adverse sequelae.

Culture of a high vaginal swab from women in SPTL between 26 and 34 weeks of gestation revealed 26 different organisms. In a control group of women who were not in labour but who were delivered electively at a similar gestational age between 26 and 34 weeks for fetomaternal indications, 15 different organisms were isolated.[40] This emphasises the fact that abnormal genital tract flora in pregnancy is a polymicrobial condition and selective attempts to isolate individual organisms are unhelpful unless these are pathogens. Equally, the presence or absence of an organism in qualitative cultures may not be as helpful as quantitative analysis. In women in SPTL between 26 and 34 weeks of gestation, significantly more women were colonised by *Ureaplasma urealyticum* (86%) than women in a control group delivered electively over the same gestational age range at which time nearly half (46%) were colonised ($P<0.01$). Similar numbers of women from study and control group were colonised by *M. hominis* but, when only those colonised with high numbers were considered, 18% of

Table 12.2. Suggested classification of abnormal vaginal flora in pregnancy

Classification	Type of organism	Examples
I	Pathogens	*Neisseria gonorrhoeae*
		Chlamydia trachomatis
		Trichomonas vaginalis
II	Group B haemolytic streptococcus	
II	Enteropharyngeal organisms	*Escherichia coli*
		Streptococcus faecalis
IV	BV-related organisms	*Gardnerella vaginalis*
		Mobiluncus spp.
		Mycoplasma hominis
		Ureaplasma urealyticum
		Anaerobes

the study group and 0% of the control group were colonised ($P<0.05$).[41] Owing to the deficiency of defining what is normal or abnormal genital tract flora, a simplistic classification of abnormal flora in pregnancy is proposed in Table 12.2. The significance of the presence of enteropharyngeal organisms is relative. Up to 5% of asymptomatic women, delivered electively preterm because of fetal or maternal indications, may be colonised by *E. coli*.[40] If these organisms are present alone and in small numbers with no cellular inflammatory response in an otherwise asymptomatic woman, this should probably be considered as normal flora. If, on the other hand, *E. coli* is detected in high numbers with polymorphonuclear leucocytes and other enteropharyngeal organisms or BV-related organisms in symptomatic women, then this should be considered abnormal.

Longitudinal data

In women with BV in early pregnancy, 50% of those who achieve a gestational age beyond 33 completed weeks will still have BV (16.4% will deliver before 33 completed weeks[9]). Conversely, only 2% of those without BV in early pregnancy will have the condition in late pregnancy.[42]

Diagnosis

Clinical diagnosis

Women may present with classic symptoms of an adherent homogeneous vaginal discharge which may be malodorous postcoitally or following vaginal bleeding, both circumstances in which the pH of the vagina is elevated. Unfortunately, 50% of women with BV may be asymptomatic. Pruritus and vulvovaginitis are uncommon symptoms and should lead to consideration of another cause such as candidiasis.

Composite clinical criteria

In 1983, Amsel *et al*.[43] developed a set of composite clinical criteria which for many years were the gold standard for comparison in clinical practice and research. The diagnosis of BV is made by finding three of the following four signs:

- homogeneous vaginal discharge
- an elevated vaginal pH above 4.5
- clue cells on wet preparation of vaginal secretions
- an amine odour ('positive whiff test') on addition of a 10% solution of the alkali potassium hydroxide to a sample of vaginal secretions.

The assessment of vaginal discharge is the most subjective, with poor sensitivity and specificity, but correlates better with the physician's impression of an abnormal discharge rather than the woman's own impression.[44]

A low vaginal pH virtually excludes BV. An elevated pH is the most sensitive but least specific since this can be due to menstruation, recent sexual intercourse or infection with *Trichomonas vaginalis*. As a single entity, the 'whiff test' has a positive predictive value of 90% and specificity of 70%.[45] Clue cells are desquamated vaginal epithelial cells so densely surrounded by adherent coccobacilli that their borders are indiscrete. The detection of clue cells on direct microscopy is the single most sensitive and specific criterion for BV but is operator-dependent[46] since debris and degenerated cells may be mistaken for clue cells.

Gram stain of vaginal secretions

The use of composite criteria is subjective, clumsy, unpleasant and irreproducible. As a result, a Gram stain of an air-dried smear of vaginal secretions quantified according to Nugent's criteria[47] provides a quick, simple, cheap, reproducible and objective method which corresponds with and has therefore replaced composite criteria as the gold standard measure of diagnosing BV.[48–50] This method also identifies a less florid but nevertheless abnormal vaginal flora which is genuinely intermediate in character.[51,52] The grade of Gram stain, Nugent score, and relationship with background flora is shown in Table 12.3. By examining the detailed microbiology of different grades of genital tract flora according to grade of Gram stain, a different distribution of bacterial species can be observed. The ability to isolate some organisms such as *Lactobacillus* spp. decreases linearly from 91% in Gram stain grade I to 66% in grade II and 38% in grade III. Some organisms, such as α-haemolytic streptococcus or *Corynebacterium* spp., show a linear increase in colonisation from 9 to 36 to 56% and 36 to 56 to 84% respectively. Some organisms, such as coagulase-negative *Staphylococcus* spp., were isolated from a similar number of women with Gram stain grade I (58%), grade II (78%) and grade III (74%). Some organisms, such as *G. vaginalis* and *M. hominis* and many anaerobes, were isolated rarely in grade I and grade II and were only fully manifested with high isolation rates in grade III Gram stain. In this way, it is possible, using a rapid, cheap and simple method such as Gram stain of vaginal secretions to predict the likelihood of the presence of a particular organism (Table 12.4). New and rapid tests for BV have been developed but these are used for research purposes only. These tests, such as gas–liquid chromatography, measure metabolic products from anaerobic bacteria[53] or are based on DNA gene probes, for example AFFIRM VPIII, which detects gene sequences from *G. vaginalis*.[54] Cytopathologists commonly report the presence of clue cells as an incidental finding on endocervical smears but while Pap smears are a reasonable means of diagnosing BV, they are not as accurate as a Gram stain of vaginal secretions.[55]

Table 12.3. Diagnosis of bacterial vaginosis

Grade of Gram stain	Nugent score[47]	Description of background flora	Proportion of women in NPH[a] study[12] in each group
I (normal)	1–3	Predominantly lactobacilli morphotypes	80%
II (intermediate)	4–6	Reduced lactobacilli morphotypes mixed with other bacterial morphotypes	5%
III (bacterial vaginosis)	7–10	Few or no lactobacilli morphotypes with greatly increased numbers of *G. vaginalis* and other morphotypes	15%

[a] Northwick Park Hospital, London, UK

Table 12.4. Isolation of different organisms from women with grade III flora (bacterial vaginosis) and grade I flora (normal) following Gram stain of vaginal secretions; adapted from Rosenstein et al.[51]

Organism	Grade I flora (normal) (%)	Grade III flora (bacterial vaginosis) (%)
Pathogenic organisms		
Chlamydia trachomatis	0	12
Microaerophilic flora		
Lactobacillus spp.	91	38
Gardnerella vaginalis	5	72
Aerobic flora		
Corynebacterium spp.	36	84
Coagulase-negative staphylococcus	58	7
Staphylococcus aureus	9	14
Haemolytic streptococcus	9	56
β-haemolytic streptococcus	0	4
Gram-negative rods	0	12
Candida spp.	21	14
Ureaplasma/mycoplasma		
Mycoplasma hominis	6	58
Ureaplasma urealyticum	42	68
Anaerobes		
Gram-positive cocci (e.g. Peptococcus spp. and Peptostreptococcus spp.)	15	74
Gram-negative rods (e.g. Bacteroides spp., Prevotella spp. and Fusobacterium spp.)	9	66
Bifidobacterium spp.	12	94
Other Gram-positive rods (e.g. Mobiluncus spp. and Propionibacterium spp.)	15	48

Adverse sequelae of BV in gynaecology and obstetrics

In gynaecology, BV has been associated with cervical intraepithelial neoplasia,[56,57] pelvic inflammatory disease,[58,59] infertility,[60,61] post-hysterectomy vaginal cuff infection,[62,63] post-abortal sepsis,[64–66] urethral syndrome[67] and first trimester miscarriage.[68] In obstetrics, apart from SPTL and PTB, BV has been associated with postpartum endometritis.[69,70] While the relationship between BV and SPTL and PTB will be covered in depth in this review, the reader is referred to a recent comprehensive review of BV in which these other adverse sequelae in both obstetrics and gynaecology are covered in much greater depth.[71]

BV and acquisition of HIV

BV is not an ulcerative or cellular inflammatory genital tract condition so it is difficult to postulate a mechanism for BV increasing the rate of positive sero-conversion to HIV. Nevertheless, there have been suggested mechanisms. *In vitro* data have demonstrated the ability of hydrogen peroxide-producing lactobacilli to kill HIV.[72] The authors postulated that at a lower pH the production of CD4 lymphocytes is reduced whereas at the higher pH associated with BV, HIV survival is enhanced. In a study of female commercial sex workers in Thailand, women with BV were 2.7 times more likely (95% CI 1.3–5.0) to be sero-positive for HIV.[73] They later postulated that this was due to an increased concentration of interleukin-10 (IL-10), an anti-inflammatory cytokine present in endocervical secretions in women with BV which increases macrophage susceptibility to HIV infection.[74] In Uganda, in women with severe BV, HIV was found to be twice as common when compared with those women without BV ($P < 0.0001$).[75] In a longitudinal study of nearly 1200 pregnant and postnatal women in Malawi, BV was significantly associated with antenatal and postnatal positive sero-conversion rates (OR 3.7 and 2.3 respectively).[76,77] BV-related organisms such as *M. hominis* can increase the activity of an HIV inducing factor which increases HIV expression.[78] Genital tract infection with *G. vaginalis* and other BV-related organisms has also been shown to be able to stimulate HIV production and increase the likelihood of sexual transmission.[79] HIV may promote abnormal genital tract flora or BV may enhance the acquisition of HIV through sexual transmission. The available evidence supports a causal relationship between BV and HIV, and BV may be an independent risk factor or co-factor for transmission of HIV infection. These studies suggest that women with disturbance of vaginal flora have an increased risk of HIV acquisition or sero-positive conversion and that the severity of the depletion of lactobacilli, i.e. the degree of BV, is directly correlated with the increased risk of sero-positivity.

BV and late miscarriage

Second trimester miscarriages occur significantly more frequently in women with BV compared with those without. In a UK study[9] there was a 5-fold increased risk of late miscarriage and this was confirmed by an American study from Denver[10] which showed a 3-fold increased risk. BV has also been associated with previous second trimester miscarriage but not with recurrent early miscarriage.[80] Since late miscarriage is on a continuum with extremely early PTB, the mechanism by which BV is associated with late miscarriage is assumed to be similar to those outlined for PTB.

Cytokines

Women in SPTL of infectious aetiology are likely to have increased concentrations of pro-inflammatory cytokines such as IL-1, IL-6 and IL-8 in amniotic fluid (AF) compared with those women in SPTL of non-infectious aetiology.[81] These cytokines are present in greater concentrations in the AF and cervical vaginal fluids of women with BV compared with controls.[82] Babies born preterm to those women with intra-amniotic infection are significantly more likely to suffer lung and brain white matter tissue damage as a result of bronchopulmonary dysplasia[83] and periventricular leukomalacia[84] than those born preterm due to non-infectious aetiology. Those babies born preterm in the presence of increased concentrations of white cells, IL-6 and IL-8 in AF were found at long-term follow-up to have a statistically significant increased incidence of cerebral palsy.[85] This may link BV indirectly to cerebral palsy.

BV in the prediction and prevention of preterm birth

The aetiology of SPTL and PTB is multifactorial although infection is thought to be a causal factor in up to 40% of cases.[86] Unfortunately, this information may be unhelpful in managing SPTL since, by the time a woman presents in SPTL, there may already be irreversible changes in the uterine cervix that render futile those attempts to reverse the process. The information that infection may be a cause of SPTL may be of more help in identifying a group of women at risk of SPTL and PTB and perhaps intervening with antibiotics to reduce the incidence of PTB.

Using different methodologies and different diagnostic techniques, eight cohort studies from Europe, the USA and the Far East[9,87-94] and three case–controlled studies from Sweden, the USA and Australia[95-97] have examined the association between BV or BV-related organisms and the adverse outcome of pregnancy. The majority of these studies showed a statistically significant association between abnormal genital tract flora indicated by the detection of BV and adverse outcome of pregnancy, e.g. late miscarriage or PTB. Screening was carried out at different gestational ages in pregnancy and the earlier that abnormal genital tract flora was detected, the greater was the subsequent risk of PTB (Table 12.5). A positive result at 26 to 32 weeks of gestation was associated with a statistically significant 1.4- to 1.9-fold increased risk of PTB.[87,88,91,94] In contrast, a positive result from screening in the second trimester was associated with a 2.0- to 6.9-fold increased risk of an adverse outcome.[9,89,92,93] In a longitudinal study of women in Indonesia,[92] women with BV in early pregnancy had a 21% risk of an adverse outcome compared with only 11% in those who developed the condition later in pregnancy. Using a multiple regression analysis, BV diagnosed before 16 weeks of gestation was associated with a 5-fold increased risk of late miscarriage or PTB independent of recognised risk factors associated with PTB such as previous PTB, black race and smoking.[9]

A number of studies have examined the use of antibiotics for the prevention of SPTL and PTB due to infection although they have employed different antibiotics in different dosages by different routes of administration and different dose regimens to women with varying degrees of risk and, not surprisingly, different outcomes. Intervention studies can be subdivided into those with pregnancies classified as high risk or unselected (Table 12.6).

Studies of BV in women at high risk of PTB

Three studies have treated BV in women at high risk of PTB and all have been criticised for either small sample size or design flaws. In the first published study,[98] 80 pregnant women with BV diagnosed by Amsel clinical composite criteria were randomised to receive either 250 mg of metronidazole orally three times a day for seven days or placebo. These women were considered to be at high risk of PTB because of a previous PTB or PPROM. Women in the treatment group were

Table 12.5. Risk of adverse outcome according to maximum gestational age at screening

Study	Maximum gestational age at screening (weeks)	Relative risk (95% CI)
Gravett et al.[91] (1986)	32	2.0 (1.1–3.5)
McDonald et al.[97] (1992)	28	1.8 (1.0–3.2)
Hillier et al.[87] (1995)	26	1.4 (1.2–1.8)
McGregor et al.[93] (1994)	24	2.0 (1.1–6.5)
Joesoef et al.[92] (1993)	20	2.0 (1.0–3.9)
Hay et al.[9] (1994)	20	5.5 (2.3–13.3)
Kurki et al.[89] (1992)	17	6.9 (2.5–19.0)

Table 12.6. Published trials of antibiotic treatment for bacterial vaginosis (BV) in pregnancy: modified with permission from Hay[11]

Study	Design	Population	Diagnosis	Intervention	Active drug	Control	P
Systemic treatment							
Morales et al.[98] (1994)	RDBPCT 13–20 weeks	Prior PTB and BV	Amsel	Metronidazole 250 mg tds 7 days	n = 44 PTL: 27% PTB: 18%	n = 36 PTL: 78% PTB: 39%	<0.05 <0.05
Hauth et al.[99] (1995)	RDBPCT 22–24 weeks	Prior PTB or weight <50 kg	Amsel	Metronidazole 250 mg tds and erythromycin 333 mg tds 7 days Repeated[a]	n = 426 PTB: 26%	n = 190 PTB: 36%	=0.01
McDonald et al.[102] (1997)	RPCT 16–26 weeks	Asymptomatic BV	Gram stain or GV > 10^7/ml	Metronidazole 400 mg bd 2 days Repeated	n = 429 PTB: 7.2% SPTB: 4.7% PPROM: 2.8%	n = 428 PTB: 7.5% SPTB: 5.6% PPROM:3.3%	=0.9 =0.5 =0.7
Carey et al.[103] (2000)	RDBPCT 23 weeks	Asymptomatic BV	Gram stain	Metronidazole 2 g day 1 and 3 Repeated	n = 946 PTB: 12.2% <32 wk: 2.3%	n = 955 PTB: 12.4% <32 wk: 2.6%	>0.05 >0.05
McGregor et al.[10] (1995)	Prospective cohort 22–29 weeks	All women	Modified Amsel and Gram stain	Clindamycin 300 mg bd 7 days for women with BV	n = 559 PTB: 12.2% <30 wk: 0.9% PPROM: 3.4%	n = 579 PTB: 12.4% <30 wk: 1.8% PPROM:3.4%	=0.1 =0.9
Ugwumadu et al.[3] (2003)	RDBPCT 12–22	All BV	Gram stain	Clindamycin 300 mg bd 5 days	n = 244 PTB: 5%	n = 241 PTB: 12%	=0.001
Topical treatment							
McGregor et al.[93] (1994)	RDBPCT 16–27 weeks	All BV	Modified Amsel and Gram stain	Clindamycin cream od 7 days	n = 60 PTB: 15% PPROM: 15%	n = 69 PTB: 7.2% PPROM:16.2%	=0.16 =0.85
Joesoef et al.[105] (1995)	RDPCT 14–26 weeks	All BV	Gram stain and pH >4.5	Clindamycin cream od 7 days	n = 340 PTB: 15%	n = 341 PTB: 13.5%	=0.6
Lamont et al.[2] (2003)	RDBPCT 13–20 weeks	All BV	Gram stain	Clindamycin cream od 3 days 7 day repeat course	n = 208 PTB: 4%	n = 201 PTB: 10%	=0.03

[a] treatment repeated after 2–4 weeks in women with persistent BV: od = once daily: PPROM = preterm prelabour rupture of the membranes; PTB = preterm birth: PTL = preterm labour: RDBPCT = randomised double-blind placebo-controlled trial: RPCT = randomised placebo-controlled trial: SPTB = spontaneous preterm birth: tds = three times daily; bd = twice daily: GV = concentration of *Gardnerella vaginalis* in vaginal fluid: RDPCT = randomised placebo-controlled trial

significantly less likely to be admitted in SPTL (27% versus 78%; $P<0.05$), to deliver preterm (18% versus 39%; $P<0.05$) or to develop PPROM (14% versus 33%).

In a second intervention study,[99] self-critical for having used a non-prespecified subgroup analysis, 624 women were randomised to use metronidazole and erythromycin or placebo. The women were considered to be at high risk of PTB because of a previous PTB and/or maternal weight less than 50 kg. Women who received antibiotics were statistically significantly less likely to give birth preterm (31% versus 49%; $P<0.006$).

In a nonrandomised study[10] of 1138 women with a high prevalence of BV and STIs, the study was carried out in two phases. In the observational (control) phase of the trial, symptomatic women with BV were treated with clindamycin 300 mg twice a day orally. In the treatment phase, all women were screened for BV and *T. vaginalis* and treated orally with clindamycin 300 mg twice a day and metronidazole respectively. The rate of PTB in women in the treatment phase was half of those in the observation phase (9.8% versus 18.8%).

As a result of these studies, the Centers for Disease Control and Prevention[100] and the *Drug and Therapeutics Bulletin*[101] recommend that it is reasonable to screen and treat BV in women in pregnancy who are at high risk of preterm birth.

Studies of BV in low-risk unselected women

Six studies have addressed the problem in unselected pregnancies. In a large, randomised controlled trial using oral metronidazole 400 mg for two days, 60% of women required repeat therapy because of initial treatment failure.[102] Women at high risk of PTB were not randomised because they were usually treated by their obstetrician. A subgroup analysis showed that treatment was beneficial in women with a previous PTB who adhered to the medication.[102] In the largest randomised controlled trial of treatment of asymptomatic women with BV no benefit of treatment of BV with 2 g of oral metronidazole was evident although there was a nonsignificant trend towards a reduction in the incidence of very low birthweight babies with treatment.[103] The study has been criticised for a number of limitations:[104]

- Women with asymptomatic BV were excluded.
- Only a small percentage of women with BV were included. Of 29,625 women considered for screening, 6540 had BV but no *T. vaginalis* yet only 1953 were randomised. Among the reasons for exclusion were ineligible (3339), refused consent (651), missed appointments (421), results not available (193), and a very high number (999) excluded for 'other reasons'.
- Forty-seven per cent of women responded to placebo, which is at odds with other studies that regularly showed approximately 10% placebo response.
- Eight weeks could elapse from diagnosis of abnormal flora to randomisation by which time 25% had experienced a change in the grade of Gram stain of vaginal secretions.
- The majority of women were treated after 20 weeks of gestation and few, if any, were treated before 16 weeks of gestation.
- Metronidazole was used which although active against anaerobes does not have a spectrum of activity against significant aerobes and some of the more fastidious organisms associated with BV such as *M. hominis* or *U. urealyticum*.

In view of the last two above, metronidazole may be considered to be 'too little, too late'. Four studies in women at low risk used clindamycin vaginal cream (CVC),[2,93,105,106] in three of which[93,105,106] no benefit was shown. In all three of these, the majority of women were treated late in pregnancy (greater than 20 weeks of gestation). In one study,[106] none of those women who delivered preterm had BV, so it is a self-fulfilling prophecy that antibiotics would be of no benefit.[107] CVC was implicated as causing more harm than good[108] but by using CVC late in pregnancy, rather than correcting abnormal flora, it is likely that Vermeulen *et al.* were producing adverse events by decimating normal flora.[109] Vermeulen *et al.*[108] quoted three studies to support the use of clindamycin in pregnancy yet in all three studies pregnancy and lactation were contraindications to study entry. In one study, recruitment was from a sexually transmitted infection clinic and in another 14% of the women had had a hysterectomy. Two studies in unselected women showed benefit from the use of antibiotics.[2,3] In one study,[3] oral clindamycin produced a significant reduction in the incidence of PTB, from 12% with placebo to 5% with clindamycin ($P<0.001$). In the other study,[2] CVC reduced the incidence of PTB from 10% with placebo to 4% with clindamycin ($P<0.02$). The differences in these studies and in those that showed no benefit are likely to be due to the early gestational age at which treatment was introduced. In the four studies that showed no benefit, the majority of women were treated after 20 weeks and few, if any, before 16 weeks. In contrast, in the two more recent studies,[2,3] the mean gestation at treatment was 16 weeks. Few, if any, were treated after 20 weeks and approximately 50% were treated before 16 weeks.

A Cochrane systematic review[1] has confirmed the recommendation that high-risk women should be treated but was equivocal with respect to unselected low-risk women. Unfortunately, the two recent studies[2,3] were not included in the systematic review, which might have affected the recommendation in low-risk women.

The benefit of early treatment is well supported by a subgroup analysis of the study by Lamont *et al.*[2] Women who initially had abnormal flora (grade II or III on Gram stain) but who subsequently reverted to normal flora (revertants) were not included in the intervention study but were followed up. Those women who always had normal flora on Gram stain had a 3% incidence of adverse outcome; the revertants had an adverse outcome in 24% which was similar to those women with BV who were randomised to receive placebo treatment.[110] This suggests that whatever adverse sequelae occur as a result of abnormal genital tract flora, these occur early in pregnancy and even if vaginal flora subsequently reverts to normal, the damage is already done. In addition, when the degree of abnormal flora was measured against response to treatment and outcome, those women with the greatest degree of abnormal genital tract flora BV (grade III Gram stain) responded better and had fewer adverse effects than those with intermediate grade II Gram stain or abnormal flora (grade II and III Gram stain) (Table 12.7).[110]

Changes in the micro-ecosystem of the genital tract induce abnormal colonisation. Synergistic growth leads to large numbers of potentially pathogenic organisms that adhere to cell surfaces and invade the tissues causing infection. Part of the host response involves release of inflammatory cytokines that may cause cell death and tissue damage. This leads to poor organ function, morbidity and possibly mortality. Antibiotics given late in pregnancy or to women in preterm labour may be given too late in this process at a time when it is already irreversible and this may explain why many of the antibiotic studies of late administration have proven unsuccessful.

Conclusions

Infection is an important cause of SPTL and PTB. Abnormal genital tract flora manifested as BV is a useful predictor of PTB and the earlier in pregnancy at which

Table 12.7. Adverse outcome of pregnancy according to Gram stain grading and treatment group

Gram stain grading	Adverse outcome			
	CVC	Placebo	Untreated	P value
Grade I (control)	–	–	3%	–
Grade I (revertant)	–	–	24%	–
Grade II (intermediate)	28%	16%	–	NS
Grade II+III (Abnormal)	17%	30%	–	0.03
Grade III (bacterial vaginosis)	19%	27%	–	NS

CVC = clindamycin vaginal cream; NS = not significant

abnormal flora is detected the greater is the risk of an adverse outcome. Antibiotics have the potential to reduce the incidence of PTB but these must be used early in pregnancy before inflammation and tissue damage occurs. The antibiotics chosen should be active against BV or BV-related organisms and are most likely to be successful if given to women with the greatest degree of abnormal genital tract flora before the host has mounted a damaging immune response.

References

1. McDonald H, Brocklehurst P, Parsons J, Vigneswaran R. Antibiotics for treating bacterial vaginosis in pregnancy. *Cochrane Database Syst Rev* 2003;(2):CD000262.
2. Lamont RF, Duncan SLB, Mandal D, Bassett P. Intravaginal clindamycin cream to reduce preterm birth in women with abnormal genital tract flora. *Obstet Gynecol* 2003;101:516–22.
3. Ugwumadu A, Manyonda I, Reid F, Hay PE. Effect of early oral clindamycin on late miscarriage and preterm delivery in asymptomatic women with abnormal vaginal flora and bacterial vaginosis: a randomized controlled trial. *Lancet* 2003;361:983–8.
4. Gardner HL, Dukes CD. New etiologic agent in non-specific bacterial vaginosis. *Science* 1954;120:853.
5. Spiegel CA, Amsel R, Eschenbach D, Schoenknecht F, Holmes KK. Anaerobic bacterial in non-specific vaginitis. *N Engl J Med* 1980;303:601–6.
6. Blackwell A, Barlow D. Clinical diagnosis of anaerobic vaginosis: a practical guide. *Br J Vener Dis* 1982;58:387–93.
7. Eschenbach DA, Hillier S, Critchlow C, Stevens C, DeRouen T, Holmes KK. Diagnosis and clinical manifestations of bacterial vaginosis. *Am J Obstet Gynecol* 1988;158:819–28.
8. Kent HL. Epidemiology of vaginitis. *Am J Obstet Gynecol* 1991;165:1168.
9. Hay PE, Lamont RF, Taylor-Robinson D, Morgan DJ, Ison C, Pearson J. Abnormal bacterial colonisation of the genital tract as a marker for subsequent preterm delivery and late miscarriage. *BMJ* 1994;308:295–8.
10. McGregor JA, French JI, Parker R, Draper D, Patterson E, Jones W, *et al*. Prevention of premature birth by screening and treatment for common genital tract infections: results of a prospective controlled evaluation. *Am J Obstet Gynecol* 1995;173:157–67.
11. Hay P. Bacterial vaginosis and pregnancy. In: MacLean A, Regan L, Carrington D, editors. *Infection and Pregnancy*. London: RCOG Press; 2001. p. 158–171.
12. Royce RA, Jackson TP, Thorp JM Jr, Hillier SL, Rabe LK, Pastore LM, *et al*. Race/ethnicity, vaginal flora patterns and pH during pregnancy. *Sex Transm Dis* 1999;26:96–102.
13. Berger BJ, Kolton S, Zenilman JM, Cummings C, Feldman J, McCormack WM. Bacterial vaginosis in lesbians: a sexually transmitted disease. *Clin Infect Dis* 1995;21:1402–5.
14. Skinner CJ, Stokes J, Kirlew Y, Kavanagh J, Forster GE. A case–controlled study of the sexual health needs of lesbians. *Genitourin Med* 1996;72:277–80.
15. McCaffrey M, Varney PA, Evans B, Taylor-Robinson D. A study of bacterial vaginosis in lesbians. *Int J STD AIDS* 1997;8:11.
16. Nilsson U, Hellberg D, Shoubnikova M, Nilsson S, Mardh PA. Sexual behaviour risk factors associated with bacterial vaginosis and *Chlamydia trachomatis* infection. *Sex Transm Dis* 1997;24:241–6.

17. Vejtorp M, Bollerup AC, Vejtorp L, Fanoe E, Nathan E, Reiter A, et al. Bacterial vaginosis: a double-blind randomised trial of the effect of treatment of the sexual partner. Br J Obstet Gynaecol 1988;95:920–6.

18. Moi H, Erkkola R, Jerve F, Nelleman G, Bymose B, Alaksen K, et al. Should male consorts of women with bacterial vaginosis be treated? Genitourin Med 1989;65:263–8.

19. Colli E, Landoni M, Parazzini F. Treatment of male partners and recurrence of bacterial vaginosis: a randomised trial. Genitourin Med 1997;73:267–70.

20. Pavlova S, Kilic AO, Mou SM, Tao L. Phage infection in vaginal Lactobacilli: an in vitro study. Infect Dis Obstet Gynecol 1997;5:36–44.

21. Tao L, Pavlova S, Mou SM, Ma W, Kilic AO.. Analysis of Lactobacilli products for phages and bacteriocins that inhibit vaginal Lactobacilli. Infect Dis Obstet Gynecol 1997;5:244–51.

22. Hay PE, Ugwumadu A, Chowns J. Sex, thrush and bacterial vaginosis. Int J STD AIDS 1997;8:603–8.

23. Larsen B, Galask RP. Influence of estrogen and normal flora on vaginal candidiasis in the rat. J Reprod Med 1984;29:863–8.

24. Kinsman OS, Pitblado K, Coulson CJ. Effect of mammalian steroid hormones on the germination of Candida albicans and implications for vaginal candidiasis. Mycoses 1988;31:617–26.

25. Taylor-Robinson D, Hay PE. The pathogenesis of the clinical signs of bacterial vaginosis and possible reasons for its occurrence. Int J STD AIDS 1998;8:13–6.

26. Furr PM, Taylor-Robinson D. Oestradiol-induced infection of the genital tract of female mice by Mycoplasma hominis. J Gen Microbiol 1989;135:2743–9.

27. Furr PM, Taylor-Robinson D. The establishment and persistence of Ureaplasma urealyticum in oestradiol treated mice. J Med Microbiol 1989;29:111–4.

28. Taylor-Robinson D, Furr PM, Hetherington CM. Neisseria gonorrhoeae colonises the genital tract of oestradiol-treated germ-free female mice. Microb Pathog 1990;9:369–74.

29. Furr PM, Taylor-Robinson D. The influence of hormones on the bacterial flora of the murine vagina and implications for human disease. Microb Ecol Health Dis 1991;4:141–8.

30. Howe L, Wiggins R, Soothill PW, Millar MR, Horner PJ, Coorfield AP. Mucinase and sialidase activity of the vaginal microflora: implications in the pathogenesis of preterm labour. Int J STD AIDS 1999;10:442–7.

31. Skarin A, Sylwan F. Vaginal Lactobacilli inhibiting growth of G vaginalis, Mobiluncus and other bacterial species cultured from vaginal content of women with bacterial vaginosis. Acta Pathol Microbiol Immunol Scand [B] 1987;94:399–403.

32. Masfari AN, Duerden BI, Kinghorn GI. Quantitative studies of vaginal bacteria. Genitourin Med 1986;62:256–63.

33. Barefood SF, Klaenhammer TR. Detection and activity of lactacin B, a bacteriocin produced by Lactobacillus acidophilus. Appl Environ Microbiol 1983;45:1808–15.

34. Hamden IY, Mikolajcik EM. Acidolin: an antibiotic produced by Lactobacillus acidophilus. J Antibiot (Tokyo) 1974;27:632–6.

35. Eschenbach DA, Davick PR, Williams BL, Klebanoff SJ, Young-Smith K, Critchlow CM, et al. Prevalence of hydrogen peroxide-producing Lactobacilli in normal women and women with bacterial vaginosis. J Clin Microbiol 1989;27:251–6.

36. Piot P, Van Dyke E, Godts P, Vanderheyden J. The vaginal microbial flora in non-specific vaginitis. Eur J Clin Microbiol 1982;1:301–6.

37. McCormack WM, Hayes CH, Rosner B, Evrard JR, Crockett VA, Alpert S, et al. Vaginal colonisation with Corynebacterium vaginale (Haemophilus vaginalis). J Infect Dis 1977;136:740–5.

38. Roberts MC, Hillier SL, Schoenknecht FD and Holmes KK. Comparison of Gram stain DNA probe and culture for the identification of species of Mobiluncus in female genital specimens. Infect Dis 1985;152:74–7.

39. Chen KCS, Forsyth PS, Buchanan TM and Holmes KK. Amine content of vaginal fluid from untreated and treated patients with non-specific vaginitis. J Clin Invest 1979;63:825–35.

40. Lamont RF, Taylor-Robinson D, Newman M, Wigglesworth JS, Elder MG. Spontaneous early preterm labour associated with abnormal genital bacterial colonisation. Br J Obstet Gynaecol 1986;93:804–10.

41. Lamont RF, Taylor-Robinson D, Wigglesworth JS, Furr PM, Evans RT and Elder MG. The role of mycoplasmas, ureaplasmas and chlamydiae in the genital tract of women presenting in spontaneous early preterm labour. J Med Microbiol 1987;24:253–7.

42. Hay PE, Morgan DJ, Ison CA, Bhide SA, Romney M, McKenzie P, et al. A longitudinal study of bacterial vaginosis during pregnancy. Br J Obstet Gynaecol 1994;101:1048–53.

43. Amsel R, Totten P, Spiegel CA, Chen KC, Eschenbach DA, Holmes KK. Non-specific vaginitis: diagnostic criteria and microbial and epidemiological associations. Am J Med 1983;74:14–22.

44. Hay PE, Taylor-Robinson D, Lamont RF. Diagnosis of Bacterial vaginosis in a gynaecology clinic. Br J Obstet Gynaecol 1992;98:63–6.

45.   Erkkola R, Jarvinen H, Terho P, Meurman O. Microbiological flora in women showing symptoms of non-specific vaginosis: applicability of KOH test for diagnosis. *Scand J Infect Dis* 1983;40:59–63.

46.   Easmon CS, Hay PE, Ison CA. Bacterial vaginosis: a diagnostic approach. *Genitorun Med* 1992;68:134–8.

47.   Nugent RP, Krohn MA, Hillier SL. Reliability of diagnosing bacterial vaginosis is improved by a standardized method of Gram stain interpretation. *J Clin Microbiol* 1991;29:297–301.

48.   Hillier SL, Krohn MA, Nugent RP, Gibbs RS. Characteristics of three vaginal flora patterns assessed by Gram stain among pregnant women. *Am J Obstet Gynecol* 1992;166:938–44.

49.   Schwebke JR, Hillier SL, Sobel JD, McGregor JA, Sweet RL. Validity of the vaginal Gram stain for the diagnosis of bacterial vaginosis. *Obstet Gynecol* 1996;88:573–6.

50.   Platz-Christensen JJ, Larsson PG, Sundstrom E, Wiqvist N. Detection of bacterial vaginosis in wet mount, Papanicolaou stained vaginal smears and in Gram stained smears. *Acta Obstet Gynecol Scand* 1995;74:67–70.

51.   Rosenstein IJ, Morgan DJ, Sheehan M, Lamont RF, Taylor-Robinson D. Bacterial vaginosis in pregnancy – distribution of bacterial species in different Gram-stain categories of the vaginal flora. *J Med Microbiol* 1996;45:120–6.

52.   Taylor-Robinson D, Lamont RF. Relation between gram stain and clinical criteria for diagnosing bacterial vaginosis with special reference to Grade II evaluation. *Int J STD AIDS* 2003;14:6–10.

53.   Thomason JL, Gelbart SM, Wilcoski LM, Peterson AK, Jilly BJ, Hamilton PR. Proline aminopeptidase activity as a rapid diagnostic test to confirm bacterial vaginosis. *Obstet Gynecol* 1988;71:607–11.

54.   O'Dowd TC, West RR, Winterburn PJ, Hewlins MJ. Evaluation of a rapid diagnostic test for bacterial vaginosis. *Br J Obstet Gynaecol* 1996;103:366–70.

55.   Lamont RF, Hudson EA, Hay PE, Morgan DJ, Modi V, Ison CA, *et al.* A comparison of the use of Papanicolaou-stained cervical cytological smears with Gram-stained vaginal smears for the diagnosis of bacterial vaginosis in early pregnancy. *Int J STD AIDS* 1999;10:93–7.

56.   Platz-Christensen JJ, Sundstrom E, Larsson PG. Bacterial vaginosis and cervical intraepithelial neoplasia. *Acta Obstet Gynecol Scand* 1994;73:586–8.

57.   Mead PA. Cervical-vaginal flora of women with invasive cervical cancer. *JAMA* 1978;52:601–4.

58.   Eschenbach DA. Bacterial vaginosis: emphasis on upper genital tract complications. *Obstet Gynecol Clin North Am* 1989;16:593–610.

59.   Mardh P-A, Westrom L. Tubal and cervical cultures in acute salpingitis with special reference to *Mycoplasma hominis* and T-strain Mycoplasmas. *Br J Vener Dis* 1970;46:179–86.

60.   Llahi-Camp JM, Ison CA, Regan L, Taylor-Robinson D. The association between bacterial vaginosis and infertility. *Int J STD AIDS* 1997;8:23–4.

61.   Morgan DJ, Wong SJ, Trueman G, Priddy P, Lamont RF, Kapembwa MS, *et al.* Can bacterial vaginosis influence fertility? Its increased prevalence in a subfertile population. *Int J STD AIDS* 1997;8:19–20.

62.   Soper DE, Bump RC, Hurt WG. Bacterial vaginosis and Trichomoniasis vaginitis are risk factors for cuff cellulitis after abdominal hysterectomy. *Am J Obstet Gynecol* 1990;163:1016–23.

63.   Larsson PG, Platz-Christensen JJ, Forsum U, Pahlson C. Clue cells in predicting infections after abdominal hysterectomy. *Obstet Gynecol* 1991;77:450–3.

64.   Larsson PG, Bergman B, Forsum H, Platz-Christensen JJ, Pahlson C. Mobiluncus and clue cells as predictors of PID after first trimester abortion. *Acta Obstet Gynecol Scand* 1989;68:217–20.

65.   Larsson PG, Platz-Christensen JJ, Thejls H, Forsum U, Pahlson C. Incidence of pelvic inflammatory disease after first trimester legal abortion in women with bacterial vaginosis after treatment with Metronidazole: a double blind randomised study. *Am J Obstet Gynecol* 1992;166:100–3.

66.   Larsson PG, Platz-Christensen JJ, Dalaker K, Eriksson K, Fahraeus L, Irminger K, *et al.* Treatment with 2% clindamycin vaginal cream prior to first trimester surgical abortion to reduce signs of postoperative infection: a prospective, double-blinded, placebo-controlled, multicenter study. *Acta Obstet Gynecol Scand* 2000;79:390–6.

67.   Stamm WE, Wagner KF, Amsel R, Alexander ER, Turck M, Counts GW, *et al.* Causes of the acute urethral syndrome in women. *N Engl J Med* 1980;303:409–15.

68.   Ralph SG, Rutherford AJ, Wilson JD. Influence of bacterial vaginosis on conception and miscarriage in the first trimester: cohort study. *BMJ* 1999;319:220–3.

69.   Watts D, Krohn MA, Hillier SL, Eschenbach DA. Bacterial vaginosis as a risk factor for post caesarean endometritis. *Obstet Gynecol* 1990;75:52–8.

70.   Newton ER, Prihoda TJ, Gibbs RS. A clinical and microbiologic analysis of risk factors for puerpereal endometritis. *Obstet Gynecol* 1990;75:402–6.

71.   Boyle DCM, Adinkra PE, Lamont RF. Bacterial vaginosis. In: Studd J, editor. *Progress in Obstetrics and Gynaecology.* Vol 15. London: Churchill Livingstone; 2003. p. 185–210.

72. Klebanoff SJ, Coombs RW. Viricidal effect of *Lactobacillus acidophilus* on human immuno-deficiency virus type 1: possible role in heterosexual transmission. *J Exp Med* 1991;174:289–92.

73. Cohen CR, Duerr A, Pruithithada N, Rugpao S, Hillier S, Garcia P, *et al.* Bacterial vaginosis and HIV seroprevalence among female commercial sex workers in Chiang Mai, Thailand. *AIDS* 1995;9:1093–7.

74. Cohen CR, Plummer FA, Mugo N, Maclean I, Shen C, Bukusi EA, *et al.* Increased interleukin-10 in the the endocervical secretions of women with non-ulcerative sexually transmitted diseases: a mechanism for enhanced HIV-1 transmission? *AIDS* 1999;13:327–32.

75. Sewankambo N, Gray RH, Wawer MJ, Paxton L, McNaim D, Wabwire-Mangen F, *et al.* HIV-1 infection associated with abnormal vaginal flora morphology and bacterial vaginosis. *Lancet* 1997;350:546–9.

76. Taha TE, Gray RH, Kumwenda NI, Hoover DR, Mtimavalye LA, Liomba GN, *et al.* HIV infection and disturbances of vaginal flora during pregnancy. *J Acquir Immune Defic Syndr Hum Retrovirol* 1999;20:52–9.

77. Taha TE, Hoover DR, Dallabetta GA, Kumwenda NI, Mtimavalye LA, Yang LP, *et al.* Bacterial vaginosis and disturbances of vaginal flora: association with increased acquisition of HIV. *AIDS* 1998;12:1699–706.

78. Al-Harthi L, Roebuck KA, Olinger GG, Landay A, Sha BE, Hashemi FB, *et al.* Bacterial vaginosis-associated microflora isolated from the female genital tract activates HIV-1 expression. *J Acquir Immune Defic Syndr* 1999;21:194–202.

79. Hashemi FB, Ghassemi M, Roebuck KA, Spear GT. Activation of human immuno-deficiency virus type 1 expression by *Gardnerella vaginalis*. *J Infect Dis* 2000;179:924–30.

80. Llahi-Camp JM, Rai R, Ison C, Regan L, Taylor-Robinson D. Association of bacterial vaginosis with a history of second trimester miscarriage. *Hum Reprod* 1996;11:1575–8.

81. Romero R, Gomez R, Mazor M, Ghezzi F, Yoon BH. The preterm labor syndrome. In: Elder MG, Lamont RF, Romero R, editors. *Preterm Labor.* New York: Churchill Livingstone; 1997. p. 29–49.

82. Platz-Christensen JJ, Mattsby-Baltzer I, Thomsen P, Wiqvist N. Endotoxin and interleukin-1 alpha in the cervical mucus and vaginal fluid of pregnant women with bacterial vaginosis. *Am J Obstet Gynecol* 1993;169:1161–6.

83. Yoon BH, Romero R, Jun JK, Park KH, Park JD, Ghezzi F, *et al.* Amniotic fluid cytokines (interleukin-6, tumor necrosis factor-alpha, interleukin-1 beta, and interleukin-8) and the risk for the development of bronchopulmonary dysplasia. *Am J Obstet Gynecol* 1997;177:825–30.

84. Yoon BH, Romero R, Yang SH, Jun JK, Kim IO, Choi JH, *et al.* Interleukin-6 concentrations in umbilical cord plasma are elevated in neonates with white matter lesions associated with periventricular leukomalacia. *Am J Obstet Gynecol* 1996;174:1433–40.

85. Yoon BH, Romero R, Park JS, Kim CJ, Kim SH, Choi JH, *et al.* Fetal exposure to an intra-amniotic inflammation and the development of cerebral palsy at the age of three years. *Am J Obstet Gynecol* 2000;182:675–81.

86. Lettieri L, Vintzileos AM, Rodis JF, Albini SM, Salafia CM. Does 'idiopathic' preterm labor resulting in preterm birth exist? *Am J Obstet Gynecol* 1993;168:1480–5.

87. Hillier SL, Nugent RP, Eschenbach DA, Krohn MA, Gibbs RS, Martin DH, *et al.* Association between bacterial vaginosis and preterm delivery of a low-birth-weight infant. The Vaginal Infections and Prematurity Study Group. *N Engl J Med* 1995;333:1737–42.

88. Meis PJ, Goldenberg RL, Mercer B, Moawad A, Das A, McNellis D, *et al.* The preterm prediction study: significance of vaginal infections. National Institute of Child Health and Human Development Maternal-Fetal Medicine Units Network. *Am J Obstet Gynecol* 1995;173:1231–5.

89. Kurki T, Sivonen A, Renkonen OV, Savia E, Ylikorkala O. Bacterial vaginosis in early pregnancy and pregnancy outcome. *Obstet Gynecol* 1992;80:173–7.

90. Gratalos E, Figueras F, Barranco M, Vila J, Cararach V, Alonso PL, *et al.* Spontaneous recovery of bacterial vaginosis during pregnancy is not associated with an improved perinatal outcome. *Acta Obstet Gynecol Scand* 1998;77:37–40.

91. Gravett MG, Nelson HP, DeRouen T, Critchlow C, Eschenbach DA, Holmes KK. Independent associations of bacterial vaginosis and Chlamydia trachomatis infection with adverse pregnancy outcome. *JAMA* 1986;256:1899–903.

92. Joesoef RM, Hillier SL, Utomo B, Wiknjosastro G, Linnan M, Kandun N. BV and prematurity in Indonesia: association in late and early pregnancy. *Am J Obstet Gynecol* 1993;169:175–8.

93. McGregor JA, French JI, Jones W, Milligan K, McKinney PJ, Patterson E, *et al.* Bacterial vaginosis is associated with prematurity and vaginal fluid mucinase and sialidase: results of a controlled trial of topical clindamycin cream. *Am J Obstet Gynecol* 1994;170:1048–60.

94. Wennerholm UB, Holm B, Mattsby-Baltzer I, Nielsen T, Plats-Christiansen JJ, Sundell G, *et al.* Fetal fibronectin, endotoxin, bacterial vaginosis and cervical length as predictors of preterm birth and neonatal morbidity in twin pregnancies. *Br J Obstet Gynaecol* 1997;104:1398–404.

95. Holst E, Goffeng AR, Anersch B. Bacterial vaginosis and vaginal microorganisms in idiopathic

premature labor and association with pregnancy outcome. *J Clin Microbiol* 1994;32:176–86.

96.   Eschenbach DA, Gravett MG, Chen KC, Hoyme UB, Holmes KK. Bacterial vaginosis during pregnancy. An association with prematurity and postpartum complications. *Scand J Urol Nephrol Suppl* 1984;86:213–22.

97.   McDonald HM, O'Loughlin JA, Jolley P, Vigneswaran R, McDonald PJ. Prenatal microbiological with factors associated with preterm birth. *Br J Obstet Gynaecol* 1992;99:190–6.

98.   Morales WJ, Schorr S, Albritton J. Effect of metronidazole in patients with preterm birth in preceding pregnancy and bacterial vaginosis: a placebo-controlled, double-blind study. *Am J Obstet Gynecol* 1994;171:345–7.

99.   Hauth JC, Goldenberg RL, Andrews WW, DuBard MB, Copper RL. Reduced incidence of preterm delivery with metrondiazole and erythromycin in women with bacterial vaginosis. *N Engl J Med* 1995;333:1732–6.

100.   Centers for Disease Control and Prevention. 1998 guidelines for treatment of sexually transmitted diseases. *MMWR Morb Mortal Wkly Rep* 1998;47:1–111.

101.   Anonymous. Management of bacterial vaginosis. *Drug Ther Bull* 1998;36:33–5.

102.   McDonald HM, O'Loughlin JA, Vigneswaran R, Jolley PT, Harvey JA, Bof A, *et al.* Impact of metronidazole therapy on preterm birth in women with bacterial vaginosis flora (*Gardnerella vaginalis*): a randomized, placebo controlled trial. *Br J Obstet Gynaecol* 1997;104:1391–7.

103.   Carey JC, Klebanoff MA, Hauth JC, Hillier SL, Thom EA, Ernest JM, *et al.* Metrondiazole to prevent preterm delivery in pregnant women with asymptomatic bacterial vaginosis. *N Engl J Med* 2000;342:534–40.

104.   Lamont RF. Antibiotics for the prevention of preterm birth. *N Engl J Med* 2000;342:581–3.

105.   Joesoef MR, Hillier SL, Wiknjosastro G, Sumampouw H, Linnan M, Norojono W, *et al.* Intravaginal clindamycin treatment for bacterial vaginosis: effects on preterm delivery and low birth weight. *Am J Obstet Gynecol* 1995;173:1527–31.

106.   Vermeulen GM, Bruinse HW. Prophylactic administration of clindamycin 2% vaginal cream to reduce the incidence of spontaneous preterm birth in women with an increased recurrence risk. *Br J Obstet Gynaecol* 1999;106:652–7.

107.   Mason MR, Adinkra PE, Lamont RF. Prophylactic administration of clindamycin 2% vaginal cream to reduce the incidence of spontaneous preterm birth in women with an increased recurrence risk. *Br J Obstet Gynaecol* 1999;107:295–6. Letter.

108.   Vermeulen GM, van Zwet AA, Bruinse HW. Changes in vaginal flora after 2% clindamycin vaginal cream in women at high risk of preterm birth. *Br J Obstet Gynaecol* 2001;108:697–700.

109.   Lamont RF. Changes in vaginal flora after 2% clindamycin vaginal cream in women at high risk of preterm birth. *Br J Obstet Gynaecol* 2003;110:788–9. Letter.

110.   Rosenstein IJ, Morgan DJ, Lamont RF, Sheehan M, Doré CJ, Hay PE, *et al.* Effect of intravaginal clindamycin cream on pregnancy outcome and an abnormal vaginal microbial flora of pregnant women. *Inf Dis Obstet Gynecol* 2000;8:158–65.

111.   Lamont RF, Morgan DJ, Wilden SD, Taylor-Robinson D. Prevalence of bacterial vaginosis in women attending one of three general practices for routine cervical cytology. *Int J STD AIDS* 2000;11:495–8.

112.   Bump RC, Buesching WJ. Bacterial vaginosis in virginal and sexually active adolescent females: evidence against exclusive sexual transmission. *Obstet Gynecol* 1988;158:935–9.

113.   Blackwell AL, Thomas PD, Wareham K, Emery SJ. Health gains from screening for infection of the lower genital tract in women attending for termination of pregnancy. *Lancet* 1993;342:206–10.

114.   Paxton LA, Sewankambo N, Gray R, Serwadda D, McNairn D, Li C, *et al.* Asymptomatic non-ulcerative genital tract infections in a rural Ugandan population. *Sex Transm Infect* 1995;74:421–5.

115.   Embree J, Caliando JJ, McCormack WM. Non-specific vaginitis among women attending a sexually transmited diseases clinic. *Sex Transm Dis* 1984;11:81–4.

Chapter 13

Preterm labour and the cervicovaginal fetal fibronectin test

Honest and Khalid S Khan

Introduction

Spontaneous preterm birth accounts for only 3–4% of births before 34 weeks of gestation but accounts for the majority of neonatal deaths of normally formed infants born before this gestation.[1] Many of the surviving preterm infants, especially those from the earlier gestations, suffer serious morbidity such as bronchopulmonary dysplasia, intra-ventricular haemorrhage, retrolental fibroplasia, neurodevelopmental problems and cognitive difficulties.[2-4] Although progress in perinatal health care has not altered the incidence of spontaneous preterm birth, effective management can reduce the associated complications. For example, the landmark Cochrane review showed that the use of antenatal steroids significantly reduced morbidity and mortality.[5] Timely use of such therapy in clinical practice depends on accurate prediction of spontaneous preterm birth.

The majority of women who present with symptoms of preterm labour, such as uterine tightening or contractions in the absence of cervical changes or advanced dilatation (less than 2–3 cm), do not progress to spontaneous preterm birth. Herein lies the dilemma for caregivers: how to identify confidently the minority of women who will go on to deliver spontaneously preterm. For women that are likely to progress to spontaneous preterm birth, the timely instituting of steroid therapy (and adjunct tocolytic therapy or *in utero* transfer to optimise care and to allow maximum benefit to the fetus), will reduce the likelihood of neonatal morbidity and mortality due to prematurity.

The fibronectin test

Fetal fibronectin is a glycoprotein found in amniotic fluid, placental tissue and the extracellular substance of the decidua basalis next to the placental intervillous space. It is released into the cervicovaginal milieu through mechanical or inflammatory-mediated damage to the membranes or placenta before birth.[6] Swabs taken from either the ectocervix or posterior vaginal fornix, using an enzyme-linked immunosorbent assay (ELISA) containing FDC-6 monoclonal antibody, to detect fetal fibronectin[6] can be used as a test to predict spontaneous preterm birth.[7] This subject has been comprehensively reviewed.[8]

Predicting spontaneous preterm birth

There are two target populations of pregnant women that need to be tested for the risk of preterm birth. The first is the population of antenatal asymptomatic women receiving routine care. These women are generally in a healthy state and anticipate a normal course of pregnancy. Antecedent factors or current history may increase the risk of preterm birth. If testing could predict spontaneous preterm birth among these women, interventions such as cervical cerclage may be more appropriately targeted as a preventive measure. Birth before 37 weeks of gestation is the general 'textbook' definition of preterm birth. However, the complications of prematurity are significantly reduced after birth at 32–34 weeks of gestation.[9] Birth before 34 weeks of gestation is thus a more clinically meaningful outcome for asymptomatic women receiving routine antenatal care. The value of testing for this population is outside the scope of this chapter.

The second population group is that of symptomatic women who present with threatened preterm labour. For these women, there is a need to identify those who will go on to deliver preterm. In this chapter, we assess whether cervicovaginal fetal fibronectin testing can predict imminent spontaneous preterm birth among these women before advanced cervical dilatation, so that a therapy such as antenatal steroid administration may be used judiciously. Among symptomatic women, the key clinical decisions following testing are related to immediate management and outcome. Birth within one week of testing is thus a clinically meaningful outcome in this situation. Antenatal steroids also have maximum effectiveness in preventing complications of prematurity among neonates born within two to seven days after administration.[5]

A test's accuracy or performance is usually assessed in tables of true and false positives and negatives, which can be used to calculate the sensitivity and specificity of the test. However, a number of studies have shown that test sensitivity and specificity are often not well understood by clinicians.[10–12] Thus neither of these measures of accuracy are helpful to clinicians in assessing the value of the test. Likelihood ratios, on the other hand, allow healthcare providers to estimate the post-test probabilities of spontaneous preterm birth, given information on fibronectin test results and some knowledge of the baseline (or pre-test) probabilities of spontaneous preterm birth in women symptomatic of preterm labour.[13,14]

Methods

A decision-making framework for generating therapeutic recommendations using diagnostic information from test results is used.[15–17] The framework is constructed using the following components:

- rates of the target disorder, as predicted by test results, that the treatment was designed to prevent
- evidence of therapeutic benefit, with number needed to treat as the effect measure, tailored according to the rates predicted by testing.

The approach used here is based on systematic reviews[18] and integration of the results as described in detail elsewhere.[16]

Fibronectin's predictive accuracy: systematic review

In order to assess how accurate the cervicovaginal fetal fibronectin test is in predicting spontaneous preterm birth in those women who present with threatened preterm labour, we need to generate post-test probabilities from the available literature. A systematic review of the accuracy of the fetal fibronectin test in predicting spontaneous preterm birth was thus undertaken.[8] We examined the accuracy of cervicovaginal fibronectin testing in predicting spontaneous preterm birth in women who presented with symptoms of preterm labour before advanced cervical dilatation. Fibronectin's accuracy in predicting preterm birth among asymptomatic women was also examined but that is not discussed in this chapter. We found that cervicovaginal fetal fibronectin is an accurate test for predicting delivery within seven days of testing in women who present with symptoms of threatened preterm labour but before advanced cervical dilatation.[8]

Steroids and number needed to treat to prevent neonatal respiratory distress syndrome following fibronectin testing: integration of evidence

For any chosen clinical endpoint, the number needed to treat (NNT) is the reciprocal of the absolute risk difference or the event rate difference between treated and untreated groups in a clinical trial. In order to assess how useful the fibronectin test is in aiding the decision to use antenatal steroid treatment to prevent respiratory distress syndrome (RDS) (clinical endpoint), information regarding the accuracy of cervicovaginal fetal fibronectin testing[8] needs to be integrated with information on therapeutic effectiveness of maternal antenatal corticosteroid administration,[5] to calculate the NNT to prevent one case of neonatal RDS. We explain this concept and its assumptions in depth elsewhere,[8,16] but Table 13.1 shows how this calculation may be undertaken when using data from meta-analyses.

Results

Our systematic review of test accuracy shows that, among women presenting with symptoms of preterm labour at 31 weeks of gestation, about 4.5% deliver within one week of first presentation to hospital. However, for those with a negative fibronectin test, only 1% deliver within one week of testing. In contrast, 20% of those with a positive fibronectin test deliver within one week of testing (Figure 13.1). The therapeutic benefits of testing become clearer when fibronectin is used to inform the decision whether to administer maternal antenatal corticosteroids to women who present with symptoms of threatened preterm labour. If the cervicovaginal fetal fibronectin test result is positive, on average 20 women with symptoms of threatened preterm labour at 31 weeks of gestation without advanced cervical dilatation need to be treated to prevent one case of neonatal RDS. On the other hand, when fibronectin testing is not used, 93 women who present with symptoms of threatened preterm labour would need antenatal corticosteroid administration to prevent one case of neonatal RDS. An even larger number (346 women) who present with symptoms of threatened preterm labour with a negative fibronectin test result would need to be treated with antenatal corticosteroids to prevent one case of neonatal RDS.

Discussion

Every clinical management decision represents a trade-off between risks and benefits, and increasingly requires cost justification. In managing women who present with symptoms of threatened preterm labour but before advanced dilatation, clinicians are often faced with a dilemma: a decision has to be made whether to initiate therapeutic measures, such as antenatal corticosteroids, tocolysis or *in utero* transfer, or simply to observe the women. Many clinicians would err on the side of caution and deploy the

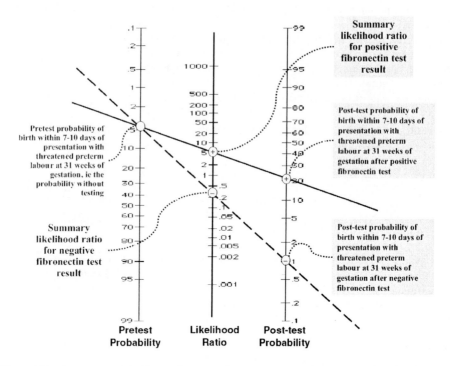

Figure 13.1. The accuracy of the fibronectin test result among symptomatic women at 31 weeks of gestation for predicting spontaneous preterm birth within 7–10 days of testing; based on the meta-analysis by Honest *et al*.[8]

therapeutic measures, which, in the vast majority of cases, are unnecessary. The availability of a cervicovaginal fetal fibronectin test, an accurate test that can predict spontaneous preterm birth within seven days of testing, should assist clinicians in their management of threatened preterm labour.

Probability information is helpful in itself and may be used as follows to assess the implications of *in utero* transfer. If no testing is carried out among mothers with symptoms of preterm labour at 31 weeks of gestation, only one in 20 transferred women will suffer premature birth. If a fibronectin test is positive, among women transferred according to this criterion, one in five will deliver within a week of transfer. If a fibronectin test is negative, and *in utero* transfer is withheld according to this criterion, only one out of 100 women not transferred will deliver within a week of presentation. On balance, considering other clinical features, clinicians would probably be much less inclined to organise *in utero* transfer for women with negative fibronectin tests.

More detailed analysis (Table 13.1) also shows the value of testing for rational and timely deployment of antenatal steroids to optimise neonatal outcome. As described earlier, if no fibronectin testing is used to guide decision making about administration of steroids in cases of threatened preterm labour at 31 weeks of gestation, the number of women needing to be treated to prevent one case of RDS in infants born within a week of presentation would be 93. On the other hand, the NNT would be 20 if a fibronectin test were positive and 346 if negative.

Table 13.1. Cervicovaginal fetal fibronectin testing in symptomatic women at 31 weeks of gestation and the number of women needed to treat (NNT) with antenatal steroids to prevent one case of neonatal respiratory distress syndrome (RDS) associated with spontaneous preterm birth within 7–10 days of testing; modified with permission from Honest et al.[8]

Fibronectin test result at 31 weeks of gestation	Probability of spontaneous preterm birth within 7–10 days of testing (%)	Risk of neonatal RDS among babies born at 32 weeks of gestation (%)	Rate of RDS[c] at 32 weeks of gestation among those with symptoms at 31 weeks of gestation (%)	NNT[d]
No testing	4.5[a]	53	2.0	93
Test positive	20.6[b]	53	11.0	20
Test negative	1.0[b]	53	0.4	346

[a] Pre-test probability of spontaneous preterm birth within 7–10 days of testing for symptomatic pregnant women presenting at 31 weeks of gestation[21–30];
[b] Information on the calculation of probabilities using likelihood ratios (LRs):
The pre-test probability of spontaneous preterm birth within 7–10 days for women presenting at 31 weeks of gestation is 4.5%
This value is converted to pre-test odds: 4.5/(100−4.5)=0.047
Post-test odds for spontaneous preterm birth among women with a positive test = pre-test odds × LR+
=0.047 × 5.45 = 0.26
This is then converted to post-test probability: 0.26/(0.26+1)=0.206 (20.6%)
LR+ is the likelihood ratio for a positive test result; its value is generated from meta-analysis[8]
(A similar calculation may be carried out for the negative test result.)
[c] The rate of RDS is calculated as follows:
The probability of spontaneous preterm birth at 32 weeks of gestation (31 weeks + 7–10 days), following a positive fibronectin test, is 20.6%
The risk of RDS at this gestation is 53%[19,20]
Therefore, the probability of a neonate's suffering from RDS when the mother had tested positive is 20.6% × 53% = 11%
(A similar calculation may be carried out for the negative test result.)
[d] An example calculation of NNT to prevent one case of neonatal RDS for women who tested positive:
The rate of RDS at 32 weeks of gestation is 11%
This value is converted to odds of RDS without treatment: 11/(100−11)=0.12
Odds of treatment benefit = 0.12 × 0.53 = 0.064 (where 0.53 is the odds ratio [OR] for treatment benefit of antenatal steroids, obtained from the Cochrane review,[5] which is coincidentally the same figure as the risk for RDS at 32 weeks of gestation)
This is then converted to the rate of RDS following antenatal steroid treatment: 0.064/(1+0.064)=0.059
The risk difference of RDS between treatment and without antenatal steroid treatment is 0.11–0.059 = 0.051
The NNT is thus 1/0.051 = 20
This means that with a positive fibronectin test, 20 symptomatic pregnant women who present at 31 weeks of gestation need to be treated with antenatal steroids to prevent one case of neonatal RDS
(A similar calculation may be carried out for the negative test result.)

We have here described how test accuracy information that we have generated for cervicovaginal fetal fibronectin testing can be combined with therapeutic effectiveness information from Cochrane reviews to inform decision making and thereby allow judicious use of limited healthcare resources.

Acknowledgement

This work was supported by a research grant from WellBeing.

References

1. Maternal and Child Health Consortium. *6th Annual Report: Confidential Enquiries into Stillbirths and Deaths in Infancy (CESDI)*. London: HMSO; 1999.
2. Paneth NS. The problem of low birth weight. *Future Child* 1995;5:19–34.
3. Stewart AL, Rifkin L, Amess PN, Kirkbride V, Townsend JP, Miller DH, *et al*. Brain structure and neurocognitive and behavioural function in adolescents who were born very preterm. *Lancet* 1999;353:1653–7.
4. Wolke D, Meyer R. Cognitive status, language attainment, and prereading skills of 6-year-old very preterm children and their peers: the Bavarian Longitudinal Study. *Dev Med Child Neurol* 1999;41:94–109.
5. Prophylactic corticosteroids for preterm birth. *Cochrane Database Syst Rev* 2000;(2):CD000065.
6. Matsuura H, Takio K, Titani K, Greene T, Levery SB, Salyan ME, *et al*. The oncofetal structure of human fibronectin defined by monoclonal antibody FDC-6. Unique structural requirement for the antigenic specificity provided by a glycosylhexapeptide. *J Biol Chem* 1988;263:3314–22.
7. Lockwood CJ, Senyei AE, Dische MR, Casal D, Shah KD, Thung SN, *et al*. Fetal fibronectin in cervical and vaginal secretions as a predictor of preterm delivery. *N Engl J Med* 1991;325:669–74.
8. Honest H, Bachmann LM, Gupta JK, Kleijnen J, Khan KS. Accuracy of cervicovaginal fetal fibronectin test in predicting risk of spontaneous preterm birth: systematic review. *BMJ* 2002;325:301.
9. Seubert DE, Stetzer BP, Wolfe HM, Treadwell MC. Delivery of the marginally preterm infant: what are the minor morbidities? *Am J Obstet Gynecol* 1999;181:1087–91.
10. Bachmann LM, Steurer J, ter Riet G. Simple presentation of test accuracy may lead to inflated disease probabilities. *BMJ* 2003;326:393.
11. Hoffrage U, Lindsey S, Hertwig R, Gigerenzer G. Medicine. Communicating statistical information. *Science* 2000;290:2261–2.
12. Steurer J, Fischer JE, Bachmann LM, Koller M, ter Riet G. Communicating accuracy of tests to general practitioners: a controlled study. *BMJ* 2002;324:824–6.
13. Jaeschke R, Guyatt GH, Sackett DL. Users' guides to the medical literature. III. How to use an article about a diagnostic test. B. What are the results and will they help me in caring for my patients? The Evidence-Based Medicine Working Group. *JAMA* 1994;271:703–7.
14. Jaeschke R, Guyatt G, Sackett DL. Users' guides to the medical literature. III. How to use an article about a diagnostic test. A. Are the results of the study valid? Evidence-Based Medicine Working Group. *JAMA* 1994;271:389–91.
15. Coomarasamy A, Braunholtz D, Song F, Taylor R, Khan KS. Individualising use of aspirin to prevent pre-eclampsia: a framework for clinical decision making. *BJOG* 2003;110:882–8.
16. Khan KS, Honest H, Bachmann LM. A generic framework for making clinical decisions integrating diagnostic and therapeutic research evidence in preterm birth. *Fetal Maternal Med Rev* 2003;14:239–49.
17. Khan KS, Chien PF. Seizure prophylaxis in hypertensive pregnancies: a framework for making clinical decisions. *Br J Obstet Gynaecol* 1997;104:1173–9.
18. Khan KS, Kunz R, Kleijnen J, Antes G. Five steps to conducting a systematic review. *J R Soc Med* 2003;96:118–21.
19. Sinclair JC. Meta-analysis of randomized controlled trials of antenatal corticosteroid for the prevention of respiratory distress syndrome: discussion. *Am J Obstet Gynecol* 1995;173:335–44.
20. Usher RH, Allen AC, McLean FH. Risk of respiratory distress syndrome related to gestational age, route of delivery, and maternal diabetes. *Am J Obstet Gynecol* 1971;111:826–32.
21. Bartnicki J, Casal D, Kreaden US, Saling E, Vetter K. Fetal fibronectin in vaginal specimens predicts preterm delivery and very-low-birth-weight infants. *Am J Obstet Gynecol* 1996;174:971–4.
22. Benattar C, Taieb J, Fernandez H, Lindendaum A, Frydman R, Ville Y. Rapid fetal fibronectin swab-test in preterm labor patients treated by betamimetics. *Eur J Obstet Gynecol Reprod Biol* 1997;72:131–5.
23. Giles W, Bisits A, Knox M, Madsen G, Smith R. The effect of fetal fibronectin testing on admissions to a tertiary maternal–fetal medicine unit and cost savings. *Am J Obstet Gynecol* 2000;182:439–42.
24. Iams JD, Casal D, McGregor JA, Goodwin TM, Kreaden US, Lowensohn R, *et al*. Fetal fibronectin improves the accuracy of diagnosis of preterm labor. *Am J Obstet Gynecol* 1995;173:141–5.
25. LaShay N, Gilson G, Joffe G, Qualls C, Curet L. Will cervicovaginal interleukin-6 combined with fetal fibronectin testing improve the prediction of preterm delivery? *J Matern Fetal Med* 2000;9:336–41.
26. Leeson SC, Maresh MJA, Martindale EA, Mahmood T, Muotune A, Hawkes N, *et al*. Detection of fetal fibronectin as a predictor of preterm delivery in high risk asymptomatic pregnancies. *Br J*

Obstet Gynaecol 1996;103:48–53.

27.   Lopez RL, Francis JA, Garite TJ, Dubyak JM. Fetal fibronectin detection as a predictor of preterm birth in actual clinical practice. *Am J Obstet Gynecol* 2000;182:1103–6.

28.   Lukes AS, Thorp JM Jr, Eucker B, Pahel-Short L. Predictors of positivity for fetal fibronectin in patients with symptoms of preterm labor. *Am J Obstet Gynecol* 1997;176:639–41.

29.   Malak TM, Sizmur F, Bell SC, Taylor DJ. Fetal fibronectin in cervicovaginal secretions as a predictor of preterm birth. *Br J Obstet Gynaecol* 1996;103:648–53.

30.   McKenna DS, Chung K, Iams JD. Effect of digital cervical examination on the expression of fetal fibronectin. *J Reprod Med* 1999;44:796–800.

Chapter 14

Screening and diagnosis II

Discussion

Romero: I have two queries for Dr Lamont: you have used metronidazole and also clindamycin and you hinted that you wanted to say something about that.

Lamont: Yes, we do not know the right answer, what is best between metronidazole and clindamycin. The clindamycin studies seem to be better than metronidazole. There is one theory that we still do not know what causes bacterial vaginosis (BV). However, there is some evidence that it may be due to a phage virus in some circumstances. A phage virus is, of course, a parasitic virus of the lactobacilli and so they will either kill off the lactobacilli or reduce the ability of the lactobacilli to produce hydrogen peroxide which is toxic to bacteria. That is one of the protective effects of lactobacilli. People have said for many years: let's use metronidazole because it preserves the lactobacilli. We want to preserve as near to normal a vaginal ecosystem as possible. If phage viruses are an important factor in the development of BV and therefore abnormal flora then maybe we are doing the worst possible thing by preserving the lactobacilli. Maybe we ought to be using clindamycin which decimates and kills everything including the lactobacilli and then you would kill off phage viruses too. That is a theoretical reason between the two and the other thing of course is that metronidazole does not target some of the very important aerobes associated with BV. BV, basically, is just another way of saying abnormal vaginal flora.

Crowley: Just how good is the evidence from randomised trials that screening and treating BV reduces preterm delivery?

Lamont: There are data just recently published that I have not yet had a chance to peruse. I spoke to Helen Macdonald when she was putting it together and I have just had a quick look at the data and from what I can see it does not look as if there is a strong case to be made. What I do not know is whether Helen has addressed the question of screening early in pregnancy.

Romero: I have two comments. First, I would like to express my doubts about the diagnosis of BV. According to different studies, the prevalence of BV is as high as 20%. I have difficulties believing that a condition present in 20% of pregnant women is really a pathological condition. Perhaps what we have here is another example of heterogeneity. If you look at the profile for cytokines in patients who have BV, there are two groups: one that has high concentrations of inflammatory cytokines and another that does not. Maybe this is clouding some of the results of the studies. The second comment I want to share with you refers to a paper in press in the *American*

Journal of Obstetrics and Gynecology addressing the questions of gene–environment interaction in BV. Jerry Strauss's group at the University of Pennsylvania reported the results of a case–control study examining the effects of BV, carriage of a polymorphism for tumour necrosis factor-α (TNF-α) and preterm delivery in a population of African-American women in the US. They found that while BV and carriage of the TNF polymorphism each had a modest association with preterm delivery, the combination of the two significantly increased the risk of preterm delivery. This is an example of a gene–environment interaction in preterm birth.

Lamont: This is a point we made two or three years back. We need to get better at diagnosing BV. It is interesting that its called vaginosis because there is no cellular inflammatory response, otherwise it would be called bacterial vaginitis. In clinical practice it is very difficult when somebody comes back with recurrent BV. It is difficult to treat them and you end up giving them both a combination of intravaginal and systemic treatment on a cyclical basis. Interestingly enough, there is some suggestion that progesterone actually helps.

Nicolaides: I have a series of points. First, it looks as if there is a non-infective consequence of BV that predisposes a patient to premature delivery especially when this non-infected event occurs at eight weeks of gestation. The second point is directed to you, Dr Lamont, on the question you raised about the need for the one major study that will sort out the issue because even when that study is published in Europe there will be almost certainly be a repeat of that study in the USA. We are always sceptical about evidence based on one study but the trend is to find more believable a series of studies that may be even crossing the line individually, but overall are producing a final result that does not cross the line. If at the end of the day whoever writes the reports on evidence-based medicine in a sense ignores the individual studies and looks at the meta-analysis.

In relation to Dr Khan's presentation, we must link the effectiveness of a test we conduct to the consequences of our action. So, for example, in the very recent document from NICE on antenatal care, it says that we must not screen people with Doppler of the uterus for pre-eclampsia in one part of the document. However it does say it is important to use much less adequate methods of screening for risk for pre-eclampsia, for example, asking the women whether they are black, finding out if this is their first pregnancy. This is because the consequences of screening in this instance will modify the type of care that they will receive. They will be seen and presumably we will measure their blood pressure. One of the points that you raised quite correctly is when we have a woman presenting with threatened preterm delivery and we know from several studies that 90% of them will not deliver in the next seven days. Secondly, we know that the only reason for which we would treat these women, on the basis of existing evidence, is to give them steroids. We also know, however, that if you do give them steroids there are increasing concerns that that in itself may have some adverse effects especially if you need to repeat the steroids. I want to finish by saying that actually if you fail to screen and distinguish between the 90% that will not deliver and the 10% who will deliver and adopt an attitude of giving steroids to everybody, in the presence of the existing attitudes and giving a woman steroids today, if she does not deliver you are depriving her of steroids at the later gestation when they would have been beneficial.

Critchley: I think you have raised several very important areas for discussion. In terms of the size of trials I would be grateful for comments by Professors Smith and Nielson.

Nicolaides: What should the endpoint of a new study be to prove in itself that it is a significant change or to modify the meta-analysis as an end point?

Smith: I am very interested in your comments, Professor Nicolaides. To me if you are setting out to do a study you want your study to have the power to answer the questions that you are interested in, and to set out to do a study hoping that someone else will do studies so eventually there will be a meta-analysis that allows you to have adequate power, I think is rather difficult. For me I could not engage in a study where I could not assure myself that the study had the power to produce conclusions on the outcome that I was interested in. I do not think any ethics committee would pass it.

Nielson: Well I think you have to be pretty pragmatic about this. Dr Lamont was talking about an application to the Medical Research Council – they funded one single trial in the whole of medicine last year. If the only way we are going to make progress is by doing Rolls-Royce, big multicentre trials then we are not going to make much progress at all and I think that would be unfortunate. I think this is the point Professor Nicolaides is making: I think it would be unfortunate if people were deterred from doing more modest studies because that actually does contribute to the sum total of knowledge. I think he is right in highlighting that and I think sometimes people feel if it is not going to be the definitive study then it is not worth doing and I would not agree with that.

Romero: If I understand correctly, Professor Nicolaides, the practical implication is how we calculate sample size. I say, then, that the effort of doing the next trial may be considerably less than undertaking a mega trial, and that has implications for the conduct and the design of the study, and also the financial burden it represents. So I think this is a very relevant point.

Gardosi: This is a very important issue because what has emerged is that the big prize is to do the trial that will reach significance. There are several examples where in my opinion at least the systematic review was overtly influenced by one particular study which had a huge amount of power but was not particularly well done. I think the Cochrane reviews have become better over the years, but it would be a pity if they were to discourage the conduct of good studies that address a particular, maybe local or generalisable issue. To me, the gold standard for a particular clinical question still is the one good study, designed properly, with the power to address the issue which hopefully then is also repeated elsewhere and therefore validated. That is how it used to be and I hope researchers will maintain the primary focus to say that we have a question within our clinical practice we want to address.

Romero: I wanted to address the second point that Professor Nicolaides raised, which has to do with infection. Although infection and inflammation are clearly causally related to premature labour and delivery, particularly in women who deliver preterm at an early gestational age (before 28 week), there are noninfectious inflammatory processes which may be present in premature labour. Moreover, among women who have inflammation, there are probably two groups: one in which infection is the primary event responsible for inflammation, and a second group in which infection is secondary to another pathological process. These two conditions may require different strategies for identification, treatment and prevention.

Shennan: Just adding to that debate I have a lot of sympathy for what Professor Smith is saying here because the reality is if you are going after money, in the cost constraints of charities or research organisations and funding bodies, you would never convince them. You would never convince a funding body without a package that has a result that you would be able to do a trial. The important issue I think from what Professor Nicolaides is saying is we should be looking at all the endpoints. You know your primary endpoint may have to be properly powered and costed for a result but the perinatal mortality and all the other issues which are very difficult to power for are the real key things to add to the meta-analysis. Unless you are brave enough to put them forward and say we are going to look at these and it is OK to look at them even though they are not powered for it will not happen and looking through the papers it is clear that people are not presenting evidence that allows a meta-analysis.

Critchley: Professor Nicolaides, you raised the issue of the importance of linking the effectiveness of a test to the consequences of the action.

Nicolaides: And the adverse effects of not giving the treatment.

Critchley: Does the argument apply to fibronectin?

Nicolaides: In the context of premature labour, 90% will not deliver and 10% will deliver. We give steroids to all, if steroids are cheap and do no harm, or we stratify who does and who does not need steroid treatment. The next point that I raised is that by giving steroids, because it is cheap and harmless today, whether that prevents you from giving steroids in three weeks when somebody is really in premature labour and are you depriving them of the benefits of three weeks down the line.

Gardosi: I would direct the discussion to another treatment, which is *in utero* transfer. It is a form of treatment and I believe that Dr Khan's work and the underlying studies on fibronectin are particularly relevant in the negative predictive value for premature labour. In other words, adding to Professor Nicolaides's point that most pregnancies presenting with threatened preterm labour are in fact not. We feel that the evidence is so clear that in the West Midlands, the Perinatal Institute and the Feto-Maternal Medicine Group want to now introduce a protocol that there shall not be *in utero* transfer arranged between units in the Region unless the fibronectin test is shown not to be negative.

Smith: We have published on that[1] because transfer *in utero* is a big problem in Australia. We certainly adopt that policy.

Thornton: The other add-on is tocolysis and you may wish to delay transfer until later.

Khan: What we really want, as Professor Nicolaides was highlighting earlier, is to be as close to 100% post-test probability as possible with a positive test result or as close to 0% post-test probability as possible with a negative test result (Figure 13.1), so we can confidently give or withhold treatment when we are certain about presence or absence of possibility of preterm birth. Unfortunately, the studies of test accuracy that allows us to evaluate this information very often only look at one test or one feature at a time. As highlighted earlier, there is overlap of information between different tests and features. So for example those women who have short cervix may be more likely to be fibronectin-positive and those who have BV may be likely to be other test positive. This overlap of information is almost never taken into account in studies but is a daily reality faced by clinicians and patients. One reason for this is that studies are too small to allow powerful multivariable analysis. I think multicentre studies with a large number of patients where all these characteristics/tests are measured and a multivariable analysis is undertaken can allow us to understand the value of combination of tests. Another solution to this problem lies in individual patient data meta-analysis of diagnostic studies where raw data instead of the reported data are pooled to undertake multivariable analyses.

Lamont: There is another issue and that is that patients who are positive for fibronectin and negative for fibronectin, or short cervix and long cervix, may not all have the same benefit from having an intervention. How do you deal with this?

Khan: This is a general problem with all medical research: how to estimate external validity or generalisability of findings to patients in real life outside the trials. An average patient in a randomised trial does not necessarily represent a patient in front of you in the clinic. We have to make several assumptions and have to ask whether this patient represents an average patient in the trial or the meta-analysis. Considering additional features of the patient in front of us, e.g. fibronectin test being negative or positive, we actually have the opportunity to tailor treatment according to this test result. If we have additional information, for example, on the historical risk factors or BV from early screening, or ultrasound cervical length, we can be much more rational in tailoring treatment in the light of all that information.

Lamont: The other important variable, as you say seven days, will be an outcome variable, but seven days at 24 weeks of gestation means much more than seven days at 34 weeks.

Khan: I think to my mind the key feature is birth within the next 48 hours after symptomatic presentation. For that outcome there are actually only three studies that provide the data in our meta-analysis.

Reference

1.   Giles W, Bisits A, Knox M, Madsen G, Smith R. The effect of fetal fibronectin testing on admissions to a tertiary maternal-fetal medicine unit and cost savings. *Am J Obstet Gynecol* 2000;182:439–42.

SECTION 4

MANAGEMENT I

Chapter 15

Fetal membrane rupture

Stephen C Bell and Penny C McParland

Introduction

In the majority of pregnancies, rupture of the gestational sac or 'fetal membranes', that is, failure of its structural integrity, follows the onset of labour-associated contractions at term. This is referred to as spontaneous rupture of membranes (SROM). In 5–10% of term deliveries, rupture of membranes occurs before clinically apparent contractions, that is, prelabour rupture of membranes (PROM). In contrast, if iatrogenic deliveries are excluded, PROM occurs in approximately 50% of preterm deliveries and represents a major cause of preterm birth; hence, it is a subject of considerable interest.[1-4]

Although progress in this area has been made, several fundamental questions still remain:

- What are the cellular and molecular features that underlie the structural integrity of the membranes?
- By what mechanisms may they be comprised?
- Is the clinical distinction between membrane rupture occurring in the presence (SROM) and absence (PROM) of labour-associated contractions reflected by fundamentally different mechanisms of rupture; in other words, are they distinct clinical conditions with distinct aetiopathologies?
- Are different mechanisms involved in PROM when presenting at different gestational periods?
- Why do women present with either preterm PROM or labour when similar clinical risk factors and associations for these conditions are involved?

Fetal membranes, development and rupture

'Fetal membranes' as applied to post-delivery recovered membranes are composed of true fetal membranes, the amnion and chorion, attached to a maternal decidua layer. This indicates that, *in vivo*, the amnion, chorion and decidua represent an intimately fused 'amniochorial–decidual unit'. However, this relationship changes during pregnancy and therefore may be reflected by gestation period-specific susceptibilities for, and aetiopathologies underlying, their rupture (Figure 15.1).

Development of the 'amniochorial–decidual unit'

During early pregnancy the amnion and the chorion are distinct entities. The amnion,

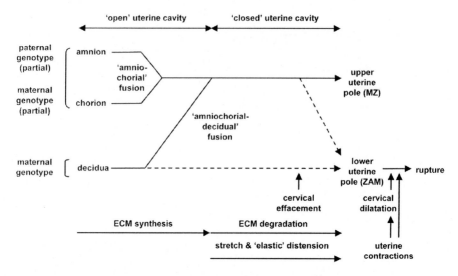

Figure 15.1. Development of the 'fetal membranes' during pregnancy and of their anatomical regionalisation in structure. The fusion of the amniochorion to the decidua parietalis represents a key transition in the development of the fetal membranes. The anatomically defined regional alteration in the membranes present prior to labour at term may arise because of the absence of, or partial, amniochorial–decidual fusion in the lower uterine pole and/or the development of the lower uterine segment and cervical effacement (dotted lines); ECM = extracellular matrix; MD = mid-zone; ZAM = zone of altered morphology

consisting of an epithelial layer attached to its basement membrane, faces the amniotic cavity. This overlies connective tissue layers, an essentially cell-free compact layer and an underlying fibroblast layer composed of monocytic and fibroblastic populations. The chorion, the chorionic laeve, is composed of cytotrophoblastic cells attached to its basement membrane facing, but separated from, the uterine cavity by the degenerating decidua capsularis. Its connective tissue layer, the reticular layer, also possesses monocytic and fibroblastic populations. The connective tissue layers of the amnion and chorion are separated by the extra-embryonic coelum. At week 12, the extra-embryonic coelum disappears and the connective tissue layers of the amnion and chorion fuse via its remnant, the essentially cell-free spongy layer.

Crucially, between weeks 20 and 25, the amniochorion undergoes fusion with the decidua parietalis, obliterating the uterine cavity, except possibly for an area over the internal os of the cervix. This fusion involves proliferation and superficial invasion of the cytotrophoblast into the decidua. The cytotrophoblast develops into a multicellular layer with basement membrane attached basal cells overlain by superficial cytotrophoblasts that may intermingle with decidual cells. These populations exhibit phenotypic differences, reflecting their differential interactions with their extracellular matrices (ECM).[5] The cytotrophoblastic–decidual interface must be stable, as evidenced by the presence of maternal decidua in the recovered fetal membranes.

Rupture of the membranes

The amniochorion is subject to increasing lateral distensional forces, particularly during the latter half of pregnancy, and this is countered by its tensile strength and elasticity. Thus, the initial site of rupture, wherever it occurs anatomically, either over the cervix or ectopically, outside this area, represents a site of failure of their structural integrity in the lateral axis to produce a vertical tear. However, after amnio-chorial–decidual fusion after mid-pregnancy, outside the area of the amniochorion over the cervix, structural failure must also occur in its vertical integration to produce a lateral cleavage plane to connect the vertical tear site with the cervix. This would either require a dissociation of the stable cytotrophoblastic–decidual interface or a structural failure within the decidua. Cleavage between the amnion and chorion with the appearance of gelatinous material in the expanded spongy layer has also been proposed to be important in rupture of the membranes creating a two-component rupture behaviour.[6]

The structural integrity and biophysical properties of the amniochorion reflect the nature of the ECM of the mesenchymal tissue layers, since epithelial components are normally 'stress shielded'. Rupture of the membranes could involve a passive physical failure of the ECM when subjected to deformation. However, the amniochorion contains cells that, in response to a variety of factors, have the capacity to degrade the ECM via secretion of enzymes such as matrix metalloproteinases (MMPs).[7] Thus, the rupture of membranes may also involve 'active' processes.

Extracellular matrices of the fetal membranes

Characterisation of the ECM of the fetal membranes has been the subject of much investigation[5,8–10] but our knowledge is still scant, particularly with respect to the changes during pregnancy.

The amnion is characterised by the dense packing of the fibrillar collagens I/III in the compact layer beneath the amniotic epithelium. The fibres are arranged parallel to the epithelium in the lateral axis, providing strength in its lateral axis, decorin is also present at high concentrations and is presumably involved in the organisation and stability of these collagen fibres. The unbanded filamentous collagens V and VI, involved in stabilising fibrillar collagens and in anchoring basement membranes to their connective tissue layers, form an extensive network. Collagen VII appears to be involved in 'rivet' structures connecting the collagen IV and laminin-containing amniotic basement membrane, transversely through the connective tissue layers. In the chorionic connective tissue reticular layer fibrillar collagens are less organised and densely packed and the chorionic cytotrophoblast not as firmly attached to its collagen IV and merosin-containing basement membrane. This looser matrix also contains presence of hyaluronan. Both connective tissue layers contain fibrillin-1, orientated in the lateral axis either side of the spongy layer, and vertically in the amnion from the basement membrane to the fibroblastic layer. This corresponds to an extensive microfibrillar network present as long, laterally orientated intermeshing bundles found intermingled with collagen fibres and in close association with mesenchymal cells. Elastin is deposited upon fibrillin-1 containing microfibrils, Thin elastic fibres and sheets have been isolated from the amniochorion.

The fused superficial cytotrophoblastic–decidual interface is associated with a matrix reflecting its stability with the deposition of fetal fibronectin and fibrillar collagens. This is reflected by the intregrin profile of the superficial as compared with the basal lamina ECM associated with the 'basal' cytotrophoblastic layer. The ECM of the decidua contains fibrillar collagens I/III and hyaluronan, and the decidual cells, unusual for mesenchymal cells, possess basal lamina components that are associated with sheaths of fibrillin-1.

The composition and organisation of these ECM would account for the relative elastic and tensile properties of the amnion and chorion in the lateral axis, with the density and organisation of the collagen fibres bestowing more rigidity and tensile strength to the former. Collagens V–VII also appear to bestow a vertical integration of these collagen fibres. The nature of the ECM is also relevant to an understanding of the potential differential effects of MMPs, which exhibit differential substrate specificities. Given its nature, it may be argued that activities of the fibrillar collagen-degrading MMPs, such as MMP-1, would be of most relevance to the tensile strength of the membranes. However, equally important are MMPs that may degrade components such as fibril-associated collagens and proteoglycans and that stabilise fibrillar matrices.

Mechanisms underlying spontaneous rupture of membranes

A critical distinction is made between whether membrane rupture occurs in the presence (SROM) or absence (PROM) of labour. Knowledge of the mechanisms that underlie SROM may provide insight into how the membranes may rupture in the absence of labour.

Pregnancy-associated biophysical stretch and extracellular matrix turnover

The fusion of the amniochorion to the decidua parietalis at mid-pregnancy appears to mark a transition in its biophysical behaviour. Studies comparing *in vivo* to post-delivery surface areas indicate that *in vivo* at mid-pregnancy membranes are not distended. However, from mid-pregnancy they respond to the increase in intrauterine volume and the increasing lateral distensional force by undergoing increasing elastic distension and, hence, are under increasing lateral tension or stretch.[11] This elastic distension has a limit, since *in vitro* term membranes exhibit viscoelasticity whereby under deformation they undergo elastic distension but, upon removal of the deformational force, exhibit only a partial elastic recovery, termed its 'elastic extension'.[12,13] The nonrecoverable component is termed the creep extension, suggesting a readjustment of its ECM, loss of components or of structural organisation bestowing its elasticity. When the elastic extension is exhausted at the limit of creep extension, the membrane is rigid and rupture occurs when the nonelastic modified ECM fails under increasing lateral force.

Table 15.1. Phenotype of the mesenchymal cell populations of the connective tissue 'reticular' layer of the chorion during pregnancy.[19] The percentage of mesenchymal cells expressing intermediate filaments V, VD, VA and VAD in the connective tissue layer of the chorion during pregnancy as assessed by immunocytochemistry. During the third trimester VA and VAD cells loose expression of α-smooth muscle actin (α-SMA) such that at term the majority of cells express V and VD, excepting in the zone of altered morphology (ZAM) region where VD cells express α-SMA.

Marker	1st/2nd trimester (n=9) (%)	3rd trimester (n=20) (%)	Term 'mid-zone' (n=10) (%)	Term 'ZAM' (n=10) (%)
Macrophages	5.32 ± 1.36	11.63 ± 1.47	7.87 ± 2.16	4.21 ± 0.74
Vimentin (V)	5.67 ± 2.34	22.09 ± 2.37	29.74 ± 6.35	26.12 ± 4.63
Vimentin Desmin (VD)	0	42.52 ± 4.22	57.56 ± 6.27	10.03 ± 4.41
Vimentin α-SMA (VA)	23.13 ± 4.29	0	0	8.58 ± 4.44
Vimentin Desmin α-SMA (VAD)	70.29 ± 3.79	23.76 ± 4.17	5.20 ± 1.75	60.19 ± 5.92

This transition is reflected by changes in ECM turnover since, particularly after 35 weeks, a switch from ECM synthesis to degradation occurs and may be reflected by its decrease in tensile strength after 39 weeks.[14] Synthesis of the major collagens, and of enzymes involved in their assembly, is highest during the first half of pregnancy[15] and subsequently further declines after 35 weeks.[16] Some reports also indicate a decline in collagen content during the final five to eight weeks. Thus, the properties of the membranes and limit of elastic distension may be set by mid-pregnancy. Amniotic fluid levels of MMP-1,[17] able to degrade fibrillar collagens, and MMP–7,[18] able to degrade elastin and basal lamina components, increase during the third trimester, particularly after 35 weeks, and, if membrane-derived, could underlie the phenomena of loss of elasticity and creep extension. The transition could reflect the switch in the phenotype of cells in the post-fusion chorion (Table 15.1)[19] and their response to increasing stretch.

Labour-associated changes

Biophysical forces associated with labour may be sufficient to cause rupture of the membranes. The rupture site at term SROM normally always involves the dependent membranes overlying the cervix and in 78% of women rupture occurs at a cervical dilatation of greater than 8 cm.[1] If the membranes outside this region are firmly attached to the uterine wall, contractions would further increases in lateral distensional forces in this unsupported area. This may be sufficient to bring the membrane to its limit of elastic distension and hence structural failure. Indeed, *in vitro* studies have demonstrated that repeated deformation of the amnion results in loss of elastic extension, termed strain hardening, and a reduction of their bursting pressure.[20] This may account for membrane rupture during pressure below the maximal pressure to which they have been exposed in labour.

Global cellular and biochemical changes in the levels of the MMPs associated with labour could act in concert with these local biophysical forces to cause the rupture of the membranes. Although expression of MMP-1 is unaffected, labour increases the expression of MMP-9.[21] Labour-affected membranes exhibit increased secretion of pro and active MMP–9.[22–26] This appears to represent a selective response of the amniotic epithelium, since it only expresses MMP-9 and the connective tissue layer only MMP-2.[25,26] Increased secretion of active MMP-2 in the decidua may be involved in the breakdown of the cytotrophoblast–decidual interface.[25,26] A critical role has therefore been proposed for MMP-9[27] and, although there is an inverse correlation between its concentrations and the tensile strength of the amniochorion,[28] its substrate specificity would indicate a role in degradation of basal lamina and not of fibrillar collagens.

A zone of localised morphological and cellular phenotypic changes and SROM

The dependent membranes over the cervix exhibit unusual changes in their morphology and cellular phenotype compared with normal fetal membranes. This was originally described in terms of an area of the membranes confined to a portion of the rupture tear, termed the zone of altered morphology (ZAM).[29] This area is almost devoid of decidua, the cytotrophoblastic layer attenuated with cells exhibiting apoptosis, swollen connective tissue layers of the amnion and particularly the chorion, gelatinous material in the spongy layer, and appearance of a range of abnormal amniotic epithelial cells. The dissociation of the collagenous matrix at the ultrastructural level may explain the observation that a marked variation in content occurs around the post-rupture tear.[30] The mesenchymal cells in the chorion of this area exhibit an activated myofibroblast phenotype (Table 15.1)[31] and the ECM characterised by increased expression of the matricellular proteins osteonectin and tenascin-C.[32,33] In some patients this cellular and extracellular matrix phenotype is also found in the associated amnion. That many of these features are exhibited by the membranes in the lower uterine pole prior to labour supports the concept that it may represent an area of increased susceptibility to rupture and that may proceed to rupture, even in the absence of labour.[34]

Mesenchymal activated myofibroblast phenotype

The differentiation of the activated myofibroblast in the chorion may play a key role in SROM. When the ECM can no longer stress shield mesenchymal cells, these cells respond by undergoing myofibroblastic differentiation.[35] Myofibroblasts then produce a counteractive contractile force to stress shield the ECM. If the loss of stress shielding occurs because of extreme tissue distension during this phase these, or other local cells, then actively remodel the ECM to provide a distended matrix and dissipate the distensional force. If loss of stress shielding is due to a weakened matrix, ECM synthesis is upregulated. In the chorion myofibroblasts are associated with matricellular proteins that are involved in the upregulation of MMP-9 expression. Myofibroblastic differentiation is co-dependent upon stretch and TGF-β.[35] The prelabour changes in the lower uterine pole, i.e. lower uterine segment development and effacement of the cervix, could provide this increased stretch and initiate local myofibroblast differentiation. Additionally, a direct effect of stretch may be involved in weakening the ECM, degrading collagens either directly or indirectly through hyaluronan, to lose stress shielding. Stretch *in vitro* causes a change in the pattern of gene expression by the amniochorion, and increased secretion of interleukin-8 (IL-8) and collagenase activity.[36,37] The appearance of the connective tissue layers of gelatinous material in the spongy layer suggests a change in hyaluronan metabolism in the ZAM. IL-8 in the cervix increases synthesis of hyaluronan, which stimulates collagenase and gelatinase activity.[38] However, stretch has also been reported to upregulate the synthesis of low molecular weight hyaluronan.[39] Such species have been reported to stimulate inflammatory cytokines and, in amnion cells, prostaglandin production.[40]

Cytotrophoblastic–decidual involution

The other key feature of the ZAM is the involution of the cytotrophoblastic–decidual interface. This could be produced by the changes in the lower uterine pole stripping the amniochorion from the decidua, equivalent to a tissue wounding, and/or indirectly through active involution of the decidua involving upregulation of active MMP-2.[26] This change may actually be involved in myofibroblastic differentiation. This phenotype represents reappearance of a phenotype seen in the pre-fusion amniochorion, where the cytotrophoblast is also attenuated and not attached to viable deciduas (Table 15.1).[19] *In vitro* physical damage to the cytotrophoblastic layer, which, as in other epithelial cells, could release TGF-β, may also induce this phenotype. Exogenous application of TGF-β but not IL-1, IL-6 or TNF-α, induces myofibroblast activation and involution of the epithelium.[19] Whether necrosis or apoptotic mechanisms in the cytotrophoblastic layer are associated with this induction is unknown but the ZAM region is associated with higher rates of apoptosis in the cytotrophoblastic layer[41,42] and amniotic epithelium.[42] TGF-β is also anti-apoptotic for myofibroblasts[43] but pro-apoptotic for certain epithelial cell types.[44] However, apoptosis could represent an epiphenomenon associated with degradation of its basement membrane, since, in other systems, disruption of integrin-mediated attachment to basal lamina induces apoptosis.[45]

Thus, a normal tissue response to extreme distension and/or tissue wounding, in a tissue dependent upon its ECM for its basic function, could paradoxically lead to a compromised ECM and, under increasing local distension, predispose them to rupture. The exact temporal and causal relationships between these components in this 'apoptotic/activated myofibroblastic' SROM pathway and the key elements whose failure underlie rupture may be crucial to an understanding of mechanisms underlying PROM.

Relevance to labour

As well as their function in the maintenance of the stability and strength of the gestational sac, cells of the fetal membranes are also implicated in the modulation of paracrine–endocrine mediators involved in the control of labour. The local mechanism proposed to underlie its structural breakdown is intimately linked with the parturition-associated changes in the lower uterine pole involving relaxation and ripening of the lower uterine segment and cervix. It could be possible that these regional differences in the amniochorial–decidual unit in the upper and lower poles are also associated with regional changes in its endocrine–paracrine function. For example, the attenuated apoptotic cytotrophoblast layer would imply lowered production of its uterotonin-degrading activities but loss of oxytocin production in the lower pole.

Preterm prelabour rupture of membranes

PROM is essentially failure of the structural integrity of the membranes in the absence of uterine contractions, that it, in the presence of normal intra-amniotic pressures. However, difficulties beset studies into the potential mechanisms underlying prelabour rupture of membranes, particularly when occurring preterm (PPROM), and the interpretation of their results.

Studies need to consider the following:

- Membranes are normally obtained long after the primary event and changes may represent 'post-event' changes acquired *in utero*.
- The aetiopathology of PROM may be gestation period-related and studies need to stratify data according to gestation date.
- Rupture may result from 'global' or 'local' changes and in the latter case changes may be missed by restricted biopsy sampling.
- A major clinical association with preterm PROM (PPROM) is intrauterine 'subclinical' infection which is often associated with major histological and biochemical alterations in the membranes. To elucidate other mechanisms of PROM, it may be crucially important to distinguish between these two major groups.
- Since complex interactive factors underlie the structural integrity and development of the membranes, PROM could result from the interaction of 'extrinsic' or sociobiological factors and 'intrinsic' genetic factors and be patient- or patient group-specific. This may be reflected by the wide range of histological patterns detected in membranes delivered after PPROM.[46] It may be argued that, as in other

complex multifactorial clinical conditions, to elucidate the mechanisms underlying PPROM, large patient bases are required to enable recognition of individual pathways or we need to focus upon specific clinical conditions associated with PPROM. At present, we are restricted in our interpretation by small group sized studies.

- The most significant clinical risk factors and clinical associations are also associated with preterm labour;[47] a fundamental question arises as to how these may underlie mechanisms leading to divergent clinical presentations. The problem is how to distinguish changes in the membranes that may be associated with preterm labour; analogous to the situation leading to SROM at term, from any specific changes leading to PROM, since as such they may just be a question of degree.

ECM degradation and apoptosis

PPROM may reflect a compromised ECM and, indeed, decreased collagen content has been reported to be associated with PPROM.[30] Although this may result from defective ECM synthesis during early pregnancy, most studies have implicated the involvement of active degradation by MMPs. PPROM, as compared with preterm labour membranes, exhibit increased expression of MMP-2, MMP-9, membrane type 1 MMP (MT1-MMP) and decreased tissue inhibitor of matrix metalloproteinase 2 (TIMP-2).[48] PPROM is associated with increased amniotic fluid levels of MMP-1,[17] and pro- and active MMP-9,[27,49] and although in not all studies, active MMP-2.[48,49] Some of these changes have been linked with the increased apoptosis and DNA fragmentation in the cytotrophoblastic and epithelial layers reported in PPROM.[50,51] Thus, PPROM as compared with preterm labour membranes exhibits increased expression of markers of the intrinsic pathway, p53 and bax and of the extrinsic pathway, Fas, TRADD and initiator caspase 8, and higher levels of the pro-apoptotic cytokine IL-18. However, it is possible that apoptosis may be associated with chorioamnionitis in these studies and also that changes in MMPs cause apoptosis via the action of these MMPs upon their basal lamina.[45]

Preterm PROM or labour

These changes appear analogous to those seen in the ZAM at term, albeit presumably affecting the membranes globally, and similarly suggest a link with the role of membranes in labour. Hypothetically, PPROM could arise from mechanisms that lead to failure of their structural integrity without any activation of activities associated with their role in labour. Such mechanisms could involve decidual involution, suboptimal synthesis and assembly of amniochorial ECM or increased activities of endogenous and exogenous enzymes able to degrade the ECM without altering the production of paracrine/endocrine mediators involved in the control of labour. Alternatively, these mechanisms could additionally be associated with the extensive apoptotic loss of cells associated with the production of these paracrine/endocrine mediators.

Alternatively, factors that activate production of paracrine/endocrine mediators, in the absence of cellular activities leading to ECM breakdown and apoptosis, would lead to preterm labour. More likely factors could induce both cellular activities with the clinical outcome dependent upon the relative activation of these activities together with the relative responses of tissues to those activities, e.g. the myometrium. Amniotic fluid levels of the ECM-degrading MMP-1 and -9 tend to be higher in PPROM, whereas the levels of inflammatory cytokines IL-1β, tumour necrosis factor alpha (TNF-α), IL-6 and IL-8, which are able to induce prostaglandin production by membranes,[52] are higher in preterm labour.[53] However, if these activities were anatomically restricted, the pathway to rupture of the membranes would be favoured, since the production of paracrine/endocrine factors from such a restricted site may not be sufficient to lead to labour. Interestingly, it has been suggested that this relative response may be related to the expression of TNF-α receptors, with responses mediated via TNFR1 predisposing to PROM but through TNFR2 to preterm labour.[54]

Clinical risk factors, clinical associations and mechanisms of PPROM

PPROM is associated with a range of clinical risk factors such as vaginal bleeding during the index pregnancy, cigarette smoking, previous preterm delivery[47] and clinical associations, e.g. clinical chorioamnionitis. Consideration of these factors may illuminate pathways leading to PPROM.

Intrauterine 'subclinical' infection

Microorganisms may be cultured from the membranes in cases of PPROM and preterm labour and these are associated with a maternal innate immune response, i.e. infiltration of neutrophils derived from the decidua into the amniochorion, recognised histologically as chorioamnionitis. Although infection in membranes may occur in the absence of chorioamnionitis, this does not imply absence of a maternal response, since the response could be restricted to the decidua, i.e. deciduitis (Figure 15.2a, b).[19] In a proportion of cases, organisms may gain access to amniotic fluid. Chorioamnionitis would appear to be preferentially associated with PPROM but the latency period in these cases could be associated with further infection spread, 'post-rupture' acquisition of infection and development of chorioamnionitis. A strong gestational effect is apparent in that intrauterine infection and chorioamnionitis is associated with the majority of cases of early preterm birth, whether PPROM or labour. This effect may reflect the potential access of infective organisms to the whole surface of the amniochorion and decidua prior to their fusion and obliteration of the uterine cavity at weeks 20–25. Indeed, their presence and the response of the chorion and decidua may prevent the fusion process and the fusion-associated change in chorionic phenotype. The association of chorioamnionitis with large areas of the fetal membranes supports the presence of infection pre-fusion and the potential global effect upon the decidua and amniochorion.

The structural stability of the amniochorion may be compromised by multiple mechanisms that act by inducing the immunoinflammatory/innate immune system. Upon access to the cavity, microorganisms may infect both the decidual and the chorionic cytotrophoblastic layer and then migrate into chorion connective tissue and amnion. These organisms may directly compromise the ECM if they possess enzymes able to degrade ECM components. Both the decidua and amniochorion can respond to the recognition of pathogen-associated molecules such as lipopolysaccharide (LPS), through the production of proinflammatory cytokines such as TNF-α, IL-1, IL-6 and the chemokines such as IL-8.[52] These factors could directly upregulate the local synthesis of MMPs in membranes, i.e. LPS upregulates MMP-2 and -9 expression,[55] IL-6 and IL-1 upregulate MMP-9 expression[54] and, in the case of TNF-α, additionally upregulate active MMP-9,[54] and thus may induce degradation of the ECM.

However, it more likely that the infiltration of neutrophils into the decidua and subsequently into the chorionic cytotrophoblastic interface and connective tissue

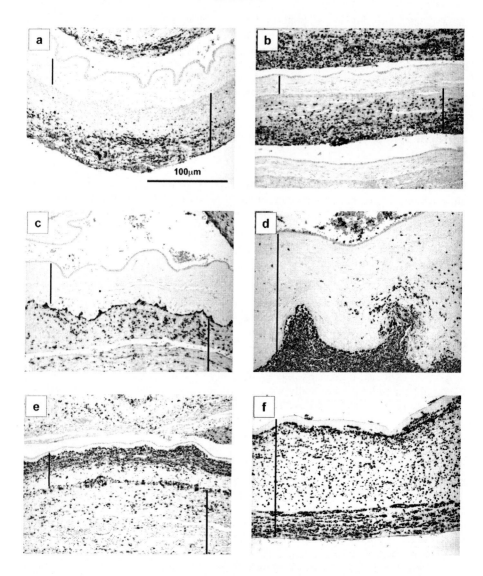

Figure 15.2. Immunocytochemical localisation of neutrophil elastase in fetal membranes obtained from patients who presented with delivered by preterm prelabour rupture of the membranes (PPROM) during weeks 25–32.[19] The vertical bars on the left hand side of the figures indicate the connective tissue layers of the amnion and chorion, and on the right hand side, if present, the chorionic cytotrophoblastic layer and the decidua. Histopathological reports for patients a and b indicated absence of chorioamnionitis. In c and d, neutrophils have not penetrated the cytotrophoblastic basal lamina except at a patch in d. In e and f, extensive infiltration is detected extending into the connective tissue layers up to the compact layer of the amnion. The amniotic epithelium is lost in f. Figures c and f reproduced with permission from McParland and Bell[4]

layers, resulting from increased synthesis of infection-induced chemoattractants IL-8, TNF-α and IL-1, is involved in ECM degradation. Neutrophils possess an armoury of mechanisms including preformed molecules in their granules, e.g. neutrophil collagenase MMP-8, MMP-9, neutrophil gelatinase-associated lipocalin MMP-9 and elastase and, upon activation, the production of free radicals which follows induction, enabling them to destroy pathogens. However, these may be released and under conditions causing their excessive infiltration or increased lifespan, the local protective mechanisms provided by resident cells, including production of antiproteases such as secretory leucocyte protease inhibitor (SLPI),[56] and of enzymes involved in the removal of free radicals,[57] may be overwhelmed and lead to direct ECM degradation and cellular apoptosis. Lower levels of SLPI are found in amniotic fluid from women with PPROM.[56] These enzymes are potentially able to degrade all components of the ECM. Free radicals may also have direct damaging effects upon components such as collagens and hyaluronan and, *in vitro*, may directly increase the secretion of MMP-9 by membrane explants.[58] Chorioamnionitis is associated with apoptosis in the cytotrophoblast and amniotic epithelium.[42,59] This could arise from a direct effect of infection since both LPS and TNF-α induce the intrinsic and extrinsic pathways of apoptosis in membranes *in vitro*.[55,60] However, apoptosis may represent an epiphenomenon reflecting the action of these enzymes upon their basal lamina.

As previously discussed, the extent of this apoptosis could underlie whether infection at the maternofetal interface gives rise to PPROM or preterm labour. Intrauterine infection has been proposed to be associated with preterm labour via the link between the inflammatory cytokine response and uterotonin production.[52] Whether infection leads to PPROM or preterm labour may depend upon the nature and relative response of the decidua and amniochorion to pathogens. This would affect the balance between the production of inflammatory cytokines and ECM degradation and cellular apoptosis as apoptosis affects those cells associated with the production of those inflammatory cytokines. Indices of activation of apoptotic pathways in membranes from women presenting with PPROM are increased compared with those in preterm labour, although the potential effects of the latency period of three to four weeks in this study has to be considered.[48] Often overlooked is the range of histological presentations of chorioamnionitis and its relationship to these parameters (Figure 15.2).[19]

Many interactive factors will be involved in the access of organisms to the uterus through the cervix. These include the properties of the organisms themselves, defects in cervical immunity, and cervical physical status. Additionally, since the decidua and chorion produce a range of antimicrobial products, such as β-defensins,[61] intrauterine infection and chorioamnionitis may only occur when it is compromised or overwhelmed.

Maternal uterocervical factors

A range of factors associated with the uterine, cervical and decidual components is linked with both PPROM and preterm labour and it is the co-presence of other factors that dictates the clinical outcome and presentation.

Multifetal gestation

Preterm delivery is associated with multiple pregnancy.[62] It is assumed that accelerated increases in intrauterine volume prematurely precipitate processes associated with term parturition, with the effects preferentially affecting the fetal membrane and cervical components. That PROM most often affects the presenting sac, which would encompass the 'dependent' membrane, supports this view. If the increase in lateral tension is premature, the development of the chorionic cytotrophoblastic layer during its fusion to the decidua, with the associated change in chorionic phenotype, may be affected and the membranes prematurely switch to excessive degradation of the ECM.

Cervical factors

Cervical weakness represents a continuum of cervical dysfunction from funnelling of the internal to full cervical dilatation in the absence of contractions. As such, these alterations in the cervical support and cleavage from the decidua could generate changes associated with term birth, i.e. ZAM generation, which could proceed to rupture of the membranes without increased intra-amniotic pressures. However, such changes would also expose the fetal membranes in the uterine cavity to ascending infections, if present prior to fusion, and those over the cervix, if present after fusion, and be classified as infected cases of PPROM. Women with both a shortened cervix and bacterial vaginosis have the highest risk of preterm delivery and the majority with advanced cervical dilatation in the absence of contractions also have colonisation of the amniotic cavity with bacteria.[63]

Decidual factors

The decidua fulfils a critical role in the establishment and maintenance of the stable interface with the amniochorion and of its functional behaviour. Factors that affect decidual function *per se* will affect the process of fusion during mid-pregnancy and be required to maintain the structural integrity of the amniochorion. The relative functional responses of macrophages within the decidua to bacterial products, as compared with those in the amniochorion, may affect the production of local immunoinflammatory cytokines and prostaglandins and influence the outcome of intrauterine infection.[52] Decidual cells have been proposed to be able to switch to a cell producing a range of mediators of ECM degradation, such as MMP-1, -3, -9, tissue plasminogen activator and urokinase-type plasminogen activator.[64] This pathway is normally suppressed by progesterone. Local failure in progesterone action or supply, perhaps through vascular defects, could result in upregulation of this pathway. Elevation of decidual relaxin production has been reported to be associated with PPROM[65] and the *in vitro* demonstration that relaxin decreases the tensile strength of membrane supports a causal role. Decidual relaxin, whose production is normally suppressed by progesterone,[66] also upregulates expression of these mediators and its receptors are found in the decidua and chorion.[67,68] Decidual haemorrhage is also associated with PPROM and it has been proposed that thrombin acting upon decidual receptors can upregulate these activities of the decidual cell leading to local ECM degradation and ROM.[69]

Nutritional and behavioural factors

Two nutritional/behavioural factors have been linked with PPROM: ascorbate levels and smoking. These potentially interact, since smoking independently affects the peripheral levels of ascorbate. However studies indicate an association with lowered amniotic fluid ascorbate levels and not with maternal levels or consumption.[70,71] Lowered amniotic fluid ascorbate levels could reflect defective maternal–fetal transport or increased consumption within the fetus and amniotic cavity and this could account for the link between lowered maternal ascorbate levels in women with a high risk of pre-eclampsia,[72] a condition not associated with PROM. Ascorbate is directly involved as a coenzyme in the synthesis and assembly of major ECM components of the amniochorion, i.e. fibrillar collagens and elastin. Thus, deficiency of ascorbate in the amniotic cavity and extraembryonic coelum could result in an ECM of suboptimal strength and elasticity. Low ascorbate levels result in increased MMP-1, -2 and -9 secretion by membrane explants[73] and this effect *in vivo* could therefore further reduce the tensile strength and elasticity of the membranes, rendering them particularly susceptible to rupture during the second half of pregnancy. Ascorbate also plays a key role in removal of free radicals and a local deficiency in the membranes and amniotic fluid could interact with the effects of the neutrophil infiltration associated with infection in the amniochorion.[74]

Genetic factors

PPROM exhibits recurrence rates of 21–32%,[75,76] and in women presenting with recurrent PROM, 62% of PPROM births are preceded by PPROM birth.[77] This supports a genetic contribution, which could act at multiple, interactive levels.

ECM synthesis

No studies have determined the association between polymorphisms affecting genes encoding the components of the ECM and enzymes responsible for their assembly. However, clinical conditions arising from such mutations have been specifically associated with PPROM. Pregnancy in women with Ehlers–Danlos syndrome has been reported to be associated with a higher incidence of PPROM delivery[78] but the highest risk for preterm delivery has been suggested to result from fetal carriage.[79] This condition arises owing to mutations in collagen I, III and V genes affecting their structure, in activities of enzymes responsible for their assembly, and from mutations in other ECM molecules involved in ECM assembly, including the matricellular proteins such as tenascin-X and small leucine-rich proteoglycans such as decorin.[80] Mutations affecting the structure of other ECM components, such as fibrillin-1 and elastin, might also exhibit a unique predisposition to PPROM. It is also possible that, owing to unique aspects of the composition of or unique pressures to which this tissue is exposed, mutations in these genes may affect the stability of the amniochorion but not be associated with any other clinical condition. As failure of amniochorial structure may occur without activation of immunoinflammatory mediator/prostaglandin production, this group could represent mechanisms unique to PPROM.

ECM degradation

Functional polymorphisms in the promoters of the MMPs that result in their enhanced production and catalytic activity have been reported.[81] Fetal carriage, i.e. expression by cells of the amniochorion, of polymorphisms associated with enhanced production of MMP-1,[82] and of MMP-9,[83] are associated with a higher risk of PPROM in African American mothers as compared with term birth. It would be of interest to determine whether these polymorphisms are specifically associated with PPROM.

Immunoinflammatory pathways

Many polymorphisms exist in genes encoding components of pathways involved in the cellular responses to bacterial products such as LPS and the production of immunoinflammatory mediators such as IL-1β and TNF-α, and are associated with a number of chronic inflammatory conditions. Any specific association with PPROM may provide insights into infection-mediated pathways that lead to either PPROM or labour. One such polymorphism in Nod2 has been reported to be absent in neonates born by PPROM in African American mothers as compared with term births, and its absence has been suggested to protect against PPROM.[84] Polymorphisms exist in genes encoding IL-1β, such as IL1B+3953*2, which is associated with elevated levels of IL-1β, and of its antagonist IL-1ra, such as ILRN*2, which is associated with elevated levels of both IL-1β and IL-1ra.[85] Absence of either fetal or maternal carriage of IL1B+3953*2 in an African American population was found to be associated with preterm delivery, whereas fetal but not maternal carriage of ILRN*2 was found to be specifically associated with a higher risk of PPROM in a Hispanic American population. Similarly, maternal or fetal carriage of a polymorphism associated with increased production of TNF-α, TNFA*2, has been reported to be specifically associated with PPROM in some populations.[86] Although the potential co-association with infection has not been examined, they imply that TNF-α, for example, plays a key role in infection-mediated pathways leading to PPROM in some populations.

Conclusions

The mechanism by which membrane rupture occurs both before and during labour is largely unknown. More information is needed about the nature of the molecular architecture and assembly of its ECM, and the role of cellular constituents in these processes and of the factors that regulate these activities. We require more information about the phenotypic responses of their cellular constituents to a range of factors to which they are exposed under normal and pathological situations, for example stretch and infection, especially in terms of ECM remodelling, immunoinflammatory cytokines, chemokines and growth factors, and the factors involved in local innate immunity. The membranes represent a functioning amniochorial–decidual unit, with interactions between the cellular components, and therefore between the maternal and fetal genomes in the decidual and amniochorial compartments.

Since the structural integrity of the membranes may be affected by multiple interactive factors and mechanisms and be differentially susceptible to those factors at different gestation periods, PPROM must represent a multifactorial clinical condition involving complex interactions between environmental, behavioural and genetic factors, and be potentially patient- or patient-population-specific. An understanding of the factors that predispose women to PPROM and their interactions is critical if progress is to be made in identifying such women and developing therapies to reduce its incidence since, unlike spontaneous labour where the process may conceivably be reversed or delayed, at its clinical presentation PPROM has already occurred.

Acknowledgements

The authors wish to thank Wellbeing and Tommy's Campaign for financial support for their studies.

References

1.   Romero R, Athayde N, Maymon E, Pacora P, Bahado-Singh R. Premature rupture of the membranes. In: Reece EA, Hobbins JC, editors. *Medicine of the Fetus and Mother.* 2nd ed. Philadelphia: Lippincott-Raven Publishers; 1999. p. 1581–625.
2.   Lee T, Silver H. Etiology and epidemiology of preterm premature rupture of the membranes. *Clin Perinatol* 2001;28:721–34.
3.   Mercer BM. Preterm premature rupture of the membranes. *Obstet Gynecol* 2003;101:178–93.
4.   McParland PC, Bell SC. The fetal membranes and mechanisms underlying their labour-associated and pre-labour rupture during pregnancy. *Fetal Maternal Medicine Review* 2004;15: 1–36.

5.   Bell SC, Malak TM. Structural and cellular biology of the fetal membranes. In: Elder MG, Romero R, Lamont RF, editors. *Preterm Labor*. New York and London: Churchill Livingstone; 1997. p. 401–28.

6.   Oxlund H, Helmig R, Halabert JT, Uldbjerg N. Biomechanical analysis of human chorioamniotic membranes. *Eur J Obstet Gynecol Reprod Biol* 1990;34:247–55.

7.   Stamenkovic I. Extracellular matrix remodelling: the role of matrix metalloproteinases. *J Pathol* 2003;200:448–64.

8.   Ockleford CD, Mongan L, Hubbard ARD. Techniques of advanced light microscopy and their applications to morphological analysis of human extra-embryonic membranes. *Microsc Res Tech* 1997;38:153–64.

9.   Bryant-Greenwood GD. The extracellular matrix of the human fetal membranes: structure and function. *Placenta* 1998;19:1–11.

10.   Meinert M, Eriksen GV, Petersen AC, Helmig RB, Laurent C, Uldbjerg N, *et al.* Proteoglycans and hyaluronan in human fetal membranes. *Am J Obstet Gynecol* 2001;184:679–85.

11.   Millar LK, Stollberg J, DeBuque L, Bryant-Greenwood G. Fetal membrane distention: determination of the intrauterine surface area and distention of the fetal membranes preterm and at term. *Am J Obstet Gynecol* 2000;182:128–34.

12.   Lavery JP, Miller CE. The viscoelastic nature of chorioamniotic membranes. *Obstet Gynecol* 1977;50:467–72.

13.   Lavery JP, Miller CE. Deformation and creep in the human chorioamniotic sac. *Am J Obstet Gynecol* 1979;134:366–75.

14.   Pressman EK, Cavanaugh JL, Woods JR. Physical properties of the chorioamnion throughout gestation. *Am J Obstet Gynecol* 2002;187:672–5.

15.   Casey ML, MacDonald PC. Interstitial collagen synthesis and processing in human amnion: a property of the mesenchymal cells. *Biol Reprod* 1996;55:1253–60.

16.   Meirowitz NB, Smulian JC, Hahn RA, Zhou P, Shen-Schwarz S, Lambert GH, *et al.* Collagen messenger RNA expression in the human amniochorion in premature rupture of membranes. *Am J Obstet Gynecol* 2002;187:1679–985.

17.   Maymon E, Romero R, Pacora P, Gervasi MT, Bianco K, Ghezzi F, *et al.* Evidence for the participation of interstitial collagenase (matrix metalloproteinase 1) in preterm premature rupture of membranes. *Am J Obstet Gynecol* 2000;183:914–20.

18.   Maymon E, Romero R, Pacora P, Gervasi MT, Edwin SS, Gomez R, *et al.* Matrilysin (matrix metalloproteinase 7) in parturition, premature rupture of membranes, and intrauterine infection. *Am J Obstet Gynecol* 2000;182:1545–53.

19.   McParland PC, Bell SC. Unpublished data.

20.   Lavery JP, Miller CE, Knight RD. The effect of labor on the rheologic response of chorioamniotic membranes. *Obstet Gynecol* 1982;60:87–92.

21.   Bryant-Greenwood GD, Yamamoto SY. Control of peripartal collagenolysis in the human chorion-decidua. *Am J Obstet Gynecol* 1995;172:63–70.

22.   Vadillo-Ortega F, Gonzalez-Avila G, Furth EE, Lei H, Muschel RJ, Stetler-Stevenson WG, *et al.* 92-kd type IV collagenase (matrix metalloproteinase-9) activity in human amniochorion increases with labor. *Am J Pathol* 1995;146:148–56.

23.   Tsatas D, Baker MS, Rice GE. Gene expression of plasminogen activation cascade components in human term gestational tissues with labor onset. *J Reprod Fertil* 1999;116:43–9.

24.   McLaren J, Taylor DJ, Bell SC. Increased concentration of pro-matrix metalloproteinase-9 in term fetal membranes overlying the cervix prior to labour: implications for membrane remodeling and rupture. *Am J Obstet Gynecol* 2000;182:409–16.

25.   Xu P, Alfaidy N, Challis JRG. Expression of matrix metalloproteinase (MMP)-2 and MMP-9 in human placenta and fetal membranes in relation to preterm and term labor. *J Clin Endocrinol Metab* 2002;87:1353–61.

26.   Goldman S, Weiss A, Eyali V, Shalev E. Differential activity of the gelatinases (matrix metalloproteinases 2 and 9) in the fetal membranes and decidua, associated with labour. *Mol Hum Reprod* 2003;9:367–73.

27.   Athayde N, Edwin SS, Romero R, Gomez R, Maymon E, Pacora P, *et al.* A role for matrix metalloproteinase-9 in spontaneous rupture of the fetal membranes. *Am J Obstet Gynecol* 1998;179:1248–53.

28.   Uchide K, Ueno H, Inoue M, Sakai A, Fujimoto N, Okada Y. Matrix metalloproteinase-9 and tensile strength of fetal membranes in uncomplicated labor. *Obstet Gynecol* 2000;95:851–5.

29.   Malak TM, Bell SC. Structural characteristics of term human fetal membranes (amniochorion and decidua): a novel zone of extreme morphological alteration within the rupture site. *Br J Obstet Gynaecol* 1994;101:375–86.

30.   Hampson V, Liu D, Billett E, Kirk S. Amniotic membrane collagen content and type distribution in women with preterm premature rupture of the membranes in pregnancy. *Br J Obstet Gynaecol*

1997;104:1087–91.

31.   McParland PC, Taylor DJ, Bell SC. Myofibroblast differentiation in the connective tissues of the amnion and chorion of term human fetal membranes: implications for fetal membrane rupture and labour. *Placenta* 2000;21:44–53.

32.   McParland PC, Bell SC, Pringle JH, Taylor DJ. Regional and cellular localization of osteonectin/SPARC expression in connective tissue and cytotrophoblastic layers of human fetal membranes at term. *Mol Hum Reprod* 2001;7:463–74.

33.   McParland PC, Pringle JH, Bell SC. Tenascin and the fetal membrane wound hypothesis – programming for fetal membrane rupture? *Br J Obstet Gynaecol* 1998;105:1223–4.

34.   McParland PC, Taylor DJ, Bell SC. Mapping of zones of altered morphology and chorionic connective tissue cellular phenotype in human fetal membranes (amniochorion and decidua) overlying the lower uterine pole and cervix before labor at term. *Am J Obstet Gynecol* 2003;189:1481–8.

35.   Tomasek JJ, Gabbiani G, Hinz B, Chaponnier C, Brown RA. Myofibroblasts and mechano-regulation of connective tissue remodelling. *Nat Rev Mol Cell Biol* 2002;3:349–63.

36.   Maradny EE, Kanayama N, Halim A, Maehara K, Terao T. Stretching of fetal membranes increases the concentration of interleukin-8 and collagenase activity. *Am J Obstet Gynecol* 1996;174:843–9.

37.   Nemeth E, Millar LK, Bryant-Greenwood GD. Fetal membrane distension. II. Differentially expressed genes regulated by acute distension *in vitro*. *Am J Obstet Gynecol* 2000;182:60–7.

38.   El Maradny E, Kanayama N, Kobayashi H, Hossein B, Khatun S, Liping S, *et al*. The role of hyaluronic acid as a mediator and regulator of cervical ripening. *Hum Reprod* 1997;12:1080–8.

39.   Dowthwaite GP, Ward AC, Flannely J, Suswillo RF, Flannery CR, Archer CW, *et al*. The effect of mechanical strain on hyaluronan metabolism in embryonic fibrocartilage cells. *Matrix Biol* 1999;18:523–32.

40.   Kobayashi H, Sun GW, Terao T. Production of prostanoids via increased cyclo-oxygenase-2 expression in human amnion cells in response to low molecular weight hyaluronic acid fragment. *Biochim Biophys Acta* 1998;1425:369–76.

41.   McLaren J, Taylor DJ, Bell SC. Increased incidence of apoptosis in non-labor affected cytotrophoblast cells in term fetal membranes overlying the cervix: implications for preterm birth. *Hum Reprod* 1999;14:2895–900.

42.   Kataoka S, Furita I, Yamada H, Kato EH, Ebina Y, Kishida T, *et al*. Increased apoptosis of human fetal membranes in rupture of the membranes and chorioamnionitis. *Placenta* 2002;23:224–31.

43.   Zhang HY. Phan SH. Inhibition of myofibroblast apoptosis by transforming growth factor beta(1). *Am J Respir Cell Mol Biol* 1999;21:658–65.

44.   Schuster N, Krieglstein K. Mechanisms of TGF-beta-mediated apoptosis. *Cell Tissue Res* 2002;307:1–14.

45.   Frisch SM, Francis II. Disruption of epithelial cell-matrix interaction induces apoptosis. *J Cell Biol* 1994;124:619–26.

46.   Bendon RW, Faye-Petersen O, Qureshi F, Elder N, Das A, Hauth J, *et al*. Histologic features of chorioamnion membrane rupture: development of methodology. *Pediatr Pathol Lab Med* 1997;17:27–42.

47.   Harger JH, Hsing AW, Tuomala RE, Gibbs RS, Mead PB, Eschenbach DA, *et al*. Risk factors for preterm premature rupture of fetal membranes: a multicenter case–control study. *Am J Obstet Gynecol* 1990;163:130–7.

48.   Fortunato SJ, Menon R. Distinct molecular events suggest different pathways for preterm labor and premature rupture of membranes. *Am J Obstet Gynecol* 2001;184:1399–406.

49.   Maymon E, Romero R, Pacora P, Gervasi MT, Gomez R, Edwin SS, *et al*. Evidence of *in vivo* differential bioavailability of the active forms of matrix metalloproteinases 9 and 2 in parturition, spontaneous rupture of membranes, and intra-amniotic infection. *Am J Obstet Gynecol* 2000;183:887–94.

50.   Fortunato SJ, Menon R, Lombardi SJ. Programmed cell death (apoptosis): a possible pathway to metalloproteinase activation and fetal membrane degradation in PROM. *Am J Obstet Gynecol* 2000;182:168–72.

51.   Sagol S, Sagol O, Ozkal S, Asena U. Role of apoptosis, bcl-2 and bax protein expression in premature rupture of fetal membranes. *J Reprod Med* 2002;47:809–15.

52.   Gomez R, Romero R, Mazor M, Ghezzi F, David C, Yoon BH The role of infection in preterm labor and delivery. In: Elder MG, Romero R, Lamont RF, editors. *Preterm Labor*. New York and London: Churchill Livingstone; 1997. p. 85–125.

53.   Romero R, Chaiworapongsa T, Espinoza J, Gomez R, Yoon BH, Edwin S, *et al*. Fetal plasma MMP-9 concentrations are elevated in preterm premature rupture of the membranes. *Am J Obstet Gynecol* 2002;187:1125–30.

54.   Fortunato SJ, Menon R, Lombardi SJ. Role of tumor necrosis factor-alpha in the premature rupture of membranes and preterm labor pathways. *Am J Obstet Gynecol* 2002;187:1159–62.

55. Fortunato SJ, Menon R, Lombardi SJ. Support for an infection-induced apoptopic pathway in human fetal membranes. *Am J Obstet Gynecol* 2001;184:1392–8.

56. Helmig R, Romero R, Espinoza J, Chaiworapongsa T, Bujold E, Gomez R, *et al.* Neutrophil elastase and secretory leukocyte protease inhibitor in prelabor rupture of the membranes, parturition and intra-amniotic infection. *J Matern Fetal Neonatal Med* 2002;12:237–46.

57. Telfer JF, Thomson AJ, Cameron IT, Greer IA, Norman JE. Expression of superoxide dismutase and xanthine oxidase in myometrium, fetal membranes and placenta during normal human pregnancy and parturition. *Hum Reprod* 1997;12:2306–12.

58. Buhimschi IA, Kramer WB, Buhimschi CS, Thompson LP, Weiner CP. Reduction-oxidation (redox) state regulation of matrix metalloproteinase activity in human fetal membranes. *Am J Obstet Gynecol* 2000;182:458–64.

59. Murtha AP, Auten R, Herbert WNP. Apoptosis in the chorion laeve of patients with histologic chorioamnionitis. *Infect Dis Obstet Gynecol* 2002;10:93–6.

60. Menon R, Lombardi SJ, Fortunato SJ. TNF-alpha promotes caspase activation and apoptosis in human fetal membranes. *J Assist Reprod Genet* 2002;19:201–4.

61. Ganz T. Defensins: antimicrobial peptides of innate immunity. *Nat Rev Immunol* 2003;3:710–20.

62. Dube J, Dodds L, Armson BA. Does chorionicity or zygosity predict adverse perinatal outcomes in twins? *Am J Obstet Gynecol* 2002;186:579–83.

63. Romero R, Salafia CM, Athanassiadis AP, Hanaoka S, Mazor M, Sepulveda W, *et al.* The relationship between acute inflammatory lesions of the preterm placenta and amniotic fluid microbiology. *Am J Obstet Gynecol* 1992;166:1382–28.

64. Lockwood CJ, Krikun G, Hausknecht VA, Papp C, Schatz F. Matrix metalloproteinase and matrix metalloproteinase inhibitor expression in endometrial stromal cells during progestin-initiated decidualization and menstruation-related progestin withdrawal. *Endocrinology* 1998;139:4607–13.

65. Bogic LV, Yamamoto SY, Millar LK, Bryant-Greenwood G. Developmental regulation of the relaxin genes in the decidua and placenta: overexpression in the preterm premature rupture of the membranes. *Biol Reprod* 1997;57:908–20.

66. Bryant-Greenwood G, Millar LK. Human fetal membranes: their preterm premature rupture. *Biol Reprod* 2000;63:1575–9.

67. Qin X, Garibay-Tupas J, Chua PK, Cachola L, Bryant-Greenwood GD. An autocrine/paracrine role of human decidual relaxin. I. Interstitial collagenase (matrix metalloproteinase-1) and tissue plasminogen activator. *Biol Reprod* 1997;56:800–11.

68. Qin X, Chua PK, Ohira RH, Bryant-Greenwood GD. An autocrine/paracrine role of human decidual relaxin. II. Stromelysin-1 (MMP-3) and tissue inhibitor of matrix metalloproteinase-1 (TIMP-1). *Biol Reprod* 1997;56:812–20.

69. Rosen T, Schatz F, Kuczynski E, Lam H, Koo AB, Lockwood CJ. Thrombin-enhanced matrix metalloproteinase-1 expression: a mechanism linking placental abruption with premature rupture of the membranes. *J Matern Fetal Neonatal Med* 2002;11:11–7.

70. Barrett BM, Sowell A, Gunter E, Wong M. Potential role of ascorbic acid and beta-carotene in prevention of preterm rupture of fetal membranes. *Int J Vitam Nutr Res* 1994;64:192–7.

71. Kim YH, Ahn BW, Yang SY, Song TB, Byun J. Antioxidant vitamins of amniotic fluid in pregnant women with preterm labor and intact membranes and with preterm premature rupture of membranes. *J Soc Gynecol Investig* 2000;7:254A.

72. Chappell LC, Seed PT, Kelly FJ, Briley A, Hunt BJ, Charnock-Jones DS, *et al.* Vitamin C and E supplementation in women at risk of preeclampsia is associated with changes in indices of oxidative stress and placental function. *Am J Obstet Gynecol* 2002;187:777–84.

73. Vadillo Ortega F, Pfeffer Burak F, Bermejo Martinez ML, Hernandez Miranda MA, Beltran Montoya J, Tejero Barrera E, *et al.* [Dietetic factors and premature rupture of fetal membranes. Effect of vitamin C on collagen degradation in the chorioamnion.] [Spanish]. *Ginecol Obstet Mex* 1995;63:158–62.

74. Woods JR. Reactive oxygen species and preterm premature rupture of the membranes – a review. *Placenta* 2001;22 Suppl A:S38–44.

75. Naeye RL, Peters EC. Causes and consequences of premature rupture of fetal membranes. *Lancet* 1980;1:192–4.

76. Asrat T, Lewis DF, Garite TJ, Major CA, Nageotte MP, Towers CV, *et al.* Rate of recurrence of preterm premature rupture of membranes in consecutive pregnancies. *Am J Obstet Gynecol* 1991;165:1111–5.

77. Doody DR, Patterson MQ, Voigt LF, Mueller BA. Risk factors for the recurrence of premature rupture of the membranes. *Paediatr Perinat Epidemiol* 1997;11:96–106.

78. Barabas AP. Ehlers–Danlos syndrome: associated with prematurity and premature rupture of foetal membranes; possible increase in incidence. *BMJ* 1966;5515:682–4.

79. Lind J, Wallenburg HC. Pregnancy and the Ehlers–Danlos syndrome: a retrospective study in a Dutch population. *Acta Obstet Gynecol Scand* 2002;81:293–300.

80.   Mao JR, Bristow J. The Ehlers–Danlos syndrome: on beyond collagens. *J Clin Invest* 2001;107:1063–9.

81.   Ye S. Polymorphism in matrix metalloproteinase gene promoters: implication in regulation of gene expression and susceptibility of various diseases. *Matrix Biol* 2000;19:623–9.

82.   Fujimoto T, Parry S, Urbanek M, Sammel M, Macones G, Kuivaniemi H, *et al.* A single nucleotide polymorphism in the matrix metalloproteinase-1 (MMP-1) promoter influences amnion cell MMP-1 expression and risk for preterm premature rupture of the fetal membranes. *J Biol Chem* 2002;277:6296–302.

83.   Ferrand PE, Parry S, Sammel M, Macones GA, Kuivaniemi H, Romero R, *et al.* A polymorphism in the matrix metalloproteinase-9 promoter is associated with increased risk of preterm premature rupture of membranes in African Americans. *Mol Hum Reprod* 2002;8:494–501.

84.   Ferrand PE, Fujimoto T, Chennathukuzhi V, Parry S, Macones GA, Sammel M, *et al.* The CARD15 2936insC mutation and TLR4 896 A>G polymorphism in African Americans and risk of preterm premature rupture of membranes (PPROM). *Mol Hum Reprod* 2002;8:1031–4.

85.   Genc MR, Gerber S, Nesin M, Witkin SS. Polymorphism in the interleukin-1 gene complex and spontaneous preterm delivery. *Am J Obstet Gynecol* 2002;187:157–63.

86.   Roberts AK, Monzon-Bordonaba F, Van Deerlin PG, Holder J, Macones GA, Morgan MA, *et al.* Association of polymorphism within the promoter of the tumor necrosis factor alpha gene with increased risk of preterm premature rupture of the fetal membranes. *Am J Obstet Gynecol* 1999;180:1297–302.

Chapter 16

Clinical management of preterm prelabour rupture of membranes

Sara Brigham and James P Neilson

Introduction

Spontaneous preterm prelabour rupture of the membranes (PPROM) complicates approximately 2% of all pregnancies and accounts for up to 30% of all preterm deliveries.[1,2] The potential maternal and perinatal complications and their relative importance vary at different gestational ages, with the main risks for the fetus balanced between premature delivery and infection. However, other complications include fetal distress, cord compression, orthopaedic deformities and pulmonary hypoplasia. Maternal consequences of PPROM include increased risk of infection, both before and after birth – the postpartum infection risk is up to 12%.[3,4] In the report of the UK Confidential Enquiry into Maternal Deaths[5] covering the period 1997 to 1999, there were three maternal deaths related to infection and PPROM: one was with ruptured membranes at 21 weeks with a cervical suture, one at 30 weeks, and one in 'mid-pregnancy'. In addition to the risk of infection, there is also an increased caesarean section rate due to fetal distress, abruption and malpresentations associated with prematurity.

In some cases, management will be dictated by overt signs of infection, fetal compromise or advanced labour at presentation. However, in cases of PPROM where there is no immediate indication for delivery at presentation, optimal management remains controversial.

Outcome following PPROM

The most frequent consequence of PPROM is preterm delivery. Most large series report similar pregnancy outcomes following PPROM of 50% delivery within one week, 70–75% by two weeks, and 80–85% or more within one month.[6] With sophisticated neonatal intensive care, 50% of infants born at 24 weeks will survive, with greater than 70% surviving at 26 weeks of gestation. The main complications of prematurity other than death are respiratory distress syndrome, intraventricular haemorrhage, necrotising enterocolitis, retinopathy of prematurity and chronic lung disease. Limited data suggest that delivery due to PPROM does not affect these incidences.[7]

In pregnancies complicated by PPROM, the main causes of neonatal death are pulmonary hypoplasia and severe prematurity. Postnatal survival is directly related to gestational age at PPROM and gestational age at delivery (57% at 24–28 weeks and 96% for those greater than 32 weeks).[8] For cases of PPROM occurring at less than 23 weeks of gestation, the outlook is poor with only a 13% perinatal survival rate, rising to 50% at 24–26 weeks.[9]

Pulmonary hypoplasia has a mortality rate among neonates as high as 70%. The development of pulmonary hypoplasia has been shown to be directly related to the gestational age at PPROM and it is unlikely to occur after 24 weeks of gestation, the incidence ranges between 0 and 24%.[7] The estimated risk of pulmonary hypoplasia is around 50% at 19 weeks of gestation, falling to about 10%+ at 25 weeks.[10]

As well as gestational age at PPROM, the amount of amniotic fluid present following rupture is important for the development of pulmonary hypoplasia. If there is a pool of amniotic fluid greater than or equal to 2 cm, the incidence of pulmonary hypoplasia dramatically reduces.[11] In addition to pulmonary hypoplasia, severe orthopaedic deformities have been described with PPROM from less than 20 weeks, with the reported incidence varying between 0% and 35%.[11] The severity of orthopaedic deformities is related to the degree of oligohydramnios and, as would be expected, there is also a strong association between pulmonary hypoplasia and the extent of skeletal deformities.[10]

Initial management

Confirmation of membrane rupture

Because of the prognostic implications of PPROM, and subsequent management challenges, an accurate initial diagnosis is necessary. In more than 90% of cases, a diagnosis can be made from taking a careful history and by performing a physical examination.[12] Sterile speculum examination will confirm the diagnosis with visualisation of clear fluid passing through the cervix or a pool of fluid in the posterior fornix. It will also enable the taking of swabs and amniotic fluid for microscopy and culture. Digital examinations should be avoided because of the increased risk of infection.[13] If the diagnosis remains in doubt, a swab can be taken from the posterior fornix, and smeared onto a microscope slide and allowed to dry: the presence of ferning confirms membrane rupture.[14] Ultrasound may also be useful to help in the diagnosis, in the presence of oligohydramnios with an appropriately grown normal baby and a history suggestive of PPROM.

Initial maternal and fetal assessment

Initial assessment should identify indications for immediate delivery such as fetal compromise, intra-amniotic infection and advanced labour. An ultrasound examination may give insight into gestational age (if not already known), estimated fetal weight and presentation, and may also exclude fetal malformations. At the time of speculum examination, vaginal swabs and vaginal amniotic fluid should be taken for microscopy and culture, which should include full bacteriological screening.

Once the diagnosis of PPROM has been confirmed, all women should receive two doses of corticosteroids 12 hours apart to reduce the incidence of neonatal respiratory distress syndrome.[15] If delivery is not imminent and a decision has been made to pursue conservative management, women should also be started on antibiotics. A Cochrane review[16] of 19 trials including over 6000 women has shown antibiotic administration following PPROM to be associated with a delay in delivery and a reduction in major markers of neonatal morbidity. The choice of which antibiotic to use is less clear, however. It appears that co-amoxiclav is associated with an increased risk of necrotising enterocolitis and should therefore be avoided in women at risk of preterm delivery. From the evidence presented in the review, it would seem that erythromycin is a better choice. Therefore, once PPROM has been confirmed, a ten-day course of oral erythromycin should be prescribed. The presence of group B haemolytic streptococcus in swabs, liquor or urine should be treated accordingly and consideration given to the appropriateness of conservative management versus expediting delivery.

Conservative management versus delivery

There is little consensus of opinion as to the exact point in gestation when the risk of infection with expectant management outweighs the risk of prematurity with active delivery of the fetus. The available data suggest that, with proper management in the previously uninfected patient, the risk of serious infection with expectant management is low.[17] There is little doubt over the appropriate conservative management of PPROM at less than 34 weeks of gestation. The management of ruptured membranes at greater than 37 weeks is also not in question. However, between 34 and 37 weeks there is a great deal of controversy and clinicians use various arbitrary cut-offs between these gestations. Some use amniocentesis to assess fetal lung maturity and if there is documented lung maturity then labour is induced.[18,19] However, evidence does suggest that pregnancies greater than or equal to 34 weeks of gestation have fewer infections and equally good outcomes if delivered immediately.[20,21]

Conservative management

Inpatient versus outpatient care for women with PPROM

Traditionally, women with PPROM are managed on an inpatient basis – mainly due to the short latency period and high complication rate, particularly of infection. Recently, however, the time from rupture to delivery has increased.

Criteria for outpatient management have been proposed which include various parameters that need to be fulfilled prior to embarking on outpatient management.[22] Initially, there should be a period of inpatient monitoring (48–72 hours) with no signs of infection. The woman should have social circumstances compatible with such a policy, with good transport and living within a short distance of the hospital (not greater than 20 minutes away), and the fetus should have a cephalic presentation. The women must have the ability to check their pulse and temperature every six hours and perform a fetal kick count daily. Twice-weekly cardiotocography and blood investigations, with weekly ultrasound for presentation and amniotic fluid index, should be performed and the deepest pool must be maintained greater than 2 cm.

A randomised controlled trial showed that only a very small proportion of cases of PPROM met these strict criteria as described above.[23] However, for those who did meet the criteria, there was no significant difference in any of the measured outcomes. The only significant difference between randomised groups was in the cost of inpatient care. Another (unpublished) randomised trial found similar results but with an increased caesarean section rate and longer hospital stay for the inpatient management group.

This information would suggest that it may be possible to manage certain highly selected women on an outpatient basis. However, this is based on only two small randomised controlled trials and therefore further larger randomised trials are needed to clarify issues of safety.

Monitoring for infection in PPROM

In the UK, the majority of units use clinical signs such as white cell count and C-reactive protein (CRP), vaginal swabs, vaginal liquor and biophysical profile to predict intra-amniotic infection. However, in some units, amniocentesis to identify infection is performed on admission as standard practice.

Clinical signs, maternal white cell count and CRP

Symptoms and signs of chorioamnionitis include raised temperature, uterine tenderness, fetal or maternal tachycardia, foul-smelling discharge, raised white cell count and the presence of contractions. Studies looking at the values of these various parameters in the prediction of intrauterine infection have reported a wide range of true positive and false positive rates.

Elevated white cell count has always been the gold standard for significant systemic infection, but it is also nonspecific. In a review of women with PPROM, there was a range of sensitivities and specificities for diagnosing intrauterine infection.[24] The positive predictive value ranged from 40% to 75% and the negative from 52% to 89%. Although white cell count has a high specificity for significant infection, the sensitivity and positive predictive values were too low for the prediction of histological chorioamnionitis, positive amniotic fluid cultures or clinical intrauterine infection. At least 55% of women with PPROM have histological signs of infection at delivery.[25]

CRP is a product of the hepatic acute-phase reaction to infection. Its production is also nonspecific and there is a wide variation in the positive and negative predictive values of the test.[24] However, one small study has shown that an increased CRP level 30% above baseline appears to be the most promising predictor of intrauterine infection.[26]

Attempts at refining the prediction of intrauterine infection (as defined by positive amniotic fluid or fetal blood cultures) have been made by combining maternal heart rate, temperature, leucocyte count and CRP. A study by Carroll et al.[27] showed that, even in combination, heart-rate and temperature changes together with relatively noninvasive blood investigations have poor sensitivity for intra-amniotic infection – this may be due to the fact that the majority of intra-amniotic infections in pregnancies complicated by PPROM are subclinical. This variation of sensitivities in prediction of intra-amniotic infection has also been shown in 23 other studies as identified by Carroll (Table 16.1).

Subclinical infection, as described above, is an important factor to consider when deciding the management of women with PPROM. Despite the apparent lack of clinical or biochemical signs, the inflammatory process has already been triggered, mediated by cytokines. Cytokines are small glycoproteins produced by many cell types, in particular those of the immune system. They have been directly linked to the development of periventricular leukomalacia and chronic lung disease in the neonate.[28] As a result of the association between subclinical infection and cytokines, studies have been conducted looking at maternal serum and amniotic fluid cytokine levels to try to identify a more sensitive marker of subclinical infection. In one study,[29] maternal serum interleukin-6 (IL-6) concentrations greater than 8 pg/ml were shown to be highly predictive of intra-amniotic infection (positive predictive value of 96%, negative predictive value of 95%). At present, serum interleukins are only available for research purposes and not as a commercial investigation. Amniotic fluid cytokines will be discussed below.

Table 16.1. Sensitivities of maternal pyrexia, leucocytosis and raised C-reactive protein in prediction of intra-amniotic infection; data from Carroll *et al.*[27]

	Sensitivity (%)
Pyrexia ≥ 38 °C	17–56
Leucocytosis	6–83
C-reactive protein	46–100

Lower genital tract swabs

Organisms from the lower genital tract have been implicated in both the aetiology and adverse neonatal sequelae for women with PPROM. In more than 75% of cases of PPROM with positive amniotic fluid cultures, the same organisms were recovered from vaginal and/or endocervical swabs.[30] However, it was also shown that the incidence of positive cultures from the lower genital tract in women with PPROM was similar to that in normal pregnancies. Positive genital tract cultures predict 40% of positive fetal blood and 53% of positive amniotic fluid cultures. From this it can be concluded that lower genital tract cultures are poor predictors of intrauterine infection but, once infection is present, they may be useful for determining the causative organisms.

Amniotic fluid

Amniotic fluid investigations are the tests that are most likely to give an accurate representation of the intrauterine environment. However, of all the tests so far discussed, they are the most invasive and, in the presence of PPROM, the most technically challenging. Evaluation of amniotic Gram stain, culture, white cell count and glucose have all been studied in an attempt to identify and predict the presence of intra-amniotic infection. The majority of these studies have, however, been undertaken in the presence of intact membranes.

The most widely used method for rapid detection of microbial invasion of the amniotic cavity is the Gram stain. However, this has been shown in several studies to have sensitivities of 50% to 60%.[31,32] Despite this, Gram stain is very specific for positive amniotic fluid culture (99.1%). The amniotic fluid culture is perhaps the gold standard, with 77% of women in the study by Garite *et al.*[32] with a positive amniotic fluid culture developing amnionitis, endometritis or neonatal infection.

Low fluid glucose concentrations have been associated with infection in studies of samples from different bodily sites.[24] It would therefore seem appropriate to examine amniotic fluid glucose concentrations. However, these concentrations must be interpreted in relation to gestational age, as the levels alter from a mean of 46 mg/dl at 16 weeks of gestation to 16 mg/dl at term.[33] Studies looking at the value of this in determining intra-amniotic infection have shown poor sensitivities and positive predictive values when using a cut-off of 14–15 mg/dl.[30,34] The sensitivities may be low because glucose metabolism may be organism-dependant, for example, *Mycoplasma* species do not use glucose as a substrate.[35]

As with maternal serum, other tests on amniotic fluid have now included cytokine assays of IL-6, IL-1b, tumour necrosis factor and IL-8. Most of the work has been performed on women in preterm labour with intact membranes. Using a cut-off of

11.3 ng/ml for amniotic fluid IL-6 has shown this test to be highly sensitive and specific (sensitivity of 100%, specificity of 82.6%) for the detection of intra-amniotic infection, which is even better than the sensitivities obtained for Gram stain, glucose and white cell count.[30] Again, as with maternal serum cytokine assays, these tests are still only available for research purposes.

Fetal assessment

Studies have suggested that intra-amniotic infection may cause vasoconstriction of the umbilical and chorionic vessels, reducing fetal circulation and oxygenation.[36,37] This would therefore affect fetal behaviour and should be identified with fetal heart rate monitoring and ultrasound.

Various studies have examined the role of the biophysical profile and the cardiotocograph in detecting intra-amniotic infection in PPROM. As with all the methods previously described, there is a wide range of sensitivities and specificities due to the differing endpoints of, for example, positive fetal blood samples or histological chorioamnionitis.

Studies that have examined the association between a nonreactive cardiotocograph and infection have shown that intra-amniotic infection is significantly associated with a nonreactive cardiotocograph (sensitivities between 78% and 86%).[37,38]

Biophysical profile scoring was initially introduced for high-risk pregnancy monitoring using methods described by Manning et al.[39] Following this, the association between an abnormal biophysical profile and intrauterine infection was described by Vintzileos et al.[40] This group accurately identified neonates who subsequently developed sepsis using daily biophysical examinations. In a further study, intervention for biophysical profile scores less than 8, despite a reduction in neonatal and maternal infection with prompt delivery, showed no documented improved neonatal survival.[41] However, low biophysical profile scores do seem to predict positive amniotic fluid cultures accurately: 100% sensitivity for a score of 2, 85% for a score of 4.[42] Of all the factors studied in the biophysical profile, fetal breathing movements appear to be the most useful. Goldstein et al.[43] showed that normal fetal breathing had a negative predictive value of 100% for a positive amniotic fluid culture.

The first randomised trial[44] of daily nonstress testing versus daily biophysical profile showed that neither cardiotocography nor the biophysical profile had good sensitivities for predicting infection, with sensitivities of 39.1% and 25% respectively. The conclusions from this study were that, despite the poor sensitivities of both nonstress testing and daily biophysical profile scoring, the specificities and negative predictive values were acceptable, and a normal test was reassuring. Therefore, it may be more worthwhile and cost-effective to perform daily nonstress testing, using biophysical profile for an abnormal test. Addition of fetal breathing evaluation to an abnormal nonstress test significantly improves the positive predictive value for intrauterine infection.[32]

Tocolysis for women with PPROM

Tocolysis has been used to delay delivery in women with PPROM and potentially reduce perinatal complications. Studies have examined the use of tocolytics either prophylactically or in women with uterine activity. A meta-analysis identified four randomised controlled trials, of which two were rejected, that addressed the question of whether tocolytics prolong pregnancies with PPROM beyond 24 hours without any serious adverse effects.[45] The studies were of small sample size but showed that there was no evidence to support the use of tocolytics after 24 hours – the time required to administer the full course of steroids.

This finding has been supported by a randomised trial[46] where 145 women were recruited to either aggressive tocolysis or no tocolysis. The results showed that women with PPROM do not have a significantly improved perinatal outcome if aggressive tocolysis is used. Another study[47] has suggested that long-term tocolysis may actually result in an increased risk of maternal and intrauterine infection. (Table 16.2).

Amnioinfusion in the management of PPROM

The intact, fluid-filled amniotic sac fulfils a variety of functions for the fetus during gestation, including bacteriostasis, development of fetal lung, intrauterine temperature homeostasis, protection from external trauma and umbilical cord protection. Apart from labour, the two most important problems that may occur following PPROM are umbilical cord compression and chorioamnionitis. More chronic problems include pulmonary hypoplasia and fetal deformities such as hand/foot abnormalities. The incidence and severity of these fetal deformations is inversely proportional to the gestational age at time of PPROM.[48]

Amnioinfusion was first proposed as a method of infusing antibiotics directly into the amniotic sacs of women with chorioamnionitis.[49] It has since been described in two further applications: to reduce the incidence of pulmonary hypoplasia and of cord compression.

Amnioinfusion to reduce the incidence of pulmonary hypoplasia

Gestational age at membrane rupture, latency period and either initial (pool depth less than 2 or less than 1 cm in the latency period) or average amniotic fluid index have been shown to have significant impact on the development of pulmonary hypoplasia and are significant factors in predicting perinatal death.[50]

A study by Locatelli *et al.*[51] examined the role of amnioinfusion in the management of PPROM at less than 26 weeks of gestation. This was a small study that did not have a control group, and only 30% of the women retained the infused solution. However, the results suggest that there may be improved perinatal outcome with serial amnioinfusions maintaining the depth of amniotic fluid at greater than 2 cm. Further larger randomised controlled trials are needed prior to including this in everyday clinical practice for management of women with PPROM.

Table 16.2. Short-term versus long-term prophylactic tocolysis for women with PPROM; data from Decavalas *et al.*[47]

	Short-term	Long-term
Number of women	105	136
Average inpatient days	5.5	6.8
Number with chorioamnionitis	12	40
Number with endometritis	20	45
Number of perinatal deaths	3	3

Amnioinfusion to reduce umbilical cord compression

Most of the work on cord compression has been performed to reduce the incidence of fetal heart-rate abnormalities caused by intrapartum cord compression in the term fetus. Miyazaki and Nevarez[52] found that amnioinfusion produced complete resolution of variable decelerations in approximately 50% of the study group. A Cochrane systematic review by Hofmeyr[53] identified one trial[54] of amnioinfusion for PPROM that included 66 women. The review found no significant difference in perinatal outcomes for the groups. However, there was a reduction in the number of severe fetal heart-rate decelerations per hour and the umbilical artery pH was increased.

New techniques in the treatment of PPROM

Iatrogenic rupture of the membranes

The incidence of iatrogenic PPROM is approximately 1% after genetic amniocentesis, 3–5% after diagnostic fetoscopy and 5–8% after operative fetoscopy.[55]

The first successful treatment of iatrogenic PPROM following operative fetoscopy was described in 1996.[56] This involved the intra-amniotic injection of a single autologous unit of platelets and a unit of cryoprecipitate. This technique mimicked that performed for cerebrospinal fluid leakage and spinal headache after spinal anaesthesia. Immediate clot formation was noted on ultrasound within the amniotic cavity. The woman experienced no further leakage and delivered at term. This technique was called the 'amniopatch'.[57]

Luks et al.[58] have developed a technique in ovine and primate models utilising gelatin sponge to seal fetoscopy port sites. At the end of the procedure, a pre-cut piece of gelatin sponge is introduced into the shaft of the cannula using an applicator. This technique has been described in one human case of membrane rupture at 17 weeks of gestation following fetoscopic treatment for a twin pregnancy, with one twin being acardiac. The procedure was initially performed at 19 weeks of gestation, following an amnioinfusion. Twenty-four hours after the procedure, the woman reported leakage of fluid and passage of the sponge. The procedure was then repeated at 21 weeks of gestation following insertion of a McDonald cerclage. The woman was delivered at 36 weeks of gestation with no abnormality in the baby other than clubbed feet.

Surgical approach to the treatment of spontaneous PPROM

Endoscopic assessment of spontaneous rupture of membranes by Quintero et al.[59] showed that the site of rupture in women with spontaneous PPROM was over the internal os, but was located elsewhere in women with iatrogenic PPROM. It was also found that 'spontaneous' PPROM does not undergo spontaneous healing, unlike iatrogenic PPROM. This is reflected in the ability of the amniopatch to seal iatrogenic PPROM. Due to the large size of the membrane defect and the location over the internal os, it was speculated that spontaneous PPROM would require surgical grafting – the 'amniograft'.[60] They report a case of spontaneous PPROM at 16 weeks and 4 days of gestation. The membrane defect was assessed endoscopically and a square of Biosis, a collagen-based graft, was passed down the shaft of the trocar. Laser welding of the graft to the amnion proved unsuccessful and it was subsequently fixed with fibrin glue. Further leakage of amniotic fluid occurred two weeks after the procedure. The woman was delivered at 30 weeks of gestation and at 12 months of age the infant was doing well.

A similar technique to the one described above has been used by Sciscione et al.[61] They describe the use of transvaginally applied intracervical fibrin sealant (using a commercial fibrin tissue sealant) for PPROM at less than 24 weeks. The fibrin was introduced using a double lumen catheter with the tip sitting in the internal os under ultrasound guidance. Injection was continued until a clot was seen. If no increase in amniotic fluid was seen then the procedure was repeated. Of the 12 women reported, the mean gestational age at delivery was 27 weeks and 4 days, with most of the women going into spontaneous labour. Only one woman had chorioamnionitis. Seven of the 13 neonates survived. (One pregnancy was a twin pregnancy: the second twin was born 13 days after the first and died of a Gram-negative sepsis.) There was no evidence of adhesions, fetal swallowing or disturbance in the fetal coagulation system.

The small studies and case reports described above suggest that there may be a role in clinical practice to try to seal the site of membrane rupture. However, these techniques need to be assessed further in larger randomised trials.

Acknowledgements

Sara Brigham's fellowship to study cytokine profiles in PPROM was funded by a grant from the Research & Development Programme of the Liverpool Women's Hospital NHS Trust.

References

1. Mercer BM, Lewis R. Preterm labor and preterm premature rupture of the membranes. Diagnosis and management. *Infect Dis Clin North Am* 1997;11:177–201.
2. Kaltreider DF, Kohl S: Epidemiology of preterm delivery. *Clin Obstet Gynecol* 1980;23:17.
3. Mercer BM. Management of premature rupture of membranes before 26 weeks' gestation. *Obstet Gynecol Clin North Am* 1992;19:339–51.
4. Garite TJ, Freeman RK. Chorioamnionitis in the preterm gestation. *Obstet Gynecol* 1982;59:539–45.
5. Lewis G, Drife J, editors. Why Mothers Die 1997–1999. The Fifth Report of the Confidential Enquiries into Maternal Deaths in the United Kingdom. London: RCOG Press, 2001.
6. Schucker JL, Mercer BM: Midtrimester premature rupture of the membranes. *Semin Perinatol* 1996;20:389–400.
7. Kilbride HW, Thibeault DW. Neonatal complications of preterm premature rupture of membranes. Pathophysiology and management. *Clin Perinatol* 2001;28:761–85.
8. Carroll SG, Blott M, Nicolaides KH: Preterm prelabor amniorrhexis: outcome of live births. *Obstet Gynecol* 1995;86:18–25.
9. Moretti M, Sibai BM. Maternal and perinatal outcome of expectant management of premature rupture of membranes in the midtrimester. *Am J Obstet Gynecol* 1988;159:390–6.
10. Rotschild A, Ling EW, Puterman ML, Farquharson D. Neonatal outcome after prolonged preterm rupture of the membranes. *Am J Obstet Gynecol* 1990;162:46–52.
11. Vergani P, Ghidini A, Locatelli A, Cavalione M, Ciarla I, Capellini A, et al. Risk factors for pulmonary hypoplasia in second trimester premature rupture of membranes. *Am J Obstet Gynecol* 1994;170:1359–64.
12. Smith RP. A technique for the detection of rupture of the membranes. A review and preliminary report. *Obstet Gynecol* 1976;48:172–6.
13. Schutte MF, Treffers PE, Kloosterman GJ, Soepatmi S. Management of premature rupture of membranes: the risk of vaginal examination to the infant. *Am J Obstet Gynecol* 1983;146:395–400.
14. Reece EA, Chervenak FA, Moya FR, Hobbins JC. Amniotic fluid arborisation: effect of blood, meconium, and pH alterations. *Obstet Gynecol* 1984;64:248–50.
15. Crowley P. Prophylactic corticosteroids for preterm birth. *Cochrane Database Syst Rev* 2000;(2):CD000065.
16. Kenyon S, Boulvain M, Neilson J. Antibiotics for preterm rupture of membranes. *Cochrane Database Syst Rev* 2003;(2):CD001058.
17. Kennedy KA, Clark SL. Premature rupture of the membranes: management controversies. *Clin*

Perinatol 1992;19:385–97.

18.   Capeless EL, Mead PB. Management of preterm premature rupture of membranes: lack of a national consensus. *Am J Obstet Gynecol* 1997;157:11–2.

19.   Mercer BM, Crocker LG, Boe NM, Sibai BM. Induction versus expectant management in premature rupture of the membranes with mature amniotic fluid at 32 to 36 weeks: a randomized trial. *Am J Obstet Gynecol* 1993;169:775–8.

20.   Naef RW 3rd, Allbert JR, Ross EL, Weber BM, Martin RW, Morrison JC. Premature rupture of membranes at 34 to 37 weeks' gestation: aggressive versus conservative management. *Am J Obstet Gynecol* 1998;178:126–30.

21.   Spinnato JA, Shaver DC, Bray EM, Lipshitz J. Preterm premature rupture of the membranes with fetal pulmonary maturity present: a prospective study. *Obstet Gynecol* 1987;69:196–201.

22.   Bartfield MC, Carlan SJ. The home management of preterm premature ruptured membranes. *Clin Obstet Gynecol* 1998;4:503–14.

23.   Carlan SJ, O'Brien WF, Parsons MT, Lense JJ. Preterm premature rupture of membranes: a randomized study of home versus hospital management. *Obstet Gynecol* 1993;8:61–4.

24.   Greig PC. The diagnosis of intrauterine infection in women with preterm premature rupture of the membranes (PPROM). *Clin Obstet Gynecol* 1998;41:849–86.

25.   Romero R, Quintero R, Oyarzun E, Wu YK, Sabo V, Mazor M. Intraamniotic infection and the onset of labor in preterm premature rupture of the membranes. *Am J Obstet Gynecol* 1988;159:661–6.

26.   Romem Y, Artal R. C-reactive protein as a predictor for chorioamnionitis in cases of premature rupture of the membranes. *Am J Obstet Gynecol* 1984;150:546–50.

27.   Carroll SG, Papaioannou S, Davies ET, Nicolaides KH. Maternal assessment in the prediction of intrauterine infection in preterm prelabour amniorrhexis. *Fetal Diagn Ther* 1995;10:290–6.

28.   Edwards AD, Duggan PJ. Placental inflammation and brain injury in preterm infants. In: Kingdom J, Jauniaux E, O'Brien PMS, editors. *The Placenta: Basic Science and Clinical Practice.* London: RCOG Press; 2000.

29.   Murtha AP, Greig PC, Jimmerson CJ, Roitman-Johnson B, Allen J, Herbert WNP. Maternal serum interleukin-6 concentrations in patients with preterm premature rupture of membranes and evidence of infection. *Am J Obstet Gynecol* 1996;175:966–9.

30.   Carroll SG, Papaionnou S, Ntumazah IL, Philpott-Howard J, Nicolaides KH. Lower genital tract swabs in the prediction of intrauterine infection in preterm prelabour amniorrhexis. *Br J Obstet Gynaecol* 1996;103:54–9.

31.   Romero R, Yoon BH, Mazor M, Gomez R, Diamond MP, Kenney JS, *et al.* The diagnostic and prognostic value of amniotic fluid white blood cell count, glucose, interleukin-6 and Gram stain in patients with preterm labor and intact membranes. *Am J Obstet Gynecol* 1993;169:805–15.

32.   Garite TJ, Freeman RK, Linzey EM, Braly P. The use of amniocentesis in patients with premature rupture of membranes. *Obstet Gynecol* 1979;54:226–30.

33.   Weiss PA, Hoffman H, Winter R, Purstner P, Lichtenegger W. Amniotic fluid glucose values in normal and abnormal pregnancies. *Obstet Gynecol* 1985;65:333–9.

34.   Coultrip LL, Grossman JH. Evaluation of rapid diagnostic tests in the detection of microbial invasion of the amniotic cavity. *Am J Obstet Gynecol* 1992;167:1231–42.

35.   Carroll SG, Sebire NJ, Nicolaides KH. Preterm prelabour amniorrhexis: detection of infection. In: Nicolaides KH, editor. *Preterm Prelabour Amniorrhexis.* London: Parthenon; 1996. p. 87–123.

36.   Hyde S, Smotherman J, Moore J, Altshuler G. A model of bacterially induced umbilical vein spasm, relevant to fetal hypoperfusion. *Obstet Gynecol* 1989;73:966–70.

37.   Vintzileos AM, Campbell WA, Rodis JF. Tests of fetal well-being in premature rupture of the membranes. *Obstet Gynecol Clin North Am* 1992;19:281–307.

38.   Goldstein I, Copel JA, Hobbins JC. Fetal behaviour in preterm premature rupture of the membranes. *Clin Perinatol* 1989;16:735–54.

39.   Manning FA, Platt LD, Sipos L. Antepartum fetal evaluation: development of a fetal biophysical profile score. *Am J Obstet Gynecol* 1980;136:787–95.

40.   Vintzileos AM, Campbell WA, Nochimson DJ, Connolly ME, Fuenfer MM, Hoehn GJ. The fetal biophysical profile in patients with premature rupture of membranes – an early predictor of infection. *Am J Obstet Gynecol* 1985;152:510–6.

41.   Vintzileos AM, Knuppel RA. Fetal biophysical assessment in premature rupture of the membranes. *Clin Obstet Gynecol* 1995;38:45–58.

42.   Gauthier DW, Meyer WJ, Bieniarz A. Biophysical profile as a predictor of amniotic fluid culture results. *Obstet Gynecol* 1992;80:102–5.

43.   Goldstein I, Romero R, Merrill S. Fetal body and breathing movements as predictors of intraamniotic infection in preterm premature rupture of membranes. *Am J Obstet Gynecol* 1988;159:363–8.

44.   Lewis DF, Adair D, Weeks J, Barrileaux P, Edwards M and Garite T. A randomized clinical trial of daily nonstress testing versus biophysical profile in the management of preterm premature rupture

of membranes. *Am J Obstet Gynecol* 1999;181:1495–9.

45. Ohlsson A. Treatment of preterm premature rupture of the membranes: a meta-analysis. *Am J Obstet Gynecol* 1989;160:890–906.

46. How HY, Cook CR, Cook VD, Miles DE, Spinnato JA. Preterm premature rupture of membranes: aggressive tocolysis versus expectant management. *J Matern Fetal Med* 1998;7:8–12.

47. Decavalas G, Mastrogiannis D, Papadopoulos V, Tzingounis V. Short-term versus long-term prophylactic tocolysis in patients with preterm premature rupture of membranes. *Eur J Obstet Gynecol Reprod Biol* 1995;55:143–7.

48. Strong TH Jr. Amnioinfusion with preterm, premature rupture of membranes. *Clin Perinatol* 1992;19:399–409.

49. Goodlin RC. Intra-amniotic antibiotic infusion. *Am J Obstet Gynecol* 1981;139:975.

50. Winn HN, Chen M, Amon E, Leet TL, Shumway JB, Mostello D. Neonatal pulmonary hypoplasia and perinatal mortality in patients with midtrimester rupture of the amniotic membranes – a critical analysis. *Am J Obstet Gynecol* 2000;182:1638–44.

51. Locatelli A, Vergani P, Pirro GD, Doria V, Biffi A, Ghidini A. Role of amnioinfusion in the management of premature rupture of the membranes at <26 weeks' gestation. *Am J Obstet Gynecol* 2000;183:878–82.

52. Miyazaki FS, Nevarez F. Saline amnioinfusion for relief of repetitive variable decelerations: a prospective randomized study. *Am J Obstet Gynecol* 1985;153:301–6.

53. Hofmeyr GJ. Amnioinfusion for preterm rupture of membranes. *Cochrane Database Syst Rev* 2000;(2):CD000942.

54. Nageotte MP, Freeman RK, Garite TJ, Dorchester W. Prophylactic intrapartum amnioinfusion in patients with preterm premature rupture of membranes. *Am J Obstet Gynecol* 1985;153:557–62.

55. Quintero RA. New horizons in the treatment of preterm premature rupture of membranes. *Clin Perinatol* 2001;28:861–75.

56. Quintero RA, Romero R, Dzieczkowski J, Mammen E, Evans MI. Sealing of ruptured amniotic membranes with intra-amniotic platelet cryoprecipitate plug [letter]. *Lancet* 1996;347:1117.

57. Quintero RA, Morales WJ, Allen M, Bornick PW, Arroyo J, LeParc G. Treatment of iatrogenic previable premature rupture of membranes with intra-amniotic injection of platelets and cryoprecipitate (amniopatch): preliminary experience. *Am J Obstet Gynecol* 1999;181:744–9.

58. Luks IL, Deprest MD, Koen HE, Peers KHE, Steegers EAP, Van Der Wildt B. Gelatin sponge plug to seal fetoscopy port sites: technique in ovine and primate models. *Am J Obstet Gynecol* 1999;181:995–6.

59. Quintero R, Morales W, Kalter CS, Allen M, Mendoza G, Angel JL, et al. Transabdominal intra-amniotic endoscopic assessment of previable premature rupture of membranes. *Am J Obstet Gynecol* 1998;179:71–6.

60. Quintero R, Morales W, Bornick P Allen M, Garabelis N. Surgical treatment of spontaneous rupture of membranes: the amniograft – first experience. *Am J Obstet Gynecol* 2002;186:155–7.

61. Sciscione A, Manley J, Pollock M, Maas B, Shlossman PA, Mulla W, et al. Intracervical fibrin sealants: a potential treatment for early preterm premature rupture of the membranes. *Am J Obstet Gynecol* 2001;184:368–73.

Chapter 17

Antimicrobials in the management of preterm parturition

David J Taylor

Introduction

Approximately 13 million preterm births occur annually worldwide. The incidence ranges from 5.6% in Oceania to 11% in North America.[1] The majority of preterm neonates in developing countries die. In developed countries, preterm birth is the most common cause of perinatal and neonatal death, neonatal morbidity and childhood disability. Approximately one-third of preterm birth in developed countries is the result of medical intervention for maternal and fetal disease, either by induction of labour or caesarean section, one-third results from spontaneous preterm labour, and one-third from preterm prelabour rupture of the fetal membranes (PPROM). There is a significant body of evidence to implicate subclinical infection of the intrauterine space via the decidua, chorion and amnion in the genesis of both spontaneous preterm labour and PPROM. This evidence comes from animal studies, human observational studies and human experimental studies.

Animal studies[2–7] have shown that administration of bacterial endotoxin and the intrauterine or intracervical inoculation of bacteria cause pregnancy loss. Furthermore, the incidence of these losses can be reduced by the administration of antibiotics and antiprostaglandins.

Human studies have demonstrated an excess of abnormal cervicovaginal pathogens in women presenting with spontaneous preterm labour or PPROM.[8] Furthermore, women who have abnormal colonisation of the cervicovaginal environment during the prenatal period are more likely to go on to deliver preterm.[8] Histological chorioamnionitis is found more often after preterm birth than term birth and the frequency of this pathology increases with decreasing gestational age.[9–11] A positive microbial culture from the amniotic fluid is found more frequently in women who present in either spontaneous preterm labour or PPROM. Gomez et al.[12] showed in their overview of the literature that microbial invasion of the amniotic fluid is found in approximately 13% of women in spontaneous preterm labour and in 35% of women who present with PPROM.

Cohort studies and case–control studies have associated a large number of microorganisms with spontaneous preterm labour and PPROM (Table 17.1). The strongest associations are with bacterial vaginosis and *Gardnerella vaginalis*, *Ureaplasma urealyticum*, and the sexually transmitted organisms *Chlamydia trachomatis* and *Neisseria gonorrhoeae*. In addition, asymptomatic bacteriuria in the first trimester is associated with a doubling of the risk of subsequent delivery of a low-birthweight infant.[13]

Table 17.1. Microorganisms associated with preterm birth and PPROM; reproduced with permission from McDonald[8]

Organism	Preterm birth		PPROM	
	During pregnancy	Labour	During pregnancy	Labour
Bacterial vaginosis	++	++	++	++
Gardnerella vaginalis[a]	++	++		
Bacteriodes	+	++	+	+
Ureaplasma urealyticum	+		+	++
Mycoplasma hominis	+		++	+
Group B streptococcus	+		+	+
Escherichia coli		+	+	+
Klebsiella		+		
Haemophilus influenzae		+		+
Chlamydia trachomatis	++	++	++	+
Neisseria gonorrhoeae	++		++	
Trichomonas vaginalis			+	
Listeria monocytogenes		+		
Asymptomatic bacteriuria	++	++		

[a] heavy concentrations; + = some evidence for association but inconclusive; ++ = strong evidence for association

Prenatal intervention

Since abnormal microbial colonisation of the genital tract during pregnancy is associated with subsequent preterm birth, attempts have been made to prevent preterm birth by antibiotic intervention during the prenatal period. However, the association between abnormal cervicovaginal colonisation by pathogenic microorganisms and subsequent preterm birth is not strong: the odds ratios lie between one and two. Some of the organisms are common in the genital tract. For example, 80% of healthy pregnant women carry Ureaplasma urealyticum,[8] while bacterial vaginosis is present in up to 20% of women during pregnancy.[14] Screening for abnormal colonisation of the cervix and vagina in the general pregnant population would therefore have low positive predictive value and specificity. However, such screening and subsequent antibiotic treatment may be of value in groups of women who are at increased risk of preterm birth.

Asymptomatic bacteriuria

One intervention that has been demonstrated to reduce the risk of delivery of a low-birthweight infant is antibiotic treatment of asymptomatic bacteriuria. A meta-analysis[13] of randomised trials of this intervention shows a reduction in the odds of delivery of a low-birthweight infant by 40% (OR 0.60; 95% CI 0.45–0.80). It is possible that antibiotics given for this condition prevent delivery by reducing the risk of an acute urinary tract infection. Up to one-third of women will develop symptomatic urinary tract infection after having been identified as having asymptomatic bacteriuria. However, another possible explanation is that asymptomatic bacteriuria is a marker of genitourinary colonisation by pathogens. Treatment with antibiotics in early pregnancy would eliminate these pathogens from the lower genital tract, thereby reducing the risk of ascending infection in the chorio-decidual space, and subsequent preterm parturition. This theory is supported by the observation that women with a history of urinary tract infection have a vaginal colonisation rate with *Escherichia coli* two to three times times higher than those with no such history.[15]

Bacterial vaginosis

Antibiotic treatment of other markers of genital tract colonisation has focused on bacterial vaginosis identified during pregnancy. In the most recent meta-analysis,[16] ten trials involving 4249 women were included. Two trials were of vaginal clindamycin cream, one of metronidazole with erythromycin, and the other trials were of metronidazole. Antibiotic therapy was effective in eradicating bacterial vaginosis during pregnancy (OR 0.21; 95% CI 0.18–0.24), but did not significantly reduce the risk of preterm birth before 37 weeks of gestation (OR 0.95, 95% CI 0.82–1.10) (see Figure 17.1). Treatment did significantly decrease the risk of PPROM (OR 0.32; 95% CI 0.15–0.67). In women with previous preterm birth, treatment did not affect the risk of subsequent preterm birth (OR 0.83; 95% CI 0.59–1.17) but it did decrease the risk of PPROM (odds ratio 0.14; 95% CI 0.05–0.38) and low birthweight (OR 0.31; 95% CI 0.13 – 0.75). This overview demonstrated that antibiotic treatment can eradicate bacterial vaginosis in pregnancy but does not prevent preterm birth and its consequences. However, for women with previous preterm birth, screening and treatment of bacterial vaginosis may prevent a future preterm birth but more research is required. There is more secure evidence that it does reduce the subsequent risk of PPROM and the risk of low birthweight.

Further trials are required in high-risk groups, as are trials that attempt to treat the whole range of pathogens that have been implicated in preterm birth, rather than focusing only on bacterial vaginosis.

Review: Antibiotics for treating bacterial vaginosis in pregnancy
Comparison: 01 Any antibiotic versus placebo/no treatment
Outcome: 05 Preterm birth < 37 weeks

Study	Treatment n/N	Control n/N	Relative Risk (Fixed) 95% CI	Weight (%)	Relative Risk (Fixed) 95% CI
01 general population					
Joesoef 1995	51/340	46/341		15.8	1.11 [0.77, 1.61]
Kekki 1999	9/187	7/188		2.4	1.29 [0.49, 3.40]
McDonald 1997	16/242	18/238		6.3	0.87 [0.46, 1.67]
NICHD MFMU 2000	116/953	121/966		41.4	0.97 [0.77, 1.23]
Odendaal 2002	12/66	13/82		4.0	1.15 [0.56, 2.34]
Subtotal (95% CI)	204/1788	205/1815		69.9	1.02 [0.85, 1.22]
Test for heterogeneity chi-square=0.92 df=4 p=0.9219					
Test for overall effect=0.17 p=0.9					
02 high risk population					
Hauth 1995	54/172	42/86		19.3	0.64 [0.47, 0.88]
Morales 1994	8/44	16/36		6.1	0.41 [0.20, 0.85]
Odendaal 2002	30/70	12/51		4.8	1.82 [1.04, 3.20]
Subtotal (95% CI)	92/286	70/173		30.1	0.78 [0.61, 1.00]
Test for heterogeneity chi-square=13.25 df=2 p=0.0013					
Test for overall effect=-1.93 p=0.05					
Total (95% CI)	296/2074	275/1988		100.0	0.95 [0.82, 1.10]
Test for heterogeneity chi-square=17.83 df=7 p=0.0128					
Test for overall effect=-0.74 p=0.5					

```
        .1    .2         1         5    10
          Favours treatment    Favours control
```

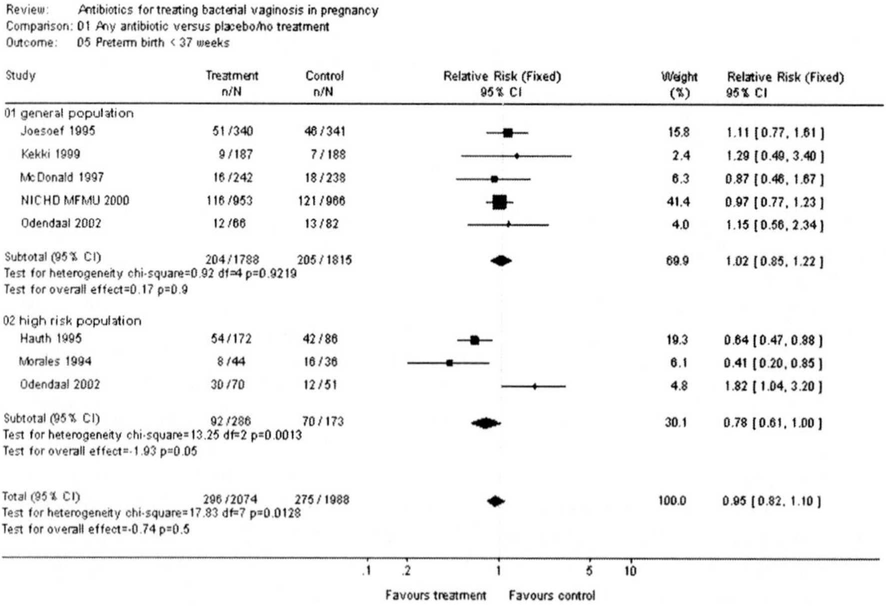

Figure 17.1. The effect of antibiotics for bacterial vaginosis on preterm birth rate; reproduced with permission from McDonald *et al.*[16]

Intrapartum intervention

Before the recently completed MRC ORACLE trials,[17,18] trials of antibiotics in spontaneous preterm labour demonstrated no health benefit, whereas those in PPROM had demonstrated prolongation of pregnancy with uncertain health benefits.

Spontaneous preterm labour

The most recent meta-analysis of prophylactic antibiotics for inhibiting preterm labour with intact membranes by King and Flenady[19] has included 11 trials where 7428 women were enrolled. Antibiotics did not demonstrate any benefit in delaying delivery by 48 hours or seven days (Figure 17.2). The only health benefit demonstrated by these trials was a reduction in maternal infection (RR 0.74; 95% CI 0.64–0.87). These data suggest that further research is required to determine the significance of the 10–12% of positive amniotic fluid cultures found in spontaneous preterm labour.

Preterm prelabour rupture of the fetal membranes

There is now good evidence to support the routine administration of antibiotics after PPROM as this intervention delays delivery and reduces the number of major markers of neonatal morbidity. The most recent meta-analysis reviewed 19 trials,[20] which included over 6000 women. This review demonstrated that the use of antibiotics following PPROM was associated with a significant reduction in chorioamnionitis (RR 0.57; 95% CI 0.37–0.86). There was a reduction in the number of babies born within 48 hours (RR 0.71; 95% CI 0.58–0.87) (Figure 17.3) and born within seven days (RR

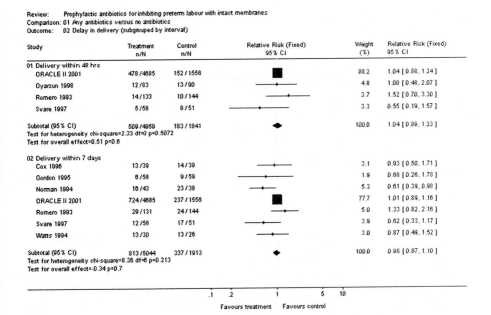

Figure 17.2. The effect of antibiotics in spontaneous preterm labour on prolongation of pregnancy; reproduced with permission from King and Flenady[19]

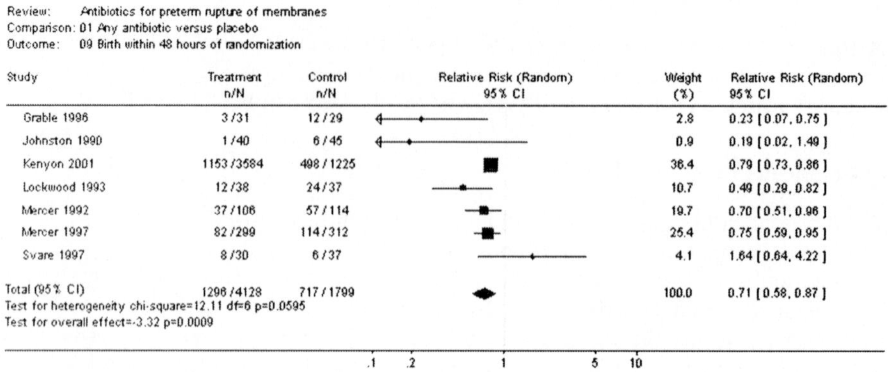

Review: Antibiotics for preterm rupture of membranes
Comparison: 01 Any antibiotic versus placebo
Outcome: 09 Birth within 48 hours of randomization

Study	Treatment n/N	Control n/N	Relative Risk (Random) 95% CI	Weight (%)	Relative Risk (Random) 95% CI
Grable 1996	3 / 31	12 / 29		2.8	0.23 [0.07, 0.75]
Johnston 1990	1 / 40	6 / 45		0.9	0.19 [0.02, 1.49]
Kenyon 2001	1153 / 3584	498 / 1225		36.4	0.79 [0.73, 0.86]
Lockwood 1993	12 / 38	24 / 37		10.7	0.49 [0.29, 0.82]
Mercer 1992	37 / 106	57 / 114		19.7	0.70 [0.51, 0.96]
Mercer 1997	82 / 299	114 / 312		25.4	0.75 [0.59, 0.95]
Svare 1997	8 / 30	6 / 37		4.1	1.64 [0.64, 4.22]
Total (95% CI)	1296 / 4128	717 / 1799		100.0	0.71 [0.58, 0.87]

Test for heterogeneity chi-square=12.11 df=6 p=0.0595
Test for overall effect=-3.32 p=0.0009

.1   .2   1   5   10

Figure 17.3. The effect of antibiotics for preterm prelabour rupture of the fetal membranes on prolongation of pregnancy for 48 hours; reproduced with permission from Kenyon et al.[20]

0.80; 95% CI 0.71–0.90) (Figure 17.4). The following markers of neonatal morbidity were reduced: neonatal infection (RR 0.68; 95% CI 0.53–0.87), use of surfactant (RR 0.83; 95% CI 0.72–0.96), oxygen therapy (RR 0.88; 95% CI 0.81–0.96) and abnormal cerebral ultrasound scan prior to discharge from hospital (RR 0.82; 95% CI 0.68–0.98). Co-amoxiclav in this review was associated with an increased risk of neonatal necrotising enterocolitis (RR 4.60; 95% CI 1.98–10.72). Table 17.2 shows the numbers of women needed to treat with antibiotics to prevent a variety of outcomes.[21] Relatively few women are required to prevent significant outcomes in the infants.

Conclusions

Although there is evidence that two antibiotic interventions can prevent preterm birth and its consequences, i.e. screening for and antibiotic treatment of asymptomatic

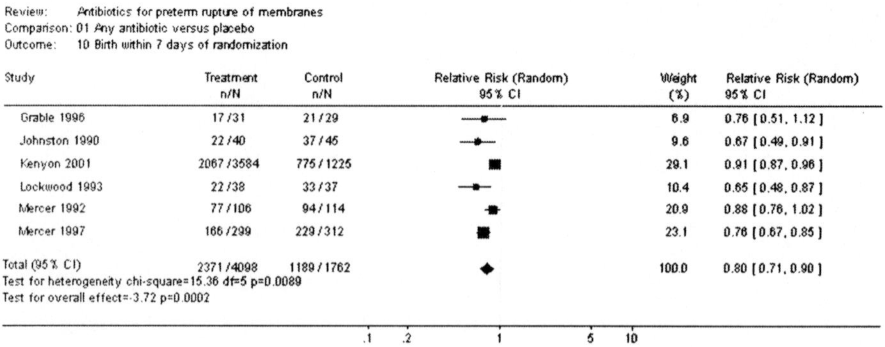

Review: Antibiotics for preterm rupture of membranes
Comparison: 01 Any antibiotic versus placebo
Outcome: 10 Birth within 7 days of randomization

Study	Treatment n/N	Control n/N	Relative Risk (Random) 95% CI	Weight (%)	Relative Risk (Random) 95% CI
Grable 1996	17 / 31	21 / 29		6.9	0.76 [0.51, 1.12]
Johnston 1990	22 / 40	37 / 45		9.6	0.67 [0.49, 0.91]
Kenyon 2001	2067 / 3584	775 / 1225		29.1	0.91 [0.87, 0.96]
Lockwood 1993	22 / 38	33 / 37		10.4	0.65 [0.48, 0.87]
Mercer 1992	77 / 106	94 / 114		20.9	0.88 [0.76, 1.02]
Mercer 1997	166 / 299	229 / 312		23.1	0.76 [0.67, 0.85]
Total (95% CI)	2371 / 4098	1189 / 1762		100.0	0.80 [0.71, 0.90]

Test for heterogeneity chi-square=15.36 df=5 p=0.0089
Test for overall effect=-3.72 p=0.0002

.1   .2   1   5   10

Figure 17.4. The effect of antibiotics for preterm prelabour rupture of the fetal membranes on prolongation of pregnancy for 7 days; reproduced with permission from Kenyon et al.[20]

Table 17.2. Numbers of women needed to treat (all antibiotics versus placebo) to avoid one additional unfavourable outcome in their babies; reproduced with permission from Kenyon *et al.*[21]

Outcome	Number needed to treat
Chorioamnionitis	9
Born within 48 hours	9
Born within 7 days	8
Neonatal infection	19
Abnormal cerebral ultrasound prior to discharge	59

bacteriuria and antibiotic prophylaxis for PPROM, extensive research is still required, particularly in the following areas:

- the significance of abnormal intrauterine microbial flora and associated phenomena in spontaneous preterm labour
- the role of amniocentesis as a diagnostic test in preterm parturition, particularly spontaneous preterm labour
- clinical trials of antibiotics for all genitourinary pathogens in the prenatal period.

References

1.   Hall M, Danielian P, Lamont RF. The importance of preterm birth. In: Elder MG, Romero R, Lamont RF, editors. *Preterm Labor*. New York: Churchill Livingstone; 1997.
2.   Zahl PA. Bjerknes C. Induction of decidua-placental hemorrhage in mice by the endotoxins of certain gram-negative bacteria. *Proc Soc Exp Biol Med* 1943;54:329–32.
3.   Rious-Darrieulat F, Parant M, Chedid L. Prevention of endotoxin-induced abortion by treatment of mice with antisera. *J Infect Dis* 1978;137:7–13.
4.   Skarnes RC, Harper MJK. Relationship between endotoxin-induced abortion and the synthesis of prostaglandin F. *Prostaglandins* 1972;1:191–201.
5.   Kullander S. Fever and parturition. An experimental study in rabbits. *Acta Obstet Gynecol Scand Suppl* 1977;66:77–85.
6.   Dombroski RA, Woodard DS, Harper MJK, Gibbs RS. A rabbit model for bacteria-induced preterm pregnancy loss. *Am J Obstet Gynecol* 1990;163:1938–43.
7.   Heddleston L, McDuffie RS, Gibbs RS. A rabbit model for ascending infection in pregnancy: intervention with indomethacin and delayed ampicillin-sulbactam therapy. *Am J Obstet Gynecol* 1993;169:708–12.
8.   McDonald H. The role of vaginal flora in normal pregnancy and in preterm labor. In: Elder MG, Romero R, Lamont RF, editors. *Preterm Labor*. New York: Churchill Livingstone; 1997. p. 65–83.
9.   Russell P. Inflammatory lesions of the human placenta. I. Clinical significance of acute chorioamnionitis. *Am J Diagn Gynecol Obstet* 1979;2:127–37.
10. Naeye RL, Peters EC. Causes and consequences of premature rupture of fetal membranes. *Lancet* 1980;i:192–4.
11. Guzick DS, Winn K. The association of chorioamnionitis with preterm delivery. *Obstet Gynecol* 1985;65:11–5.
12. Gomez R, Romero R, Mazor M, Ghezzi F, David C, Yoon BH. The role of infection in preterm labor and delivery. In: Elder MG, Romero R, Lamont RF, editors. *Preterm Labor*. New York: Churchill Livingstone; 1997.
13. Smaill F. Antibiotics for asymptomatic bacteriuria in pregnancy. *Cochrane Database Syst Rev* 2001;(2):CD000490.
14. Lamont RF, Fisk NM. The role of infection in the pathogenesis of preterm labour. In: Studd, JWW, editor. *Progress in Obstetrics and Gynaecology*. London: Churchill Livingstone; 1993. p. 135–58.
15. Chow AW, Percival-Smith R, Bartlett KH, Goldring AM, Morrison BJ. Vaginal colonization with *Escherichia coli* in healthy women. Determination of relative risks by quantitative culture and multivariate statistical analysis. *Am J Obstet Gynecol* 1986;154:120–6.

16.   McDonald H, Brocklehurst P, Parsons J, Vigneswaran R. Antibiotics for treating bacterial vaginosis in pregnancy. *Cochrane Database Syst Rev* 2003;(2):CD000262.

17.   Kenyon S, Taylor DJ, Tarnow-Mordi W. Broad-spectrum antibiotics for spontaneous preterm labour: the ORACLE II randomised trial. ORACLE Collaborative Group. *Lancet* 2001;357:989–94.

18.   Kenyon S, Taylor DJ, Tarnow-Mordi W. Broad-spectrum antibiotics for preterm, prelabour rupture of fetal membranes: the ORACLE I randomised trial. ORACLE Collaborative Group. *Lancet* 2001;357:979–988. Erratum in *Lancet* 2001;358:156.

19.   King J, Flenady V. Prophylactic antibiotics for inhibiting preterm labour with intact membranes. *Cochrane Database Syst Rev* 2002;(4):CD000246.

20.   Kenyon S, Boulvain M, Neilson J. Antibiotics for preterm rupture of membranes. *Cochrane Database Syst Rev* 2003;(2):CD001058.

21.   Kenyon S, Boulvain M, Neilson J. Antibiotics for preterm rupture of the membranes: a systemic review. Submitted for publication.

Chapter 18

Management I

Discussion

Shennan: Could I ask Professor Taylor about the meta-analysis on screening for bacterial vaginosis in a high-risk group? I'm sure that that is the one question people are going to seek an answer for in this book because that is such a key thing. Do you think that we should say categorically that high-risk women should be screened and treated?

Taylor: You can only base your decisions on the evidence that is available and I think the evidence now is that high-risk women should be screened and treated but there still needs to be further work. I am sure Dr Lamont would have a much more vigorous view.

Lamont: I think I would go along with that. I also think that symptomatic women should also be treated.

Steer: One item which I think should be discussed is the potential long-term disadvantages of the very widespread use of antibiotics that we are now seeing. I think our recommendations should not be confined to when to use antibiotics but to encourage people to think twice before using them. I think the evidence is now becoming very substantial that we are seeing the tip of a rapidly growing iceberg of major antibiotic-resistant organisms. I think there is a danger that all this advantage that we have seen demonstrated could be lost in the next 10 years if we are not very careful and we will simply be back where we started with a whole set of antibiotics that will be of very little use.

Bennett: Would Professor Shennan like to comment on the PREMET trial result?

Shennan: There seem to be different circumstances. There are other trials that I am aware of, including ours, which have used different criteria to select for antibiotic use, for example, detection of fetal fibronectin in the vagina. Studies from the USA[1] where women at high risk of preterm delivery, who are positive for fibronectin, showed a significant increase in preterm delivery with combined metronidazole and erythromycin treatment. I think the risk was almost doubled. We found exactly the same thing in our PREMET trial (which is not yet published). So there are three randomised controlled trials that I know of where metronidazole has been associated with a doubling of preterm delivery. That worries me in terms of suggesting routine antibiotic treatment but, as you say, the data as it stands suggest that we should treat at least for bacterial vaginosis.[2]

Neilson: I am intrigued by resealing of the fetal membranes [in cases of PPROM] as a spontaneous phenomenon and I wondered about Professor Bell's thoughts about the ability of the membranes to repair injuries and what therapeutic interventions might be possible in the future.

Bell: An area to think about in this context is the change in phenotype that the fetal membranes undergo after full chorion–decidual fusion. Membranes seem more likely to reseal if the rupture is early in pregnancy before fusion. Perhaps if we could recreate the pre-fusion phenotype we might be able to get it to repair spontaneously. Other important factors include the size of the tear, and whether it is in the region overlying the cervix or elsewhere. A small tear away from the cervix is more likely to reseal than a large tear over the cervix.

Romero: I would like to add to that discussion from the experience of those of us who are involved in fetoscopy. We know that when we put in one trochar the membranes rupture about 10% of the time. Putting in a trochar is quite an injury and in 90% of cases membranes repair so I presume from that experience, and from the more recent experience where we put multiple instruments in the uterus, that there must be a capacity to repair the membranes. Also, we have looked embryoscopically at a group of women who have spontaneous membranes ruptured and another group who have membranes ruptured after surgical procedures. The membranes in the two groups look very different and we have published pictures of this. The womb is very clean after a surgical procedure and is completely different to how the membranes appear when there has been spontaneous ruptured membranes and inflammation.

Calder: I wonder if I could make a general observation about membrane rupture? I found Professor Bell's paper absolutely fascinating in looking for mechanisms that apply at term to explain what happens in the preterm situation. I think that we tend to forget that, although obstetricians and midwives cannot keep their fingers off membranes and they rupture them early often for good clinical purposes, in two out of three women with the membranes left intact in labour at term, they will remain intact until very nearly the second stage of labour. That is in a situation where there are high pressures being generated and yet the membranes remain intact whereas in the preterm situation in 50% of cases the membranes rupture before labour starts and presumably without those pressures really adding to the aetiology of the membrane rupture. So presumably there is a more advanced process taking place in these preterm ruptures, or it is a different mechanism?

Bell: There must be a balance in terms of the response of the tissue to distensional forces. A tissue response involves matrix remodelling, matrix breakdown and actual laydown of a new matrix. I envisage that in some circumstances the new extracellular matrix is actually quite effective in terms of collagen deposition. Indeed, the area that ruptures at term is actually characterised by a net increase in synthesis of collagen although obviously at some point this response is not sufficient to resist rupture. The membrane only exhibits tensional force from about mid-pregnancy when the fetal membrane essentially exhibits a different phenotype. Fusion of the amniochorion to the decidua can be considered as a critical timing event in terms of endocrine interactions, and we consider it is also a crucial transitional event in terms of the nature of the membrane's response to distensional forces. We have pointed out that preterm rupture may involve the premature activation of the mechanism involved with rupture at term, but also different mechanisms, such that is associated with infection-linked inflammation.

Calder: I just wonder if the fetal head in late pregnancy which is smooth and well applied across the membranes and against the tissues actually confers a degree of protection. As a young clinician, I was told that where the membranes ruptured early in the process at term you should be on the lookout for an occipito-posterior position of the vertex which is a less well fitting presenting part. Over the years I have seen that that often is the case and I wonder if in the absence of a nice smooth application of the presenting part against the membranes more stress or pressure is somehow delivered to the membranes which makes it more likely to rupture and that would certainly apply in earlier stages of pregnancy when there is not going to be the same situation.

López Bernal: I have a point in relation to the tension. I wanted to remind the group of some studies from Australia[3,4] that demonstrated that surfactant increases the resistance to tension of the fetal membranes. I think it is no coincidence that at 25 weeks of gestation, when there is very little surfactant, the fetus and membranes not only are thin but also the surface area is less resistant to stretch than at term when they have a nice coating of surfactant because this has been delivered into the amniotic cavities with fetal breathing movements. So I believe that surfactant coating of the amniochorionic epithelium is an important factor to give extra resistance to the fetal membranes.

Gardosi: There is a lot of argument for the finding that the membranes stay intact as long as possible. You could almost argue that intact membranes transmit pressure much better to actually add a dilatation component to the cervix. Also, we have talked about the effect of infection on membranes. I am also interested in what happens in cases of fetal growth restriction. Is there anything in the literature that compares the quality of the membranes between normal and growth-restricted fetuses?

Bell: There is a dearth of literature in this area. There are studies looking at fetal membrane pathology in preterm birth and in pre-eclampsia but not, as far as I know, in intrauterine growth restriction (IUGR).

Gardosi: Is there a database that you retrospectively could look at in terms of fetal size for gestation?

Bell: We do not have one but it would be useful if there were one. The other problem of course that we have had relates to the anatomy. It is very difficult to get biopsies from different sites and to maintain the structural relationships between different tissues. This is where animal models can be useful. Superficially, animal models may not seem to represent the human but, if you look more deeply into the physiology, you can actually see comparative aspects between a human and the animal. Mapping where the tissue has come from is very important. Mashing a piece of tissue up and doing microarrays or whatever will miss information that can be had from intact tissue histology and histopathology. With placentas and fetal membranes, a single biopsy may not be representative of the whole patient and so the problem with fetal membranes and I would say also with the placenta is actually getting the appropriate mapping procedure. I do not know of any collection representing that.

Calder: Professor Nathanielsz might know better than anyone whether premature rupture of the membranes is a phenomenon that is peculiar to the human.

Nathanielsz: That is a very interesting question. Certainly in our non-human primate models, in a group setting in as normal an environment as you can get, they do tend to have quite a lot of premature labour and they do abort quite frequently. They are very stress-dependent. So, for example, if you have workmen working near to the cages this might lead the animals to abort. I do not know about premature rupture of the membranes but they do seem to have some of the pathologies of premature labour.

Saade: In view of the high rate of infection or inflammation with PPROM already present and with the data from Dr Romero's group about outcome is there room now to go back and perform some type of evaluation on the amniotic fluid to decide whether to keep these babies in or not?

Romero: I think there is. Professor Taylor mentioned this afternoon that probably there is a need to ascertain better the infection status of women who have PPROM. In our clinical actions we are treating all women with PPROM alike. We know that at presentation 30% of them have an infection and I agree with the point Dr Norman made that if you observe patients over time and do repeated amniocentesis up to 75% of the women at the time of onset of labour will have infections. So I believe that we need to find ways to make a diagnosis of the infection. I think if we do that then one of the questions that is going to be on the table is, if we know that a patient is infected is it better to leave that patient (that fetus) *in utero* or to deliver? And what is the effect of steroids and antibiotics in those who are infected and those who are not infected? Now that presents us with a tremendous problem, an ethical challenge, because today we are only allowed to run an invasive procedure if that particular fetus upon whom we are performing the invasive procedure can benefit. It poses a challenge for us to think about the ethics and interventions of the human fetus.

Saade: The control group would be the usual management. It was also suggested this morning that we should do amniocentesis before (rescue) cerclage. So if that is ethical why would it not be ethical in PPROM?

Romero: Because if we found infection in a woman who has acute cervical weakness we would change the management and not put in a cerclage. But if you find an infection in a fetus with premature labour and you went to randomise that fetus to expectant management or immediate delivery, thinking about antibiotics or steroids or the combination of them, that creates a major challenge.

Steer: Can I just comment that nobody has actually mentioned the issue of the differential bactericidal or bacteriostatic properties of the amniotic fluid? It has been known for a long time that 40 to 50% of women have amniotic fluid which actively suppresses bacterial growth. It occurs to me that one way that we could try to minimise the use of antibiotics might be to do an amniocentesis, not only to do a culture but actually to compare the activity of that amniotic fluid against the woman's own vaginal organisms. We know that a lot of women will have ruptured membranes for months and not get infected. Perhaps it is the women who have got bactericidal fluid that we could safely leave without antibiotics whereas, if we found that their bugs grow furiously in their amniotic fluid, we ought to give them antibiotics.

References

1. Andrews WW, Sibai BM, Thom EA, Dudley D, Ernest JM, McNellis D, et al., National Institute of Child Health & Human Development Maternal–Fetal Medicine Units Network. Randomized clinical trial of metronidazole plus erythromycin to prevent spontaneous preterm delivery in fetal fibronectin-positive women. *Obstet Gynecol* 2003;101(5 Pt 1):847–55.
2. Odendaal HJ, Popov I, Schoeman J, Smith M, Grove D. Preterm labour – is bacterial vaginosis involved? *S Afr Med J* 2002;92:231–4.
3. Hills BA, Cotton DB. Premature rupture of membranes and surface energy: possible role of surfactant. *Am J Obstet Gynecol* 1984;149:896–902.
4. Hills BA. Further studies of the role of surfactant in premature rupture of the membranes. *Am J Obstet Gynecol* 1994;170(1 Pt 1):195–201.

SECTION 5

MANAGEMENT II

Chapter 19

Antiphospholipid syndrome and preterm birth

May Backos and Lesley Regan

Introduction

Preterm birth (PTB) is defined as occurring before 37 completed weeks of gestation[1] and thus includes pregnancies delivering between 22 weeks and 36 weeks with significant differences in neonatal outcome. In the UK the incidence of PTB is 7% and in developing countries the scale of the problem is much greater.[2]

The aetiology of PTB is diverse and the eventual outcome for the baby is invariably determined by both gestational age at delivery and the prenatal factors which precipitate PTB.[3] Four circumstances may lead to PTB:

- uncomplicated spontaneous preterm labour
- prelabour rupture of membranes (PROM)
- complicated emergency preterm delivery (e.g. placental abruption, eclampsia)
- elective preterm delivery, usually resulting from severe pre-eclampsia (PET) or intrauterine fetal growth restriction (IUGR).

Antiphospholipid syndrome (APS), when originally described in the late 1980s, referred to the association of antiphospholipid antibodies (aPL) with recurrent fetal loss, vascular thrombosis and thrombocytopenia.[4] More recently, the definition of APS has been expanded to include a wide range of pregnancy morbidity, including:

- recurrent first trimester miscarriage
- one or more morphologically normal fetal deaths after the 10th week of gestation
- one or more preterm births before the 34th week of gestation due to severe PET, eclampsia or placental insufficiency.[5]

Most data on the association between APS and PTB come from treated series of APS pregnancies. The reported incidence of PTB in treated APS pregnancies is in excess of 20%.[6-8] However, there are no prospective data published to determine the prevalence of aPL in women with PTB, and the incidence of PTB in untreated APS pregnancies remain unknown.

Antiphospholipid antibodies

The aPL are a family of approximately 20 antibodies directed against negatively charged phospholipid binding proteins. If a value greater than the 95th centile is used to define positivity, an individual will have a 64% chance of a positive test result from one of these 20 antibodies. However, in the aetiology of pregnancy morbidity, only the lupus anticoagulant (LA) and anticardiolipin antibodies (aCL) (IgG and IgM subclass, but not IgA) have been shown to be of clinical significance. Testing for aPL other than LA or aCL is noninformative.[9]

The detection of aPL is subject to considerable interlaboratory variation. This is due to temporal fluctuation of aPL titres in individual woman, transient positivity secondary to infections, suboptimal sample collection and preparation, and lack of standardisation of laboratory tests for their detection. It is therefore important that the laboratory assays are performed according to established international guidelines.[5] While no single test will detect all LA, the dilute Russell's viper venom time (dRVVT) test together with the platelet neutralisation procedure is more sensitive and specific than either the activated partial thromboplastin time (aPTT) or the kaolin clotting time (KCL) test.[10] A standardised enzyme-linked immunosorbent assay (ELISA) is used to detect aCL. To diagnose APS it is mandatory to have at least two positive tests six weeks apart for either LA or aCL of IgG and/or IgM class present in medium or high titre.

Using the strict criteria above, aPL are present in 15% of women with recurrent first trimester miscarriage and in 21% of women with one or more midtrimester miscarriage.[10] By comparison, the prevalence of aPL in women with a low-risk obstetric history is less than 2%.[11]

Mechanisms of aPL-related pregnancy morbidity

The mechanisms by which aPL cause pregnancy morbidity are varied, reflecting, in part, the heterogeneity of aPL antibodies. Historically, the pathogenesis of aPL-related pregnancy loss focused on placental thrombosis.[12,13] However, recent research has provided new insights into the mechanisms of aPL-related pregnancy failure and suggests that defective decidualisation of the endometrium and abnormality of early trophoblastic function and differentiation may be the primary pathological mechanisms.[14-17]

Invasion of the extravillous trophoblast into the spiral arteries is a central event in placentation.[18] Defective trophoblastic invasion of the spiral arteries, an indicator of abnormal placentation, is well described in association with early pregnancy failure,[19] PET,[20] IUGR,[21] placental abruption,[22] preterm prelabour rupture of membranes (PPROM)[23] and preterm labour.[24] In normal early pregnancy, trophoblast 'plugging' of the maternal circulation plays an important part in limiting the extent of intervillous blood flow. This limits the developing placenta from exposure to high-velocity blood flow and oxidative stress.[25] In women with APS, it would appear that the interaction of aPL with invading trophoblast or the endothelium in maternal decidual vessels inhibits the normal endovascular trophoblast invasion from occurring and resulting in fetal loss.[17] In less severely affected cases, the pregnancy may remain viable into the second or third trimester but abnormalities of the uteroplacental vasculature may then lead to an increased risk of later pregnancy complications such as IUGR, PET and PTB.[6,8]

Treatment of APS and preterm birth

In untreated pregnancies the prospective fetal loss of women with recurrent miscarriage associated with aPL is as high as 90%.[26] Several treatment modalities have been tried to improve the pregnancy outcome of these women. The use of steroids during pregnancy does not further improve pregnancy outcome when compared with other treatment modalities but is associated with a significant increase in prematurity (RR 4.83; 95% CI 2.8–8.2) and maternal morbidity.[27]

The current treatment of choice for pregnant women with APS is low-dose aspirin in combination with low-dose heparin commencing as soon as pregnancy is confirmed. Since the majority of aPL-related miscarriages occur before 14 weeks of gestation, delay in commencement of treatment may compromise pregnancy outcome. A recent meta-analysis has shown that aspirin plus heparin treatment reduces pregnancy loss by 54%.[27] The therapeutic benefits of heparin are based on the ability of this compound to bind to aPL, thereby improving trophoblast invasiveness and differentiation, resulting in successful placentation.[28,29] This is in addition to its anticoagulant effect in later pregnancy, which reduces the risk of placental thrombosis and infarction. The therapeutic benefit of aspirin is related to its ability to reduce platelet adhesiveness, thereby preventing placental thrombosis.

However, despite the improvement in fetal survival, aPL pregnancies treated with aspirin and heparin remain at risk of late pregnancy complications due to impaired placentation (e.g. PET, IUGR and placental abruption), which often results in PTB.[7–9] It is possible therefore that aspirin and heparin therapy does not eradicate the underlying pathological process but merely reduces the severity or modifies disease expression. In a study of 150 consecutive women with aPL-related recurrent miscarriage treated with aspirin plus heparin, 24% of babies were born preterm (before 37 weeks of gestation).[8] The causes of PTB were spontaneous preterm labour (24%), PPROM (20%), elective PTB for severe PET and/or IUGR (32%), and emergency PTB for abruption or fetal distress (24%). Interestingly, the majority of preterm deliveries (69%) occurred between 34 and 36 weeks of gestation, which accounted for the excellent infant survival noted in the study. The apparent temporal relationship between the discontinuation of treatment at 34 weeks of gestation and an increased number of babies born between 34 and 36 weeks was further investigated in a randomised controlled trial.[30] This RCT has reported that continuation of the treatment up until delivery rather than until 34 weeks of gestation does not significantly reduce the risk of late pregnancy complications and PTB. This is not surprising since normal placentation should be completed by the 22nd to the 24th week of gestation[31] and the benefit of any therapeutic intervention in preventing pregnancy complications related to defective placentation should be achieved during the first and second trimester of pregnancy. The benefit of treatment thereafter is thought to be protection against thrombosis of the uteroplacental circulation.

Using an alternative strategy, a pilot study of pregnant women with APS who were enrolled into a placebo-controlled trial examined the benefit of the addition of intravenous immune globulin (IVIg) treatment to aspirin and heparin therapy.[32] In this study the authors found that IVIg did not improve the obstetric or neonatal outcomes beyond those achieved by aspirin plus heparin alone. Indeed, the PTB rate was significantly higher in the IVIg group, but this was explained by the inclusion of two elective PTBs in the IVIg group, due to previous third trimester intrauterine fetal death. When these cases were excluded from the analysis, the difference between the two groups was no longer significant. Nonetheless, this small study did report fewer cases of IUGR and admission to neonatal intensive care unit among those treated with IVIg, a finding that requires further investigation.

The subtypes of aPL vary in their risk of late pregnancy complications and PTB. In a large series of women with aPL-related recurrent pregnancy loss (n = 170) treated with aspirin and heparin, the PTB rate in pregnancies associated with LA (19%; 6/31) was similar to that in IgG aCL (17%; 8/48) and LA + aCL pregnancies (17%; 2/12), but significantly higher than in those pregnancies associated with IgM aCL in isolation

(7%; 5/76).[33] This may be due to the varying severity of the disease process caused by the different subtypes of aPL, with LA at the most severe end of the spectrum and IgM aCL at the least severe end.

Summary

Preterm birth is a major clinical feature of APS. Treatment with aspirin and heparin improves fetal survival among women with aPL-related pregnancy loss. Nonetheless, these pregnancies remain at risk of late pregnancy complications and PTB. Continuation of treatment until the time of delivery (rather than until 34 weeks of gestation) and the addition of IVIg to the treatment regimen does not appear to improve perinatal outcome. Further research is needed to define the role of alternative adjunctive therapies. At present the identification of aPL pregnancies as being at increased risk of perinatal complications necessitates close antenatal surveillance and planned delivery in a unit with neonatal intensive care facilities.

References

1.   World Health Organization. *Manual of the International Classification of Diseases, Injuries and Causes of Death.* Geneva: World Health Organization; 1977.
2.   Steer P, Flint C. Preterm labour and premature rupture of membranes. *BMJ* 1999;318:1059–62.
3.   Wariyar U, Richmond S, Hey E. Pregnancy outcome at 24-31 weeks' gestation: mortality. *Arch Dis Child* 1989;64:670–7.
4.   Harris EN: Sydrome of the black swan. *Br J Rheumatol* 1987;26:324–6.
5.   Wilson WA, Gharavi AE, Koike T, Lockshin MD, Branch DW, Piette JC, *et al.* International consensus statement on preliminary classification criteria for definite antiphospholipid syndrome: report of an international workshop. *Arthritis Rheum* 1999;42:1309–11.
6.   Branch DW, Silver RM, Blackwell JL, Reading JC, Scott JR. Outcome of treated pregnancies in women with antiphospholipid syndrome: an update of the Utah experience. *Obstet Gynecol* 1992;80:614–20.
7.   Rai R, Cohen H, Dave M, Regan L. Randomised controlled trial of aspirin and aspirin plus heparin in pregnant women with recurrent miscarriage associated with phospholipid antibodies (or antiphospholipid antibodies). *BMJ* 1997;314:253–7.
8.   Backos M, Rai R, Baxter N, Chilcott IT, Cohen H, Regan L. Pregnancy complications in women with recurrent miscarriage associated with antiphospholipid antibodies treated with low-dose aspirin and heparin. *Br J Obstet Gynaecol* 1999;106:102–7.
9.   Branch DW, Silver R, Pierangeli S, Van LI, Harris EN. Antiphospholipid antibodies other than lupus anticoagulant and anticardiolipin antibodies in women with recurrent pregnancy loss, fertile controls, and antiphospholipid syndrome. *Obstet Gynecol* 1997;89:549–55.
10. Rai RS, Regan L, Clifford K, Pickering W, Dave M, Mackie I, *et al.* Antiphospholipid antibodies and beta 2-glycoprotein-I in 500 women with recurrent miscarriage: results of a comprehensive screening approach. *Hum Reprod* 1995;10:2001–5.
11. Lockwood CJ, Romero R, Feinberg RF, Clyne LP, Coster B, Hobbins JC. The prevalence and biologic significance of lupus anticoagulant and anticardiolipin antibodies in a general obstetric population. *Am J Obstet Gynecol* 1989;161:369–73.
12. Out HJ, Kooijman CD, Bruinse HW, Derksen RH. Histopathological findings in placentae from patients with intra-uterine fetal death and anti-phospholipid antibodies. *Eur J Obstet Gynecol Reprod Biol* 1991;41:179–86.
13. Peaceman AM, Rehnberg KA. The effect of immunoglobulin G fractions from patients with lupus anticoagulant on placental prostacyclin and thromboxan production. *Am J Obstet Gynecol* 1993;169:1403–6.
14. Mak IY, Brosens JJ, Christian M, Hills FA, Chamley L, Regan L, *et al.* Regulated expression of signal transducer and activator of transcription, Stat5, and its enhancement of PRL expression in human endometrial stromal cells *in vitro. J Clin Endocrinol Metab* 2002;87:2581–8.
15. Katsuragawa H, Kanzaki H, Inoue T, Hirano T, Mori T, Rote NS. Monoclonal antibody against phosphatidylserine inhibits *in vitro* human trophoblastic hormone production and invasion. *Biol*

Reprod 1997;56:50–8.

16. Di Simone N, Castellani R, Caliandro D, Caruso A. Antiphospholid antibodies regulate the expression of trophoblast cell adhesion molecules. *Fertil Steril* 2002;77:805–11.

17. Sebire NJ, Fox H, Backos M, Rai R, Paterson C, Regan L. Defective endovascular trophoblast invasion in primary antiphospholipid antibody syndrome-associated early pregnancy failure. *Hum Reprod* 2002;17:1067–71.

18. Pijnenborg R, Dixon G, Robertson WB, Brosens I. Trophoblastic invasion of human decidua from 8 to 18 weeks of pregnancy. *Placenta* 1980;1:3–19.

19. Hustin J, Jauniaux E, Schaaps JP. Histological study of the materno–embryonic interface in spontaneous abortion. *Placenta* 1990;11:477–86.

20. Pijnenborg R, Anthony J, Davey DA, Rees A, Tiltman A, Vercruysse L, *et al*. Placental bed spiral arteries in hypertensive disorders of pregnancy. *Br J Obstet Gynaecol* 1991;98:648–55.

21. Khong TY, Wolf FD, Robertson WB, Brosens I. Inadequate maternal vascular response to placentation in pregnancies complicated by pre-eclampsia and by small-for-gestational age infants. *Br J Obstet Gynaecol* 1986;93:1049–59.

22. Dommisse J, Tiltman AJ. Placental bed biopsies in placental abruption. *Br J Obstet Gynaecol* 1992;99:651–4.

23. Kim YM, Chaiworapongsa T, Gomez R, Bujold E, Yoon BH, Rotmensch S, *et al*. Failure of physiologic transformation of the spiral arteries in the placental bed in preterm premature rupture of membranes. *Am J Obstet Gynecol* 2002;187:1137–42.

24. Arias F, Rodriquez L, Rayi SC, Kraus FT. Maternal placental vasculopathy and infection: two distinct subgroups among patients with preterm labor and preterm ruptured membranes. *Am J Obstet Gynecol* 1993;168:585–91.

25. Jauniaux E, Hempstock J, Greenwold N, Burton GJ. Trophoblastic oxidative stress in relation to temporal and regional differences in maternal placental blood flow in normal and abnormal early pregnancies. *Am J Pathol* 2003;162:115–25.

26. Rai RS, Clifford K, Cohen H, Regan L. High prospective fetal loss rate in untreated pregnancies of women with recurrent miscarriage and antiphospholipid antibodies. *Hum Reprod* 1995;10:3301–4.

27. Empson M, Lassere M, Craig JC, Scott JR. Recurrent pregnancy loss with antiphospholipid antibody: a systematic review of therapeutic trials. *Obstet Gynecol* 2002;99:135–44.

28. Di Simone N, Ferrazzani S, Castellani R, De Carolis S, Mancuso S, Caruso A. Heparin and low-dose aspirin restore placental human chorionic gonadotrophin secretion abolished by antiphospholipid antibody-containing sera. *Hum Reprod* 1997;9:2061–5.

29. Di Simone N, Caliandro D, Castellani R, Ferrazzani S, De Carolis S, Caruso A. Low-molecular weight heparin restores *in-vitro* trophoblast invasiveness and differentiation in presence of immunoglobulin G fractions obtained from patients with antiphospholipid syndrome. *Hum Reprod* 1999;14:489–95.

30. Backos M, Rai R, El-Gaddal S, Regan L. Effect of the duration of aspirin plus heparin treatment on the rate of preterm birth in women with antiphospholipid syndrome: A randomised controlled trial [abstract]. *J Soc Gynecol Investig* 2004;11:201.

31. Robertson WB, Khong TY, Brosens I, De Wolf F, Sheppard BL, Bonnar J. The placental bed biopsy: review from three European centres. *Am J Obstet Gynecol* 1986;155:401–12.

32. Branch DW, Peaceman AM, Druzin M, Silver RK, El-Sayed Y, Silver RM, *et al*. A multicenter, placebo-controlled pilot study of intravenous immune globulin treatment of antiphospholipid syndrome during pregnancy. The Pregnancy Loss Study Group. *Am J Obstet Gynecol* 2000;182(1 Pt 1):122–7.

33. Venkat-Raman N, Backos M, Teoh TG, Lo WT, Regan L. Uterine artery Doppler in predicting pregnancy outcome in women with antiphospholipid syndrome. *Obstet Gynecol* 2001;98:235–42.

Chapter 20

Steroids

Patricia Crowley

Introduction

In the 1960s, while studying the effect of corticosteroids on the initiation of parturition in the ewe, Liggins[1] observed that lambs exposed *in utero* to maternally administered corticosteroids demonstrated accelerated lung maturity when delivered preterm. Subsequently, a randomised, placebo-controlled trial of betamethasone administration in women who were expected to give birth preterm found a statistically significant reduction in the frequency of respiratory distress in babies born before 32 weeks of gestation and a halving in neonatal mortality among preterm babies born after maternal corticosteroid administration compared with those exposed to placebo.[2]

Obstetricians were slow to incorporate this intervention into clinical practice. Further randomised trials took place throughout the 1970s and 80s. Antenatal steroids finally became an established part of the management of preterm birth in the 1990s. This chapter reviews the biological effects of antenatal corticosteroids, the evidence from randomised trials and systematic reviews on which current practice is based, and explores current areas of uncertainty with respect to the number of doses and the choice of drug.

Biological effects of antenatal corticosteroids

An understanding of some of the biological effects of antenatal corticosteroids in both humans and animals helps to inform current debates relating to safety and efficacy of single and repeat doses of antenatal steroids.

Extrapulmonary effects

Glucocorticoids have been shown to accelerate cytodifferentiation and protein and enzyme synthesis in a variety of tissues, including liver, pancreas, kidney, intestine, adrenal, skin and myocardium. The accelerated maturation of the fetal intestine may account for the reduced incidence of necrotising enterocolitis observed in corticosteroid-treated neonates. Accelerated maturation of fetal skin may result in reduced insensible water loss.[3] Effects on the myocardium and on catecholamine responsiveness may explain the reduced incidence of intraventricular haemorrhage seen in extremely preterm infants that appeared to be independent of any effect on respiratory distress syndrome (RDS).[4]

Pulmonary effects

The most well-known effect of antenatal corticosteroid therapy is a receptor-mediated effect on all components of the surfactant system, including phospholipids, lipogenic enzymes and surfactant-associated proteins. However, structural development is also affected, resulting in an increase both in lung compliance and in maximum volume that is independent of surfactant. Protein leak from vessels and airways is reduced and clearance of lung liquid at delivery is accelerated.[3] In some animal species, glucocorticoid treatment causes precocious increases in activity of the antioxidant enzymes superoxide dismutase, glutathione peroxidase and catalase.[3]

The relative contributions of the enhanced surfactant production and the changes in lung structure to the ultimate clinical outcome are likely to vary depending on the gestational age at which steroids are administered, the number of courses of treatment and the interval between treatment and delivery. The acute structural changes involving thinning of mesenchyma and a decrease in alveolar septation[5,6] result in improved lung compliance and better gas exchange, but the arrest of alveolar septation could be viewed as a form of lung injury and altered lung development.[7]

In theory, an acute decrease in alveolar septation could be clinically relevant as a reduction in alveolar septation appears to be the primary pathology in preterm infants who develop severe bronchopulmonary dysplasia.[8]

In a study on the effects on the monkey neonatal lung of varying the timing and duration of maternal glucocorticoid therapy, Johnson et al.[9] found that daily maternal treatments with about 0.3 mg/kg betamethasone for three days before preterm delivery increased maximal lung gas volumes almost two-fold. The same dose of betamethasone given for 13 days increased lung volumes but not surfactant.[10] The lung gas volumes of the glucocorticoid-exposed fetuses were higher than those of controls when both were delivered preterm but lower when delivery occurred at term.[10] The explanation proposed for this variable effect on fetal lung volume was that glucocorticoids had an acute effect on the lung by decreasing the amount of lung interstitium, increasing the airspaces but inhibiting alveolar septation. In this model of prolonged antenatal steroid exposure, the physiological changes were primarily changes in lung connective tissue and not the surfactant system. Other workers demonstrated that a high dose of steroids given for three consecutive days at various stages of lung development made the lung parenchymal structure appear more mature.[11] However, the alveoli were less numerous and larger, resulting in an 'emphysematous'-appearing lung. These experiments with monkeys demonstrated large and persistent effects on lung structure resulting from high-dose and/or prolonged fetal exposures to maternal glucocorticoids, even at early gestational ages. Accelerated lung maturity may be purchased at the price of alveolar septation. This adverse effect remains evident at term. The relevance of these observations to the human is unclear because in general the glucocorticoid doses and durations of treatment differed from those used clinically. Animal models such as those cited show what can happen in humans, not necessarily what does happen. However, these animal experiments raise theoretical concerns about repeated or prolonged corticosteroid therapy.

On the other hand, a considerable body of animal evidence points towards potential benefits on neonatal pulmonary performance from repeated courses of antenatal steroids. Two recent reports using animals with short gestations have attempted to model repetitive dosing strategies. Stewart et al.[12] found in mice that multidose betamethasone resulted in more effective breathing and better lung saccular development than did a single treatment. In the rabbit, Pratt et al.[13] found that the more treatments the rabbits received, the greater the induction of the surfactant proteins.

However, fetal weight was decreased proportionately to the number of doses of maternal betamethasone, and the effects on birthweight were more striking for late gestational treatments. Ikegami *et al.*[14] have performed a series of experiments in sheep using repetitive weekly maternal glucocorticoid treatments beginning as early as 104 days of gestation (term is 150 days). A dose of 0.5 mg/kg maternal weight of a mixture of betamethasone acetate and phosphate was used. This dose induces lung maturation and is approximately equivalent to the combined two 12 mg dose schedule used clinically. Their results demonstrate that the improvements in lung function induced by maternal betamethasone last for at least a week. The measurements of compliance and lung gas volume indicate that the response is larger after a two- or seven-day interval than a 21-day interval. The amount of surfactant was increased after the seven-day interval but not increased very much after a 21-day interval. These results demonstrate that treatments given earlier in gestation are less effective than treatments given closer to delivery. There are no data to answer the question of why the longer interval has less effect on lung function or surfactant. Possible explanations are that the more immature lung is less responsive to the stimulus or that some of the glucocorticoid effects are reversible. Whatever the explanation, the result supports the possibility that repeated treatments may be of benefit.

The evidence on which current clinical practice is based

The response of obstetricians to the outcome of the first randomised trial[2] of antenatal steroid therapy in 1972 was surprising: the incorporation of antenatal corticosteroid therapy into clinical practice occurred remarkably slowly. Published reports reveal that the use of antenatal corticosteroids in women with threatened preterm delivery increased from 8% in 1985 to 20% in 1990, 52% in 1995, and 75% in 2000.[15] Given the magnitude of the beneficial effects demonstrated in this first randomised trial, it is surprising that a further eighteen randomised trials of antenatal corticosteroid therapy were conducted, the latest as recently as 1998.[16] Fifteen of these trials were placebo-controlled and reported clinically relevant outcomes[4,17–32] A systematic review of these trials was conducted according to standard methods for literature searching[33] and statistical analysis.[34] This was first published in journal form in 1990[35] and subsequently updated.[36,37] This evidence forms the basis for the recommendation by professional bodies such as the Royal College of Obstetricians and Gynecologists, The American College of Obstetricians and Gynaecologists and the Society of Obstetricians and Gynaecologists of Canada that a single course of either beta-methasone or dexamethasone should be given to all pregnant women between 24 and 34 weeks of gestation who are at risk of preterm delivery within seven days.

Effect of antenatal corticosteroids on relevant clinical outcomes

Neonatal mortality

Table 20.1 summarises the effects of a single course of antenatal corticosteroid therapy on the odds ratio of neonatal death. Antenatal corticosteroid therapy is associated with a reduction in neonatal mortality (typical OR 0.60, 95% CI 0.48–0.76). The magnitude of this effect is greatest in trials conducted before 1980 when the case-fatality rate for RDS was higher. The reduction in neonatal mortality is mainly due to a significant reduction in two important causes of neonatal death – RDS and intraventricular haemorrhage.

Table 20.1. Effects of antenatal steroids on neonatal death; reproduced with permission from Crowley[37]

Review: Prophylactic corticosteroids for preterm birth
Comparison: 01 Corticosteroids versus placebo or no treatment
Outcome: 02 Neonatal death

Study	Treatment n/N	Control n/N	Peto Odds Ratio 95% CI	Weight (%)	Peto Odds Ratio 95% CI
01 Neonatal death (all babies)					
AMSTERDAM 1980	3/64	12/58		4.4	0.23 [0.08, 0.67]
AUCKLAND 1972	36/532	60/538		29.3	0.58 [0.38, 0.89]
BLOCK 1977	1/69	5/61		1.9	0.22 [0.04, 1.12]
DORAN 1980	4/81	11/63		4.5	0.26 [0.09, 0.77]
GAMSU 1989	14/131	20/137		10.0	0.70 [0.34, 1.44]
GARITE 1992	9/40	11/42		5.1	0.82 [0.30, 2.24]
KARI 1994	6/95	9/94		4.7	0.64 [0.22, 1.84]
MORALES 1986	7/121	13/124		6.2	0.54 [0.22, 1.33]
MORRISON 1978	3/67	7/59		3.1	0.37 [0.10, 1.33]
PAPAGEORGIOU 1979	1/71	7/75		2.6	0.22 [0.05, 0.91]
PARSONS 1988	0/23	1/22		0.3	0.13 [0.00, 6.52]
SCHMIDT 1984	5/49	4/31		2.6	0.77 [0.19, 3.15]
TAUESCH 1979	8/56	10/71		5.1	1.02 [0.37, 2.76]
US STEROID TRIAL	32/371	34/372		20.2	0.94 [0.57, 1.56]
Subtotal (95% CI)	129/1770	204/1747		100.0	0.60 [0.48, 0.75]
Test for heterogeneity chi-square=14.70 df=13 p=0.3265					
Test for overall effect=-4.42 p=0.0000					
02 Neonatal death in babies treated before 1980					
AMSTERDAM 1980	3/64	12/58		7.3	0.23 [0.08, 0.67]
AUCKLAND 1972	36/532	60/538		48.1	0.58 [0.38, 0.89]
BLOCK 1977	1/69	5/61		3.2	0.22 [0.04, 1.12]
DORAN 1980	4/81	11/63		7.3	0.26 [0.09, 0.77]
GAMSU 1989	14/131	20/137		16.4	0.70 [0.34, 1.44]
MORRISON 1978	3/67	7/59		5.1	0.37 [0.10, 1.33]
PAPAGEORGIOU 1979	1/71	7/75		4.2	0.22 [0.05, 0.91]
TAUESCH 1979	8/56	10/71		8.4	1.02 [0.37, 2.76]
Subtotal (95% CI)	70/1071	132/1062		100.0	0.51 [0.38, 0.68]
Test for heterogeneity chi-square=9.20 df=7 p=0.2384					
Test for overall effect=-4.60 p<0.00001					
03 Neonatal death in babies treated after 1980					
GARITE 1992	9/40	11/42		13.1	0.82 [0.30, 2.24]
KARI 1994	6/95	9/94		11.9	0.64 [0.22, 1.84]
MORALES 1986	7/121	13/124		15.8	0.54 [0.22, 1.33]
PARSONS 1988	0/23	1/22		0.9	0.13 [0.00, 6.52]
SCHMIDT 1984	5/49	4/31		6.6	0.77 [0.19, 3.15]
US STEROID TRIAL	32/371	34/372		51.7	0.94 [0.57, 1.56]
Subtotal (95% CI)	59/699	72/685		100.0	0.78 [0.54, 1.12]
Test for heterogeneity chi-square=2.12 df=5 p=0.833					
Test for overall effect=-1.33 p=0.19					

                        .1   .2   1   5   10

Respiratory distress syndrome

Overall, the risk of neonatal RDS is reduced by about 50% (typical OR 0.53; 95% CI 0.44–0.63). A secondary analysis, stratified by time interval between trial entry and delivery, indicates that babies delivered between 24 hours and seven days after corticosteroid administration show a more marked benefit (typical OR of RDS 0.38; 95% CI 0.25–0.57). The odds ratios for RDS in those delivered less than 24 hours after administration (OR 0.70; 95% CI 0.43–1.16) do not show a statistically significant treatment effect. Babies delivered more than seven days after trial entry experienced a low level of RDS and so the point estimate (0.41) for the odds ratio for respiratory distress is surrounded by wide confidence intervals (95% CI 0.18–0.98).

Contrary to opinions expressed in previous reviews of this subject,[38] the beneficial effect of corticosteroids is not confined to babies delivered between 30 and 34 weeks of gestation. Seven trials supply data allowing a secondary analysis of the risk of RDS in babies born at less than 30 weeks of gestation. This shows an unambiguous reduction in the risk of RDS in this high-risk group (typical OR 0.48; 95% CI 0.30–0.77). Only 35 babies, from eight trials, developed RDS after 34 weeks of gestation, so the typical odds ratio of 0.65 is surrounded by wide confidence limits (95% CI 0.33–1.29) and is thus compatible with either a beneficial effect or a chance variation.

Effect of gender

There is no evidence, from the few trials that refer to it, that the gender of the infant determines its likelihood of benefiting from antenatal corticosteroids. The typical odds ratio for males is 0.43 (95% CI 0.29–0.64) and for females it is 0.36 (95% CI 0.23–0.57).

Postnatal surfactant

The reduction in RDS associated with antenatal corticosteroid therapy may seem less important in the post-surfactant era. This is not the case. Apart from the evident medical and economic advantages of preventing rather than treating RDS, there is evidence that antenatal exposure to corticosteroids potentiates the response to postnatally administered surfactant. Table 20.2 summarises a secondary analysis of data from two multicentre trials of postnatal surfactant therapy showing how adverse neonatal outcomes are lowest in the subgroup of babies exposed antenatally to corticosteroids and postnatally to surfactant.[39]

Intraventricular haemorrhage

Corticosteroid therapy causes a highly significant reduction in the odds of periventricular haemorrhage. Because of the potential confounding effect of the differential in neonatal mortality on the diagnosis of intraventricular haemorrhage, this outcome is analysed by diagnosis at autopsy (typical OR 0.29; 95% CI 0.14–0.61) and by ultrasound (typical OR 0.48; 95% CI 0.32–0.72).

Table 20.2. Effects of the combined use of antenatal corticosteroids and postnatal surfactant; adapted with permission from Jobe et al.[39]

	No steroids and no surfactant	Steroids only	Surfactant only	Steroids and surfactant
Number	566	46	555	57
Birthweight (g ± SD)	1021 ± 281	1013 ± 226	1013 ± 284	989 ± 201
Gestational age (weeks ± SD)	27.1 ± 2.6	27.5 ± 1.7	27.2 ± 2.6	27.4 ± 1.7
Air leaks (%)	44.4	21.7	47	27.6
Patent ductus (n)	44.2	21.7	47	27.6
Severe intraventricular haemorrhage (n)	22.6	10.9	24.6	6.9
Death from RDS (n)	19.6	6.5	7.2	0
Death < 28 days (%)	24.9	15.2	17.7	0

This benefit may in part reflect a domino effect of the reduced incidence of RDS, but the profound effect on intraventricular haemorrhage seen in the absence of a reduction in the risk of RDS in the Garite *et al.* trial[4] points to an independent benefit.

Necrotising enterocolitis

A profound effect (OR 0.32; 95% CI 0.15–0.68) on the incidence of necrotising enterocolitis was reported in association with corticosteroid use in the US Collaborative Trial.[40] In the systematic review the typical odds ratio was 0.59 (95% CI 0.32–1.09). No effect on the incidence of patent ductus arteriosus or of bronchopulmonary dysplasia was seen. Only one trial reported on the incidence of neonatal jaundice and the result suggests a reduction in neonatal hyperbilirubinaemia in corticosteroid-treated babies compared with controls.

Long-term effects on children

Lessons learned from medical history dictate caution in the use of hormonal preparations during pregnancy[41] and underline the importance of long-term follow-up studies of children exposed to antenatal corticosteroids. Children from three large trials have been followed in childhood.[42–44] Follow-up data have been published on physical growth and development up to three years of age in children from the US trial,[43] up to six years of age in children from the Auckland trial[42] and up to 12 years of age in children from the Amsterdam trial.[44] None of these studies indicates that antenatal corticosteroid therapy has any effect on these parameters, nor is there any evidence that lung growth is affected. A variety of psychometric tests have been applied to survivors of these three trials at the ages already mentioned. There is no evident difference in the scores achieved by those exposed to antenatal steroids versus the unexposed controls, despite the fact that the preferential neonatal survival of children born after corticosteroid administration might be expected to have increased their risk of long-term neurological sequelae. In fact, the available evidence suggests that, if anything, antenatal corticosteroids administration may protect against neurological abnormality (hemiparesis, diplegia, quadriplegia, etc.).

Adverse maternal effects

Maternal infection

An increased risk of infection in mothers or an altered immunological response to an infectious process is one potential hazard of therapy. Eleven trials reported this outcome. The pooled odds ratio of 1.30 (95% CI 0.99–1.73) suggests a small increase in maternal infection, which just stops short of statistical significance.

Maternal pulmonary oedema

Instances of pulmonary oedema have been reported in women being treated with corticosteroids in combination with intravenous fluids and other drugs, typically tocolytics.[45] Case reports of such adverse events are important but lack denominators on which incidence rates can be based. Morales *et al.*[25] reported two cases of pulmonary oedema in women who were exposed to both corticosteroids and magnesium sulphate – an incidence rate of 1.6%, Reports of cases of pulmonary oedema in women treated with corticosteroids and betamimetics are numerous. Katz *et al.*[46] reported an incidence rate of 5%. Fluid overload, the presence of underlying heart disease and multifetal pregnancy are significant risk factors.[47,48] There appear to be no reports of the condition occurring in women treated with corticosteroids only.

Economic effects of antenatal corticosteroid therapy

Both the cost and duration of neonatal hospital stay are substantially reduced by antenatal corticosteroid therapy.[4,18,20,25] Using contemporary estimates of the cost of neonatal hospitalisation and of the number of babies at risk of RDS, Avery[49] estimated a potential annual saving to the USA of $35 million. Present-day estimates of the economic implications of antenatal corticosteroid therapy are altered by the availability of neonatal surfactant therapy, and by the possibility of using it either as prophylaxis or as treatment of RDS. Only one trial[24] reports on the effect of antenatal corticosteroid therapy on surfactant usage, showing a reduced use of surfactant in treated babies (OR 0.41; 95% CI 0.19–0.90). Mugford *et al.*[50] have attempted to estimate the cost implications of antenatal corticosteroid therapy in eligible women based on a study of the cost of caring for neonates with and without RDS at a variety of gestational ages. Using odds ratios for reduction in RDS similar to those quoted in this chapter, and allowing for those deliveries that take place soon after admission to hospital, they estimate that a policy of intending to administer antenatal corticosteroids prior to delivery of all babies of less than 35 weeks of gestation would result in a reduction in the average cost/baby of 10% with a 14% reduction in the average cost/survivor. Applied only to mothers of babies with gestational ages of less than 31 weeks, antenatal administration of corticosteroids would increase total costs by 7% because of the greater cost of caring for babies of this gestation who would otherwise not have survived, but this policy would have reduced the cost/survivor by 9%.

Corticosteroids in specific clinical situations

Preterm prelabour rupture of the membranes

Preterm prelabour rupture of the membranes (PPROM) occurs in only one percent of all pregnancies, but precedes preterm delivery in 33% of babies born before 29 weeks.[51] The proportion of preterm births associated with PPROM is even higher if one excludes preterm births following elective preterm labour, twins and intrauterine fetal death. The effect of PPROM on fetal lung maturation is controversial, with some authors reporting an acceleration of fetal lung maturation and some disputing this.[52-54] The confusion here may relate to difficulties in choosing an appropriate control group with which to compare babies born preterm following prelabour rupture of the membranes (PROM). Notwithstanding any effect that PROM itself may have on fetal pulmonary maturity, the evidence derived from a meta-analysis of randomised trials of corticosteroid therapy following PPROM indicates that the incidence of RDS is substantially reduced by corticosteroid administration (typical OR 0.44; 95% CI 0.32–0.60).[55] There has been concern that the inherent susceptibility to infection of women with PROM might be increased or that the signs of infection might be masked, thereby causing a delay in its diagnosis. Fifteen randomised controlled trials reported on the overall incidence of fetal or neonatal infection in corticosteroid cases compared with placebo-treated controls. No increase in perinatal infection was evident (typical OR 0.82; 95% CI 0.57–1.19). The results of these meta-analyses support the use of corticosteroids to prevent RDS following PPROM. The use of corticosteroids combined with antibiotic prophylaxis in women with PPROM is also supported by current evidence.[56]

Maternal diabetes

Maternal diabetes predisposes the preterm infant to RDS, especially when poorly controlled diabetes gives rise to fetal hyperinsulinism that blocks surfactant production by type 2 pulmonary cells. Tight control of diabetes mellitus in pregnancy reduces the incidence of respiratory distress. The results of the randomised trials reviewed above do not permit an authoritative statement on the efficacy and safety of antenatal corticosteroids in women with insulin-dependent diabetes as only 35 diabetic women were randomised across all available randomised controlled trials. Glucocorticoid therapy is likely to provoke insulin resistance and deterioration in diabetic control, which could potentially cause cortisol resistance in the fetal lung. A protocol has been proposed for improving glycaemic control during corticosteroid therapy in women with diabetes.[57]

Maternal hypertensive disease

Hypertensive disease constitutes one of the main indications for elective preterm delivery. RDS is a major problem in the infants of hypertensive mothers and the evidence does not support the hypothesis that pre-eclampsia accelerates fetal lung maturation. Ninety women with hypertension were included in the first randomised trial of antenatal corticosteroid therapy.[23] Twelve intrauterine fetal deaths occurred in 47 treated women compared with three among 43 controls (OR 3.75; 95% CI 1.24–11.30). This, understandably, led to a great reluctance to administer antenatal corticosteroid therapy to women with hypertension. Subsequent analysis of these fetal deaths revealed that they occurred in women with proteinuria of greater than 2 g per day for more than 14 days. Women with hypertensive disease were included in three other trials[20,22,26] but only two[20,22] of these were able to provide a secondary analysis of intrauterine fetal deaths in this subgroup of women. No deaths occurred in either treatment or control arms of these trials. Observational data have not reproduced an excess risk of fetal death in association with corticosteroid therapy in women with pre-eclampsia.[58]

Multifetal pregnancy

Babies born preterm following multiple pregnancy are at increased risk of RDS, with second twins being at particular risk. Two groups of investigators conducted a secondary analysis of the effect of corticosteroid therapy in reducing RDS in multifetal pregnancies.[22,59] Burkett et al.[59] have quoted data from the Collaborative Group study[20] to indicate that the effect of antenatal corticosteroid therapy is suboptimal in this situation. However, the odds ratio (0.79; 95% CI 0.33–1.91) quoted for the risk of RDS in this group of babies is compatible with a treatment effect of equal magnitude to that seen in singleton babies. The apparently diminished treatment effect may represent a type II error, may be due to the subtherapeutic maternal plasma corticosteroid levels,[59] or may indicate that the benefits of corticosteroid therapy are offset by the effects of perinatal hypoxia in second twins.

Single versus multiple doses of corticosteroid therapy

Given that the systematic reviews of antenatal steroid therapy indicate that up to 50% of babies delivered following antenatal steroid therapy still develop RDS, it is imperative that alternative treatment schedules are evaluated. The course of threatened preterm labour is variable and unpredictable. All randomised trials of interventions such as tocolysis and antenatal corticosteroids report significant numbers of both treatment and control subjects who remain undelivered one week or more following trial entry. Given the significant morbidity associated with prematurity even in those treated with a single course of corticosteroids, it was inevitable that the question of repeat courses would arise. Unfortunately, a policy of repeating antenatal steroid therapy crept into practice before undergoing rigorous evaluation. Following the slow adoption of antenatal corticosteroid therapy as the standard of care in women expected to delivery preterm, the use of repeated courses of treatment became common during the 1990s. Ninety-eight percent of British obstetric units surveyed in 1997 indicated that they prescribed repeated courses of corticosteroids to women who remain undelivered more than one week after treatment.[60] Non-randomised cohort studies reported adverse effects after repeat doses of steroids on measures of growth at birth,[61] risk of neonatal infection, fetal pituitary–adrenal axis function and childhood behaviour.[62] Pulmonary effects were equivocal. Long-term follow-up studies on growth, development and behaviour of children exposed prenatally to repeated courses of steroids are limited and to date have been based on non-randomised designs. Results are conflicting, with evidence of adverse effects on development[63] and behaviour[62] from some studies while others have shown no difference between corticosteroid-exposed children and controls.[62,64,65] An additional, albeit hypothetical, long-term potential adverse outcome is the possible effect of single or repeat doses of antenatal steroids on cardiovascular settings in the fetus leading to adult hypertension.[66] Repeated courses of antenatal steroids also carry theoretical maternal risks of adrenal insufficiency, impaired glucose tolerance, osteoporosis and dysphoria.

Clinicians have responded to this clinical dilemma by initiating a number of randomised controlled trials of single versus repeated courses of antenatal corticosteroids. Three trials,[67-69] which recruited a total of 551 women, have been published and form the basis of a systematic review.[70] Two of the trials were conducted in the USA[68,69] and the other in Canada.[67] In addition, multicentre trials of single versus repeat courses of antenatal steroids are recruiting in Canada (the MACS trial), the USA (NIH trial), the UK (TEAMS trial), Finland, and Australia and New Zealand (ACTORDS trial).

The systematic review of the trials published to date[70] (see Table 20.3) indicates that fewer infants in the repeat dose(s) of corticosteroids group had severe lung disease compared with infants in the placebo group (RR 0.64; 95% CI 0.44–0.93, one trial;[68] 500 infants). No statistically significant differences were seen for any of the other primary outcomes, which included other measures of respiratory morbidity, small-for-gestational-age at birth, perinatal death, periventricular haemorrhage, periventricular leukomalacia and maternal infectious morbidity. The mean birthweight of steroid-treated babies is lower but this deficit is not statistically significant. The outcome of further randomised trials of repeat versus single courses of steroids is awaited with interest. Until then, repeat courses should only be given either in the context of randomised trials or after careful discussion, in those women where extreme prematurity at the time of anticipated delivery puts their babies at the risk of greatest morbidity.

Table 20.3. Effects of repeat versus single courses of antenatal corticosteroids on the severity of any lung disease; reproduced with permission from Crowther et al.[70]

Review: Repeat doses of prenatal corticosteroids for women at risk of preterm birth for preventing neonatal respiratory disease
Comparison: 01 Repeat doses of corticosteroids versus single course (all trials)
Outcome: 02 Severity of any lung disease

Study	Treatment n/N	Control n/N	Relative Risk (Fixed) 95% CI	Weight (%)	Relative Risk (Fixed) 95% CI
Guinn 2002	38 / 255	57 / 245		100.0	0.64 [0.44, 0.93]
Total (95% CI)	38 / 255	57 / 245		100.0	0.64 [0.44, 0.93]

Test for heterogeneity chi-square=0.00 df=0
Test for overall effect=-2.35 p=0.02

.1   .2   1   5   10

Favours treatment   Favours control

Betamethasone versus dexamethasone

The glucocorticoid regimens that have been explored in randomised trials in humans are four doses of dexamethasone 6 mg at 12-hour intervals or two doses of betamethasone 12 mg intramuscularly at 24-hour intervals. Despite the fact that the structures of the two drugs are stereoisomeric, varying only in the configuration of the 16 methyl group, the non-genomic effects of the two agents appear to vary. The effects on RDS are similar – dexamethasone odds ratio 0.56 (95% CI 0.43–0.73) and betamethasone odds ratio 0.49 (95% CI 0.39–0.63).[37] The effects on fetal state appear to differ both in animals and in humans. Three randomised trials reported reduced heart-rate variability following betamethasone while they found no consistent effect following dexamethasone.[71-73]

In a non-randomised cohort study of 883 liveborn preterm infants born in France between 1993 and 1996, Baud et al.[74] studied the 357 babies who received no steroids, 361 exposed to betamethasone and 165 to dexamethasone. It was found that maternal betamethasone reduced the incidence of periventricular leukomalacia (OR 0.5; 95% CI 0.2–0.9) whereas dexamethasone had no protective effect.

This report must be treated with caution because of the non-randomised design. The reported effects may relate to the sulphiting agents used as preservatives in some intramuscular steroid preparations. In France betamethasone is preservative-free while dexamethasone contains sulphites. The opposite situation applies in the UK. The author of the original observational study has shown that sulphites and sulphited steroids are neurotoxic in vitro while no such effect is seen with pure preparations of either dexamethasone or betamethasone.[75]

Conclusions

There is robust clinical evidence that the structure and function of many fetal organs and systems is amenable to accelerated maturation. This has already resulted in substantial benefits to preterm babies without adverse effects on safety. In the future, it may be possible to manipulate structural or functional maturity in a more precise way. For the present, clinicians should continue to use antenatal corticosteroids in a manner that ensures that wherever possible preterm babies are exposed to a single course of corticosteroids prior to delivery. Repeat courses should be the exception outside the context of randomised trials, until further evidence is available in relation to efficacy and long-term safety. Provided the preparation is nonsulphited, either dexamethasone or betamethasone can be used.

References

1.   Liggins GC. Premature delivery of fetal lambs infused with glucocorticoids. *J Endocrinol* 1969;45:515–23.

2.   Liggins GC, Howie RN. A controlled trial of antepartum glucocorticoid treatment for prevention of the respiratory distress syndrome in premature infants. *Pediatrics* 1972;50:515–25.

3.   Ballard R, Ballard P. Scientific basis for antenatal steroid use. In: *National Institutes of Health Report of the Consensus Development Conference on the Effect of Corticosteroids for Fetal Maturation on Perinatal Outcomes.* NIH Publication No 95-3784. Bethesda, MD: NIH; 1995. p. 27–9.

4.   Garite TJ, Rumney PJ, Briggs GG, Harding JA, Nageotte MP, Towers CV, *et al.* A randomized placebo-controlled trial of betamethasone for the prevention of respiratory distress syndrome at 24 to 28 weeks' gestation. *Am J Obstet Gynecol* 1992;166:646–51.

5.   Jobe AH, Ikegami M. Fetal responses to glucocorticoids. In: Mendelson CR, editor. *Endocrinology of the Lung.* Totawa: Humana Press; 2000. p. 45–57.

6.   Massaro DJ, Massaro GD. The regulation of the formation of pulmonary alveoli. In: Bland RD, Coalson JJ, editors. *Chronic Lung Disease in Early Infancy.* New York: Marcel Dekker, Inc.; 2000. p. 479–92.

7.   Jobe AH. Animal models of antenatal corticosteroids: clinical implications. *Clin Obstet Gynecol* 2003;46:174–89.

8.   Jobe AH. The new BPD: An arrest of lung development. *Pediatr Res* 1999;46:641–3.

9.   Johnson JWC, Mitzner W, London WT, Palmer AE, Scott R, Kearney K. Glucocorticoids and the rhesus fetal lung. *Am J Obstet Gynecol* 1978;132:905–16.

10.   Johnson JWC, Mitzner W, Beck JC, London WT, Sly DL, Lee PA, *et al.* Long-term effects of betamethasone on fetal development. *Am J Obstet Gynecol* 1981;141:1053–61.

11.   Bunton TE, Plopper CG. Triamcinolone-induced structural alterations in the development of the lung of the fetal rhesus macaque. *Am J Obstet Gynecol* 1984;150:203–15.

12.   Stewart JD, Sienko AE, Gonzalez CL, Christensen HD, Rayburn WF. Placebo-controlled comparison between a single dose and a multidose of betamethasone in accelerating lung maturation of mice offspring. *Am J Obstet Gynecol* 1998;179:1241–7.

13.   Pratt L, Magness RR, Phernetton T, Hendricks SK, Abbott DH, Bird IM. Repeated use of betamethasone in rabbits: effects of treatment variation on adrenal suppression, pulmonary maturation, and pregnancy outcome. *Am J Obstet Gynecol* 1999;181:995–1005.

14.   Ikegami M, Jobe AH, Newnham J, Polk DH, Willet KE, Sly P. Repetitive prenatal glucocorticoids improve lung function and decrease growth in preterm lambs. *Am J Respir Crit Care Med* 1997;156:178–84.

15.   Meadow WL, Bell A, Sunstein CR. Statistics, not memories: what was the standard of care for administering antenatal steroids to women in preterm labor between 1985 and 2000? *Obstet Gynecol* 2003;102:356–62.

16.   Fekih M, Chaieb A, Sboui H, Denguezli W, Hidar S, Khairi H. Value of prenatal corticotherapy in the prevention of hyaline membrane disease in premature infants. Randomized prospective study. *Tunis Med* 2002;80:260–5.

17.   Block MF, Kling OR, Crosby WM. Antenatal glucocorticoid therapy for the prevention of respiratory distress syndrome in the premature infant. *Obstet Gynecol* 1977;50:186–90.

18.   Carlan SJ, Parsons M, O'Brien WF, Krammer J. Pharmacological pulmonary maturation in preterm premature rupture of membranes. *Am J Obstet Gynecol* 1991;164:371.

19.   Cararach V, Sentis J, Botet F, De Los Rios. A multi-centric prospective randomized study in premature rupture of membranes (PROM): respiratory and infectious complications in the newborn. In: *Proceedings of the Twelfth European Congress of Perinatal Medicine.* Lyon: European Association of Perinatal Medicine; 1990.

20.   Collaborative Group on Antenatal Steroid Therapy. Effect of antenatal steroid administration on prevention of respiratory distress syndrome. *Am J Obstet Gynecol* 1981;141:276–87.

21.   Doran TA, Swyer P, MacMurray B, Mahon W, Enhorning G, Bernstein A, *et al.* Results of a double-blind controlled study on the use of betamethasone in the prevention of respiratory distress syndrome. *Am J Obstet Gynecol* 1980;136:313–20.

22.   Gamsu HR, Mullinger BM, Donnai P, Dash CH. Antenatal administration of betamethasone to

prevent respiratory distress syndrome in preterm infants: report of a UK multicentre trial. *Br J Obstet Gynaecol* 1989;96:401–10.

23. Howie RN, Liggins GC. Clinical trial of antepartum betamethasone therapy for prevention of respiratory distress in preterm infants. In: Anderson ABM, Beard R, Brudenell J, Dunn PM, editors. *Preterm Labour.* Proceedings of the Fifth Study Group of the Royal College of Obstetricians and Gynaecologists. London: RCOG Press; 1977. p. 281-289.

24. Kari AM, Hallman M, Eronen M. Prenatal dexamethasone in conjunction with rescue therapy of human surfactant – a randomised placebo-controlled multicentre study. *Pediatrics* 1994;93:730–6.

25. Morales WJ, Diebel ND, Lazar AJ, Zadrozny D. The effect of antenatal dexamethasone on the prevention of respiratory distress syndrome in preterm gestation with premature rupture of membranes. *Am J Obstet Gynecol* 1986;154:591–5.

26. Morrison JC, Whybrew WD, Bucovaz ET, Schneider JM. Injection of corticosteroids to the mother to prevent neonatal respiratory distress syndrome. *Am J Obstet Gynecol* 1978;13:358–66.

27. Papageorgiou AN, Desgranges MF, Masson M, Colle E, Shatz R, Gelfand MM. The antenatal use of betamethasone in the prevention of respiratory distress syndrome. A controlled double-blind study. *Pediatrics* 1979;63:73–9.

28. Parsons MT, Sobel D, Cummiskey K, Constantine L, Roitman J. Steroid, antibiotic and tocolytic versus no steroid, antibiotic and tocolytic management in patients with preterm PROM at 25–32 weeks. In: *Proceedings of the Eighth Annual Scientific Meeting of the Society of Perinatal Obstetricians.* Las Vegas: Society of Perinatal Obstetricians; 1988. p. 44.

29. Schutte MF, Treffers PE, Koppe JG, Breur W. The influence of betamethasone and orciprenaline on the incidence of respiratory distress syndrome in the newborn after premature labour. *Br J Obstet Gynaecol* 1980;87:127–31.

30. Schmidt PL, Sims ME, Strassner HT, Paul RH, Mueller E, McCart D. Effect of antepartum glucocorticoid administration upon neonatal respiratory distress syndrome and perinatal infection. *Am J Obstet Gynecol* 1984;148:178–86.

31. Tauesch HW, Frigoletto F, Kitzmiller J. Risk of respiratory distress syndrome after prenatal dexamethasone treatment. *Pediatrics* 1979;63:64–72.

32. Teramo K, Hallman M, Raivio K. Maternal glucocorticoid in unplanned premature labor. *Pediatr Res* 1980;14:326–9.

33. Chalmers I, Hetherington J, Elbourne D, Keirse MJNC, Enkin M. Materials and methods used in synthesizing evidence to evaluate the effects of care during pregnancy and childbirth. In: Chalmers I, Enkin M, Keirse MJNC, editors. *Effective Care in Pregnancy and Childbirth.* Oxford: Oxford University Press; 1989. p. 39–65.

34. Yusuf S, Peto R, Lewis T, Collins R, Sleight P. Beta blockade during and after myocardial infarction: an overview of the randomised trials. *Prog Cardiovasc Dis* 1985;27:335–71.

35. Crowley P, Chalmers I, Keirse MJ. The effects of corticosteroid administration before preterm delivery: an overview of the evidence from controlled trials. *Br J Obstet Gynaecol* 1990;97:11–25.

36. Crowley P. Antenatal corticosteroid therapy: a meta-analysis of the randomized trials, 1972 to 1994. *Am J Obstet Gynecol* 1995;173:322–35.

37. Crowley P. Prophylactic corticosteroids for preterm birth. *Cochrane Database Syst Rev* 2000;(2):CD000065.

38. Robertson NRC. Advances in respiratory distress syndrome. *BMJ* 1982;284:917–8.

39. Jobe AH, Mitchell BR, Gunkel JH. Beneficial effects of the combined use of prenatal corticosteroids and postnatal surfactant on preterm infants. *Am J Obstet Gynecol* 1993;168:508–13.

40. Bauer CR, Morrison JC, Poole WK, Korones SB, Boehm JJ, Rigatto H. *et al.* A decreased incidence of necrotizing enterocolitis after prenatal glucocorticoid therapy. *Pediatrics* 1984;73:682–8.

41. Bibbo M, Gill WB, Azizi F, Blough R, Fang VS, Rosenfield RL, *et al.* Follow-up study of male and female offspring of DES-exposed mothers. *Obstet Gynecol* 1977;49:1–8.

42. MacArthur BA, Howie RN, Dezoete JA, Elkins J. School progress and cognitive development of 6-year-old children whose mothers were treated antenatally with betamethasone. *Pediatrics* 1982;70:99–105.

43. Collaborative Group on Antenatal Steroid Therapy. Effect of Antenatal steroid administration on the infant: long-term follow-up. *J Pediatr* 1984;104:259–67.

44. Smolders-de Haas H, Neuvel J, Schmand B, Treffers PE, Koppe JG, Hoeks J. Physical development and medical history of children who were treated antenatally with corticosteroids to prevent respiratory distress syndrome: a 10- to 12-year follow-up. *Pediatrics* 1990;86:65–70.

45. Stubblefield PG. Pulmonary edema occurring after therapy with dexamethasone and terbutaline for premature labor: a case report. *Am J Obstet Gynecol* 1978;132:341–2.

46. Katz M, Robertson PA, Creasy RK. Cardiovascular complications associated with terbutaline treatment for preterm labor. *Am J Obstet Gynecol* 1981;139:605–8.

47. Finley J, Katz M, Rojas-Perez M, Roberts JM, Creasy RK, Schiller NB. Cardiovascular consequences of beta-agonist tocolysis: an electro-cardiographic study. *Obstet Gynecol* 1984;64:787–91.

48. King JF, Grant A, Keirse MJNC, Chalmers I. Beta-mimetics in preterm labour: an overview of the randomized controlled trials. *Br J Obstet Gynaecol* 1988;95:211–22.

49. Avery ME. The argument for prenatal administration of dexamethasone to prevent respiratory distress syndrome. *J Pediatr* 1984;104:240.

50. Mugford M, Piercy J, Chalmers I. Cost implications of different approaches to the prevention of respiratory distress syndrome. *Arch Dis Child* 1991;66:757–64.

51. Hoekstra RA, Jackson JC, Myers TF, Frantz ID 3rd, Stern ME, Powers WF. Improved neonatal survival following multiple doses of bovine surfactant in very premature neonates at risk for respiratory distress syndrome. *Pediatrics* 1991;88:10–8.

52. Wennergren M, Krantz M, Hjalmarson O, Karlsson K. Interval from rupture of the membranes to delivery and neonatal respiratory adaptation. *Br J Obstet Gynaecol* 1986;93:799–803.

53. Coustan DR. Clinical aspects of antenatal enhancement of pulmonary maturity. *Clin Perinatol* 1987;14:697–711.

54. Yoon JJ, Harper RG. Observations on the relationship between duration of membrane rupture and the development of idiopathic respiratory distress syndrome. *Pediatrics* 1973;52:161–8.

55. Crowley P. Corticosteroids after preterm prelabour rupture of membranes. *Obstet Gynecol Clin North Am* 1992;19:317–26.

56. Kenyon S, Boulvain M, Neilson J. Antibiotics for preterm rupture of membranes. *Cochrane Database Syst Rev* 2003;(2):CD001058.

57. Kaushal K, Gibson JM, Railton A, Hounsome B, New JP, Young RJ. A protocol for improved glycaemic control following corticosteroid therapy in diabetic pregnancies. *Diabet Med* 2003;20:73–5.

58. Lamont RF, Dunlop PDM, Levene MI, Elder MI. Use of glucocorticoids in pregnancies complicated by severe hypertension and proteinuria. *Br J Obstet Gynaecol* 1983;90:199–202.

59. Burkett G, Bauer CR, Morrison JC, Curet LB. Effect of prenatal dexamethasone administration on prevention of respiratory distress syndrome in twin pregnancies. *J Perinatol* 1986;6:304–8.

60. Brocklehurst P, Gates S, McKenzie-McHarg K, Alfirevic Z, Chamberlain G. Are we prescribing multiple courses of antenatal corticosteroids? A survey of practice in the UK. *Br J Obstet Gynaecol* 1999;106:977–9.

61. French N, Hagan R, Evans S, Godfrey M, Newnham J. Repeated antenatal corticosteroids: size at birth and subsequent development. *Am J Obstet Gynecol* 1999;180:114–21.

62. French N, Hagan R, Evans S, Godfrey M, Newnham J. Repeated antenatal corticosteroids: behaviour outcomes in a regional population of very preterm infants [abstract]. *Pediatr Res* 1998;43:214A.

63. Esplin M, Fausett M, Smith S, Oshiro B, Porter TF, Branch DW, *et al.* Multiple courses of antenatal steroids associated with a delay in long-term psychomotor development in children with birth weight <1500 grams. *Am J Obstet Gynecol* 2000;182:S24. Abstract 27.

64. Hasbargen U, Reber D, Versmold H, Schulze A. Growth and development of children to 4 years of age after repeated antenatal steroid administration. *Eur J Pediatr* 2001;160:552–5.

65. Thorp JA, Etzenhouser J, O'Connor M, Jones A, Jones P, Belden B, *et al.* Effects of phenobarbital and multiple-dose antenatal/postnatal steroid on developmental outcome at age 7 years. *Am J Obstet Gynecol* 2002;185:S87.

66. Benediktsson R, Lindsay RS, Noble J, Secki JR, Edwards CRW. Glucocorticoid exposure *in utero*: new model for adult hypertension. *Lancet* 1993;341:339–41.

67. Aghajafari F, Murphy K, Ohlsson A, Amankwah K, Matthews S, Hannah M. Multiple versus single courses of antenatal corticosteroids for preterm birth: a pilot study. *J Obstet Gynaecol Can* 2002;24:321–9.

68. Guinn DA, Atkinson MW, Sullivan L, Lee M, MacGregor S, Parilla B, *et al.* Single vs weekly courses of antenatal corticosteroids for women at risk of preterm delivery: A randomized controlled trial. *JAMA* 2001;286:1581–7.

69. McEvoy C, Bowling S, Willamson R, Lozano D, Tolaymat L, Izquierdo L, *et al.* The effect of a single remote course versus weekly courses of antenatal corticosteroids on functional residual capacity in preterm infants: a randomized trial. *Pediatrics* 2002;110:280–4.

70. Crowther CA, Harding J. Repeat doses of prenatal corticosteroids for women at risk of preterm birth for preventing neonatal respiratory disease. *Cochrane Database Syst Rev* 2003;(3):CD003935.

71. Mulder EJ, Derks JB, Visser GH. Antenatal corticosteroid therapy and fetal behaviour: a randomised study of the effects of betamethasone and dexamethasone. *Br J Obstet Gynaecol* 1997;104:1239–47.

72. Senat MV, Minoui S, Multon O, Fernandez H, Frydman R, Ville Y. Effect of dexamethasone and betamethasone on fetal heart rate variability in preterm labour: a randomised study. *Br J Obstet Gynaecol* 1998;105:749–55.

73. Rotmensch S, Liberati M, Vishne TH, Celentano C, Ben-Rafael Z, Bellati U. The effect of betamethasone and dexamethasone on fetal heart rate patterns and biophysical activities. A prospective randomized trial. *Acta Obstet Gynecol Scand* 1999;78:493–500.

74.   Baud O, Foix-L'Helias L, Kaminski M, Audibert F, Jarreau PH, Papiernik E, *et al.* Antenatal glucocorticoid treatment and cystic periventricular leukomalacia in very premature infants. *N Engl J Med* 1999;341:1190–6.

75.   Baud O, Laudenbach V, Evrard P, Gressens P. Neurotoxic effects of fluorinated glucocorticoid preparations on the developing mouse brain: role of preservatives. *Pediatr Res* 2001;50:706–11.

Chapter 21

Myometrial physiology

Andrés López Bernal

Introduction

The uterus is a fundamental organ for reproduction which performs several functions. Under the influence of ovarian steroid hormones it blocks or allows the passage of sperm through the cervical canal by varying the consistency of cervical mucus, it facilitates sperm transport through the uterine cavity and into the fallopian tube by peristaltic movements, and it accommodates the blastocyst and facilitates the blood supply to the growing conceptus. These early events in the establishment of pregnancy are followed by a remarkable period of growth by hypertrophy and hyperplasia of uterine smooth muscle.

Pregnancy demands a balance between the need for space for the growing fetus and the ability of the uterus to hold its contents. In most pregnancies this equilibrium is maintained for approximately 40 weeks. Then, a combination of changes in connective tissue that favour cervical ripening and dilatation, and changes in myometrial smooth muscle that increase the rate of spontaneous activity and coordinated contractions, leads to the onset of labour and successful delivery. In the puerperium, the uterus begins a major remodelling process that returns the organ to its basal nonpregnant state within a few weeks.

Initially, the control of uterine activity in pregnancy is likely to be under the influence of ovarian hormones, especially luteal progesterone, and, as pregnancy progresses and the corpus luteum regresses, the control is probably taken over by the placenta through its secretion of steroid and peptide hormones, including progesterone, oestrogens, placental lactogen, chorionic gonadotrophin, and many growth factor-type molecules. Our understanding of smooth muscle physiology in general and of myometrial function in particular has advanced steadily in the past decade, especially at a cellular and biochemical level, but much remains to be done before the mechanisms involved in the maintenance of pregnancy and the transition to labour are elucidated at the level of maternal–fetal physiology and endocrinology. To name but one example, the effect of progesterone on nuclear transcription factors or on cell membrane receptors is now known in considerable detail, and yet it is still unclear whether the apparently important role of this hormone in the maintenance of pregnancy in most species applies to women. In this chapter I will focus on pathways that are relevant to myometrial function and point out the many gaps that still remain in our knowledge.

Structure of the myometrium

Myometrial smooth muscle cells are arranged in bundles embedded in a matrix of connective tissue composed mainly of collagen (Figure 21.1). The collagen fibres of the matrix facilitate the transmission of the contractile forces generated by the myometrial bundles. Changes in the connective tissue (increase in collagen solubility and alterations in glycosaminoglycans of the ground substance) occur in preparation for birth throughout the uterus, but are more evident in the cervix where the ratio of collagen to smooth muscle is very high.[1] The control of extracellular matrix turnover is highly regulated and involves a specific class of proteolytic enzymes known as the matrix metalloproteinases (MMPs) and their associated locally produced tissue inhibitors (TIMPs).[2] In biopsies of lower uterine segment from women undergoing caesarean section at term, an increase in MMP-8, MMP-9 and TIMP-1 with advancing labour has been demonstrated.[3] The levels of MMP-2 and MMP-9 also increase in cervical tissue during the ripening process.[4] Interestingly, inflammatory mediators such as interleukin-1β and tumour necrosis factor-α promote the production of MMP-9 in human myometrial cells.[5]

Uterine smooth muscle cells are fusiform in shape and have a complex cytoskeletal structure designed to maximise the effect of isometric contraction.[6] The cells are rich in actin stress fibres that connect to the extracellular matrix through vinculin at focal adhesion plaques. There is a dense mesh of intermediate filaments (cytokeratin, vimentin) and a complex arrangement of microtubules.[6] During gestation there is hypertrophy and hyperplasia of myometrial cells. However, the amounts of contractile

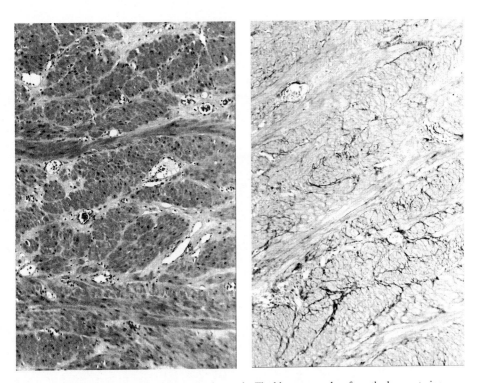

Figure 21.1. Structure of human uterine smooth muscle. The biopsy was taken from the lower uterine segment at the time of caesarean section at term. Note the compact transversal and longitudinal bundles of myometrial cells, and the vascular tissue. Haematoxylin-eosin. The right panel shows the extent of collagen distribution in red, using van Gieson stain. (Courtesy of Dr Helen Porter)

proteins actin and myosin per milligram of protein or per tissue cross-sectional area remain constant in relation to nonpregnant tissue.[7] The content of caldesmon (a smooth muscle protein associated with actin) increases with gestation.[7]

The myofilaments actin (thin filament) and myosin (thick filament) occur in long random fibres throughout the cytoplasm of uterine smooth muscle cells, in contrast to striated muscle where the myofilaments are tightly packed and organised. Myosin is both a structural protein and an enzyme capable of transforming the chemical energy of adenosine triphosphate (ATP) into mechanical energy. Myosin is a hexamer consisting of two identical heavy chains (MHC: approximately 200 kDa) and four light chains (MLC: two 20 kDa and two 17 kDa). The human genome appears to encode more than 40 different myosins: some participate in muscle contraction but others are involved in a variety of other processes. The distribution of myosin isoforms varies between tonic and phasic smooth muscles. In human myometrium (a phasic muscle) the distribution of MHC isoforms is similar in pregnant and nonpregnant tissue, comprising about one-third 204 kDa smooth muscle myosin 1 (SM1), one-third 200 kDa SM2 and one-third a nonmuscle myosin of 196 kDa.[8,9] This myosin composition allows the tissue to develop isometric tension with a force in the range 2–6 mN/mm² at a shortening velocity of 0.1–0.2 muscle length per second.[9]

Physiological basis of uterine contractions

The basis of contraction in myometrium, as in any other muscle, is the capacity of myosin to move along filaments of actin (F-actin). This is possible because of the remarkable structure of MHC – a 20 nm long head and a 140 nm long α-helical tail (Figure 21.2). In smooth muscle, myosin exists as a double-headed molecule with the

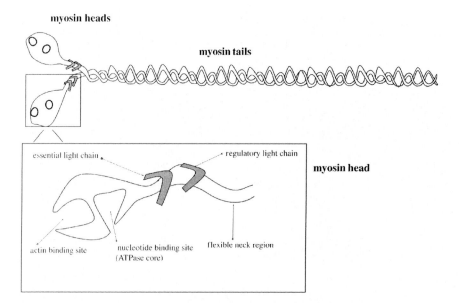

Figure 21.2. Myosin molecules have a two-headed structure with a long tail. The myosin head has an actin binding site and an ATPase core. The neck region is the binding site for the two myosin light chains

two tails forming a coiled coil-rod. The three-dimensional structure of the myosin head has been established by X-ray crystallography and it shows an actin binding cleft and an ATP binding pocket (the ATPase catalytic domain). The head and tail are connected by an α-helical 'neck' that has two important functions. Firstly, the neck domain is the site where the 17 kDa essential and the 20 kDa regulatory MLCs are noncovalently attached. Secondly, the neck domain acts as a mechanical lever arm that amplifies small conformational changes in the head into a 10 nm powerstroke.[10] Interestingly, the ATPase pocket is homologous to that found for guanosine triphosphate (GTP) in heterotrimeric (αβγ subunits) G proteins and there is great functional similarity between the two types of proteins: when the α-subunit of a G protein is bound to GTP it has low affinity for the βγ dimer, whereas the guanosine diphosphate (GDP) form has high affinity for it. Similarly, when myosin is bound to ATP it has poor affinity for actin, whereas when it is bound to adenosine diphosphate (ADP) the affinity for actin is high. Myosin converts the chemical energy of ATP into mechanical energy by cyclic interactions with F-actin polymers. The speed at which myosin moves along actin is determined by the rate of ATP hydrolysis. Thus, when myosin is detached from actin (ATP bound state) it does not generate force. The hydrolysis of ATP to ADP with the release of inorganic phosphate from the actomyosin complex provokes the attachment and force-generating reaction. This is followed by the powerstroke with the release of ADP. Finally, myosin is ready to bind ATP again and release actin (detachment reaction) to start another cycle (Figure 21.3).

Role of myosin light chains

MLCs are remarkably similar in structure to the protein calmodulin, which belongs to a family of proteins characterised by the presence of calcium or metal ion binding domains termed 'EF-helices'. MLC_{17} exists as two isoforms (A and B)[11] and there is evidence that a high content of $MLC_{17}A$ enhances shortening velocity and ATPase of

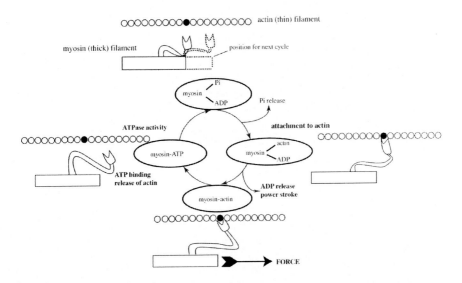

Figure 21.3. A diagram representing the cyclic actin–myosin interaction that leads to the development of force

smooth muscle cells. The 20 kDa MLC also has two isoforms, $MLC_{20}A$ and $MLC_{20}B$, with the former being predominant in adult tissues.[12] Phosphorylation of myosin is a key event in the initiation of smooth muscle contraction and there is very good correlation between the extent of MLC_{20} phosphorylation, shortening velocity and tension development.[13] MLC_{20} can be phosphorylated at two sites, serine 19 (Ser-19) and threonine 18, by a number of enzymes, including protein kinase C (PKC), Ca^{2+}-calmodulin dependent kinase II, rho-kinase, p21-activated kinase (PAK), integrin-linked kinase and leucine-zipper kinase.[14] However, from a physiological point of view the Ca^{2+}-dependent phosphorylation of MLC_{20} at Ser-19 by myosin light chain kinase (MLCK) is the most important reaction.

Myosin light chain kinase – a key enzyme in the regulation of myometrial contractility

Smooth muscle contraction is initiated by an increase in intracellular calcium ($[Ca^{2+}]_i$) and activation of MLCK, which has a key role in the regulation of myometrial contractility.[15] When Ca^{2+} is removed, dephosphorylation of myosin occurs rapidly and the muscle relaxes. MLCK rests in an autoinhibited state that can be rapidly reversed by calmodulin. Thus when $[Ca^{2+}]_i$ increases, a Ca^{2+}-calmodulin complex forms which binds to MLCK and exposes two amino acid residues in the catalytic core of the enzyme. MLCK becomes fully active, phosphorylating MLC_{20} at Ser-19 and initiating contraction. This occurs because phosphorylated MLC_{20} causes myosin to change from a folded, enzymatically inactive structure to an elongated structure with a 500-fold higher actin-activated ATPase activity. Myometrium, like other phasic smooth muscles, has rapid Ca^{2+} extrusion mechanisms that promote relaxation by lowering $[Ca^{2+}]_i$. However, there are other mechanisms to limit the action of MLCK. These occur because MLCK is itself a substrate for cyclic AMP-dependent protein kinase (PKA), PKC, PAK and the multifunctional calmodulin-dependent protein kinase II (CaM kinase II). From a physiological point of view, phosphorylation of MLCK by CaM kinase II is probably the most relevant mechanism.[16] This phosphorylation increases the concentration of Ca^{2+}-calmodulin required for activation of MLCK. The enzyme is therefore less sensitive to Ca^{2+} and loses activity at a given concentration of $[Ca^{2+}]_i$. The $[Ca^{2+}]_i$ required to effect MLCK phosphorylation is greater than that required for MLC_{20} phosphorylation, hence the initial rise in Ca^{2+} results in Ca^{2+}-calmodulin activation of MLCK. However, when $[Ca^{2+}]_i$ reaches a high level or remains elevated for too long, the Ca^{2+}-calmodulin complex activates CaM kinase II, which phosphorylates MLCK, leading to desensitisation of the enzyme.

Regulation of contractility by myosin phosphatase

Dephosphorylation of MLC_{20} by myosin light chain phosphatase (MLCP) transforms myosin into an inactive form, thus restoring relaxation of smooth muscle. The MLCP molecule is increasingly recognised as an important regulatory target. MLCP consists of two regulatory peptides of 110 kDa and 21 kDa and a catalytic subunit of 37 kDa that belongs to the protein-phosphatase-1 family.[17] The 110 kDa myosin binding subunit (MYPT1) is required to target the catalytic subunit to its substrate, the phosphorylated Ser-19 in MLC_{20}. It is important to note that MLCP is a Ca^{2+}-independent enzyme so its activity should remain constant during the phasic $[Ca^{2+}]_i$ fluctuations that influence MLCK activity so much. However, this is not the case, and many G protein-coupled receptors (GPCRs) that stimulate contractility by increasing $[Ca^{2+}]_i$ also enhance contractility through a second mechanism that involves MLCP inhibition.[18,19]

This is due to the activation of rhoA-associated kinase, an enzyme that phosphorylates MYPT1 thus decreasing the ability of MLCP to bind and dephosphorylate MLC_{20}. This mechanism is called 'calcium sensitisation' of the myofilaments because, due to the sluggish MLCP action, less Ca^{2+}-dependent MLCK activity is required to achieve the same level of MLC_{20} phosphorylation (Figure 21.4). Rho-kinase can also phosphorylate MLC_{20} directly in a Ca^{2+}-independent manner, thus potentiating its inhibitory effect on MLCP. RhoA belongs to a family of small GTP binding proteins whose role in the regulation of smooth muscle contractility is the subject of considerable interest. RhoA activates two effector enzymes, rho-kinase and phospholipase D. The latter hydrolyses phosphatidylcholine, generating phosphatidic acid which is easily dephosphorylated to diacylglycerol, resulting in PKC activation[20]. Moreover, there is strong evidence that rho-kinase is involved in oxytocin- and muscarinic-receptor induced Ca^{2+}-sensitisation in myometrium.[21,22] Contractility studies using myometrial strips obtained from pregnant women at term indicate that rho-kinase influences the tonic rather than the phasic components of contractions.[23] During pregnancy there is upregulation of PAK and rhoA-activated kinases in human myometrium.[24] It is possible that two contractile systems coexist in smooth muscle cells, one involving SM myosins, regulated primarily by MLCK and responsible for phasic contractions, and a second involving nonmuscle myosins, regulated by rho-kinase and PKC and responsible for tonic contractile activity.[14] The regulatory subunit of MLCP is also a substrate for PKC, leucine-zipper kinase and integrin-linked kinase but the role of these enzymes in human myometrial cells is not known. Experimental data suggest that in some phasic smooth muscles a cooperative mechanism between rho-kinase and CPI-17, a strong inhibitor of MLCP that is phosphorylated and thereby activated by PKC, may exist.[20,25] The relevance of the PKC/CPI-17 pathway to human myometrial smooth muscle remains to be investigated.

Role of actin-associated proteins

Caldesmon and calponin are two of a group of actin binding proteins that are involved in the regulation of myometrial contractility because they inhibit actomyosin ATPase activity. The inhibitory activities of caldesmon and calponin can, in turn, be blocked through phosphorylation by several protein kinases, including members of the mitogen-activated protein kinase (MAP kinase) group. The content of caldesmon increases significantly during pregnancy in both human and rat myometrium.[7,26] Experiments in rats suggest that caldesmon may contribute to uterine quiescence through inhibition of actomyosin interaction and decreased calcium sensitivity of myometrial tissue. This inhibition appears to be reversed at the onset of labour because caldesmon is phosphorylated (and thereby inactivated) through activation of the MAP kinase pathway.[26] It would be of great interest to investigate these mechanisms in relation to term and preterm labour in women.

Calcium as an essential second messenger

Myometrial smooth muscle has the ability to develop spontaneous activity and generate action potentials. Calcium enters the cells from the extracellular fluid when the cell membrane depolarises. In addition, most receptors that stimulate contractility provoke Ca^{2+} release from intracellular stores. In human myometrium there is a strong temporal relationship between changes in $[Ca^{2+}]_i$ and the development of force,[27] thus calcium homeostatic mechanisms are central to the regulation of myometrial activity.

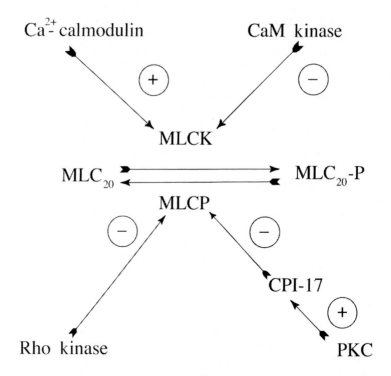

Figure 21.4. Phosphorylation of the 20 kDa regulatory light chains of myosin (MLC$_{20}$) by Ca^{2+}-calmodulin dependent myosin light chain kinase (MLCK) is a prerequisite for the interaction of actin and myosin that leads to myometrial contraction. However, when [Ca^{2+}] reaches a high level or remains elevated for too long, the Ca^{2+}-calmodulin complex activates a kinase (CaM kinase) that phosphorylates MLCK leading to desensitisation of the enzyme. Rho-kinase and protein kinase C (PKC), either singly or cooperatively, are involved in the inhibition of myosin phosphatase (MLCP). Rho-kinase phosphorylates the myosin-targeting subunit in MLCP, inhibiting enzyme activity. PKC acts by phosphorylating an endogenous 17 kDa inhibitory protein (CPI-17), which enhances the ability of this protein to bind to and inhibit the catalytic subunit of MLCP. As a result of MLCP inhibition, more MLC$_{20}$ remains phosphorylated at a given level of Ca^{2+}-calmodulin dependent MLCK activity, resulting in 'calcium sensitisation'

Calcium entry

It is generally acknowledged that voltage-dependent calcium channels (VDCCs) are the main mediators of calcium entry required for smooth muscle contraction. These channels are classified electrophysiologically and pharmacologically into five groups: L, N, T, R and P/Q. L-type Ca^{2+} channels are the most important from the point of view of myometrial physiology and pharmacology because they are crucial for excitation–contraction coupling and they are inhibited by 1,4-dihydropyridines (e.g. nifedipine) and Mg^{2+}, both of which have been used in clinical practice to inhibit uterine contractions in preterm labour.[28] The structure of VDCCs is known in fine detail. They comprise four subunits, including a pore-forming α-subunit for which at least ten genes have been identified. In smooth muscle the main pore-forming subunit, which is the target for nifedipine, has been identified as α_{1C} now known as Ca$_v$1.2.[29] The pores open when the cell membrane reaches negative potentials below –40 mV and the

Ca^{2+} floods into the cells, activating MLCK and initiating contractions. The Ca^{2+} pores close when the membrane repolarises due to K^+ channels' opening. Moreover, L-type channels are also inactivated by increased $[Ca^{2+}]_i$ through a negative feedback effect. T-type Ca^{2+} channels have been described in human myometrium and they require more negative potential (below $-60\,mV$) than L-type channels.[30] Their possible role in action potential transmission and the activity of pacemaker cells is worth investigating.

A relatively new type of Ca^{2+} entry channel, named *trp*, has been described in myometrial cells. The name derives from the transient receptor response observed in the retina of Drosophila flies with faulty vision, which led to the discovery of the *trp* gene.[31] Several *trp* protein isoforms have been described in human myometrial tissue[32] and there is increasing evidence that *trp* channels may be implicated in Ca^{2+} entry into cells in response to signals from GPCRs, arachidonic acid release and intracellular Ca^{2+} store depletion.[33]

Calcium extrusion mechanisms

In order to restore Ca^{2+} homeostasis following the influx of Ca^{2+} during excitation events, smooth muscle cells require mechanisms for the rapid removal of Ca^{2+}. Myometrial cells are thought to have at least two mechanisms in common with other types of smooth muscle. The major mechanism is the plasma membrane Ca^{2+}-ATPase (PMCA), which uses ATP energy to pump Ca^{2+} from the cytoplasm to the extracellular space against a steep electromechanical gradient. Since the extrusion of Ca^{2+} results in uptake of H^+ to maintain neutrality, the action of PMCA is compensated by ion transporters such us Na^+/H^+ exchangers. PMCAs are encoded by at least four genes and the isoform PMCA1b is the most common.[34] Unfortunately, specific inhibitors of PMCA have not been available to investigators and more research is necessary to understand their functional regulation. However, it is known that PMCAs rest as autoinhibited enzymes and become activated by Ca^{2+}-calmodulin, increasing their transport rate. The calmodulin binding site of PMCAs is a phosphorylation substrate for several protein kinases, including PKA, protein kinase G (PKG) and CaM kinases. Phosphorylation of PMCAs causes enhanced Ca^{2+} extrusion. This is likely to be a mechanism by which agonists that increase cyclic adenosine monophosphate (cAMP), e.g. ritodrine, promote uterine relaxation.

A second mechanism of rapid Ca^{2+} extrusion is through Na^+/Ca^{2+} exchangers that use energy from the electrochemical gradient across the membrane and transport three Na^+ ions while removing one Ca^{2+} ion. The relative contribution of PMCA versus Na^+/Ca^{2+} exchange in myometrial Ca^{2+} homeostasis is not known.[35]

Intracellular Ca^{2+} storage

The storage of Ca^{2+} in intracellular compartments is an important physiological mechanism. The sarcoplasmic reticulum (SR) forms a large intracellular network capable of Ca^{2+} storage and release and has a major role to play in Ca^{2+} signalling. Interestingly, much of the SR surface is closely associated with the plasma membrane so that Ca^{2+} release by the SR can influence the concentration of Ca^{2+} near the inner surface of the plasma membrane in a highly localised manner. The uptake of Ca^{2+} by the SR occurs through specialised Ca^{2+}-ATPases known as SERCA pumps. There are at least three genes encoding different SERCA isoforms[36] and myometrium expresses SERCA 2a and 2b. In women, myometrial SERCA expression increases with labour.[37] SERCA pumps are regulated by a $6\,kDa$ homopentameric protein called phospholamban that inhibits Ca^{2+}-ATPase activity.[38] The inhibitory effect of phospholamban can be blocked through phosphorylation by cyclic nucleotide-dependent protein kinases such as PKA and PKG. Thus, agonists that increase cAMP or cyclic guanosine monophosphate (cGMP) enhance Ca^{2+} uptake by the SR and contribute to smooth muscle relaxation.

Fortunately, there are relatively specific SERCA pump inhibitors (e.g. thapsigargin and cyclopiazonic acid) and investigators have been able to document the functional importance of these pumps. SERCA pumps are involved in smooth muscle relaxation by lowering $[Ca^{2+}]_i$. The pumps can generate and maintain a 10 000-fold gradient of Ca^{2+} concentration between the SR lumen and the cytoplasm.[39] This is made possible in part by the presence in the SR of calreticulin and calsequestrin, two proteins that can bind large amounts of Ca^{2+}.

Intracellular Ca^{2+} release

There are two types of channel that release Ca^{2+} from the SR: the ryanodine receptor (RyR) and the inositol trisphosphate ($InsP_3$) receptor. RyRs take their name from the plant alkaloid ryanodine to which they bind. This type of channel is activated by caffeine. Cyclic ADP-ribose (cADPR) and nicotinic acid adenine dinucleotide phosphate (NAADP) are naturally occurring nucleotides implicated in Ca^{2+} signals in many cell types. Increasing evidence suggest that cADPR and NAADP interact to enhance the Ca^{2+} sensitivity of RyRs to produce prolonged signals through 'Ca^{2+}-induced Ca^{2+} release' and to amplify highly localised Ca^{2+} signals in discrete cellular compartments.[40] Human myometrium expresses several isoforms of RyR[41] and cADPR provokes intracellular Ca^{2+} release.[42] However, neither ryanodine nor caffeine has a significant effect on the contractility of human myometrial strips.[43]

$InsP_3$ receptors ($InsP_3$Rs) are activated by many agonists that stimulate inositol phospholipid breakdown and generate $InsP_3$, notably those agonists (e.g. oxytocin, endothelin, carbachol) whose receptors operate through G proteins of the $G_{q/11}$ family (coupled to phospholipase Cβ) and by growth factor receptor tyrosine kinases (phospholipase γ). The human myometrial $InsP_3$R was first identified by binding assays.[44] Three genes encode $InsP_3$Rs and each receptor channel is made up of a tetramer of identical or different polypeptide subunits.[45] All three isoforms of $InsP_3$Rs have been described in human myometrium.[46] $InsP_3$Rs show astonishing chemical discrimination and are activated by $Ins(1,4,5)P_3$ only and not by other $InsP_3$ isomers or other inositol polyphosphates.[44] The binding of $InsP_3$ to its receptor is inhibited by heparin and tightly regulated by Ca^{2+} and Mg^{2+}. The release of Ca^{2+} from the SR triggered by agonist-mediated $InsP_3$ production is sufficient to provoke contraction, even in the absence of extracellular Ca^{2+} entry through VDCCs. However, the store is rapidly depleted unless the influx of extracellular Ca^{2+} is restored. Interestingly the activation of $InsP_3$Rs is regulated by Ca^{2+} in a biphasic manner. Initially, a rise in $[Ca^{2+}]_i$ increases the potency of $InsP_3$ in activating channel openings, but when $[Ca^{2+}]_i$ reaches more than 300 nM it has a negative feedback effect on $InsP_3$ binding and channel opening.[46] This happens because the $InsP_3$R has both stimulatory and inhibitory Ca^{2+} binding sites. High luminal $[Ca^{2+}]$ has a direct stimulatory action on $InsP_3$ channel opening.[47] The inhibition of $InsP_3$R by high cytosolic $[Ca^{2+}]_i$ appears to require calmodulin.[48] Conversely, lowering free $[Ca^{2+}]$ inside the endoplasmic reticulum store attenuates the extent of $InsP_3$-induced release, probably through activation of compensatory SERCA activity. $InsP_3$Rs are substrates for and can be regulated by PKA, PKC, CaM kinases and tyrosine kinases. The $InsP_3$R is regulated through the binding of proteins such as FK506 or chromogranin, whose role in smooth muscle is not known, and is also subject to allosteric regulation by ATP. Thus, the kinetic properties of Ca^{2+} release through the $InsP_3R$ channel are very complex. Many lines of evidence point to a central role for $InsP_3$ in the initiation of Ca^{2+} signals and in the conversion of numerous signals from the cell membrane into Ca^{2+} waves and Ca^{2+} oscillations. As Ca^{2+} imaging technology improves, the physiological significance of the $InsP_3R$ channel in the control of myometrial contractility will be studied better.

Regulation of contractility by myometrial receptors

Myometrial smooth muscle activity is driven by action potentials associated with the development of tension (electromechanical coupling). This is a property of myogenic smooth muscles. However, this intrinsic activity is modulated by both stimulatory and inhibitory receptors. Large-conductance Ca^{2+}-activated K^+ channels play a critical role in regulating myometrial contractility by controlling membrane polarisation.[49,50] Electrophysiological mechanisms are essential to control myometrial activity in pregnancy and labour and have been reviewed elsewhere.[28,51] Uterine contractions are sustained by glycogen catabolism and high energy molecules (ATP, phosphocreatine) and it is important to realise that during labour, with contractions lasting several minutes, the regular episodes of ischaemia and acidosis pose tough regulatory demands on the uterus.[52] Nevertheless, our knowledge of energy metabolism in uterine smooth muscle cells is still very limited.

G protein-coupled receptors

Myometrial activity is modulated by agonists operating through GPCRs (pharmacomechanical coupling). From a practical point of view, the study of GPCR function is important because many of the drugs used clinically to control uterine activity target GPCRs. The uterus has a bewildering variety of receptors and responds to peptide hormones, classical neurotransmitters, lipids, gonadotrophins, vasoactive peptides, inflammatory mediators, catecholamines, etc. (Table 21.1). These compounds bind to seven transmembrane domain receptors and induce a change in conformation of the receptor, allowing its third intracellular loop to interact with heterotrimeric GTP binding proteins.[53] G proteins in turn regulate the activity of various effectors, such as enzymes and ion channels (Table 21.2).

The G protein cycle

The α-subunit GTP complex and the separated βγ subunits interact independently with a variety of effector molecules initiating complex and interlinked signalling cascades (Figure 21.5). The GTPase activity inherent to the α-subunit terminates the G protein activation. The GDP formed remains bound to the α-subunit, which now re-associates with the βγ complex. This re-association renders the βγ complex inactive. The type of myometrial response that a particular receptor elicits is determined by the class of G protein to which it couples (Table 21.1).[54] Moreover, for myometrial cells to remain responsive to agonists, activated GPCRs must be rapidly desensitised. This usually involves phosphorylation of the activated receptor by a GPCR kinase (GRK) and the binding of specialised proteins called arrestins to the receptor. Arrestins block the binding of G proteins to the receptor and promote the internalisation of receptors by dynamin and clathrin. They also serve as adaptors to link the receptors to other signalling pathways such as the MAP kinases.[55] Internalised receptors can be recycled to the cell membrane, where they can be activated again, or broken down in lysosomes.

Table 21.1. Examples of G protein-coupled receptors that can modulate myometrial activity

Endogenous ligands	Receptors	G protein class	Predicted effect on myometrial contractility
Amines			
Acetylcholine	M_1, M_3	G_{q11}/G_{io}	Stimulation
Catecholamines	α_1	G_{q11}	Stimulation
	α_2	G_{io}	Stimulation
	β_2	G_s	Inhibition
	β_3	G_s	Inhibition
Histamine	H_1	G_{q11}	Stimulation
	H_2	G_s	Inhibition
Serotonin	5-HT$_1$	G_{io}	Stimulation
	5-HT$_2$	G_{q11}	Stimulation
	5-HT$_4$, 5-HT$_7$	G_s	Inhibition
Lipids			
Lysophosphatidic acid	LPA (several subtypes)	G_{io}/G_{q11}	Stimulation
Sphingosine-1-phosphate	S1P (several subtypes)	G_{io}/G_{q11}	Stimulation
Platelet activating factor	PAF	G_{q11}	Stimulation
Prostaglandin D$_2$	DP	G_s	Inhibition
Prostaglandin E$_2$	EP$_1$	G_{q11}	Stimulation
	EP$_2$, EP$_4$	G_s	Inhibition
	EP$_3$	$G_{io}/G_{q11}/G_s$	Stimulation/inhibition
Prostaglandin F$_2\alpha$	FP	G_{q11}	Stimulation
Prostacyclin	IP	G_s	Inhibition
Thromboxane A$_2$	TP	$G_{q11}/G_{12/13}$	Stimulation
Peptides			
Adrenomedullin	AM_1, AM_2	G_s	Inhibition
Amylin	AMY_1, AMY_2	G_s	Inhibition
Bombesin	BB1, BB2	G_{q11}	Stimulation
Bradykinin	$B_1 B_2$	$G_{q11}/G_{12/13}$	Stimulation
Calcitonin gene-related peptide	$CGRP_1$	G_s/G_q	Inhibition/stimulation
Chorionic gonadotrophin	LH/hCG	G_s	Inhibition
Corticotrophin-releasing hormone	CRF_1, CRF_2	G_s	Inhibition
Endothelin	ET_A	G_{q11}/G_i	Stimulation
Melatonin	MT_1, MT_2	G_{q11}/G_i	Stimulation
Oxytocin/vasopressin	OT/V$_{1a}$	G_{q11}/G_i	Stimulation
Somatostatin	Sst_1	G_{io}	Stimulation
Others			
Adenosine	A_1	G_{io}	Stimulation
Purine/pyrimidine	P2Y	G_{q11}	Stimulation
Opioid	δ, κ, μ	G_{io}	Stimulation

There are several GRK isoforms and two of them (GRKs 2 and 6) are upregulated in human myometrium during pregnancy.[56]

Two bacterial toxins that specifically interfere with the G protein cycle have been useful tools in studying GPCR signalling. Pertussis toxin (from *Bordetella pertussis*) catalyses the ADP-ribosylation of $G_{i/o}$ proteins at a C-terminal cysteine residue, resulting in the uncoupling of the receptor and the G protein. Cholera toxin (from *Vibrio cholerae*) ADP-ribosylates an internal arginine residue in G_s protein subtypes leading to constitutive activation of the α-subunit by blockade of its GTPase activity. G proteins are also modified under physiological conditions by the incorporation of

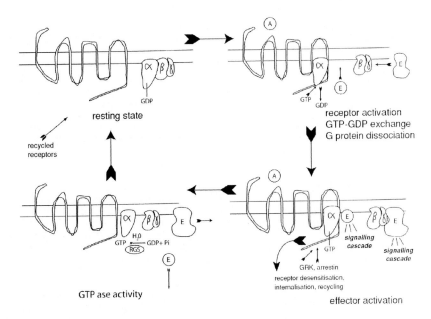

Figure 21.5. The G protein cycle. The binding of an agonist (A) to a seven transmembrane domain receptor induces a conformational change, allowing the receptor to interact with a specific heterotrimeric (αβγ subunits) G protein (see Table 21.1). This promotes GTP/GDP exchange in the α-subunit and dissociation of the βγ complex. Acting as separate functional units, α-GTP and βγ stimulate or inhibit effector molecules and initiate signalling cascades (Table 21.2). Some effectors (e.g. adenylyl cyclases) are present in neighbouring parts of the cell membrane, while other effectors (e.g. phospholipases) translocate from the cytoplasm. In the continuous presence of agonist, activated receptors may be targets for G protein receptor kinases (GRK) that phosphorylate the receptor promoting the binding of arrestin. This is a mechanism for rapid desensitisation (G protein uncoupling) of the receptor but it can also lead to receptor internalisation and stimulation of other signalling cascades (e.g. MAP kinases). Internalised receptors may be degraded or recycled back to the cell membrane. A GTPase activity inherent to the α-subunit terminates the G protein activation. The formed GDP remains bound to the α-subunit, which now re-associates with the βγ complex. Effector molecules dissociate and both receptor and αβγ return to their basal inactive state. The GTPase activity of the α-subunit is usually accelerated by the presence of the effector molecule. In addition, a family of proteins termed regulators of G protein signalling (RGS) are able to increase the GTPase rate of α-subunits, especially $G\alpha_i$ and $G\alpha_q$.

lipids. G protein α-subunits are myristoylated or palmitoylated or both near the N-terminus, whereas γ-subunits are prenylated on the C-terminus. These modifications facilitate protein–protein interactions or attachment to the cell membrane.

An important physiological regulatory mechanism occurs by several effector proteins that interact with the GTP-bound form of the α-subunits and accelerate their GTPase activity.[57] For example, the GTPase activity of $G\alpha_s$ is increased several-fold by contact with adenylyl cyclase, and phospholipase $C\beta_1$ ($PLC\beta_1$) shortens the half-life of α_q-GTP from one minute to less than one second. Other modes of regulation involve at least two different families of proteins called RGS (regulators of G protein signalling) that also increase the GTPase rate of the α-subunit,[58] and AGS (activators of G protein-mediated signalling) that modulate G protein activity in a receptor-independent manner.[59]

Table 21.2. Effectors regulated by heterotrimeric G proteins

G Protein subunit[a]	Effector	Physiological effect
$G\alpha_s$	Adenylyl cyclase (all nine isoforms)	Increased cAMP production → activation of PKA → phosphorylation of many cellular targets, including ion channels and Ca^{2+} transporters
$G\alpha_{i/o}$	Adenylyl cyclase (isoforms I, III, V, VI, VIII, IX)	Inhibition of cAMP production
$G\alpha_{q/11}$	Phospholipase C (isoform 1)	Increased hydrolysis of PIP_2 → formation of $InsP_3$ (→ mobilisation of Ca^{2+} from the sarcoplasmic reticulum) and DAG (→ activation of PKC → phosphorylation of many cellular targets, including MAP kinases, ion channels and Ca^{2+} transporters)
$G\alpha_{12/13}$	RhoGEF	Activation of RhoA → Ca^{2+} sensitisation (inhibition of MLCP by rho-kinase); cytoskeletal changes
$G\beta\gamma$	Adenylyl cyclase (isoforms II, IV, VII)	Increased cAMP production → activation of PKA → phosphorylation of many cellular targets
$G\beta\gamma$	ARF6	Modulation of PLD activity → release of choline and phosphatidic acid → generation of DAG → activation of PKC
$G\beta\gamma$	GRK	Desensitisation of G protein signalling
$G\beta\gamma$	PLCβ (isoforms 2, 3)	Increased hydrolysis of PIP_2 → formation of $InsP_3$ (→ mobilisation of Ca^{2+} from the sarcoplasmic reticulum) and DAG (→ activation of PKC → phosphorylation of many cellular targets, including MAP kinases, ion channels and Ca^{2+} transporters)
$G\beta\gamma$	PI-3-kinase	Phosphorylation of PIP_2 → increased formation of $PI(3,4,5)P_3$ → activation of several proteins, including PKC and MAP kinases → downstream effectors include Rac, Cdc42, Src and PLA_2
$G\beta\gamma$	GIRK	Stimulation of K^+ currents
$G\beta\gamma$	VDCC	Inhibition of Ca^{2+} currents

[a] $G\alpha_s$ subtypes are stimulated by cholera toxin; $G\alpha_{i/o}$ subtypes are inhibited by pertussis toxin; $G\beta\gamma$ subunits are released as a result of $G\alpha$ activation. The most abundant cellular source of $G\beta\gamma$ is $G_{i/o}$; ARF6 = ADP-ribosylation factor 6, a small GTPase; DAG = 1,2-diacylglycerol; GIRK = G protein regulated inward rectifier potassium channel; GRK = G protein-coupled receptor kinases, a universal regulatory mechanism that leads to desensitisation of G protein signalling and to the activation of alternative signalling pathways, e.g. MAP kinases; $InsP_3$ = inositol 1,4,5-trisphosphate; MAP kinases = mitogen-activated protein kinase cascade, constituted by a number of kinases such as Raf-1, extracellular signal-regulated kinases (ERKs) and MEK (MAP kinase/ERK kinase); MLCP = myosin light chain phosphatase (can be inhibited by rho-kinase which phosphorylates the myosin phosphatase-targeting subunit, MYPT1); $PI(3,4,5)P_3$= phosphatidylinositol 3,4,5-trisphosphate; PI-3-kinase = phosphatidylinositol-3-kinase, PIP_2 = phosphatidylinositol 4,5-bisphosphate; PLA_2 = cytosolic phospholipase A_2. This enzyme is also activated by many receptors that increase $[Ca^{2+}]$; PLCβ = phospholipase β isoforms contain a G protein binding domain; PLD = phospholipase D, requires PIP_2 for activity. PLD is activated by endothelin in myometrium; RhoGEF = rho guanine nucleotide exchange factor; Rac and Cdc42 are members of the Ras homologous GTPase family, which regulates p21-activated kinases (PAKs); Src = a family of tyrosine kinases involved in growth; VDCC = voltage-dependent Ca^{2+} channel

Receptors coupled to $G\alpha_s$

In general, $G\alpha_s$-coupled receptors are inhibitory. These include receptors for prostanoids (EP2, IP), chorionic gonadotrophin, corticotrophin-releasing hormone and catecholamines (Table 21.1). $G\alpha_s$ stimulates all isoforms of adenylyl cyclase to increase the rate of cAMP formation. In the uterus this results in relaxation, probably because the cAMP-dependent protein kinase A phosphorylates various targets, such as PMCAs, phospholamban and $InsP_3$ receptors, thus favouring a decrease in $[Ca^{2+}]_i$.

Activation of $G\alpha_s$ with β_2 adrenoceptor agonists (e.g. ritodrine) was until recently commonly used to inhibit uterine contractions in women in preterm labour. However, this approach causes potentially serious adverse effects due to the abundant expression of β_2 adrenoceptor in the cardiovascular system. Further work is necessary to investigate the interaction of the receptor/$G\alpha_s$ complex with individual myometrial adenylyl cyclase isoforms[60] before better uterine selectivity can be achieved with drugs that increase cAMP production. A complementary approach would be to inhibit cAMP catabolism with inhibitors selective for uterine phosphodiesterases.[61]

Receptors coupled to $G\alpha_{q/11}$

Myometrial receptors coupled to $G\alpha_{q/11}$ are stimulatory, and include the receptors for oxytocin, endothelin and prostaglandin $F_2\alpha$ (OT, ET and FP receptors, respectively), amongst others (Table 21.1). Receptor-$G\alpha_{q/11}$ complexes are usually positively coupled to PLCβ isoforms in myometrial cells.[62] Stimulation of PLCβ results in rapid InsP$_3$ release, Ca^{2+} entry, activation of PKC and a cascade of events that promotes contractility by increasing both the tone and frequency of contractions. Receptors coupled to $G\alpha_q$ may also contribute to the hypertrophy and hyperplasia of myometrial cells through activation of PKC, Src tyrosine kinases and extracellular signal-regulated kinases (ERKs).[63,64] Release of G$\beta\gamma$ subunits following activation of OT[64] or FP receptors[65] plays an important role in MAP kinase/ERK activation in myometrial cells. Pharmacological activation of the OT receptor has been used for many years for the induction and augmentation of labour, and more recently OT receptor antagonists (atosiban) have been introduced for the management of preterm labour with the advantage of similar efficacy but much better uterine selectivity than β_2 adrenoceptor agonists.[66] Progesterone compounds have been used as tocolytic agents and their beneficial effect may be related to inhibition of OT and ET receptor binding and signalling in myometrium[67] and/or inhibition of phosphodiesterase activity.[68]

Receptors coupled to $G\alpha_{i/o}$

$G\alpha_{i/o}$ subtypes are usually the most abundant heterotrimeric G proteins in cells and thus activation of $G\alpha_i$ has two consequences: the activation of the α_i-GTP complex itself, and the release of relatively large amount of G$\beta\gamma$ subunits. Coupling to $G\alpha_{i/o}$ may be partly responsible for the complex effects of catecholamine and prostaglandin receptors on myometrial contractility through their effects on K^+ channels and Na^+-K^+-ATPase pumps.[69] Inhibition of adenylyl cyclases by α_i-GTP favours contractility. G$\beta\gamma$ subunits interact with many effectors (Table 21.2), including PLCβ_3, which initiates the InsP$_3$ –Ca^{2+} pathway, and the phosphatidylinositol-3-kinase pathway with multiple signalling effects important for growth and functional differentiation of smooth muscle cells. The latter pathway has been demonstrated in myometrial cells challenged with endothelin or oxytocin.[63,64]

Receptor tyrosine kinases

Receptor tyrosine kinases (RTKs) are involved in the regulation of myometrial signalling and there is growing evidence of 'cross-talk' between GPCR and RTK pathways in myometrium. Growth factors, such as insulin, platelet-derived growth factor (PDGF) and epidermal growth factor (EGF), and cytokines bind to receptors whose extracellular domains form dimers upon binding of the agonist molecules. Dimerisation results in autophosphorylation of a number of tyrosine residues in the intracellular domains of the receptor. Tyrosine phosphorylated sites in growth factor receptors act as anchor sites for a number of proteins containing SH2 (Src homology) domains. These include effector enzymes and adaptor molecules (Table 21.3). RTKs are essential for the regulation of growth and differentiation of myometrial cells during pregnancy, and tend to use MAP kinase/ERK 1/2 cascades as final common pathways to regulate nuclear transcriptional activity. Human myometrial cells have a strong tyrosine kinase response to EGF, resulting in PLCγ activation.[62] In cultured human-derived myometrial cells, oxytocin promotes tyrosine kinase activation of the EGF receptor and ERK 1/2 phosphorylation, probably through the release of Gβγ from G_q.[64] In rat myometrial cells, activation of PDGF results in ERK stimulation and phospholipase A_2 activation, with increased release of arachidonic acid for prostaglandin synthesis.[70] This response is mimicked by oxytocin in cultured human myometrial cells.[71] The interplay between GPCRs and RTKs is clearly important for uterine adaptation to pregnancy and it is likely to have a role in the events leading to the onset of labour.

Table 21.3. Effectors and signalling pathways associated with receptor tyrosine kinases in myometrium[a]

Effector	Physiological effect
PLCγ	Increased hydrolysis of PIP_2 → formation of $InsP_3$ (→ mobilisation of Ca^{2+} from the sarcoplasmic reticulum) and DAG (→ activation of PKC → phosphorylation of many cellular targets); as a consequence of Ca^{2+} mobilisation, cytosolic PLA_2 is activated, resulting in arachidonate release and prostanoids synthesis
PI-3-kinase	Phosphorylation of PIP_2 → increased formation of $PI(3,4,5)P_3$ → activation of several proteins, including PKC and MAP kinases → downstream effectors including Src and PLA_2.
Src	Tyrosine phosphorylation of several substrates involved in the regulation of growth
Ras	Regulation of cell growth through serine/threonine protein kinases
SHP-2	SHP-2 tyrosine phosphatase plays a positive role in transducing the signal relay elicited from receptor tyrosine kinases, functioning in, amongst others, the ERK and PI-3-kinase pathways
Adaptor proteins	These include Grb2, Shc and Sos → activation of Ras → activation of MAP kinases → phosphorylation of ERK 1/2 → nuclear translocation → regulation of transcriptional activity

[a] There are many types of tyrosine kinase receptors specific for endogenous ligands such as insulin, growth factors, cytokines and interferons. These receptors usually form dimers and autophosphorylate on tyrosine residues, resulting in anchoring and activation of the effector molecules. Tyrosine kinase receptors are involved in the growth and differentiation of myometrial cells through the regulation of nuclear transcriptional activity; DAG = 1,2-diacylglycerol; Grb2 = an adaptor protein containing SH(Src homology)2 and SH3 domains; $InsP_3$ = inositol 1,4,5-trisphosphate; $PI(3,4,5)P_3$ = phosphatidylinositol 3,4,5-trisphosphate; PI-3-kinase = phosphatidylinositol-3-kinase; PIP_2 = phosphatidylinositol 4,5-bisphosphate; PLA_2 = phospholipase A_2; PLCγ = an isoform of phospholipase C containing SH2 and SH3 domains, but no G protein binding domain; Ras = a family of small GTPases; SHP-2 = an SH2 (Src homology) domain-containing protein tyrosine phosphatase; Shc = an adaptor protein (Src homology/collagen) whose tyrosine phosphorylation targets the complex Grb2-Sos to the membrane to activate Ras; Sos = a guanine nucleotide exchange factor (son of sevenless). Allows Ras to exchange GTP for GDP; Src = a family of tyrosine kinases

Conclusions

The intriguing puzzle of uterine function is steadily being assembled. Many pieces are known in great detail and they fit together well in some areas of myometrial physiology. Progress in biochemical and electrophysiological techniques (protein labelling, the use of chimeric and mutated proteins, confocal imaging, better Ca^{2+} dyes, single-channel recording, etc.) is steadily pushing functional studies on smooth muscle to the level of nanomachinery. The increasing use of genomic and proteomic methods will lead to the discovery of new genes and proteins involved in myometrial function. This will allow the integration of changes in related proteins and interacting signalling pathways in different physiological states. Although much work remains to be done, there is increasing quality and depth of research in this area. The overall picture of maternal and fetal influences on uterine physiology and the regulatory mechanisms that have a direct effect on the myometrium during pregnancy and parturition will become visible soon.

Acknowledgements

I am grateful to Jamie López Bernal for figure design and to Mrs Pam Hendry for secretarial help.

References

1. Granstrom L, Ekman G, Ulmsten U, Malmstrom A. Changes in the connective tissue of corpus and cervix uteri during ripening and labour in term pregnancy. *Br J Obstet Gynaecol* 1989;96:1198–202.
2. Curry TE Jr, Osteen KG. Cyclic changes in the matrix metalloproteinase system in the ovary and uterus. *Biol Reprod* 2001;64:1285–96.
3. Winkler M, Oberpichler A, Tschesche H, Ruck P, Fischer DC, Rath W. Collagenolysis in the lower uterine segment during parturition at term: correlations with stage of cervical dilatation and duration of labor. *Am J Obstet Gynecol* 1999;181:153–8.
4. Stygar D, Wang H, Vladic YS, Ekman G, Erikson H, Shalin L. Increased level of matrix metalloproteinases 2 and 9 in the ripening process of the human cervix. *Biol Reprod* 2002;67:889–94.
5. Roh CR, Oh WJ, Yoon BK, Lee JH. Up-regulation of matrix metalloproteinase-9 in human myometrium during labour: a cytokine-mediated process in uterine smooth muscle cells. *Mol Hum Reprod* 2000;6:96–102.
6. Yu JT, A. Lopez Bernal A. The cytoskeleton of human myometrial cells. *J Reprod Fertil* 1998;112:185–98.
7. Word RA, Stull JT, Casey ML, Kamm KE. Contractile elements and myosin light chain phosphorylation in myometrial tissue from nonpregnant and pregnant women. *J Clin Invest* 1993;92:29–37.
8. Cavaille F, Fournier T, Dallot E, Dhellemes C, Ferre F. Myosin heavy chain isoform expression in human myometrium: presence of an embryonic nonmuscle isoform in leiomyomas and in cultured cells. *Cell Motil Cytoskeleton* 1995;30:183–93.
9. Morano I, Koehlen S, Haase E, Erb G, Bultas LG, Rimbach S, *et al*. Alternative splicing and cycling kinetics of myosin change during hypertrophy of human smooth muscle cells. *J Cell Biochem* 1997;64:171–81.
10. Rayment I. The structural basis of the myosin ATPase activity. *J Biol Chem* 1996;271:15850–3.
11. Helper DJ, Lash JA, Hathaway DR. Distribution of isoelectric variants of the 17,000-dalton myosin light chain in mammalian smooth muscle. *J Biol Chem* 1988;263:15748–53.
12. Inoue A, Yanagisawa M, Takano-Ohmuro H, Masaki T. Two isoforms of smooth muscle myosin regulatory light chain in chicken gizzard. *Eur J Biochem* 1989;183:645–51.
13. Murphy RA, Walker JS, Strauss JD. Myosin isoforms and functional diversity in vertebrate smooth muscle. *Comp Biochem Physiol B Biochem Mol Biol* 1997;117:51–60.
14. Morano I. Tuning smooth muscle contraction by molecular motors. *J Mol Med* 2003;81:481–7.
15. Krueger JK, Gallagher SC, Zhi G, Greguchadze R, Persechini A, Stull JT, *et al*. Activation of myosin light chain kinase requires translocation of bound calmodulin. *J Biol Chem* 2001;276:4535–8.

16.   Tansey MG, Luby-Phelps K, Kamm KE, Stull JT. Ca(2+)-dependent phosphorylation of myosin light chain kinase decreases the Ca2+ sensitivity of light chain phosphorylation within smooth muscle cells. *J Biol Chem* 1994;269:9912–20.

17.   Somlyo AP, Somlyo AV. Signal transduction by G-proteins, rho-kinase and protein phosphatase to smooth muscle and non-muscle myosin II. *J Physiol* 2000;522:177–85.

18.   Somlyo AP, Somlyo AV. From pharmacomechanical coupling to G-proteins and myosin phosphatase. *Acta Physiol Scand* 1998;164:437–48.

19.   McKillen KS, Thornton S, Taylor CW. Oxytocin increases the [Ca2+]i sensitivity of human myometrium during the falling phase of phasic contractions. *Am J Physiol* 1999;276(2 Pt 1):E345–51.

20.   Murthy KS, Zhou H, Grider JR, Brautigan DL, Eto M, Makhlough GM. Differential signalling by muscarinic receptors in smooth muscle: m2-mediated inactivation of myosin light chain kinase via Gi3, Cdc42/Rac1 and p21-activated kinase 1 pathway, and m3-mediated MLC20 (20 kDa regulatory light chain of myosin II) phosphorylation via Rho-associated kinase/myosin phosphatase targeting subunit 1 and protein kinase C/CPI-17 pathway. *Biochem J* 2003;374:145–55.

21.   Gogarten W, Emola CW, Lindeman KS, Hirshman CA. Oxytocin and lysophosphatidic acid induce stress fiber formation in human myometrial cells via a pathway involving Rho-kinase. *Biol Reprod* 2001;65:401–6.

22.   Oh JH, You SK, Hwang MK, Ahn DS, Kwon SC, Taggart MJ, et al. Inhibition of rho-associated kinase reduces MLC20 phosphorylation and contractility of intact myometrium and attenuates agonist-induced Ca2+ sensitization of force of permeabilized rat myometrium. *J Vet Med Sci* 2003;65:43–50.

23.   Kupittayanant S, Burdyga T, Wray S. The effects of inhibiting Rho-associated kinase with Y-27632 on force and intracellular calcium in human myometrium. *Pflugers Arch* 2001;443:112–4.

24.   Moore F, Da Silva C, Wilde JI, Simarasan A, Watson SP, López Bernal A. Up-regulation of p21- and RhoA-activated protein kinases in human pregnant myometrium. *Biochem Biophys Res Commun* 2000;269:322–6.

25.   Kitazawa T, Eto M, Woodsome TP, Khalequzzamen M. Phosphorylation of the myosin phosphatase targeting subunit and CPI-17 during Ca2+ sensitization in rabbit smooth muscle. *J Physiol* 2003;546:879–89.

26.   Li Y, Je HD, Malek S, Morgan KG. ERK1/2-mediated phosphorylation of myometrial caldesmon during pregnancy and labor. *Am J Physiol Regul Integr Comp Physiol* 2003;284:R192–9.

27.   Szal SE, Repke JT, Seely EW, Graves SW, Parker CA, Morgan KG. [Ca2+]i signaling in pregnant human myometrium. *Am J Physiol* 1994;267(1 Pt 1):E77–87.

28.   Sanborn BM. Relationship of ion channel activity to control of myometrial calcium. *J Soc Gynecol Investig* 2000;7:4–11.

29.   Yamaguchi S, Khorov BS, Yoshioka K, Nagao T, Chizo H, Adachi-Akahane S, et al. Key roles of Phe1112 and Ser1115 in the pore-forming IIIS5-S6 linker of L-type Ca2+ channel alpha1C subunit (CaV 1.2) in binding of dihydropyridines and action of Ca2+ channel agonists. *Mol Pharmacol* 2003;64:235–48.

30.   Inoue Y, Nakao K, Okabe K, Izumi H, Kanda S, Kitamura K, et al. Some electrical properties of human pregnant myometrium. *Am J Obstet Gynecol* 1990;162:1090–8.

31.   Montell C, Rubin GM. Molecular characterization of the Drosophila trp locus: a putative integral membrane protein required for phototransduction. *Neuron* 1989;2:1313–23.

32.   Dalrymple A, Slater DM, Beech D, Poston L, Tribe RM. Molecular identification and localization of Trp homologues, putative calcium channels, in pregnant human uterus. *Mol Hum Reprod* 2002;8:946–51.

33.   Shlykov SG, Yang M, Alcom JL, Sanborn BM. Capacitative cation entry in human myometrial cells and augmentation by hTrpC3 overexpression. *Biol Reprod* 2003;69:647–55.

34.   Sanders KM. Invited review: mechanisms of calcium handling in smooth muscles. *J Appl Physiol* 2001;91:1438–49.

35.   Wray S, Kupittayanant S, Shmygol A, Smith RD, Burdyga T. The physiological basis of uterine contractility: a short review. *Exp Physiol* 2001;86:239–46.

36.   Wu KD, Lee WS, Way J, Bungard D, Lytton J. Localization and quantification of endoplasmic reticulum Ca(2+)-ATPase isoform transcripts. *Am J Physiol* 1995;269:C775–84.

37.   Tribe RM, Moriarty P, Poston L. Calcium homeostatic pathways change with gestation in human myometrium. *Biol Reprod* 2000;63:748–55.

38.   Arkin IT, Adams PD, Brunger AT, Smith SO, Engleman DM. Structural perspectives of phospholamban, a helical transmembrane pentamer. *Annu Rev Biophys Biomol Struct* 1997;26:157–79.

39.   van Breemen C, Saida K. Cellular mechanisms regulating [Ca2+]i smooth muscle. *Annu Rev Physiol* 1989;51:315–29.

40.   Galione A, Churchill GC. Interactions between calcium release pathways: multiple messengers and multiple stores. *Cell Calcium* 2002;32:343–54.

41. Awad SS, Lamb HK, Morgan JM, Dunlop W, Gillespie JI. Differential expression of ryanodine receptor RyR2 mRNA in the non-pregnant and pregnant human myometrium. *Biochem J* 1997;322:777–83.

42. Chini EN, Chini CC, Barata da Silva H, Zileinska W. The cyclic-ADP-ribose signaling pathway in human myometrium. *Arch Biochem Biophys* 2002;407:152–9.

43. Kupittayanant S, Luckas MJ, Wray S. Effect of inhibiting the sarcoplasmic reticulum on spontaneous and oxytocin-induced contractions of human myometrium. *BJOG* 2002;109:289–96.

44. Rivera J, López Bernal A, Varney M, Watson SP. Inositol 1,4,5-trisphosphate and oxytocin binding in human myometrium. *Endocrinology* 1990;127:155–62.

45. Patel S, Joseph SK, Thomas AP. Molecular properties of inositol 1,4,5-trisphosphate receptors. *Cell Calcium* 1999;25:247–64.

46. Morgan JM, De Smedt H, Gillespie JI. Identification of three isoforms of the InsP3 receptor in human myometrial smooth muscle. *Pflugers Arch* 1996;431:697–705.

47. Caroppo R, Colella M, Colasuonno A, DeLuisi A, Debellis L, Curci S, et al. A reassessment of the effects of luminal [Ca2+] on inositol 1,4,5-trisphosphate-induced Ca2+ release from internal stores. *J Biol Chem* 2003;278:39503–8.

48. Taylor CW, Laude AJ. IP3 receptors and their regulation by calmodulin and cytosolic Ca2+. *Cell Calcium* 2002;32:321–34.

49. Perez G, Toro L. Differential modulation of large-conductance KCa channels by PKA in pregnant and nonpregnant myometrium. *Am J Physiol* 1994;266(5 Pt 1):C1459–63.

50. Chanrachakul B, Matharoo-Ball B, Turner A, Robinson G, Boughton-Pipkin F, Arulkumaran S, et al. Immunolocalization and protein expression of the alpha subunit of the large-conductance calcium-activated potassium channel in human myometrium. *Reproduction* 2003;126:43–8.

51. Khan RN, Matharoo-Ball B, Arulkumaran S, Ashford ML. Potassium channels in the human myometrium. *Exp Physiol* 2001;86:255–64.

52. Wray S, Jones K, Kuppittayanant S, Li Y, Matthew A, Monir-Bishty E, et al. Calcium signaling and uterine contractility. *J Soc Gynecol Investig* 2003;10:252–64.

53. Hepler JR, Gilman AG. G proteins. *Trends Biochem Sci* 1992;17:383–7.

54. López Bernal A, Europe-Finner GN, Phaneuf S, Watson SP. Preterm labour: a pharmacological challenge. *Trends Pharmacol Sci* 1995;16:129–33.

55. Perry SJ, Lefkowitz RJ. Arresting developments in heptahelical receptor signaling and regulation. *Trends Cell Biol* 2002;12:130–8.

56. Brenninkmeijer CB, Price SA, López Bernal A, Phaneuf S. Expression of G-protein-coupled receptor kinases in pregnant term and non-pregnant human myometrium. *J Endocrinol* 1999;162:401–8.

57. Scholich K, Mullenix JB, Wittpath C, Poppleton HM, Pierre SC, Lindorfer MA. Facilitation of signal onset and termination by adenylyl cyclase. *Science* 1999;283:1328–31.

58. Neubig RR. Regulators of G protein signaling (RGS proteins): novel central nervous system drug targets. *J Pept Res* 2002;60:312–6.

59. Offermanns S. G-proteins as transducers in transmembrane signalling. *Prog Biophys Mol Biol* 2003;83:101–30.

60. Price SA, Pochun I, Phaneuf S, López Bernal A. Adenylyl cyclase isoforms in pregnant and non-pregnant human myometrium. *J Endocrinol* 2000;164:21–30.

61. Mehats C, Yanguy G, Paris B, Robert B, Permin N, Ferré F, et al. Pregnancy induces a modulation of the cAMP phosphodiesterase 4-conformers ratio in human myometrium: consequences for the utero-relaxant effect of PDE4-selective inhibitors. *J Pharmacol Exp Ther* 2000;292:817–23.

62. Phaneuf S, Carrasco MP, Europe-Finner GN, Hamilton CH, Lopez Bernal A. Multiple G proteins and phospholipase C isoforms in human myometrial cells: implication for oxytocin action. *J Clin Endocrinol Metab* 1996;81:2098–103.

63. Robin P, Boulven I, Desmyter C, Harbon S, Leiber D. ET-1 stimulates ERK signaling pathway through sequential activation of PKC and Src in rat myometrial cells. *Am J Physiol Cell Physiol* 2002;283:C251–60.

64. Zhong M, Yang M, Sanborn BM. Extracellular signal-regulated kinase 1/2 activation by myometrial oxytocin receptor involves Galpha(q)Gbetagamma and epidermal growth factor receptor tyrosine kinase activation. *Endocrinology* 2003;144:2947–56.

65. Ohmichi M, Koike K, Kimura A, Masuhara K, Ikegami H, Ikebuchi Y, et al. Role of mitogen-activated protein kinase pathway in prostaglandin F2alpha-induced rat puerperal uterine contraction. *Endocrinology* 1997;138:3103–11.

66. Moutquin JM, Sherman D, Cohen H, Mohide PT, Hochner-Celnikier D, Fesgin M, et al. Double-blind, randomized, controlled trial of atosiban and ritodrine in the treatment of preterm labor: a multicenter effectiveness and safety study. *Am J Obstet Gynecol* 2000;182:1191–9.

67. Fomin VP, Cox BE, Word RA. Effect of progesterone on intracellular Ca2+ homeostasis in human myometrial smooth muscle cells. *Am J Physiol* 1999;276:C379–85.

68. Kofinas AD, Rose JC, Kontnik DR, Meis PJ. Progesterone and estradiol concentrations in nonpregnant and pregnant human myometrium. Effect of progesterone and estradiol on cyclic adenosine monophosphate-phosphodiesterase activity. *J Reprod Med* 1990;35:1045–50.

69. Parkington HC, Tonta MA, Davies NK, Brennecke SP, Coleman HA. Hyperpolarization and slowing of the rate of contraction in human uterus in pregnancy by prostaglandins E2 and f2alpha: involvement of the Na+ pump. *J Physiol* 1999;514:229–43.

70. Boulven I, Palmier B, Robin P, Vacher M, Harbon S, Leiber D. Platelet-derived growth factor stimulates phospholipase C-gamma 1, extracellular signal-regulated kinase, and arachidonic acid release in rat myometrial cells: contribution to cyclic 3',5'-adenosine monophosphate production and effect on cell proliferation. *Biol Reprod* 2001;65:496–506.

71. Molnar M, Rigo J Jr, Romero R, Hertelendy F. Oxytocin activates mitogen-activated protein kinase and up-regulates cyclooxygenase-2 and prostaglandin production in human myometrial cells. *Am J Obstet Gynecol* 1999;181:42–9.

Chapter 22

Management II

Discussion

Shennan: I would like to ask Professor Regan about the survival curves. It appears to me that if you cut off the treatment at the end of the first trimester or the beginning of the second you would have the same results. Is that true? The reason I ask is because as obstetricians we often diagnose antiphospholipid syndrome through testing after booking. Is it worth then starting heparin and aspirin?

Regan: I think all the evidence shows that you do the maximum good in changing the quality of implantation or placentation by treating it in the first trimester. But, having published those data, we started another randomised trial to compare continuing until 34 weeks of gestation with stopping at 14 or 15 weeks. But we stopped the trial after the first eight women who were randomised to stopping at 15 weeks miscarried at 20 to 24 weeks. I am sure that was very unscientific but it was a very difficult situation to be in because here we were taking people who had previously never gotten past the first trimester, getting them into the second trimester, and the cohort that was going along with them who continued was going on to have a successful pregnancy. Therefore you may need a maintenance dose to continue the good progress but it would appear that the most important effect that you can have is right at the beginning of pregnancy. So I do not treat women with heparin from 13 to 14 weeks unless they have already started it earlier.

Calder: Professor López Bernal, was the film you showed of the transport of calcium between the myometrial cells in real time? For how long does the individual myometrial cell remain contracted?

López Bernal: The film is a bit accelerated. These cells were not actually contracting because they were attached. There would be shortening but it is not the best system for looking at contractility. The timing of these calcium fluxes is similar to what you would find in a contracting situation so there is a very rapid increase within 20 to 60 seconds or so.

Calder: Is it the same length that you would expect a contraction in labour to last? And is it still believed, as what I was taught, that the wave of contractility begins at pacemaker zones at the cornua of the uterus and spreads right down in a sort of peristaltic wave, or is that a naive thought?

López Bernal: I do not think there is much evidence for pacemaker zones. I have asked that question myself at meetings and nobody has an answer. I remember going to a meeting in Denmark and seeing a film of nonpregnant uterine contractility. It is quite fascinating because there are waves of contractility that have nothing to do with this idea that they come from the fundus. There are two myometrial layers, an inner part of the myometrium and another one sitting on top that, which have waves of contraction similar to the Mexican waves that we see in football matches. So I do not think there is evidence for pacemaker activity.

Nathanielsz: We have put electrodes in several positions in both the sheep and the primate. There is really no wave and, in the primate uterus in particular, provided that the cervix dilates (and we have emphasised the function of the cervix here at this meeting), there is only one way out anyway. So you do not really need a wave and I do not think there is a wave.

I personally have an aversion to this concept of a quiescent uterus. I think that why the contractions get stronger is because one or two cells start off and, if the gap junctions are there and the continuity is there, they connect together. What Bob Garfield and other people have done in highlighting the importance of producing this continuity of channels is important. The uterus is not even quiet in the nonpregnant state. We get these things which we call contractures. The uterine muscle is constantly keeping itself in trim. It goes out training every morning to keep itself fit. It just does not suddenly start to work at labour and delivery. We have recorded contractures as early as one-third of the way through gestation and I think this recruitment of more and more cells produces the coordination for something that is there all the time.

I think that contractures could be very important in terms of stretch. As I understand it, most studies looking at stretch have used static rather than intermittent stretch. If you have ever seen these contractions in a sheep uterus they are really quite phenomenal. They last three, four, five minutes, they are fairly strong and then they disappear for 20 minutes. The various tissues inside the uterus are going to be stretched backwards and forwards. None of the biochemical processes that you have been talking about are continuous, they are all switching off and on otherwise the system downregulates. So the phasic nature of uterine activity I think is extremely important.

López Bernal: There are obviously episodes of contractility during pregnancy. But we are talking, at the end, about this irreversible contractility when the membrane potential of the cells is so high that they are going to start contracting following this spontaneous change of action potential. I agree with the point that was made yesterday that the uterus is probably ready long before the beginning of labour. It is like an orchestra ready on a stage. You have all the individual players there and then they start tuning their instruments and they produce a peculiar noise but it is only when the leader and finally the conductor starts the pattern that the whole thing makes sense. So I think we need to find out who is the conductor.

Critchley: I came across quite an interesting gene array paper in August this year in *Molecular Endocrinology*.[1] Although the numbers are small, they have looked at myometrium from mice and for women. They had three women in preterm labour, three women in preterm nonlabour and three women in term labour. I think that their data support the comments that Dr Nathanielsz made about contractility. They showed downregulation of many genes, many of which are exactly the same in the preterm labour group as in the term labour group. As you go down the list you find many genes which we know are involved in labour, such as prostaglandin receptors, prostaglandin dehydrogenase, etc. It is encouraging when you see that, although they are trying to identify new candidate genes, they are finding changes in the genes that would be expected from what we already know.

López Bernal: And of course the tremendous potential of that methodology is that you can simultaneously study many genes and many proteins. However, at the moment with genomic and proteomic facilities with the capacity for high throughput, we have to be careful not to make the conclusion too complete. Many of those data will have to be confirmed by doing verifying studies with good antibodies and good functional studies. But I think we will move much faster now as a community of researchers.

Calder: On the issue of the contractile wave, you showed very nicely that at term the normal wave involves a significant period of relaxation. If you give prostaglandins to the early pregnant uterus you get coordinated contractility but with almost no relaxation. It is almost like a sound wave straight up and down. I wonder what is the explanation for that because presumably there are no gap junctions at that stage of pregnancy and yet these cells are working in a coordinated way with each other to produce that wave pattern.

López Bernal: There may be other synchronisation mechanisms through the connective tissue that do not necessarily involve gap junctions, but the other thing that was new to me, and I only read that in preparing the chapter for this meeting, is the fact that there are many forms of myosin. There are myosins that are involved in basic contractions and myosins that are involved in tonic contractions. About 30% of myosin content of the human myometrium is the nonsmooth-muscle type of myosin that is probably involved in the tonic effects. So not only do we have to worry about different receptors but also about what type of myosin is eventually a target for that particular pathway. And I think some of those effects of pharmacological agents are probably due to the fact that they are reaching paths that they normally would not reach and they are affecting myosins and other components of the cell that physiologically they would not activate.

Steer: Coming back to Professor Calder's point about the issue of pacemakers, he is probably too young to know the literature, but if you go back to the 1952 British Congress there was a whole session on myometrial activity. There were some fascinating data derived from intramyometrial balloons placed at different points in the uterus which showed very clearly that there is a phase shift in the contraction and that the contractions start near the top of the uterus. Norman Jeffcoate[2] also did quite a lot of his own work using intrauterine catheters and showed in general that you see rises in pressure near the fundus rather than lower down. Norman Smyth[3] and Reynolds[4] from Johns Hopkins, using multiple external transducers, have also very clearly shown a contraction wave which passes down the uterus. Hence this concept of fundal dominance necessary for a progressive dilatation. If you get contractions going in the reverse direction they seem to be less effective, probably because they are not mechanically so efficient.

Then finally there was a series of papers from Japan, the USA and Slovenia using electrodes on the maternal abdomen[5-7] and computer systems to construct a three-dimensional model of depolarisation within the uterus[8] which suggest that the majority of contractions in progressive labour start at the fundus and work their way down. Now if you actually do the mathematics you do not specifically have to have a pacemaker site because there is just a lot more uterine muscle at the top than at the bottom. If you just say we will pick one at random it is much more likely to be at the top of the uterus than at the bottom.

Nathanielsz: It is certainly true that there is more muscle at the fundus but whether there is actually a peristaltic wave I am not so sure.

Steer: It depends what you mean by peristalsis. I am not sure about peristalsis as such but I think there is progressive depolarisation and recruitment of muscle fibres. That is why you get the characteristic shape of the intrauterine pressure curve. It normally starts at the top of the uterus because that is where most of the muscle is. I doubt whether there is a specific pacemaker site but it probably has that effect functionally.

Bennett: You do not need a peristaltic wave in the way that you do in the gut to move things along, you just need shortening.

Steer: You need shortening but there is some evidence that if you get shortening in the lower segment it tends to push the head upwards rather than downwards. Indeed, if you look at Karl Olah and Harry Gee's work[9-11] using the intrauterine pressures in the cervix and our own work[12-16] using head–cervix force sensors you will see that if you get an abnormal pattern of contractions you can actually see a reduction in head-to-cervix force as the contraction comes on, suggesting that the head is actually being pushed up because of inappropriate contractions in the lower segment.

Nathanielsz: That is where Gordon Smith's work is so interesting because in the lower segment the predominant prostaglandin receptor is the EP_2 receptor and that protects you against contraction down at that end.

Smith: I want to ask Professor Saade what their experience was in relation to these questions about the electrical activity and pressure.

Saade: I agree with Professor Nathanielsz that there is no pacemaker in the uterus. I think contractions just start somewhere and more likely in the fundus because there are more cells there and, through the gap junctions, they just continue down and down.

López Bernal: This is isometric contractility. You do not need a strong shortening to create force. There is a cavity full of fluid so it does not matter if you put pressure on the bottom or on the sides so long as we increase the pressure that will be transmitted by the membranes or the head on the surface.

Steer: That is correct in early labour but of course once the membranes have ruptured you have venting of pressure. You actually start to register lower pressures because some of the contraction force is no longer being represented as a rise in intrauterine pressure. So there is not a direct connection between the strength of the uterine contraction and the measurement of intrauterine pressure because you have modulating factors, not the least of which is descent of the head with each contraction. So it is not actually quite correct to say that it is an isometric contraction because the retraction part of the process becomes really quite important, particularly in women who are progressing rapidly. You see some women who will deliver in an hour or two where the baby actually moves five or six centimetres with each contraction. So quite clearly there has to be some retraction as well as contraction otherwise the labour would simply stop.

López Bernal: From measurements in isolated strips it seems that the 10% contraction or shortening is enough to generate all the tension that you need.

Steer: From one contraction to the next but not over a whole labour.

López Bernal: No, of course not – the effect is additive.

Saade: I have a question on a different subject: the use of steroids. I agree that we should not give repeated courses of steroids but I have a problem completely discarding repeat doses because of the reduction in severe respiratory distress syndrome.

Crowley : I think it would be speculative to anticipate the results of the ongoing trials but there is probably going to be a subgroup of babies where it will be necessary to repeat steroids Those are likely to be the babies who were least mature when they had their first course but that is the group where we may be trading off a benefit in respiratory terms against some long-term drawback, maybe known or maybe unknown. And so the story is very, very simple. The single course is beneficial without any evidence of major long-term hazards. Multiple courses enter a murkier area where we are going to be trading off significant falls in birthweight perhaps or significant long-term drawbacks to the babies for improvement in respiratory outcome. So as well as looking at the question of single versus repeat courses we also have to look at alternative ways of accelerating fetal lung maturation.

Romero: What is the evidence that steroid effects have a window of benefit? One of the clinical problems that we now have is that we are going to give steroids early in premature labour. But that patient can come back five weeks later still with premature labour. So what is the evidence? How long will the beneficial effects last?

Crowley: It looks as if some of the effects are reversible and some are irreversible. Some of the reversibility is going to be gestation-dependent and so to find these answers we may need to go back to the original trials and perform individual patient analysis. There is evidence of some benefit at all the gestational ages and even in the least mature babies there are benefits in terms of the duration of mechanical ventilation or the severity of respiratory distress rather than respiratory distress versus no respiratory distress. But the least mature babies are the group who are more likely to need the second course and more likely to have more adverse effects from repeated courses so it is becoming much more complicated to get further improvements from where we are at the moment. The least mature babies also benefit in terms of intraventricular haemorrhage.

Nathanielsz: As part of this discussion on repeated doses and potential cost/benefit, I think it is really important to consider the dose itself. There has never to my knowledge been a dose–response trial with any single steroid, be it dexamethasone, betamethasone or hydrocortisone. What evidence do we have that currently used doses are the most appropriate?

Crowley: I think it is unfortunate that Liggins and Howie[17] did so well on their first outing because had they been unsuccessful the first time they might have investigated with many different dose regimens and maybe we would now know more from earlier on in the work. But they did look at betamethasone doses that were double those that we now use and they saw no additional benefit from that, but what they did not look at was half the dose that they initially used.

Nathanielsz: Well, I can tell you from our animal data that we see a 33% increase in fetal blood pressure within six hours of giving these doses of glucocorticoids to either the baboon or the sheep so it is not a species thing. There is a really quite powerful increase in fetal blood pressure which lasts the full 48 hours of the treatment regimen and in the sheep one-third the dose will produce exactly the same rise in blood pressure. Now if you can extrapolate, and it is a very tenuous extrapolation, that the beneficial effects on lung maturation are also going to be maximal at one-third the dose then I really think there is a need to investigate because you can see all sorts of scenarios opening. If the long-term adverse effects will be less with a smaller dose but with the same benefit perhaps you could even get away with more repeat doses.

Steer: I think we need to remember that these are relatively huge doses that we are giving. These are not the doses that we normally give to people who have medical disorders. There are now many papers showing that even up to the teens there are problems arising with hypertension, with diabetes and with other long-term adverse effects. But perhaps the thing that worries me most is that we know that no baby born before 28 weeks will be developmentally entirely normal. Psychologically and mentally there is always going to be a deficit. Newnham's work[18-23] in the sheep is perhaps the most worrying. He shows that fetal brain development is significantly delayed with these doses of steroids. Presumably development and neuronal migration must resume again at some point and it goes on as we know in the human up until the age of two but where the neurons actually end up and whether or not the connections are in exactly the right place I do not think we know yet. I think we do need to have a really detailed follow-up study on some of these babies to make sure that we are not generating a lot of behavioural problems.[24,25] I agree with Dr Nathanielsz that we ought to be looking not just at repeated doses but at whether we are using the right dose. Perhaps we are actually going for short-term survival at the expense of storing up a lot of long-term problems and I know for a fact that David Barker of the MRC Unit at Southampton University is a strong proponent of the view that we need a lot more information about this.

Saade: I agree that we need more studies, especially in multiple gestations and exploring dosage. The problem is that recruitment is very difficult. The US National Institutes of Health (NIH) study that you mentioned was stopped prematurely because of public opinion and the results will be presented in January at the Society for Maternal–Fetal Medicine group. Even large studies supported by NIH cannot be performed anymore.

Steer: No, but I think there are enough groups where we have data about babies whose mother received steroids and those whose did not. At least an observational study may give us some idea as to whether we are doing something really dangerous or not.

References

1. Bethin KE, Nagai Y, Sladek R, Asada M, Sadovsky Y, Hudson TJ, *et al.* Microarray analysis of uterine gene expression in mouse and human pregnancy. *Mol Endocrinol* 2003;17:1454–69.
2. Jeffcoate JNA. Physiology and mechanism of labour. In: *British Obstetric and Gynaecological Practice*, Claye A, Bourne A, editors. London: William Heinemann Medical Books Ltd; 1963. p. 145–83.
3. Smyth CN. The guard-ring tocodynamometer: absolute measurement of intra-amniotic pressure by a new instrument. *J Obstet Gynaecol Br Emp* 1957;64:59–66.
4. Caldeyro R, Alvarez H, Reynolds SRM. A better understanding of uterine contractility through simultaneous recording with an internal and a seven channel external method. *Surg Gynecol Obstet* 1950;91:641–50.

5.   Manabe Y, Sakaguchi M, Mori T. Distention of the uterus activates its multiple pacemakers and induces their coordination. *Gynecol Obstet Invest* 1994;38:163-98.

6.   Buhimschi C, Boyle MB, Garfield RE. Electrical activity of the human uterus during pregnancy as recorded from the abdominal surface. *Obstet Gynecol* 1997;90:102–11.

7.   Kavsek G, Pajntar M, Leskosek B. Electromyographic activity of the uterus above the placental implantation site. *Gynecol Obstet Invest* 1999;48:81–4.

8.   Andersen HF, Barclay ML. A computer model of uterine contractions based on discrete contractile elements. *Obstet Gynecol* 1995;86:108–11.

9.   Olah KS, Gee H, Brown JS. Cervical contractions: the response of the cervix to oxytocic stimulation in the latent phase of labour. *Br J Obstet Gynaecol* 1993;100:635–40.

10. Olah KS. Changes in cervical electromyographic activity and their correlation with the cervical response to myometrial activity during labour. *Eur J Obstet Gynecol Reprod Biol* 1994;57:157–9.

11. Olah KS, Gee H, Brown JS. The effect of cervical contractions on the generation of intrauterine pressure during the latent phase of labour. *Br J Obstet Gynaecol* 1994;101:341–3.

12. Allman AC, Genevier ES, Johnson MR, Steer PJ. Head-to-cervix force: an important physiological variable in labour. 2. Peak active force, peak active pressure and mode of delivery. *Br J Obstet Gynaecol* 1996;103:769–75.

13. Allman ACJ, Genevier ESG, Johnson MR, Steer PJ. Head-to-cervix force: an important physiological variable in labour. 1. The temporal relationship between head-to-cervix force and intrauterine pressure during labour. *Br J Obstet Gynaecol* 1996;103:763–8.

14. Steer PJ, Allman ACJ. Head to cervix force – a new dimension in understanding the mechanics of labour. *Int J Gynaecol Obstet* 1994;36 Suppl 3:62.

15. Antonucci MC, Pitman MC, Eid T, Steer PJ, Genevier ES. Simultaneous monitoring of head-to-cervix forces, intrauterine pressure and cervical dilatation during labour. *Medical Engineering & Physics* 1997;19:317–26.

16. Pitman M, Antonucci M, Eid T, Genevier E, Johnson M, Steer P. Head-to-cervix force: profiles beats peaks. *J Obstet Gynaecol* 1997;17 Suppl 1:S19.

17. Liggins GC, Howie RN. A controlled trial of antepartum glucocorticoid treatment for prevention of the respiratory distress syndrome in premature infants. *Pediatrics* 1972;50:515–25.

18. Sloboda DM, Moss TJ, Gurrin LC, Newnham JP, Challis JR. The effect of prenatal betamethasone administration on postnatal ovine hypothalamic-pituitary-adrenal function. *J Endocrinol* 2002;172:71–81.

19. Huang WL, Harper CG, Evans SF, Newnham JP, Dunlop SA. Repeated prenatal corticosteroid administration delays myelination of the corpus callosum in fetal sheep. *Int J Dev Neurosci* 2001;19:415–25.

20. Quinlivan JA, Beazley LD, Braekevelt CR, Evans SF, Newnham JP, Dunlop SA. Repeated ultrasound guided fetal injections of corticosteroid alter nervous system maturation in the ovine fetus. *J Perinat Med* 2001;29:112–27.

21. Quinlivan JA, Beazley LD, Evans SF, Newnham JP, Dunlop SA. Retinal maturation is delayed by repeated, but not single, maternal injections of betamethasone in sheep. *Eye* 2000;14(Pt 1):93–8.

22. Sloboda DM, Newnham JP, Challis JR. Effects of repeated maternal betamethasone administration on growth and hypothalamic-pituitary-adrenal function of the ovine fetus at term. *J Endocrinol* 2000;165:79–91.

23. Dunlop SA, Archer MA, Quinlivan JA, Beazley LD, Newnham JP. Repeated prenatal corticosteroids delay myelination in the ovine central nervous system. *J Matern Fetal Med* 1997;6:309–13.

24. Newnham JP. Is prenatal glucocorticoid administration another origin of adult disease? *Clin Exp Pharmacol Physiol* 2001;28:957–61.

25. Newnham JP, Moss TJ. Antenatal glucocorticoids and growth: single versus multiple doses in animal and human studies. *Semin Neonatol* 2001;6:285–92.

SECTION 6

MANAGEMENT III

Chapter 23

Tocolysis: for and against

Azhar Husnain Syed and John J Morrison

Introduction

The birth of infants at preterm periods of gestation is the single largest factor contributing to perinatal morbidity and mortality in current obstetric practice in developed countries. As defined by the World Health Organization,[1] this refers to the birth of an infant prior to 37 completed weeks of gestation. There is no clear international lower limit to the definition of preterm, but that often presumed is 23–24 weeks of gestation,[2] which equates approximately to an average fetal weight of 500 g. The lower limit of preterm birth as defined by the World Health Organization is 500 g.

While the overall spectrum of preterm birth refers to a gestation period of less than 37 weeks, it is those occurring prior to 32 weeks of gestation that are of most perinatal concern. While these comprise only 1–2% of all births,[3,4] it is this subgroup that accounts for the 75% of perinatal deaths that are attributed to preterm birth.[5] The adverse sequelae for these infants, in respect of both short- and long-term morbidity, are of major health importance to society. Any intervention or measures that may result in a reduction of mortality or morbidity for this group, either by preventing the birth or by preventing the associated complications, would be a welcome addition to the field of perinatal medicine. Thus far, birth of infants at this period of gestation has remained one of the most intractable problems facing obstetricians.

Attempts to address the problem of preterm birth have focused mainly on the two approaches of prediction and prevention,[2] and the latter can be considered in terms of primary prevention and secondary prevention. Primary prevention refers to prevention of the onset of the condition, whereas secondary prevention refers to therapeutic interventions to treat the condition once it has been initiated, i.e. medication to stop preterm labour. Much research effort over the last 20 years has focused on various methods of prediction and prevention.[5] This effort has been intensified by the fact that, in developed countries in the last decade, there has also been a clear increase in the incidence of preterm birth.[6] This idealistic approach of efficient prediction and prevention has been frustrated by a lack of progress with either aim. The ideal basis for developing a predictive test is that an efficient therapeutic intervention exists. Numerous predictive tests are available, including cervical ultrasound scanning, digital cervical examination, biochemical markers and fetal fibronectin.[7–10] However, no efficient therapeutic interventions exist for preterm labour and predictive tests have thus not met with expectations in terms of improving perinatal outcome. The main approach has therefore been focused on prevention, and particularly secondary prevention of preterm labour. To this end, a long list of pharmacological compounds has been investigated in the last three decades as potential tocolytic agents.

Such pharmacological compounds have various mechanisms of action but all act by relaxing or inhibiting uterine contractions. After years of research on various compounds, it remains uncertain whether or not tocolytics have a clear place in clinical practice. What is clear, however, is that the benefits derived from such use are limited and, for certain compounds, the incidence of serious adverse effects is high. The purpose of this chapter is to review tocolysis in terms of the historical perspective and the various compounds used and their different stages of evaluation, and finally to provide an overall commentary on whether or not tocolysis use is appropriate in current clinical obstetric practice.

Tocolysis: historical perspective

The chief issue of concern in obstetric practice in the first half of the 20th century was maternal mortality. By the 1950s, in developed countries with significantly reducing maternal mortality rates, a greater emphasis on perinatal mortality began to emerge. The contribution of prematurity, as it was then known, to perinatal wastage was well recognised. Attempts to inhibit the uterus's contracting in such a situation were initially made in the 1950s and the history of tocolysis began with relaxin, which was introduced by Abramson and Reid in 1955.[11] The initial study, which included five women, reported a 100% success rate with continuance of pregnancy up to 36 weeks of gestation. On repeat of this study by McCarthy et al.[12] in 1957, it was reported that relaxin did not result in any particular benefit.

Fuchs et al.[13] in New York introduced ethanol in the mid-1960s. It was demonstrated that ethanol was an efficient uterine relaxant in vitro. However, clinical use of ethanol was fraught with problems as the levels in serum required to maintain uterine relaxation had significant and deleterious central effects.

The term 'tocolysis' did not emerge until 1964 when it was coined by Mosler[14] at the Symposium on Physiology and Pathology of Uterine Contractility, from the Greek words τοκοζ (contraction) and λυειν (to untie or destroy). By the mid-1960s the issue of tocolysis, and the investigative efforts for smooth muscle relaxing compounds, had well and truly begun. In the decade that followed, compounds under investigation included magnesium sulphate,[15] calcium antagonists such as nifedipine,[16] and β-adrenergic agonists.

Throughout the 1970s and 1980s, the case reports and observational studies were followed by randomised controlled clinical trials. What initially was presumed to be a simple matter of uterine relaxation developed into a much more complex issue clinically. There were many reasons for this. Preterm birth results from a heterogeneous set of conditions or disorders, not all of which are amenable to utero-relaxant treatment. Recruitment to studies using tocolytic compounds was difficult, and different criteria were accepted for various studies. For many studies, no objective definition of preterm labour, in terms of cervical dilatation or otherwise, was laid down. It became evident that there was a major 'placebo effect' in that many women recruited into such studies for preterm labour were in fact in spurious preterm labour. It therefore became apparent that large numbers of women were required to demonstrate a benefit from the use of such drugs. From the point of view of the actual compounds used, β-adrenergic agonists were the leaders in the field, followed by calcium channel antagonists, and then magnesium sulphate.

A clearer picture began to emerge with the advent of larger multicentre randomised controlled clinical trials in the 1990s,[17] and the meta-analysis of all trials meeting certain criteria.[18] A consistent conclusion from such studies was that the use of tocolytic compounds resulted in a 24–48 hour prolongation of gestation, without conferring any benefit in terms of perinatal outcome. In other words, neonatal outcome as measured by perinatal death, respiratory distress syndrome, birthweight, patent ductus arteriosus, necrotising enterocolitis, intraventricular haemorrhage, seizures, hypoglycaemia or neonatal sepsis does not differ between women treated with tocolytic compounds and placebo. While the possibility remains that tocolytic compounds may provide a delay period for administration of corticosteroids, or allow for transfer to a tertiary referral centre for neonatology, the overall findings from the randomised controlled trials and their meta-analyses has raised the question of whether or not tocolytic drugs should be used.

Tocolytic drugs

Prior to separate evaluation of the various types of tocolytic drugs, it is appropriate to examine the risks and benefits derived from the use of such drugs in a collective sense. Gyetvai et al.[18] have reported a systematic review that involved 17 trials with a total of 2284 women. The aim of the review was to compare tocolysis with no treatment or placebo. There were confounding variables to consider as some of the trials included maintenance treatment while others did not, and some trials excluded women with ruptured membranes but in others they were included. The most frequently evaluated agent was the β-2 adrenergic agonist ritodrine. Isoxsuprine, terbutaline, magnesium sulphate, indomethacin and atosiban were also evaluated. Tocolytic drugs, when used, were associated with a reduction in the odds of delivery within 24 hours (OR 0.47; 95% CI 0.29–0.77), 48 hours (OR 0.57; 95% CI 0.38–0.83) and seven days (OR 0.60; 95% CI 0.38–0.95). This effect was statistically significant for β-agonists, indomethacin and atosiban, but not for magnesium sulphate. No statistically significant reduction in births before 30 weeks of gestation (OR 1.33; 95% CI 0.53–3.33), before 32 weeks (OR 0.81; 95% CI 0.61–1.07) or before 37 weeks of gestation (OR 0.17; 95% CI 0.02–1.62) was observed, confirming similar disappointing results in earlier studies. Finally, tocolysis was not associated with any benefit in terms of perinatal death (OR 1.22; 95% CI 0.84–1.78) or neonatal morbidity outcome measures, such as respiratory distress syndrome (OR 0.82; 95% CI 0.64–1.07) or intraventricular haemorrhage (OR 0.73; 95% CI 0.46–1.15). Similar results comparing atosiban with placebo have since been reported and will be discussed separately below.[19] There are no placebo-controlled trials of calcium channel blockers. On the basis of the best evidence available, the conclusions regarding the use of tocolytics versus no treatment are similar to those reported in the systematic review outlined above.

β-adrenergic agonists

An overview of the various pharmacological compounds under investigation as tocolytics is given in Table 23.1.[17–44] The various compounds have been investigated to different degrees, i.e. scientifically or in vitro in laboratory models, in vivo using animal studies, or by clinical studies such as case reports or randomised controlled trials. Owing to a greater understanding of the physiological and pharmacological pathways involved in regulation of the myometrial cell, this is a rapidly changing area of research. In contrast, however, clinical benefits derived from such treatments have remained depressingly static.

Throughout the 1980s, and 1990s, β-adrenergic agonists such as ritodrine were the most commonly used tocolytic agents in Europe and the USA. For this reason, it is the

Table 23.1. Pharmacological compounds and tocolysis

Tocolytic compounds	Scientific studies		Clinical studies	References
	In vitro	*In vivo*	(type)	
Atosiban	Yes	Yes	RCTs	18–22
β. agonists	Yes	Yes	RCTs	17,18,20,22–24,41
β. agonists	Yes	No		18,25
Calcium channel antagonists	Yes	Yes	RCTs	24,42
COX-2 inhibitors	Yes	Yes	CR	26,27
Glyceryl trinitrate	Yes	No	RCTs	23
Human chorionic gonadotrophin	Yes	Yes	RCTs	28–30
Indomethacin	Yes	Yes	RCTs	31
Magnesium sulphate	Yes	Yes	RCTs	32,43
Peptides				
17 Alpha-hydroxyprogesterone caproate	Yes	Yes	RCT	33,44
Parathyroid hormone-related peptide	Yes	No		34
Vasoactive intestinal peptide	Yes	Yes		35
Calcitonin gene-related peptide	Yes	No		36
Potassium channel openers	Yes	No		37
Protein kinase inhibitors	Yes	No		38
Rho-kinase inhibitors	Yes	No		39
THG 113	Yes	No		40
Tyrosine kinase inhibitors	Yes	No		38

COX-2 = cyclooxygenase 2; CR = case report; RCT = randomised controlled trial

compound that has been best evaluated in terms of clinical studies of efficacy. In placebo-controlled studies it is apparent that ritodrine is effective in reducing the number of women who deliver within 24–48 hours of commencing treatment, but it has no significant beneficial effect on perinatal mortality, neonatal morbidity, birthweight or in prolonging the pregnancy.[17,41] The Canadian preterm labour study[17] that was published in 1992 was one of the larger studies of that time where 708 women with preterm labour were randomised to receive either an intravenous infusion of ritodrine or placebo. There was no significant improvement in perinatal outcome, but there was severe maternal morbidity such as chest pain, cardiac arrhythmias and pulmonary oedema. Because of the widespread use of ritodrine in the field, and the fact that in many countries it was the only licensed product, many randomised clinical trials were designed to compare its efficacy with other novel compounds. A summary of these studies is provided below

Oxytocin antagonists

In recent years, and particularly since the introduction of the oxytocin antagonist atosiban, in many countries the use of β-adrenergic agonists as tocolytics has declined rapidly. The reason is largely the high incidence of serious maternal adverse effects associated with β-adrenergic agonists.

Romero *et al.*[19] have reported a multicentre double-blind placebo-controlled trial using atosiban. Standard tocolytics were used for rescue therapy after one hour of either placebo or atosiban if preterm labour continued. When compared with placebo, atosiban resulted in prolongation of pregnancy for periods up to seven days, but the neonatal morbidity and mortality were the same in the treatment and placebo arms of the trial. Essentially, the findings were no different from those reported from the systematic review outlined earlier.[18]

The risks and benefits of atosiban versus β-adrenergic compounds have also been evaluated. Three multinational multicentre double-blind randomised controlled trials including 733 women have compared atosiban with three different β-agonists (ritodrine, salbutamol and terbutaline).[22] There was no significant difference observed between atosiban and β-adrenergic agonists in terms of ability to delay delivery by 48 hours or seven days. Data on gestation at birth were not reported and there were too few perinatal deaths for any reliable conclusions (RR 0.53; 95% CI 0.20–1.40). Atosiban was, however, associated with fewer maternal adverse effects compared to the β-adrenergic agonists.

Calcium channel blockers

Calcium channel blockers are primarily used for treatment of hypertension, but they are known to exert a relaxant effect on uterine smooth muscle. Their benefits and limitations as tocolytic agents have been outlined in a Cochrane library review comprising 12 randomised controlled trials including 1029 women.[42] Their benefits were compared with other tocolytics and no studies comparing their efficacy versus placebo, or no treatment, have been reported. There was a statistically significant decrease in the incidence of delivery within seven days of treatment with calcium channel blockers compared to other tocolytic agents (RR 0.76; 95% CI 0.60–0.97). Maternal adverse reactions, and cessation of treatment due to maternal adverse reactions, were markedly reduced in patients treated with calcium channel blockers. There was also a reduction in the incidence of neonatal respiratory distress syndrome, necrotising enterocolitis, intraventricular haemorrhage and jaundice. It was therefore felt that when tocolytic drugs are indicated, calcium channel blockers are preferable to other compounds, particularly β-adrenergic agonists.

Magnesium sulphate

Magnesium sulphate, which is also used for the treatment and prophylaxis of eclampsia, has been widely used as a tocolytic agent in the hope of preventing preterm birth, but there is a lack of well-defined randomised control trials to support its use. The exact mechanism of action is not known. Magnesium sulphate inhibits uterine contractility by apparently altering calcium transport in smooth muscle cells. A systematic review identified 23 trials with 2000 women recruited.[43] The primary outcome measure of delivery within 48 hours of treatment was available in 11 trials with 881 women recruited. There was no difference between magnesium sulphate and control, i.e. placebo, no treatment or other tocolytic agent (RR 0.85; 95% CI 0.58–1.25). In seven trials, with 727 infants, magnesium sulphate was associated with an increase in fetal and neonatal deaths (RR 2.82; 95% CI 1.20–6.62). In one trial, with 99 children, a nonsignificant reduction in the risk of cerebral palsy was seen in follow-up to 18 months age (RR 0.14; 95% CI 0.01–2.60). In summary, magnesium sulphate is ineffective as a tocolytic and is probably associated with increased neonatal mortality.

Nitric oxide donors

In the mid-1990s it became apparent that nitric oxide (NO) had the ability to relax myometrial cells by activation of the cyclic guanosine monophosphate (cGMP) pathway. This led to an initial enthusiasm for the use of NO donors in the treatment of preterm labour. Nitric oxide donors have been evaluated more closely using randomised controlled trials.

Analysis of five randomised controlled trials[45] comparing NO donors with placebo or other tocolytic agent revealed that there was no significant reduction in the number of deliveries at less than 34 weeks of gestation. However, there was a reduction observed in deliveries at less than 37 weeks in the NO-treated group, compared with placebo or other tocolytic (RR 0.69; 95% CI 0.53–0.88). Antenatal corticosteriods were used in only one study. Headaches were a more frequent adverse effect associated with the use of NO donors. There was no significant difference in outcome between NO donors and other tocolytics or placebo. There is therefore insufficient evidence to support the routine use of NO donors as tocolytic agents.

Prostaglandin synthetase inhibitors

Owing to the central role played by prostaglandins in the onset and maintenance of human labour, the potential use of cyclooxygenase (COX) inhibitors as tocolytic agents has been extensively studied. There are two COX isoforms, COX-1 and COX-2. Initial research effort focused on COX-1 inhibitors such as indomethacin. Such compounds are as effective as β-adrenergic agonists but are associated with severe fetal adverse effects, essentially prohibiting their use.[46] The adverse effects include oligohydramnios, renal failure, premature closure of the ductus arteriosus with consequent pulmonary hypertension, persistent patent ductus arteriosus, necrotising enterocolitis and intraventricular haemorrhage. More recently, the possibility that COX-2 selective inhibitors may be useful for tocolysis has been evaluated. However, it appears that such compounds cause similar adverse fetal effects.[47]

Progesterone and preterm delivery

The basis upon which progesterone is used for management of preterm delivery is that of the progesterone withdrawal hypothesis as promoted by Csapo,[48] in which the high ratio of progesterone to oestrogen that allows the uterus to expand during pregnancy is reversed as labour approaches, thus allowing cervical ripening and uterine contractility to increase and labour to occur. This pathway has been explored in animal species[49] and many studies have investigated the role of progesterone in a human clinical setting,[50-52] despite the fact that the progesterone withdrawal hypothesis is not as clearly relevant in human as it is in animal models. The use of progesterone has recently been revived, with the report by Meis et al.[33] In this report, 17 alpha-hydroxyprogesterone caproate (17P) resulted in an absolute risk reduction of 18.6% in women with a previous preterm delivery, in comparison with a control group treated with placebo. The rate of delivery before 37 weeks of gestation was 36.3% in the treatment group and 54.9% in the control group (RR 0.66; 95% CI 0.54–0.81). In addition, the infants of women treated with 17P had significantly lower rates of necrotising enterocolitis, intraventricular haemorrhage and the need for supplemental oxygen. In other words, the suggestion from this study is that 17P confers significant benefit in terms of reducing preterm births and their associated morbidity. However, these results have raised interesting and controversial points in relation to the mechanism of action of progesterone in maintaining uterine quiescence during pregnancy. Further controversy[53] has arisen in relation to the castor oil used as the vehicle and placebo in this study. In any case, further evaluation of 17P is necessary before its use in clinical practice is advised. Interestingly, provisional results from our studies[44] using *in vitro* isometric recordings have revealed that 17P does not exert an inhibitory effect on isolated myometrial contractions. This would suggest that its potential benefit as a tocolytic compound is exerted by other mechanisms. It remains a possibility that 17P acts to prevent the onset of contractions by its genomic effects.

Tocolysis – to use or not

The debate concerning whether or not to use the currently available tocolytic drugs is now more pertinent than ever in the history of tocolysis. A decision to use such drugs is currently based on the presumptive benefits that may be obtained by delaying delivery for 24–48 hours in order to administer glucocorticoids for fetal lung maturation or to allow for *in utero* transfer to a specialist neonatal/tertiary-level centre. The evidence available in the literature is now more reliable, in terms of randomised trials and meta-analyses, and is consistently negative about the potential benefits of such drugs. As there is no clear evidence that their use improves outcome, in terms of perinatal or neonatal survival or wellbeing, it is reasonable to adopt a strategy of not using such drugs except in the context of a randomised clinical trial. The possible adverse effects associated with their use also merits close consideration. In practical terms, this relates to the serious maternal risks of β-adrenergic agonists, and the major fetal risks of COX inhibitors.

The more difficult philosophical question for tocolytics in general is whether or not prolongation of gestation in circumstances of preterm labour may actually be linked to an increased risk of neonatal morbidity. There was some evidence from the atosiban trial[19] that there was a higher incidence of fetal death at the early periods of gestation in the tocolytic arm, in comparison to the placebo arm. The EPICure Study Group[54] examined the association between extremely premature birth and consequent neurological and developmental disability in a cohort of 811 infants born between 22 and 25 weeks of gestation in the UK and Ireland.[55] Follow-up studies[54] from that group showed that tocolytics, although associated with a decrease in death before discharge (OR 0.57; 95% CI 0.41–0.79), were associated with an increase in the frequency of severe neonatal brain scan abnormalities (OR 2.02; 95% CI 1.04–3.94) and severe chronic lung disease (OR 2.53; 85% CI 1.42–4.51). The mechanisms of this are unclear but what is clear is that prolongation of gestation alone, in as much as tocolytic drugs can offer this, may not always be beneficial for the fetus or neonate.

Great disparity currently exists between different countries, and different units within the same country, in relation to which is the optimal compound for use as a tocolytic agent. Because of their adverse effects, neither ritodrine nor COX inhibitors constitute the first line of approach. Alternatives such as atosiban or nifedipine are now regarded as the drugs of choice as they display similar effectiveness in delaying birth but possess a much lesser profile of adverse effects. While the purchase price of atosiban is higher than that of nifedipine, atosiban is licensed in many European countries for tocolysis whereas nifedipine is not. However, the benefits derived from using them remain open to question. In order to answer these questions fully, much larger randomised controlled trials, enrolling thousands of women, are required.

References

1.   World Health Organization. *The Prevention of Perinatal Mortality and Morbidity*. WHO Technical Report Series 457. Geneva: World Health Organization; 1970.
2.   Morrison JJ, Rennie JM. Clinical, scientific and ethical aspects of fetal and neonatal care at

extremely preterm periods of gestation. *Br J Obstet Gynaecol* 1997;104:1341–50.

3.   McFarlane A, Cole S, Johnson A, Botting B. Epidemiology of birth before 28 weeks of gestation. *Br Med Bull* 1988;44:861–91.

4.   Slattery MM, Morrison JJ. Preterm delivery. *Lancet* 2002;360:1489–97.

5.   Lumley J. The epidemiology of preterm birth. *Baillieres Clin Obstet Gynaecol* 1993;7:477–98.

6.   Goldenberg RL, Rouse DJ. Prevention of premature birth. *N Engl J Med* 1998;339:313–20.

7.   Iams JD, Newman RB, Thom EA, Goldenberg RL, Mueller-Heubach E, Moawad A, *et al.* Frequency of uterine contractions and the risk of spontaneous preterm delivery. *N Engl J Med* 2002;346:250–5.

8.   Owen J, Iams JD, Hauth JC. Vaginal sonography and cervical incompetence. *Am J Obstet Gynecol* 2003;188:586–96.

9.   Iams JD. Prediction and early detection of preterm labor. *Obstet Gynecol* 2003;101:402–12.

10.   Goldenberg RL, Klebanoff M, Carey JC, Macpherson C, Leveno KJ, Moawad AH, *et al.* Vaginal fetal fibronectin measurements from 8 to 22 weeks' gestation and subsequent spontaneous preterm birth. *Am J Obstet Gynecol* 2000;183:469–75.

11.   Abramson D, Reid DE. Use of relaxin in treatment of threatened premature labor. *J Clin Endocrinol Metab* 1955;15:206–9.

12.   McCarthy JJ, Erving HW, Laufe LE. Preliminary report on the use of relaxin in the management of threatened premature labor. *Am J Obstet Gynecol* 1957;74:134–8.

13.   Fuchs F, Fuchs AR, Poblete VF Jr, Risk A. Effect of alcohol on threatened preterm labour. *Am J Obstet Gynecol* 1967;99:627–37.

14.   Mosler KH. Symposion über Physiologie der Wehentätigkeit. *Zentralblatt Für Gynäkologie* 1965.

15.   Dumont M. Traitement des douleurs utérine gravidiques par le lactate de magnésium. *Lyon Méd* 1965;213:1571–82.

16.   Andersson KE, Ingermarsson I, Ulmsten U, Wingerup L. Inhibition of prostaglandin-induced uterine activity by nifedipine. *Br J Obstet Gynaecol* 1979;86:175–9.

17.   The Canadian Preterm Labor Investigators Group. Treatment of preterm labor with the beta adrenergic agonist ritodrine. *N Engl J Med* 1992;327:308–12.

18.   Gyetvai K, Hannah ME, Hodnett ED, Ohlsson A. Tocolytics for preterm labor: a systematic review. *Obstet Gynecol* 1999;94:869–77.

19.   Romero R, Sibai BM, Sanchez-Ramos L, Valenzuela GJ, Veille JC, Tabor B, *et al.* An oxytocin receptor antagonist (atosiban) in the treatment of preterm labor: a randomized, double-blind, placebo-controlled trial with tocolytic rescue. *Am J Obstet Gynecol* 2000;182:1173–83.

20.   Moutquin JM, Sherman D, Cohen H, Mohide PT, Hochner-Celnikier D, Fejgin M, *et al.* Double-blind, randomized, controlled trial of atosiban and ritodrine in the treatment of preterm labor: a multicenter effectiveness and safety study. *Am J Obstet Gynecol* 2000;182:1191–9.

21.   French/Australian Atosiban Investigators Group. Treatment of preterm labor with the oxytocin antagonist atosiban: a double-blind, randomized controlled comparison with salbutamol. *Eur J Obstet Gynecol Reprod Biol* 2001;98:177–85.

22.   Worldwide Atosiban versus Beta-agonists Study Group. Effectiveness and safety of the oxytocin antagonist atosiban versus beta-adrenergic agonists in the treatment of preterm labour. *BJOG* 2001;108:133–42.

23.   Lees CC, Lojacono A, Thompson C, Danti L, Black RS, Tanzi P, *et al.* Glyceryl trinitrate and ritodrine in tocolysis: an international multicenter randomized study. GTN Preterm Labour Investigation Group. *Obstet Gynecol* 1999;94:403–8.

24.   Tsatsaris V, Papatsonis D, Goffinet F, Dekker G, Carbonne B. Tocolysis with nifedipine or beta-adrenergic agonists: a meta-analysis. *Obstet Gynecol* 2001;97:840–7.

25.   Dennedy MC, Friel AM, Gardeil F, Morrison JJ. Beta-3 versus beta-2 adrenergic agonists and preterm labour: in vitro uterine relaxation effects. *BJOG* 2001;108:605–9.

26.   Slattery MM, Friel AM, Healy DG, Morrison JJ. Uterine relaxant effects of cyclooxygenase inhibitors *in vitro*. *Obstet Gynecol* 2001;98:563–9.

27.   Peruzzi L, Gianoglio B, Porcellini MG, Coppo R. Neonatal end-stage renal failure associated with maternal ingestion of cyclo-oxygenase-type-1 selective inhibitor nimesulide as tocolytic. *Lancet* 1999;354:1615.

28.   Slattery MM, Brennan C, O'Leary MJ, Morrison JJ. Human chorionic gonadotrophin inhibition of pregnant human myometrial contractility. *BJOG* 2001;108:704–8.

29.   Kurtzman JT, Spinnato JA, Goldsmith LJ, Zimmerman MJ, Klem M, Lei ZM, *et al.* Human chorionic gonadotropin exhibits potent inhibition of preterm delivery in a small animal model. *Am J Obstet Gynecol* 1999;181:853–7.

30.   Ali AFM, Fateen B, Ezzet A, Badawy H, Ramadan A, El-tobge A. Treatment of preterm labor with human chorionic gonadotrophin: a new modality. *Obstet Gynecol* 2000;95(Suppl 1):S61.

31.   Abramov Y, Nadjari M, Weinstein D, Ben-Shachar I, Plotkin V, Ezra Y. Indomethacin for preterm labor: a randomized comparison of vaginal and rectal-oral routes. *Obstet Gynecol* 2000;95:482–6.

32. Terrone DA, Rinehart BK, Kimmel ES, May WL, Larmon JE, Morrison JC. A prospective, randomized, controlled trial of high and low maintenance doses of magnesium sulfate for acute tocolysis. *Am J Obstet Gynecol* 2000;182:1477–82.

33. Meis PJ, Klebanoff M, Thom E, Dombrowski MP, Sibai B, Moawad AH, *et al.* Prevention of recurrent preterm delivery by 17 alpha-hydroxyprogesterone caproate. *N Engl J Med* 2003;348:2379–85. Erratum in: *N Engl J Med* 2003;349:1299.

34. Slattery MM, O'Leary MJ, Morrison JJ. Effect of parathyroid hormone-related peptide on human and rat myometrial contractility *in vitro*. *Am J Obstet Gynecol* 2000;184:625–9.

35. Bajo AM, Juarranz MG, Valenzuela P, Martinez P, Prieto JC, Guijarro LG. Expression of vasoactive intestinal peptide (VIP) receptors in human uterus. *Peptides* 2000;21:1383–8.

36. Dong YL, Fang L, Kondapaka S, Gangula PR, Wimalawansa SJ, Yallampalli C. Involvement of calcitonin gene-related peptide in the modulation of human myometrial contractility during pregnancy. *J Clin Invest* 1999;104:559–65.

37. Morrison JJ, Ashford ML, Khan RN, Smith SK. The effects of potassium channel openers on isolated pregnant human myometrium before and after the onset of labor: potential for tocolysis. *Am J Obstet Gynecol* 1993;169:1277–85.

38. Morrison JJ, Dearn R, Smith SK, Ahmed A. Activation of protein kinase C is required for oxytocin-induced contractility in human pregnant myometrium. *Hum Reprod* 1996;11:2285–90.

39. Moran CJ, Friel AM, Smith TJ, Cairns M, Morrison JJ. Expression and modulation of Rho kinase in human pregnant myometrium. *Mol Hum Reprod* 2002;2:196–200.

40. Peri KG, Quiniou C, Hou X, Abran D, Varma DR, Lubell WD, *et al.* THG113: a novel selective FP antagonist that delays preterm labor. *Semin Perinatol* 2002;26:389–97.

41. King JF, Grant A, Keirse MJ, Chalmers I. Beta-mimetics in preterm labour: an overview of the ramdomised controlled trials. *BJOG* 1988;95:211–22.

42. King JF, Flenady VJ, Papatsonis DN, Dekker GA, Carbonne B. Calcium channel blockers for inhibiting preterm labour. *Cochrane Database Syst Rev* 2003;(1):CD002255.

43. Crowther CA, Hiller JE, Doyle LW. Magnesium sulphate for preventing preterm birth in threatened preterm labour. *Cochrane Database Syst Rev* 2002;(4):CD001060.

44. Sexton DJ, O'Reilly MW, Friel AM, Morrison JJ. 17 Alpha-hydroxyprogesterone caproate (17P) and human myometrial contractility *in-vitro*. *J Soc Gynecol Investig* 2004;11:81A.

45. Duckitt K, Thornton S. Nitric oxide donors for the treatment of preterm labour. *Cochrane Database Syst Rev* 2002;(3):CD002860.

46. Norton ME, Merrill J, Cooper BA, Kuller JA, Clyman RI. Neonatal complications after the administration of indomethacin for preterm labor. *N Engl J Med* 1993;329:1602–7.

47. Sawdy RJ, Lye S, Fisk NM, Bennett PR. A double-blind randomised study of fetal side effects after short-term maternal administration of indomethacin, sulindac, and nimesulide for the treatment of preterm labor. *Am J Obstet Gynecol* 2003;188:1046–51.

48. Csapo AI. The see-saw theory of parturition. In: O'Connor M, Knight J, editors. *The Fetus and Birth*. New York: Elsevier; 1977. p. 159–210.

49. Saito Y, Sakimoto H, MacKusky NJ, Naftolin F. Gap-junctions and myometrial steroid hormone receptors in pregnant and post-partum rats: a possible cellular basis for the progesterone withdrawal hypothesis. *Am J Obstet Gynecol* 1985;151:805–12.

50. Johnson JWC, Austin KL, Jones GS, Davis GH, King TM. Efficacy of 17 alpha hydroxy-progesterone caproate in the prevention of premature labor. *N Engl J Med* 1975;292:675–80.

51. Hartikainen-Sorri AL, Kauppila A, Tuimala R. Inefficacy of 17 alpha-hydroxyprogesterone caproate in the prevention of prematurity in twin pregnancy. *Obstet Gynecol* 1980;56:692–5.

52. Hauth JC, Gilstrap LC 3rd, Brekken AL, Hauth JM. The effect of 17 alpha-hydroxyprogesterone caproate on pregnancy outcome in an active-duty military population. *Am J Obstet Gynecol* 1983;146:187–90.

53. Brancazio LR, Murtha AP, Heine RP. Prevention of recurrent preterm delivery by 17 alpha-hydroxyprogesterone caproate. *N Engl J Med* 2003;349:1087–8.

54. Costeloe K, Hennessy E, Gibson AT, Marlow N, Wilkinson AR. The EPICure study: outcomes to discharge from hospital for infants born at the threshold of viability. *Pediatrics* 2000;106:659–71.

55. Wood NS, Marlow N, Costeloe K, Gibson AT, Wilkinson AR. Neurological and developmental disability after extremely preterm birth. *N Engl J Med* 2000;343:378–84.

Chapter 24

Nifedipine in the management of preterm labour: evidence from the literature

Dimitri NM Papatsonis and Guus A Dekker

Introduction

In developing countries preterm birth is the single most important cause of perinatal mortality.[1] The annual number of preterm births worldwide is estimated to be approximately 13 million.[2] Two-thirds of preterm births result from spontaneous preterm labour or preterm prelabour rupture of the membranes, and the rest are due to medical interventions for maternal or fetal indications.[3] In developed countries the incidence of preterm birth is estimated at 5–10% of all births.[4,5] The incidence has been stable over the last four decades despite remarkable improvements in perinatal care facilities, the widespread use of tocolytic agents, and the introduction of steroids to enhance fetal lung maturation. Preterm birth is responsible for 75–90% of all neonatal deaths not due to congenital anomalies, and for 50% of childhood neurological disabilities.[6]

The costs of preterm birth and its associated neonatal intensive care unit (NICU) admission include immediate and long-term costs. The weekly cost of approximately $10,000 per baby yield an estimated total cost in the USA of more than $5 billion.[7] The cost to graduate a sick infant from admission to discharge from the NICU typically ranges between $20,000 and $100,000, and up to $140,000 for those weighing less than 1000 g. Infants with severe handicaps can have long-term care costs estimated to be more than $100,000, and lifetime care as much as $450,000.[7]

The exact causes and aetiologies of preterm birth are not known. It is clear that preterm birth needs to be seen as the final common pathway of several pathophysiological pathways, including ascending infection, (utero-)placental insufficiency, and 'fetal stress'. It is therefore difficult to influence the incidence rate. Management strategies to prevent preterm birth are mainly focused on identification of those women who are at high risk for preterm delivery. Tocolytic agents are often required in women in unexplained preterm labour without signs of fetal compromise.

Perinatal outcome of preterm delivery

In recent decades we have witnessed a significant improvement in neonatal survival and serious morbidity rates in preterm infants. This improvement is due to some extent to better perinatal surveillance, but more importantly to major improvements in neonatal care. The gestational age of viability is currently around 24 weeks. In line with this, the limit of aggressive intrapartum management should be 24 weeks.[8,9] Viability requires the availability of effective clinical interventions for the immediate and longer term care of these infants.[10] The analysis of perinatal outcome should not only be based on mortality rates but also on morbidity and long-term prognosis. For the infant undergoing aggressive neonatal management, a fair balance should be maintained between clinical benefit in terms of intact survival versus mortality and impaired survival. In recent years the 50% survival rate has shifted from 26 weeks to 24 weeks of gestation.[11,12] Lumley[5] showed that the incidence of preterm births under 28 weeks is approximately 10%, but that these are responsible for 57% of perinatal mortality preterm. The incidence of preterm births under 26 weeks is approximately 7%, and these are responsible for 46% of perinatal mortality preterm. The EPICure study[13,14] investigated the outcome of infants born at less than 25 completed gestational weeks. The percentage of singleton infants who survived and were discharged from the NICU increased from 23% at 23 weeks to 38% at 24 weeks and 54% at 25 weeks. The incidence of disability in infants born at less than 25 completed weeks of gestation was 48%, and 23% of the them had severe disability.

Management of preterm labour with calcium channel blockers

While the incidence of preterm birth in developed countries has not reduced in recent decades, there are benefits in prolonging pregnancy in that this allows corticosteroids to be administered for promoting fetal lung maturation and it enables pregnant women to be transferred to a tertiary referral centre with NICU facilities.[15] A range of tocolytic agents has been used to inhibit preterm labour to gain time for such interventions to occur. The most widely used tocolytic agents are the betamimetics such as ritodrine, salbutamol and terbutaline. Betamimetics have been shown to be effective in delaying delivery by up to seven days and longer, although no impact has yet been shown on perinatal mortality.[16–18] However, betamimetics have a high frequency of unpleasant and sometimes severe maternal adverse effects, including tachycardia, hypotension, tremulousness and a range of biochemical disturbances. Furthermore, betamimetics have been associated with at least 25 maternal deaths, mainly from pulmonary oedema.[19] It is likely that if one were to try to introduce these drugs in 2004, they would not be considered acceptable because of lack of convincing benefit coupled with maternal adverse effects.

Calcium channel blockers (CCBs), or calcium entry blockers, were originally developed in the early 1960s for angina pectoris but, owing to new insights into their mechanism of action, the number of indications has expanded.[20,21] CCBs are now used for angina, hypertension, supraventricular arrhythmia, subarachnoid haemorrhage and myocardial infarction.[22] In recent years, CCBs have also been used in obstetrics and gynaecology, especially in the management of preterm labour and pre-eclampsia.[23] Their popularity in the management of preterm labour is at least partially based on the absence of tachyphylaxis and the low incidence of adverse effects in comparison with betamimetics.[24,25]

Pharmacology

CCBs act by blockage of the voltage-dependent calcium channels, thus preventing extracellular calcium influx into smooth muscle cells. The density of the channels is not affected by long-term CCB treatment and thus, in contrast to betamimetics, no tachyphylaxis or withdrawal symptoms occur when therapy is stopped.[26,27]

Tachyphylaxis occurs due to a combination of both receptor downregulation and enzyme induction with prolonged betamimetics. The absence of tachyphylaxis may be one the most important reasons for CCBs' efficacy in managing preterm labour.

Pharmacokinetics

The various CCBs have very different chemical and pharmacodynamic characteristics, but they exhibit rather similar pharmacokinetic properties. After oral administration, nifedipine is rapidly and almost completely absorbed from the gastrointestinal tract. Some of the nifedipine is metabolised into inactive metabolites because of a first-pass effect in the intestinal wall and liver.[28] CCBs are mainly metabolised in the intestinal wall, and a minor part in the liver, to inactive metabolites by oxidative pathways, especially by cytochrome P-450 CYP3A, a subgroup of the cytochrome P-450 enzyme family.[22,29–31] The biologically inactive metabolites are mainly excreted by the kidneys (70–80%), with the remainder (20–30%) excreted in the faeces.[32–34] Half-life is short and most metabolites of nifedipine are inactive.[20,35–40]

There is large inter-individual variability in the kinetics of nifedipine. The plasma levels are highly variable.[40] According to Murad,[41] the daily maximum dosage should not exceed 180 mg. Onset of action after administration of an oral dose is less than 20 minutes.[20,41,42] Maximum serum concentrations are obtained more quickly when the capsule is chewed before it is swallowed, compared with standard oral administration. After a sublingual dose of nifedipine the time for an effect 1–5 minutes.[43] The elimination half-life of nifedipine in plasma varies between 1.3 hours for 10 mg oral capsules and 6–11 hours for 20 mg sustained-release tablets (nifedipine retard).[20,38–40,44] In pregnant women, peak serum concentration and half-life of nifedipine are decreased and the clearance rate is increased compared with nonpregnant women (Table 24.1).[44,45] In order to have the same effect as in nonpregnant women, the dosage in pregnant women should therefore be higher and the interval time shorter for the same therapeutic effect. A slow-release form of nifedipine, GITS (gastrointestinal therapeutic system), has a delay of three hours after ingestion before nifedipine appears in the plasma. There is a plateau of nifedipine levels for 6 to 24 hours, after which the plasma levels decline.[46]

Kleinbloesem et al.[40] investigated the peak plasma concentration and half-life of nifedipine in six healthy male volunteers after they received intravenous nifedipine, 0.015 mg/kg body weight, 20 mg in a capsule, and 20 mg in a sustained-release tablet (nifedipine retard). After intravenous nifedipine, the half-life was 1.7 ± 0.4 hours. For the capsule, peak plasma concentration was 117 ± 15 ng/ml at 1.4 ± 0.5 hours after administration. After absorption of the sustained-release tablet (nifedipine retard), peak plasma concentration was 26 ± 10 ng/ml at 4.2 ± 0.7 hours after administration.

Ferguson et al.[39] studied the pharmacokinetics of nifedipine during preterm labour tocolysis. Thirteen women in labour received 10 mg sublingual nifedipine followed by 20 mg oral nifedipine if uterine contractions were stopped. The peak concentration of nifedipine in 12 women in whom blood samples were taken during sublingual therapy was 96.7 ± 45.3 ng/ml (range 23.4–197.9 ng/ml). The women in general had increased plasma concentrations of nifedipine after each successive dose of nifedipine. The half-life of nifedipine, calculated from plasma concentrations obtained hourly after the last sublingual dose but before the first oral dose, was 81 ± 26 minutes (range 49–137 minutes).

Although the physiological changes of pregnancy can affect absorption, distribution, metabolism and excretion of nifedipine, the pharmacokinetic parameters observed by Ferguson et al.[39] were very similar to those of nonpregnant women.

Table 24.1. Peak serum concentration, half-life and clearance rate of nifedipine (10 mg capsule) in pregnant and nonpregnant women (after Prevost et al.[44] and Foster et al.[45])

	Pregnant	Nonpregnant
Peak serum concentration (ng/ml)	38.6 ± 18	73.48 ± 17.48
Half-life (h)	1.3 ± 0.5	3.43 ± 10.6
Clearance rate (l/h/kg)	2.0 ± 0.8	0.49 ± 0.09

Values are given as mean ± one standard deviation

Prevost et al.[44] studied the pharmacokinetics of oral nifedipine in 15 women with pregnancy-induced hypertension in the third trimester. Nifedipine 10 mg capsules were administered orally every six hours. The values were assessed after at least 48 hours of dosing to achieve steady state. Nifedipine was well tolerated by all the women, with headache being the only adverse effect reported in three women. The peak serum concentration was 38 ± 18 ng/ml 40 minutes after a 10 mg oral dose. The serum half-life with 10 mg nifedipine capsules was 1.3 ± 0.5 hours (range 0.44–2.5 hours). In an earlier study with the same dose, Foster et al.[45] had found a peak serum concentration of 73.5 ± 17.5 ng/ml in nonpregnant healthy subjects. This difference could be explained by an increased first-pass effect through the liver.

Nifedipine gastrointestinal therapeutic system

Nifedipine GITS is an extended-release nifedipine tablet that slowly releases the drug in the gastrointestinal tract over a 24-hour period. The nifedipine tablet consists of a coating with a laser-drilled delivery orifice and two compartments within the coating, one containing an osmotic drug core and the other a polymer. The release mechanism involves an osmotically driven push–pull process. As water is absorbed across the semi-permeable cellulosic membrane that surrounds the bilayer tablet, nifedipine particles become suspended in solution and are then pushed into the intestinal tract as the osmotically active polymers expand.[47] The nifedipine GITS tablet (nifedipine Oros®) is designed to provide a extended- release. The GITS tablets have an oral bioavailability of 55–65% after a single dose and 75–85% at steady state.[48]

Plasma concentrations after ingestion of a single dose of nifedipine GITS are not seen before three hours and the plasma concentrations plateau approximately six hours later but continue for at least 24 hours after administration.[46,49] Drug release by nifedipine GITS is not affected by changes in pH or gastrointestinal motility.[46] As predicted in in vitro tests, the nifedipine plasma concentrations begins to decline 20 hours after administration.[46] The advantages of the nifedipine GITS are a longer duration of action and fewer adverse effects.[48] Nifedipine GITS tablets are available in 30 mg, 60 mg and 90 mg formulations. Grundy and Foster[46] found that a total daily dosage of nifedipine GITS between 30 and 180 mg did not significantly affect the heart rate in hypertensive patients. In our experience with pregnant women we do not exceed a maximum daily dosage of 160 mg.

Tocolytic efficacy

The first CCB that was used and studied in an observational study was the dihydropyridine nifedipine.[50] Nifedipine seems to be an effective tocolytic agent with minimal adverse effects.[50] Both in the Netherlands and in Australia nifedipine is

Table 24.2. Prospective randomised clinical trials with nifedipine; modified with permission from Papatsonis et al.[19]

Study	Study design	Drugs	Women (n)	Results
Read et al. (1986)[52]	Randomised placebo controlled	Nif. vs. Rit.	60	Nifedipine was more successful in delaying delivery than ritodrine and the control group (P < 0.05) and had significantly fewer maternal adverse effects
Ferguson et al. (1990)[53]	Randomised comparison	Nif. vs. Rit.	66	Nifedipine had similar tocolytic efficacy and fewer maternal adverse effects (P < 0.01)
Janky et al. (1990)[54]	Randomised comparison	Nif. vs. Rit.	62	Nifedipine had similar tocolytic efficacy
Meyer et al. (1990)[55]	Randomised comparison	Nif. vs. Rit.	58	Nifedipine had similar tocolytic efficacy and fewer maternal adverse effects
Bracero et al. (1991)[56]	Randomised comparison	Nif. vs. Rit.	49	Nifedipine had similar tocolytic efficacy, fewer maternal adverse effects and lower neonatal morbidity, especially RDS and NICU admission
Glock et al. (1993)[57]	Randomised comparison	Nif. vs. MgSO.	80	Nifedipine had similar tocolytic efficacy and similar maternal adverse effects
Smith et al. (1993)[58]	Randomised comparison	Nif. vs. Terbut.	52	Nifedipine had similar tocolytic efficacy and fewer (not significantly) maternal adverse effects
Kupferminc et al. (1993)[59]	Randomised comparison	Nif. vs. Rit.	71	Nifedipine had similar tocolytic efficacy and fewer maternal adverse effects (P < 0.001)
Papatsonis et al. (1997)[24,25]	Randomised comparison	Nif. vs. Rit.	185	Nifedipine had better tocolytic efficacy, fewer maternal adverse effects and lower neonatal morbidity, especially RDS, NICU admission and intracranial haemorrhage
Koks et al. (1998)[51]	Randomised comparison	Nif. vs. Rit.	102	Nifedipine had similar tocolytic efficacy and fewer maternal adverse effects
El-Sayed et al. (1998)[60]	Randomised comparison	Nif. vs. Dilt.	69	Randomisation after magnesium sulphate tocolysis; gestational age at birth was higher in the nifedipine group and less preterm birth occurred
Garcia-Velasco et al. (1998)[61]	Randomised comparison	Nif. vs. Rit.	52	Nifedipine had similar tocolytic efficacy and fewer maternal adverse effects
Weerakul et al. (2002)[62]	Randomised comparison	Nif. vs. Terbut.	89	Nifedipine had similar tocolytic efficacy and fewer maternal adverse effects, with a similar neonatal outcome

Dilt. = diltiazem; Nif. = nifedipine; Rit. = ritodrine; Terbut. = terbutaline; NICU = neonatal intensive care unit; RDS = respiratory distress syndrome

currently replacing betamimetics as the first-line tocolytic agent in clinical practice. Randomised trials comparing nifedipine with betamimetics, especially ritodrine, have shown that it has an equal tocolytic efficacy with fewer adverse effects.[24,51] Randomised studies comparing nifedipine with other tocolytic agents such as magnesium sulphate, terbutaline or diltiazem have shown a similar tocolytic efficacy with fewer adverse effects. Table 24.2 lists the prospective randomised trials of nifedipine for preterm labour.[24,25,51–62]

Meta-analyses have compared CCBs, mainly orally administered nifedipine, with intravenous ritodrine,[63] with other intravenous betamimetics,[64,65] and with any other tocolytic agent (mainly betamimetics).[66] In these meta-analyses the studies that were included used nifedipine capsules or nifedipine sustained-release (nifedipine retard). They showed that nifedipine has at least an equal efficacy for a delay in delivery for 48 hours,[63–66] and a better tocolytic efficacy for delay of delivery within seven days of initiation of treatment (RR 0.76; 95% CI 0.60–0.97)[66] and prior to 34 weeks of gestation (RR 0.83; 95% CI 0.69–0.99).[66] The number of maternal adverse effects in the nifedipine group is significantly lower than in the betamimetic group (RR 0.32; 95% CI 0.24–0.41),[66] and there are significantly fewer women in the nifedipine group in which cessation of treatment is needed because of severe maternal adverse effects (RR 0.14; 95% CI 0.05–0.36),[66] compared with the betamimetic group.

CCBs are not associated (probably primarily owing to a lack of power) with a reduction in perinatal mortality compared with betamimetics but are associated with decreased perinatal morbidity.[63,65,66] A Cochrane review[66] (Table 24.3) has shown that the use of CCBs (mainly nifedipine) when compared with any other tocolytic agent resulted in a statistically significant increase in gestation at birth (weighted mean difference 0.70 weeks; 95% CI 0.19–1.20), and a reduction in neonatal respiratory distress syndrome (RDS) (RR 0.63; 95% CI 0.46–0.88), necrotising enterocolitis (RR 0.21; 95% CI 0.05–0.96) and intraventricular haemorrhage (RR 0.59; 95% CI 0.36–0.98). The risk reduction for the outcome of RDS gives a number needed to treat (NNT) of 14 (95% CI 8–50) and for intraventricular haemorrhage the NNT is 13 (95% CI 7–100). Admission of neonates to a NICU was also significantly lower in the nifedipine group compared with the betamimetic group (RR 0.78; 95% CI 0.64–0.95). Less neonatal jaundice was also shown for infants whose mothers received CCBs (RR 0.73; 95% CI 0.57–0.93). No statistically significant differences were shown for the outcomes of birthweight, Apgar score less than seven at five minutes, neonatal sepsis or perinatal mortality. The largest trial investigated in these meta-analyses showed that the favourable neonatal outcomes persist even after logistic regression analysis and correction for gestational age at birth.[24,25]

Table 24.3. Calcium channel blockers for inhibiting preterm labour; data from King et al.[66]

	Relative risk	95% Confidence interval
Birth prior to 34 weeks	0.83	0.69–0.99
Birth within 48 hours	0.80	0.61–1.05
Birth within 7 days	0.76	0.60–0.97
Adverse drug reaction	0.32	0.24–0.41
RDS	0.63	0.46–0.88
Neonatal jaundice	0.73	0.57–0.93
Intraventricular haemorrhage	0.59	0.36–0.98
NICU admission	0.78	0.64–0.95

NICU = neonatal intensive care unit; RDS = respiratory distress syndrome

Adverse effects and safety of CCBs

In clinical use in normotensive women, the cardiovascular adverse effects of the CCBs, particularly nifedipine, appear to be minimal and seldom severe enough to withdraw therapy.[67,68] Tachyphylaxis is not induced by CCBs.[42,69]

Teratogenicity

Although evidence of serious adverse effects of CCBs and particularly dihydropyridines in pregnancy is absent, nifedipine, nicardipine and nimodipine are still classified in 'safety group' C.[70] This means that animal studies have revealed adverse effects on fetuses, but there are no controlled studies from women or animals. An observational study by Magee et al.[71] and a case–control study in women[72] did not show any increased risk for congenital anomalies in fetuses exposed to nifedipine in the first trimester. A drug should only be given if the potential benefit justifies the potential risk.[70] This basic tenet is even more important during pregnancy. It should be noted that the doses used in these animal studies exceed the maximum recommended human dose considerably. Also, in the majority of obstetric patients, nifedipine or other CCBs are only used after 12 weeks, when organogenesis is complete.

Cardiovascular adverse effects

Conflicting results have been reported in the literature concerning the effect of nifedipine or nicardipine on uterine blood flow in animal studies.[58,73–85] In hypertensive animals treated with nifedipine, no evidence has been found for any change in uterine blood flow or the occurrence of fetal hypoxia or acidosis.[79,82] The reason might be that the uteroplacental vasculature is not completely dilated in hypertensive animals,[79] so nifedipine can reduce uteroplacental resistance and lower perfusion pressure (maternal systemic blood pressure) without lowering uteroplacental blood flow. In normotensive animals, some studies[78,84] found a decrease in uteroplacental blood flow resulting in fetal hypoxaemia or acidosis while other studies[76,82] found the uteroplacental blood flow to remain unchanged.

The reason for the fetal acidosis in these studies is that they used intravenously administered nifedipine dissolved in ethyl alcohol. The high dose of alcohol results in maternal metabolic acidosis and subsequent fetal acidosis. Data on nifedipine-use associated acidosis in animal experiments are thus not relevant to the human situation. The problem in experimental and animal studies is how to compare the results of different species, and how to extrapolate them to the human situation. The dosage and administration route in animal studies, mainly intravenous, differ from those of clinical human studies in which the administration route is normally oral.

There have so far been no signs, based primarily upon Doppler flow investigations, that nifedipine in humans is associated with a decrease in uteroplacental blood flow.[42]

A study published in 2003 showed that nifedipine was associated with fewer maternal haemodynamic and metabolic adverse effects, in particular, lower maternal heart rate and higher diastolic blood pressure, less hypokalaemia and less hyperglycaemia compared with ritodrine after tocolysis.[86] Treatment cessation with nifedipine is rare compared with betamimetics. The most common adverse effects are tachycardia, palpitations, peripheral oedema, headaches and facial flushing. Less common adverse effects are constipation, dizziness, nausea, bradycardia, fatigue and increased liver enzymes.[19,33]

Neonatal effects

So far there have been no adverse effects reported in neonates exposed to nifedipine *in utero*. A follow-up study[87] of newborns exposed to nifedipine *in utero* because of mild to moderate hypertension in pregnancy showed no difference in development at 18 months. A long-term follow-up study of the Amsterdam nifedipine trial for children exposed *in utero* to nifedipine or ritodrine for the treatment of preterm labour is in progress. As mentioned earlier, a Cochrane meta-analysis has shown that CCBs, especially nifedipine, are associated with a lower perinatal morbidity compared with any other tocolytic agent.[66]

Contraindications for nifedipine tocolysis

The (relative) contraindications for the use of nifedipine are: allergy to nifedipine, suspected intrauterine infection, placenta praevia, placental abruption, severe intrauterine growth restriction, fetal malformation, fetal death *in utero*, significant maternal cardiac disease, hypotension, hepatic dysfunction, and concurrent use of antihypertensive medication. The concurrent use of intravenous betamimetics is not recommended because of a potential hypotensive effect and the possible occurrence of cardiac ischaemia.

The authors recommend caution when using high tocolytic doses of nifedipine (160 mg) in combination with a bolus of intravenous magnesium sulphate.[19] The risk of severe hypotension may be explained by the fact that both drugs are effective CCBs.

Costs

The daily cost of nifedipine at a dosage of 30 mg/day is £0.21 for 10 mg capsules, £0.28 for 30 mg extended-release tablets, and £0.20 for 20 mg sustained-release tablets. The daily cost of ritodrine intravenously at 200 μg/minute is £13.70. An atosiban intravenous bolus injection of 6.75 mg costs £18.12, and an atosiban maintenance dose for a maximum of 48 hours (initial loading infusion 18 mg/hour for three hours followed by a maintenance dose of 6 mg/hour for a maximum of 45 hours) costs £508.64.

Dosage

A systematic review by King *et al.*[88] found ten trials that compared oral nifedipine with other tocolytic agents. Eight of these used ritodrine as the other tocolytic. Initial tocolytic therapy used nifedipine administered orally or sublingually, as either capsules or tablets (whole, or crushed and dissolved in water). Dosage varied from 30 mg/day to 160 mg/day until uterine contractions stopped. The largest trial[34] used a higher dosage of nifedipine (up to 40 mg in the first hour) than most of the included trials. Maintenance dose in this study was 60–160 mg sustained-release nifedipine. All ten trials continued oral nifedipine after the initial treatment but three did not report the total duration of treatment. The maximum dosage of nifedipine should not exceed 160 mg/day.

Protocol for administration of nifedipine for tocolysis

Because nifedipine is not licensed for use as a tocolytic agent, it is recommended that institutions develop specific protocols for administration, including consideration of issues surrounding informed consent.

Conclusions

This literature review has shown that nifedipine is a safe and effective tocolytic agent compared with betamimetics, particularly ritodrine. The higher tocolytic efficacy of nifedipine results in a higher gestational age at birth, and lower neonatal morbidity such as NICU admission, RDS, intracranial haemorrhage and neonatal jaundice. There are significantly fewer adverse effects with nifedipine, and these effects are transient compared with ritodrine. Nifedipine should thus be considered to be the preferred first-line tocolytic agent in the management of preterm labour. Development of an optimum dosage scheme for nifedipine and long-term follow-up studies of children exposed to nifedipine are priorities for the future.

References

1.   Berkowitz GS, Papiernik E. Epidemiology of preterm birth. *Epidemiol Rev* 1993;15:414–43.
2.   Hall M, Danielian P, Lamont RF. The importance of preterm birth. In: Elder MG, Romero R, Lamont RF, editors. *Preterm Labor*. New York: Churchill Livingstone; 1997. p. 1–28.
3.   Mercer BM, Goldenberg RL, Das A, Moawad AH, Iams JD, Meis PJ, *et al*. The preterm prediction study: a clinical risk assessment system. *Am J Obstet Gynecol* 1996;174:1885–93.
4.   Villar J, Ezcurra EJ, Gurtner de la Fuente V, Campodonico L. Preterm delivery syndrome: the unmet need. In: Keirse MJNC, editor. *New Perspectives for the Effective Treatment of Preterm Labour – an International Consensus. Research and Clinical Forums*. Kent: Wells Medical Ltd; 1994. p. 9–38.
5.   Lumley J. The epidemiology of preterm birth. *Baillieres Clin Obstet Gynaecol* 1993;7:477–98.
6.   Hack M, Fanaroff AA. Outcomes of children of extremely low birthweight and gestational age in the 1990's. *Early Hum Dev* 1999;53:193–218.
7.   Morrison JC. Preterm birth: A puzzle worth solving. *Obstet Gynecol* 1990;76:5S–12S.
8.   Kilpatrick SJ, Schlueter MA, Piecuch R, Leonard CH, Rogido M, Sola A. Outcome of infants born at 24–26 weeks' gestation: I. Survival and cost. *Obstet Gynecol* 1997;90:803–8.
9.   Rennie JM. Perinatal management at the lower margin of viability. *Arch Dis Child Fetal Neonatal Ed* 1996;74:F214–8.
10.   Ahner R, Bikas D, Rabl M, Al Kouatly HB, Krauss AN, McCullough LB, *et al*. Ethical implications of aggressive obstetric management at less than 28 weeks of gestation. *Acta Obstet Gynecol Scand* 2001;80:120–5.
11.   Stevenson DK, Wright LL, Lemons JA, Oh W, Korones SB, Papile LA, *et al*. Very low birth weight outcomes of the National Institute of Child Health and Human Development Neonatal Research Network, January 1993 through December 1994. *Am J Obstet Gynecol* 1998;179:1632–9.
12.   Philip AG. Neonatal mortality rate: is further improvement possible? *J Pediatr* 1995;126:427–33.
13.   Wood NS, Marlow N, Costeloe K, Gibson AT, Wilkinson AR. Neurologic and developmental disability after extremely preterm birth. EPICure Study Group. *N Engl J Med* 2000;343:378–84.
14.   Costeloe K, Hennessy E, Gibson AT, Marlow N, Wilkinson AR. The EPICure study: outcomes to discharge from hospital for infants born at the threshold of viability. *Pediatrics* 2000;106:659–71.
15.   Crowley P. Prophylactic corticosteroids for preterm birth. *Cochrane Database Syst Rev* 2000;(2):CD000065.
16.   King JF, Grant A, Keirse MJNC, Chalmers I. Beta-mimetics in preterm labour: an overview of the randomized controlled trials. *Br J Obstet Gynaecol* 1988;95:211–22.
17.   Keirse MJNC. Betamimetic tocolytics in preterm labour. In: Enkin M, Keirse MJNC, Renfrew MJ, Neilson JP, editors. *Pregnancy and Childbirth Module of the Cochrane Database of Systematic Review*. London: BMJ Publishing Group; 1995.
18.   Gyetvai K, Hannah ME, Hodnett ED, Ohlsson A. Tocolytics for preterm labor: a systematic review. *Obstet Gynecol* 1999;94:869–77.
19.   Papatsonis DNM, Lok CAR, Bos JM, Van Geijn HP, Dekker GA. Calcium channel blockers in the management of preterm labor and hypertension in pregnancy. *Eur J Obstet Gynecol Reprod Biol* 2001;97:122–40.
20.   Sorkin EM, Clissold SP, Brogden RN. Nifedipine: a review of its pharmacodynamic and pharmacokinetic properties, and therapeutic efficacy, in ischemic heart disease, hypertension and related cardiovascular disorders. *Drugs* 1985;30:182–274.
21.   Fleckenstein A. *Calcium Antagonism in Heart and Smooth Muscle: Experimental Facts and*

Therapeutic Prospects. New York: John Wiley and Sons; 1983.

22. Abernethy DR, Schwartz JB. Calcium-antagonist drugs. *N Engl J Med* 1999;341:1447–57.

23. Fenakel K, Lurie S. The use of calcium channel blockers in obstetrics and gynecology: a review. *Eur J Obstet Gynecol Reprod Biol* 1990;37:199–203.

24. Papatsonis DN, Van Geijn HP, Ader HJ, Lange FM, Bleker OP, Dekker GA. Nifedipine and ritodrine in the management of preterm labor: a randomized multicenter trial. *Obstet Gynecol* 1997;90:230–4.

25. Papatsonis DN, Kok JH, van Geijn HP, Bleker OP, Ader HJ, Dekker GA. Neonatal effects of nifedipine and ritodrine in the management of preterm labor. *Obstet Gynecol* 2000;95:477–81.

26. Huszar G, Roberts JM. Biochemistry and pharmacology of the myometrium and labor: regulation at the cellular and molecular levels. *Am J Obstet Gynecol* 1991;142:225–37.

27. Caritis SN, Chiao JP, Moore JJ, Ward SM. Myometrial desensitization after ritodrine infusion. *Am J Physiol* 1987;253(4 Pt 1):E410–7.

28. Kolars JC, Schmiedlin-Ren P, Schuetz JD, Fang C, Watkins PB. Identification of rifampin-inducible P450IIIA4 (CYP3A4) in human small bowel enterocytes. *J Clin Invest* 1992;90:1871–8.

29. Kroemer HK, Gautier JC, Beaune P, Henderson C, Wolf CR, Eichelbaum M. Identification of P450 enzymes involved in metabolism of verapamil in humans. *Naunyn Schmiedebergs Arch Pharmacol* 1993;348:332–7.

30. Pichard L, Gillet G, Fabre I, Dalet-Beluche I, Bonfils C, Thenot JP, et al. Identification of the rabbit and human cytochromes P-450IIIA as the major enzymes involved in the N-demethylation of diltiazem. *Drug Metab Dispos* 1990;18:711–9.

31. Guengerich FP, Brian WR, Iwasaki M, Sari MA, Baarnhielm C, Berntsson P. Oxidation of dihydropyridine calcium channel blockers and analogues by human liver cytochrome P-450 IIIA4. *J Med Chem* 1991;34:1838–44.

32. Caritis SN, Darby MJ, Chan L. Pharmacologic treatment of preterm labor. *Clin Obstet Gynecol* 1988;31:635–51.

33. Ray D, Dyson DC. Calcium channel blockers. *Clin Obstet Gynecol* 1995;38:713–21.

34. Follath F, Taeschner W. Clinical pharmacology of calcium antagonists. *J Cardiovasc Pharm* 1988;12 Suppl 6:S98–100.

35. Kelly J, O'Malley K. Clinical pharmacokinetics of calcium antagonists. An update. *Clin Pharmacokinet* 1992;22:416–33.

36. Piepho R. Individualization of calcium entry-blocker dosage for systemic hypertension. *Am J Cardiol* 1985;56:105H–11H.

37. Reid J, Meredith P, Donnelly R, Elliott H. Pharmacokinetics of calcium antagonists. *J Cardiovasc Pharmacol* 1988;12 Suppl 7:S22–6.

38. Van Wisse M. Tweede generatie calcium antagonisten. *Pharma Selecta* 1991;1:13–20.

39. Ferguson JE, Schutz T, Pershe R, Stevenson DK, Blaschke T. Nifedipine pharmacokinetics during preterm labor tocolysis. *Am J Obstet Gynecol* 1989;161:1485–90.

40. Kleinbloesem CH, Van Brummelen P, Van de Linde JA, Voogd PJ, Breimer DD. Nifedipine kinetics and dynamics in healthy subjects. *Clin Pharm Ther* 1984;35:742–9.

41. Murad F. Drugs used for the treatment of angina: organic nitrates, calcium-channel blockers, and β-adrenergic antagonists. In: Hardmann JG, Limbird LE, Molinoff PB, Ruddon RW, Gilman AG, editors. *Goodman & Gillmans, the Pharmacological Basis of Therapeutics.* New York: McGraw Hill; 1996. p. 764–83.

42. Childress CH, Katz VL. Nifedipine and its indications in obstetrics and gynecology. *Obstet Gynecol* 1994;83:616–24.

43. Kirsten R, Nelson K, Kirsten D, Heintz B. Clinical pharmacokinetics of vasodilators. Part II. *Clin Pharmacokinet* 1998;35:9–36.

44. Prevost RR, Akl SA, Whybrew WD, Sibai BM. Oral nifedipine pharmacokinetics in pregnancy-induced hypertension. *Pharmacotherapy* 1992;12:174–7.

45. Foster TS, Hamann SR, Richards VR, Bryant PJ, Graves DA, McAllister RG. Nifedipine kinetics and bioavailability after single intravenous and oral doses in normal subjects. *J Clin Pharmacol* 1983;23:161–70.

46. Grundy JS, Foster RT. The nifedipine gastrointestinal therapeutic system (GITS). Evaluation of pharmaceutical, pharmacokinetic and pharmacological properties. *Clin Pharmacokinet* 1996;30:28–51.

47. Crome P, Muller FO, Wijayawardhana P, Groenewoud G, Hundt HK, Leighton G, et al. Single dose and steady-state pharmacokinetic profile of nifedipine GITS tablets in healthy elderly and young volunteers. *Drug Invest* 1993;5:193–9.

48. Scholz H. Pharmacological aspects of calcium channel blockers. *Cardiovasc Drugs Ther* 1997;10 Suppl 3:869–72.

49. Murdoch D, Brogden RN. Sustained release nifedipine formulations. An appraisal of their current uses and prospective roles in the treatment of hypertension, ischaemic heart disease and peripheral

vascular disorders. *Drugs* 1991;41:737–9.

50.   Ulmsten U, Andersson KR, Wingerup L. Treatment of premature labor with the calcium antagonist nifedipine. *Arch Gynecol* 1980;229:1–5.

51.   Koks CA, Brolmann HA, de Kleine MJ, Manger PA. A randomized comparison of nifedipine and ritodrine for suppression of preterm labor. *Eur J Obstet Gynecol Reprod Biol* 1998;77:171–6.

52.   Read MD, Wellby DE. The use of a calcium antagonist (nifedipine) to suppress preterm labour. *Br J Obstet Gynaecol* 1986;93:933–7.

53.   Ferguson JE, Dyson DC, Schutz T, Stevenson DK. A comparison of tocolysis with nifedipine or ritodrine: analysis of efficacy and maternal, fetal, and neonatal outcome. *Am J Obstet Gynecol* 1990;163:105–11.

54.   Janky E, Leng JJ, Cormier PH, Salamon R, Meynard J. A randomized study of the treatment of threatened premature labor. Nifedipine versus ritodrine. [French]. *J Gynecol Obstet Biol Reprod (Paris)* 1990;19:478–82.

55.   Meyer WR, Randall HW, Graves WL. Nifedipine versus ritodrine for suppressing preterm labor. *J Reprod Med* 1990;35:649–53.

56.   Bracero LA, Leikin E, Kirshenbaum N, Tejani N. Comparison of nifedipine and ritodrine for the treatment of preterm labor. *Am J Perinatol* 1991;8:365–9.

57.   Glock JL, Morales WJ. Efficacy and safety of nifedipine versus magnesium sulfate in the management of preterm labor: a randomized study. *Am J Obstet Gynecol* 1993;169:960–4.

58.   Smith CS, Woodland MB. Clinical comparison of oral nifedipine and subcutaneous terbutaline for initial tocolysis. *Am J Perinatol* 1993;10:280–4.

59.   Kupferminc M, Lessing JB, Yaron Y, Peyser MR. Nifedipine versus ritodrine for supression of preterm labour. *Br J Obstet Gynaecol* 1993;100:1090–4.

60.   El-Sayed YY, Holbrook RH Jr, Gibson R, Chitkara U, Druzin ML, Baba D. Diltiazem for maintenance tocolysis of preterm labor: comparison to nifedipine in a randomized trial. *J Matern Fetal Med* 1998;7:217–21.

61.   Garcia-Velasco JA, Gonzalez Gonzalez A. A prospective, randomized trial of nifedipine vs. ritodrine in threatened preterm labor. *Int J Gynaecol Obstet* 1998;61:239–44.

62.   Weerakul W, Chittacharoen A, Suthutvoravut S. Nifedipine versus terbutaline in management of preterm labor. *Int J Gynaecol Obstet* 2002;76:311–3.

63.   Oei SG, Mol BW, de Kleine MJ, Brolmann HA. Nifedipine versus ritodrine for suppression of preterm labor; a meta-analysis. *Acta Obstet Gynecol Scand* 1999;78:783–8.

64.   Ray JG. Meta-analysis of nifedipine versus beta-sympathomimetic agents for tocolysis during preterm labour. *J Soc Obstet Gynaecol Can* 1998;20:259–69.

65.   Tsatsaris V, Papatsonis DNM, Goffinet F, Dekker GA, Carbonne B. Tocolysis with nifedipine or beta-adrenergic agonists: a meta-analysis. *Obstet Gynecol* 2001;97:840–7.

66.   King JF, Flenady VJ, Papatsonis DN, Dekker GA, Carbonne B. Calcium channel blockers for inhibiting preterm labour. *Cochrane Database Syst Rev* 2003;(1):CD002255.

67.   Ferguson JE, Dyson DC, Holbrook RH Jr, Schutz T, Stevenson DK. Cardiovascular and metabolic effects associated with nifedipine and ritodrine tocolysis. *Am J Obstet Gynecol* 1989;161:788–95.

68.   Walker JJ, Mathers A, Bjornsson S, Cameron AD, Fairlie FM. The effect of acute and chronic antihypertensive therapy on maternal and fetoplacental Doppler velocimetry. *Eur J Obstet Gynecol Reprod Biol* 1992;43:193–9.

69.   Nayler WG. *Calcium Antagonists*. San Diego: Academic Press; 1989.

70.   Briggs GG, Freeman RK, Yaffe S. *Drugs in Pregnancy and Lactation*. Philadelphia: Lippincott Williams & Wilkins; 2002.

71.   Magee LA, Schick B, Donnenfeld AE, Sage SR, Conover B, Cook L, et al. The safety of calcium channel blockers in human pregnancy: a prospective, multicenter cohort study. *Am J Obstet Gynecol* 1996;174:823–8.

72.   Sorensen HT, Czeizel AE, Rockenbauer M, Steffensen FH, Olsen J. The risk of limb deficiencies and other congenital abnormalities in children exposed *in utero* to calcium channel blockers. *Acta Obstet Gynecol Scand* 2001;80:397–401.

73.   Csapo AI, Puri CP, Tarro S, Henzl MR. Deactivation of the uterus during normal and premature labor by the calcium antagonist nicardipine. *Am J Obstet Gynecol* 1982;142:483–91.

74.   Holbrook RH, Lirette M, Katz M. Cardiovascular and tocolytic effects of nicardipine HCL in the pregnant rabbit: comparison with ritodrine HCL. *Obstet Gynecol* 1987;69:83–6.

75.   Lirette M, Holbrook RH, Katz M. Effect of nicardipine HCL on prematurely induced uterine activity in the pregnant rabbit. *Obstet Gynecol* 1985;65:31–5.

76.   Veille JC, Bissonnette JM, Hohimer AR. The effect of a calcium blocker (nifedipine) on uterine blood flow in the pregnant goat. *Am J Obstet Gynecol* 1986;154:1160–3.

77.   Ducsay CA, Thompson JS, Wu AT, Novy MJ. Effects of calcium entry blocker (nicardipine) tocolysis in rhesus macaques: fetal plasma concentrations and cardiorespiratory changes. *Am J Obstet Gynecol* 1987;157:1482–6.

78. Harake B, Gilbert RD, Ashwal S, Power GG. Nifedipine: effects on fetal and maternal hemodynamics in pregnant sheep. *Am J Obstet Gynecol* 1987;157:1003–8.

79. Ahokas RA, Sibai BM, Mabie WC, Anderson GD. Nifedipine does not adversely affect uteroplacental blood flow in the hypertensive term-pregnant rat. *Am J Obstet Gynecol* 1988;159:1440–5.

80. Holbrook RH Jr, Voss EM, Gibson RN. Ovine fetal cardiorespiratory response to nicardipine. *Am J Obstet Gynecol* 1989;161:718–21.

81. Parisi VM, Salinas J, Stockmar EJ. Fetal vascular responses to maternal nicardipine administration in the hypertensive ewe. *Am J Obstet Gynecol* 1989;161:1035–9.

82. Furuhashi N, Tsujiei M, Kimura H, Nagae H, Yajima A. Effects of nifedipine on placental blood flow, placental weight and fetal weight in normotensive and spontaneously hypertensive rats. *Gynecol Obstet Invest* 1992;34:193–6.

83. Matsuda Y, Ikenoue T, Matsuda K, Sameshima H, Ibara S, Hokanishi H, et al. The effect of nicardipine on maternal and fetal hemodynamics and uterine blood flow in chronically instrumented pregnant goats. *Asia Oceania J Obstet Gynaecol* 1993;19:191–8.

84. Blea CW, Barnard JM, Magness RR, Phernetton TM, Hendricks SK. Effect of nifedipine on fetal and maternal hemodynamics and blood gases in the pregnant ewe. *Am J Obstet Gynecol* 1997;176:922–30.

85. Golichowski AM, Hathaway DR, Fineberg N, Peleg D. Tocolytic and hemodynamic effects of nifedipine in the ewe. *Am J Obstet Gynecol* 1985;151:1134–40.

86. Papatsonis DN, van Geijn HP, Bleker OP, Ader HJ, Dekker GA. Hemodynamic and metabolic effects after nifedipine and ritodrine tocolysis. *Int J Gynaecol Obstet* 2003;82:5–10.

87. Bortolus R, Ricci E, Chatenoud L, Parazzini F. Nifedipine administered in pregnancy: effect on the development of children at 18 months. *BJOG* 2000;107:792–4.

88. King JF, Flenady V, Papatsonis DNM, Dekker GA, Carbonne B. Calcium channel blockers for inhibiting preterm labour; a systematic review of the evidence and a protocol for administration of nifedipine. *Aust N Z J Obstet Gynaecol* 2003;43:192–8.

Chapter 25

Oxytocin antagonists for tocolysis

Roberto Romero, Tinnakorn Chaiworapongsa and
Luís F Gonçalves

Introduction

Treatment of preterm labour with the oxytocin receptor antagonist atosiban was
approved in January 2000 by the European Agency for the Evaluation of Medicinal
Products (EMEA). This chapter will briefly review the rationale for the use of an
oxytocin antagonist in the management of preterm labour, as well as the clinical
pharmacology of atosiban.

The role of oxytocin in labour

The precise role of oxytocin in parturition has been controversial for decades. While
some investigators have proposed that 'oxytocin is the primary maternal factor that
activates the uterus during labour in all mammals',[1] others have argued that oxytocin
may be important in the second or third stages of labour,[2] but not in the initiation of
parturition.

Fuchs[1] has proposed the primary stimulant of myometrial contractility during labour
to be:

- myometrial-specific
- available in sufficient quantities to initiate labour (i.e. be stored and available for
  immediate release)
- secreted in response to maternal and fetal stimuli
- tightly regulated in terms of its biological effects in order to avoid untimely
  initiation of labour (i.e. via availability of its receptors).

Fuchs[1] further proposed that oxytocin is the only compound to meet these
requirements. Obviously, the participation of one hormone does not exclude the role of
others. For example, oxytocin can induce the production of prostaglandins by amnion
and decidua, which in turn can mediate some of the biological effects of oxytocin in
labour.[3,4]

To date, the evidence supporting a role for oxytocin in parturition has been largely
indirect and includes the following:

1. Oxytocin is a potent stimulant of myometrial contractility capable of inducing
    labour at term. Indeed, oxytocin remains the most widespread method of
    induction of labour worldwide. However, this must be considered evidence of

feasibility rather than of actual participation in the physiological process of labour. For example, although the administration of bacterial endotoxin to pregnant animals induces labour,[5,6] this does not imply that bacterial endotoxin is a physiological mediator of parturition.

2.   Plasma concentrations of oxytocin increase during labour in animals (e.g. rabbits,[7] sheep,[8] cows,[9] rats,[10] goats,[11] pigs[12] and monkeys[13]). In non-mammalian species, the concentration of oxytocin-related peptides such as arginine vasotocin (in chickens)[14] and annetocin (in earthworms)[15] increases during oviposition. The timing of the increase in plasma concentrations varies among mammals.[16] In most species, the peak plasma oxytocin concentrations occur around the time of expulsion of the conceptus[8,9,12,13,17] while in others, such as the rat, the concentrations are increased throughout labour but peak during expulsion.[10,16]

The data on humans is contradictory and this has been attributed to three methodological issues.[16] Firstly, oxytocin is secreted in a pulsatile manner, making frequent sampling necessary to detect changes reliably in plasma concentration and characterise pulsatile changes.[18–21] Secondly, the hormone degrades in blood by the action of placental oxytocinase, also known as cysteine aminopeptidase.[22,23] Accurate determination of plasma concentrations thus requires the use of oxytocinase inhibitors to blood (e.g. EDTA and phenanthrolene). Thirdly, the specificity of the antibody used in the immunoassay for oxytocin is important because some antibodies cross-react with oxytocin precursors.[16,24]

Fuchs et al.[18] reported that oxytocin is secreted in a pulsatile manner during pregnancy (Figures 25.1 and 25.2) and that pulse frequency was higher in women in the first stage of labour than in those not in labour at term, and that a further increase in pulse frequency occurred during the second and third stages of labour (Figure 25.3). Burd et al.[21] also reported an increased pulsatile secretion of oxytocin in three of six women during the first stage of labour and that these pulses were associated with uterine contractions. Two women in the first stage did not have detectable pulsatile secretion, and one with hypocontractile labour had a non-pulsatile profile. In contrast, in a third study using a similarly rigorous technique no increase in oxytocin pulsatility was observed during the first stage of labour.[20] It is interesting to note that Fuchs et al.[18] reported that the magnitude of the pulses observed during the course of labour was similar to that created by a bolus of oxytocin of 4–16 mU which induced uterine contractions.

3.   Oxytocin gene expression has been demonstrated in decidua and fetal membranes.[25] Furthermore, an increase in oxytocin gene expression has been reported during labour in these tissues in both rats[26] and women.[25] Oxytocin receptors are present on both myometrial and decidual cells.[27] This suggests that locally synthesised oxytocin may participate as a paracrine or autocrine mediator in parturition, rather than as a circulating hormone.[28,29]

4.   The administration of the oxytocin antagonist atosiban results in a delay in delivery in women with spontaneous preterm labour[30] and suppresses uterine contractility in several species, including non-human primates.[31–33] Furthermore, atosiban eliminates the nocturnal increase in uterine activity, which precedes the spontaneous onset of labour in primates.[33]

5.   The myometrial response of oxytocin is dependent on gestational age: oxytocin sensitivity increases with advancing gestational age.[34,35] This response seems to be mediated by oxytocin receptors whose numbers, but not affinity, increase with advancing gestational age.[34] The oxytocin/oxytocin receptor system thus provides a mechanism to regulate the biological effects of oxytocin.

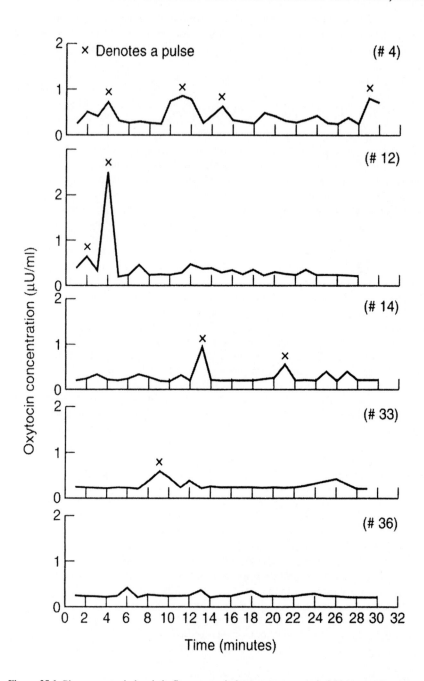

Figure 25.1. Plasma oxytocin levels in five women in late pregnancy not in labour; samples were collected at one-minute intervals from in-dwelling catheters in the right arm; data plots were chosen to show the highest and lowest pulse frequencies and amplitudes in each group; each identified pulse is denoted with a cross; reproduced with permission from Fuchs *et al.*[18]

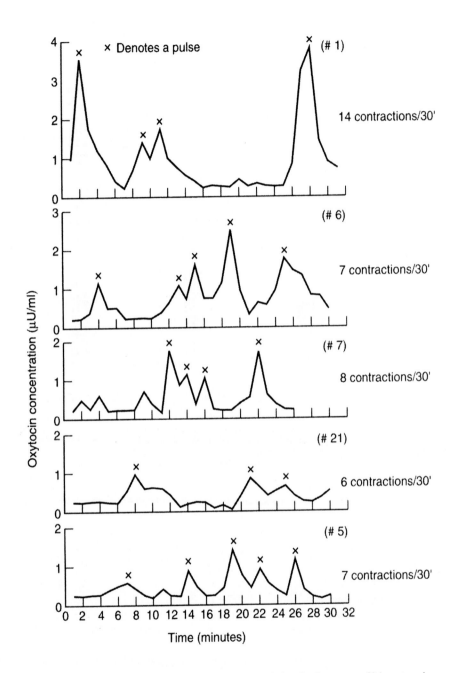

Figure 25.2. Plasma oxytocin levels in five pregnant women during the first stages of labour (cervix 2–5 cm dilated); data plots were chosen to show the highest and lowest pulse frequencies and amplitudes in each group; all women in this group had oxytocin pulses during the study period; reproduced with permission from Fuchs *et al.*[18]

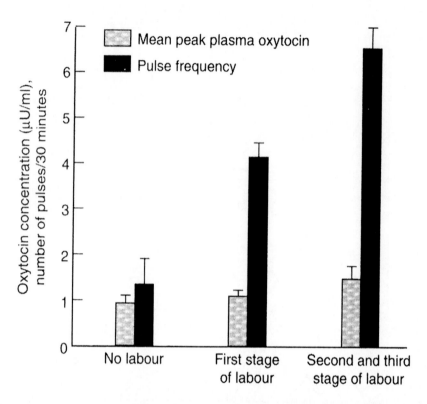

Figure 25.3. Plasma oxytocin pulse frequency and amplitude determined in women at term, not in labour (n=11), during the first stage of labour (n=13), and combined second and third stages of labour (n=8); oxytocin concentrations were measured by radioimmunoassay in samples collected at one-minute intervals for 30 minutes in each group (values greater than baseline ± 3 SD were considered a pulse); means of all pulses in individual patients were calculated – values shown represent the mean of these means ± SEM (standard error of the mean); reproduced with permission from Fuchs *et al.*[18]

6.   Oxytocin stimulates prostaglandin $F_{2\alpha}$ ($PGF_{2\alpha}$) production by the decidua[36] and PGE_2 by amnion cells.[37] This effect is relevant because considerable evidence supports the participation of these arachidonic acid metabolites in the mechanism of human parturition.[36,38–40] The effect of oxytocin on $PGF_{2\alpha}$ production is accomplished at oxytocin concentrations that are lower than those required to induce myometrial contractility. Oxytocin would therefore seem to have a dual effect in the stimulation of myometrial contractility, a direct effect on myometrium and an indirect effect mediated via prostaglandins.[36]

Of major interest have been the results of gene deletion studies. Gene deletion has thus far been reported for oxytocin but not for oxytocin receptor. Mice lacking oxytocin (-/-) deliver at term, indicating that oxytocin is not required for labour, although it is for the ejection of milk.[41,42] Nevertheless, experimental observations in wild and null mice (-/-) suggest that the oxytocin/oxytocin receptor system is important for 'focusing' the timing of the onset of labour.[43] In oxytocin-deficient mice, oxytocin administration at low doses delayed the spontaneous onset of labour, while at higher doses it induced preterm labour in the absence of progesterone withdrawal.[44] Furthermore, oxytocin-induced preterm labour could not be prevented by the administration of indomethacin, suggesting that this phenomenon is independent of prostaglandins and probably due to a direct effect of oxytocin on the myometrium.[16,44] These observations have been interpreted as indicating that the oxytocin/oxytocin receptor system is important for focusing the onset of labour.[44] The expression of the oxytocin receptor in the ovary is crucial for the production of progesterone and pregnancy maintenance (oxytocin has been demonstrated to have luteotrophic actions).[45–47] However, when luteolysis occurs, there is a decrease in the expression of oxytocin receptor in the ovary and an increase in the myometrium. The net effect of this shift is to decrease progesterone production by the ovary and stimulate uterine contractility.[16,44] However, in humans, luteolysis is not the main mechanism for progesterone withdrawal.

Fuchs et al.[48] have demonstrated that the cervical mucosa of the cow has oxytocin receptors and that their numbers increase near term. Preliminary evidence indicates that incubation of oxytocin with cervical mucosa results in the stimulation of PGE$_2$ into the media. Oxytocin may thus also play an indirect role in the process of cervical ripening.[48]

Oxytocin and oxytocin receptors in preterm labour

Even if the available evidence suggests a role for oxytocin in spontaneous parturition at term, this does not necessarily indicate that oxytocin is involved in the mechanisms of preterm labour. A small study has demonstrated that the concentration of oxytocin in plasma obtained from the mother, the umbilical artery and vein are higher in women in preterm labour than in pregnant women at term not in labour.[49] No currently available studies describe the pulsatile pattern of oxytocin in women in preterm labour. Contradictory data exist regarding the concentration of oxytocin receptors in myometrium of women in preterm labour. While Fuchs et al.[36] have reported an increase in the receptor concentration during the initiation of labour, a more recent large study by Bossmar et al.[50] did not confirm these observations. Of interest is that there was a wide variation among women in oxytocin receptor concentration.[50] Further studies are required to clarify the role of oxytocin and its receptors in preterm labour.

Atosiban – chemical structure, mechanism of action and basic pharmacology

Chemical structure and mechanism of action

Atosiban [1-deamino-2D-Tyr(OEt)-4Tyr-8-Orn]-OT is a synthetic compound derived from both arginine vasopressin (AVP) and oxytocin by a substitution of ornithine in position 8.[51,52] Atosiban is a competitive oxytocin receptor antagonist that binds to the oxytocin receptor in the myometrial cell membrane resulting in a dose-dependent inhibition of oxytocin-stimulated inositol trisphosphate (IP$_3$) production and, consequently, of calcium release from the sarcoplasmic reticulum, causing a reduction of myometrial contractility.[53,54] Atosiban also reduces the oxytocin-stimulated release of prostaglandins in the rat and human myometrial tissue in vitro.[55] Experiments in animals[33,56] and humans[57–59] have demonstrated that atosiban is a potent oxytocin antagonist with minimal vasopressor and antidiuretic activity.

Pharmacokinetics

When given by the intravenous route, the mean plasma concentration of atosiban increases linearly with the dose administered, reaching a plateau in one to two hours.[58,60-63] The pharmacokinetics of atosiban were studied in eight healthy nonpregnant subjects (five women and three men),[61] eight pregnant women not in labour[60] and eight pregnant women in labour.[58] The volume of distribution, plasma clearance and biological half-life for each group are displayed in Table 25.1. After completion of the infusion, the plasma concentration of atosiban was shown to decline in a bi-exponential manner.[58,61,62,64,65] Intranasal administration of atosiban results in a more gradual increase in plasma concentration, reaching a peak after 10 to 45 minutes, followed by a more gradual decrease, with measurable plasma concentrations two hours after administration.[1] Although atosiban crosses the placenta, the mean plasma concentrations in the umbilical vein are only 10 to 12% of the mean plasma concentration in the maternal uterine vein.[58,60]

Clinical studies in pregnant women

Pilot studies

The first clinical study designed to test the effect of an oxytocin antagonist on uterine activity in pregnant women was reported by Akerlund et al. in 1987.[66] This study demonstrated that successful tocolysis was achieved (defined as a decrease in the contraction frequency to less than two contractions per 20 minutes). The entry criteria for this study were:

- preterm gestation (gestational age 27 to 35 weeks)
- increased uterine contractility, defined as four or more uterine contractions in 20 minutes, which persisted despite two hours of bed rest
- a Westin cervical score (modified Bishop score ranging from 0 to 10 which includes dilatation, effacement, station, consistency and position of the cervix) above 3 and below 6.

Women with contraindications for tocolysis were excluded from the study (e.g. placental abruption, moderate to heavy marginal bleeding, signs of chorioamnionitis, prelabour rupture of the membranes (PROM), pre-eclampsia and uterine or fetal congenital anomalies).

Thirteen women with the diagnosis of preterm labour received an intravenous infusion of atosiban with doses ranging from 10 to 100 µg/minute in 5.5% glucose for one to ten hours. Eighty-four percent (11/13) of the women met the criteria for successful tocolysis. Over half of the women (7/11) required tocolysis with ritodrine

---

Table 25.1. Volume of distribution, plasma clearance and biological half-life of atosiban; all values are given as mean ± SD; adapted from references 58, 60 and 61

	Volume of distribution (l)	Plasma clearance (l/h)	Biological half-life (min)
8 nonpregnant subjects[61]	13.1 ± 3.8	23.5 ± 7.6	39.0 ± 4.1
8 pregnant subjects not in labour[60]	13.8 ± 5.8	41.8 ± 8.2	18.0 ± 3.0
8 pregnant subjects in labour[103]	18.3 ± 6.8	41.8 ± 0.2	18.0 ± 3.0

one to four days after discontinuation of atosiban treatment and two of these women delivered preterm. Three women were given 'prophylactic ritodrine' for over a week after atosiban administration and one delivered preterm. Three women did not receive any additional tocolysis after atosiban treatment and all delivered at term. The overall rate of preterm delivery was 23% (3/13). Although the explicit objective of the study was not to determine the optimal dose required for tocolysis, all women receiving an infusion of 25 µg/minute had a significant inhibition of uterine contractions. The total dose administered ranged from 1.5 to 5.4 mg, and the duration of the treatment ranged from 1 to 10 hours. Six of the seven women receiving a total dose of 4.7 mg or more had their uterine contractions arrested completely. No significant adverse effects were detected during atosiban infusion (including palpitations, tremor, hypo/hypertension, and maternal or fetal tachycardia).

A second phase II trial was conducted in Denmark by Andersen and co-workers.[67] This study was also designed to assess the efficacy of atosiban as a tocolytic agent in preterm labour. The primary outcomes of this study were somewhat different than those in the first phase II trial. In this case, successful tocolysis was defined as complete arrest of uterine contractions after 90 minutes of infusion and successful treatment of preterm labour (defined as pregnancy progression to term with no cervical changes). Entry criteria were similar to those in the previous study:

- preterm gestation (less than 36 weeks)
- four or more uterine contractions in 20 minutes persisting despite two hours of bed rest
- a Westin cervical score above 3 and below 7
- cervical dilatation below 4 cm
- intact membranes.

Standard contraindications for tocolysis were considered to be exclusion criteria (e.g. placental abruption, chorioamnionitis, severe pre-eclampsia and uterine and fetal malformations). Twelve women met the inclusion criteria (four women reported in this trial had been included in the first phase II report).[66]

Atosiban was administered intravenously at a rate of 25 to 100 µg/minute in 5.5% glucose. After uterine activity had been arrested for one hour, the infusion continued for 60 minutes, after which it was titrated to the lowest infusion rate able to sustain complete tocolysis during this time. Once tocolysis was achieved, all women received oral prophylactic ritodrine (10 mg) four times a day for one week. If the woman continued to contract after 90 minutes of atosiban infusion, conventional tocolysis with ritodrine was initiated. Complete tocolysis was achieved in 50% (6/12) of the women, four progressed to term and two delivered preterm (two and three weeks, respectively, after atosiban treatment). Three women (25%) experienced a reduction of uterine contractility but did not achieve total inhibition of uterine activity. This was considered to be 'partial tocolysis'. All three of these women delivered preterm; two had twin gestations. In three women, no reduction in uterine activity was achieved after 90 minutes of infusion. All three of these women were at 27 weeks and were subsequently treated with ritodrine. One woman delivered at term, and the others delivered at 36 and 28 weeks, respectively. No significant adverse effects for the mother or fetus were observed.

An early randomised, placebo-controlled trial with rescue tocolysis in women with preterm uterine contractility without cervical changes

The first placebo-controlled, double-blind, randomised clinical trial with tocolytic rescue evaluating the efficacy of intravenous atosiban on women with increased preterm uterine contractility was reported by Goodwin *et al.* in 1994.[68] Women with documented cervical change were excluded.

Inclusion criteria were:

- gestational age between 20 and 36 weeks
- the presence of four or more uterine contractions in one hour
- cervix less than 3 cm dilated, and effaced less than 80%
- no changes in the cervix following one hour of observation.

Women meeting the inclusion criteria were randomised to bed rest, hydration and atosiban (n=56) versus bed rest, hydration and placebo (n=56). Atosiban was administered for two hours (300 μg/minute) and then discontinued. The cervix and the frequency of contractions were re-evaluated at the end of the two-hour period. Women who continued to contract after the observational period were treated with either magnesium sulphate or terbutaline at the discretion of the clinician.

The administration of atosiban was associated with a significant decrease in the frequency of uterine contractions per hour (placebo group: 12 ± 7.2 contractions/hour [mean $\pm$ SD] versus atosiban group: 6.9 ± 6.2 contractions/hour; $P=0.004$). The mean percentage decrease in contraction frequency was 55.3% for women receiving atosiban, and only 26.7% for those randomised to the placebo group ($P<0.001$). Complete cessation of uterine activity occurred in 25% (14/56) of the women treated with atosiban and only 5% (3/56) of those in the placebo group ($P<0.01$). Eleven women (20%) in the atosiban group and 18 (32%) in the placebo group received tocolysis. However, there was no difference in the mean gestational age at birth between the two groups (placebo: 38.3 ± 2.1 versus atosiban: 37.8 ± 3.5). Nine percent of the women in the atosiban group (5/56) and 4% of those receiving placebo (2/56) delivered within 48 hours. Adverse effects were limited to only one woman who experienced nausea and vomiting.

An observational study of atosiban in the treatment of preterm labour

The first study aiming to determine the effect of an atosiban infusion (300 μg/minute) on the course and outcome of preterm labour was reported by Goodwin *et al.* in 1992.[69] Women were included based on the following criteria:

- 20 to 36 weeks of gestation
- six or more uterine contractions in one hour
- documented cervical change.

Women with PROM, fetal distress, evidence of systemic or uterine infection, undiagnosed vaginal bleeding, major medical disorders or prior tocolysis were excluded from the study. This study did not have a control group.

Atosiban was administered at a rate of 300 μg/minute intravenously for up to 6 hours until contractions stopped. If the investigator considered that tocolysis with atosiban was inadequate, women were given another tocolytic agent. Treatment failure was defined as either unplanned delivery within 48 hours of the beginning of atosiban infusion or the requirement for an alternative tocolytic regimen. Women who did not meet these criteria were considered treatment successes. Of the 62 women initially enrolled in the study, one had PROM one hour after the initiation of the therapy and was excluded from further analysis. Among the remaining women, 62.3% (38/61) had complete cessation of uterine contractions for 4.6 ± 3.2 hours while receiving atosiban. Eight-two percent (50/61) of the women exhibited a decrease of 50% or more in the frequency of uterine contractions. Overall, 70.5% of the women had either a prolongation of pregnancy of at least 58 hours or were not required to change to an alternative tocolytic agent. The treatment failure rate was 29.5% (18/61): 23% (14/61) received another tocolytic agent and 6.6% (4/61) delivered within 48 hours of the initiation of therapy. Seventy-eight percent (42/54) of the women with cervical dilatation below 3 cm achieved successful tocolysis. Only four women experienced adverse effects such as nausea, vomiting and chest pain.

The design of clinical trials to test the efficacy and safety of tocolysis

Treatment of preterm labour with tocolytic agents and corticosteroids has become standard obstetric practice.[70,71] The delay in delivery afforded by tocolysis is believed to contribute to the beneficial effects of corticosteroid administration in reducing the incidence of respiratory distress syndrome, intraventricular haemorrhage and perinatal mortality.[72-74] The history of tocolytic drugs was presented in detail recently by Keirse.[75] Three different study designs could be used to test the efficacy of a new agent:

- a placebo-controlled trial
- an equivalence trial (a comparison of two active agents)
- a placebo with 'rescue tocolysis' trial.

The efficacy of tocolysis in delaying delivery was established with placebo-controlled trials.[76-82] This type of trial led to the approval by the FDA of ritodrine for the treatment of preterm labour.[77,83] The last placebo-controlled trial of tocolysis was conducted by the Canadian Preterm Labor Investigators Group, which compared ritodrine versus placebo and concluded that ritodrine administration was associated with a delay in delivery of 48 hours but did not reduce perinatal morbidity and mortality.[77] However, this investigational approach is considered not acceptable by many clinicians who would not agree to participate in a trial requiring that tocolysis be withheld in a woman at risk for preterm delivery because of the substantial risks associated with prematurity. For this reason, placebo-controlled trials have not been conducted in the last ten years.

The most common alternative used in recent years has been equivalence trials of new agents against established tocolytic agents (e.g. β-adrenergic agents). While designing a clinical trial to determine the safety and efficacy of atosiban for the treatment of preterm labour for consideration of the FDA, the Robert Wood Johnson Company (USA) considered conducting an equivalence trial comparing atosiban with ritodrine to delay delivery for 48 hours. However, such a trial was not thought feasible because of the infrequent use of ritodrine in the USA (< 20% of the preterm labour cases).

The third option, a novel design in clinical trials of tocolysis, was to conduct a study in which women who met a strict definition of premature labour were allowed to receive placebo treatment for at least one hour and thereafter permitted alternative tocolytics as 'rescue therapy'. This type of trial was used for the study of the efficacy and safety of atosiban in the USA.

A placebo-controlled trial with tocolytic rescue

A large prospective randomised double-blind, placebo-controlled trial with tocolytic rescue was conducted to test the efficacy and safety of atosiban for the treatment of preterm labour.[30] Women were eligible for the trial if they had preterm labour with intact membranes, a gestational age between 20 weeks and 33 weeks and 6 days, live fetus(es), and consented to participate in the trial. The diagnosis of preterm labour required the presence of four or more uterine contractions over 30 minutes, each lasting at least 40 seconds, and documented cervical change. The cervical change criteria were met when either of the following was present:

- a single cervical examination demonstrating dilatation of 1 cm to less than 3 cm and effacement of at least 75% or dilatation of 3 cm with effacement of at least 50%
- multiple cervical examinations demonstrating a 1 cm increase in cervical dilatation, or an increase in effacement of 50%.

Women were randomly assigned to receive intravenous therapy with atosiban or matching placebo for at least one hour. Assigned short-term treatment was planned for up to 48 hours, followed by maintenance therapy with the assigned treatment. Active drug and placebo were administered at the same volume and rate. Short-term intravenous therapy began with a bolus of the initial study drug (6.75 mg for atosiban) administered over one minute. This was immediately followed by an infusion of 300 μg/minute of atosiban for three hours, then 100 μg/minute of atosiban for up to 45 hours. Intravenous treatment was discontinued when uterine quiescence, progression of labour, or rupture of membranes occurred. Uterine quiescence was defined as either 12 consecutive hours of four or fewer contractions per hour (lasting 40 seconds or more) or 48 hours of intravenous infusion without progression of labour requiring the use of an alternative tocolytic. Labour was considered to have progressed and the woman became eligible for rescue tocolysis if either of the following occurred after at least one hour of observation during intravenous treatment:

- cervical effacement of 75% or more (0.5 cm or less) with no decrease in the frequency or intensity of contractions and continued cervical change (at least a 1 cm change in dilatation or effacement)
- cervical dilatation of 4 cm or more with a 1 cm increase since the previous cervical examination.

Women could receive rescue therapy with an alternative tocolytic of the investigator's choice after discontinuation of the study drug. To receive rescue therapy women were to meet the criteria for progression of labour while receiving their assigned intravenous drug. Atosiban was not used as rescue therapy for women allocated to the placebo group. Women who achieved uterine quiescence received maintenance therapy via a subcutaneous infusion of either atosiban or matching placebo.

Maintenance therapy began as a subcutaneous infusion of 0.004 ml/minute (30 μg/minute for atosiban) to the end of the 36th week of gestation, the time of delivery or the progression of labour necessitating an alternative tocolytic, whichever occurred first. Once maintenance began, alternative tocolytics were permitted only after a subsequent intravenous study drug infusion when progression of labour was observed. Intravenous therapy for additional episodes of preterm labour was permitted. Other tocolytic agents were not permitted concomitantly with the study drug.

The primary endpoint was the time (days) to delivery or therapeutic failure (progression of labour necessitating an alternative tocolytic), whichever occurred first. The secondary endpoints were the proportion of women successfully treated up to 24 hours, 48 hours and seven days after the start of acute intravenous therapy. Maternal and fetal adverse events and infant outcomes at delivery were also assessed. Figure 25.4 describes the disposition of women enrolled into the trial.

There was no significant difference in the time elapsed from start of treatment to delivery or therapeutic failure between atosiban and placebo groups (median: 25.6 days versus 21 days, respectively; $P=0.6$) (Figure 25.5). The proportions of women remaining undelivered and not requiring an alternative tocolytic agent at 24 hours, 48 hours and seven days were significantly higher in the atosiban group than in the control group (all $P<0.008$) (Table 25.2).

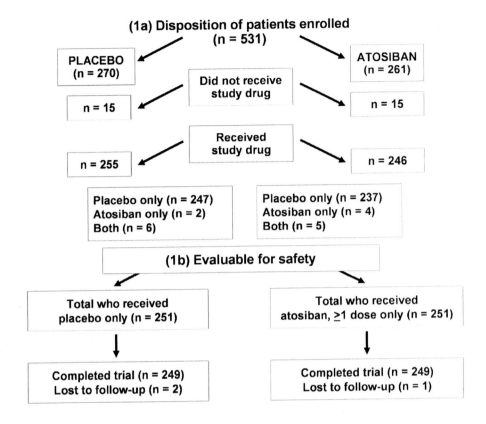

Figure 25.4. Disposition of patients enrolled in a randomised double-blind, placebo-controlled trial of atosiban with tocolytic rescue; reproduced with permission from Romero *et al.*[30]

Two features of this clinical trial are noteworthy. First, although this trial is placebo-controlled with regard to the primary efficacy endpoint (time to delivery or therapeutic failure), it is not a placebo-controlled trial with respect to infant outcomes (or time to delivery), since all women were permitted to receive 'rescue therapy' after only one hour of study drug infusion (atosiban or placebo) if criteria for progression of labour were met. Second, the subgroup of women with failure of assigned treatment with placebo who received an alternative tocolytic as 'rescue therapy' are biologically different from the subgroup of women with failure of assigned treatment with atosiban who received an alternative tocolytic as rescue therapy. These features have important implications for the interpretation of our results.

The placebo-controlled primary efficacy endpoint of this trial was the time elapsed between the beginning of treatment and delivery or therapeutic failure. Statistical significance for this endpoint was not achieved. However, an implicit assumption in the selection of this endpoint was that a tocolytic agent should be able to prolong pregnancy and prevent preterm birth. Regrettably, despite the use of a wide range of

Table 25.2. Percentages of women who remained undelivered and did not receive alternative tocolytic agents at 24 hours, 48 hours, and 7 days; reproduced with permission from Romero et al.[30]

Time	Placebo (n = 255)		Atosiban (n = 246)		Statistical significance[a]
	Proportion	%	Proportion	%	
24 hours	148/255	58	179/246	73	$P < 0.001$
48 hours	142/255	56	165/246	67	$P = 0.008$
7 days	125/254	49	153/246	62	$P = 0.003$

[a] determined by Cochran–Mantel–Haenszel test, stratified by centre

pharmacological approaches (such as multiple β-adrenergic receptor agents, magnesium sulphate, prostaglandin synthase inhibitors and calcium channel blockers), there is little evidence that this goal can be achieved.[74] Previous studies have demonstrated that short-term tocolysis with ritodrine can prolong pregnancy for up to seven days.[77] However, parenteral administration of this drug is associated with a significant rate of adverse effects, which appear to have limited its clinical utility. The observations reported suggest that a similar prolongation of pregnancy can be accomplished with atosiban with a lower rate of maternal adverse effects. The consistent inability of tocolytic agents – regardless of their mechanism of action – to reduce the rate of preterm birth is a reflection that this strategy (tocolysis) addresses only one of the clinical manifestations of preterm parturition (uterine contractility) rather than the underlying physiologic process causing preterm labour and birth.[84] The clinical advantages of short-term prolongation of pregnancy (seven days) are related to the time gained either to allow administration of corticosteroids or permit transfer of the woman to an institution with an intensive care nursery, or both of these, interventions that can reduce the risk of perinatal morbidity and mortality.[85]

Tocolytic failure in the first day of therapy has a potentially worse prognosis for infant survival than failure after weeks of treatment. An examination of the survival curves for the primary endpoint (Figure 25.5) reveals that they are completely separated for at least the first 15 days of treatment and that the atosiban curve is above the placebo curve for approximately 45 days from the initiation of treatment. The results of the early endpoints of 24 hours, 48 hours, and seven days are consistent with the early separation in the survival curves.

A significant interaction was noted between treatment and gestational age at entry for the time to delivery or therapeutic failure and the proportion of women who remained undelivered and did not receive an alternative tocolytic at 48 hours and seven days after the start of treatment. Results favoured atosiban over placebo for women at higher gestational ages but not at lower. For both the 48 hour and seven day time points, an advantage of atosiban over placebo was observed at gestational ages of 28 weeks or more at admission (Table 25.3). Two possible explanations have been invoked to explain this finding. First, the existence of a different pathologic mechanism involved in preterm labour at different gestational ages. Specifically, the frequency of intrauterine infection, which renders tocolysis less effective, has been reported to be greater when the gestational age at presentation is lower.[86] Second, oxytocin receptor expression is thought to increase with gestational age. The agent may thus be less effective when the receptor density is lower. It is noteworthy that in this study and others about 80% of enrolled women were at 28 weeks or more of gestational age. Therefore, most women in preterm labour eligible for tocolysis are in the gestational age range at which there is benefit from atosiban.

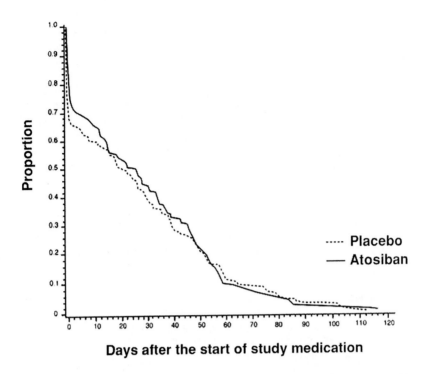

Days after the start of study medication

Figure 25.5. Survival curve for time to delivery interval or therapeutic failure in intent-to-treat subjects who received the study drug; reproduced with permission from Romero *et al.*[30]

The frequency of fetal/infant death was higher in women allocated to atosiban than in the control group (13 in the atosiban group and five in the control group). Table 25.4 displays the characteristics of the infant/neonatal death. This finding is probably related to an imbalanced allocation to the study groups. A greater number of women who had an early gestational age (less than 26 weeks) and advanced preterm labour (as

Table 25.3. Percentages of women who remained undelivered and did not receive alternative tocolytic agents at 24 hours, 48 hours, and 7 days, by gestational age at study admission; reproduced with permission from Romero *et al.*[30]

Endpoint	Placebo (n = 255)		Atosiban (n = 246)		Difference[a]
	Proportion	%	Proportion	%	and 95% CI (%)
24 hours					
< 28 weeks	20/34	59	29/43	67	9 (−14 to 32)
≥ 28 weeks	128/221	58	150/203	74	16 (7 to 25)
48 hours					
< 28 weeks	20/34	59	25/43	58	−1 (−24 to 23)
≥ 28 weeks	122/221	55	140/203	69	14 (4 to 23)
7 days					
< 28 weeks	20/34	59	22/43	51	−8 (−31 to 16)
≥ 28 weeks	105/220[b]	48	131/203	65	17 (7 to 26)

[a] percentage in atosiban group minus that in placebo group; [b] one patient was lost to follow-up before the conclusion of the 7-day time period

judged by the modified Bishop score) were randomised to receive atosiban. Seven of the ten infant deaths in the atosiban group (with or without rescue) were among women enrolled at less than 24 weeks who delivered infants with birthweight less than 650 grams. Five of the ten infants who died did not receive any immediate delivery room resuscitation, suggesting that they were considered nonviable by the paediatrician in attendance. Chorioamnionitis was diagnosed in three of seven cases and may have played a role in the deaths. A toxic effect of atosiban is considered unlikely given that in a randomised clinical trial of atosiban maintenance infants exposed to the higher doses of atosiban had better outcomes than those with the least exposure. Furthermore, no differences in fetal/infant deaths were reported in the comparative trial of atosiban versus β-adrenergic agents. Finally, standard toxicity studies in pregnant animals revealed no demonstrable adverse events at atosiban concentrations in the fetuses that were three times higher than those observed in human fetuses.

The investigators concluded that atosiban treatment resulted in prolongation of pregnancy for up to seven days in women with a gestational age at or greater than 28 weeks, while the efficacy and infant outcome data at less than 28 weeks was inconclusive.

Comparative trials

Three large randomised clinical trials compared the efficacy and safety profile of atosiban versus β-adrenergic agents using the same diagnostic criteria for preterm labour, gestational age at enrolment, and primary outcome (see Table 25.5). The β-adrenergic agent used for tocolysis varied among trials. Ritodrine was used in one trial,[87] terbutaline in another[88] and salbutamol in the third.[89] A pooled analysis of these comparative studies has been published,[90] as well as a systematic review.[91] The diagnosis of preterm labour required all the following criteria to be met:

- regular uterine contractions (longer than 40 seconds in duration, at a rate of four or more contractions within 30 minutes, confirmed by external tocography)
- cervical dilatation of 0–3 cm for nulliparous women or 1–3 cm for primiparous or multiparous women
- cervical effacement of 50% or greater.

Enrolment was restricted to women with a gestational age at entry between 23 and 33 weeks. Twin gestations were eligible for participation, but women with triplets or higher orders of multiple gestations were excluded. The exclusion criteria were the same across the trials as was the atosiban treatment regimen with one exception. The maximum duration of the acute treatment was 18 hours in two trials[87,88] and 48 hours in the other.[89] The treatment regimen for β-adrenergic agents by trial is described in Table 25.5.

The clinical trials were designed to test effectiveness and safety as primary outcomes. 'Tocolytic effectiveness' was assessed by calculating the proportion of women who had not delivered at 48 hours and at seven days. The entire population (intent-to-treat group) was used for this calculation. 'Safety' was assessed by the rate of maternal and neonatal morbidity. The primary outcome also included 'tocolytic efficacy and tolerability', which was defined as the proportion of women who were not delivered and who did not require alternative tocolysis at 48 hours and at seven days after initiation of therapy, in addition to an assessment of the progression of labour. The investigators included 'tolerability' as part of the primary outcome because many investigators were reluctant to participate in a study that did not allow administration of an alternative tocolytic drug in the event of progression of labour (if treatment

Table 25.4. Clinical characteristics of pregnancies leading to fetal or infant death; reproduced with permission from Romero et al.[30]

	Placebo with or without rescue (No. of deaths)	Atosiban with or without rescue (No. of deaths)	Difference[a] and 95% CI (%)
Gestational age at admission			
<26 weeks	0/16[b] (0%)	10/27[b] (37%)	37 (16 to 58)
≥26 to <28 weeks	1/26[b] (4%)	0/26[b] (0%)	−4 (−13 to 5)
≥28 to <32 weeks	2/125[b] (2%)	2/126[b] (2%)	0 (−4 to 3)
≥32 weeks	2/128[b] (2%)	1/109[b] (1%)	−1 (−4 to 3)
Time of death			
Before delivery	3 (0[c])	3 (1[c])	
Neonatal			
0–7 days	1 (0[c])	6 (3[c])	
8–28 days	1	2	
Postneonatal	0	2	
Findings in association with death			
Fetal-neonatal weight <500 g			
With infection	0	1 (1[d])	
Without infection	0	2 (2[d])	
Extreme prematurity			
With infection	0	5 (5[d])	
Without infection	0	1 (1[d])	
Cord accident	1	1 (1[d])	
Placental abruption	2	1	
Congenital anomaly	1	1	
Endocarditis	0	1	
Unable to resuscitate	1	0	

[a] percentage in atosiban group minus that in placebo group; [b] per total number; [c] number of stillbirths and early neonatal deaths (0–7 days) associated with infection; [d] number of deaths with gestational age at admission <26 weeks

failure had occurred). The consequence is that the efficacy endpoint of these trials included components of efficacy as well as tolerability to treatment.

The secondary outcomes included changes in the mean frequency of uterine contractions after treatment, mean gestational age at delivery, the proportion of infants born at different gestational age or birthweight, as well as the number of infants requiring neonatal intensive care (see Table 25.5).

Progression of labour was evaluated at the end of the infusion, or optionally at six or 12 hours after initiation of therapy. Progression of labour was diagnosed if two of the three following criteria were met:

- a contraction rate of four or more per hour
- an increase in cervical dilatation of 1 cm or more from the initial measurement
- an increase in cervical effacement of 25% or more from the initial measurement.

If labour was diagnosed to have progressed or there were intolerable adverse events, the study treatment was stopped and alternative tocolysis was considered. Women who had been successfully tocolysed and had another episode of preterm labour were allowed to receive treatment with the same agent originally used provided that the eligibility criteria were met, the gestational age was below 34 weeks, and no alternative tocolysis had been given in the previous episode of preterm labour. Concomitant tocolysis was not prohibited.

Table 25.5. Comparative trials: diagnostic criteria for preterm labour, gestational age at enrolment, dosage regimens of the study drugs and outcomes of the trials

Trial	Women (n)	Definition of preterm labour	Gestational age (weeks)	Atosiban	β-adrenergic agent	Outcomes
Moutquin et al.[87]	247	Regular uterine contractions at least 30 s in duration, at a rate of at least 4 in 30 min and cervical dilatation of 0–3 cm in nulliparous women and 1–3 cm in primiparous and multiparous women and at least 50% of cervical effacement	23–33	Atosiban 6.75 mg bolus; 300 μg/min for 3 h, then 100 μg/min for as long as 18 h	Ritodrine 0.10–0.35 mg/min; increase every 10 minutes; treatment up to 18 h	*Primary* 1. Tocolytic effectiveness 2. Tocolytic safety (maternal adverse effects and neonatal morbidity) 3. Tocolytic efficacy and tolerability *Secondary* 1. The change in uterine contraction rate with time 2. The mean gestational age at delivery 3. The proportion of infants born at <1500 grams and 1500 to <2500 grams 4. The number of infants requiring neonatal intensive care
European Atosiban Study[88]	249	Regular uterine contractions at least 30 s in duration, at a rate of at least 4 in 30 min and cervical dilatation of 0–3 cm in nulliparous women and 1–3 cm in primiparous and multiparous women and at least 50% of cervical effacement	23–33	Atosiban 6.75 mg bolus; 300 μg/min for 3 h, then 100 μg/min for up to 18 h	Terbutaline 10–25 μg/min; treatment up to 18 h	*Primary* 1. Tocolytic effectiveness 2. Tocolytic safety (maternal adverse effects and neonatal morbidity) 3. Tocolytic efficacy and tolerability *Secondary* 1. The change in uterine contraction rate with time 2. The mean gestational age at delivery 3. The proportion of women re-treated with study medication 4. The proportion of infants born at different gestational age 5. The number of infants requiring neonatal intensive care
French/Australian Atosiban Investigators Group[89]	241	Regular uterine contractions at least 30 s in duration, at a rate of at least 4 in 30 min and cervical dilatation of 0–3 cm in nulliparous women and 1–3 cm in primiparous and multiparous women and at least 50% of cervical effacement	23–33	Atosiban 6.75 mg bolus; 300 μg/min for 3 h, then 100 μg/min for up to 48 h	Salbutamol 5–25 μg/min (France); 2.5–45 μg/min (Australia); treatment up to 48 h	*Primary* 1. Tocolytic effectiveness 2. Tocolytic safety (maternal adverse effects and neonatal morbidity) 3. Tocolytic efficacy and tolerability *Secondary* 1. The change in uterine contraction rate with time 2. The mean gestational age at delivery 3. The proportion of women re-treated with study medication 4. The proportion of infants born at different birthweight 5. The number of infants requiring neonatal intensive care

The pooled analysis was based on data from 742 women, of whom 362 were randomised to atosiban and 379 to β-adrenergic agents.[90] The proportion of women who delivered after 48 hours of treatment or seven days was similar between women randomised to atosiban and β-adrenergic agents (for 48 hours: 88.1% versus 88.9%; $P=0.9$, for 7 days: 79.7% versus 77.6%; $P=0.2$). There was no significant difference in the mean gestational age at delivery (35.8 ± 3.9 weeks versus 35.5 ± 4.1 weeks) and mean birthweight (2491 ± 813 grams versus 2461 ± 831 grams) between the two groups. There were no differences in neonatal and infant outcomes between women allocated to tocolysis with atosiban and those allocated to β-adrenergic agents. In contrast, maternal adverse events were more common among women randomised to β-adrenergic agents than those in the atosiban group (81.2% versus 8.3%; $P<0.001$). The rate of discontinuation of therapy due to adverse effects was also greater in women randomised to β-adrenergic agents than in those in the atosiban group (15.4% versus 1.1%; $P<0.0001$). The most common adverse events were of a cardiovascular nature and included maternal tachycardia, palpitations, hypotension and chest pain. There were three cases with pulmonary oedema in the analysis. Two cases occurred in women receiving β-adrenergic agents. The other case was observed in a woman initially allocated to atosiban who did not respond to the agent and received 'rescue' tocolysis with β-adrenergic agents for seven days.

For the endpoint of 'efficacy and tolerability', atosiban was superior to β-adrenergic agents in singleton pregnancy. 'Therapeutic failure', defined as delivery within 48 hours or seven days or the need for alternative tocolysis, was more common in women randomised to β-adrenergic agents than those in the atosiban group (for 48 hours: 29.9% versus 23.4%; $P=0.03$, for seven days: 51.4% versus 38.9%; $P=0.004$). This difference was not observed in twin gestations.

Analysis of the endpoint of 'efficacy and tolerability' after seven days by β-adrenergic agents indicated that a significant difference was observed with ritodrine ($P=0.029$) and salbutamol ($P=0.02$) but not terbutaline ($P=0.07$) (see Figure 25.6). Heterogeneity was not detected among the three clinical trials that contributed to the pooled analysis or among centres.[90]

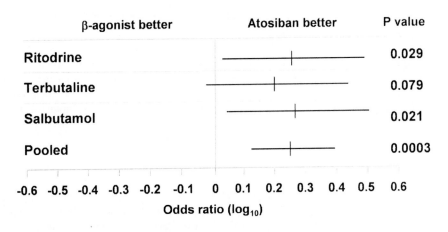

Figure 25.6. Centre-stratified $\log_{10}$ odds ratios (with 95% CI) for the proportion of women undelivered and not requiring alternative tocolysis after seven days of starting treatment in the three β-agonist trials and the pooled analysis; reproduced with permission from The Worldwide Atosiban versus Beta-agonists Study Group[90]

An interesting observation was that among twins tocolytic effectiveness at 48 hours was greater for women allocated to β-adrenergic agents than to the atosiban group (93.3% versus 75%; $P=0.003$) but this difference did not reach significance at seven days (76.7% versus 61.4%; $P=0.07$). The reasons for this are unclear.

There were 18 fetal or infant deaths during the study period. Six deaths were reported in the atosiban group (four singletons and two twins) and 12 in the β-adrenergic group (five singletons and seven twins). Consequently, the perinatal mortality rate was 14.7 per 1000 in the atosiban group and 26.7 per 1000 in the β-adrenergic group. The stated causes of death were complications associated with prematurity, such as infection/sepsis, respiratory distress syndrome, necrotising enterocolitis and intraventricular haemorrhage. Of these deaths, three were intrauterine deaths, two in the β-adrenergic group, and one in the atosiban group. One unexplained stillbirth in the atosiban group occurred 11 weeks after treatment. Two stillbirths occurred in the β-adrenergic group two days after initiating therapy, and had no obvious relationship to the administration of the study drug.[90]

Coomarasamy et al.[91] conducted a systematic review of comparative trials of atosiban versus β-adrenergic agents. In this review, one additional study[92] was included in the meta-analysis. This study[92] was conducted and designed primarily to determine the lowest effective dose regimen of atosiban but included a comparison with ritodrine. Meta-analysis of the four trials for the endpoint of delivery within 48 hours demonstrated no significant difference between atosiban and β-adrenergic agents (relative risk 1.07; 95% CI 0.98–1.17).[91] However, for the endpoint of efficacy and tolerability the results are the same as those reported by the Worldwide Atosiban versus Beta-agonists Study Group.[90]

Maintenance treatment of preterm labour with atosiban

Recurring episodes of preterm labour are treated either episodically by intravenous or subcutaneous routes in response to recurrent preterm labour, or prophylactically by continuous administration of a tocolytic agent.[93] The latter approach has taken several forms, including oral administration of tocolytic agents (terbutaline, magnesium), subcutaneous administration with an infusion pump (terbutaline), and long-term intravenous suppression in hospital (magnesium).[94] Despite the widespread use of maintenance therapy, only a few studies support its efficacy.[95–97]

A multicentre, double-blind, placebo-controlled, randomised clinical trial was conducted to compare the efficacy and safety of atosiban with those of placebo for maintenance therapy in women with preterm labour who achieved uterine quiescence with intravenous atosiban.[98] Women were eligible for participation if they met the same criteria as those in the randomised clinical trial of atosiban versus placebo with tocolytic rescue reported by Romero et al.[30] Eligible women were treated with intravenous infusion of atosiban until uterine quiescence was achieved. Uterine quiescence was defined as either 12 consecutive hours with four or fewer contractions per hour or 48 hours of intravenous infusion without progression of labour requiring the use of an alternative tocolytic agent. Acute treatment used the regimen as reported by Romero et al.[30] Responders (women who achieved uterine quiescence with atosiban) were subsequently randomly selected to receive subcutaneous maintenance therapy with either atosiban or matching placebo.

The assigned maintenance agent, either atosiban or placebo, was delivered by a 3 ml subcutaneous infusion pump to provide a continuous atosiban infusion of 6 ml/hour (30 μg/min). The endpoints of maintenance therapy were 36 completed weeks of gestation, delivery, or progression of labour requiring an alternative tocolytic agent, whichever occurred first. Compliance was assessed by patient diary cards and drug use, and supported by home health care with daily nursing contact for all women (home uterine activity monitoring was not used). All women assigned to maintenance were to be discharged from the hospital. Subsequent intravenous treatment with atosiban for any additional episode of preterm labour was given, and subcutaneous maintenance therapy with the assigned study drug was resumed if uterine quiescence was again achieved. Women were to be reassessed in the hospital if contractions of six to eight per hour returned, and re-treatment with atosiban could be given when contractions reached ten or more contractions per hour. Other tocolytic agents were not permitted during treatment with the study drug. Antibiotic therapy and steroid therapy were allowed for standard clinical indications.

The primary endpoint was the number of days from the start of maintenance therapy until the first recurrence of labour, whether it occurred before or at term. Time to the next episode of labour was chosen as the primary endpoint for two reasons:

1. It is the initial measurable endpoint in the clinical progression from successful acute tocolysis to preterm delivery.
2. In a study design that permits active therapy for all subsequent episodes of preterm labour, it is the only placebo-controlled endpoint.

The authors conducted a *post hoc* analysis of the number of days from the start of maintenance therapy to the next occurrence of preterm labour. A secondary endpoint was the percentage of women who had at least one subsequent intravenous atosiban treatment.

The median time from the start of maintenance treatment to the first recurrence of labour was 32.6 days with atosiban and 26.6 days with placebo ($P = 0.02$). At least one subsequent intravenous atosiban treatment was needed by 61 atosiban patients (23%) and 77 placebo patients (31%). Except for injection site reactions, adverse event profiles of atosiban and placebo were comparable. There were four neonatal deaths reported in the atosiban group and five in the placebo group after the start of maintenance therapy. Infant outcomes (including birthweight) were comparable between maintenance and treatment groups. The authors concluded that maintenance therapy with the oxytocin receptor antagonist atosiban can prolong uterine quiescence after successful treatment of an acute episode of preterm labour with atosiban. Treatment was well tolerated.

The results of this study indicate that women who respond to early intravenous treatment with atosiban achieve a delay in the period from the start of maintenance therapy to the next episode of preterm labour, or term labour, when given continuous subcutaneous treatment with atosiban, in comparison with placebo. Moreover, women allocated to the atosiban group had a 25% decrease in the need for intravenous re-treatment, a difference that fell short of reaching statistical significance.

The goals of maintenance tocolysis are to reduce the frequency of recurrent episodes of preterm labour, the need for hospitalisation, re-treatment with intravenously administered tocolytic agents, and preterm birth.[95–97,99] However, only two of seven studies have shown clinical efficacy.[95,96] Several potential explanations can be invoked to account for this apparent failure. Compliance with oral therapy is much lower than with some other drug delivery modalities. Treatment via a subcutaneous infusion pump should result in much better treatment compliance than oral therapy, as problems with gastrointestinal absorption are eliminated. Orally administered β-sympathomimetic drugs, the most frequently prescribed maintenance tocolytics, have a relatively short half-life and thus result in the need for frequent dosing at night to maintain adequate blood levels. Frequent oral dosing coupled with common cardiovascular adverse effects leads to a lack of compliance and therefore, predictably, to a lack of efficacy. Switching from one agent for intravenous tocolysis to another for maintenance also accounts for this apparent failure. The drug chosen for maintenance treatment may not be as effective in a particular woman as the drug that was successful in achieving tocolysis during the acute episode of preterm labour.

The success of maintenance treatment with an oxytocin receptor antagonist reported in this trial may be attributed to improved compliance with the use of a subcutaneous infusion pump and therapeutic consistency both in the treatment of the acute episode of preterm labour and during the maintenance period. The requirement that women achieve successful acute tocolysis with atosiban was a criterion for randomisation in this trial. This can be considered a therapeutic trial that may have identified women most likely to benefit from maintenance treatment with this agent. Finally, a therapy aimed at the pharmacological control of the biological actions of oxytocin and its receptor may be more appropriate in the long-term control of uterine contractility and parturition than one directed toward adrenergic receptors' biological effects.

A challenge in evaluating the role of maintenance therapy in the treatment of women at risk of preterm delivery is the absence of a single, well-accepted efficacy endpoint. Investigators have used several endpoints, including time to the next episode of labour,[30] number of recurrent episodes of preterm labour,[96] time to delivery,[95,99] percentage of women with preterm delivery,[100] gestational age at delivery,[101] and proportion of women delivered within seven days of initiation of maintenance therapy.[102] The order of measurable events in the progression from successful acute tocolysis to recurrent preterm labour and delivery begins with the loss of uterine quiescence, which leads to subsequent hospital admissions, re-treatments, preterm birth, and neonatal morbidity. Success with maintenance treatment should result in a reduction in the number of women progressing along this path. A prerequisite for accomplishing this goal is the maintenance of uterine quiescence after arrest of an acute episode of preterm labour. This study was designed to compare the efficacy of atosiban with that of placebo in suppressing uterine activity, as measured by the time from the start of treatment to the next episode of labour. The results indicate that atosiban maintenance was successful. The primary endpoint for this study was uterine quiescence, rather than the percentage of women requiring subsequent intravenous treatment or the percentage of women with preterm delivery. The authors estimated that 1000 women would be required for a conclusive study, given the assumptions of power and certainty similar to those of this study.

An important observation in this study was that the rate of fetal and infant deaths was comparable in the two study groups. Of the fetal and infant deaths in each study group, three of the five had evidence of infection and extreme prematurity. The single fetal death occurred at 34 weeks of gestation after treatment with fenoterol and betamethasone and, subsequently, atosiban for 10 days. This result is reassuring in terms of the safety of long-term administration of atosiban.

Conclusions

Treatment of premature labour with an oxytocin receptor antagonist has become an important therapeutic choice. Treatment with atosiban results in the delay of preterm delivery compared with placebo-initiated therapy, and the adverse event profile compares favourably with that reported with the use of β-adrenergic agents. Comparative trials with other agents such as calcium channel blockers or with novel oxytocin receptor antagonists are warranted.

References

1. Fuchs AR. Oxytocin and oxytocin receptors: maternal signals for parturition. In: Garfield RD, editor. *Uterine Contractility*. Massachusetts: Serono Symposia; 1990. p. 177–90.

2. MacDonald PC. Parturition: biomolecular and physiologic processes. In: Cunningham FC, MacDonald PC, Leveno KJ, Gant ND, Gilstrap LC, editors. *William's Obstetrics*. Connecticut: Appleton and Lange; 1993. p. 297–361.

3. Fuchs AR, Husslein P, Fuchs F. Oxytocin and the initiation of human parturition. II. Stimulation of prostaglandin production in human decidua by oxytocin. *Am J Obstet Gynecol* 1981;141:694–7.

4. Wilson T, Liggins GC, Whittaker DJ. Oxytocin stimulates the release of arachidonic acid and prostaglandin F2 alpha from human decidual cells. *Prostaglandins* 1988;35:771–80.

5. Romero R, Mazor M, Tartakovsky B. Systemic administration of interleukin-1 induces preterm parturition in mice. *Am J Obstet Gynecol* 1991;165:969–71.

6. Fidel PL Jr, Romero R, Wolf N, Cutright J, Ramirez M, Araneda H, et al. Systemic and local cytokine profiles in endotoxin-induced preterm parturition in mice. *Am J Obstet Gynecol* 1994;170:1467–75.

7. Fuchs AR, Dawood MY. Oxytocin release and uterine activation during parturition in rabbits. *Endocrinology* 1980;107:1117–26.

8. Glatz TH, Weitzman RE, Eliot RJ, Klein AH, Nathanielsz PW, Fisher DA. Ovine maternal and fetal plasma oxytocin concentrations before and during parturition. *Endocrinology* 1981;108:1328–32.

9. Landgraf R, Schulz J, Eulenberger K, Wilhelm J. Plasma levels of oxytocin and vasopressin before, during and after parturition in cows. *Exp Clin Endocrinol* 1983;81:321–8.

10. Higuchi T, Tadokoro Y, Honda K, Negoro H. Detailed analysis of blood oxytocin levels during suckling and parturition in the rat. *J Endocrinol* 1986;110:251–6.

11. Currie WB, Gorewit RC, Michel FJ. Endocrine changes, with special emphasis on oestradiol-17 beta, prolactin and oxytocin, before and during labour and delivery in goats. *J Reprod Fertil* 1988;82:299–308.

12. Gilbert CL, Goode JA, McGrath TJ. Pulsatile secretion of oxytocin during parturition in the pig: temporal relationship with fetal expulsion. *J Physiol* 1994;475:129–37.

13. Hirst JJ, Haluska GJ, Cook MJ, Novy MJ. Plasma oxytocin and nocturnal uterine activity: maternal but not fetal concentrations increase progressively during late pregnancy and delivery in rhesus monkeys. *Am J Obstet Gynecol* 1993;169:415–22.

14. Koike TI, Shimada K, Cornett LE. Plasma levels of immunoreactive mesotocin and vasotocin during oviposition in chickens: relationship to oxytocic action of the peptides *in vitro* and peptide interaction with myometrial membrane binding sites. *Gen Comp Endocrinol* 1988;70:119–26.

15. Oumi T, Ukena K, Matsushima O, Ikeda T, Fujita T, Minakata H, et al. Annetocin: an oxytocin-related peptide isolated from the earthworm, *Eisenia foetida*. *Biochem Biophys Res Commun* 1994;198:393–9.

16. Blanks AM, Thornton S. The role of oxytocin in parturition. *BJOG* 2003;110 Suppl 20:46–51.

17. Fuchs AR, Dawood MY. Oxytocin release and uterine activation during parturition in rabbits. *Endocrinology* 1980;107:1117–26.

18. Fuchs AR, Romero R, Keefe D, Parra M, Oyarzun E, Behnke E. Oxytocin secretion and human parturition: pulse frequency and duration increase during spontaneous labor in women. *Am J Obstet Gynecol* 1991;165:1515–23.

19. Fuchs AR, Behrens O, Liu HC. Correlation of nocturnal increase in plasma oxytocin with a decrease in plasma estradiol/progesterone ratio in late pregnancy. *Am J Obstet Gynecol* 1992;167:1559–63.

20. Thornton S, Davison JM, Baylis PH. Plasma oxytocin during the first and second stages of spontaneous human labour. *Acta Endocrinol (Copenh)* 1992;126:425–9.

21. Burd JM, Davison J, Weightman DR, Baylis PH. Evaluation of enzyme inhibitors of pregnancy associated oxytocinase: application to the measurement of plasma immunoreactive oxytocin during human labour. *Acta Endocrinol (Copenh)* 1987;114:458–64.

22. Davison JM, Sheills EA, Philips PR, Barron WM, Lindheimer MD. Metabolic clearance of vasopressin and an analogue resistant to vasopressinase in human pregnancy. *Am J Physiol* 1993;264:F348–53.

23. Thornton S, Vatish M, Slater D. Oxytocin antagonists: clinical and scientific considerations. *Exp Physiol* 2001;86:297–302.

24. Amico JA, Hempel J. An oxytocin precursor intermediate circulates in the plasma of humans and rhesus monkeys administered estrogen. *Neuroendocrinology* 1990;51:437–43.

25. Chibbar R, Miller FD, Mitchell BF. Synthesis of oxytocin in amnion, chorion, and decidua may influence the timing of human parturition. *J Clin Invest* 1993;91:185–92.

26. Lefebvre DL, Giaid A, Bennett H, Lariviere R, Zingg HH. Oxytocin gene expression in rat uterus. *Science* 1992;256:1553–5.

27.   Zingg HH, Laporte SA. The oxytocin receptor. *Trends Endocrinol Metab* 2003;14:222–7.
28.   Mitchell BF, Fang X, Wong S. Oxytocin: a paracrine hormone in the regulation of parturition? *Rev Reprod* 1998;3:113–22.
29.   Miller FD, Chibbar R, Mitchell BF. Synthesis of oxytocin in amnion, chorion and decidua: a potential paracrine role for oxytocin in the onset of human parturition. *Regul Pept* 1993;45:247–51.
30.   Romero R, Sibai BM, Sanchez-Ramos L, Valenzuela GJ, Veille JC, Tabor B, *et al*. An oxytocin receptor antagonist (atosiban) in the treatment of preterm labor: a randomized, double-blind, placebo-controlled trial with tocolytic rescue. *Am J Obstet Gynecol* 2000;182:1173–83.
31.   Honnebier MB, Figueroa JP, Rivier J, Vale W, Nathanielsz PW. Studies on the role of oxytocin in late pregnancy in the pregnant rhesus monkey: plasma concentrations of oxytocin in the maternal circulation throughout the 24-h day and the effect of the synthetic oxytocin antagonist [1-beta-Mpa(beta-(CH2)5)1,(Me(Tyr2, Orn8] oxytocin on spontaneous nocturnal myometrial contractions. *J Dev Physiol* 1989;12:225–32.
32.   Giussani DA, Jenkins SL, Mecenas CA, Winter JA, Barbera M, Honnebier OM, *et al*. The oxytocin antagonist atosiban prevents androstenedione-induced myometrial contractions in the chronically instrumented, pregnant rhesus monkey. *Endocrinology* 1996;137:3302–7.
33.   Nathanielsz PW, Honnebier MB, Mecenas C, Jenkins SL, Holland ML, Demarest K. Effect of the oxytocin antagonist atosiban (1-deamino-2-D-tyr(OET)-4-thr-8-orn-vasotocin/oxytocin) on nocturanl myometrial contractions, maternal cardiovascular function, transplacental passage, and fetal oxygenation in the pregnant baboon during the last third of gestation. *Biol Reprod* 1997;57:320–4.
34.   Fuchs AR, Fuchs F, Husslein P, Soloff MS. Oxytocin receptors in the human uterus during pregnancy and parturition. *Am J Obstet Gynecol* 1984;150:734–41.
35.   Takahashi K, Diamond F, Bieniarz J, Yen H, Burd L. Uterine contractility and oxytocin sensitivity in preterm, term, and postterm pregnancy. *Am J Obstet Gynecol* 1980;136:774–9.
36.   Fuchs AR, Fuchs F, Husslein P, Soloff MS, Fernstrom MJ. Oxytocin receptors and human parturition: a dual role for oxytocin in the initiation of labor. *Science* 1982;215:1396–8.
37.   Mitchell MD, Stundin-Schiller SL. Mode of action of prostaglandins in myometrial cells. In: Garfield RD, editor. *Uterine Contractility – Mechanisms of Control*. Massachussetts: Serono Symposia; 1990.
38.   Romero R, Baumann P, Gonzalez R, Gomez R, Rittenhouse L, Behnke E, *et al*. Amniotic fluid prostanoid concentrations increase early during the course of spontaneous labor at term. *Am J Obstet Gynecol* 1994;171:1613–20.
39.   Romero R, Gonzalez R, Baumann P, Behnke E, Rittenhouse L, Barberio D, *et al*. Topographic differences in amniotic fluid concentrations of prostanoids in women in spontaneous labor at term. *Prostaglandins Leukot Essent Fatty Acids* 1994;50:97–104.
40.   Romero R, Munoz H, Gomez R, Parra M, Polanco M, Valverde V, *et al*. Increase in prostaglandin bioavailability precedes the onset of human parturition. *Prostaglandins Leukot Essent Fatty Acids* 1996;54:187–91.
41.   Nishimori K, Young LJ, Guo Q, Wang Z, Insel TR, Matzuk MM. Oxytocin is required for nursing but is not essential for parturition or reproductive behavior. *Proc Natl Acad Sci U S A* 1996;93:11699–704.
42.   Young WS 3rd, Shepard E, Amico J, Hennighausen L, Wagner KU, LaMarca ME, *et al*. Deficiency in mouse oxytocin prevents milk ejection, but not fertility or parturition. *J Neuroendocrinol* 1996;8:847–53.
43.   Gross GA, Imamura T, Luedke C, Vogt SK, Olson LM, Nelson DM, *et al*. Opposing actions of prostaglandins and oxytocin determine the onset of murine labor. *Proc Natl Acad Sci U S A* 1998;95:11875–9.
44.   Imamura T, Luedke CE, Vogt SK, Muglia LJ. Oxytocin modulates the onset of murine parturition by competing ovarian and uterine effects. *Am J Physiol Regul Integr Comp Physiol* 2000;279:R1061–7.
45.   Wuttke W, Jarry H, Knoke I, Pitzel L, Spiess S. Luteotropic and luteolytic effects of oxytocin in the porcine corpus luteum. *Adv Exp Med Biol* 1995;395:495–506.
46.   Wuttke W, Jarry H, Pitzel L, Knoke I, Spiess S. Luteotrophic and luteolytic actions of ovarian peptides. *Hum Reprod* 1993;8 Suppl 2:141–6.
47.   Einspanier A, Jurdzinski A, Hodges JK. A local oxytocin system is part of the luteinization process in the preovulatory follicle of the marmoset monkey (*Callithrix jacchus*). *Biol Reprod* 1997;57:16–26.
48.   Fuchs AR, Chang SM, Fields MJ. Oxytocin receptors in cervical mucosa and endometrium are differently regulated during pregnancy. Chicago: Soc Gynecol Invest Symposium; 1994. (Abstract).
49.   Fuchs AR, Fuchs F. Endocrinology of human parturition: a review. *Br J Obstet Gynaecol* 1984;91:948–67.
50.   Bossmar T, Akerlund M, Fantoni G, Szamatowicz J, Melin P, Maggi M. Receptors for and

myometrial responses to oxytocin and vasopressin in preterm and term human pregnancy: effects of the oxytocin antagonist atosiban. *Am J Obstet Gynecol* 1994;171:1634–42.

51. Melin P. Oxytocin antagonists in preterm labor and delivery. *Clin Obstet Gynecol* 1993;7:577–600.

52. Goodwin TM, Zograbyan A. Oxytocin receptor antagonists. Update. *Clin Perinatol* 1998;25:859–71,vi.

53. Lopez BA, Phipps SL, Rosevear SK, Turnbull AC. Mechanism of action of the oxytocin antagonist 1-deamino-2-D-Tyr-(OEt)-4-Thr-8-Orn-oxytocin. *Br J Obstet Gynaecol* 1989;96:1108–10.

54. Thornton S, Gillespie JI, Anson LC, Greenwell JR, Melin P, Dunlop W. The effect of the oxytocin antagonists, CAP 476 and F327, on calcium mobilisation in single cultured human myometrial cells. *Br J Obstet Gynaecol* 1993;100:581–6.

55. Chan WY, Powell AM, Hruby VJ. Antioxytocic and antiprostaglandin-releasing effects of oxytocin antagonists in pregnant rats and pregnant human myometrial strips. *Endocrinology* 1982;111:48–54.

56. Manning M, Miteva K, Pancheva S, Stoev S, Wo NC, Chan WY. Design and synthesis of highly selective *in vitro* and *in vivo* uterine receptor antagonists of oxytocin: comparisons with Atosiban. *Int J Pept Protein Res* 1995;46:244–52.

57. Hauksson A, Akerlund M, Melin P. Uterine blood flow and myometrial activity at menstruation, and the action of vasopressin and a synthetic antagonist. *Br J Obstet Gynaecol* 1988;95:898–904.

58. Valenzuela GJ, Craig J, Bernhardt MD, Holland ML. Placental passage of the oxytocin antagonist atosiban. *Am J Obstet Gynecol* 1995;172:1304–6.

59. Lamont RF. The development and introduction of anti-oxytocic tocolytics. *BJOG* 2003; 110 Suppl 20:108–12.

60. Abrams LS, Goodwin TM, Miller TM, Wegelein RC, Kalamarides D, North L, *et al.* Pharmacokinetics of Atosiban in pregnant women. *Pharm Res* 1993;10:S335.

61. Lundin S, Akerlund M, Fagerstrom PO, Hauksson A, Melin P. Pharmacokinetics in the human of a new synthetic vasopressin and oxytocin uterine antagonist. *Acta Endocrinol (Copenh)* 1986;112:465–72.

62. Lundin S, Broeders A, Melin P. Pharmacokinetic properties of the tocolytic agent [Mpa1, D-Tyr(Et)2, Thr4, Orn8]-oxytocin (antocin) in healthy volunteers. *Clin Endocrinol (Oxf)* 1993;39:369–74.

63. Snyder CL, Merriman R, Abrams L, Blank MS. *Safety and tolerance evaluation of 12 hour infusion of atosiban (RWJ 22164) in normal female volunteers (protocol 188-084).* Document ID No. 200769. RWJPRI Full Clinical and Statistical Report No. MR-92068. 1993.

64. Akerlund M, Kostrzewska A, Laudanski T, Melin P, Vilhardt H. Vasopressin effects on isolated non-pregnant myometrium and uterine arteries and their inhibition by deamino-ethyl-lysine-vasopressin and deamino-ethyl-oxytocin. *Br J Obstet Gynaecol* 1983;90:732–8.

65. Snyder CL, Merriman R, Abrams L. *Rising dose tolerance and safety evaluation of atosiban (RWJ 22164) in normal female subjects (Protocol 988-012).* Document ID No. 301824. RWJPRI Full Clinical and Statistical Report No. MR-92067. 1993

66. Akerlund M, Stromberg P, Hauksson A, Andersen LF, Lyndrup J, Trojnar J, *et al.* Inhibition of uterine contractions of premature labour with an oxytocin analogue. Results from a pilot study. *Br J Obstet Gynaecol* 1987;94:1040–4.

67. Andersen LF, Lyndrup J, Akerlund M, Melin P. Oxytocin receptor blockade: a new principle in the treatment of preterm labor? *Am J Perinatol* 1989;6:196–9.

68. Goodwin TM, Paul R, Silver H, Spellacy W, Parsons M, Chez R, *et al.* The effect of the oxytocin antagonist atosiban on preterm uterine activity in the human. *Am J Obstet Gynecol* 1994;170:474–8.

69. Goodwin TM, Paul RH, Millar L, Valenzuela GJ, Silver H, Chez R. *et al.* Effect of the oxytocin antagonist Atosiban on preterm labor – initial US trial. San Antonio: Soc Gynecol Invest; 1992. (Abstract).

70. Goldenberg RL. The management of preterm labor. *Obstet Gynecol* 2002;100:1020–37.

71. ACOG Practice Bulletin. Clinical management guidelines for obstetrician-gynecologist. Number 43, May 2003. Management of preterm labor. *Obstet Gynecol* 2003;101:1039–47.

72. Goldenberg RL, Rouse DJ. Prevention of premature birth. *N Engl J Med* 1998;339:313–20.

73. Keirse MJNC, Grant A, King JF. Preterm labour. In: Chalmers I, Enkin MW, Keirse MJNC, editors. *Effective Care in Pregnancy and Childbirth.* Oxford: Oxford University Press; 1989. p. 194–202.

74. Smith GN. What are the realistic expectations of tocolytics? *BJOG* 2003;110 Suppl 20:103–6.

75. Keirse MJ. The history of tocolysis. *BJOG* 2003;110 Suppl 20:94–7.

76. Wesselius-de Casparis A, Thiery M, Yo IS, Baumgarten K, Brosens I, Gamisans O, *et al.* Results of double-blind, multicentre study with ritodrine in premature labour. *BMJ* 1971;3:144–7.

77. The Canadian Preterm Labor Investigators Group. Treatment of preterm labor with the beta-adrenergic agonist ritodrine. *N Engl J Med* 1992;327:308–12.

78. Spellacy WN, Cruz AC, Birk SA, Buhi WC. Treatment of premature labor with ritodrine: a randomized controlled study. *Obstet Gynecol* 1979;54:220–3.

79.	Christensen KK, Ingemarsson I, Leideman T, Solum T, Svenningsen N. Effect of ritodrine on labor after premature rupture of the membranes. *Obstet Gynecol* 1980;55:187–90.
80.	Howard TE Jr, Killam AP, Penney LL, Daniell WC. A double blind randomized study of terbutaline in premature labor. *Mil Med* 1982;147:305–7.
81.	Leveno KJ, Klein VR, Guzick DS, Young DC, Hankins GD, Williams ML. Single-centre randomised trial of ritodrine hydrochloride for preterm labour. *Lancet* 1986;i:1293–6.
82.	Larsen JF, Eldon K, Lange AP, Leegaard M, Osler M, Olsen JS, et al. Ritodrine in the treatment of preterm labor: second Danish Multicenter Study. *Obstet Gynecol* 1986;67:607–13.
83.	Caughey AB, Parer JT. Tocolysis with beta-adrenergic receptor agonists. *Semin Perinatol* 2001;25:248–55.
84.	Romero R, Mazor M, Munoz H, Gomez R, Galasso M, Sherer DM. The preterm labor syndrome. *Ann N Y Acad Sci* 1994;734:414–29.
85.	National Institutes of Health. *Report of the Consensus Development Conference of the effect of corticosteroids for fetal maturation on perinatal outcomes.* NIH Publication No. 95-3784. Washington, NIH; 1994.
86.	Romero R, Sirtori M, Oyarzun E, Avila C, Mazor M, Callahan R, et al. Infection and labor. V. Prevalence, microbiology, and clinical significance of intraamniotic infection in women with preterm labor and intact membranes. *Am J Obstet Gynecol* 1989;161:817–24.
87.	Moutquin JM, Sherman D, Cohen H, Mohide PT, Hochner-Celnikier D, Fejgin M, et al. Double-blind, randomized, controlled trial of atosiban and ritodrine in the treatment of preterm labor: a multicenter effectiveness and safety study. *Am J Obstet Gynecol* 2000;182:1191–9.
88.	European Atosiban Study Group. The oxytocin antagonist atosiban versus the beta-agonist terbutaline in the treatment of preterm labor. A randomized, double-blind, controlled study. *Acta Obstet Gynecol Scand* 2001;80:413–22.
89.	French/Australian Atosiban Investigators Group. Treatment of preterm labor with the oxytocin antagonist atosiban: a double-blind, randomized, controlled comparison with salbutamol. *Eur J Obstet Gynecol Reprod Biol* 2001;98:177–85.
90.	The Worldwide Atosiban versus Beta-agonists Study Group. Effectiveness and safety of the oxytocin antagonist atosiban versus beta-adrenergic agonists in the treatment of preterm labour. *BJOG* 2001;108:133–42.
91.	Coomarasamy A, Knox EM, Gee H, Khan KS. Oxytocin antagonists for tocolysis in preterm labour – a systematic review. *Med Sci Monit* 2002;8:RA268–73.
92.	Goodwin TM, Valenzuela GJ, Silver H, Creasy G. Dose ranging study of the oxytocin antagonist atosiban in the treatment of preterm labor. Atosiban Study Group. *Obstet Gynecol* 1996;88:331–6.
93.	Higby K, Xenakis EM, Pauerstein CJ. Do tocolytic agents stop preterm labor? A critical and comprehensive review of efficacy and safety. *Am J Obstet Gynecol* 1993;168:1247–56.
94.	Kosasa TS, Busse R, Wahl N, Hirata G, Nakayama RT, Hale RW. Long-term tocolysis with combined intravenous terbutaline and magnesium sulfate: a 10-year study of 1000 patients. *Obstet Gynecol* 1994;84:369–73.
95.	Brown SM, Tejani NA. Terbutaline sulfate in the prevention of recurrence of premature labor. *Obstet Gynecol* 1981;57:22–5.
96.	Creasy RK, Golbus MS, Laros RK, Jr., Parer JT, Roberts JM. Oral ritodrine maintenance in the treatment of preterm labor. *Am J Obstet Gynecol* 1980;137:212–9.
97.	Holleboom CA, Merkus JM, van Elferen LW, Keirse MJ. Double-blind evaluation of ritodrine sustained release for oral maintenance of tocolysis after active preterm labour. *Br J Obstet Gynaecol* 1996;103:702–5.
98.	Valenzuela GJ, Sanchez-Ramos L, Romero R, Silver HM, Koltun WD, Millar L, et al. Maintenance treatment of preterm labor with the oxytocin antagonist atosiban. The Atosiban PTL-098 Study Group. *Am J Obstet Gynecol* 2000;182:1184–90.
99.	How HY, Hughes SA, Vogel RL, Gall SA, Spinnato JA. Oral terbutaline in the outpatient management of preterm labor. *Am J Obstet Gynecol* 1995;173:1518–22.
100.	Rust OA, Bofill JA, Arriola RM, Andrew ME, Morrison JC. The clinical efficacy of oral tocolytic therapy. *Am J Obstet Gynecol* 1996;175:838–42.
101.	Parilla BV, Dooley SL, Minogue JP, Socol ML. The efficacy of oral terbutaline after intravenous tocolysis. *Am J Obstet Gynecol* 1993;169:965–9.
102.	Lewis R, Mercer BM, Salama M, Walsh MA, Sibai BM. Oral terbutaline after parenteral tocolysis: a randomized, double-blind, placebo-controlled trial. *Am J Obstet Gynecol* 1996;175:834–7.
103.	Valenzuela GJ. Atosiban passage through the placenta; result of an investigator sponsored IND study [unpublished work]. 2003.

Chapter 26

Management III

Discussion

Thornton: If I were to choose questions of importance, they would be: should we use progesterone prophylaxis, should we give tocolysis at all, and, if we give tocolytics, which drug should be used? I would love to get a consensus on these but I know for sure that we could not. However, I would like to judge the general feeling for the last two questions.

Smith: I guess my colleagues in Australia have not had the opportunity of seeing everything presented today but I can report that virtually everyone is switching over to nifedipine from betasympathomimetics in Australia, with the possible exception of Perth. So many people were distressed by pulmonary oedema cases and just how awful it is for women to be on betasympathomimetics with very little evidence that they provide neonatal benefit. We were persuaded by the data on nifedipine: that it was safer and that the evidence appeared to indicate it was better for the neonate. Most people have switched but there is still concern that it is not as effective as anticipated. I also have to state an interest. In Australia we have set up a study called 'BORN' (birth outcomes with rofecoxib and nifedipine). This is a multicentre trial at 22–28 weeks of gestation. There is stratification within gestational ages and for singletons versus twins. We are hoping to get a thousand women in the early preterm labour group. It is powered to look at the outcomes at two years.

Regan: Professor Morrison, I think you mount a very powerful argument for not using tocolysis. Have you managed to persuade your colleagues in your unit not to use tocolysis and what is your protocol?

Morrison: We use atosiban, which is licensed in Ireland and the UK. Nifedipine is not licensed in either country. So atosiban is our protocol although we use tocolysis very little.

Bennett: I must make a point about licensing. My understanding is that, in Europe, the purpose of the licence is to enable a pharmaceutical company to advertise and promote a drug for a particular indication. It does not in any way stop a clinician from prescribing that drug for a clinical indication and so I think the fact that nifedipine does not have a licence does not mean that we should discount it or not consider using it.

Morrison: Most of what we use in pregnancy does not have a licence.

Bennett: Exactly. Steroids do not have a licence for use in pregnancy.

Smith: It reflects the interests of the drug companies in making money. If there is no money to be made, no company is going to take it up.

Saade: I have heard repeatedly in the last three days that clinically apparent labour is a late event in the process. If you look at uterine electrical activity, it starts a few hours before clinically evident labour. We have also heard that cervical changes start much earlier, so it seems to me that the effort to stop uterine contractility may be futile and you should be looking at something earlier to diagnose the cervical changes and act on that. I think that cerclage may be an option, or even local treatment with prostaglandin inhibitors, which we have successfully used in animals. Other issues are that any treatment to stop contractions that work on ion channels should raise the question as to the effect on vascular smooth muscle. The sensitivity of vascular smooth muscle to ion channel inhibitors is much higher than the myometrium and so you may give enough medication to cause hypotension or placental insufficiency.

Smith: I would like to discuss how the agents are working and go back to what Professor López Bernal talked about in the myometrium. Atosiban and betasympathomimetics both work through seven transmembrane receptors that desensitise or downregulate. Dr Romero, I am surprised that your study was able to show the value of persistent atosiban. I do not know what the oxytocin receptor does after continual exposure to its agonist but we know that betasympathomimetics cause a pronounced downregulation. The attractiveness of the cyclooxygenase 2 inhibitor is that it works by inhibiting the synthesis of the agent rather than via a receptor that may be dysregulated.

Saade: No one is talking about cyclooxygenase inhibitors at this meeting. I guess they are not used in the UK but we have used them. We have used them up to 32 weeks of gestation, for 72 hours. There was no effect on the Dopplers or amniotic fluid and there were minimal maternal and fetal adverse effects. I think they are another option, particularly with their effects on the cervix.

Nathanielsz: I would like to address several of these points because I do think this is an area where the basic science can really help. Listening to Dr Romero give a masterful description of what happened and having been at the US Food and Drug Administration (FDA) review, I have thought a lot about it since then. What I tried to say in my talk, and I would have enlarged upon it if there had been more time, is the concept that parturition is a continuum. We are all looking for the triggers and the clocks for parturition but I think we have got it all wrong, including myself. If there is any single trigger to parturition it is fertilisation, without any question whatsoever. After that the trajectory of development determines the time of labour and delivery. Oestrogen rises from 28 weeks onwards and recruits different mechanisms. One of them is the oxytocin system. It would seem that the early preterm labours are infected and after 26–28 weeks you have a system that is accelerating faster than it should be. The salivary oestrogens tell that story too. You have a system that is accelerating faster than it should be and you recruit the oxytocin system. Now whether that is the signal or is just a major participant is not known. I think we have to stop focusing on a single trigger.

In my view, atosiban is such a powerful agent after 26–27 weeks because you have a system in which oestrogen is rising, perhaps because the fetal and maternal adrenals have been recruited due to stress. This results in more androgen and oestrogen production . Providing there is no risk to the fetus, the goal should be to break that circle – whether you are breaking a trigger or not does not matter. Atosiban is extraordinarily powerful in our hands in the animal model and I am told by Murph Goodwin at the University of Southern California that you can not blind atosiban after 28 weeks. The response is so pronounced that you will immediately know which women have been receiving atosiban: they will rapidly say that the contractions have decreased, whereas the placebo patients will not. If you give atosiban to a pregnant baboon or a pregnant rhesus monkey it wipes out contractions – we have published data showing that.[1] Providing you define the right patient after 26–28 weeks, atosiban and other oxytocin antagonists will be extraordinarily powerful. I would like to comment on receptor downregulation with atosiban, which is very important question. We have shown the 24 hour cycle in oxytocin is driven by oestrogen. If you are going to use an oxytocin antagonist you do not have to give it to the patient 24 hours a day. It will be just as beneficial to give the antagonist at 4 o'clock in the afternoon to abolish the diurnal variation. I think if you wanted to use prophylactic atosiban, it should be given every afternoon for six or seven hours to stop that night's episode of uterine activity.

Professor Saade, you said that we have learned that labour is a long-term process and yet some things start late. I think the first is right and the second wrong. I think it is a long process. If you can break the vicious circle of nocturnal uterine activity for two or three hours early in the process, that will be more effective. So we have to think about prophylactic tocolysis very seriously. As far as downregulation is concerned, we can avoid it by giving for five or six hours each day. Actually, you don't have to worry about downregulation because if you downregulate the receptor you have done something you would like to achieve.

One of the things we have worried about in our nonhuman primate work is whether we were going to get significant haemorrhage when we remove the placenta at caesarean section in animals that have received the oxytocin antagonist. We do not need to worry. When we give oxytocin, the uterus contracts beautifully. Atosiban is a very safe agent. We have given it to pregnant sheep and infused it into the fetus for up to 15 days. So would you let your wife, daughter or daughter-in-law be treated with an oxytocin antagonist? I certainly would after 28 weeks. I think if we modify our therapeutic regimens we could use it prophylactically. I think it was a tragedy when the FDA did not allow the drug to go forward.

López Bernal: That is a very good point about desensitisation. Agonists stimulate the receptor and promote desensitisation but antagonists do not. There is another question about the clinical use of oxytocin. It will induce receptor desensitisation because it is an agonist. Regarding tocolytics, I think we should not forget the recommendation that the College has made that there is a place for them in order to transfer the baby to somewhere with good neonatal facilities. I think paediatricians would be devastated if we said that we do not want to use tocolytics. I think we must promote the idea that we need safe drugs to relax the uterus even for a short time.

Azzopardi: I want to make the comment that I think all the presentations I've heard today have focused on the neonatal outcome, which I think is great, but I doubt whether these studies were powered to look at the neonatal outcome. When you are talking about neonatal outcome you are usually talking about babies below 26 weeks of gestation because those are the ones with the highest morbidity and mortality. These are relatively small numbers of pregnancies. So it is not surprising that you get spurious results. Some of the major morbidity that you have mentioned, such as necrotising enterocolitis, is notoriously difficult to study even when you have a hundred cases. let alone when you have five or six. It is interesting that the Australian study will follow up for two years but I think that demonstrating an effect will be dependent on the gestational age of your population. Once you get beyond 26 weeks I would be very surprised if you would see any changes in outcome at two years.

Lamont: Prophylactic tocolysis is, I think, the wrong terminology. Tocolysis means to destroy contractions and we are actually giving something to prevent the contractions. The second thing is the short delay for steroids. We keep mentioning 48 hours and I think if Mark Keirse were here, he would point out that when he did the meta-analysis he tried to find ways to compare the different studies. The one common factor was 48 hours so they chose that as the standard. Since that time it has become carved in stone that tocolytics only works for 48 hours but many studies show that tocolysis works for more than 48 hours.

Gardosi: In relation to Dr Azzopardi's point, I would like to reinforce that the numbers are small at early gestational ages but a great deal of morbidity is caused at later gestations. This is because delivery is more common at later gestational ages. These babies can still have significant morbidity.

Lamont: There are two areas we haven't addressed in the last couple of days. One is the health economics: not just the cost of neonatal intensive care but the cost of care in the first five to ten years of life. The second thing is what we should do at the extremes of viability (22–25 weeks).

Thornton: There is a clash in the dates of this meeting with another and we intended to have the financial aspect represented. Can I go on to the presentation on nifedipine? Looking at the data included in the meta-analyses, none were blinded, some women were already on ritodrine and some were given very high ritodrine concentrations, which one presumes causes maternal adverse effects. I just worry whether we can really draw conclusions from such trials.

Papatsonis: I think that is a problem. Normally studies are included where patients are randomised between tocolytics but there was no exclusion of tocolysis prior to randomisation. That is a little bit of a flaw. There were about eight studies excluded from the meta-analysis because it was not clear how randomisation was done or maintenance agents were used. Our study was the biggest study included. We gave higher doses of nifedipine in the first hour and the maintenance dose was higher. We could not find a significant difference in favour of the higher dose but all the studies are a little bit different in dosage so it was difficult to compare them.

Lamont: The other problem with some of the nifedipine studies is that it is not clear whether they are a single agent or double agent and whether they are first- or second-line therapy. I guess particularly with oral administration sometimes people don't want to wait for the effect so they start intravenous betasympathomimetics first of all. The other thing I find difficult is to work out which nifedipine studies use capsules, tablets, slow release and so on, because these are often given in different doses.

The other thing is that because most of the studies on nifedipine have been quite small they relied on meta-analyses. If you take the largest paper out there is no significance in terms of safety or efficacy.

Neilson: I don't know enough about the individual trials in the meta-analysis but I have been very interested in the presentations. If we didn't use any tocolytic drug at all, and

Professor Morrison was perhaps right in suggesting that we should not, do Dr Romero or Dr Papatsonis think that the evidence in favour of atosiban or calcium channel blockers would persuade us to start using these drugs?

Romero: I don't think the atosiban trials were designed to answer that question but it is effective in delaying delivery and that is a desirable goal. Remember that the standard was not to improve neonatal morbidity for the first tocolytic agent to be approved. We are probably convinced from today's discussion that we should do placebo-controlled trials of tocolytics but when we go to clinicians and try to involve patients we find a great deal of obstacles. How many of you who treat women with premature labour would enrol your patients in a randomised trial of steroids plus placebo and any tocolytic plus steroids?

Lamont: At 30 to 34 weeks people might do it but at 26 to 30 weeks they might not. The other point that Professor Morrison made was that no study has shown any benefit of tocolysis in neonatal outcome but they have not been powered to do it.

Smith: Dr Papatsonis's study shows benefits for neonatal outcome of nifedipine compared to betasympathomimetics. Dr Lamont keeps saying that short-term treatment must be an advantage to allow for transfer and steroids but this does not appear in the trials. This suggests that it is a misapprehension.

Bennett: There is no evidence that delaying delivery improves neonatal outcome and you can't extrapolate from cross-sectional studies that you get 3% improvement in death rates.

Lamont: I agree that it is a leap of faith but we know that steroids significantly reduce perinatal mortality and morbidity. We also know that neonatal transfer reduces perinatal mortality.

Reference

1.   Nathanielsz PW, Honnebier MB, Mecenas C, Jenkins SL, Holland ML, Demarest K. Effect of the oxytocin antagonist atosiban (1-deamino-2-D-tyr(OET)-4-thr-8-orn-vasotocin/oxytocin) on nocturnal myometrial contractions, maternal cardiovascular function, transplacental passage, and fetal oxygenation in the pregnant baboon during the last third of gestation. *Biol Reprod* 1997;57:320–4.

SECTION 7

MANAGEMENT IV

Chapter 27

Mode of preterm delivery: caesarean section versus vaginal delivery

Philip J Steer

Introduction – the systematic review

There has been little new information published about the advantages and disadvantages of abdominal versus vaginal delivery since the systematic review by Grant, Penn and Steer published in 1996.[1] Currently, authors often quote the Cochrane Collaboration review, which states that 'This review should be cited as: Grant A, Glazener CMA. Elective caesarean section versus expectant management for delivery of the small baby (Cochrane Review). In: The Cochrane Library, Issue 3, 2003. Oxford: Update Software.' This gives the misleading impression that there has been a recent advance in knowledge on this topic. In fact, the 2003 review states that the most recent substantive amendment was on 13 December 2000, and the review is simply an amplified version of the 1996 paper. We have thus not really moved forward scientifically in the views that we can hold on this topic over the past seven years.

The analysis in the Grant systematic review is based upon six randomised trials comparing a policy of elective caesarean delivery with expectant management with recourse to caesarean section. Three of these trials compared elective caesarean section versus expectant management for babies with cephalic presentations only (two published trials[2,3] and one unpublished abandoned trial), and the other three with breech presentations only.[4-6] Most of the data come from the 1980s and there have been substantial improvements both in the operative techniques for caesarean section and in the care of the preterm neonate since that time. The numbers randomised were 38, 4 and 2, and 27, 38 and 13 respectively. The number of cases on which we can base our management is thus only 44 and 78 respectively. Consequently, any conclusions that we can draw from this data must be treated with great caution.

As a result of the small numbers of cases randomised, only a few of the differences between the groups by mode of delivery reach statistical significance, if considered by the frequentist approach. A formal Bayesian analysis, incorporating prior probabilities, has not been performed using this data but nonetheless Lilford et al.[7] have pointed out that even nonsignificant differences in outcome in trials that are methodologically sound can be used to refine our clinical judgement. In the comments that follow, the two groups will for simplicity be referred to as the 'caesarean section group' and the 'vaginal delivery group', although the former does contain a few cases where the delivery was vaginal because it occurred unexpectedly quickly, and the latter contains some babies delivered by caesarean section for specific obstetric indications.

Perhaps the most important issue is the relative likelihood of fetal intrapartum/neonatal death. The results overall showed that caesarean section was associated with a lower risk of death by a factor of 75% (2/62 versus 8/60). However, two of the eight in the vaginal delivery group were associated with lethal congenital anomalies (hypoplastic left heart syndrome and pulmonary hypoplasia).[6] If these two cases are disregarded, the difference in risk is no longer statistically significant. Nonetheless, the Peto odds ratio is still 0.32, thus indicating, on a Bayesian interpretation, that for every 15 additional caesarean sections that we perform we will save one fetal/neonatal death. Most clinicians and parents would probably consider this to be a clinically significant difference. Reductions in the incidence of cord prolapse, neonatal seizures, the need for neonatal intubation, and low five-minute Apgar scores, although not statistically significant, were all also in the expected direction, favouring caesarean section. However, an unexpected finding was that there was a statistically significantly lower need for maternal blood transfusion in the caesarean section group (OR 0.02; $P = 0.03$).

Also as expected, major maternal morbidity was much more likely in the caesarean section group (Peto OR 6.4; $P = 0.01$). Possibly as a result, breastfeeding was much more likely to occur if the delivery was vaginal rather than by caesarean section. Postpartum haemorrhage rates were lower with vaginal delivery (despite the need for more blood transfusions in this group than in those delivered by caesarean section, a paradoxical finding). However, a surprising finding was that the incidence of acidosis in the baby at birth was much lower following vaginal delivery than caesarean section (Peto OR 10.8; $P = 0.01$). This may account for the lower likelihood of the need for mechanical ventilation following vaginal delivery. Another counterintuitive finding was that head entrapment was more likely at caesarean section than at vaginal delivery, perhaps giving the clinical message, which also applies to term breech delivery, that an adequate abdominal incision needs to be made in order to avoid difficulty in delivering the head.

What of the longer term outcome? As so often with obstetric interventions, there was no obvious difference. Intracranial pathology (Peto OR 0.86; $P = 0.8$), other birth trauma (OR 1.18; $P = 0.9$), abnormal follow-up in childhood (OR 0.8; $P = 0.7$), neonatal stay longer than 10 days (OR 0.86; $P = 0.7$) and maternal stay longer than 10 days (OR 1.3; $P = 0.7$) were all similar in the two groups.

Management in the light of the systematic review

In general, the findings of the systematic review agree with the subjective impressions of most obstetricians, which is that caesarean section is safer for the baby but riskier for the mother. Thus, when faced with a mother in preterm labour, we have to balance the two risks. Different mothers, and different fathers, will have a different perspective on this situation. Most clinicians will have encountered cases where the mother is willing to take additional risks to safeguard her baby but the father has the opposite view, and *vice versa*. In these situations, the most we can do is to provide accurate information, encourage parents to explore their personal priorities, and support them in the choice that they make. Whether we should take into account socio-economic issues is another difficult question. For example, is it better for a very young socially disadvantaged mother to keep her uterus intact and risk losing her very preterm baby, or potentially compromise her future reproductive performance to save a baby that may survive but be severely handicapped?

Will further randomised trials shed any light on this situation? It seems unlikely that such trials will now be carried out. There was no fundamental problem in obtaining women's consent to randomisation of mode of delivery; antenatal consent was obtained from 70% of women in several of the trials.[5,8] The major problem was persuading obstetricians to allocate randomly what they perceived as a major decision; they were likely to be influenced by individual factors associated with each case.[5,9,10]

Some specific clinical management points emerge from the trials. For example, a significant proportion of babies were not of the expected presentation when the delivery was actually carried out. In one of the trials, babies thought to be in breech presentation actually turned out to be cephalic at delivery.[5] In the same trial, one woman recruited who was allocated to elective caesarean section turned out not to be in labour: she was eventually delivered three weeks after trial entry, indicating that a policy of elective caesarean section may occasionally result in unnecessary preterm caesarean delivery.

Recent nonrandomised studies

Since the systematic review was carried out, there have been a few nonrandomised studies which have reported interesting results. For example, Topp et al.[11] have suggested that caesarean section might even increase the risk of long-term cerebral palsy, rather than reducing it. Wolf et al.[12] compared two centres in relation to how they delivered women with babies of gestational age 26 to 31 weeks, one with a 17% caesarean section rate (n = 305) and one with an 85% rate (n = 162). They found no differences in the rates of perinatal death, respiratory distress syndrome, intracranial bleeding or handicap at two years or later. Grisaru-Granovsky et al.[13] showed no difference in immediate neonatal outcome for babies whose mothers had been delivered for chorioamnionitis, according to whether they were delivered vaginally or by caesarean section. Bauer et al.[14] studied the mode of delivery of 48 extremely preterm infants (less than 26 weeks of gestation): 44% were delivered by caesarean section. As with the systematic review, babies born by caesarean section had significantly lower umbilical cord blood artery pHs. Moreover, their survival rate was only 43%, compared with 78% for babies born vaginally. However, the mean birthweight of babies born by caesarean section was only 655 g, compared with 751 g for those born vaginally ($P < 0.05$). Although they concluded that extremely immature preterm infants had a more favourable outcome if they were born vaginally when compared with infants delivered by caesarean section, the substantial and significant difference in birthweight between the two groups and the fact that the mode of delivery was not randomised must make this conclusion doubtful.

Wadhawan et al.[15] followed up 1606 babies weighing 401–1000 g born by caesarean section between 1995 and 1997 inclusive. Controlling in a multivariate analysis for known risk factors, they found no significant difference according to whether or not the caesarean section was done electively or during labour, in intraventricular haemorrhage, periventricular leukomalacia, and neurodevelopment scores. They concluded that, of itself, labour did not have a deleterious effect on these very small babies.

Current practice in the UK – data from the North West Thames database

What about current practice in the UK? I have interrogated the North West Thames perinatal database to answer this question, at least for this region of London. There were 585 291 pregnancies between 1988 and 2000 inclusive. Of these, 517 381

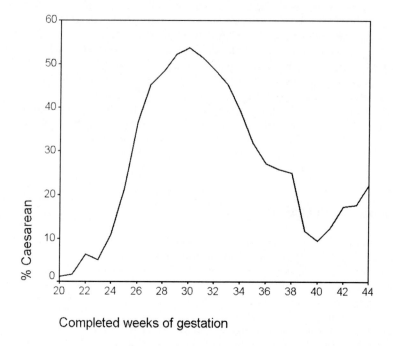

Completed weeks of gestation

Figure 27.1. The caesarean section delivery rate for gestations from 20 to 44 weeks in 517 381 pregnancies that progressed far enough to have a birthweight recorded in North West Thames (a region of London, UK) from 1988 to 2000

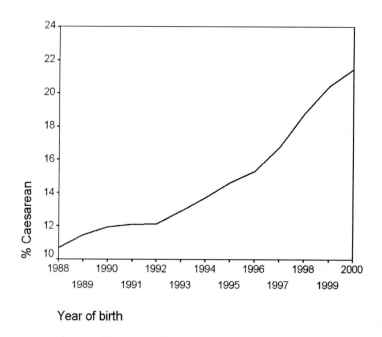

Year of birth

Figure 27.2. Change in the caesarean section rate for pregnancies with a gestation of 37 weeks or more from 1988 to 2000

Figure 27.3. Change in the caesarean section rate for pregnancies with a gestation of 32 to 36 weeks inclusive from 1988 to 2000

Figure 27.4. Change in the caesarean section rate for pregnancies with a gestation of 27 to 31 weeks inclusive from 1988 to 2000

pregnancies progressed far enough to have a birthweight recorded. Figure 27.1 shows the caesarean section rate for gestations from 20 to 44 weeks. As it can be difficult to distinguish between elective and emergency caesarean sections at early gestations, for the purposes of this analysis I have included both. It can be seen that before 24 weeks of gestation, the caesarean section rate was less than 10%, rising to over 50% between 29 and 32 weeks. Thereafter, the caesarean section rate declined again, reaching a nadir of less than 10% at 40 weeks. It then rose again to 20% by 44 weeks.

We also know that the overall caesarean section rate has been rising steadily during this period. Figure 27.2 shows that the caesarean section rate in term and post-term pregnancies rose from under 11% in 1988 to over 20% by the year 2000. Similarly, the rate between 32 and 36 weeks inclusive rose from just under 25% to over 40% (Figure 27.3). However, the rate from 27 to 31 weeks inclusive stayed stable at below 50% until 1994, when it started to rise and then stabilise between 50% and 60% (Figure 27.4). In contrast to the term caesarean section rate, the rate at 24 to 26 weeks inclusive has not altered consistently and has fluctuated between 13% to just over 40% with no clear trend (Figure 27.5).

I have also looked at the rate of perinatal mortality in relation to caesarean section. I have excluded antepartum stillbirths as these cannot be affected by mode of delivery, but have included intrapartum stillbirths as many of these might be preventable by a policy of routine caesarean section. Figure 27.6 shows a steady decline in intrapartum and neonatal perinatal mortality from 1988 to 2000, from just over 3.4 per thousand to 2.2 per thousand. Figure 27.7 shows the same intrapartum and neonatal perinatal mortality aggregated over the whole period, and classified by mode of delivery. It should be noted that, between 22 and 38 weeks, the fall in perinatal mortality is linear

Figure 27.5. Change in the caesarean section rate for pregnancies with a gestation of 24 to 26 weeks inclusive from 1988 to 2000

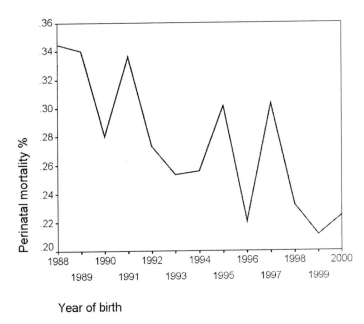

Figure 27.6. Perinatal mortality rate from 1988 to 2000, excluding antepartum stillbirths but including intrapartum stillbirths and one-week neonatal deaths

on a log scale. The perinatal mortality is remarkably similar by mode of delivery, suggesting that either the mode of delivery has no influence on perinatal mortality or the increased risk that prompts the caesarean section is exactly balanced by the improved outcome produced by this mode of delivery. It is also interesting to note that perinatal mortality rises sharply again from 39 weeks onwards in babies born by caesarean section, whereas in babies born vaginally a rising perinatal mortality is not evident until 42 weeks. This is likely to be due to the 'treatment paradox', whereby caesarean section is performed for babies showing signs of intrapartum dysfunction, who accordingly have a higher perinatal mortality rate.

Conclusions

The systematic review of the mode of preterm delivery suggests that caesarean section benefits the baby but carries an increased risk for the mother. However, recently published papers, and our own data, cast considerable doubt on the benefit to the baby from being born by caesarean section. This may be due to the improvements in neonatal intensive care in the 15 years since most of the babies in the systematic review were born. As caesarean section carries a risk of significant morbidity for the mother, the appropriate conclusion therefore seems to be that caesarean section in preterm labour should be reserved for specific indications, such as signs of fetal dysfunction (abnormal heart rate patterns), or other risk factors such as antepartum haemorrhage, prolapsed cord or abnormal presentation. Whether abnormal presentation includes all babies presenting by the breech remains unclear. Where labour is progressing rapidly

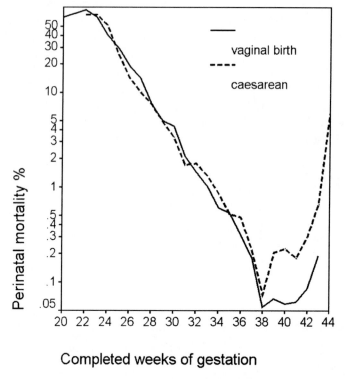

Figure 27.7. Perinatal mortality rate from 1988 to 2000, excluding antepartum stillbirths but including intrapartum stillbirths and one-week neonatal deaths, by mode of delivery

and straightforward vaginal delivery appears likely, it is probably inappropriate to perform a caesarean section solely because the fetus is in breech presentation. In particular, the risk of head entrapment has probably been overstated in the past. It seems to be most unlikely in cases where the membranes remain intact until full dilatation. If the presentation is cephalic, then most obstetricians currently favour a policy of aiming for vaginal delivery, with close fetal and maternal monitoring. The gestation at which the baby is sufficiently viable for the mother to be counselled about the option of caesarean section remains a matter of judgement. It must depend upon the local facilities (for example, availability of high-quality neonatal intensive care), upon the skill and experience of the obstetrician, and perhaps most of all upon the properly informed preferences of the parents regarding the balance between increasing the chance of survival for the baby versus increasing the risk of morbidity for the mother. Currently, most obstetricians would treat babies of less than 24 weeks of gestation as previable and those of 26 weeks or more as viable, relying on assessment of the specific circumstances at 24 and 25 weeks.

In relation to vaginal birth, the appropriate instrument to use to expedite delivery at full dilatation in cases of fetal dysfunction (for example, an abnormal fetal heart-rate trace) remains controversial. Complications reported with ventouse delivery include cerebral haemorrhage[16,17] and leptomeningocoele.[18] However, one study of babies weighing 1500 g to 2499 g found no excess morbidity from the use of the silicone rubber vacuum extractor,[19] and a similar study of 56 neonates weighing less than 2000 g also found no excess morbidity from the use of this instrument.[20] Evidence relating to the use of a metal or plastic 'Bird' type cup, which produces substantially more chignon, is currently lacking. Until more data is forthcoming, many obstetricians currently favour the use of forceps at less than 34 weeks of gestation, on the principle that they form a protective cage around the fetal head and minimise head compression.

References

1. Grant A, Penn ZJ, Steer PJ. Elective or selective caesarean delivery of the small baby? A systematic review of the controlled trials. *Br J Obstet Gynaecol* 1996;103:1197–200.

2. Wallace RL, Schifrin BS, Paul RH. The delivery route for very-low-birth-weight infants. A preliminary report of a randomized, prospective study. *J Reprod Med* 1984;29:736–40.

3. Lumley J, Lester A, Renou P, Wood C. A failed RCT to determine the best method of delivery for very low birth weight infants. *Control Clin Trials* 1985;6:120–7.

4. Viegas OA, Ingemarsson I, Sim LP, Singh K, Cheng M, Ratnam SS, *et al.* Collaborative study on preterm breeches: vaginal delivery versus caesarean section. *Asia Oceania J Obstet Gynaecol* 1985;11:349–55.

5. Penn ZJ, Steer PJ, Grant A. A multicentre randomised controlled trial comparing elective and selective caesarean section for the delivery of the preterm breech infant. *Br J Obstet Gynaecol* 1996;103:684–9.

6. Zlatnik FJ. The Iowa premature breech trial. *Am J Perinatol* 1993;10:60–3.

7. Lilford RJ, Thornton JG, Braunholtz D. Clinical trials and rare diseases: a way out of a conundrum. *BMJ* 1995;311:1621–5.

8. Lumley J. Method of delivery for the preterm infant. *BJOG* 2003;110 Suppl 20:88–92.

9. Penn ZJ, Steer PJ. How obstetricians manage the problem of preterm delivery with special reference to the preterm breech. *Br J Obstet Gynaecol* 1991;98:531–4.

10. Penn ZJ, Steer PJ. Reasons for declining participation in a prospective randomized trial to determine the optimum mode of delivery of the preterm breech. *Control Clin Trials* 1990;11:226–31.

11. Topp M, Langhoff-Roos J, Uldall P. Preterm birth and cerebral palsy. Predictive value of pregnancy complications, mode of delivery, and Apgar scores. *Acta Obstet Gynecol Scand* 1997;76:843–8.

12. Wolf H, Schaap AH, Bruinse HW, Smolders-de Haas H, van Ertbruggen I, Treffers PE. Vaginal delivery compared with caesarean section in early preterm breech delivery: a comparison of long term outcome. *Br J Obstet Gynaecol* 1999;106:486–91.

13. Grisaru-Granovsky S, Schimmel MS, Granovsky R, Diamant YZ, Samueloff A. Cesarean section is not protective against adverse neurological outcome in survivors of preterm delivery due to overt chorioamnionitis. *J Matern Fetal Neonatal Med* 2003;13:323–7.

14. Bauer J, Hentschel R, Zahradnik H, Karck U, Linderkamp O. Vaginal delivery and neonatal outcome in extremely-low-birth-weight infants below 26 weeks of gestational age. *Am J Perinatol* 2003;20:181–8.

15. Wadhawan R, Vohr BR, Fanaroff AA, Perritt RL, Duara S, Stoll BJ, *et al.* Does labor influence neonatal and neurodevelopmental outcomes of extremely-low-birth-weight infants who are born by cesarean delivery? *Am J Obstet Gynecol* 2003;189:501–6.

16. Choudhari K, Choudhari Y. Posterior fossa haemorrhage in a preterm infant following vacuum assisted delivery. *BJOG* 2003;110:787.

17. Kent A, Lemyre B, Loosley-Millman M, Paes B. Posterior fossa haemorrhage in a preterm infant following vacuum assisted delivery. *BJOG* 2001;108:1008–10.

18. Stewart KJ, Acolet D, Peterson D. Leptomeningocoele: a rare complication of ventouse delivery. *BJOG* 2000;107:1173–5.

19. Morales R, Adair CD, Sanchez-Ramos L, Gaudier FL. Vacuum extraction of preterm infants with birth weights of 1,500–2,499 grams. *J Reprod Med* 1995;40:127–30.

20. Thomas SJ, Morgan MA, Asrat T, Weeks JW. The risk of periventricular-intraventricular hemorrhage with vacuum extraction of neonates weighing 2000 grams or less. *J Perinatol* 1997;17:37–41.

Chapter 28

Postmortem examination and placental pathology in relation to preterm birth

Neil J Sebire

Introduction

Postmortem examination and/or pathological examination of the placenta should be considered a routine component of patient management in cases of preterm birth since such examination may provide important additional information for the management of either the current or future pregnancies. There are several issues that pathological examination in this context should address, including determination of the underlying cause of spontaneous preterm birth, definition of the underlying pathological process in cases of iatrogenic preterm birth, identification of complications related to prematurity, identification of iatrogenic complications secondary to medical care of the premature infant and provision of a summary of the pathophysiological processes in relation to the clinical course. This chapter provides an overview of these issues; further details are available from the specialist references provided.

The postmortem/placental examination

Numerous studies have reported the value of perinatal postmortem examination in providing useful clinical information in addition to that known prior to the autopsy, for various indications including termination of pregnancy for prenatally diagnosed fetal abnormality, intrauterine fetal death and neonatal deaths.[1,2] (Table 28.1[3–15]) All studies demonstrate similar results, with additional clinically relevant information being generated in about one-third of the cases. Furthermore, this figure is similar for all the examined clinical indications, including cases from neonatal intensive care units in which extensive premortem investigation may have been carried out. The additional information gained from postmortem examination may be related to the underlying cause of the pregnancy complication and its evolution, or it may reveal previously unknown factors, which may nevertheless have an impact on patient management. Most of these studies were, however, based on postmortem examination performed by specialist paediatric/perinatal pathologists in specialist centres. It has been reported that the quality and usefulness of information obtained at perinatal autopsy is strongly related to the expertise of the pathologist performing the procedure, with the minimum acceptable criteria for adequate reports, as determined by the Royal College of Pathologists, being achieved in only about half of cases carried out by general pathologists compared with almost 100% in cases performed by specialist paediatric

Table 28.1. Studies reporting on the value of postmortem examination following intrauterine, perinatal and neonatal deaths and terminations of pregnancy for fetal abnormality

Study	Women (n)	Indication	Additional information obtained[a] (%)
Yeo et al.[15] (2002)	88	ToP	36
Hefler et al.[14] (2001)	139	IUD	56
Kabra et al.[13] (2001)	240	NND	39
Faye-Petersen et al.[12] (1999)	139	IUD, ToP, NND	26 (51 for ToP)
Barr et al.[11] (1999)	91	NND	30
Tennstedt et al.[10] (1998)	183	ToP	22
Dhar et al.[9] (1998)	338	NND	18
Rajashekar et al.[8] (1996)	1594	IUD, NND	60
Cartlidge et al.[7] (1995)	232	IUD, ToP, NND	39
Saller et al.[6] (1995)	125	IUD, NND	34
Chescheir et al.[5] (1994)	133	IUD, ToP, NND	39
Shen-Schwarz et al.[4] (1989)	61	ToP anomalies	46
Meier et al.[3] (1986)	139	IUD, ToP, NND	48
Total	3502	IUD, ToP, NND	39[b]

IUD = intrauterine death; NND = neonatal death; ToP = termination for prenatally diagnosed fetal abnormality; [a] percentage of cases in which clinically useful additional information was obtained from the postmortem examination which was not previously known; [b] non-weighted

pathologists.[16-22] Magnetic resonance imaging (MRI) has been suggested as a possible alternative to postmortem examination but it has a low sensitivity for major malformations (56%)[23] and cannot detect histological features that may be diagnostic for specific conditions. Adjunctive postmortem MRI examination may, however, have a role in the assessment of central nervous system malformations.[24]

Similarly, clear guidelines for cases requiring examination of the placenta by a pathologist have been approved by the College of American Pathologists, the Royal College of Obstetricians and Gynaecologists and the Royal College of Pathologists.[25-28] Essentially, all cases of severe preterm birth or other pregnancy complications are included in the indications, which will represent around 5–10% of deliveries in most obstetric units, depending upon their patient population. Placental examination provides useful clinical information in the majority of cases with appropriate indications, since even negative results may be useful for planning future care.[29] The proportion with positive findings will vary according to the indication for examination and gestational age. For example, severe preterm labour is much more likely to be associated with pathological lesions of the placenta than preterm labour at 36 weeks of gestation in an otherwise uncomplicated pregnancy. Many pathological lesions of the placenta have been assessed and most demonstrate acceptable inter-and intra-observer reproducibility among experienced pathologists,[30-32] even among archival specimens,[33] but, as with perinatal postmortem practice, studies examining diagnostic entities of the placenta have demonstrated that the usefulness of the report varies with the degree of specialisation of the pathologist. In about 40% of cases reported by general pathologists with limited experience in placental pathology, compared with specialist pathologists, there are diagnostic discrepancies including both missed and erroneously diagnosed conditions.[34]

An important factor in allowing the pathologist to produce meaningful reports of either postmortems or placental examinations is the provision of adequate clinical information since, as the fetus and placenta are dynamic and show varying appearances throughout gestation, the interpretation of many findings depends upon their context.

A clinical summary should be provided for all cases and any specific questions posed by the obstetrician should be highlighted. The use of specific request forms may significantly improve provision of clinical information, particularly for placental pathology requests, which may be completed by the midwives on labour ward using an appropriate proforma.[35] Labour ward and risk management protocols should include procedures for determining whether postmortem and/or placental examination is required in all deliveries.[36]

Causes of spontaneous preterm birth

Preterm birth may be iatrogenic, induced on the basis of fetal or maternal indications, or spontaneous. Several studies examining the underlying pathological features of the placenta in cases of preterm birth have reported that approximately one-third to one-half of cases (depending on gestational age; see below) will demonstrate inflammatory lesions, one-third of cases will show features of uteroplacental disease and the remainder will show either other specific entities or no pathological lesions.[37-41]

Choriodecidual inflammation

Inflammatory lesions due to ascending infection from the lower genital tract are the single largest group of pathologies causing preterm delivery.[40-46] The inflammatory process may be highly localised to the region of membranes overlying the cervix or may be more generalised, and may affect just the choriodecidual zone (choriodecidual inflammation) or involve the amniotic cavity itself (chorioamnionitis). The syndrome of clinical chorioamnionitis represents only a small minority of cases in which an inflammatory lesion is the underlying pathology, since in most cases a localised inflammatory reaction occurs that stimulates uterine contractions leading to preterm delivery before either frank amniotic fluid infection or maternal symptoms have developed.[47,48] Several studies have reported that there is a relationship between more severe prematurity and increasing frequency of inflammatory lesions.[48-54] Figure 28.1 shows that the majority of spontaneous pregnancy losses at 20–24 weeks of gestation are a consequence of inflammatory processes whereas the frequency falls as gestation advances. In common with most pathological entities, there is an issue of sampling adequacy in detection of focal choriodecidual inflammation or chorioamnionitis. The membrane rupture site should be extensively sampled since, in all cases, this is the area of maximal inflammatory infiltrate. It is not uncommon to identify severe inflammation of the membranes in one area while other areas, closer to the placental margin, may show no inflammatory infiltrate at all.[55]

The high frequency of placental inflammatory lesions in cases of spontaneous severe preterm birth also has implications for methods of screening for severe preterm delivery, such as measurement of cervical length by transvaginal ultrasound examination. The finding of a short cervix at 22–24 weeks of gestation with such methodologies is predictive of subsequent severe preterm delivery.[56-59] It remains unclear whether a short cervix predisposes to ascending infection or whether a localised, low-grade inflammatory response leads to cervical shortening but there is a reported association between the finding of a short cervix on ultrasound examination and the presence of acute inflammatory lesions of the placenta demonstrated by pathological examination.[60] Furthermore, the application of cervical cerclage does not appear to reduce the frequency of inflammatory lesions identified in these cases, suggesting that any inflammatory reaction present in women with a short cervix may

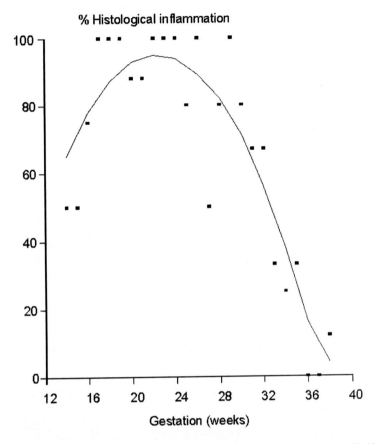

Figure 28.1. Prevalence of histological inflammation in placentas delivering spontaneously at 12–40 weeks of gestation; modified with permission from Sebire *et al.*[48]

already be established, although low-grade, at the time cervical shortening is recorded.[60,61] Several studies have examined the association between placental histopathological findings and amniotic fluid culture results and have reported that the relationship is not strong, with about 25% of culture+ cases showing no histological inflammation and vice versa.[62] The interpretation of these results is complicated by sampling issues, since inflammation may be focal, and the presence of organisms such as mycoplasmas, which may initiate less of an inflammatory cascade than other pathogenic bacteria. Furthermore, since many cases of preterm labour due to inflammatory lesions may be mediated via stimulation of uterine contractions via localised release inflammatory mediators in the supracervical region, rather than frank amniotic fluid infection, it is not surprising to find cases of preterm labour in which marked localised histological inflammation is identified but in which amniotic fluid cultures are negative.[47] In addition to representing a direct cause of preterm labour through the initiation of inflammatory cascades, inflammation of the decidua and chorion may also rarely be associated with the development of placental abruption, the postulated mechanism being inflammatory cell destruction/damage to vascular walls within the decidua.[63–65]

Placental inflammation may therefore initiate preterm labour with the associated potential complications to the neonate of severe premature birth (see later section). In addition, placental histopathological findings in such cases may have prognostic and epidemiological benefits since several studies have reported an association between the presence of chorioamnionitis and the development of more severe perinatal brain injury in these preterm infants. The release of inflammatory mediators, such as interleukin-6, may mediate neuronal injury in association with altered expression of adhesion molecules and inflammatory cell recruitment.[66–69]

Uteroplacental disease

Severe uteroplacental disease leading to local or widespread reduction in uteroplacental intervillous flow is the most common underlying mechanism in pregnancies complicated by intrauterine growth restriction (IUGR) or pre-eclampsia leading to iatrogenic preterm delivery (see later section). In addition, it has been suggested that up to one-third of cases of spontaneous preterm labour may be associated with uteroplacental disease.[39,40] The precise mechanism whereby placental ischaemia results in uterine contractions is not known but may be related to localised release of inflammatory mediators as the final common pathway.

Polyhydramnios/fetal abnormality

A minority of spontaneous preterm births are a consequence of congenital abnormalities leading to either polyhydramnios or idiopathic preterm labour.[70] The majority of polyhydramnios-associated cases have prenatally diagnosable fetal structural defects such as duodenal atresia or fetal tumour but several distinct abnormality syndromes may present with preterm labour in the absence of an obvious reason such as polyhydramnios, including fetal Bartter syndrome,[71] Fryns syndrome[72] and many others.[73] Pathological examination of the placenta is usually unremarkable but pregnancies with lethal fetal anomalies should be offered postmortem examination to confirm the defect and detect additional syndromic features important for counselling for future pregnancies.

Placental abruption

Around 1–5% of spontaneous preterm births are estimated to be a direct consequence of premature placental separation.[74–76] In some such cases, underlying predisposing factors such as uteroplacental vasculopathy or choriodecidual inflammation may be identifiable and should direct counselling for recurrence risks. Acute placental abruptions may show minimal or no abnormal histopathological findings and therefore negative histological examination does not exclude the diagnosis of placental abruption. Indeed, fewer than 50% of women with a history of acute placental abruption demonstrate the diagnostic pathological feature of retroplacental haematoma.[77] Conversely, only about one-third of histologically demonstrable placental abruptions have a clinical history of antepartum vaginal bleeding.[77] In those cases in which the haematoma has been present for a longer time, there may be a depression in the maternal surface of the placenta with marked villus congestion of the overlying parenchyma (Figure 28.2), fibrinous or organising retroplacental haematoma and acute parenchymal placental infarction.[77–79]

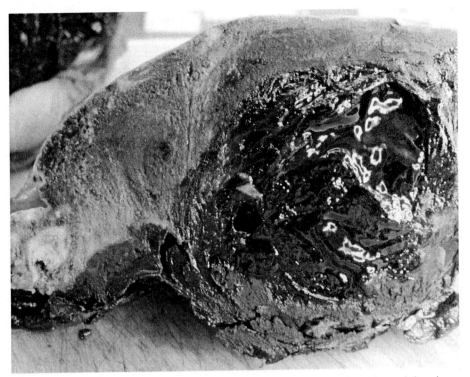

Figure 28.2. Macroscopic photograph of a placenta delivering preterm due to a large placental abruption; retroplacental haematoma can be seen with compression of the overlying parenchyma

Disorders of placentation

Several minor abnormalities of placentation have been described, some of which have been associated with a small number of cases of otherwise idiopathic preterm labour, usually near term. Such entities include circumvallate placenta, in which the basal plate is larger than the chorionic plate and hence is a form of placenta extrachorialis, and placenta praevia, in which an otherwise histologically normal placenta is abnormally inferiorly in the uterus with part of the placenta inserted over the cervical os. Further details on such entities are provided in standard texts on placental pathology.[80,81]

Multiple pregnancies

Multiple pregnancies account for 1–2% of births, of which at least 5–10% are severely preterm, with the proportion increasing with fetal number.[82] The risk of preterm delivery before 32 completed weeks of gestation is about 5% for dichorionic twins, 10% for monochorionic twins, due to the additional development of twin-to-twin transfusion syndrome (TTTS), and 30% for triplet pregnancies.[83,84] The role of the pathologist in such cases is to accurately determine both chorionicity (Figure 28.3) and the presence of associated multiple-pregnancy-related complications, in addition to all the features relevant to preterm birth in singleton pregnancies.[85,86] Although the proportion of multiple pregnancies delivering preterm with no histopathological

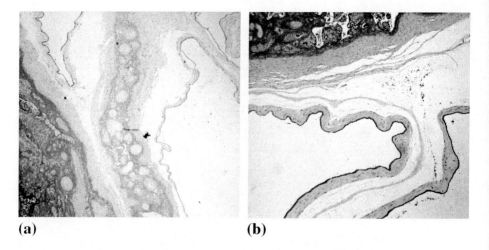

(a)   **(b)**

Figure 28.3. Histological sections of the junction of the placental disk and the intertwin membrane of dichorionic (a) and monochorionic (b) twin pregnancies; in dichorionic pregnancies there is extension of chorionic tissue between the amniotic layers of the intertwin membrane (H&E, original magnifications ×25)

placental abnormality is greater than for singletons, presumably because many cases of spontaneous preterm labour are secondary to uterine distension, the relationship between severe preterm delivery and chorioamnionitis remains and, in essentially all such cases, it is the membranes of the presenting fetus that are inflamed.[87,88] Additionally, about 10–15% of monochorionic pregnancies may be complicated by severe TTTS.[83] Placental examination in such cases should determine the extent of placental share and the vascular anastomotic pattern in relation to pregnancy course, and the effects of intrauterine therapy such as endoscopic laser ablation of placental vessels should be assessed; marked localised changes secondary to chorionic vessel occlusion such as extensive villus hypovascularity and fibrosis are usually seen following laser ablation.[89,90] Pathological examination should be carried out as part of the evaluation of all such intrauterine procedures.

Pathology of iatrogenic preterm birth

The pathology of iatrogenic preterm birth is obviously related to the underlying disease indicating delivery. In this context, the main roles of pathological examination are to confirm the prenatal findings and to provide additional information regarding the pathophysiology of the condition in relation to prenatal findings to aid the management of future pregnancies with similar complications.

Uteroplacental disease (IUGR, pre-eclampsia)

The most common indication for iatrogenic preterm delivery is chronic uteroplacental disease manifesting as IUGR and /or pre-eclampsia.[37] The decision regarding timing of delivery of pregnancies undergoing antenatal surveillance is now usually based on ultrasound findings, in particular fetal and umbilical Doppler flow velocity waveform indices.[91] The underlying pathophysiological event in such pregnancies is essentially defective trophoblastic invasion and inadequate conversion of uterine spiral arteries, with resultant suboptimal intervillous blood flow, which becomes more marked as the pregnancy advances.[92,93] In cases resulting in intrauterine death, postmortem examination can confirm the degree of fetal growth restriction with indices such as the brain/liver weight ratio, and may show additional features not detected antenatally such as erythroblastosis and intrauterine periventricular white matter damage.[94] Placental examination usually demonstrates features of uteroplacental disease including placental parenchymal infarction and villus changes secondary to severely reduced intervillous flow, including villus hypovascularity and increased trophoblastic syncytial knot formation in association with stem vessel vasoconstrictive changes.[95] On rare occasions, direct evidence of vascular disease such as atherosis of basal plate vessels may be demonstrated in the delivered placenta (Figure 28.4).[96] Rare cases of severe early-onset IUGR may not be associated with classical uteroplacental disease but demonstrate small poorly vascularised chorionic villi, and a primary defect in placental development has been suggested as a possible underlying pathological mechanism in these cases.[97]

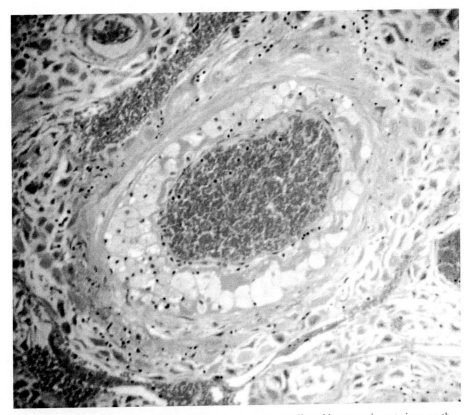

Figure 28.4. Photomicrograph of the basal plate of a placenta complicated by severe intrauterine growth restriction (IUGR) demonstrating changes of acute atherosis of the maternal vessels with accumulation of intimal lipid-laden macrophages; these changes indicate severe uteroplacental disease (H&E, original magnification ×200)

In most cases of severe IUGR the primary event is reduction of maternal intervillous blood flow due to uteroplacental abnormalities. The placental villus morphological and umbilical artery Doppler changes are progressive and probably represent secondary changes in response to the reduced oxygen delivery. Progressive stem vessel vasoconstriction occurs in response to reduced intervillous flow as a placental autoregulatory mechanism to maximise oxygen extraction and this is the probable cause of the increased vascular flow resistance identified as absent or reversed end-diastolic flow in the umbilical arteries.[98,99] Our understanding of the mechanisms and hence the diagnostic usefulness and pitfalls of abnormal umbilical artery flow in IUGR has been based on pathological examination of the placentas in cases with well-documented prenatal findings.[99] More recently, *in vitro* dual perfusion experiments in conjunction with patch clamping and gene expression studies have demonstrated the main site of placental hypoxic vasoconstriction to be at the level of the subchorial stem arteries.[100]

Other unusual cases of IUGR may be associated with specific placental pathologies unrelated to uteroplacental disease (see below).

Specific placental pathologies

Massive perivillous fibrin deposition/maternal floor infarction (MPVFD/MFI)

These entities represent a spectrum of disease with the underlying pathological mechanism being excessive deposition of fibrinous material within the intervillous space, which surrounds and entraps chorionic villi reducing their gas exchange and nutrient transfer function.[101,102] Some degree of perivillous fibrin deposition is normal in uncomplicated pregnancies but when excessive it may be associated with pregnancy loss, IUGR or intrauterine death.[102] Maternal floor infarction is associated with extensive fibrin deposition in and around the basal plate which focally extends throughout the placenta resulting in a characteristic macroscopic appearance (Figure 28.5).[102] The aetiological factors for development of MPVFD/MFI remain unknown but there is an apparent association with autoimmune diseases and recurrence in future pregnancies is well documented in 10–50% of cases.[102–108] Prenatal diagnosis by ultrasound has been reported.[103]

Chronic histiocytic intervillositis

This condition is characterised by extensive infiltration of the placental intervillous space by maternal inflammatory cells, predominantly histiocytes.[109,110] Similar infiltrates may be observed in specific infective conditions such as maternal malarial infection, in which additional features, including presence of malarial pigment, are usually apparent.[111] In the absence of known infective aetiologies, the diagnosis of chronic histiocytic intervillositis (CHI) is most appropriate. There is an association with IUGR and intrauterine death in addition to idiopathic preterm delivery. The pathophysiology of the underlying stimulus resulting in the inflammatory response is not known but affected cases have been reported in association with autoimmune disease including lupus. A recurrence rate of more than 50% has been reported.[109,110]

Fetal abnormality/fetal hydrops

A wide range of fetal abnormalities may result in iatrogenic preterm birth for either fetal or maternal indications. These will not be discussed further here other than to reiterate the role of postmortem and placental examination in the final diagnosis of any

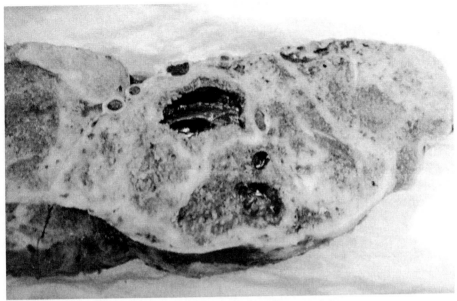

Figure 28.5. Macroscopic photograph of a section of a placenta from a pregnancy delivered preterm due to maternal floor infarction (MFI); the parenchyma appears solid with numerous pale areas extending from the basal to chorionic plates, giving the placenta a 'marbled' appearance, representing areas of massive fibrin deposition

prenatally diagnosed abnormality. The postmortem examination, procedures and investigations for specific prenatally diagnosed conditions, such as fetal hydrops or skeletal dysplasias, are targeted to the nature of the abnormality and may be extensive. These are well described in standard paediatric pathology texts.[112–114]

Procedure-related iatrogenic preterm birth

Ultrasound-guided diagnostic or therapeutic intrauterine procedures, such as amniocentesis, chorionic villus sampling and thoracoamniotic shunt insertion, are now relatively commonplace in fetomaternal medicine practice. All intrauterine needling procedures have an associated procedure-related risk of causing miscarriage or preterm delivery although, almost by definition, in the majority of cases the indication for intervention itself places the pregnancy at high risk for complications making assessment of the true procedure-related risk difficult. In pregnancies resulting in miscarriage, intrauterine death or severe preterm birth following a previous intrauterine procedure, pathological examination is indicated. The main role of the pathologist in this context is similar to that following an intraoperative event in adulthood, namely to identify any complications that are likely to have arisen as a direct consequence of the procedure. Examples include development of amniotic fluid leak, amniotic infection syndrome or fetal trauma following incorrect placement of a shunt.[115] Similarly, if no such findings are apparent, it is important that the pathologist report that the cause of the loss is unlikely to be directly related to the procedure but may be a consequence of the underlying disease. Only by investigation of post-procedure complications in this way can the true direct procedure-related complication rates be calculated.

Pathology of prematurity-related complications

In addition to the effects of prenatal factors that may have led to the preterm delivery, infants delivered prematurely are at risk of developing a wide range of complications related to the immaturity of various organ systems, and this may be compounded by the effects of treatment. Common prematurity-related neonatal complications include respiratory distress syndrome, chronic lung disease of prematurity, air leaks, necrotising enterocolitis, retinopathy of prematurity, germinal matrix haemorrhage and periventricular leukomalacia. The pathology of these lesions is well described in standard texts and thus only specific points of current interest will be described below.[112–114,116]

Periventricular leukomalacia/germinal matrix haemorrhage

The pattern of central nervous system damage in infants is related to the gestational age, with periventricular leukomalacia (white matter damage) and germinal matrix haemorrhage (periventricular/intraventricular haemorrhage) being characteristic for the preterm infant. Although classical patterns of brain damage for preterm and term infants have been described the distinction is not absolute and preterm infants may also demonstrate other forms of central nervous system injury.[117] The most common category of injury is hypoxic-ischaemic, which preferentially affects the periventricular white matter in preterm infants but may also occur prenatally. This area appears vulnerable at this gestation due to a combination of factors including relatively low blood flow and vessel density in this area in conjunction with intrinsic vulnerability of these neurons to hypoxic-ischaemic injury, in particular the effects of excitatory neurotransmitters such as glutamate.[117] Furthermore, it has been reported that placental histopathological features of inflammation and/or elevation of proinflammatory cytokine concentrations may increase the severity of white matter damage and intracranial haemorrhage in such cases.[118–120] There is white matter necrosis that undergoes subsequent remodelling by tissue macrophages resulting in areas of neuronal loss, dystrophic calcification and/or cyst formation. Furthermore, in gestations below 36 weeks, the periventricular germinal matrix, from which developing cortical neurons arise, has not yet involuted, it has an architecture of poorly supported delicate blood vessels and there is prematurity-related impaired autoregulatory ability, all of which may result in the development of germinal matrix haemorrhage with secondary 'venous infarction' of surrounding tissue and/or rupture into the ventricular system with intraventricular haemorrhage and obstructive hydrocephalus.[117] It has been reported that more subtle areas of neuronal damage that are difficult to identify with routine examination methods may be highlighted by the use of beta amyloid precursor protein (BAPP) immunohistochemistry, which provides a highly sensitive method of detecting foci of hypoxic-ischaemic type brain injury in a variety of clinical settings.[121–125]

Hyaline membrane disease, chronic lung disease of prematurity and pulmonary air leak

The major complication related to preterm birth is the development of clinical respiratory distress syndrome due to hyaline membrane disease (HMD).[126] The underlying pathophysiology is related to lung surfactant deficiency and structural lung immaturity, which may be complicated by patent ductus arteriosus. There is poor lung expansion and hence oxygenation resulting in alveolar wall and capillary damage with exudation of oedema fluid and formation of hyaline membranes composed of fibrin, necrotic debris and exudates lining air spaces, which further impairs oxygenation.[127] Modern treatment is with surfactant replacement therapy, and mechanical ventilation where required, which reduces both the frequency and severity of HMD. Positive-pressure ventilation is often required with the associated risk of pulmonary air leak development manifesting as either acute interstitial pulmonary emphysema (AIPE), pneumothorax or persistent interstitial pulmonary emphysema (PIPE), in which the interstitial air elicits a foreign-body type inflammatory response (Figure 28.6).[126] A consequence of bronchiolar obstruction and the subsequent irregularity in lung expansion, in conjunction with oxygen therapy required in HMD, may be the development of long-standing structural lung abnormality. These changes were originally termed bronchopulmonary dysplasia (BPD), the features being widespread bronchial and bronchiolar epithelial metaplasia and alternating areas of collapse and hyperexpansion with interstitial fibrosis. However, since the widespread introduction of surfactant replacement therapy to treat HMD, 'classical' BPD is rarely observed in infants with long-standing lung sequelae of HMD, the features usually being predominant acinar simplification with reduced numbers of overexpanded alveoli, features much more pathologically subtle than those previously reported. Nevertheless, such changes, now termed chronic lung disease of prematurity, may be associated with significant respiratory morbidity and even mortality including sudden unexpected death.[126]

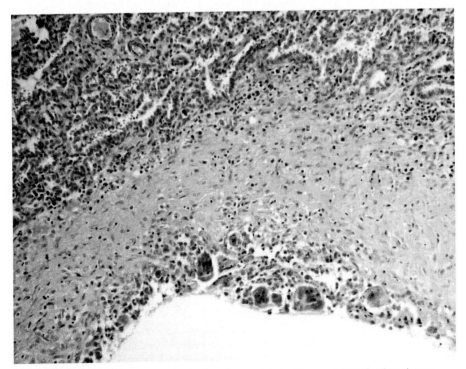

Figure 28.6. Photomicrograph demonstrating lung from an infant with prematurity-related respiratory complications including persistent interstitial pulmonary emphysema (PIPE) in which an air leak into the interstitial tissues elicits a foreign-body type inflammatory reaction with numerous giant cells (H&E, original magnification × 200)

Pathology of iatrogenic complications of medical care of the preterm infant

The birth of the preterm infant may be traumatic and medical management of several prematurity-related complications entails use of therapeutic strategies that may themselves result in complications. The list of such reported pathologies is wide and details can be found reported in specialist publications.[115,116] The more serious and common complications reported include subgaleal haematoma, occipital osteodiastasis, spinal cord injuries, endotracheal intubation-related trauma, lung trauma secondary to chest drain insertion, ischaemic lesions distal to arterial cannulae, sepsis due to venous cannulae, thromboembolic phenomena secondary to umbilical cannulae, hexachlorophene-induced brain damage, skin damage secondary to alcohol cleansing products, extracorporeal membrane oxygenation (ECMO)-related complications, total-parenteral nutrition (TPN)-associated liver disease, retinopathy of prematurity and other sepsis. The pathologist plays an important role in the accurate identification of such complications, many of which may only be recognised after death, in order that the risk may be minimised in future cases.

Summary

Pathological examination of the placenta and/or postmortem examination should be an integral part of the management protocol of pregnancies complicated by severe preterm delivery. These investigations may provide diagnostic and prognostic information regarding management of the neonate and improve our understanding of the underlying pathophysiological processes in order to facilitate planning of rational future intervention studies.

References

1.   Husain AN, O'Conor GT. The perinatal autopsy: a neglected source of discovery. *IARC Sci Publ* 1991;(112):151–62.
2.   Naeye RL. The epidemiology of perinatal mortality. The power of the autopsy. *Pediatr Clin North Am* 1972;19:295–310.
3.   Meier PR, Manchester DK, Shikes RH, Clewell WH, Stewart M. Perinatal autopsy: its clinical value. *Obstet Gynecol* 1986;67:349–51.
4.   Shen-Schwarz S, Neish C, Hill LM. Antenatal ultrasound for fetal anomalies: importance of perinatal autopsy. *Pediatr Pathol* 1989;9:1–9.
5.   Chescheir NC, Reitnauer PJ. A comparative study of prenatal diagnosis and perinatal autopsy. *J Ultrasound Med* 1994;13:451–6.
6.   Saller DN, Lesser KB, Harrel U, Rogers BB, Oyer CE. The clinical utility of the perinatal autopsy. *JAMA* 1995;273:663–5.
7.   Cartlidge PH, Dawson AT, Stewart JH, Vujanic GM. Value and quality of perinatal and infant postmortem examinations: cohort analysis of 400 consecutive deaths. *BMJ* 1995;310:155–8.
8.   Rajashekar S, Bhat BV, Veliath AJ, Ratnakar C. Perinatal autopsy – a seven-year study. *Indian J Pediatr* 1996;63:511–6.
9.   Dhar V, Perlman M, Vilela MI, Haque KN, Kirpalani H, Cutz E. Autopsy in a neonatal intensive care unit: utilization patterns and associations of clinicopathologic discordances. *J Pediatr* 1998;132:75–9.
10. Tennstedt C, Chaoui R, Bollmann R, Korner H, Dietel M. Correlation of prenatal ultrasound diagnosis and morphological findings of fetal autopsy. *Pathol Res Pract* 1998;194:721–4.
11. Barr P, Hunt R. An evaluation of the autopsy following death in a level IV neonatal intensive care unit. *J Paediatr Child Health* 1999;35:185–9.
12. Faye-Petersen OM, Guinn DA, Wenstrom KD. Value of perinatal autopsy. *Obstet Gynecol* 1999;94:915–20.
13. Kabra NS, Udani RH. Correlation between clinical diagnoses at the time of death and autopsy

findings in critically sick neonates at a regional neonatal intensive care unit in India. *J Trop Pediatr* 2001;47:295–300.

14. Hefler LA, Hersh DR, Moore PJ, Gregg AR. Clinical value of postnatal autopsy and genetics consultation in fetal death. *Am J Med Genet* 2001;104:165–8.

15. Yeo L, Guzman ER, Shen-Schwarz S, Walters C, Vintzileos AM. Value of a complete sonographic survey in detecting fetal abnormalities: correlation with perinatal autopsy. *J Ultrasound Med* 2002;21:501–10.

16. Wigglesworth JS. Quality of the perinatal autopsy. *Br J Obstet Gynaecol* 1991;98:617–9.

17. Waldron G. Perinatal and infant postmortem examination. Quality of examinations must improve. *BMJ* 1995;310:870.

18. Vujanic GM, Cartlidge PHT, Stewart JH, Dawson AJ. Perinatal and infant postmortem examinations – how well are we doing. *J Clin Pathol* 1995;48:998–1001.

19. Wright C, Cameron H, Lamb W. A study of the quality of perinatal autopsy in the former Northern region. The Northern Perinatal Mortality Survey Steering Group. *Br J Obstet Gynaecol* 1998;105:24–8.

20. Vujanic GM, Cartlidge PH, Stewart JH. Improving the quality of perinatal and infant necropsy examinations: a follow up study. *J Clin Pathol* 1998;51:850–3.

21. Fox R. A study of the quality of perinatal autopsy in the former Northern region. *Br J Obstet Gynaecol* 1998;105:1040.

22. Bjugn R, Berland J. Quality of fetal, perinatal and infant autopsy reports. An audit of all reports of postmortem examinations following fetal, perinatal and infant death in Rogaland County, Western Norway, 1997–1999. *APMIS* 2002;110:746–52.

23. Alderliesten ME, Peringa J, Van der Hulst V, Blaauwgeers HL, Van Lith LM. Perinatal mortality: clinical value of postmortem magnetic resonance imaging compared with autopsy in routine obstetric practice. *BJOG* 2003;110:378–82.

24. Huisman TA, Wisser J, Stallmach T, Krestin GP, Huch R, Kubik-Huch RA. MR autopsy in fetuses. *Fetal Diagn Ther* 2002;17:58–64.

25. Altshuler G, Deppisch M. College of American Pathologists Conference XIX on the Examination of the Placenta: Report of the Working Group on Indications for Placental Examination. *Arch Pathol Lab Med* 1991;115:701–3.

26. Bove KE, Baker PB, Bjornsson J, Davis GJ, Froede RC, Hanzlick RL, *et al.* Practice guidelines for autopsy pathology – The perinatal and pediatric autopsy. *Arch Pathol Lab Med* 1997;121:368–76.

27. Langston C, Kaplan C, Macpherson T, Manci E, Peevy K, Clark B, *et al.* Practice guideline for examination of the placenta: developed by the Placental Pathology Practice Guideline Development Task Force of the College of American Pathologists. *Arch Pathol Lab Med* 1997;121:449–76.

28. Kingdom J, Jauniaux E, O'Brien S. *The Placenta: Basic Science and Clinical Practice.* London: RCOG Press; 2000.

29. Larsen LG, Graem N. Morphological findings and value of placental examination at fetal and perinatal autopsy. *APMIS* 1999;107:337–45.

30. Khong TY, Staples A, Moore L, Byard RW. Observer reliability in assessing villitis of unknown aetiology. *J Clin Pathol* 1993;46:208–10.

31. Khong TY, Bendon RW, Qureshi F, Redline RW, Gould S, Stallmach T, *et al.* Chronic deciduitis in the placental basal plate: definition and interobserver reliability. *Hum Pathol* 2000;31:292–5.

32. Beebe LA, Cowan LD, Hyde SR, Altshuler G. Methods to improve the reliability of histopathological diagnoses in the placenta. *Paediatr Perinat Epidemiol* 2000;14:172–8.

33. Grether JK, Eaton A, Redline R, Bendon R, Benirschke K, Nelson K. Reliability of placental histology using archived specimens. *Paediatr Perinat Epidemiol* 1999;13:489–95.

34. Sun CC, Revell VO, Belli AJ, Viscardi RM. Discrepancy in pathologic diagnosis of placental lesions. *Arch Pathol Lab Med* 2002;126:706–9.

35. Sebire NJ, Regan L, Goldin RD. Introduction of specialised placental pathology request forms is associated with appropriate requests and significantly improved clinical information provision. *J Pathol* 2002;198:23A.

36. Lavery JP. The role of placental examination and its pathology in obstetric risk management. *J Healthc Risk Manag* 1997;17:15–20.

37. Salafia CM, Vogel CA, Vintzileos AM, Bantham KF, Pezzullo J, Silberman L. Placental pathologic findings in preterm birth. *Am J Obstet Gynecol* 1991;165:934–8.

38. Lettieri L, Vintzileos AM, Rodis JF, Albini SM, Salafia CM. Does "idiopathic" preterm labor resulting in preterm birth exist? *Am J Obstet Gynecol* 1993;168:1480–5.

39. Salafia CM, Mill JF. The value of placental pathology in studies of spontaneous prematurity. *Curr Opin Obstet Gynecol* 1996;8:89–98.

40. Germain AM, Carvajal J, Sanchez M, Valenzuela GJ, Tsunekawa H, Chuaqui B. Preterm labor: placental pathology and clinical correlation. *Obstet Gynecol* 1999;94:284–9.

41. Lockwood J, Kuczynski E. Risk stratification and pathological mechanisms in preterm delivery.

Paediatr Perinat Epidemiol 2001;15:78–89.

42.   Odibo AO, Rodis JF, Sanders MM, Borgida AF, Wilson M, Egan JF, *et al*. Relationship of amniotic fluid markers of intra-amniotic infection with histopathology in cases of preterm labor with intact membranes. *J Perinatol* 1999;19:407–12.

43.   Hansen AR, Collins MH, Genest D, Heller D, Schwarz S, Banagon P, *et al*. Very low birthweight infant's placenta and its relation to pregnancy and fetal characteristics. *Pediatr Dev Pathol* 2000;3:419–30.

44.   Van Hoeven KH, Anyaegbunam A, Hochster H, Whitty JE, Distant J, Crawford C, *et al*. Clinical significance of increasing histologic severity of acute inflammation in the fetal membranes and umbilical cord. *Pediatr Pathol Lab Med* 1996;16:731–44.

45.   Hameed C, Tejani N, Verma UL, Archbald F. Silent chorioamnionitis as a cause of preterm labor refractory to tocolytic therapy. *Am J Obstet Gynecol* 1984;149:726–30.

46.   Perkins RP, Zhou SM, Butler C, Skipper BJ. Histologic chorioamnionitis in pregnancies of various gestational ages: implications in preterm rupture of membranes. *Obstet Gynecol* 1987;70:856–60.

47.   Sebire NJ. Choriodecidual inflammatory syndrome (CoDIS) is the leading, but underrecognised, cause of early preterm delivery and second trimester miscarriage. *Med Hypotheses* 2001;56:497–500.

48.   Sebire NJ, Goldin RD, Regan L. Histological chorioamnionitis in relation to clinical presentation at 14-40 weeks of gestation. *J Obstet Gynecol* 2001;21:242–5.

49.   Mueller-Heubach E, Rubinstein DN, Schwarz SS. Histologic chorioamnionitis and preterm delivery in different patient populations. *Obstet Gynecol* 1990;75:622–6.

50.   Perkins RP, Zhou SM, Butler C, Skipper BJ. Histologic chorioamnionitis in pregnancies of various gestational ages. II: Implications in preterm labor. *Am J Perinatol* 1988;5:300–3.

51.   Romen Y, Greenspoon J, Artal R. Clinical chorioamnionitis–analysis of the incubation period in patients with preterm premature rupture of membranes. *Am J Perinatol* 1985;2:314–6.

52.   Guzick DS, Winn K. The association of chorioamnionitis with preterm delivery. *Obstet Gynecol* 1985;65:11–6.

53.   Hameed C, Tejani N, Verma UL, Archbald F. Silent chorioamnionitis as a cause of preterm labor refractory to tocolytic therapy. *Am J Obstet Gynecol* 1984;149:726–30.

54.   Garite TJ, Freeman RK. Chorioamnionitis in the preterm gestation. *Obstet Gynecol* 1982;59:539–45.

55.   Sebire NJ, Goldin RD. Distribution of histological chorioamnionitis in placental membranes: does a membrane roll provide additional information? *J Pathol* 2001;195:18A.

56.   To MS, Skentou C, Liao AW, Cacho A, Nicolaides KH. Cervical length and funneling at 23 weeks of gestation in the prediction of spontaneous early preterm delivery. *Ultrasound Obstet Gynecol* 2001;18:200–3.

57.   Guzman ER, Walters C, Ananth CV, O'Reilly-Green C, Benito CW, Palermo A, *et al*. A comparison of sonographic cervical parameters in predicting spontaneous preterm birth in high-risk singleton gestations. *Ultrasound Obstet Gynecol* 2001;18:204–10.

58.   Naim A, Haberman S, Burgess T, Navizedeh N, Minkoff H. Changes in cervical length and the risk of preterm labor. *Am J Obstet Gynecol* 2002;186:887–9.

59.   Carvalho MH, Bittar RE, Brizot ML, Maganha PP, Borges da Fonseca ES, Zugaib M. Cervical length at 11-14 weeks' and 22-24 weeks' gestation evaluated by transvaginal sonography, and gestational age at delivery. *Ultrasound Obstet Gynecol* 2003;21:135–9.

60.   Guzman ER, Shen-Schwarz S, Benito C, Vintzileos AM, Lake M, Lai YL. The relationship between placental histology and cervical ultrasonography in women at risk for pregnancy loss and spontaneous preterm birth. *Am J Obstet Gynecol* 1999;181:793–7.

61.   Rust OA, Atlas RO, Reed J, Van Gaalen J, Balducci J. Revisiting the short cervix detected by transvaginal ultrasound in the second trimester: why cerclage therapy may not help. *Am J Obstet Gynecol* 2001;185:1098–105.

62.   Carroll SG, Sebire NJ, Nicolaides KH. Preterm prelabour amniorrhexis: detection of infection. In: Carroll SG, Sebire NJ, Nicolaides KH, editors. *Preterm Prelabour Amniorrhexis*. Carnforth: Parthenon Press; 1996. p. 87–124.

63.   Darby MJ, Caritis SN, Shen-Schwarz S. Placental abruption in the preterm gestation: an association with chorioamnionitis. *Obstet Gynecol* 1989;74:88–92.

64.   Rana A, Sawhney H, Gopalan S, Panigrahi D, Nijhawan R. Abruptio placentae and chorioamnionitis – microbiological and histologic correlation. *Acta Obstet Gynecol Scand* 1999;78:363–6.

65.   Salafia CM, Lopez-Zeno JA, Sherer DM, Whittington SS, Minior VK, Vintzileos AM. Histologic evidence of old intrauterine bleeding is more frequent in prematurity. *Am J Obstet Gynecol* 1995;173:1065–70.

66.   Tauscher MK, Berg D, Brockmann M, Seidenspinner S, Speer CP, Groneck P. Association of histologic chorioamnionitis, increased levels of cord blood cytokines, and intracerebral hemorrhage

in preterm neonates. *Biol Neonate* 2003;83:166–70.

67. Rezaie P, Dean A. Periventricular leukomalacia, inflammation and white matter lesions within the developing nervous system. *Neuropathology* 2002;22:106–32.

68. Kadhim H, Tabarki B, Verellen G, De Prez C, Rona AM, Sebire G. Inflammatory cytokines in the pathogenesis of periventricular leukomalacia. *Neurology* 2001;56:1278–84.

69. Placental inflammation and brain injury in preterm infants. *Dev Med Child Neurol Suppl* 2001;86:16–7.

70. Boylan P, Parisi V. An overview of hydramnios. *Semin Perinatol* 1986;10:136–41.

71. Ernst LM, Parkash V. Placental pathology in fetal bartter syndrome. *Pediatr Dev Pathol* 2002;5:76–9.

72. Ramsing M, Gillessen-Kaesbach G, Holzgreve W, Fritz B, Rehder H. Variability in the phenotypic expression of fryns syndrome: A report of two sibships. *Am J Med Genet* 2000;95:415–24.

73. Online Mendelian Inheritance in Man [www.ncbi.nlm.nih.gov/omim/].

74. Sheiner E, Shoham-Vardi I, Hadar A, Hallak M, Hackmon R, Mazor M. Incidence, obstetric risk factors and pregnancy outcome of preterm placental abruption: a retrospective analysis. *J Matern Fetal Neonatal Med* 2002;11:34–9.

75. Kyrklund-Blomberg NB, Gennser G, Cnattingius S. Placental abruption and perinatal death. *Paediatr Perinat Epidemiol* 2001;15:290–7.

76. Ananth CV, Berkowitz GS, Savitz DA, Lapinski RH. Placental abruption and adverse perinatal outcomes. *JAMA* 1999;282:1646–51.

77. Fox H. Macroscopic abnormalities of the placenta: retroplacental haematoma. In: Fox H, editor. *Pathology of the Placenta.* London: WB Saunders; 1997. p. 125–30.

78. Harris RD, Cho C, Wells WA. Sonography of the placenta with emphasis on pathological correlation. *Semin Ultrasound CT MR* 1996;17:66–89.

79. Gruenwald P, Levin H, Yousem H. Abruption and premature separation of the placenta. The clinical and the pathologic entity. *Am J Obstet Gynecol* 1968;102:604–10.

80. Fox H. Abnormalities of placentation. In: Fox H, editor. *Pathology of the Placenta.* London: WB Saunders; 1997. p. 54–76.

81. Benirschke K, Kaufmann P. Placental shape aberrations. In: Benirschke K, Kaufmann P, editors. *Pathology of the Human Placenta.* New York: Springer; 1995. p. 378–403.

82. Taffel SM. Demographic trends in twin births. In: Keith LG, Papiernik E, Keith DM, Luke B, editors. *Multiple Pregnancy.* Carnforth: Parthenon Press; 1995. p. 133–44.

83. Sebire NJ, Snijders RJM, Hughes K, Sepulveda W, Nicolaides KH. The hidden mortality of monochorionic twin pregnancies. *Br J Obstet Gynaecol* 1997;104:1203–7.

84. Sebire NJ, D'Ercole C, Sepulveda W, Hughes K, Nicolaides KH. Effects of reduction from trichorionic triplets to twins. *Br J Obstet Gynaecol* 1997;104:1201–3.

85. Sepulveda W, Sebire NJ, Hughes K, Odibo A, Nicolaides KH. The lambda sign at 10–14 weeks of gestation as a predictor of chorionicity in twin pregnancies. *Ultrasound Obstet Gynecol* 1996;7:421–3.

86. Carroll SG, Soothill PW, Abdel-Fattah SA, Porter H, Montague I, Kyle PM. Prediction of chorionicity in twin pregnancies at 10–14 weeks of gestation. *BJOG* 2002;109:182–6.

87. Phung DT, Blickstein I, Goldman RD, Machin GA, LoSasso RD, Keith LG. The Northwestern Twin Chorionicity Study: I. Discordant inflammatory findings that are related to chorionicity in presenting versus nonpresenting twins. *Am J Obstet Gynecol* 2002;186:1041–5.

88. Mizrahi M, Furman B, Shoham-Vardi I, Vardi H, Maymon E, Mazor M. Perinatal outcome and peripartum complications in preterm singleton and twins deliveries: a comparative study. *Eur J Obstet Gynecol Reprod Biol* 1999;87:55–61.

89. Machin GA, Keith LG. How to examine twin and higher order multiple pregnancy placentas. In: Machin GA, Keith LG, editors. *An Atlas of Multiple Pregnancy: Biology and Pathology.* Carnforth: Parthenon Press; 1997. p. 55–60.

90. VanPeborgh P, Rambaud C, Ville Y. Effect of laser coagulation on placental vessels: histological aspects. *Fetal Diagn Ther* 1997;12:32–5.

91. Nicolaides KH, Rizzo G, Hecher K. Doppler studies in fetal hypoxemic hypoxia. In: Nicolaides KH, Rizzo G, Hecher K, editors. *Placental and Fetal Doppler.* Carnforth: Parthenon Press; 2000. p. 67–88.

92. Brosens I, Dixon HG, Robertson WB. Fetal growth retardation and the arteries of the placental bed. *Br J Obstet Gynaecol* 1977;84:656–63.

93. Brosens IA. Morphological changes in the utero-placental bed in pregnancy hypertension. *Clin Obstet Gynaecol* 1977;4:573–93.

94. Gordijn SJ, Erwich JJ, Khong TY. Value of the perinatal autopsy: critique. *Pediatr Dev Pathol* 2002;5:480–8.

95. Fox H. The placenta in abnormalities and disorders of the fetus. In: Fox H, editor. *Pathology of the Placenta.* London: WB Saunders; 1997. p. 241–8.

96.   Rogers BB, Bloom SL, Leveno KJ. Atherosis revisited: current concepts on the pathophysiology of implantation site disorders. *Obstet Gynecol Surv* 1999;54:189–95.

97.   Kingdom J. Adriana and Luisa Castellucci Award Lecture 1997. Placental pathology in obstetrics: adaptation or failure of the villous tree? *Placenta* 1998;19:347–51.

98.   Sebire NJ, Talbert D. Cor placentale: placental intervillus/intravillus blood flow mismatch is the pathophysiological mechanism in severe intrauterine growth restriction due to uteroplacental disease. *Med Hypotheses* 2001;57:354–7.

99.   Sebire NJ. Umbilical artery Doppler revisited: pathophysiology of changes in intrauterine growth restriction revealed. *Ultrasound Obstet Gynecol* 2003;21:419–22.

100.   Hampl V, Bibova J, Stranak Z, Wu X, Michelakis ED, Hashimoto K, *et al.* Hypoxic fetoplacental vasoconstriction in humans is mediated by potassium channel inhibition. *Am J Physiol Heart Circ Physiol* 2002;283:H2440–9.

101.   Naeye RL. Maternal floor infarction. *Hum Pathol* 1985;16:823–8.

102.   Katzman PJ, Genest DR. Maternal floor infarction and massive perivillous fibrin deposition: histological definitions, association with intrauterine fetal growth restriction, and risk of recurrence. *Pediatr Dev Pathol* 2002;5:159–64.

103.   Mandsager NT, Bendon R, Mostello D, Rosenn B, Miodovnik M, Siddiqi TA. Maternal floor infarction of the placenta: prenatal diagnosis and clinical significance. *Obstet Gynecol* 1994;83:750–4.

104.   Andres RL, Kuyper W, Resnik R, Piacquadio KM, Benirschke K. The association of maternal floor infarction of the placenta with adverse perinatal outcome. *Am J Obstet Gynecol* 1990;163:935–8.

105.   Bendon RW, Hommel AB. Maternal floor infarction in autoimmune disease: two cases. *Pediatr Pathol Lab Med* 1996;16:293–7.

106.   Adams-Chapman I, Vaucher YE, Bejar RF, Benirschke K, Baergen RN, Moore TR. Maternal floor infarction of the placenta: association with central nervous system injury and adverse neurodevelopmental outcome. *J Perinatol* 2002;22:236–41.

107.   Sebire NJ, Backos M, Goldin RD, Regan L. Placental massive perivillous fibrin deposition associated with antiphospholipid antibody syndrome. *BJOG* 2002;109:570–3.

108.   Bane L, Gillan JE. Massive perivillous fibrinoid causing recurrent placental failure. *BJOG* 2003;110:292–5.

109.   Jacques SM, Qureshi F. Chronic intervillositis of the placenta. *Arch Pathol Lab Med* 1993;117:1032–5.

110.   Boyd TK, Redline RW. Chronic histiocytic intervillositis: a placental lesion associated with recurrent reproductive loss. *Hum Pathol* 2000;31:1389–96.

111.   Sullivan AD, Nyirenda T, Cullinan T, Taylor T, Lau A, Meshnick SR. Placental haemozoin and malaria in pregnancy. *Placenta* 2000;21:417–21.

112.   Keeling J. *Fetal and Neonatal Pathology.* 3rd ed. London: Springer; 2001.

113.   Wigglesworth JS, Singer DB. *Textbook of Fetal and Perinatal Pathology.* 2nd ed. London: Blackwell Science; 1998.

114.   Stocker JT, Dehner LP, editors. *Pediatric Pathology.* 2nd ed. Philadelphia: Lippincott Williams and Wilkins; 2001.

115.   Howatson A. Iatrogenic complications. In: Keeling J, editor. *Fetal and Neonatal Pathology.* 3rd ed. London: Springer; 2001. p. 349–80.

116.   De Sa DJ. *Pathology of Neonatal Intensive Care: an Illustrated Reference.* London: Chapman and Hall Medical; 1995.

117.   Squier W. Pathology of fetal and neonatal brain damage: identifying the timing. In: Squier W, editor. *Acquired Damage to the Developing Brain: Timing and Causation.* London: Arnold; 2002. p. 110–27.

118.   Tauscher MK, Berg D, Brockmann M, Seidenspinner S, Speer CP, Groneck P. Association of histologic chorioamnionitis, increased levels of cord blood cytokines, and intracerebral hemorrhage in preterm neonates. *Biol Neonate* 2003;83:166–70.

119.   Hemorrhagic-ischemic cerebral injury in the preterm infant: current concepts. *Clin Perinatol* 2002;29:745–63.

120.   Shalak LF, Laptook AR, Jafri HS, Ramilo O, Perlman JM. Clinical chorioamnionitis, elevated cytokines, and brain injury in term infants. *Pediatrics* 2002;110:673–80.

121.   Yam PS, Takasago T, Dewar D, Graham DI, McCulloch J. Amyloid precursor protein accumulates in white matter at the margin of a focal ischaemic lesion. *Brain Res* 1997;760:150–7.

122.   Yam PS, Patterson J, Graham DI, Takasago T, Dewar D, McCulloch J. Topographical and quantitative assessment of white matter injury following a focal ischaemic lesion in the rat brain. *Brain Res Brain Res Protoc* 1998;2:315–22.

123.   Irving A, Bentley DL, Parsons AA. Assessment of white matter injury following prolonged focal cerebral ischaemia in the rat. *Acta Neuropathol (Berl)* 2001;102:627–35.

124.   Baiden-Amissah K, Joashi U, Blumberg R, Mehmet H, Edwards AD, Cox PM. Expression of

amyloid precursor protein (beta-APP) in the neonatal brain following hypoxic ischaemic injury. *Neuropathol Appl Neurobiol* 1998;24:346–52.

125.   Koistinaho J, Pyykonen I, Keinanen R, Hokfelt T. Expression of beta-amyloid precursor protein mRNAs following transient focal ischaemia. *Neuroreport* 1996;7:2727–31.

126.   Stocker JT. Respiratory tract. In: Stocker JT, Dehner LP. editors. *Pediatric Pathology.* 2nd ed. Philadelphia: Lippincott Williams and Wilkins; 2001. p. 455–518.

Chapter 29

Management IV

Discussion

Shennan: There appears to be a serious shortage of perinatal pathologists, especially in London. I do not know if that is a more general problem.

Sebire: The current situation in the country is that there are approximately 40 UK consultant posts for paediatric and perinatal pathology of which 15 are vacant. There was a big problem at the time of the Alder Hey scandal in getting trainees. However, now there are actually quite a few good trainees, most of whom have done higher examinations in either obstetrics or paediatrics prior to training in pathology. I think this problem has to some extent resolved. But perinatal pathology still needs to be made more attractive. We saw this in other aspects of pathology. When it was decided that all cancer services had to have a dedicated expert pathologist suddenly there was a lot more funding for these training posts, and the services and the posts were made more attractive. Now there is no problem at all getting your cancer pathology done.

Shennan: A question I had for Professor Steer relates to the North West Thames database. Do you have the data on iatrogenic versus spontaneous delivery? We know from CESDI that 50% of 27- and 28-week deliveries are iatrogenic, which is a huge confounder for caesarean sections.

Steer: The data distinguishes between elective and emergency but there is always a problem with what is elective and what is emergency. So, for example, if a woman is booked for an elective section but she comes in in the middle of the night this is very often classified as an emergency section, which you could argue is invalid. On the other hand, you could have a woman in the opposite situation where really it had been in your mind to do a caesarean section for a long time and then something starts to go wrong so you do what is classified as an emergency section but in a sense it was pre-planned. So it is very difficult to know with that degree of precision. What we can do is categorise the mode of delivery by associated conditions such as pre-eclampsia. Thus we know, for example, that one-third of all the preterm deliveries before 32 weeks of gestation are associated with pre-eclampsia. That is one of the major causes of preterm delivery so we can look at that group separately. Whether you consider those caesareans as elective or emergency becomes a moot point: if a woman suddenly develops a rapid rise in blood pressure and you decide to go for a section, is that elective or is it an emergency?

Morrison: A question for Dr Sebire: I am interested in the very high incidence of histological evidence of chorioamnionitis in the preterm group and I have noticed it anecdotally in a lot of our patients. What has puzzled me is that even in women who have no evidence of infection or have delivered electively by caesarean section the same findings often appear and I had wondered if it was our pathology service or if it was a post-delivery issue. In other words, is it inflammation that occurred in the dying process between the time of the placenta leaving us and getting to the pathologist?

Romero: I wanted to speak a little bit on the recommendations that Dr Sebire has formulated. The placenta has been considered to be the largest human biopsy and it is very surprising to me that there is no interest in examining this organ. In our unit we are trying to establish placental pathology as a research unit and we are coming across the same problem, which is that there are very few specialists. I believe part of the reason for that is that in other disciplines, for example, if you have someone who is diagnosed with cancer, it makes a big difference if you can diagnose breast cancer or prostate cancer, but if you examine the placenta there seems to be very little consequence to that. So I would like to make a plea for supporting the recommendation that placentas be examined. I think placental pathologists need to be able to show that the diagnoses they make are reproducible, there should be a dictionary of the lesions and what they mean, and they need to demonstrate that that information makes a difference.

Gardosi: I wonder how reliable placental pathology is in the diagnosis of chorio-amnionitis or growth restriction?

Sebire: I would suggest that a significant proportion of growth restriction, even with abnormal umbilical artery Doppler, without doing morphometric studies, can be very difficult to diagnose. The severe cases of pre-eclampsia and intrauterine growth restriction that present in the early third trimester nearly always have morphological abnormalities. The cases where delivery is at 35 weeks and above are very much more difficult.

Saade: When you are looking at placentas to categorise the cause of preterm birth, how do you differentiate between what happened before the woman went into labour and what happened during that period of time, i.e. contractions, labour, medication, one or two days, ruptured membranes, and so on.

Sebire: It is an interesting point and we do not know because there are no data. What we need are simple studies comparing placental findings, for example, in patients who have not had tocolysis, who have not had this, that or the other intervention. There are very few systematic studies of the placenta. My main worry is not so much whether simple morphological examination can be particularly useful but that, in view of the increasing use of things such as gene array and proteomic technologies, it is very important they are done but it is important they are done knowing what tissue you are looking at.

Regan: I would like to ask Dr Sebire about what samples the pathologist should take from the placenta. I am asking that question because when we worked for several years in the same hospital we got into a system where the placenta went sent off and we published several papers about the various abnormalities that we found in women who have miscarried. Although we are now sending slides of blocks from the placentas over to him at Great Ormond Street, he has not found an abnormality for at least a year, suggesting that the way that they are being sampled is not very effective.

Sebire: In practice it is difficult because what you really should examine in the placenta are samples from areas that appear morphologically normal in given sites and from areas that appear to be morphologically abnormal. The difficulty is that, while in some cases it is very obvious, in a lot of cases there is a subtle distinction as to what is normal and what is abnormal. I would like to highlight the point that pathology, particularly histopathology, is a very interpretative thing. It is seen very much as being a right or a wrong answer but for a huge amount of things, and this is true whether you are looking at diagnosis of bronchial carcinoma, or of placental anomalies, there is an error rate and there is an interpretational aspect. That is very difficult to put on paper. I would be happy to include some basic guidelines for block taking if required.

Regan: Now that there are so few paediatric pathologists, many clinicians are going to have to rely on sending slides for an opinion to someone such as yourself. So I think it would be particularly helpful, even if they were very rough guidelines, to have those guidelines included in our recommendations.

Sebire: One of the problems is that pathologists are seen as pathologists, and obstetricians must not touch the placenta because they are obstetricians. I think one of the ways of moving forward here is to have much more modular training. I see no reason why if people are interested they could not easily spend one day a week to train in placental pathology. You could have an obstetrician or a fetal medicine specialist who spends four days a week doing ultrasound scanning, high risk obstetrics and on one day a week does post mortems and placental examination. I think trying to get pathologists interested in obstetric issues is extremely difficult because most pathologists are not interested in obstetrics.

Lamont: How much of a problem in getting perinatal pathologists is the thought of litigation? Eighty percent of litigation is currently in obstetrics. Are the pathologists frightened that they are going to put themselves into that arena by getting involved in the diagnostic process?

Sebire: I do not think that is the case at all. My own impression of the problem is that, in general, pathologists go into pathology because they are interested in disease processes and actually just from anecdotal experience most of them do not like doing obstetrics because they have to get their hands dirty and do things.

Bennett: Infection does not appear to be a major aetiological factor in early pregnancy loss. Is that right? Do women lose pregnancies before 12 weeks from infection?

Regan: In sporadic miscarriage there is a massive cull from infection. It is predominantly maternal viraemia. Whether it is the actual virus or specific organism or whether it is the general illness that that woman is experiencing is unclear. What is also not clear is what the contribution of infection is to recurrent pregnancy loss because, for an organism to be the cause of recurrent episodes, it has to be a pretty extraordinary bug. It has to be able to avoid detection or be immune to 21st century antibiosis, and presumably not cause too many symptoms either.

Lamont: The organism that would fit in with that is *Mycoplasma hominis*, which is not easily detectable, does not respond to the normal set of antibiotics and is associated with bacterial vaginosis.

SECTION 8

CONSENSUS VIEWS

Consensus views arising from the 46th Study Group: Preterm Birth

Health education and policy

- The public and medical professionals need to be aware that it is still not known what initiates the spontaneous onset of labour in women. This makes the prevention and management of preterm labour difficult.
- There is a need to inform the public of the requirement for clinical research and make women aware at the time of the booking that they might be invited to participate in clinical studies.
- The pharmaceutical industry needs to know that it is worthwhile to invest in the development of novel uterine-specific drugs to control uterine activity.
- An improved awareness of the early signs of impending preterm labour is important to improve steroid exposure.
- Regulatory authorities need to be aware that an increase in administrative regulations can impede research and patient care.

Future research

General

- Interdisciplinary research networks should be established.
- Animal research is vital for understanding of the normative process of labour. In addition, animals provide the only means of conducting carefully controlled perturbation challenges that address the pathophysiology of infection, maternal stress and undernutrition, as they impact upon preterm delivery.
- Important lessons can be learned from animal models.
- The elucidation of the physiological pathways of normal delivery is essential. This is a prerequisite for understanding pathological delivery.
- Multidisciplinary approaches are essential for a complete understanding of function at the gene, protein and mechanistic systems levels. Many studies indicate that the time course of changes cannot be followed at a single level.
- Clinical studies are essential to translate the findings from experimental studies into real improvements in clinical care.
- Regulations regarding the use of patient information can impede their use in many ways. This may be detrimental to the consumer. Concerns about protection of

information limit the use of such information. This may prevent evaluation of care that patients need in order to make treatment-related decisions.

Clinical

- There is a crisis in clinical research.
- There is a lack of high-quality clinical studies in preterm labour and delivery.
- The quality of clinical care is improved by clinical research and, if studies are inhibited, the care of women in preterm and term labour will be impaired.
- Measures, such as translational research, need to be encouraged to help bridge the gap between scientific understanding and clinical studies in women at risk of preterm labour.
- Any benefits of tocolysis should be investigated in a randomised placebo-controlled trial.
- Trials should investigate which tocolytic should be used (if appropriate).
- There are no trials comparing the tocolytic efficacy of atosiban with that of nifedipine. Future research should encourage a randomised placebo-controlled trial.
- The role for progesterone in the management of preterm birth needs to be critically evaluated. Further research should address dose, mode of administration and potential benefits/risks. Current use should be restricted to randomised controlled trials.
- Future clinical trials need to be adequately powered to address neonatal/infant outcome.
- More work is required to evaluate noninvasive methods of monitoring myometrial activity.
- There are ethical issues in clinical studies in preterm labour and neonatology, such as the need to obtain immediate consent. Gaining truly informed consent in emergency situations may be difficult but, equally, it is impractical to consent all patients in order to include a very small proportion that are ultimately eligible for a particular study.

The cervix

- Further investigation on the physiology of cervical ripening at term is likely to be useful in understanding the pathophysiology of preterm delivery.
- Cervical biochemistry and biomechanics should be studied in women with 'cervical dysfunction'. The development of noninvasive techniques such as the colloscope may be useful.

The myometrium

- There is a need to promote basic research into the physiology of the human myometrium.
- Investigations into the mechanisms for the spontaneous onset of labour at term are required. This is a prerequisite for investigating how preterm labour deviates from physiological term labour.
- Targets for effector enzymes (e.g. protein kinases) in human myometrium should be identified. This will help to explain the relative quiescence of the uterus during pregnancy and the transition into labour.

Predisposing factors

- Research is needed to explore additional therapies to reduce the preterm birth rate in women with antiphospholipid syndrome.
- The significance of abnormal intrauterine microbial flora and associated phenomena in spontaneous preterm labour requires further study.
- The role of amniocentesis as a diagnostic test in preterm parturition, particularly spontaneous preterm labour, needs to be evaluated.
- Clinical trials of antibiotics for all genitourinary pathogens in the prenatal period are required.
- No benefit has been shown to date for antibiotic treatment of bacterial vaginosis in low-risk women. However, antibiotics were administered late in pregnancy and further research should address their use earlier in pregnancy.
- Research on the maternal ability to produce an inflammatory response as a result of abnormal colonisation is lacking.
- There is a need to evaluate methods to identify babies infected as a result of abnormal colonisation.
- The outcome of bacterial vaginosis intervention studies should be noninfected mothers and babies rather than numbers of preterm deliveries or days gained.
- Improved understanding of the repair processes in fetal membranes could lead to innovative therapies for preterm prelabour rupture of membranes in the future.

Other interventions

Studies are needed to:

- determine the risks and benefits of repeat steroids
- investigate selective modulation of pulmonary steroid receptors
- clarify which steroid effects are reversible
- evaluate the safety of home-based care of women with preterm prelabour rupture of membranes
- determine the optimal timing for induction of labour in women with preterm prelabour rupture of membranes
- investigate the place of repeated amnioinfusion in early preterm prelabour rupture of membranes to try to prevent fetal pulmonary hypoplasia.

Index

acidosis, fetal 342
actin 259–61
actin-associated proteins 263
acute interstitial pulmonary emphysema (AIPE) 361
adaptive response, preterm labour as 33, 36–7, 66, 91–2
adaptor proteins 272
adrenal gland, fetal 7, 15–16, 19, 32
adrenocorticotrophic hormone (ACTH) 15, 16, 32
African American women 207–8
Afro-Caribbean women 61, 62, 164
alcohol consumption 62
allergy-induced preterm labour 41–2
allograft reaction, abnormal 40–1
amines, in vaginal secretions 167, 168
amniocentesis
      before cervical cerclage 158
      in PPROM 215, 234
      research needs 375
amniochorial–decidual unit 195–6
amniograft, in PPROM 220
amnioinfusion, in PPROM 219–20
amnion 195–6
      extracellular matrix 197
      prostaglandins 8, 23
amniopatch 220
amniotic fluid
      bactericidal properties 234
      culture 217, 353
      tests, in PPROM 217–18
      volume, after PPROM 214
anaerobes, vaginal 166
androgens 7
androstenedione 7
anencephaly 32
angiogenin 35
animal models 373
      antenatal steroids 245–6
      control of gestation length 3–12, 13–17
      PPROM 233–4
      rationale for using 3–4
      role of oxytocin 309
      see also primates, non-human
antenatal corticosteroids 181, 244–57, 281–2
      adverse maternal effects 249–50
      biological effects 244–6
      choice of agent 253
      clinical decision making 189, 191
      dose regimens 281–2
      economic effects 250

evidence for benefits 78, 246–51
fetal fibronectin testing 182, 183, 184, 185
indications 134
long-term effects on children 249, 282
in maternal diabetes 251
in maternal hypertensive disease 251
in multifetal pregnancy 251
in PPROM 214, 250
research needs 375
single vs multiple doses 251–2, 253, 281
antibiotics 224–30
      adverse effects 231
      in bacterial vaginosis 172–5, 176, 188, 226
      cervical cerclage with 157–8
      intrapartum 227–8
      in PPROM 214–15, 227–8
      prenatal, to prevent preterm birth 225–6
      in preterm labour 227
      research needs 375
anticardiolipin antibodies (aCL) 240, 241–2
antiphospholipid antibodies (aPL) 147, 239–40
antiphospholipid syndrome (APS) 239–43, 277, 375
      diagnosis 240
      mechanisms of pregnancy morbidity 240
      pregnancy morbidity 239
      treatment 240–2
antiprogesterones 89, 106–7, 109
apoptosis
      in cervical ripening 109
      in intrauterine infection 205
      in membrane rupture 32, 200–1, 202
arrestins 267
ascorbate levels, and PPROM 206–7
Asian women 61, 62
aspirin, in antiphospholipid syndrome 241
assisted conception pregnancies 96
atherosis, maternal vessels 357
atosiban 293, 309, 313–28, 333–6
      chemical structure 313
      clinical studies 289, 290–1, 314–28
            comparative trials 322–6
            early randomised placebo-controlled trial 315–16
            maintenance therapy 326–8, 334, 335
            observational study 316–17
            pilot studies 314–15
            placebo-controlled, with tocolytic rescue 317–22
            trial design 317, 337
      costs 303

mechanism of action 313, 334
pharmacokinetics 314
safety and tolerability 325, 326, 327, 328
ATP 261

baboons *see* primates, non-human
bacterial vaginosis (BV) 163–80, 224, 225
adverse sequelae 170–1
aetiology 164–5
associated factors 164
diagnosis 168–9, 188–9
frequency 163–4, 165
gene interaction 37–8, 189
history 163
HIV acquisition and 170–1
longitudinal data 168
microbiology 166
nomenclature 163
pathophysiology 166–7
in prediction and prevention of preterm birth
171–5, 188, 226, 231
research needs 375
bacteriophages, bacterial vaginosis and 164–5
bacteriuria, asymptomatic 224, 225–6
Bacteroides spp. 166–7
Bartter syndrome 354
behavioural factors, in PPROM 206–7
behavioural problems 80
β-adrenergic agonists (betamimetics) 288,
289–90, 333
adverse effects 290, 297, 325
mechanism of action 271
vs other tocolytics 291, 301, 322–6
beta amyloid precursor protein (BAPP) 360
betamethasone, antenatal 253
biglycan 30, 100, 103
biophysical profile, in PPROM 218
birthweight
antenatal steroids and 246
discordant twin 69
distribution, preterm infants 64–5
for gestation, dating error and 66, 67
body mass index 62
BORN study 333
brain development
after antenatal steroids 282
postnatal, preterm babies 79
brain injury, preterm babies 78–9, 360
breastfeeding 342
breathing movements, fetal, in PPROM 218
breech presentation 343, 347–8
bronchopulmonary dysplasia (BPD) 76, 361
see also chronic lung disease of prematurity
BV *see* bacterial vaginosis

Ca²⁺-ATPase, plasma membrane (PMCA) 265
caesarean section
elective *vs* emergency 368
rates 73, 344, 345, 346
recommended use 347–8
vs vaginal delivery 341–9
caesarean section hysterectomy, animal models 7
calcitonin gene-related peptide 290
calcium (Ca²⁺)
entry 264–5
extrusion mechanisms 265
intracellular ([Ca²⁺]) 262
release 266–7
storage 265–6
myometrial function 263–7, 277

sensitisation 263, 264
calcium (Ca²⁺)-calmodulin 262, 264
calcium channel blockers (CCBs) 290, 297–304
adverse effects and safety 302–3
historical perspective 288
pharmacokinetics 298–9
pharmacology 271, 297–8
tocolytic efficacy 291, 299–301
see also nifedipine
calcium channels, voltage-dependent (VDCCs)
264–5, 297
caldesmon 260, 263
calmodulin 262, 265, 266
calmodulin-dependent protein kinase II (CaM
kinase II) 262, 264
calponin 263
cardiotocography, in PPROM 218
cerclage *see* cervical cerclage
cerebral palsy 73, 80
bacterial vaginosis and 171
intrauterine infection and 78–9
mode of delivery and 343
multiple pregnancy and 73
cerebral white matter injury 78, 360
cervical cerclage 140–50, 157–60
adverse effects 147
antibiotic cover 157–8
cervical length and *see under* cervical length
elective 142–3, 155, 158–60
emergency 'rescue' 145, 158, 159
mechanisms of effect 152, 153–4
in multiple pregnancy 146
placental pathology and 352–3
preconception 145–6
repeat 145
timing of suture removal 147
transabdominal (TAC) 145–6
types 146–7, 153
ultrasound-indicated 143–5
cervical dysfunction 99, 102, 152–3
cervical effacement 119, 120
cervical insufficiency (weakness; incompetence)
42, 99
biochemical changes 102
cervical cerclage *see* cervical cerclage
definition 140
incidence 141–2
mechanism of PROM 206
terminology 152–3
cervical length (shortness) 31, 33, 125–37, 140,
155
after cervical cerclage 154
in asymptomatic pregnancies 125–31
high-risk women 125–7
low-risk women 126, 127–9
fetal fibronectin and 129, 136–7
indicating cervical cerclage 143–5, 155, 156,
158–9
placental pathology and 352–3
post cervical cerclage 145
preterm PROM and 135–6
sonographic measurement 124–39
acceptability 125
techniques 124–5
in threatened preterm labour 131–6
after tocolysis 132, 133
delivery within 7 days and 132, 133–4
fetal fibronectin and 134, 135
at presentation 130, 131
in twin pregnancies 133, 136

in triplet pregnancies 127, 130, 131, 136,
    146
in twin pregnancies 127, 128, 129–31, 136,
    146
    fetal fibronectin and 131
    threatened preterm labour 133, 136
cervical mucus plug 153
cervical ripening 28, 99
    induction *in vivo* 109
    inflammatory hypothesis 30, 116–21, 154
    mechanisms 30–1, 104–9, 151–2, 154–5
    methods of studying 99–100
    research needs 374
    structural changes during 102–4
cervix 99–114
    anatomy 100, 101
    continuum of integrity model 140–1
    inflammatory mediators 115–23
    innervation 118
    prostaglandin synthesis 8
    prostanoid receptors 9, 151
    research needs 374
    short *see* cervical length
    structural composition 100–2
        in disordered function 102
        normal 100–1
        during ripening 102–4
children born preterm 80–1
    effects of antenatal steroids 249, 252, 282
    mode of delivery and 342
    social and educational interventions 81
Chlamydia trachomatis 224, 225
cholera toxin 268
chondroitin sulphates 100
chorioamnionitis 224
    clinical signs 216, 217
    histopathology 352, 368–9
    mechanisms of PPROM 203–5
    mode of delivery 343
    multiple pregnancy 356
    neurological complications and 78–9
    see also intrauterine infection
choriodecidual inflammation 352–4
chorion 195–6
    extracellular matrix 197, 198
chorionicity, postnatal determination 355–6
chronic lung disease of prematurity 75, 76, 360–1
circadian rhythms, myometrial activity 6, 29, 335
clindamycin, in bacterial vaginosis 173, 174–5,
    176, 188, 226
clinical guidelines, care of preterm babies 74
clue cells 165, 168–9
co-amoxiclav 214–15, 228
Cochrane Collaboration 74
collagen(s)
    cervical 30, 100–1
        breakdown 104, 118–19
        in cervical weakness 102
        during ripening 102–3
    fetal membranes 197, 198
        in PPROM 201
        in process of rupture 31–2, 198, 199
    gene mutations 207
    myometrium 259
collagenases 32, 104
    see also matrix metalloproteinases
colloscope 103
connexin 43 29–30, 40
consent, informed 93–5, 374
continuous positive airway pressure (CPAP), nasal

75
contraction-associated proteins 30
corticosteroids 244–57
    antenatal *see* antenatal corticosteroids
    antiphospholipid syndrome 240–1
    preterm infants 76, 79
corticotrophin-releasing hormone (CRH)
    maternal plasma levels 17, 28, 92
    receptors, myometrium 19
    regulation of placental expression 17–18
    role in onset of labour 15, 16, 19, 24, 32
cortisol
    fetal secretion 5, 7, 15, 32
    initiating labour in sheep 16
    maternal plasma 28
costs, economic
    antenatal steroids 250
    preterm birth 296
    tocolysis 303, 336
CPI-17 263, 264
C-reactive protein (CRP) 216, 217
creep extension 198–9
cyclic ADP-ribose (cADPR) 266
cyclooxygenase 2 (COX-2; PGHS-2)
    inhibitors 290, 292, 334
    in initiation of labour 21, 23, 43
    prelabour increase in levels 8, 23
cysteine aminopeptidase 309
cystic periventricular leukomalacia 78
cytokines 36–7, 81, 156–7
    amniotic fluid 217–18
    in bacterial vaginosis 171, 188
    cervical ripening 105–6, 109, 118
    maternal serum, in PPROM 216
cytotrophoblast 196
cytotrophoblastic–decidual involution 200–1

databases
    informed consent issues 94–5
    quality of data 90–1
dating, pregnancy
    birthweight for gestation and 66, 67
    errors 62–4
    menstrual–scan discrepancy 62, 64
decidua 195–6
    role in PPROM 206
decidual/fetal membrane activation 28, 31–2
decorin
    cervix 30, 100, 101, 103
    fetal membranes 197
    gene mutations 207
deformities, after PPROM 214, 219
dehydroepiandrosterone sulphate (DHEA-S) 19,
    32
    cervical ripening and 108, 109
delivery
    mode of preterm *see* mode of preterm
        delivery
    vs conservative management, in PPROM 215
deprivation, socioeconomic 61, 95
dermatan sulphate 30, 100
developing countries 296
dexamethasone, antenatal 31, 253
diabetes mellitus, antenatal steroids 251

economic costs *see* costs, economic
educational achievement 80
educational interventions 81
Ehlers–Danlos syndrome 207
elastic fibres 102, 197

elasticity, fetal membranes 198–9
elastin 32, 197
    mutations 207
endocrine changes
    bacterial vaginosis and 165
    preparturitional 5, 14, 15–16
endocrine disorders, preterm parturition 42–4
endothelin (ET) receptors 10, 271
engineering perspective, human parturition 157
enzymes, in bacterial vaginosis 165
eosinophils 41, 117
EPICure study 80, 293, 297
epidemiology
    preterm birth 61–72, 89–90
    routine data collection 94–5
epidermal growth factor (EGF) 272
EP receptors 9, 151
equivalence trials 317
ERKs 271, 272
erythromycin 215, 231
Escherichia coli 166, 168
ethanol, for tocolysis 288
ethics committees 93, 94–5
ethnic differences
    bacterial vaginosis 164
    PPROM susceptibility 207–8
    preterm birth 61, 62, 91
evidence-based guidelines, preterm babies 74
evolution, parturition strategies 13–14
extracellular matrix (ECM)
    cervix 30
    fetal membranes 197–8
        changes underlying rupture 199–201
        degradation 32, 198–9, 202
        genetic influences 207
        infection-associated changes 203–5
        in PPROM 201–3
    myometrium 259

fasting 29
fetal abnormality 354, 358–9
fetal assessment, in PPROM 214–15, 218
fetal fibronectin test 33, 181–7
    cervical length and 129, 136–7
        in threatened preterm labour 134, 135
        in twin pregnancies 131
    predictive accuracy 182–5
    technique 181
fetal growth, preterm birth and 64–9
fetal growth restriction (IUGR)
    in antiphospholipid syndrome 241
    membrane rupture and 233
    multifetal pregnancies 68–9
    neonatal survival and 66, 67
    pathological features 356–8, 369
    pre-eclampsia 66–8
    preterm birth and 64–6
fetal hypothalamic–pituitary–adrenal (HPA) axis
    15–16, 32
fetal inflammatory response syndrome (FIRS) 37,
    96
fetal membranes see membranes, fetal
fetoscopy, PPROM after 220, 232
fetus
    intrauterine infection involving 33, 36
    role in onset of labour 32
fibrillin-1 197, 207
fibrin tissue sealant, in PPROM 221
fibroblasts, cervical 103, 106, 109
fibromodulin 100, 101

fibronectin
    fetal see fetal fibronectin test
    oncofetal 32
forceps delivery 349
c-fos mRNA, stretch-induced expression 40
FP receptors 9, 271
free radicals 205
Fryns syndrome 354
fundus, uterine
    origin of contractions 279–80
    prostaglandins 8, 9
fungal infections, preterm babies 77
funisitis 37

$G\alpha_{i/o}$ coupled receptors 268, 271
$G\alpha_{q/11}$ coupled receptors 268, 271
$G\alpha_s$ 19, 20, 269
    coupled receptors 268, 270–1
gap junctions, myometrial 29–30, 278, 279
Gardnerella vaginalis
    association with preterm birth 224, 225
    bacterial vaginosis and 163, 166, 167, 169
gelatinases 32, 104
gelatin sponge 220
gender differences, effects of antenatal steroids
    248
gene–environment interactions
    bacterial vaginosis 37–8, 189
    intrauterine infection 33, 37–8
genes
    upregulated in labour 22, 91
    uterine 278–9
genetic conflict hypothesis 13–14
genetic factors, PPROM 207–8
germinal matrix haemorrhage 78, 360
gestational age
    errors in estimating 62–4
    outcome of PPROM and 213–14
    physiological variation 91
    survival by 79–80
    tocolytic efficacy of atosiban and 320, 321
    viability 296–7
gestation length, control of 13–27
    animal studies 3–12
    humans 17–24
        vs mammals 13–17
    single trigger/clock concept 4–5
    see also onset of parturition
glucocorticoids
    placental CRH expression and 17–18
    role in onset of labour 24
    see also corticosteroids; cortisol
glucose, amniotic fluid 217
glyceryl trinitrate 290
glycosaminoglycans (GAGs), cervical 100–1,
    108–9
G protein(s)
    cycle 267–9
    effectors regulated by 270
G protein-coupled receptors (GPCRs) 262–3,
    267–71, 272
Gram stain
    amniotic fluid, in PPROM 217
    vaginal secretions 169, 170
GRK (GPCR kinase) 267–8
group B streptococcus (GBS)
    maternal carriage 166, 215
    maternal screening 77
    neonatal early-onset infection 77
growth factors

receptors 271–2
therapy 77

head entrapment 342, 348
Health and Social Care Act 2001 94
health education and policy 373
height, maternal 62
heparin, in antiphospholipid syndrome 241, 277
high-risk pregnancy
    bacterial vaginosis 171–4, 226, 231
    cervical length assessment 125–7
histiocytic intervillositis, chronic 358
HIV infection, bacterial vaginosis and 170–1
hospitalisation
    indications 134
    in PPROM 215
house dust mite allergy 41
human chorionic gonadotrophin 290
Hunter, William 101, 119, 120
hyaline membrane disease (HMD) 360–1
hyaluronan 197, 200
hydrops, fetal 358–9
17α-hydroxylase 15
17 alpha-hydroxyprogesterone caproate (17P) 44,
    89, 290, 292–3
hypersensitivity reaction, type I 41–2
hypertensive disease of pregnancy, antenatal
    steroids 251
hypothalamic–pituitary–adrenal (HPA) axis, fetal
    15–16, 32
hypoxaemia, fetal 40
hypoxic-ischaemic brain injury 79, 360

IgE 41
immune response
    neurological complications and 79
    polymorphisms affecting 207–8
immunoglobulin, intravenous (IVIg) 77, 241
indemnity cover 93
indomethacin 289, 290, 292
infections
    associated with preterm birth 224, 225
    in early pregnancy loss 370
    intrauterine see intrauterine infection
    maternal, antenatal steroids and 249
    preterm babies 77
inflammation 116–17, 156–7
    acute vs chronic 156, 157
    cervical ripening and 30, 116–21, 154
    choriodecidual 352–4
    neurological complications and 79
    physiological vs pathological 156–7
    role in onset of labour 21–2
    role in preterm labour 34, 35, 96, 190
inflammatory cells
    chemotaxis 117
    infiltrating ripening cervix 104, 109, 117
    mechanism of cervical infiltration 118
    role in cervical ripening 118–19
inflammatory mediators 156–7
    in cervical ripening 105–6, 108
    cervix 115–23
    intrauterine infection 35
    polymorphisms affecting production 207–8
    in preterm parturition 36–7
initiation of parturition see onset of parturition
inositol trisphosphate receptors (InsP₃Rs) 266–7
instrumental vaginal delivery 348–9
interleukin-1 (IL-1; IL-1β)
    in cervical ripening 105–6, 108, 118

polymorphisms 208
    in preterm parturition 36–7
interleukin-2 (IL-2) soluble receptor 41
interleukin-6 (IL-6)
    amniotic fluid 35, 38, 156, 217–18
    in cervical ripening 105, 106, 118
    fetal plasma 37, 38
    maternal serum 35, 216
interleukin-8 (IL-8) 22
    in cervical ripening 30, 109, 118
    in membrane rupture 200
intermediate filaments 259
intervillositis, chronic histiocytic 358
intrauterine growth restriction see fetal growth
    restriction
intrauterine infection 33–8, 224
    cervical cerclage in presence of 158
    cervical cerclage in prevention 153
    cervical insufficiency and 42, 141
    cervical length and 155
    chronic nature 35
    clinical signs 216, 217
    delayed delivery of second twin and 146
    fetal involvement 33, 36
    frequency in spontaneous preterm birth 34–5
    gene–environment interactions 33, 37–8
    labour as adaptive response 33, 36–7, 91–2
    neurological complications and 78–9
    placental pathology 352–4
    in PPROM 35, 135
        aetiological role 203–5
        fetal assessment 218
        monitoring 216–18, 234
    research needs 375
    subclinical 203–5, 216, 224
    see also chorioamnionitis
intravenous immunoglobulin (IVIg) 77, 241
intraventricular haemorrhage
    antenatal steroids and 248–9
    germinal matrix 78, 360
    nifedipine tocolysis and 301
in utero transfer 335
    fetal fibronectin testing and 184, 191
in vitro fertilisation (IVF) pregnancies 96
in vitro studies 3
isoxsuprine 289

Lactobacillus spp. 163, 166, 169
    phage viruses 164–5, 188
    during pregnancy 167
lesbians 164
leucocytes
    in cervical ripening 117, 118–19, 154
    see also inflammatory cells; neutrophils
licensing, drug 333–4
likelihood ratios 182
litigation, medico-legal 93, 370
lower genital tract swabs, in PPROM 214, 217
lower uterine segment
    prostaglandin synthesis 8
    prostanoid receptors 9, 280
    vs cervix 100, 152
low-risk pregnancy
    bacterial vaginosis 174–5
    cervical length assessment 126, 127–9
lung
    air leaks 360–1
    complications, preterm infants 75–6
    effects of antenatal steroids 245–6
    pathology 360–1

lupus anticoagulant (LA) 240, 241–2

macrophages
  decidual, in PPROM 206
  in ripening cervix 117, 118
magnesium (Mg^{2+}) 264
magnesium sulphate 288, 289, 290, 291
  and nifedipine therapy 303
magnetic resonance imaging (MRI)
  brain of preterm babies 78, 79
  postmortem 351
malaria 358
mammals, parturition in 13–17
MAP kinases 263, 267, 271, 272
massive perivillous fibrin deposition/maternal floor
  infarction (MPVFD/MFI) 358, 359
mast cells 41
maternal age 62
maternal factors, predicting preterm birth 61, 62
matrix metalloproteinase-1 (MMP-1) 39
  in cervical ripening 106, 108, 118–19
  in membrane rupture 32, 90, 199, 202
matrix metalloproteinase-2 (MMP-2) 199, 202,
  259
matrix metalloproteinase-7 (MMP-7) 199
matrix metalloproteinase-8 (MMP-8) 32, 35, 104,
  118–19
matrix metalloproteinase-9 (MMP-9)
  in cervical ripening 104, 118, 259
  in membrane rupture 32, 199, 200, 202
matrix metalloproteinase-13 (MMP-13) 118
matrix metalloproteinases (MMPs) 259
  cells producing 118–19
  in cervical ripening 104, 120–1
  in decidual/membrane activation 32, 90
  endogenous regulators of cervical 105–8
  fetal membrane degradation 198
  genetic polymorphisms 207
  in intrauterine infection 203, 204–5
  in membrane rupture 199, 202
McDonald sutures 146–7
membranes, fetal 195–6
  control of labour 201
  development 195–6
  effects of stretch 40, 152, 198–9, 200
  extracellular matrix see under extracellular
    matrix
  labour-associated changes 199
  prolapsed, short cervix 145, 155, 158–9
  prostaglandin production 23
  rupture see rupture of membranes
  zone of altered morphology 31, 198,
    199–201
  see also decidual/fetal membrane activation
menstrual history
  date, discrepancy with scan date 62, 64
  pregnancy dating 62–4
menstruation–conception interval 64
meta-analysis 189, 190, 191
methicillin-resistant Staphylococcus aureus 77
metronidazole
  adverse effects 231
  in bacterial vaginosis 172–4, 188, 226
microorganisms 224, 225
mifepristone 106–7, 109
miscarriage
  bacterial vaginosis and 171
  previous 61, 62
  recurrent, in antiphospholipid syndrome 240
  role of infection 370

Mobiluncus spp. 166
mode of preterm delivery 341–9, 368
  clinical management issues 342–3
  current practice in UK 343–7
  recent nonrandomised studies 343
  recommendations 347–9
  systematic review 341–2
mRNA, tissue measurements 9–10
multicentre research ethics committees (MREC)
  93, 95
multifetal pregnancy 68–9
  antenatal steroids 251
  cervical cerclage 146
  increased rates 73
  mechanism of PROM 205
  placental pathology 355–6
multiparae 62, 63
Mycoplasma hominis 35, 370
  in bacterial vaginosis 165, 166, 167–8, 169
Mycoplasmas, genital 35
myofibroblasts
  cervical 103–4, 109
  fetal membranes 200–1
myometrial activity (contractility) 258–76,
  277–81
  circadian rhythm 6, 29, 335
  functional progesterone withdrawal and 20–1
  methods of studying 3, 4
  oxytocin actions 308–9, 312
  pacemaker zones 277–8, 279–80
  physiology 260–3
  pregnant non-human primates 6–7
  in preterm parturition 28–30
  receptor-mediated regulation 267–72
  research needs 374
  role of calcium 263–7, 277
  stretch and 40, 278
  structural basis 258–60
myosin 260–1, 279
myosin binding subunit (MYPT1) 262, 263
myosin heavy chain (MHC) 260
myosin light chain kinase (MLCK) 262, 263, 264
myosin light chains (MLC) 260, 261–2, 264
myosin phosphatase (MLCP) 262–3

Na$^+$/Ca^{2+} exchangers 265
Naegele's rule 63
National Institute for Clinical Excellence (NICE)
  189
necrotising enterocolitis 76
  antenatal steroids and 244, 249
  co-amoxiclav-related risk 215, 228
  nifedipine tocolysis and 301
Neisseria gonorrhoeae 165, 224, 225
neonatal care
  at birth 74–5
  improving quality 81
  pathology of iatrogenic complications 362
  protocol-directed 74
  respiratory management after birth 75
neonatal intensive care
  costs 296
  nifedipine tocolysis and 301
  in utero transfer see in utero transfer
neonatal mortality 73
  antenatal steroids and 246, 247
  see also perinatal mortality
neonatal sepsis 77
neurodevelopmental outcomes, long-term 80–1
neurological complications 78–9

antenatal steroids and 78, 249, 253
    mode of delivery and 342, 343
neutrophils
    infiltrating ripening cervix 104, 117
    in PPROM 203–5
    role in cervical ripening 118–19
nifedipine 293, 297–304, 333
    adverse effects and safety 302–3
    contraindications 303
    costs 303
    dosage 303
    gastrointestinal therapeutic system (GITS)
      298, 299
    pharmacokinetics 298–9
    pharmacology 297–8
    tocolytic efficacy 299–301, 336–7
nitric oxide (NO)
    in cervical ripening 31, 106, 118, 120
    CRH interactions 18, 19
nitric oxide donors 109, 291–2
nitric oxide synthase (NOS), in cervical ripening
    105–6, 107
Nod2 polymorphism 207–8
North West Thames perinatal database 343–7, 368
nuclear factor kappa B (NFκB) 43, 152
Nugent score 169
nulliparae 62, 63
numbers needed to treat (NNT)
    after fetal fibronectin testing 183, 184, 185
    antibiotics 229
    nifedipine tocolysis 301
nutritional state
    length of gestation and 23, 29
    PPROM and 206–7

obesity 61, 62
oestrogen
    bacterial vaginosis and 165
    cervical ripening and 30, 107, 109
    placental CRH expression and 18
    preparturitional increase 5, 7
    profiles during pregnancy 14
    role in onset of labour 7, 15, 16, 19, 20–1,
      42
oestrogen:progesterone ratio 5, 7
oestrogen receptors (ER) 43
    α (ERα) 20–1, 43, 107
    β (ERβ) 107
oligohydramnios 214
onapristone 107
onset of parturition
    in humans 17–24, 28–32, 115–16
    in mammals 15–16
    in non-human primates 7–9, 16–17
    role of fetus 32
orthopaedic deformities, after PPROM 214, 219
outpatient care, in PPROM 215
oxygen therapy 77–8
oxytocin
    gene deletion studies 312–13
    mechanism of action 272
    plasma levels in labour 309, 310, 311, 312
    in preterm labour 313
    role in labour 29, 115, 308–13
oxytocin antagonists 271, 290–1, 308–32
    see also atosiban
oxytocinase, placental 309
oxytocin receptors (OTr) 271, 309, 312–13
    in control of parturition 20–1, 29
    downregulation 334, 335

methods of studying 3–4
    in preterm labour 313
    stretch-induced expression 40

p21-activated kinase (PAK) 262, 263
pacemakers, myometrial 277–8, 279–80
parathyroid hormone-related peptide 290
parity 62, 63
parturition
    common pathway of term and preterm 28–32
    continuum concept 334–5
    engineering perspective 157
    evolution of strategies 13–14
    mammals vs humans 13–17
    onset of see onset of parturition
paternal–maternal conflict hypothesis 13–14
pathological examination 350–67, 368–70
pathologists
    shortages 368, 370
    variation in expertise 350–1
Peptostreptococcus spp. 166–7
perinatal mortality 288, 296–7
    after PPROM 213–14
    atosiban tocolysis and 321–2, 323, 326, 327,
      328
    mode of delivery and 342, 346–7, 348
    very preterm infants 79–80, 297
    see also postmortem examination
periventricular leukomalacia
    antenatal steroids and 253
    cystic 78
    pathological features 360
persistent interstitial pulmonary emphysema
    (PIPE) 361
pertussis toxin 268
phage viruses, bacterial vaginosis and 164–5, 188
phosphatidylinositol-3-kinase (PI-3-kinase) 271,
    272
phospholamban 265–6
phospholipase Cβ (PLCβ) 269, 271
phospholipase Cγ (PLCγ) 272
placebo-controlled trials
    atosiban 315–16, 317–22
    tocolytics 317, 337
placenta
    chronic histiocytic intervillositis 358
    circumvallate 355
    massive perivillous fibrin deposition/maternal
      floor infarction (MPVFD/MFI) 358, 359
placental abruption 39, 241
    pathological features 354, 355
placental pathology 350–67, 368–70
    choriodecidual inflammation 352–4
    iatrogenic preterm birth 356–8
    indications 351
    multifetal pregnancy 355–6
    uteroplacental disease 354, 356–8
placental sulphatase deficiency 92
placenta praevia 355
placentation disorders 355
plasma membrane Ca²⁺-ATPase (PMCA) 265
plasmin 32, 39
platelet activating factor (PAF) 106, 118
platelet-derived growth factor (PDGF) 272
pneumothorax 361
polyethylene bag 75
polyhydramnios 354
positive-pressure ventilation 75, 361
postmortem examination 350–67
    iatrogenic preterm birth 358–9

prematurity-related complications 360–2
uteroplacental disease 357
value 350, 351
postpartum haemorrhage 342
post-test probability 182–3, 191
potassium channel openers 290
potassium (K⁺) channels, Ca²⁺-activated 267
prediction of preterm birth 287
bacterial vaginosis 171–5
cervical length assessment 124–39
fetal fibronectin test 181–5
maternal plasma CRH 17
prepregnancy factors 61, 62
study design and power 189–92
pre-eclampsia (PET) 66–8, 368
antenatal steroids 251
in antiphospholipid syndrome 241
pathological features 356–8
prelabour rupture of membranes (PROM) 195,
201
preterm see preterm prelabour rupture of
membranes
prematurity
complicating PPROM 213–14
definition 91
neonatal survival and 66, 67
PREMET trial 231
presentation, fetal 343, 347–8
preservatives, in steroid preparations 253
preterm birth (PTB)
bacterial vaginosis and 171–5
causes 239, 352–6
clinical problem 13, 239, 287
definition 182, 239, 287
distinction from PPROM 90–1
frequency 73–4, 296
iatrogenic, pathology 356–8
prediction see prediction of preterm birth
prevention see prevention of preterm birth
previous history 61, 62
preterm infants 73–87
after PPROM 213–14
complications 75–9
management 74–5
see also neonatal care
mode of delivery see mode of preterm
delivery
postmortem examination see postmortem
examination
strategies for improving outcome 81
survival and outcome 79–81, 296–7
see also children born preterm
preterm labour 78
as adaptive response 33, 36–7, 66, 91–2
components of pathway 28–32
as syndrome with multiple aetiologies see
preterm parturition syndrome
threatened see threatened preterm labour
preterm parturition syndrome 28, 32–45, 92–3
abnormal allograft reaction 40–1
allergy-induced preterm labour 41–2
cervical insufficiency 42
endocrine disorders 42–4
intrauterine infection 32–8
uterine overdistension 40
uteroplacental ischaemia 38–40
preterm prelabour rupture of membranes (PPROM)
195, 213–23
as adaptive response to infection 33, 36–7
after cervical cerclage 147

amnioinfusion 219–20
in animal models 233–4
antenatal steroids 214, 250
antibiotic therapy 214–15, 227–8
cervical length assessment 135–6
clinical risk factors and associations 203–8
genetic factors 207–8
intrauterine infection 35, 203–5
maternal uterocervical factors 205–6
nutritional and behavioural factors
206–7
conservative management 215
conservative management vs delivery 215
distinction from preterm birth 90–1
fetal assessment 214–15, 218
iatrogenic 220, 232
initial management 214–15
inpatient vs outpatient care 215
mechanisms 31–2, 38–40, 90, 201–8, 232–4
monitoring for infection 216–18, 234
new treatment techniques 220–1
outcome 213–14
recurrence 159–60, 207
research needs 375
surgical treatment 220–1
tocolysis 218–19
prevention of preterm birth 287, 334
antibiotic therapy 225–6, 277
bacterial vaginosis therapy 171–5, 188, 226,
231
cervical cerclage see cervical cerclage
progesterone therapy see under progesterone
see also tocolysis
primates, non-human 16–17
advantages of studying 5–7
antenatal steroids 245
atosiban tocolysis 335
myometrial activity 6–7
PPROM 233–4
role of oestrogen 7
role of prostaglandins 8–9
probability, post-test 182–3, 191
procedure-related iatrogenic preterm birth 359
progesterone 258
anti-inflammatory action 22
bacterial vaginosis and 165
cervical ripening and 30, 31, 106–7, 108–9
functional withdrawal in humans 15
cervical ripening and 107
mechanisms 20–1, 22, 24, 42–3
in PPROM 206
preparturitional changes 5
research needs 374
role in onset of labour 7, 15, 16
treatment to prevent preterm birth 22, 43–4,
88–9, 95, 292–3
vaginal, prophylactic therapy 44, 89
withdrawal, in mammals 14–15, 42, 292
progesterone receptors (PR) 20–1, 43, 89
full-length (PR-B) 20, 43
PR-A/PR-B ratio 20–1, 22, 43
truncated (PR-A) 20–1, 22, 23, 24, 43
prostaglandin dehydrogenase (PGDH) 8, 118, 120
prostaglandin E₂ (PGE₂)
cervical ripening 31, 108, 118, 120
oxytocin stimulation of production 312, 313
production by fetal membranes 23
uterine responsiveness in late gestation 9
prostaglandin endoperoxide H synthase-2 (PGHS2)
see cyclooxygenase 2

prostaglandin F₂α
    in cervical ripening 106
    oxytocin stimulation of production 312
    receptors (FP receptors) 9, 271
prostaglandins (PGs)
    in cervical ripening 31, 106, 108, 151
    from fetal membranes 23
    induction of cervical ripening *in vivo* 109
    receptors 8–9, 151, 280
    regulation of cervical MMPs 105–6
    role in onset of labour 8–9, 22, 23, 24
prostaglandin synthetase inhibitors 292
protein kinase C (PKC) 262, 263, 264
proteoglycans, cervical 30, 100–1, 103
protocol-directed clinical care, preterm babies 74
pulmonary hypoplasia 214, 219
pulmonary oedema, maternal 249–50, 333
pyrexia, maternal 216, 217

quality of life, children's perceptions 80–1

Ras 272
receptor tyrosine kinases (RTKs) 271–2
reductionist approach 5
relaxin 108, 109
    administration 288
    in PPROM 206
renin–angiotensin system 39
research
    clinical 93–5, 374
    future requirements 373–5
respiratory distress syndrome, (RDS), neonatal 76, 360–1
    antenatal steroids and 246, 247–8, 250–1, 281
    fetal fibronectin testing and 183
    nifedipine tocolysis and 301
    postnatal prophylaxis 75, 248
respiratory support, preterm babies 75
retinopathy of prematurity (ROP) 74, 77–8
retroplacental haematoma 40, 354, 355
rhesus monkeys *see* primates, non-human
rhoA-associated kinase 263, 264
rho-kinase inhibitors 290
ritodrine 289–90
    costs 303
    placebo-controlled trial 317
rofecoxib 333
rupture of membranes 195, 196–208
    cellular phenotypic changes 198, 199–201
    diagnosis 214
    initial site 197, 199
    mechanisms 31–2, 198–9, 232–3
    pathological examination of site 352
    prelabour *see* prelabour rupture of membranes
    research needs 375
    spontaneous *see* spontaneous rupture of membranes
    uterine contractility and 280
    zone of altered morphology *see* zone of altered morphology
ryanodine receptors (RyR) 266

sarcoplasmic reticulum (SR) 265
school performance 80, 81
secretory leucocyte protease inhibitor (SLPI) 205
sepsis, preterm babies 77
SERCA pumps 265–6
sex, fetal 96

sexual transmission, bacterial vaginosis 164
sheep, pregnant
    antenatal steroids 246
    myometrial activity 6
    preparturitional endocrine changes 5, 14, 15–16
Shirodkar suture 146–7, 153
SHP-2 272
small-for-gestational-age (SGA) infants 39, 64
    neonatal survival 66, 67
    pre-eclampsia and 66–8
smoking, cigarette
    PPROM and 206–7
    preterm labour and 61, 62
smooth muscle cells, uterine 259–60
social class 61, 95
social interventions, children born preterm 81
spiral arteries, defective trophoblast invasion 39, 240
spontaneous rupture of membranes (SROM) 195
    cellular phenotypic changes 198, 199–201
    mechanisms 198–9
Src 272
staphylococci, coagulase-negative 77
Staphylococcus aureus infections 77
steroids *see* corticosteroids
stillbirths 65–6, 326, 346–7
strain hardening 199
streptococcus, group B *see* group B streptococcus
stress shielding, in fetal membranes 197, 200
stretch
    cervical 108
    fetal membranes 40, 152, 198–9, 200
    uterine 23, 40, 278
study design and power 189–92, 317, 335–6
succinate 166
sulphiting agents, in steroid preparations 253
surfactant
    antenatal steroids and 245–6
    membrane rupture and 233
    postnatal therapy 75, 248
suture materials, cervical cerclage 147
systems synthetic approach 5

tachyphylaxis 297–8
temperature, body 216, 217
tenascin 31
teratogenicity, calcium channel blockers 302
terbutaline 289
TH-2 CD4⁺ T cells 41
THG 113 290
threatened preterm labour 191
    cervical length assessment *see under* cervical length
    clinical decision making 182–3, 189, 191
    fetal fibronectin test 182–5
thrombin 39–40, 206
thrombin/antithrombin (TAT) complexes 39, 90
thrombosis 90
    placental 240, 241
thyroid hormones, preterm babies 79
tissue inhibitors of metalloproteinases (TIMPs) 32, 104, 106–7, 259
tissue type plasminogen activator (tPA) 39
tocolysis 287–95, 333–7
    cervical length assessment after 132, 133
    costs 303
    historical perspective 288–9
    indications 134
    maintenance, with atosiban 326–8

in PPROM 218–19
progesterone therapy and 95
research needs 374
whether or not to use 293, 333, 336–7
tocolytic agents 271, 287–8, 289–93
design of clinical trials 317, 335–6
'rescue therapy,' atosiban studies 315–16, 317–22
transabdominal cervical cerclage (TAC) 145–6
transforming growth factor-β (TGF-β) 200–1
transvaginal cervicoisthmic cerclage 146
triplet pregnancies
cervical cerclage 146
cervical length 127, 130, 131, 136
trp channels 265
tumour necrosis factor-α (TNF-α) 35, 36–7
in cervical ripening 105–6
polymorphism 38, 189, 208
receptors 203
twin pregnancy
atosiban tocolysis 322, 326
cervical cerclage 146
cervical length assessment see under cervical length
fetal growth restriction 68–9
monochorionic vs dichorionic 90
placental pathology 355–6
twins
cervical cerclage after delivery of one 146
delayed delivery of second 95
twin-to-twin transfusion syndrome (TTTS) 355, 356
tyrosine kinase inhibitors 290

ultrasound
dating 62–4
measurement of cervical length see cervical length, sonographic measurement
in PPROM 214
umbilical cord compression, after PPROM 219, 220
Ureaplasma urealyticum 35, 167, 224, 225
urinary tract infection, prevention 225
urokinase type plasminogen activator (u-PA) 39
uterine activity see myometrial activity
uterine artery Doppler velocimetry 39
uterine contractions
physiological basis 260–3, 277–81
switch to, from contractures 6–7, 28–30
see also myometrial activity
uterine contractures 6, 28, 278

switch to contractions 6–7, 28–30
uteroplacental blood flow, calcium channel blockers and 302
uteroplacental ischaemia (disease)
pathological features 354, 356–8
in preterm parturition 38–40
uterus 258
gene microarrays 278–9
overdistension 40
prostanoid receptors 9
stretch, in initiation of labour 23, 40, 278
zonal prostaglandin synthesis 8

vaginal bleeding 40
vaginal delivery
instrumented 348–9
recommendations 348–9
vs caesarean section 341–9
vaginal discharge, in bacterial vaginosis 168
vaginal examination, in PPROM 136, 214
vaginal flora 166
in bacterial vaginosis 169, 170
history and nomenclature 163
in pregnancy 167–8
vaginal pH 166, 168
vaginal swabs, in PPROM 214, 217
vascular endothelial growth factor (VEGF) 151–2
vascular lesions 38–40
vasoactive intestinal peptide 290
ventilation, mechanical 75, 361
ventouse delivery 348–9
versican 100, 103
very low birthweight infants, survival 79–80
very premature babies
mode of delivery 343
survival and outcome 79–80, 297
viability, fetal 296–7, 348
villitis 40–1
voltage-dependent calcium channels (VDCCs) 264–5, 297

weight, maternal 62
'whiff test' 168
white cell count, maternal 216, 217

Yom Kippur effect 29

zone of altered morphology (ZAM) 31, 198, 199–201
cytotrophoblastic–decidual involution 200–1
myofibroblast phenotype 200